Agent Technology for e-Commerce

Maria Fasli

University of Essex

BICENTENNIAL

1807

WILEY

2007

BICENTENNIAL

John Wiley & Sons, Ltd

Other Wiley Editorial Offices

John Wiley & Sons Inc., 111 River Street, Hoboken, NJ 07030, USA

Jossey-Bass, 989 Market Street, San Francisco, CA 94103-1741, USA

Wiley-VCH Verlag GmbH, Boschstr. 12, D-69469 Weinheim, Germany

John Wiley & Sons Australia Ltd, 42 McDougall Street, Milton, Queensland 4064, Australia

John Wiley & Sons (Asia) Pte Ltd, 2 Clementi Loop #02-01, Jin Xing Distripark, Singapore 129809

John Wiley & Sons Canada Ltd, 6045 Freemont Blvd, Mississauga, ONT, L5R 4J3, Canada

Wiley also publishes its books in a variety of electronic formats. Some content that appears in print may not be available in electronic books.

Library of Congress Cataloging-in-Publication Data

Fasli, Maria.
 Agent technology for e-commerce / Maria Fasli.
    p. cm.
  ISBN 978-0-470-03030-1 (pbk. alk. paper)
1. Electronic commerce. 2. Intelligent agents (Computer software) I. Title.
HF5548.32.F375 2007
658.8'72028563 – dc22

                    2006032523

British Library Cataloguing in Publication Data

A catalogue record for this book is available from the British Library

ISBN 978-0-470-03030-1

Typeset in 9/12 Sabon by Laserwords Private Limited, Chennai, India
Printed and bound in Great Britain by Bell & Bain, Glasgow
This book is printed on acid-free paper responsibly manufactured from sustainable forestry in which at least two trees are planted for each one used for paper production.

C
10/01/08

A
f

 University of
Chester

This book is to be returned on or before the last date stamped below. Overdue charges will be incurred by the late return of books.

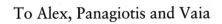

To Alex, Panagiotis and Vaia

Contents

List of Figures   xv

List of Tables   xvii

Preface   xix

C H A P T E R 1 – Introduction   1
1.1   A paradigm shift   3
        1.1.1   A brief history   5
        1.1.2   The novelty in agents   8
        1.1.3   Agent applications   9
1.2   Electronic commerce   10
        1.2.1   E-commerce and organizations   12
        1.2.2   E-commerce and the individual   14
1.3   Agents and e-commerce   16
1.4   Further reading   18
1.5   Exercises and topics for discussion   19

C H A P T E R 2 – Software Agents   21
2.1   Characteristics of agents   22
2.2   Agents as intentional systems   25
2.3   Making decisions   26
        2.3.1   Environments   26
        2.3.2   Performance measure and rationality   30
        2.3.3   Rational decision-making and optimal policies   32
        2.3.4   Optimal policies in MDPs   34
2.4   Planning   37
2.5   Learning   38
2.6   Agent architectures   41
        2.6.1   Logic-based architecture   41
        2.6.2   Reactive architecture   45
        2.6.3   Belief-Desire-Intention architecture   49
        2.6.4   Hybrid architecture   54
2.7   Agents in perspective   57
        2.7.1   Agents and objects   58
        2.7.2   Agents and expert systems   59
        2.7.3   Agents, Web Services and the Semantic Web   60

2.8	Methodologies and languages	62
	2.8.1 Methodologies	62
	2.8.2 Agent-oriented methodologies	62
	2.8.3 Object-oriented based methodologies	66
	2.8.4 Knowledge-engineering based and other methodologies	67
	2.8.5 Programming languages and environments	67
	2.8.6 From legacy systems to agents	69
2.9	Further reading	71
2.10	Exercises and topics for discussion	72

CHAPTER 3 – Multi-agent Systems   **75**

3.1	Characteristics of multi-agent systems	76
	3.1.1 Potential and challenges	77
	3.1.2 Closed multi-agent systems	79
	3.1.3 Open multi-agent systems	79
3.2	Interaction	80
	3.2.1 Elements of interactions	80
	3.2.2 Modes of interaction	81
	3.2.3 Interaction protocols	83
3.3	Agent communication	84
	3.3.1 Speech Act theory	85
	3.3.2 Agent communication languages	85
	3.3.3 Knowledge and Query Manipulation Language (KQML)	86
	3.3.4 FIPA ACL	90
	3.3.5 Comparing KQML and FIPA ACL	93
	3.3.6 Knowledge Interchange Format Language (KIF)	93
	3.3.7 Dialogues	94
	3.3.8 A layered model of communication	95
3.4	Ontologies	97
	3.4.1 Explicit ontologies	98
	3.4.2 Developing ontologies	99
	3.4.3 OWL	100
3.5	Cooperative problem-solving	103
	3.5.1 Task decomposition and distribution	104
	3.5.2 The ContractNet Protocol	104
3.6	Virtual organizations as multi-agent systems	107
3.7	Infrastructure requirements for open multi-agent systems	108
3.8	Further reading	111
3.9	Exercises and topics for discussion	111

CHAPTER 4 – Shopping Agents   **115**

4.1	Consumer buying behaviour model	116
4.2	Comparison shopping	117
4.3	Working for the user	119

4.4	How shopping agents work	120
4.5	Limitations and issues	122
4.6	Further reading	125
4.7	Exercises and topics for discussion	125

C H A P T E R 5 – Middle Agents   **127**

5.1	Matching	128
	5.1.1 Middle agent architecture	129
	5.1.2 Interacting through a middle agent	130
5.2	Classification of middle agents	131
	5.2.1 Matchmaker	132
	5.2.2 Broker	134
	5.2.3 Broadcaster	135
	5.2.4 FIPA Directory Facilitator	136
5.3	Describing capabilities	136
5.4	LARKS	137
	5.4.1 Matching in LARKS	139
	5.4.2 Matching methods	140
5.5	OWL-S	144
5.6	Further reading	147
5.7	Exercises and topics for discussion	147

C H A P T E R 6 – Recommender Systems   **149**

6.1	Information needed	151
6.2	Providing recommendations	152
6.3	Recommendation technologies	153
6.4	Content-based filtering	153
6.5	Collaborative filtering	155
	6.5.1 How collaborative filtering systems work	155
	6.5.2 Neighbourhood-based algorithms	156
	6.5.3 Problems in collaborative filtering	158
	6.5.4 Collaborative filtering systems	159
6.6	Combining content and collaborative filtering	161
6.7	Recommender systems in e-commerce	162
6.8	A note on personalization	163
6.9	Further reading	165
6.10	Exercises and topics for discussion	165

C H A P T E R 7 – Elements of Strategic Interaction   **167**

7.1	Elements of Economics	168
	7.1.1 A simple market economy	168
	7.1.2 Consumption bundles and preferences	173
	7.1.3 Utilities	177
	7.1.4 Equilibrium	178

7.2	Elements of Game Theory	180
	7.2.1 Strategic games	181
	7.2.2 Extensive form representation	183
	7.2.3 Information	184
	7.2.4 Categories of games	185
	7.2.5 Solution concepts	185
	7.2.6 Mixed strategies	188
	7.2.7 The prisoner's dilemma	191
	7.2.8 Repeated games	193
	7.2.9 Dynamic games	194
	7.2.10 Bayesian Nash games	196
	7.2.11 Beliefs and sequential rationality	200
7.3	Further reading	203
7.4	Exercises and topics for discussion	204

CHAPTER 8 – Negotiation I   **209**

8.1	Negotiation protocols	211
8.2	Desired properties of negotiation protocols	212
8.3	Abstract architecture for negotiating agents	213
8.4	Auctions	215
8.5	Classification of auctions	217
8.6	Basic auction formats	220
	8.6.1 English auction	220
	8.6.2 Dutch auction	221
	8.6.3 First-price sealed-bid auction	222
	8.6.4 Vickrey auction	222
	8.6.5 Allocation and revenue comparisons	223
	8.6.6 Disadvantages of auctions	225
8.7	Double auctions	228
	8.7.1 Mth and $(M + 1)$st price rules	229
	8.7.2 Implementation of the Mth and $(M + 1)$st price rules	231
8.8	Multi-attribute auctions	234
8.9	Combinatorial auctions	236
8.10	Auction platforms	239
	8.10.1 AuctionBot	239
	8.10.2 e-Game	240
	8.10.3 Trading agent competition	242
	8.10.4 Online auctions	243
8.11	Issues in practical auction design	244
8.12	Further reading	247
8.13	Exercises and topics for discussion	248

CHAPTER 9 – Negotiation II   **251**

9.1	Bargaining	252

9.1.1	Bargaining power	253
9.1.2	Axiomatic bargaining	255
9.1.3	Strategic bargaining	256
9.1.4	The Strategic Negotiation Protocol	258
9.2	Negotiation in different domains	260
9.2.1	Task-oriented domains	260
9.2.2	Worth-oriented domains	266
9.3	Coalitions	267
9.3.1	Coalition formation	267
9.3.2	Coalition structure generation	268
9.3.3	Division of payoffs	271
9.4	Applications of coalition formation	272
9.4.1	Customer coalitions	273
9.4.2	Coalition Protocols	275
9.4.3	Post-negotiation protocol	277
9.4.4	Pre-negotiation protocol	278
9.4.5	Distribution of costs and utility	279
9.4.6	Other applications	280
9.5	Social choice problems	280
9.5.1	Making a social choice	281
9.5.2	Voting protocols	282
9.5.3	Maximizing social welfare	286
9.6	Argumentation	287
9.6.1	Generating arguments	289
9.6.2	The PERSUADER system	291
9.6.3	Logic-based argumentation	293
9.6.4	Negotiation as dialogue games	295
9.7	Further reading	299
9.8	Exercises and topics for discussion	300
CHAPTER 10 – Mechanism Design		**305**
10.1	The mechanism design problem	306
10.2	Dominant strategy implementation	308
10.3	The Gibbard–Satterthwaite Impossibility Theorem	311
10.4	The Groves–Clarke mechanisms	312
10.4.1	Quasilinear environments	312
10.4.2	The Groves mechanism	313
10.4.3	The Clarke mechanism	314
10.4.4	The Generalized Vickrey Auction	315
10.4.5	Inducing truth-telling in voting mechanisms	318
10.5	Mechanism design and computational issues	319
10.6	Further reading	322
10.7	Exercises and topics for discussion	322

C H A P T E R 11 – Mobile Agents   **325**
11.1   Introducing mobility   326
11.2   Facilitating mobility   328
        11.2.1 Migration   329
        11.2.2 Modes of migration   330
11.3   Mobile agent systems   331
        11.3.1 Non-Java mobile agent systems   332
        11.3.2 Java-based mobile agent systems   333
11.4   Aglets   335
        11.4.1 Programming model   336
        11.4.2 Communication   337
        11.4.3 Security   338
11.5   Mobile agent security   339
        11.5.1 Threats   340
        11.5.2 Security services   343
        11.5.3 Protecting the host   344
        11.5.4 Protecting the mobile agent   345
        11.5.5 Dealing with the perpetrators   347
11.6   Issues on mobile agents   348
11.7   Further reading   350
11.8   Exercises and topics for discussion   350

C H A P T E R 12 – Trust, Security and Legal Issues   **351**
12.1   Perceived risks   353
12.2   Trust   355
12.3   Trust in e-commerce   356
        12.3.1 Trust in agent technology   357
        12.3.2 Trust in the marketplace   359
12.4   Electronic institutions   360
        12.4.1 Norms, institutions and organizations   361
        12.4.2 From norms to institutions   362
        12.4.3 Formalizing norms   364
        12.4.4 Agents in electronic institutions   365
12.5   Reputation systems   366
        12.5.1 Reputation systems in practice   367
        12.5.2 Issues and problems   369
12.6   Security   370
12.7   Cryptography   373
        12.7.1 Symmetric cryptosystems   374
        12.7.2 Asymmetric cryptosystems   375
        12.7.3 Applications of public key cryptography   376
        12.7.4 Digital signatures   378
        12.7.5 Digital certificates   380

12.8	Privacy, anonymity and agents	381
	12.8.1 Agents and privacy	381
	12.8.2 Anonymity	383
	12.8.3 Protecting privacy	384
12.9	Agents and the law	386
12.10	Agents as legal persons	389
12.11	Closing remarks	391
12.12	Further reading	392
12.13	Exercises and topics for discussion	394
APPENDIX A – Introduction to Decision Theory		**395**
A.1	Probability theory	396
	A.1.1 Prior probability	397
	A.1.2 Conditional probability	397
	A.1.3 Independence	398
	A.1.4 Bayes' rule	398
A.2	Making decisions	399
	A.2.1 Non-probabilistic decision-making under uncertainty	401
	A.2.2 Probabilistic decision-making under uncertainty	403
A.3	Utilities	403
	A.3.1 Preferences	404
	A.3.2 Utility functions	405
	A.3.3 Utility and money	407
	A.3.4 Multi-attribute utility functions	411
A.4	Further reading	411
Bibliography		**413**
Index		**445**

List of Figures

1.1	Agents and multi-agent systems: an interdisciplinary area	8
2.1	An agent and the interaction with its environment	26
2.2	The grid world problem	35
2.3	The grid world problem: (a) utilities; (b) optimal policy	37
2.4	The Maze World	43
2.5	Reactive architecture: mapping of perceptions (situations) to actions	46
2.6	Subsumption relation between behaviours in the distant planet exploration scenario	48
2.7	The BDI architecture for agents	51
2.8	Information and control flow in horizontal and vertical layered architectures: (a) horizontal layering; (b) vertical one-pass; (c) vertical two-pass. Source (Müller et al. 1995, p. 265) with kind permission of Springer Science and Business Media	54
2.9	The architecture of TouringMachines	55
2.10	The architecture of InterRRaP	57
2.11	Working together: Agents and Web Services on the Semantic Web	61
2.12	Agentification methods: (a) transducer; (b) wrapper; (c) rewrite	70
3.1	Elements and modes of interaction	82
3.2	A layered model for agent communication	96
3.3	The exchange of messages between manager and contractor agents in the ContractNet protocol	105
3.4	Infrastructure requirements for open MASs	108
4.1	How current shopping agents work	123
5.1	The components of a middle agent	129
5.2	The matchmaker	133
5.3	The broker	134
5.4	The broadcaster	135
5.5	The OWL-S service description	145
6.1	The recommender	151
7.1	The demand curve for the market of flats	170
7.2	The supply curve in the short term for the market of flats	171
7.3	Equilibrium price in the market of flats: supply meets demand	172
7.4	Indifference curve and weakly preferred set	176
7.5	Properties of well-behaved preferences: (a) monotonicity: more is always preferred to less; (b) convexity: average bundles are preferred to extremes	176
7.6	Extensive form representation of the simple game	183
7.7	The sequential version of the prisoner's dilemma game	195
7.8	The entrant-incumbent game	196

7.9	Example game	201
7.10	Dynamic game for Exercise 6	206
8.1	Negotiation protocols enable the transition from one state in a market to another	210
8.2	Abstract architecture for negotiating agents	214
8.3	Auction typology	218
8.4	Example of buy and sell bids in a double auction	229
8.5	Determining the Mth and $(M + 1)$st clearing prices	230
8.6	The organization of bids into four ordered lists	232
8.7	(a) The four ordered lists after the insertion of the new sell bid 5. (b) The four ordered lists after the removal of buy bid 8	233
8.8	The architecture of AuctionBot	239
8.9	The architecture of e-Game	240
9.1	A typical bargaining situation	253
9.2	The alternating offers bargaining situation as an extensive form game	257
9.3	The Monotonic Concession Protocol	262
9.4	Binary voting protocols: different agendas may lead to different outcomes	284
9.5	Abstract architecture for argumentation-based negotiating agents	291
11.1	Hierarchical structure for mobile agent creation and execution	329
11.2	The process of migration	330
11.3	Statefull migration	331
11.4	Stateless migration	331
11.5	The Oasis execution environment	335
12.1	The relationships between norms, institutions and organizations	362
A.1	Tree diagram for the umbrella example	400
A.2	Utility function for money	408
A.3	The utility function of a risk-averse agent	409
A.4	The utility function of a risk-prone agent	410
A.5	The utility function of a risk-neutral agent	410

List of Tables

3.1	Reserved keywords in KQML	88
3.2	FIPA ACL Communicative Acts	91
3.3	A classification of dialogues based on Walton and Krabbe (1995)	95
5.1	A LARKS specification for finding information on laptops	138
6.1	Example of user-item matrix	156
6.2	User-item matrix	166
7.1	Example of assigning utilities to consumption bundles	178
7.2	Normal form representation of the simple game	182
7.3	Game with a dominant strategy equilibrium	186
7.4	The battle of the sexes (BoS) game	187
7.5	The prisoner's dilemma game	191
7.6	The battle of the sexes game: (a) Sally is a basketball fan; (b) Sally is a shopping fan	199
7.7	The normal form representation of the example game	201
7.8	The game for Exercise 3	205
7.9	The game for Exercise 4	205
7.10	The game for Exercise 5	205
7.11	The battle of the sexes game for Exercise 7: (a) Kevin is a basketball fan; (b) Kevin is a shopping fan	206
7.12	The battle of the sexes game for Exercise 8: (a) Kevin is a basketball fan; (b) Kevin is a shopping fan	207
8.1	Common auction terminology	216
9.1	Coalition structures for four agents	270
9.2	Example preferences	283
9.3	Borda voting protocol example	284
9.4	Locutions in the dialogue game protocol of McBurney et al. (2003)	298
11.1	Aglet events	338
A.1	Payoff table for the umbrella example	399
A.2	Loss table for the umbrella example	400
A.3	Payoff table for the stocks example	401
A.4	Payoff table for the modified stocks example	402
A.5	Loss table for the modified stocks example	402
A.6	Utilities for the umbrella example	407

Preface

Agents are computational systems that are capable of autonomous, reactive and proactive behaviour, endowed with the ability to interact with other agents. This ability to interact is fundamental, as agents live and act in complex and dynamic multi-agent environments trying to achieve their goals having limited capabilities and resources. Consequently, they need to be able to coordinate their actions with those of other agents, be it human or artificial. Coordination can take two forms: cooperation to solve a complex problem or perform a difficult task, and negotiation to resolve conflicts, reach agreements or allocate resources and other commodities.

With the advent of the World Wide Web and in an increasingly interconnected and networked world, more and more individuals and organizations choose to do business online. Agents are well-suited for intricate, fast-changing and constrained environments such as electronic marketplaces. Software agents representing individuals and organizations can interact with each other in virtual marketplaces and coordinate and plan their activities so that they can further their owners' objectives. Essential in this process are the abilities to locate other agents who can be partners, competitors or providers, and negotiate and reach deals with them. Electronic commerce in general, and software agents in particular, offer enormous flexibility in this respect, as they open up new possibilities for organizations and individuals to gain access and take advantage of markets that have never before been possible due to geographical and other constraints. An agent representing a company in the UK can negotiate the terms of a contract with the representative agent of another company whose base is in Argentina. As continuously running entities, agents can conduct business on behalf of their users and are able to respond to changes as and when they happen – agents never sleep. If a company in the UK needs to make some urgent changes in its order from a company in Thailand, having agents re-negotiate the deal is much more efficient and cost-effective than arranging meetings and flying people over to one country or the other.

The field of agents and multi-agent systems is relatively new even in the short history of Computer Science. It has gained momentum since the mid-1990s as it has been recognized as offering a new software engineering paradigm that will help us build systems for inherently distributed problems and domains, such as the Internet. Agent behaviour in the context of markets has traditionally been the subject of Economics and its sub-discipline Game Theory. In the last few years there has been a lot of activity in the field, emanating mainly from two communities: economists and game theorists on the one hand, and computer scientists on the other. Economists and game theorists are mainly interested in theoretical aspects of strategic interaction in marketplaces and the design of protocols with well-defined properties. On the other hand, computer scientists, whilst still interested in theoretical aspects of electronic markets and strategic interaction, also look at the problem from a computational point of view. Namely, the problem of providing computationally efficient protocols for electronic markets as well as effective and efficient trading strategies for operating in constrained and dynamic environments. This has resulted in cross-fertilization of ideas emanating from the two disciplines.

My intention in writing this book is to introduce the main theory behind and the applications of agent technology in e-commerce in a way that will be accessible to anyone with a basic background in computer science. My aim is to bring together principles from economics and game theory, which are traditionally the disciplines studying the behaviour of agents within marketplaces, with software agents. My effort is to present the material in such a way as to be comprehensible to computer science students or practitioners who do not necessarily have the background or foundations to delve too deeply into topics in economics and game theory. Nevertheless, I believe that a fundamental understanding of such concepts is essential.

The first part of the book, Chapters 1–3 inclusive, provide a general introduction to the discipline, the nature of agents and how such systems can be built, as well as multi-agent systems and in particular interactions among agents. Chapters 4–6 discuss how agent technology can assist users by providing recommendations and searching for and finding goods and services in the vast expanse of the Internet. Chapter 7 presents an essential introduction to principles of economics and game theory that are necessary to comprehend agent interaction in the context of the dynamic, complex and competitive environments that markets are. My aim is to provide the necessary concepts at a level which is appropriate to computer science students. The next two chapters deal with one of the most fundamental issues in electronic commerce, which is that of negotiation. In particular, I decided to devote the entire first part of this exposition to auctions. This was partly due to the fact that auctions have been widely used in electronic commerce, and partly because there has been an immense research effort into such protocols which cover a lot of different types of negotiation situations. Multi-dimensional auctions are also discussed in this context. Chapter 9 delineates the second part on negotiation which describes bargaining, the strategic negotiation protocol, task and worth-oriented domains, coalitions as well as the problem of making social choices in a society of self-interested agents. I close the topic of negotiation with a discussion on argumentation. Chapter 10 provides an introduction to the problem of mechanism design, namely how we can design efficient and individual rational protocols to facilitate strategic interaction among self-interested agents. The following chapter is devoted to the technology of mobile agents. Despite some potential misgivings, mobile agents seem to be offering yet more possibilities for higher interconnection and interoperation, hence my decision to include this topic. The book culminates with a discussion on trust, security and legal issues in a complex multi-agent world populated by self-interested agents developed by different individuals and organizations. I have also provided a short introduction to decision theory as an Appendix to allow readers who are not familiar with the topic to gain a basic understanding.

The book is addressed mainly to middle to advanced undergraduate and graduate students in computer science or information technology degrees. However, the way the book has been written and presented should make it accessible to computing and IT professionals who would like to become acquainted with the new and exciting discipline of agents and multi-agent systems and learn more about their application in the field of e-commerce, in particular. Furthermore, it could also be a valuable resource to students studying economics who are interested in computer science as it provides a bridge between the two disciplines and shows how Economics and Multi-agent Systems can work together.

Prerequisites

I have made the assumption that the audience of the book will have a basic knowledge of computer science obtained in the first couple of years of a computer science or information technology degree. Thus, the necessary knowledge to comprehend the contents and follow the book includes:

- an understanding of the principles of programming in high-level languages, such as C# or Java
- an understanding of the basic concepts and issues in artificial intelligence, such as knowledge representation, search and intelligent problem-solving
- an understanding of probability theory and familiarity with its notation
- familiarity with basic set theory and logic notation.

How to use this book

The book has been written primarily as a text book that could accompany a middle to advanced undergraduate, or graduate course on agents and multi-agent systems, with a particular emphasis on the applications of agent technology in e-commerce.

The book partly follows the structure of a graduate course that I have been teaching in Agent Technology for E-commerce at the University of Essex since 2001. The course does not assume any prior knowledge on agents and multi-agent systems or economics and game theory. Thus, these topics need to be covered to some extent in order to enable students to understand issues, in particular, in relation to electronic marketplaces and negotiation which are examined in more detail.

The book consists of eight units:

- an introduction to the themes of agents and e-commerce (Chapter 1)
- an introduction to agents and multi-agent systems (Chapters 2–3)
- an introduction to agent technology that can assist users by providing recommendations and finding goods and services in the vast expanse of the Internet (Chapters 4–6)
- an introduction to elements of strategic interaction and a discussion of various negotiation protocols (Chapters 7–9)
- an introduction to mechanism design (Chapter 10)
- an introduction to mobile agents (Chapter 11)
- a discussion on trust, security and legal issues that emanate from the use of agent technology in e-commerce (Chapter 12)
- an introduction to basic concepts and principles of decision theory (Appendix A).

Individual teachers may choose to omit or cover particular units or chapters in more detail, depending on the specific course delivered and its emphasis. To this end, suggestions for further reading are provided at the end of each chapter.

Although an introduction to agents and multi-agent systems is provided, this is not the main theme of the book. Further references are provided for those who would like to gain a deeper understanding of agents as an emerging technology. However, I tried to cover most recent developments regarding agent-oriented methodologies, programming languages and environments.

I have included a chapter on mechanism design (Chapter 10), although individual teachers may decide to leave this aside as it delves into more advanced topics, which may not be covered as part of an undergraduate course.

Chapter 11 is devoted to mobile agents. Some colleagues may not feel particularly sanguine about this technology, nevertheless I decided to include it as, despite some potential misgivings, it seems to offer yet more possibilities in the context of electronic marketplaces. However, the entire chapter can be left out, if individual teachers decide that they do not see any benefit from exposing their students to this kind of technology.

Chapter 12 discusses trust, security and legal issues that arise, in particular with regards to agent technology in e-commerce. Depending on the emphasis of a particular course this chapter can be left out. However, I feel that it is important for both undergraduate and graduate students to be exposed to the issues surrounding the use of such technology and the potential for misuse.

The introduction to decision theory which is provided as an appendix has been included to allow readers who are not familiar with the topic to gain a basic understanding. The Appendix can be used in combination with Chapter 2, or alternatively with Chapter 7 and, in particular, after reading the first part of the chapter on elements of economics.

Structure of chapters

Each chapter begins with a list of learning objectives, i.e., what the students are expected to be able to do after having studied the respective chapter and understood its contents. The presentation of the relevant topics follows. At the end of each chapter there is a further reading section which provides pointers to other works that examine concepts and approaches in more detail or from a more technical point of view than is possible here. I have tried to be objective in my suggestions for further reading, but nevertheless the reader should be aware that the material suggested of course reflects my own preferences. Finally, at the end of each chapter there is a set of exercises and topics for class discussion.

Lecture slides, exam questions and other relevant material can be found at:

http://www.wileyeurope.com/college/fasli

I would welcome any additional material, exercises, exam questions or other topics for discussion. These will be made available on an open source basis. Suggestions can be emailed to:

mfasli@essex.ac.uk

Omissions and errors

It is unavoidable that certain issues could not be covered in the context of this book. This does not mean that such topics are unimportant, but in writing a textbook one discovers that some hard decisions need to be made and material needs to be left out. For instance, agent architectures are only discussed briefly in order to provide the basic concepts and principles to the reader. Other textbooks on agents and multi-agent systems provide a more thorough coverage of this topic as suggested in the respective Further Reading section. Belief-desire-intention (BDI) agents are only briefly covered in the context of agent architectures. Formal aspects of BDI agents are not discussed, but the interested reader could follow the suggested reading material in the respective chapter. Other topics, which are only briefly presented, are planning and learning. As these are fundamental topics in Artificial Intelligence, there are a number of texts that cover them extensively. Markov decision processes (MDPs) are only briefly discussed. Sources for further reading on all these topics are provided in the respective chapter.

Also, this book is about e-commerce and not e-business. As such, I have decided to leave out and not discuss at all topics such as business models and processes, as these topics are beyond the scope of this book.

Notably, this book does not provide any code examples nor does it provide specific instruction on how to program agents as pieces of software. Although I would have liked that, the purpose of this book is not to teach students how to program agents, but to explain the underlying principles, concepts and current technologies and applications in e-commerce.

I have strived to provide an accurate and complete list of references as part of this book. I have made extensive use of CiteSeer (2006), DBLP (2006) and the ACM Portal (2006) to obtain the references and to check their accuracy. Nevertheless, there are bound to be some mistakes. Web references have been checked and were working at the time of writing. However, it may occasionally be the case that some of them are no longer working when you happen to read this book.

Finally, although a textbook by its nature describes the work of others, the final product reflects the author's own biases, preferences and subjective point view. It is almost certain that this book contains omissions, mistakes and oversights. I may have omitted a significant reference or may have missed some aspect that others consider fundamental in this field. In any case, I would welcome comments, suggestions and corrections on any part of this work.

Conventions

As this book refers mainly to computational agents, I will use ''it'' to refer to such an entity. In some of the examples described, and where it is clear that I refer to human agents, I will use ''she''.

The terms 'business', 'organization' and 'company' are used invariably throughout the book to refer to the same class of entities. Also, the terms 'vendor' and 'merchant' are used interchangeably.

Acknowledgments

A number of people have generously given me their time and commented on various aspects of this book. I am indebted to Magnus Boman for providing detailed and insightful comments on an earlier draft of this book. I would also like to thank David Parkes for his feedback on the book as well as his detailed and helpful suggestions on the Mechanism Design chapter. Nick Jennings also provided helpful suggestions on an earlier draft. Nikos Vlassis gave me useful feedback on the chapter on software agents and, in particular, on rational decision-making. Julian Padget and Frank Dignum offered me much-appreciated suggestions on electronic institutions. I would also like to thank the anonymous reviewers for their helpful comments and suggestions on earlier drafts of various chapters as well as the book in its entirety.

I would also like to thank all the students who attended my course on Agent Technology for E-commerce since 2001 at the University of Essex. Their feedback and suggestions have been invaluable in shaping the contents of this book. I have taught the material on auctions at tutorials at the Intelligent Agent Technology Conference 2005 (Compiegne, France) and the European Agent Systems Summer School 2006 (Annecy, France). The participants have provided me with much useful feedback.

The work on the e-Game platform has been joint work with Michael Michalakopoulos, who I would like to thank for the hard work and enthusiasm put into this project, as well as for his help with checking the references.

I would also like to thank my editor at Wiley, Jonathan Shipley, as well as Claire Jardine for their much-appreciated help and support during this project. Special thanks go to project editor David Barnard for all his help and patience during the final production stages of this book.

My mentors Alexandros Tomaras and Ray Turner deserve special thanks for their continuous support and encouragement throughout my career.

A number of friends have supported me throughout this endeavour. Special thanks go to Rania, Marisa, Udo and Naomi.

My parents have been a source of inspiration and support throughout my life. They always kept their positive outlook in the face of life's adversities – this was their most important gift and my late father's legacy to me.

Finally, I would like to thank my husband Alex for his love and belief in me and especially for his unconditional support during the writing of this book.

Maria Fasli

CHAPTER 1

Introduction

LEARNING OBJECTIVES

After reading and completing this chapter, you should be able to:

- Describe the various phases in computing and explain what led to each paradigm shift.
- Discuss how the current technological advancements are leading us to a new paradigm shift and the role envisaged for agent technology.
- Differentiate between e-business and e-commerce.
- Discuss the impact of e-commerce on individuals and organizations.
- Discuss the role envisaged for agent technology in e-commerce.

It is 14:45 on a Friday afternoon and John, who works for a big bank in the City of London, is frantically preparing for a very important meeting with clients which is expected to last at least a couple of hours. The phone rings and it is Sarah, John's wife. While on the phone, John realizes that he has forgotten something very important: it is Sarah's 33rd birthday on Saturday. Busy as he is, it has completely slipped his mind. He realizes that he does not have the time to go shopping and buy her a nice present as the meeting is due to start in only a few minutes. But all is not lost. John instructs his personal software agent – Neo – to make all the necessary arrangements for a surprise trip to Paris leaving later that evening and returning on Sunday. John also instructs Neo to book tickets to the ballet or a classical concert performance for Saturday evening followed by a romantic dinner in a nice restaurant. He then rushes into the meeting.

While the meeting is well under way, John's agent is busy trying to accomplish the task that was delegated to it. First Neo contacts a yellow pages agent and enquires about travel agents that specialize in European short breaks. The yellow pages agent provides Neo with a list of travel agents, airline agents and auction houses that auction last-minute deals. Neo gets in touch with a travel agent and enquires about the availability of Eurostar tickets to Paris on the prescribed dates and times. Neo also enquires at one of the auction houses auctioning last-minute deals. A number of first-class seats are currently under auction and the price is considerably lower than the price indicated by the travel agent. Neo places the necessary bids and, after a few rounds of competing against other human and software agents, it wins two first-class tickets by Eurostar to Paris for the usual price of standard-class tickets. Next, Neo enquires at a travel agent based in Paris about five-star hotels according to John's preferences – no expenses spared. The travel agent returns a list of five-star hotels and Neo chooses one in Montmartre with views over Sacré Coeur and the whole of Paris, for John and his wife. Next, Neo enquires at the travel agent for restaurants and entertainment options and it obtains a list of restaurants overlooking the river, plus a list of ballet performances and classical concerts that take place on Saturday night. Knowing John's expressed preference for the ballet, Neo books two tickets for Swan Lake and also books a table for two in a restaurant with views over the river Seine that has an excellent recommendation for a romantic dinner before the performance. It is now 4.45 pm and, while still in the meeting, John receives a notification on his PDA from Neo informing him that the trip has been arranged. He glances at the details of the trip and authorizes Neo to pay for all goods and services booked. He then sends an email to Sarah telling her to prepare her things for a short surprise trip. John takes a deep breath and relaxes knowing that, yet again, his personal agent did a phenomenal job!

This is a glimpse of the not-so-distant future where users are represented by highly personalized and sophisticated pieces of software called 'agents' that know their preferences and can take such actions on their behalf as find and recommend products and services, negotiate the terms of transactions, and make payments. We are not quite there yet.

Agent technology has an immense potential in e-commerce, but it is still early days. There is a lot of work to be done if we want to reach the stage in which such autonomous agents proliferate the Internet and make our lives easier. Nevertheless, the signs of change are evident and agents have already started making an impact.

This book looks at the applications of agent technology in e-commerce and, in particular, it discusses:

- the nature of agents, their characteristics, and methodologies and architectures for designing and building them
- multi-agent systems and elements of agent interaction
- communication languages
- agents that can help users with and enhance their shopping experience
- middle agents that enable connections among service requesters and providers
- basic elements of economics and game theory
- agent-based negotiation and protocols, including auctions, bargaining, coalition formation, voting and argumentation
- issues on mechanism design
- mobile agents
- issues and concerns regarding the use of agent technology in e-commerce and potential ways of addressing them.

The purpose of this first chapter is to set the scene for the rest of the book, by providing a general discussion on the themes of agents and e-commerce.

1.1 A PARADIGM SHIFT

Computers have come a long way from the colossal machines of the early 1950s consisting of electronic switches in the form of vacuum tubes occupying entire rooms, to the minute transistor chips in today's modern computers. Throughout the short history of computing there have been changes in how people think about and use computer systems. When such changes are major and have a significant impact on people's lives and way of thinking, they constitute a *paradigm shift*. Such paradigm shifts typically bring about changes to the status of computers within our society. There have been two major paradigm shifts widely acknowledged in the design and development of computer systems, and consequently in how people use and regard computers (Weiser and Brown 1997).

During the first phase of computing, users worked on big mainframes. Each mainframe supported a number of users and was characterized by a single Central Processing Unit (CPU) which was shared by all of them. Users communicated with such systems through rigid command line interfaces. Such systems were typically used as powerful calculation and data administration tools.

In the second phase, the size of transistor chips was reduced considerably and their manufacturing became cheaper, thus allowing a significant number of individual users to obtain personal computers (PCs) which are small in size and affordable. PCs at home are used in a number of applications ranging from simple word processing to computer games, image manipulation and also for educational purposes. The rigid command line interfaces have given way to more user-centred and friendly window-based interfaces. Computers are regarded as personal tools.

The third phase of computing, ubiquitous computing, which is slowly dawning upon us, is characterized by the ever-present digital and other computational technologies, such as nanotechnologies and quantum computing. Users are increasingly surrounded by numerous tiny processing units, while computing is everywhere and it becomes part of nearly every human activity.

The signs of this new paradigm shift abound around us today. We are increasingly surrounded by computational devices as chips have made their way into a number of appliances that we use in our everyday lives, from washing machines to mobile phones. The huge growth of the Internet since the middle 1990s has meant increased connectivity and the flourishing of distributed and concurrent systems. The Internet has redefined the role of computers as windows to the world: they provide us with a new means of communication and interaction as well as access to information, resources and services on a scale never before possible or imaginable (Rieder 2003).

Nevertheless, despite information being at one's fingertips, users increasingly require assistance, guidance and support in the vast information space of the Internet. Inherently, the users' needs have changed: the standard user-computer interaction model, which is based on the direct manipulation metaphor, i.e., a single instruction either through a command line or by clicking a button on a window interface which triggers a single action, does not suffice any more. Instead of *acting upon* computer systems, we are increasingly *delegating to* and *interacting with* them in more complex, conversational ways. Thus, the nature of computation has changed from mere calculation to delegation and continuous interaction. New theoretical models and software engineering methodologies are required to support the design and development of systems that reflect this shift in the nature of computation.

This trend to view computation more as a delegation of our goals and continuous interaction with computer systems, assumes building systems that can act on one's behalf. In addition, the tasks being delegated are increasing in complexity, thus demanding the building of ever smarter systems that can anticipate and learn from their users' needs and actively seek to further their goals, but by acting almost autonomously without constant and direct intervention from the users. Such systems observe their environment and respond to any changes that occur and which will affect the achievement of their goals. In looking after the user's interests, a smart computer system may interact with or seek the assistance or the services of other computer systems. Thus, in order to successfully achieve their goals, such smart systems must communicate and interact not only with the user, but also with each other.

The natural metaphor for such inevitably intricate and complex systems that aid us in our everyday lives and can react, learn and adapt to their environment and have the ability to interact with each other is that of an *agent*. Put simply, an agent is a computer system that acts on behalf of its user and attempts to achieve the user's goals and objectives by acting autonomously. An agent is usually not an isolated entity: it is embedded within an environment and it continuously interacts with it as well as with other entities, including agents and humans. A multi-agent system comprises a number of agents that communicate and interact with each other to solve a complex problem or to further their users' goals. What distinguishes agents from other pieces of software is that computation is not simply calculation, but delegation and interaction; users do not act upon agents as they do with other software programs, but they delegate tasks to them and interact with them in a conversational rather than in a command mode. Intrinsically, agents enable the transition from simple static algorithmic-based computation to dynamic interactive delegation-based service-oriented computation.

Agents can provide the means to mask the underlying complexity of our use of computers nowadays, facilitating the achievement of our tasks and goals with the minimum effort. As such, agents have the potential to render Information Technology more friendly and accessible even to the most novice of users, by rendering the information itself more comprehensible and manageable. They can filter, organize and restructure information before presenting it, in an appropriate and easily digestible form, to the user.

As digital technology becomes increasingly embedded in devices and appliances that we use in our everyday lives and spans a variety of activities ranging from the more mundane ones (daily chores) to more creative ones (art and personal recreation), agents will permeate such static and mobile devices to facilitate integration of services and assist and support the user. In the not-so-distant future we will not only talk about intelligent computer systems, but also smart cars and even smart homes which will feature embedded agents that will be able to aid us by interacting with us and each other. Substantial progress has already been made in this direction. Undoubtedly, agent technology plays a prominent role in this vision of pervasive and ubiquitous computing.

1.1.1 A brief history

From a historical point of view, agents and multi-agent systems have their roots in Artificial Intelligence (AI) and Distributed Artificial Intelligence (DAI). The idea of an intelligent computer system was clearly present in the early AI, an example being the Advice Taker as described by McCarthy (1958). Nevertheless, the notion of a multi-agent system only began to emerge and gain in importance in the 1980s. In fact, research into individual agents progressed largely separate from research into multi-agent systems until the 1990s.

Since its inception, the predominant objective of AI has been to understand intelligence and to devise intelligent systems. Yet, research in intelligent systems in AI developed into separate strands that concentrated on specific aspects of intelligence, such as representation and reasoning, planning, learning, problem solving and natural language processing, amongst others. Within these strands, research was conducted independently of each other, trying to solve problems and developing systems that demonstrated only certain aspects of intelligence. Attempts to bring together these different aspects of intelligent behaviour in one system were very limited in number.

Most AI researchers advocated a symbolic approach to intelligence, i.e., intelligence is the product of manipulating symbolic representations of the world. As a result of this stance, the idea of deliberative or cognitive systems emerged, and dominated the scene of AI. But this created systems that were heavy and cumbersome and whose interaction with their environment was rather limited and could only solve specific problems in restricted domains known as *microworlds*. A typical example of a microworld is the blocks world which consists of a number of blocks placed on a table or other surface. Tasks in this world involve re-arranging the blocks in a particular way using a robotic arm. Some researchers started rejecting this idea of intelligence as symbolic representation and manipulation and advocated a more radical approach to intelligence, which culminated with Brooks' behavioural thesis in the mid 1980s: that intelligence can emerge from the interaction with one's environment through simple behaviours. This created a rift in AI, splitting the community into those defending a symbolic approach, and those rejecting symbolic representation altogether and advocating a behavioural approach. Nowadays, it is generally recognized that, in order to build intelligent systems, the truth lies somewhere in-between. Both deliberative and behavioural or reactive components are required to achieve effective and flexible behaviour from intelligent systems in complex and dynamic environments.

The concept of an agent as an entity, which is part of a bigger system able to communicate, makes its appearance in the Actor model of Hewitt in the early days of research into DAI in the 1970s (Hewitt et al. 1973, Hewitt 1977). In this model, Hewitt proposed a computational system called Actor which is a self-contained, interactive and concurrently-executing object. Actors have an internal state and they are both social and reactive: they can send messages to other Actors and they can carry out computations in response to messages from others. Moreover, Actors can carry out their actions concurrently.

The blackboard systems that emerged in the 1970s can be considered to be among the first prototypical multi-agent systems. The idea behind blackboard systems is that a set of experts with different areas of knowledge can work together in order to solve a complex problem, which each individual is unable to solve on its own (Newell 1962). Such systems work on the principle that there is a shared data structure called a blackboard that all computational entities (knowledge sources) use in order to communicate with each other via reading and writing messages. Each computational entity has some expert knowledge and monitors the blackboard and contributes partial problem solutions, as necessary. One of the best known blackboard systems is Hearsay, for speech understanding, which was developed in the early 1970s (Reddy et al. 1973). A similar approach based on the metaphor of a community of problem-solving experts was used in the ETHER system (Kornfeld 1979).

Another seminal approach to solving complex problems by using a number of computational entities, was developed by Reid Smith. This approach which is known as the ContractNet emulates the contracting mechanism used by businesses. Computational entities (nodes) solve problems by delegating (subcontracting) subproblems to other entities (Smith 1977, 1980a,b), and then synthesize the partial solutions. This is one of the best known protocols of DAI and it has been used extensively up to this day and constitutes the basis of other approaches. The ContractNet introduces a number of fundamental issues in DAI, such as task distribution and synthesis as well as delegation.

Work in multi-agent systems in the form of DAI began to flourish in the early 1980s with the establishment of dedicated venues such as the Distributed Artificial Intelligence workshops in the US and the publication of a number of works that contained core papers in the area such as (Huhns 1987, Gasser and Huhns 1989, Bond and Gasser 1988). In Europe in the late 1980s and under the ARCHON and MAGMA projects, research into DAI and multi-agent systems began to take shape and it was supported by dedicated workshops such as Modelling Autonomous Agents in a Multi-Agent World (MAAMAW), while in Japan dissemination of research was through the Multi-Agent and Concurrent Computing (MACC) workshops (Ferber 1999).

With the growth of the Internet and the emergence of the Web, research into multi-agent systems went from strength to strength in the 1990s, as it was recognized that agents and multi-agent systems can play a pivotal role in the development of distributed, complex and open systems. During this time a significant amount of both theoretical and practical works have been produced. The emphasis has been on autonomous rational agents (Rao and Georgeff 1991, Wooldridge and Jennings 1995), multi-agent systems (Gasser 1995, Jennings et al. 1996, Ferber 1999, Sycara et al. 2003) interaction standards such as communication languages (Labrou and Finin 1998), strategic interactions among agents (Rosenchein and Zlotkin 1994, Kraus 2001) and learning in multi-agent systems (Stone 2000) to name just a few – this list is by no means exhaustive or indicative of the most important works in this area. During this period the International Conference on Multi-Agent Systems (ICMAS) along with the Agent Theories, Architectures and Languages (ATAL) and Autonomous Agents conferences, were established. The three were brought together in 2002 under the Autonomous Agents and Multi-Agent Systems (AAMAS) conference. The Foundation for Intelligent Physical Agents (FIPA) (FIPA 2006) was also established during this period in an effort to promote and impose standards. FIPA currently operates under the auspices of IEEE. Organizations such as FIPA and networks such as AgentLink (AgentLink 2006a) in Europe have also been encouraging research and education in agent-based and multi-agent systems and promoting the wider adoption of agent technology.

Agents and multi-agent systems are now a well-established areas of research and development with a number of potential applications. Indeed, agents and multi-agent systems is one of the most rapidly advancing areas of computing technology. The most recent initiative of the Semantic Web and the emergence of Web Services further enforce the relevance and the strength of the agent paradigm, as agents can facilitate the seamless interaction and integration of Semantic Web Services (Singh and Huhns 2005).

The discipline of agents and multi-agent systems which evolved out of AI and DAI is very interdisciplinary. It is a fusion of ideas and concepts from other disciplines as diverse as mathematics, sociology, biology, computer science, philosophy and ethology, to mention just a few, Figure 1.1. Multi-agent systems facilitate the cross-fertilization of ideas amongst all these disciplines.

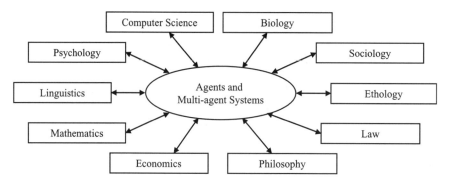

Figure 1.1: Agents and multi-agent systems: an interdisciplinary area

1.1.2 The novelty in agents

So what is it that makes agents different, over and beyond other software? Whereas traditional software applications need to be told explicitly what it is that they need to accomplish and the exact steps that they have to perform, agents need to be told what the goal is but not how to achieve it. Then, being 'smart', they will actively seek ways to satisfy this goal, acting with the minimum intervention from the user. Agents will figure out what needs to be done to achieve the delegated goal, but also react to any changes in the environment as they occur, which may affect their plans and goal accomplishment, and then subsequently modify their course of action.

So what do agents have to offer? Why should we consider using the agent-based approach to solving problems? As explained in (Jennings and Wooldridge 1998), for any new technology to be considered useful, it must enable us to solve problems that, so far, we have been unable to solve with other technologies; or allow us to solve problems that we can already solve with other technologies, but in a significantly better, more efficient, faster, more natural way. Agent technology allows us to do both.

First, agents can solve problems that are beyond the scope of other methodologies or programming paradigms such as, for instance, open systems (Hewitt 1986). In such systems the components are not known in advance, their structure and topology may change, and the individual components are inherently heterogeneous as they may be implemented by different developers using different languages and technologies. Such an example of an open system is the Internet. Agents are particularly well-suited for very large and complex systems, as using the abstraction and modularity that agents offer may be the only way that such systems can be made to work. Such complex systems can be seen as a loosely coupled network of entities, each possessing its own problem-solving abilities, expertise and resources. These entities can then interact and work together on problems that may be beyond the scope and the capabilities of any of the entities individually. To this end, agents are suitable for dynamic, uncertain, information-rich and process-rich environments.

Second, agents can also be used to solve problems that can be solved using other methodologies, but in a significantly better, faster, cheaper and more natural way. For instance, problems where data, control and expertise or resources are inherently distributed will be appropriate for agent-based solutions. Agents with different expertise and computational resources which may be distributed over a network can come together and coordinate to solve a complex task. The agent metaphor is a natural abstraction for such problems and thus a collection of agents can be viewed as a society of agents. Agents can also be used as a means to interoperate and interact with legacy components or systems. Legacy components are technologically obsolete pieces of software which are a part of organizations and are essential for their functionality, but are difficult to replace.

1.1.3 Agent applications

Agent technology has been rapidly recognized as the new software engineering paradigm for developing complex and open systems in a variety of application domains. Such smart computational systems can help us to organize our email, find news articles and scientific papers that are of interest to us, control the manufacturing process in a factory or guide spacecraft and explore distant worlds. Some indicative application domains are:

- **Process control**. Process control is a typical application for agents and multi-agent systems, as process controllers are themselves autonomous reactive systems. One of the most well-known approaches is ARCHON which is a software platform accompanied by a methodology for developing multi-agent systems (Jennings et al. 1996). ARCHON has been used to develop several applications, including electricity transportation management and particle accelerator control.

- **Operations management.** A cluster of factories that coordinate their inputs and outputs can be naturally modelled as elements of a multi-agent system. A number of systems have been developed for production planning and scheduling and manufacturing control (Marik and McFarlane 2005). One of the first such systems was YAMS (Van Dyke Parunak 1987) which made use of the ContractNet protocol. More recent examples are the system produced by Eurobios for SCA Packaging (AgentLink 2006b) and ExPlanTech (Pechoucek et al. 2002).

- **Information management.** Although the Internet has offered us almost unlimited access to information, this has resulted in information overload. In essence, there is too much information out there for an individual to sift through. Agents can be used for information filtering to help users find useful information, i.e., news articles, papers or web pages that are of interest to them (Maes 1994, Lieberman et al. 2001). The required information may be scattered across the World Wide Web. Agents can facilitate information gathering, that is, they can help us collect and collate information which meets our requirements.

- **Entertainment.** Agents have the potential to be used in the entertainment industry in computer games as well as movies (Bates 1992, Hayes-Roth and Doyle 1998, Wavish 1996, Wavish and Connah 1997). Game characters can be naturally seen as agents, as their properties perfectly fit the agent concept, as was briefly explained earlier. Such characters can learn and adapt to the user's abilities and so provide them with challenges, making games more realistic and responsive and ultimately more fun. For instance, Haunt 2 involves believable AI characters that have needs and drives (Magerko et al. 2004). Another game that was built using agent techniques is Creatures (Grand and Cliff 1998). In the movie industry, the 'Lord of the Rings' made extensive use of believable agents, namely artificial characters, in creating all those epic scenes of battles. The proprietary software program developed by Weta Digital (Weta Digital 2006) called 'Massive' (Massive 2006) enabled thousands of artificial characters or agents who were endowed with a 'brain' to make decisions and react to their environment and each other.

- **Education.** Agents can be used for educational purposes (Jafari 2002). The concept of an intelligent tutoring system can be expanded to that of a partner in learning (Chan 1996); an artificial educator that teaches the user, but also learns and adapts to her individual needs.

1.2 ELECTRONIC COMMERCE

Businesses have long taken advantage of networking in order to improve communications and the efficiency of their operations. The idea of conducting transactions electronically is not new; many companies have integrated their systems with those of their suppliers and distributors using proprietary networks for electronic data interchange (EDI), called value-added networks (VAN), since the 1970s. But such networks are static and therefore inflexible: should a company decide to change a supplier or distributor, a new and perhaps costly EDI connection needs to be established. In addition, the cost involved in building such proprietary networks is prohibitive for smaller businesses.

The immense growth of the Internet has had a profound impact on business environments. Companies need not build their own private/proprietary VANs to be able to perform transactions electronically. The Internet can serve as the medium allowing them to do so. The relatively low cost of the underlying IT infrastructure which is required to be in place to enable electronic transactions has meant that even smaller companies can take advantage of this new medium.

The result of this revolution in the way that companies conduct their business and transactions has given birth to a new phenomenon. This phenomenon is called *e-commerce* and the term is often used to describe all kinds of commercial dealings in the digital world, such as contract negotiations, procurement, transactions, market research and even delivery of services. E-commerce invariably involves the conduct of economic-related activities that take place between at least two parties who interact electronically. Such activities cross organizational boundaries.

In conjunction with e-commerce, another frequently used term is that of *e-business*. Although there are no universally accepted definitions for the two terms, they are customarily perceived to be closely related, but distinctly different (van Slyke and Belanger 2003). E-business includes an organization's internal operations as well as operations that are related to third parties, i.e., customers, suppliers and distributors. Consequently, e-business enables companies to integrate and streamline their intra and interbusiness processes more efficiently and effectively to better satisfy the needs and expectations of their customers. In practice, this may involve the introduction of e-commerce systems to expand and better serve one's market base, or knowledge management systems to improve efficiency. Thus, e-commerce is always e-business, but not the other way round.

The overall goal is to integrate e-commerce into existing business processes in such a way that a processing order moves smoothly through existing accounting, order processing and inventory systems no matter how or where the transaction was initiated, e.g., direct sales, online sales, retail outlet. The seamless integration of online sales with back end-business process and information systems introduces a variety of technical and business challenges as well as opportunities.

Undoubtedly, e-commerce has had an impact both on organizations as well as individuals (van Slyke and Belanger 2003). It has instigated changes in the market structures, the products and services available, and the parties involved. Nowadays we are talking about a 24-hour economy in a digital world.

1.2.1 E-commerce and organizations

The Internet offers global and constant access to information through a fundamental technology, which is freely available to everyone, namely web browsers. Essentially, web browsers constitute the most basic e-commerce-enabling technology. As a result, e-commerce is an opportunity available to organizations irrespective of size.

The true global nature of the Internet and the inherent lack of geographical barriers has meant that new markets have opened up to all those willing to embrace e-commerce. Organizations can expand their target market and reach potential customers all around the world. The Internet enables geographically dispersed buyers and sellers to come together. For instance, a bookstore's web site is globally accessible, thereby allowing purchases to be made by customers who may reside in a different country or even a different continent than that of the bookstore. New opportunities have opened up, allowing companies to get in touch with potential partners from all around the world and not be confined by geographical boundaries. It is perfectly possible for a product manufacturer in Australia to be partners with a product designer in Italy. Communication can be done through email and teleconferencing.

One of the advantages of using the Internet and e-commerce technology is that organizations are in a position to streamline their operations with their business partners, such as suppliers as well as clients. Organizations can interact with other partners seamlessly, and thus increase their effectiveness and efficiency. For instance, the various operations involved in supply chain management, i.e., keeping track of supply and demand, procuring raw materials, inventory tracking and order management, can greatly benefit from the use of e-commerce systems. This leads to improved relations between business partners.

In today's highly dynamic business world, organizations need to be agile and innovative in order to be able to respond to the constantly changing needs of the market and the customer force, and to withstand competition. This has lead to the emergence of virtual organizations. A virtual organization, often referred to as a virtual or agile enterprise, comprises a number of partners that forge a consortium dynamically in order, for instance, to meet customer demand, offer new or improved services or exploit a niche in the market. The partners may have common, compatible, overlapping or complementary goals, therefore joining forces and operating under one hood enables them to achieve these goals. Streamlining, coordination and integration of operations are central to the concept of a virtual organization.

Internet-based companies have sprung up, companies that do not maintain physical 'brick and mortar' stores, but simply operate and trade online. A classic and successful example of such a business is Amazon (Amazon 2006). However, the success of such ventures depends on the underlying business models and their viability and soundness. The demise of dot com companies in 2000 was due to this reason, namely the lack of realistic and sustainable business models.

New types of services have emerged, e-services, that are offered to companies as well as individuals. Such services are usually information or other digital-form services, for instance, music or software downloads or providing comparative information on products. Many traditional, 'brick-and-mortar' companies have recognized the opportunities in such niche markets and have begun to invest in e-commerce web sites.

The application of e-commerce technologies may have, as an effect, the reduction of transaction costs, thus improving economic efficiency. In a perfectly efficient economy transaction, costs are zero. Typically, every transaction performed involves some cost, that is, a transaction is not without 'friction'. For instance, when an order is placed via the phone, the assistant who answers the call and handles the order has a cost. E-commerce technologies have the potential to reduce some of these transaction costs. An order placed via the vendor's web site, which is passed on directly to the order fulfillment system, does not involve a person. Thus, the original friction cost is eliminated. The savings could be potentially passed on to consumers through lower prices. In general, when the transaction costs are minimized, a portion of the inefficiencies in the economy disappears, resulting in a more efficient economy. Nevertheless, building, introducing and maintaining an e-commerce system as part of one's business model does involve a certain cost which may be nontrivial.

Organizations that deploy e-commerce have another advantage: they can potentially know who is accessing their sites and requesting information on their products and services. Knowing the identity of the potential customer provides an organization with the opportunity to offer personalized services. Organizations can gradually build profiles of their clientele and employ them to offer tailor-made services and even personalize the prices that they are offering, which is usually referred to as dynamic pricing or price discrimination (Vulkan 2003). Thus, having built a profile enables a vendor to measure the customer's desire to purchase a certain item and charge them accordingly. Different customers can be charged different prices for the same item.

As customers shopping online are often engaged in 'considered' and not 'impulse' shopping, vendors need to find ways to induce more trade. However, a customer who knows exactly what she wants will not easily be influenced by advertising. Vendors need to find other ways to entice these careful buyers into buying more than what they originally intended, while at the same time gaining an edge over their competitors and differentiating themselves. Bundling goods and services, that is, offering combinations of products and services rather than selling them on their own, may help towards this objective. Bundling in e-commerce does not cost the organization anything, as the material commodities do not have to be physically bundled until they actually have to be shipped, and bundling services or other types of commodities, such as pieces of software or music, is easy. If the bundle represents value for money for the customer, the likelihood is that they will return to this vendor.

Organizations can also use the Internet as a means to find out about their competition and the prices that they are charging. This information can then be used, on the one hand, to adjust their prices to remain competitive, but on the other, this can also lead to an implicit price collusion among sellers, allowing them to charge higher prices.

E-commerce has also brought about changes in the market structures. For instance, the way that traditional stock markets used to operate would discourage individuals from investing small amounts in stocks (van Slyke and Belanger 2003). Traders would require a considerable fee as commission for their services, inevitably eating into a small investor's potential profit. However, e-commerce has enabled companies to operate online with smaller fees, enabling individuals to trade in the stock exchange markets.

Finally, the Internet has offered the means for new business models to develop such as, for instance, the facilitation of consumer-to-consumer commerce (C2C). Consumer-to-consumer commerce allows consumers to trade goods with others via e-commerce systems using simple negotiation protocols such as auctions. A well-known example of such a successful site that enables millions of consumer-to-consumer transactions is eBay (eBay 2006).

Despite the positive effects of e-commerce on organizations, such as creating new markets and increasing efficiency, it has also brought up new competition. The same technology that allows an organization to enter and exploit new markets, also enables competitors to enter the market. This competition may come from newly founded businesses, from existing competitors or even from existing businesses that diversify or expand their remit and services. To make matters worse, the competition now crosses geographical borders. Organizations need to be flexible and embrace and cope with constant change in order to survive in such a competitive climate.

1.2.2 E-commerce and the individual

E-commerce has also had a tremendous impact on individuals. In particular, e-commerce in combination with the expanse of the Internet and the availability of broadband services, has resulted in a shift in the individual consumer's attitudes towards purchasing goods and services. The nature of business-to-consumer commerce (B2C) has changed dramatically over the last few years. Organizations have realized the potential of the Internet and what it can offer to individual consumers and as a result, e-commerce sites flourish, offering a wide range of services and products nowadays. The traditional shopping trip has been replaced by a virtual one.

E-commerce offers a lot of flexibility and great convenience to consumers. One can shop from the comfort and convenience of one's own home, at any time during the day or night without having to worry about store opening times. Shopping online of course has its disadvantages as, for certain products, one may not be able to grasp all the physical aspects.

Consumers may also be able to profit from the greater economic efficiency that e-commerce brings about. If some of the friction costs that are involved in transactions are reduced, some of these savings can be passed on to the consumers. For instance, airlines offer discounted prices for consumers who book their flights directly with them and not through a travel agent, i.e., the travel agent's commission is passed on as a saving to the consumer. Moreover, the Internet and the Web have empowered consumers in the sense that they have alleviated *information asymmetry*. Information asymmetry is the term used by economists to describe the situation that often occurs in economic interactions in which one party has more information than the other. Consumers are no more ignorant or uninformed about their potential options on products and services and even vendors. Information on specifications can easily be found and so consumers are no more disadvantaged. Indeed, their negotiation position has significantly improved as they can now make informed choices and are able to demand better deals.

Moreover, e-commerce offers increased choice to the consumer. One's shopping trip is no longer confined by geographical proximity. Virtual shopping trips can involve vendors that are based in different cities, countries or even continents. Vendors all over the world are within easy reach, just a few clicks away. In addition, individuals may also benefit from service and product personalization as well as the bundling of goods and services.

Shopping online also saves time for the consumer. Typically, a consumer looking for a particular item may have to visit several vendors that provide similar quality and specification products in order to get a good idea of what is available in the market, and then make an informed decision based on their own criteria. Without doubt, it is less time-consuming to visit the vendor's e-commerce sites and look for the products in which one is interested, rather than to make the actual shopping trip.

The increasing number of vendors who choose to do business online also means increased competition, which can also benefit the consumer in terms of lower prices. Vendors wanting to attract customers have an incentive to be competitive. The consumers are now in a position to perform extensive product searches and find the best deals available.

Finally, e-commerce and the Internet have opened up new opportunities for individual users as well. Users can now become sellers if they feel that they own an item that other people may value. C2C commerce has expanded immensely in the last few years. Individuals can trade goods with others via e-commerce systems using mechanisms such as auctions. eBay (eBay 2006), Yahoo!Auctions (YahooAuctions 2006), and

Amazon.comAuctions (Amazon 2006) among others, offer the means for millions of individuals to trade items ranging from collectibles to books and spare parts.

Despite e-commerce having a number of advantages and positive effects on individual consumers, it has also raised a number of issues. In particular, e-commerce can only benefit those with access to computer systems and the Internet (van Slyke and Belanger 2003). The number of people who do not have access to such facilities and stand on the other side of the *digital divide* is significant. In developed countries, there is still a large number of people who do not have access to computing facilities, and in developing countries, only the better off can afford such facilities. Thus, in reality, the largest part of the population actually loses out. The effect of this may not be insignificant as people without access to e-commerce, in essence, pay higher prices. To make matters worse, the people who pay higher prices are actually those that can less afford it (van Slyke and Belanger 2003).

E-commerce as traditional commerce is also plagued by fraud; both old and new types of fraud. Fraudulent and untrustworthy individuals and vendors abound in the digital world. Scams involving bogus e-commerce web sites often make the headlines. E-commerce is also vulnerable to credit-card fraud, although not more so than traditional commerce. Fraud in consumer online auctions is also possible.

The Internet and e-commerce also brought about increased risks regarding the invasion of one's privacy. As information on consumers is gathered at an increasing pace, individuals are rightly worried about who has access to their personal information. User profile building, unbeknown to the user, is another potential and serious problem. These user profiles may be used to offer personalized services to users, but they may also be used to operate price-discrimination schemes. Finally, although on the one hand the Internet and e-commerce have offered increased choice, there are simply too many potential choices for individuals to handle. Information overload is an undisputed fact.

1.3 AGENTS AND E-COMMERCE

Despite its name, e-commerce is not fully automated. Typically, online transactions require a significant level of human intervention. Humans undertake the search for products, services, potential vendors and business partners. They evaluate alternatives, decide what goods to buy and when, from which vendor, and how much they are willing to pay for them. They engage in potential negotiations, carry out the transactions and so on. In essence, all the decision-making is done by humans. But, in principle, there is no reason why some aspects of commerce, if not all in some cases, cannot be automated. The concept of an agent as a computational system that can act on the user's behalf seems particularly suitable for e-commerce applications. It is natural, then, to consider delegating some of the decision-making to agents.

Indeed, the potential for agents in e-commerce is immense; e-commerce is considered by some researchers and technology analysts as the potential killer application for agents (Ulfelder 2000). Others purport that this kind of technology will revolutionize commerce. There has already been some headway in this direction, although the scenario described in the opening of this chapter is still some way ahead. Nevertheless, the technology exists for agents to:

- find, recommend and compare products, vendors, or services
- participate in electronic markets and negotiate the price/terms of transactions or contracts with other participants
- perform transactions on behalf of their users
- track the user's interests and offer personalized services
- monitor conditions and provide notifications
- retrieve, filter, and mine information and knowledge
- produce and deliver e-services, such as information gathering, processing and management.

Partially or fully automating some of the processes involved in e-commerce will bring about significant cost savings. Although the choices and opportunities for individuals and organizations have increased dramatically, unless they can actually locate these opportunities – clients, markets, potential partners, openings in the market – they will be unable to take advantage of them. Using agents, an organization can truly do business 24 hours a day and take advantage of opportunities as they arise, even if they present themselves in different time zones or continents. As a software agent can search tirelessly for the best matches globally, the costs of searching for partners or products can be minimized and efficiency can thereby increase. The searches that these agents can perform on behalf of the user can be intelligent searches, involving visiting a number of sites in order to extract the required information, match the user's preferences and find the best possible deal. Such agents can undertake one of the most time-consuming tasks, which is that of negotiating the terms of the transactions and contracts. Agents can make good decisions fast, again minimizing costs and improving overall economic efficiency without necessarily involving humans. Agents can also be used to offer personalized services to users.

As the technology matures, more and more complex tasks will be delegated to software agents, who will become an indispensable part of an increasingly open, free-market information economy. Agent technology can reduce the costs of trading and thus, increase market efficiency and profitability, trading volumes, as well as the speed of trading. Agents can enable the move from traditional brick and mortar companies to intelligent and ubiquitous digital business. The vision is that agents will evolve from being simple facilitators to complex and autonomous decision makers handling incomplete, inconsistent information in real-time and making complex but good decisions.

Agent technology is also instrumental in the realization of virtual organizations. Agents representing different entities such as manufacturers, suppliers, service providers, brokers and other partners, can take advantage of new opportunities and changing circumstances in markets and organize themselves into virtual organizations or enterprises to achieve temporary objectives. Although consisting of a number of autonomous and independent partners, the virtual organization acts and appears as a single conceptual entity to any other third party that will be dealing with it, therefore integration and coordination are fundamental issues. Agility and the ability to respond to constant change in an unpredictable environment is what characterizes virtual organizations.

For this vision to materialize, we need knowledge-based agents that can reason under uncertainty and with incomplete information, goal-driven agents that can plan, and agents that can learn and adapt to their environment. Without doubt, agents play an instrumental role in the vision of a borderless digital 24-hour information economy, but users need to trust them first.

The rest of this book will explore this vision, what agent technology is and how it can be used in e-commerce, as well as the potential barriers and misgivings.

1.4 Further Reading

A collection of papers discussing the impact of technology on our lives and what is yet to come can be found in (Denning and Metcalfe 1997). Although a bit out of date, (Negroponte 1995) still makes very good reading. Rieder (2003) provides an illuminating discussion on the role of agents in a networked society.

More detailed accounts of the history of agents and multi-agent systems are provided in (Ferber 1999) and (Wooldridge 2002) while (Russell and Norvig 2003) provide an overview of the history of AI. Three collections of papers (Huhns 1987, Bond and Gasser 1988, Gasser and Huhns 1989) although now dated, present a thorough account of the issues and problems of DAI.

A number of books discuss e-commerce and e-business technologies in more detail (Stanford-Smith and Kidd 2000, van Slyke and Belanger 2003). In their book (van Slyke and Belanger 2003) discuss the distinction between the two terms, as well as the impact of e-commerce and e-business on organizations and individuals. Vulkan (2003) also provides an insightful discussion, albeit from an economist's point of view. The discussion on e-commerce and its impact here is mainly based on these two works.

The papers by Farhoodi and Fingar (1997a,b) present the industry's perspective and provide a convincing account of the role of agent technology in e-commerce and e-business, as well as how we can move from object-oriented to agent-oriented engineering.

1.5 Exercises and Topics for Discussion

1. Discuss the shift in the nature of computation from mere calculation to delegation and interaction. How have the users' perceptions and expectations of computer systems changed in particular in the last few years?

2. Multi-agent systems is a multi-disciplinary research area taking input as well as providing output to a number of other disciplines, some of which are illustrated in Figure 1.1. Can you think of any other disciplines that may be relevant to multi-agent systems research and how? What do you think ethology[1], philosophy and psychology have to contribute to multi-agent systems and vice versa?

3. Discuss how e-commerce impacts on your everyday life as an individual consumer. Is the overall impact on you positive or negative? Why?

4. Consider the potential implications of automating commercial and financial transactions by delegating such tasks to software agents. How comfortable would you feel entrusting the task of booking a flight to a software travel agent who would have access to your credit card details?

---

[1]Ethology is a branch of zoology and is the study of animal behaviour. Ethologists have a special interest in genetically-programmed behaviours, i.e., instincts.

CHAPTER 2

Software Agents

LEARNING OBJECTIVES

After reading and completing this chapter, you should be able to:

- Describe what a software agent is and its main characteristics.
- Distinguish among different types of environments and explain how they impact on agent design and decision-making.
- Explain the process of decision-making for agents.
- Describe and compare the various types of architectures for building software agents and their relative advantages and disadvantages.
- Compare and contrast agent-based systems with other types of software and explain their differences.
- Name current agent-enabling technologies and software engineering methodologies.

The aim of this chapter is to provide a succinct introduction to agents and architectures for building them, as well as an overview of agent-enabling technologies and methodologies. In the simplest form, the term 'agent' as is used in Computer Science describes a piece of software or a combination of software and hardware that acts on behalf of the user. But this in itself does not say much, as all pieces of software (and/or hardware) do something on behalf of the user: they do it faster and more efficiently, this is the purpose of technology in the first place.

The type of agents that we are interested in are more than simple pieces of software. Unfortunately, what exactly is an agent defies a universally accepted definition, despite the area of agents having been active for almost three decades now. Different people have different views as to what exactly an agent may be, and what are its essential characteristics and properties. This stems from the fact that agents are used in a variety of domains with different characteristics and inherently different requirements on the agents' behaviour. For some application domains, the ability to adapt is important, whereas for others this is not a strict requirement. Although it is not the purpose of this book to provide a unique definition, I will briefly discuss various definitions of agents and identify the most important characteristics through them.

2.1 CHARACTERISTICS OF AGENTS

Several researchers have attempted to provide specific definitions of what an agent is, with each definition emphasizing different aspects of agency. The starting point of our discussion will be the well-known definition of (Russell and Norvig 2003, p.32):

> An agent is anything that can be viewed as perceiving its environment through sensors and acting upon that environment through effectors.

This definition is quite generic as, accordingly, anything that can be viewed as perceiving the environment and acting upon it via some form of sensors and effectors, is described as an agent. So a thermostat in a room is an agent: it senses the environment, the temperature in this case, and then it can affect the environment (by turning the heating on or off). These are useful 'agents', but they are not *intelligent* agents.

According to (Huhns and Singh 1997, p.1):

> Agents are active, persistent (software) components that perceive, reason, act and communicate.

This definition provides a clearer idea of what an agent may be and explicitly describes agents as being software components. Also agents are able to perceive, reason, act and communicate. In this sense, the thermostat, is not an agent: it is not a software component, but rather its decision-making mechanism is built into wires and switches. Furthermore, the abilities of the thermostat are rather limited. It may be able to perceive its environment, but it can do so only with respect to one aspect of the environment: the temperature. If someone turns off the light, the thermostat will not be able to perceive this. Nevertheless, this may be important for the functionality of the thermostat itself: switching off the light may mean that the room is no longer occupied and thus there is no reason to have the heating on. But the thermostat has no way of perceiving this or reasoning about its implications. The thermostat can only perform a single action and has no way of communicating with humans or indeed other agents – although someone could argue that the thermostat, by turning on or off the heating, actually manages to convey its intention to keep the temperature at a certain level (see discussion on intentional stance later in this chapter).

Another view along the same lines is that an agent is:

> . . . an entity that functions continuously and autonomously in an environment in which other processes take place and other agents exist. (Shoham 1997, p. 271–2).

A new characteristic added to the notion of agency is that of autonomy, while agents are also described as entities that are situated in an environment, perhaps with other agents, and function continuously in it.

> Autonomous agents are computational systems that inhabit some complex, dynamic environment, sense and act autonomously in this environment, and by doing so realize a set of goals or tasks that they are designed for. (Maes 1995, p. 108).

Autonomy, as well as the environment that the agents inhabit, again feature prominently in this definition. In particular, the environment is described as complex and dynamic and the agents, whilst operating in it, are trying to achieve their design objectives or goals by performing actions.

There are many more definitions in the literature and it would take many more pages to simply note them all down. The definitive list of properties that a piece of software should possess in order to be characterized as an agent is still an issue of debate. Nevertheless, there seems to be a core set of properties that appear to be central to the idea of agency and feature in most definitions (Wooldridge and Jennings 1995).

- **Autonomy**. The concept of autonomy is difficult to pin down. In general, autonomy describes how self-ruled the agent really is. An autonomous agent is one that can interact with its environment without the direct intervention of other agents and has control over its own actions and internal state. The less predictable an agent is, the more autonomous it appears to be to an external observer. However, such absolute autonomy, in the sense of complete unpredictability, is rarely useful in the design of an agent system, as agents typically must serve some purpose which inadvertently constrains them. Full autonomy may even be undesirable; if I instruct my trading agent to book me a flight specifying a maximum budget for the transaction, I would not want it to exceed this budget, simply because it decided to exercise its autonomy. Consequently, some control over the agent's behaviour would be preferable, which may be in terms of design objectives, budget restrictions or other preferences.

An agent that lives, acts and interacts in an environment with other agents may have its autonomy restricted if it has to comply with social norms (Huhns and Singh 1997). Nevertheless, an agent that is sociable and responsible can still be autonomous. It would attempt to coordinate with others when appropriate and honour its commitments. But it would exercise its autonomy in entering into those commitments in the first place. Albeit, an agent exhibiting autonomy may decide not to abide by the social norms and rules, risking being left out.

- **Proactiveness.** An intelligent agent is capable of exhibiting proactive behaviour. We build proactive systems, which are systems capable of teleonomic, goal-directed behaviour when we write functions, procedures or methods in programming languages (Wooldridge 2002). Thus, the design objectives to be satisfied are built into the system. When we write a procedure, we describe the preconditions which the procedure needs to satisfy in order to be executed, as well as the effect of the execution of the procedure or, in other words, the postconditions. If the preconditions are met and the procedure executes correctly, then the postconditions specified will be true. This is goal-directed behaviour in its simplest form. Intelligent agents are expected to have their own goals either built in or specified during run-time by the user and they attempt to accomplish them by taking the initiative, planning courses of action and having appropriate alternatives to various situations.

- **Reactiveness.** Simply exhibiting goal-directed behaviour is not enough, as such behaviour may be a necessary but not a sufficient condition (in most cases) for 'smart' behaviour to ensue. Goal-directness, as epitomized via the execution of a simple procedure, has two inherent limitations (Wooldridge 2002). First, it assumes that, while the procedure is executing, the preconditions remain valid, i.e., the environment does not change. Second, it also presupposes that the goal and the conditions for pursuing this goal (and thus executing the procedure), remain valid at least until the procedure terminates. Both these assumptions are not realistic in complex, dynamic and inherently uncertain environments in which other agents may perform actions that can change the state of the world while an agent is executing. Therefore, agents should not only blindly attempt to achieve their own goals, but they should be able to perceive their environment and the changes that occur in it and respond accordingly. Changes in the environment may actually affect the agent's own goals and limit the available options and courses of action that it can take in order to satisfy them. Building a system that simply responds to the changes that occur in the environment is not difficult. However, what turns out to be incredibly difficult is to build an agent that strikes the right balance between seeking to satisfy its own goals, while at the same time reacting to the environment. We do not want an agent continuously reacting to the environment and constantly replanning how to achieve its own goals: the agent may end up spending all of its time and computational resources simply replanning without actually doing anything. On the other hand, an agent which blindly attempts to execute a goal while the reasons for such a goal may no longer be relevant is barely a useful or smart agent.

- **Social ability**. Agents may live and act in an environment along with other agents, human or artificial. Although computer systems communicate every day in a more mundane way by exchanging millions of bits, true social ability is much more complex than that. Social ability means being able to operate in a multi-agent environment and coordinate, cooperate, negotiate and even compete with others in order to achieve one's objectives. Coordinating with other agents even though they may not share exactly the same goals, negotiating and reaching complex agreements with them requires very complex skills. This social dimension of the notion of agency must address many difficult situations which are not yet fully understood, even in the context of human social behaviour.

2.2 AGENTS AS INTENTIONAL SYSTEMS

The term 'agent', as will be used in the rest of the text, describes a software system that is capable of independent action and rational behaviour in an open and often unpredictable environment. This implies that such systems are highly complex and trying to understand and analyze their behaviour in a natural, intuitive and efficient way, is a nontrivial task. For instance, trying to analyze the behaviour of an intelligent agent which is responsible for patient monitoring by making reference to its hardware and software elements and how the content of the memory registers changes over time may be possible, but it is also strenuous, impractical and may not even provide any insight as to why the agent behaves the way it does. Sometimes it is more convenient and practical to describe the actions and the reasons for action of a particular system by adopting methods that abstract us away from its mechanistic and design details.

A convenient way of determining a complex system's behaviour is by ascribing to it mental attitudes such as knowledge, beliefs, desires, goals and obligations. Thus, the system is described as an *intentional* one and its behaviour is interpreted in terms of folk psychology (Dennett 1987, Newell 1982). The legitimacy of such an attribution of human mentalistic characteristics to machines (anthropomorphism) is controversial. But as McCarthy explains (McCarthy 1979, p.161):

> To ascribe certain 'beliefs', 'knowledge', 'free will', 'intentions', 'consciousness', 'abilities' or 'wants' to a machine or computer program is legitimate when such an ascription expresses the same information about the machine that it expresses about a person. It is useful when the ascription helps us understand the structure of the machine, its past or future behaviour, or how to repair or improve it.

Despite any potential misgivings, the intentional stance does seem to provide us with a powerful abstraction tool. In particular, it seems to work very well when used to describe the behaviour of systems whose structure is unknown, or when other methods, such as the physical and the design or even the biological stance, are not practically available or do not offer any real insight into the functions of the system. Returning to the patient monitoring agent, it seems more intuitive to say that the agent notified the doctor because it believed that the temperature of the patient started rising, than to say that the doctor was notified because at cycle t_{1000} the content of a particular register was 11101001.

In accordance with the intentional stance, computer systems or programs are treated as rational agents. An agent possesses knowledge or beliefs about the world it inhabits, it has desires and intentions and it is capable of performing a set of actions. The behaviour of the agent is then explained by the principle of rationality, that is the agent, using practical reasoning and based on its information about the world (knowledge or beliefs) and its chosen desires and intentions, will select an action which will lead to the achievement of one of its goals.

2.3 MAKING DECISIONS

Ultimately we would like software agents to be 'smart' enough so that tasks can be delegated to them and they can then make decisions and take actions so as to successfully bring about these tasks. Being able to make good decisions is essential in any domain or environment, but in particular in the context of electronic markets that we will be considering in this book, where an agent needs to remain within a set budget, or carry out profitable transactions for its user. But, endowing an agent with the ability to make good decisions is a nontrivial issue and it depends on a number of factors, including the kind of environment in which the agent operates.

2.3.1 Environments

An intelligent agent is typically situated with other similar, or not, agents in an environment. The most simple view of an agent is given in Figure 2.1. The agent perceives the environment and the changes that occur in it through the sensory information that it obtains, and in turn it affects the environment through actions which are the result of its decision-making process.

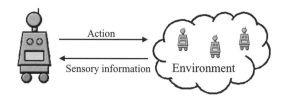

Figure 2.1: An agent and the interaction with its environment

From an abstract point of view, the environment can be regarded as being in a particular state s at each point in time. The set of states $S = \{s_1, s_2, \ldots\}$ that the environment can be in are called the environment or world states. As an agent perceives its environment through its sensors, the sensory function *see* maps environment states into percepts:

$$see : S \rightarrow P$$

An agent can be in a particular internal state and the set of internal states is indicated by *IS*. This internal state or memory of the agent is updated through a function *next* which is a mapping from internal states and percepts to internal states:

$$next : IS \times P \rightarrow IS$$

An agent can then be viewed as performing a set of actions $A = \{a_1, a_2, \ldots\}$ through which it affects its environment. Hence, an action is a function from internal states to actions:

$$action : IS \rightarrow A$$

The effects of the agent's actions are captured by a function *do* which maps an action performed in a particular state into the resulting state:

$$do : A \times S \rightarrow S$$

Consequently, an agent decides what actions to perform based upon a sequence of environment states, which intuitively represent the experience that the agent has accumulated so far. According to this simple view, the control loop of an agent program would appear as follows:

```
// control loop for Simple-Agent
begin
    IS:=IS_0; // initial internal state
    while true do
        p:=get-percept();
        IS:=update(IS,p);
        action:=choose-best-action(IS);
        execute(action);
    end-while
end
```

The agent's internal state **IS** is updated given the new percept **p** and the old internal state. The best action **action** is then selected based on the new internal state and subsequently it is executed. This agent has an explicit representation of the world built into its **IS**, in other words it has a world model. There are other types of agents that do not have such an internal representation of the world and thus there is no world model that needs to be updated (Genesereth and Nilsson 1987). Instead, a percept is mapped directly into an action.

The characteristics of the environment have a direct impact on the design of an agent and its decision-making process. Intrinsically, the nature of the environment imposes constraints on an agent's behaviour and prescribes the properties and attributes that the agent needs to possess to be successful in this environment. According to Russell and Norvig (2003) the environment can be characterized as:

- **Fully observable or partially observable.** Observability intuitively describes access to information about the current state of the world. In a fully observable environment, an agent has complete access to its state and can also perceive all changes as they occur in it. Practically speaking, this is impossible in most realistic environments as uncertainty is inevitably present and an agent may not be able to perceive or have access to all information that is relevant to its own goals and decision-making. A good agent, as we will see in this chapter, is an agent that always does the right thing, namely it always chooses and performs the best action. But to be able to always do the right thing, one needs accurate information about the current state of the world. The more complete the information about the state of the world, the easier it is for the agent to identify the best action to perform. If little or insufficient information is available, i.e., the environment is only partially observable, the agent may not be able to choose the right action, and as a consequence it may not be successful in bringing about its goal.

  Partial observability could be attributed to noise in the agent's sensors or perceptual aliasing (Vlassis 2003). In the former case, if for instance the agent's sensors are malfunctioning, the same state may generate different perceptions at different times. In the latter case, different states may produce identical perceptions at different times, e.g., two cars may look exactly the same to the agent. As a result, it is easier to build agents for fully observable environments, whereas partially observable environments are more complex to deal with. Furthermore, partial observability is an important issue in multi-agent systems as it affects not only what an agent knows about the world, but also what it knows about the other agents' knowledge.

- **Deterministic or stochastic.** In a deterministic environment the next state is completely determined by the current state and the actions performed by the agent. To put it simply, the outcome or effect of any action performed by the agent is uniquely defined. If there is no doubt about the effect of an action performed by the agent, then there is no need to stop and reconsider its goals or course of action to achieve them. However, most realistic environments are stochastic; the agent has limited control over the environment, including other agents. Therefore, in a stochastic environment an agent appears as having a *limited sphere of influence* (Wooldridge 2002) and the effects of its actions are not known in advance. Instead, there is a random element that decides how the world changes as a result of an action, and an agent's actions can even fail. Clearly, stochasticity further complicates the design of agents.

- **Static or dynamic.** In a static environment, the world only changes by the performance of actions by the agent itself. This in turn means that, if an agent perceives the environment at time t_0 and performs no action between t_0 and t_1, then the environment will not change. However, in a dynamic environment the world constantly changes and thus it cannot be guaranteed that the state of the world at time t_1 will be the same.

Therefore, the agent needs to continuously gather information in order to determine the best possible action according to the situation at hand. Even while the agent is executing an action with a precondition p that holds true before the execution, p may not hold true at some point during the execution. In dynamic environments, the outcome of an agent's own actions cannot be guaranteed to be the desired one as other agents, and the environment itself which can be thought of as simply another agent, may interfere.

It is inherently more complex and more difficult to design and implement agents for dynamic environments. In a static environment, an agent need only do information gathering once, whereas in a dynamic environment, this needs to be done often enough so as to guarantee that the agent always has up-to-date information about the state of the world to enable it to choose the best action possible. How often this needs to be done depends on the particular environment and its rate of change, namely how fast the environment changes. Finally, in a dynamic environment, an agent needs to take into account the other agents present and synchronize or coordinate its actions with theirs in order to avoid interference and conflicts.

- **Episodic or sequential**. In an episodic environment, a cycle of perception and then action is considered to be a separate episode. The performance of the agent depends only on the episode itself and there is no connection between the performance of the agent in different episodes. Thus, an agent need not worry about the effects of its actions on subsequent episodes, as these are unrelated. Agents operating in episodic environments need not think ahead, they only have to decide the best course of action given the current episode. An example of an episodic environment is taxi driving. Each trip is a separate episode and does not affect the next one. The agent need only worry about the best move (route) in the current trip as this does not affect its course of action in the next one. However, if one looks at the individual trips, then the environment appears to be sequential, i.e., each decision made, for instance which road to take, affects the next decision. Therefore at times, how an environment is characterized depends on the level of abstraction. Chess is an example of a sequential environment: the performance of the agent within a game is affected by every move that it performs, and a move now will have an effect on the agent's position later on.

- **Discrete or continuous**. In a discrete environment, there is a fixed, finite number of actions and percepts, while in a continuous environment the number of states may be infinitely long. Chess and driving a car are examples of a discrete and a continuous environment respectively. In a game of chess there is a finite number of states, while in driving a car the speed and location of the car and the other vehicles have a range of continuous values. In principle, in finite discrete state environments, it is feasible to enumerate all possible states and the optimal action to perform in each of these. However, such an approach to agent design and implementation is impractical.

- **Single-agent or multi-agent**. Essentially, in a single-agent environment there is only one agent operating, whereas in a multi-agent one there are many agents that interact with each other. Nevertheless, one needs to be careful with this simple distinction.

There may be circumstances in which objects that we would not normally consider as agents, may have to be modelled as such. For instance, it is very often the case that Nature needs to be modelled as an agent within a system, as chance events may affect the environment and thus the agent that operates in it. A useful way to determine which objects need to be characterized or modelled as agents is to consider whether or not they affect or influence the behaviour of the agent under consideration. Whether in a competitive or a cooperative environment, any other object that affects an agent and the successful achievement of its goals needs to be regarded as another agent.

Clearly, the most complex general class of environments are those that are partially observable, stochastic, dynamic, sequential, continuous and multi-agent. Such environments are often referred to as *open* (Hewitt 1986).

2.3.2 Performance measure and rationality

The idea of having an intelligent agent do things on our behalf is very attractive: all we have to do is simply tell it what we want, and then the agent being autonomous, proactive, reactive and social, will find a way to achieve the goal. The objective is to design and develop agents that perform well in their environments. How can we measure how well an agent is doing, how successful it is? A good or successful agent is obviously one that always does the right thing, but then how do we define the right thing? The term performance measure is used to indicate how successful an agent is, i.e., the set of criteria that determine its success. There are two aspects to measuring performance: *how* and *when* (Russell and Norvig 2003).

Clearly, different performance measures will have to be used for different types of agents. For trading agents operating in the stock exchange market, one possible performance measure could be how successful their portfolios are, how much profit they have made, how many clients they have, etc. For a vacuum-cleaning agent, the performance measure can be how much dirt it has managed to clean or how fast it can clean a particular area. We could presumably ask human agents how happy or how successful they are, perhaps in terms of wealth accumulation, or even social status. This is a subjective performance measure, and as it turns out it can be highly unreliable as human agents lie or misrepresent their performance measure. We cannot use such a subjective performance measure for software agents, as we cannot really ask them how successful they feel they are. Instead an objective performance measure is required, one that is defined by us, as external observers, to establish a standard of what it means for an agent to be successful in an environment (Russell and Norvig 2003).

When performance is evaluated is also very important. When do you assess the success of a trading agent in the stock exchange, after an hour of operation, a day, a year or ten years? If you measure its performance after an hour, the agent may be deemed unsuccessful, but if you let it operate in the market for a year and then evaluate its performance the results may be quite different. Performance can be measured continually, periodically, or one-shot.

One possible way to measure how well an agent is doing is by assessing whether or not it has achieved its goals. If we take the vacuum-cleaning agent for instance, one possible way of measuring its success is to check if it has achieved its goal, i.e., to clean a particular area. In order for an agent to satisfy its goals, whether these are formulated on the fly or are pre-defined, it may have to do some complicated reasoning, including planning a sequence of actions that will lead it to achieve its goals. As there may be a number of different sequences of actions that will enable the agent to achieve its goals, in certain cases goal achievement may not indicate a successful performance. Returning to our example, the vacuum-cleaning agent, depending on which route it follows around a particular area, may finish vacuum cleaning within 30 minutes or one hour. A good performance measure should allow the comparison of different world states (or sequences of states).

Since there may be a number of different sequences of actions that will enable an agent to achieve a particular goal, agents have preferences over different goal states. For instance, an agent bidding in an auction prefers a state in which it wins and acquires the item, although it prefers states in which it wins the auction and it does not have to pay its true valuation but a much lower price. One way to formalize the notion of preference over states is to associate with each state s a utility[1] $u(s)$ for each particular agent. The utility of a state is a real number which in essence indicates the desirability of that state for the agent: the larger the utility of s, the better that state for the agent. For two distinct states s and s', agent i prefers s to s' if and only if $u(s) > u(s')$, while the agent is indifferent between the two states if and only if $u(s) = u(s')$. In a multi-agent system though, a state that may be good for one agent, may, at the same time, be undesirable to another one; winning an auction is typically unpleasant to one's opponents. The objective of the agent then is to bring about states of the environment that maximize its utility. Thus, an agent needs to choose its next action from a set of actions in such a way so that it gains the maximum utility. But in a stochastic environment, the performance of an action may bring about any one of a number of different outcomes. The expected utility $EU(a)$ of an action a is calculated by multiplying the utility of each possible resulting state with the probability of indeed reaching this state and then summing up the terms:

$$EU(a) = \sum_{s'} P(s'|s, a) u(s')$$

where $P(s'|s, a)$ is the probability[2] of reaching state s' when action a is performed in s. This is the expected utility of an action a given the agent's current situation. The agent

---

[1]Utilities and preferences are examined in more detail in Chapter 7 and they are also discussed in the context of decision theory in Appendix A.

[2]Readers who are not familiar with the concepts and notation of probability theory are referred to Appendix A.

then chooses to perform the action a^* which has the maximum expected utility. The principle of Maximum Expected Utility (MEU) takes the form:

$$a^* = \arg \max_{a \in A} \sum_{s'} P(s'|s, a)u(s')$$

Having a complete specification of the utility function allows rational decisions when (Russell and Norvig 2003):

- There are conflicting goals, only some of which can be accomplished; the utility function indicates the appropriate tradeoff.

- There are several goals that the agent can endeavour to achieve, but none of which can be achieved with certainty; the utility provides a way in which the likelihood of success can be evaluated against the importance of the goals.

This leads us to the definition of an ideal rational agent:

> **Definition 1** *An ideal rational agent performs actions that are expected to maximize its performance measure.*

What is rational at any given time depends on:

- the performance measure that determines the degree of success
- everything that the agent has perceived so far
- what the agent expects to perceive and happen in the future
- what the agent knows about the environment
- the actions that the agent can perform.

A rational agent should, for each possible percept sequence, do whatever actions will maximize its performance measure based on the percept sequence, and its built-in and acquired knowledge. However, in deciding the best action, the agent will have to make use of computational power, memory and of course computation takes time. In this sense, all agents are resource-bounded and this has an impact on their decision-making process. Given that in any realistic environment an agent will have to decide on an action within a reasonable amount of time and its resources are limited, optimal decision-making may not be possible. Therefore, ideal rationality may be difficult to achieve. Alternatively, bounded rationality can be accepted and thus restrictions on the types of options are imposed; the time/computation for option consideration is limited or the search space is pruned. The option selected is inevitably strategically inferior to the one that would have been produced under ideal rationality and it may be far from optimal.

2.3.3 Rational decision-making and optimal policies

From the previous discussion we can surmise that the successful performance of an agent is inextricably linked with the type of environment in which the agent operates. Assume an agent is situated in an environment where there may be other agents operating as well. Time can be measured in discrete time points $T = \{1, 2, \ldots\}$. The environment is in a particular state s_t at time t and the set of all possible environment or world states is denoted by S. At each time point the agent perceives its environment through a percept p_t which encapsulates information about the state of the world. Subsequently, the agent affects its environment by choosing and performing an action a_t from a finite set of actions A. In this setting, a *policy* π is a complete mapping from states to actions. Thus, given a state, the policy tells the agent what action to perform.

To decide on the best action to perform, it seems reasonable to suggest that an agent's policy should take into account both information about the past as well as about the future (Vlassis 2003). Information about the past is contained in the history of percept-action pairs (p_t, a_t). Thus, for an agent to take into account the past history, its policy should map the complete history of percept-action pairs up to time point t to an optimal action a_t:

$$\pi((p_1, a_1), (p_2, a_2), \ldots, p_t) = a_t$$

But defining and implementing such a policy is problematic. First, the complete history of percept-action pairs may be very large and thus it may be difficult to store the entire sequence, and second, even if the agent has a large enough memory to store all percept-action pairs, computing the policy π from a computational complexity point of view would be nontrivial.

In some problem domains, the state of the world at time t provides a complete description of the history before t, and thus the agent need not take into account its entire history in its decision-making process. In such a fully observable environment the current percept p_t provides the agent with complete information about the current state, in other words, $s_t = p_t$. This, in turn, means that the agent, through the percept p_t, obtains all the information that is necessary in order to decide on the optimal action. Such a world state that encapsulates all relevant information about the past in a particular task is said to be Markov or to have the Markov property. An agent's policy then is a mapping from the current percept to an action $\pi(p_t) = a_t$ or, alternatively, from the current world state to an action $\pi(s_t) = a_t$. Such an agent, which ignores its entire past history except for the last percept, is called reactive, and its policy reactive or memoryless.

Optimal decision-making should take into account not only the past but the future as well, i.e., what the agent expects to happen after t. In a discrete world, as the agent performs an action a at each time point, the world changes as a result of this at the next time point. A *transition model* or a *world model* $T(s, a, s')$, describes how the world s changes as a result of an action a being performed. If the environment is deterministic, namely the next state is completely determined by the current state and the actions performed by the agent, the transition model simply maps a state-action pair (s, a) to a single resulting state s'. On the other hand, if the world is stochastic, there is uncertainty with regard to the resulting state. In this case, the transition model maps a state-action pair (s, a) to a probability distribution $P(s'|s, a)$ over states where s' is a random variable that can take all possible values in S, each with probability $P(s'|s, a)$, in other words $T(s, a, s') \equiv P(s'|s, a)$.

In a deterministic world, planning an optimal policy through a state space that would lead to the accomplishment of a goal, can be reduced to a graph search problem for which a number of approaches exist (Russell and Norvig 2003). But in a stochastic world, planning by simple graph search is not applicable since there is uncertainty about the transitions between states. This uncertainty needs to be taken into account in determining the optimal policy. The problem of calculating an optimal policy in a fully observable, stochastic environment with a transition model that satisfies the Markov property, i.e., the transitions depend only on the current state and not its history, is called a Markov decision problem (MDP).

In a partially observable environment, the percept p_t provides limited information about the environment and the agent cannot determine in which state the world really is. This inadvertently affects its decision-making process. A Partially Observable Markov Decision Problem (POMDP) is the problem of calculating an optimal policy in a partially observable environment. In this case, instead of maintaining the current state, the agent's incomplete information about the world can be modelled in terms of a distribution of conditional probabilities over S which is called the belief state. The set of all possible belief states forms the belief space. The optimal policy of a POMDP problem is a function $\pi(b)$ where b is the belief state. Methods used for solving MDP problems are not directly applicable to POMDP problems.

2.3.4 Optimal policies in MDPs

Given a Markov decision problem, one can calculate a policy from the transition model, i.e., the probabilities, and the utility function. Indeed, since each state of the world has a corresponding utility value, the agent can compute an optimal action. Consider a stochastic, but for simplicity single-agent, world with transition model $P(s'|s, a)$. The agent should choose an optimal action a^* such that this action maximizes its expected utility:

$$a^* = \arg \max_{a \in A} \sum_{s'} P(s'|s, a)u(s')$$

If $u^*(s)$ is a set of optimal utilities and, since the transition model is known, we are in a position to calculate the optimal policy as follows:

$$\pi^*(s) = \arg \max_a \sum_{s'} P(s'|s, a)u^*(s')$$

But to be able to compute the optimal policy we need to know the utilities of all states.

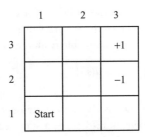

Figure 2.2: The grid world problem

Consider the grid world of Figure 2.2 (adapted from Russell and Norvig 2003). The agent can move around this world by choosing one of the actions {North (↑), South (↓), West (←), East (→)}. Bumping into the walls does not change the position of the agent. The environment is fully observable, i.e., the agent always knows where it is. The initial position of the agent is (1,1) and there are two terminal states, a desired and an undesired one, marked +1 and −1 respectively. If the environment is deterministic, then each time the agent performs an action the outcome of the action is guaranteed to be the intended one. If the environment is stochastic, there is an element of uncertainty with regard to the outcome of the agent's actions: every action to an intended direction succeeds with probability 0.8, but with probability 0.2 the agent moves at right angles towards the intended direction. For example, if the agent is in state (2,1) and performs the action North, it may reach the intended state (3,1) with probability 0.8, but it may also reach state (2,2) with probability 0.1 or bump into the wall and remain in the same state with probability 0.1.

In this problem, the calculation of an optimal policy is complicated by the fact that the only utilities known are those for the terminal states. Clearly, the utility of a state depends on where you can get from that state. As a consequence we have to base the utility function on a state sequence $u([s_0, \ldots, s_n])$ instead of a single state, i.e., an environment history. Moreover, as we want to be able to use utilities in the context of the MEU principle, we require that the utility function of a state sequence has the property of separability. A utility function $u([s_0, \ldots, s_n])$ is separable if we can find a function f such that:

$$u([s_0, \ldots, s_n]) = f(s_0, u([s_1, \ldots, s_n]))$$

An example of a separable utility function is the additive:

$$u([s_0, \ldots, s_n]) = R(s_0) + u([s_1, \ldots, s_n])$$

where $R(s_0)$ is called the reward function. Suppose the immediate reward for each of the nonterminal states in the grid world is −0.04 which can be perceived as the cost of moving from one square to another.

As the utility of a state depends on the utilities of a sequence of states, therefore, the utility $u(s)$ of state s is defined as being the reward value for that state, plus the maximum expected utility of the state sequences possible from that state:

$$u(s) = R(s) + \max_{a \in A} \sum_{s'} [P(s'|s,a)u(s')]$$

Put differently, the utility of a state is the immediate reward of the state plus the value of the best action which represents a history, or a state sequence. In order to generate a history, the utility equation above is used iteratively so that the rewards of the terminal states can be propagated out through all the other states, thus resulting in a history from each state to each terminal state. The above equation is also known as the Bellman equation (Bellman 1957) and forms the basis of dynamic programming. In dynamic programming, the problem of calculating the utilities is formulated as an n-step decision problem, where the states reached after n steps are considered to be terminal states. First the utilities at step $n - 1$ are calculated in terms of the terminal state utilities. The calculation of the utilities at step $n - 2$ follows, and so on. Although dynamic programming gives exact utility values right away, it can be quite costly in large state spaces.

Two other methods for calculating optimal policies in MDPs are value iteration and policy iteration (Russell and Norvig 2003). Both of these methods try to modify the utilities of the neighbouring states in such a way so that they will satisfy the utility equations. If this local update process is repeated at each state in the state space, and provided that a sufficient number of iterations are performed, the utilities of the individual states will eventually converge to static values. Starting with a transition model and a reward function, the idea underlying the value iteration method is to calculate a utility for each state, and then to use these utilities to create a policy. In contrast, the idea behind the policy iteration method is to start with some policy, and then to repeatedly calculate the utility function for that policy, and then use it to calculate a new policy, and so on. The second method exploits the fact that the policy often converges long before the utility function does. A detailed description of the value and policy iteration methods can be found in Russell and Norvig (2003).

Let us now return to the grid world problem. The immediate reward function in this world is -0.04 for the non-terminal states and $+1$ and -1 for the two terminal states respectively. Using the value iteration method the final utilities have been calculated and are shown in Figure 2.3 (a). As the utilities, actions and transition model are known we can now calculate the optimal policy which is shown in Figure 2.3 (b). Note that the suggested policy in state (2,2) is to move West and not North which could presumably bring the agent closer to the desired state. However, by performing the action North the agent could accidentally end up in the undesired terminal state -1, whereas the action West avoids this risky situation.

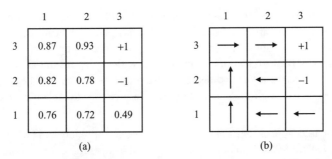

Figure 2.3: The grid world problem: (a) utilities; (b) optimal policy

2.4 PLANNING

Planning is a key ability for intelligent behaviour as it increases an agent's flexibility, enabling it to construct sequences of actions to achieve its goals. Intuitively, planning is deciding *what* to do. Goals that are delegated to software agents may be quite complex and not necessarily achievable by executing a single action. Thus, to solve a goal intelligently, an agent needs to consider what it will do now and in the future. Planning is closely related to scheduling as the later is deciding *when* to do an action.

Planning can be thought of as determining all the small tasks that must be carried out in order to accomplish a goal. The agent may have to plan a number of tasks and achieve a number of subgoals in order to bring about the desired state of affairs. For instance, consider the goal: 'Arrange a weekend trip to Paris' being delegated to a software agent. This goal involves a number of subgoals and tasks that need to be performed in order to be considered as successfully completed. Such planning problems are certainly nontrivial and they involve search and problem-solving strategies, task or goal decomposition and the use of knowledge representation schemes. Hence, an agent will have to figure out a list of steps and subsequent actions that it will have to perform to reach a state in which it will have successfully arranged a weekend trip to Paris. Among such actions may be to enquire travel agents for tickets and hotels, visit auction sites and bid in auctions that provide goods or services of interest.

There have been a number of different approaches that attempt to solve the problem of planning:

- **Logic-based approaches.** Such planning algorithms take as input descriptions in a formal language such as first-order logic. States and goals are represented as sets of sentences and actions are represented by logical descriptions of preconditions and effects. In this way the planning algorithm can make direct connections between states and actions. One of the best known logic-based approaches to planning is Situation Calculus which reduces planning to a first-order implication proof.

- **Case-based approaches.** In case-based planning (CBP), previously generated plans are stored as cases and can be reused to solve similar planning problems in the future. Thus, given a new problem, a goal and a description of an initial state, the agent looks in the library of plans to identify a similar case, with analogous initial and goal states. The plan retrieved is then modified to suit the new problem. The key to CBP is to find good similarity metrics. Such techniques can save considerable time over planning from scratch.

- **Operator-based approaches.** The best-known such approach is STRIPS (Fikes and Nilsson 1971) In STRIPS, actions are represented as operators, which consist of three components: the action description which is the name of the operator; the precondition, which is a conjunction of atoms (positive literals) that assert what must be true before the operator is applied; and the effect of an operator, which is a conjunction of literals (positive or negative) that describe how the situation changes after the application of the operator. An operator can be applied if all the preconditions are true, and following its application all the effects that are specified in the respective component are true.

- **Planning as search.** Planning can be regarded as conducting a search through a space of possibilities. There are two main approaches:
  - **Situation space search.** A situation space planner searches through the space of possible situations. The planning problem is to find a path from the initial state to the goal state. There are two methods:
    1. **Progression.** The planner searches forward from the initial situation to the goal situation.
    2. **Regression.** The planner searches backward from the goal state by finding actions the effects of which satisfy one or more of the posted goals, and then posting the chosen action's preconditions as goals (goal regression).
  - **Plan space search.** A plan space planner searches through the space of possible plans. One can search for a plan with a totally-ordered sequence of actions (total order planning), or a plan with a partially-ordered set of actions (partial-order planning or least-commitment planning).

Apart from individual planning, agents that work together as members of multi-agent systems need to formulate joint plans to achieve a complex goal or perform a difficult task (Durfee 1999).

2.5 LEARNING

Learning is important in the open, dynamic and constantly evolving environments that electronic marketplaces are. An agent may have to learn, for example, how a new negotiation protocol works, adapt to changing trends in the marketplace or learn from other agents and modify its behaviour to better respond to their strategies in order to maximize its utility.

Learning refers to the process of acquiring knowledge, skills, or attitudes through experience, imitation, or teaching, which then causes changes in the behaviour. An agent learns whenever it changes its structure, code or data in such a manner that its future performance improves (Nilsson 1996).

Learning has a prominent role in AI and there are several reasons why the ability to learn is important. First, if we succeed in endowing agents and other software systems with the ability to learn, this might offer us important insights into how we humans and other animals learn. Second, most of the time it is impractical or even impossible to specify agent systems correctly and completely at the time of design and implementation. This presupposes that a designer/developer knows in advance in what type of environment an agent will be operating, how this environment is likely to change, what other entities will be present and all the possible ways in which they could potentially interact with and affect the system currently under consideration. This difficulty can be alleviated if agents are endowed with the ability to learn and thus adapt to their environment. Third, it may not be practical to design and build into the agent all intelligence in advance. For some tasks, although we may only be able to specify input/output pairs, the precise relationship between these may not be known or easy to formulate. Nevertheless, we would like agents to be able to approximate the desired outputs when provided with an adequate number of examples. Fourth, it is possible that there are hidden important relationships and correlations among huge amounts of data which may not be easy to discern. Machine learning methods can often identify these relationships and extract patterns. Another reason is that it is often the case that the systems produced do not work as well as desired or expected in the environments in which they are used. As often happens, during the design and development stage, not all of the environment's characteristics are known. Learning techniques can be used to improve the functionality and performance of systems already in operation. In some cases, although knowledge about certain tasks may already be available, it may simply be too large to be explicitly encoded in a system by humans. Agents that learn this knowledge gradually might be able to capture more of it than humans would be able to encode. Let us also not forget that agents may be operating in a dynamic environment which constantly changes. In this sense, any initial knowledge and skills encoded into the agent at the development phase with time will become useless or out-of-date as the environment changes. For an agent to continue to be successful, it needs to be able to adapt to the constant changes within the environment. Furthermore, although the agent may have been designed with one task in mind, the nature of the task might change or the nature of the environment may change in such a way that it demands changes to the agent's goals. Responding to these changes can only be achieved in practical terms if systems are endowed with the ability to learn and adapt, and not through constant system redesign.

Learning takes place as a result of the interaction between an agent and the environment and from observing one's own decision-making process. Such environments may also include other agents (multi-agent systems). Agents can learn on their own (isolated or centralized learning) or they can learn in conjunction with others (Sen and Weiss 1999). Learning with others can take many forms, such as cooperative learning, social learning, etc., or, as is often mentioned, decentralized or interactive learning. To be more specific, centralized learning refers to learning that is being done by a single agent and does not require any interaction with other agents, that is, the agent acts as if it is on its own. In decentralized or interactive learning, on the other hand, several agents are engaged in the learning process. Decentralized learning can occur in different ways, for instance, all agents may be learning in parallel or, by interacting with each other, they may be learning the same or different things, etc.

Learning is primarily characterized by the method used to achieve learning and the form that the feedback provided to the learner (if any) takes (Sen and Weiss 1999). The learning method can take the following forms:

- **Learning through knowledge acquisition (rote, memorization)**. One can learn through acquiring and storing knowledge without any further processing of this knowledge.
- **Learning from instruction and through advice taking**. Knowledge acquired in this way needs to be transformed, operationalized and internalized to be used effectively.
- **Learning from examples and by practice**. Humans are able to classify things in the world by way of being presented with positive and negative examples without knowing explicit rules. Such methods usually involve a trainer or instructor to aid and oversee the learning process.
- **Learning by analogy**. If an agent can recognize similarities in information already stored, then it may be able to transfer some knowledge to improve the solution of a similar, but unsolved, task.
- **Learning through problem-solving**. When engaging in problem-solving, one may learn from the experience. The next time a similar problem arises, it can be solved more efficiently. This process does not usually involve gathering new knowledge, but may involve reorganization of data or remembering how to reach a solution.
- **Learning by discovery**. One learns independently from a teacher by gathering new knowledge and skills on one's own, by making observations, generating and testing hypotheses or theories and performing experiments. This is the most difficult type of learning to implement in software agents.

The learner may be provided with some form of feedback in order to improve the learning process:

- In supervised learning, the feedback specifies the desired activity and the objective is to match this desired action as closely as possible.
- In reinforcement learning, the feedback only specifies the utility of the learner's activity and the goal is to maximize this utility.
- In unsupervised learning, no explicit feedback is provided and the objective is to learn useful and desired skills, and activities or acquire knowledge through a process of trial and error.

A number of machine-learning algorithms have been developed in the literature. However, an extended discussion of these methods is beyond the scope of this book.

2.6 AGENT ARCHITECTURES

Thus far, agents have been described more from an abstract point of view. In the following sections we will look at agent architectures and how agents can be built.

2.6.1 Logic-based architecture

The logic-based architecture is inspired by the 'traditional' symbolic artificial intelligence approach to building intelligent systems (Genesereth and Nilsson 1987). Accordingly, the agent possesses a symbolic representation of its environment and rules on how it should behave and what actions it can take. The behaviour of the system is then generated by syntactic manipulation of the symbolic representations. The symbolic representations are usually in the form of logical formulas and then syntactic manipulation corresponds to logical deduction or theorem proving.

The idea of agents as theorem provers is very attractive (Wooldridge 2002). Suppose there is some theory ϕ that explains how an agent should behave, how goals are generated, and how the agent can take action to satisfy them. This theory could be viewed as the agent's specification. In traditional software engineering one would have to take this specification and, through a series of refinements, create the design and finally proceed to the implementation of the agent. But in logic-based agent architectures no such intermediate steps are required, the theory ϕ can be executed directly to produce the agent's behaviour.

Building on the notation introduced in Section 2.3.1, the agent's internal state is now described by a knowledge base of sentences in a logical language such as first-order predicate calculus. Let $\mathcal{L}$ be the set of sentences in first-order logic that describe an environment and let $\mathcal{KB} = \mathcal{P}(\mathcal{L})$ be the set of sets (powerset) of $\mathcal{L}$. The internal state of an agent at every time point is then an element of $\mathcal{KB}$ which is denoted by $KB, KB_1, \dots$. As previously, the set of world states is $S = \{s_1, s_2, \dots\}$ and the agent can perform a set of actions $A = \{a_1, a_2, \dots\}$. The agent's sensory function *see* and the function *do*, which capture the effects of its actions on the environment, remain the same.

The knowledge base, which intuitively holds an agent's information about the world, is updated through a function *next* which maps a knowledge base and a percept to a new knowledge base:

$$next : \mathcal{KB} \times P \rightarrow \mathcal{KB}$$

An action is now a function that maps a knowledge base to an action:

$$action : \mathcal{KB} \rightarrow A$$

The agent's decision-making process is modelled through the rules of inference ρ. If the formula ϕ can be proven through the rules of inference ρ and the internal state of the agent KB, then we write $KB \vdash_\rho \phi$. The action that can be performed at each moment in time is defined by the inference rules. The agent programmer will have to encode the inference rules ρ in such a way that, if a formula of the form $Do(a)$, where a is a term that denotes an action, can be proven from the inference rules and the agent's knowledge base, then a is the best action to perform (Wooldridge 2002). The control loop for a logic-based agent would take the following form:

```
// control loop for LogicBased-Agent
begin
     KB:=KB₀; // initial knowledge base
     while true do
          action:=null;
          p:=get-percept();
          KB:=update(KB,p);
          // prove Do(a) from the KB
          for every a ∈ A
               if KB⊢ρ Do(a) then
                    action:=a;
                    break;
               end-if
          end-for
          // if Do(a) cannot be proven, find an action that is consistent with the KB
          if action==null then
               for every a ∈ A
                    if KB⊬ρ ¬Do(a) then
                         action:=a;
                         break;
                    end-if
               end-for
          end-if
          execute(action);
     end-while
end
```

Accordingly, the agent perceives its environment and decides what to do next by taking every one of its available actions a and trying to prove – using its rules of inference and knowledge base – that it can $Do(a)$. If the agent can prove $Do(a)$, a is returned as the action to be executed next. However, if the agent fails to prove $Do(a)$, it attempts to find an action a which is consistent with its knowledge base, that is, it cannot derive $\neg Do(a)$ from the rules of inference and the knowledge base. If such an action can be determined, then this is returned as the action to be executed next, otherwise the action returned is null.

The Maze World

Suppose that we would like to build an agent for the Maze World depicted in Figure 2.4 (this example has been adapted from Genesereth and Nilsson (1987) and Wooldridge (2002)). In this world, an agent has the task of moving around a two-dimensional grid in order to find a stack of gold, collect it and then get it to the exit (2,2). If we want to develop such an agent using the logic-based architecture, we have to encode the world in some logical language that would then allow us to apply rules of inference. In this example, the knowledge base of the agent consists of logical formulas in classical first-order logic. The agent is equipped with a sensor which returns the percept *gold* in the presence of gold or the percept *null* indicating no special information. The agent can perceive its position in the grid and also has a sense of its direction which can be North, South, East or West. The environment is partially observable as the agent can only sense what is in the square that is currently positioned and cannot detect the location of gold in neighbouring squares. The state of the world and the agent are described using the following predicates:

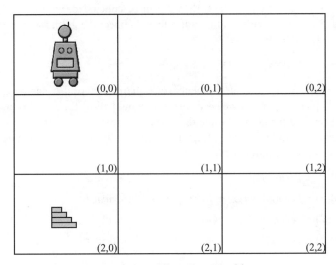

Figure 2.4: The Maze World

In(x, y) the agent is in square with coordinates (x, y).

Gold(x, y) there is gold in square (x, y).

Facing(d) the agent is facing in direction d, where d ∈ {North, South, East, West}.

The agent can pick up the gold when it is co-located in the same square, it can move forward and it can change direction by turning 90° clockwise. If the agent bumps onto the walls, its position remains unchanged. So the repertoire of possible actions is $A = \{pick - up, forward, turn\}$. The function *next* must take the perceptual information from the environment and generate a new knowledge base which includes this information. Of course, old information which is not accurate as it does not represent the current state of the world, must also be deleted from the knowledge base. Let $old(KB)$ denote the set of old information in the knowledge base which we want the function *next* to update and $new(KB, p)$ denote the new information which we want to add. The *next* function is then defined as follows:

$$next(KB, p) = (KB - old(KB)) \cup new(KB, p)$$

For instance, from the knowledge base containing the predicates $In(2, 0)$ and *Facing* (*South*) and the new percept *gold*, the *next* function would generate the new knowledge base which would describe the world by the predicates $In(2, 0)$, $Facing(South)$, $Gold(2, 0)$.

The rules that govern the agent's behaviour have the form $\phi(\ldots) \rightarrow \psi(\ldots)$, where ϕ and ψ are predicates over some arbitrary list of constants and variables. Accordingly, if ϕ matches the agent's knowledge base, then ψ can be concluded, with all variables in ψ instantiated. Since the agent's goal is to locate and collect the gold, the first rule should allow it to do just that:

$$In(x, y) \land Gold(x, y) \rightarrow Do(pick - up)$$

This rule intuitively says that if an agent is in square (x, y) and it has perceived gold, then it should pick it up. Next we need rules that would allow the agent to move around the grid in search of the gold. Assume that the agent always starts at position (0,0) and moves subsequently to (0,1), (0,2), (1,2), (1,1), (1,0), (2,0), (2,1) and terminates in square (2,2). The rules are as follows:

$$In(0, 0) \land Facing(East) \land \neg Gold(0, 0) \rightarrow Do(forward)$$
$$In(0, 1) \land Facing(East) \land \neg Gold(0, 1) \rightarrow Do(forward)$$
$$In(0, 2) \land Facing(East) \land \neg Gold(0, 2) \rightarrow Do(turn)$$
$$In(0, 2) \land Facing(South) \land \neg Gold(0, 2) \rightarrow Do(forward)$$

$\ldots$

In the same way the rest of the rules for the agent's navigation around the Maze can be written. These rules together with the functions *old*, *new*, and *next* will generate the desired behaviour.

Advantages and disadvantages

The advantages of using a logic-based architecture for building agents are evident. If there is a theory ϕ that describes the agent's behaviour, all we have to do is execute this specification. Such an approach is therefore elegant, intuitive and with clear semantics. However, the example discussed here is that of an over-simplified world that can be described in simple rules that are very few in number. Most real-world application domains are far more complex than that.

In building intelligent agents based on the traditional symbolic AI approach, there are two fundamental problems that need to be addressed (Wooldridge 2002): the transduction and the representation/reasoning problems. The former has to do with translating the real world into a precise, detailed and meaningful symbolic model of the world at the right abstraction level and in time for that model to be useful. The latter is the problem of representing information in a symbolic form suitable for the agents to reason with and in time for the results of the reasoning to be useful. Building a robotic agent using a logic-based architecture to explore, locate and collect precious rocks in a terrain, would involve using sensors such as cameras and radars to obtain information from the environment. This input would then have to be transformed in some way into a set of declarative statements that correspond and describe the environment precisely enough for the agent to be able to function in it. How to realize this mapping of the environment onto a set of symbolic percepts is an open issue. Moreover, writing down all the rules that would allow the agent to explore such a complex environment seems unrealistic.

Even if we were able to write down all the rules, we still have a problem. Imagine that at time t_1, as the agent moves around, it perceives a stack of gold in a particular location and applying the rules of inference and using its knowledge base comes up with the optimal action that can be performed, *pick – up*. The problem is that some time will have elapsed from t_1 until the agent's function *action* returns an action at t_2. In this time, call it t_e, the world may have changed and the action that the agent has decided is the optimal one may not be so in the new situation. Perhaps another agent has already picked up the gold, while the agent was trying to prove $Do(pick – up)$ thus, making the action *pick – up* no longer optimal or simply irrelevant. If t_e is infinitesimal, that is, decision-making is instantaneous, we can disregard this problem. However, using theorem proving as the decision-making process for an agent is not infinitesimal. The computational complexity of theorem proving is always a problem and although propositional logic is decidable, first-order predicate calculus is only semi-decidable, which means that even if there is a proof, the theorem prover may fail to terminate. The assumption that the world is not going to change in a significant way while an agent is deliberating what to do is known as *calculative rationality*. But this is not a characteristic of most real-world domains. As a consequence, such architectures are not suitable for building agents to operate in complex and dynamic environments. Finally, representing temporal information, changes in time, and reasoning about them, is very hard using logical formalisms.

2.6.2 Reactive architecture

The logic-based type of architecture is based on the idea that information about the environment and an agent's own objectives and actions are explicitly modelled in the form of logical formulas or relations in an internal knowledge base. Then intelligent behaviour arises by syntactic manipulation of the knowledge base. However, such architectures and types of agents may not be appropriate for complex and dynamic environments in which a real-time response is required and the assumption of calculative rationality may not hold.

Breaking with the 'traditional' AI approach to building agents, some researchers have propounded the idea of reactive or behaviour-based architectures. In essence, the use of an internal mental representation and decision-making based on it, is rejected. Instead, 'smart' behaviour is linked directly to the environment that the agent inhabits and it can be generated by simply responding to the environment and the changes that occur in it. The agent does not have an internal representation of the environment and its own goals and abilities, but the representation of the world is built into the agent's sensory and effectory capabilities. As a result, intelligence emerges from the interaction of various simple behaviours. In a reactive agent, perceptual input is mapped directly to actions as shown in Figure 2.5.

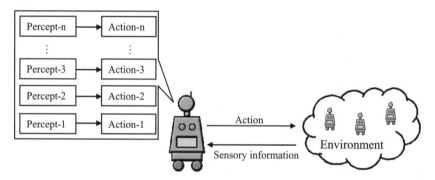

Figure 2.5: Reactive architecture: mapping of perceptions (situations) to actions

Brooks, who was the first to reject the idea of a symbolic model, (Brooks 1986, 1990), advocated that 'real' intelligence is situated in the world and not in disembodied systems and therefore intelligent behaviour arises as a result of the agent interacting with its environment. Brooks' position can be summarized as follows (Brooks 1991a,b): intelligence is an emergent property; intelligent behaviour can be generated without an explicit internal mental representation and without explicit reasoning, but by the interaction of simple behaviours.

Brooks' proposed architecture is called the Subsumption Architecture (Brooks 1986, Ferber 1996). In the subsumption architecture, the agent's decision-making is performed by a set of Task Accomplishing Behaviours (TABs), where a TAB can be a finite state machine or a rule of the type *situation → action*. Each behaviour achieves a particular task and can be thought of as an individual action function which takes sensory input and maps it to an action to be performed. Many behaviours can 'fire' at the same time and action selection is based on a subsumption hierarchy: behaviours are arranged in layers. The lower the layer, the higher the priority. Usually the low layer is related to behaviours that deal with situations that are critical for the survival of the agent such as, for instance, avoiding obstacles, etc., whereas higher layers may achieve other tasks such as exploring. For instance, Percept-1→Action-1 in Figure 2.5 would encode a behaviour to avoid obstacles, Percept-2→Action-2 would enable the agent to wander, and so on.

The Luc Steels scenario

The advantages of the reactive type of architecture are elegantly demonstrated in the exploration of a distant planet scenario described by Luc Steels (Steels 1990). Imagine that a mission to a distant planet has as a goal the gathering of samples of rocks and other minerals. Although the locations of these samples are not known in advance, what is known is that they are typically gathered in certain locations. There is no detailed map of the environment, but it is known that the surface of the planet is not homogeneous and, apart from plateaus, it includes many obstacles such as valleys and hills. Therefore, communication through message exchange is unreliable and has been ruled out. A vehicle can drive around the planet and collect the samples and later transport them back to the spacecraft.

Steels suggests that the task can be performed by a number of robotic agents who can move around, collect samples and return them to the vehicle. He convincingly argues that building the agents with a logic-based architecture is totally impractical for this particular scenario. Instead, he proposes the use of the reactive type of architecture. Accordingly, agents are equipped with simple behaviours for obstacle avoidance, random movement and behaviours that allow them to identify, pick up samples and return to the vehicle. These behaviours are arranged in a subsumption hierarchy. To enable the agents to locate the vehicle easily without high-level communication, Steels introduces the gradient field mechanism. The vehicle generates a radio signal and as the agents move away from the vehicle, the strength of the signal decreases and conversely, as they move towards it, the signal increases. To find the direction of the vehicle, an agent simply has to travel up the gradient following the signal's strength. The signal itself does not carry any other information.

In the experiments that he conducted Steels proved that a number of such agents working in parallel could carry out the task. Although the behaviour of the system is robust and fault-tolerant, its effectiveness would be further improved if the agents could cooperate. Communication would be ideal as, having found a deposit, an agent could alert others as to its location, and speed up the collection process. But, as direct communication is not possible, Steels proposes a second mechanism. The agents carry 'radioactive crumbs' which they can drop, pick up and detect. The basic idea is that an agent who finds a deposit of rocks and minerals, having already picked up a sample and following up the gradient on its way back to the vehicle, will leave behind it two radioactive crumbs. As a result, this creates a trail which leads back to the deposit of the rocks and minerals. As another passing agent detects the radioactive crumbs, it will follow the trail down the gradient, while picking up some of the crumbs along the way. When it finds the deposit, it picks up a sample and starts following up the gradient leaving its own trail of radioactive crumbs.

These simple behaviours will enable the agents to explore the terrain, cooperatively gather samples, and transport them back to the vehicle. Cooperation among the agents, for instance, is facilitated by the following simple rules:

> *if detect crumb → pick up 1 and travel down the gradient*
>
> *if carrying samples and not at the base → drop 2 crumbs and travel up the*
> *   gradient*

The behaviours are arranged in a subsumption hierarchy as illustrated in Figure 2.6 and each behaviour may encompass more than one *situation → action* rules.

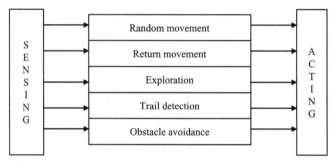

Figure 2.6: Subsumption relation between behaviours in the distant planet exploration scenario

Hence, complex behaviour can be achieved through the interaction of very simple ones without requiring an explicit model of the environment. Such a configuration is cheap in terms of the computational power required by the individual agents. It is also robust and fault-tolerant; even if individual agents have 'accidents' along the way or their power source fails, this will not affect the behaviour of the system as a whole in a significant way as the rest of the agents will keep moving around looking for and gathering samples. Agents are able to self-organize and accomplish a complex task through the interaction of simple behaviours. The interested reader is referred to (Steels 1990) for the full details.

Advantages and disadvantages

Steels' example of the use of reactive agents demonstrates the advantages of this type of architecture: it is simple and elegant, an agent's behaviour is computationally tractable and very robust against failure. Although individual reactive agents are simple, the power lies in numbers, and complex tasks can be accomplished by a group of such agents. Most fundamentally, complex behaviours emerge from the interaction of simpler behaviours.

However, without a model of the environment, agents need sufficient information about their current state in order to determine an action. Reactive agents are short-sighted and have no planning capabilities, which may limit decision quality. Learning from experience is difficult to achieve, since there is no symbolic representation of the environment, objectives, capabilities or what happened in the past. Although in this example a complex pattern of cooperative behaviour emerged from the interaction of simpler individual behaviours, in reality, *emergence* or *emergent behaviour* is not yet fully understood and it is even more difficult to engineer (Odell 1998). Consequently, it is difficult to build task-specific agents, since the behaviour of the agent emerges from the interaction of component behaviours.

2.6.3 Belief–Desire–Intention architecture

The Belief-Desire-Intention (BDI) architecture has its origins in the philosophical theory of practical reasoning (Bratman 1987). Practical reasoning is different from theoretical reasoning since the former has to do with the process of deciding what to do, while the latter is the process of deriving knowledge or reaching conclusions using one's beliefs and knowledge.

Practical reasoning involves two aspects: deciding what we want to achieve, also known as *deliberation*, and deciding how we are going to achieve it, also known as *means-ends reasoning* or planning. We constantly use practical reasoning in our every day lives to make decisions on what we are going to do next.

To illustrate how practical reasoning works, consider the following example. Maria is a Ph.D. student. She has just seen a call for papers for a very prestigious conference in her discipline, the deadline of which is in about a month's time. She considers writing and submitting a paper. At the same time she is also considering taking a two-week holiday. Currently, these are Maria's options or desires. She may want to achieve both of them, i.e., write a good paper and go on a holiday; however, in this particular case one prevents the other from being accomplished. Thus, if she decides to have a holiday, she will not be able to work on the paper and have it ready in time for submission. Maria will consider her options and weigh them against each other: having a paper accepted in this prestigious conference is far more important at this stage in her Ph.D. than having a holiday. Her chosen option to write the paper then becomes an intention, meaning that she has committed to submitting a paper and consequently she is going to take the necessary steps to bring it about. Maria's intention is closely related to her beliefs about the future. She believes she will actually submit the paper, or at least she stands a good chance of submitting it, otherwise it would not have been rational on her behalf to commit to something that she does not believe is feasible. Under normal circumstances, you would expect Maria to actually work towards the achievement of her intention, perform experiments and analyze the results. Even though time is limited, you would expect her to do her best to finish the paper. Moreover, this commitment further restricts her practical reasoning and future options. So for instance, you would not expect Maria to go playing golf all day long, given that she has decided to work on the paper. This option or desire is inconsistent with her intention to finish the paper. One would also expect that Maria's intention persists over time, so she would not capriciously change her mind and drop her intention to write and submit a paper. That is, unless she has some very good reason for doing so. If she realizes that this intention is no longer feasible, perhaps there is not enough time for her to analyze the results of the experiments and present them in an appropriate way, she may decide to drop that intention. Another reason for dropping an intention would be if the initial motivation behind the intention no longer exists, for instance, if Maria has been offered a job in a company and has decided to abandon her Ph.D. studies.

Intentions are key in practical reasoning. They describe states of affairs that the agent is actually committed to bringing about and as a result they are action-inducing: an intention constitutes a reason for action and it is a conscious wish to carry out an act. The concept of intention characterizes both the mind and the actions of an agent, and it involves a distinctive kind of commitment in that intentions resist reconsideration, are volitional and reasoning-centered, and one intention leads to further intentions being generated. Hence, intentions provide strong reasons for action, reasons that are over and above ordinary desire and belief reasons together.

Forming intentions is critical for an agent's success. This is because an agent is resource-bounded and it cannot continually weigh its options, but it must settle on a state of affairs and decide what to do next. Moreover, an agent needs to coordinate its future actions and commit itself to a course of actions. According to Bratman (1987), intentions play three characteristic functional roles in an agent's behaviour:

- an agent needs to determine ways to achieve its intentions
- an agent's intentions lead it to adopt or refrain from adopting further intentions
- an agent is interested in succeeding in its intentions and thus it keeps track of its attempts to do so.

BDI architecture components

Following the theory of practical reasoning, there are three main aspects to the BDI paradigm: beliefs, desires and intentions. Beliefs represent an agent's information about the environment, which may not necessarily be correct, thus giving it an inaccurate picture of the world. Desires represent the agent's motivation or possible options, while intentions represent an agent's commitments, namely options that the agent has committed itself to bringing about.

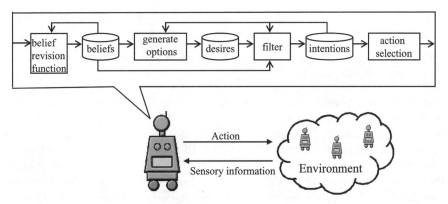

Figure 2.7: The BDI architecture for agents

The BDI architecture illustrated in Figure 2.7 consists of seven main components (Wooldridge 1999):

- A *belief revision function*, which updates the agent's current beliefs based on new perceptual information and the old beliefs held by the agent.

- A set of current *beliefs* about the environment which represent the agent's current information about the state of the world.

- An *option generation function* which determines the agent's available options (desires) based on its current beliefs and intentions. This function is responsible for the means-ends reasoning of the agent, that is how to achieve intentions. In essence, the option generation function progressively refines intentions starting from an abstract one which, as it is fed back into the option generation function, becomes more concrete until it reaches a state where it corresponds to an executable action. The options generated must be consistent with the agent's beliefs and the previously held intentions. Furthermore, such a function should be able to recognize changes in the environment that would lead the agent to achieve its intentions in a different way, or to achieve intentions that were unachievable before.

- A set of *desires* which correspond to the possible options or courses of action that the agent could follow.

- A *filter function*, which determines new intentions based on current beliefs, desires and old intentions. This filter function plays the role of the deliberation process, namely deciding what to do. It is responsible for dropping any intentions which are not achievable, or the original reason for forming the intention is no longer present, or it is no longer cost-effective to try to achieve the intention. On the other hand, the filter function should maintain intentions that have not been achieved, but they are expected to contribute to the agent's utility. Finally, it is the responsibility of the filter function to adopt new intentions in order to further existing ones and exploit new opportunities.

- A set of current *intentions*, which are the options the agent is committed to bringing about.

- An *action selection function*, which selects the action to be performed next, based on the current set of intentions.

The content of the belief, desires and intentions knowledge bases can be in logical or some other form. Whatever the form, there needs to be some consistency between the content of these knowledge bases. For instance, intentions should be consistent with beliefs as we clearly saw earlier in the example. There is no point in Maria holding an intention to write a paper, if she believes that she is not going to achieve this intention. If the three sets consist of logical formulas, then the three functions can be formally defined (Wooldridge 1999). Assume that the sets of all possible beliefs, desires and intentions are *Beliefs*, *Desires* and *Intentions* respectively. The state of the agent at any moment in time is then defined as a triplet (B, D, I) where $B \subseteq$ *Beliefs*, $D \subseteq$ *Desires* and $I \subseteq$ *Intentions*. The agent's belief-revision function is a mapping from the current beliefs and percepts to a new set of beliefs:

$$brf : \mathcal{P}(Beliefs) \times P \rightarrow \mathcal{P}(Beliefs)$$

The option generation function, which represents the agent's means-ends reasoning process, maps a set of beliefs and a set of intentions to a set of desires (options):

$$options : \mathcal{P}(Beliefs) \times \mathcal{P}(Intentions) \rightarrow \mathcal{P}(Desires)$$

The filter function which represents the agent's deliberation process, maps a set of beliefs, desires and intentions to a new set of intentions:

$$filter : \mathcal{P}(Beliefs) \times \mathcal{P}(Desires) \times \mathcal{P}(Intentions) \rightarrow \mathcal{P}(Intentions)$$

The resulting set of intentions can either be previously held intentions or newly adopted options, that is the filter function needs to satisfy the condition $filter(B, D, I) \subseteq I \cup D$.

The action selection function returns any intentions that correspond directly to actions:

$$asf : \mathcal{P}(Intentions) \rightarrow A$$

The control loop for such an agent would have the general form:

```
// control loop for BDI-Agent
begin
    B:=B₀; // initial beliefs
    I:=I₀; // initial intentions
    while true do
        p:=get-percept();
        B:=brf(B,p); // update beliefs
```

```
            D:=options(B,I) // generate options
            I:=filter(B,D,I) // determine intentions
            action:=asf(I) // select an intention to be executed
            execute(action)
        end-while
    end
```

Advantages and disadvantages

Having its roots in practical reasoning, the BDI architecture is clear and intuitive as we all have a basic understanding of practical reasoning, and the role of beliefs, desires and intentions in an agent's decision-making is familiar. Moreover, there is a clear functional decomposition of the subsystems that comprise an agent in the BDI architecture. Another advantage is that it is easy to study the formal properties of such agents as a lot of work has been done into developing logics that are capable of formalizing the properties of rational agents based on practical reasoning. Rao and Georgeff (1991, 1998) have developed a family of BDI logics that provide for the formal semantics of BDI architectures in terms of the mental attitudes of belief, desires and intentions and their possible interrelations (Rao and Georgeff 1991, 1998, Fasli 2003).

However, there are problems with the BDI architecture. Although the decomposition of the subsystems is clear, how to efficiently implement their functionality is not. A BDI agent needs to achieve a balance between commitment and reconsideration. How often an agent stops and reconsiders its intentions can be crucial for the successful performance of the agent. This depends on the rate of environment change. In particular, there are two kinds of agents: bold and cautious. The former never stop to reconsider while the latter constantly stop to do so. Kinny and Georgeff (1991) performed a number of experiments with the dMARS BDI agent framework and their results regarding the trade-off between commitment and reconsideration can be summarized as follows. If the rate of environment change is low, then bold agents seem to be doing better than cautious agents, as the latter waste time reconsidering their commitments too often. If, on the other hand, the rate of environment change is high, then cautious agents tend to do better in comparison to bold agents. The former are able to detect when their intentions are out-of-date or no longer relevant, as well as when new opportunities arise.

A number of agent-based and multi-agent systems have been built, based on the BDI architecture. Among the most well known such systems are the Procedural Reasoning System (PRS) (Georgeff and Lansky 1987, Georgeff and Ingrand 1989) and dMARS (d'Inverno et al. 2004).

2.6.4 Hybrid architecture

Reactivity and proactiveness feature prominently among the list of desirable properties for agents. Ideally we would like agents to react to changes in the environment in a timely fashion, as well as exhibit proactive behaviour, to further their goals. An obvious solution is to combine the strengths of each approach and create hybrid agents with deliberative and reactive components. The deliberative component would then be responsible for maintaining a model of the world, taking decisions using symbolic reasoning and constructing plans to achieve the agent's goals, while the reactive component would enable the agent to react to external stimuli promptly. One way of accomplishing this is via a hierarchy of interacting layers – at least two for reactive and proactive behaviour. Then decision-making is performed via a separation into several software layers and each layer reasons at a different level of abstraction (Müller et al. 1995). There are two ways of organizing the different layers: horizontally and vertically.

Horizontal layered architecture

In horizontal layering, each layer connects to sensory input and action output directly, as is shown in Figure 2.8 (a). For n different behaviours, n layers need to be implemented which inevitably compete with each other in order to take control of the agent. This competition amongst layers for the agent's control can result in incoherent behaviour. Consistency can be achieved by incorporating a function which achieves mediation between the layers. This mediator function is exponentially complete: if there are n layers capable of suggesting m possible actions, there are m^n interactions that have to be considered from the design perspective. Hence, introducing a mediator function or a central control system can cause a bottleneck in the agent's decision-making.

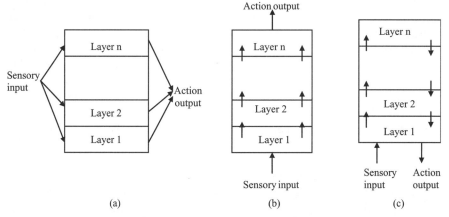

Figure 2.8: Information and control flow in horizontal and vertical layered architectures: (a) horizontal layering; (b) vertical one-pass; (c) vertical two-pass. Source (Müller et al. 1995, p. 265) with kind permission of Springer Science and Business Media

An example of a system based on the horizontal layered architecture is TouringMachines (Ferguson 1992a,b). TouringMachines consists of three layers called *activity producing layers* shown in Figure 2.9. Each layer is an approximate machine and may include its own incomplete world model:

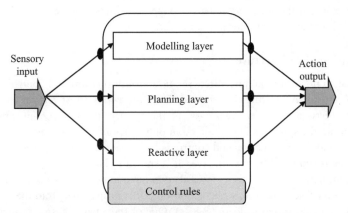

Figure 2.9: The architecture of TouringMachines

- **Reactive layer.** This acts as a reactive agent and responds to changes that occur in the environment. It is implemented through situation-action rules, as in the subsumption architecture and, similarly, this layer does not have a model of the world. The rules in this layer can only use information about the current state of the environment and they produce an action. If a rule fires, this simply means that an action is suggested; there is no model of the environment to be updated. Moreover, every time a situation-action rule fires, the modelling layer is also notified so that it can assess whether the resulting action and its potential consequences may prevent the agent from achieving its goals.

- **Planning layer.** This layer achieves the agent's proactive behaviour. It generates and executes plans for achieving its goals. These plans are based on a library of plan templates or schemas that the agent's planning layer elaborates during run time as part of its decision-making process.

- **Modelling layer.** It endows the agent with reflective and predictive capabilities. Entities at this level, including the agent itself, are modelled as having a configuration, beliefs, desires and intentions. The modelling layer uses these models to predict potential conflicts with other agents as well as within the agent itself. It then generates goals which are associated with conflict-resolution strategies in order to resolve them. Subsequently, these are propagated down to the planning layer, which uses its library of plans to determine ways to implement them.

The issue of which layer takes control over the agent at a given point in time is addressed by enveloping the three layers into a control subsystem which is responsible for assigning the control of the agent to one of the layers. The control rules act as filters and can either suppress sensor information to the layers or else inhibit action output from the layers. Such control rules prevent a particular layer from ever receiving a piece of sensory information. For example, although another agent could be considered as an obstacle, the most appropriate layer to deal with this information is the modelling layer and not the reactive one, as the agent may have to cooperate with this other agent, in which case avoiding it is not an appropriate action to take.

Vertical layered architecture

In contrast to horizontal architectures, the flow of information and control within the system in vertical architectures is restricted. There are two types of vertical architectures: vertical one-pass and vertical two-pass. In the former, the flow of information and control within the system is in one direction only: sensory input is only received by the lower level and the information and control is being passed to the other levels upwards, while action is produced by the nth layer as is shown in Figure 2.8 (b). In the latter, the flow of information and control is towards two directions. Sensory input is first passed from the lower level upwards, while action output is propagated from the higher layer downwards, as illustrated in Figure 2.8 (c). One of the advantages of vertical layering is low complexity. If there are n layers, there are $n-1$ interfaces between them. If each layer is capable of suggesting m possible actions, then there are at most $m^2(n-1)$ interactions to be considered between layers from the design perspective. Since there is no central control, there is no bottleneck in the agent's decision-making. However, the vertical layered architecture is less flexible and fault-tolerant as control must pass between each different layer in order to reach a decision. If one layer fails, the agent's execution will most likely halt or its decision-making process will be severely affected.

An example of a system based on a vertical layered architecture is INTERRAP (Fischer et al. 1994, Müller 1997). The INTERRAP system consists of three main components: the world interface (WIF), the control unit (CU) and a hierarchical knowledge base (KB).

The control unit is based on a vertically layered two-pass architecture and consists of three layers, Figure 2.10. The lower layer called the behaviour-based layer is responsible for the reactive behaviour of the agent. The next layer, namely the local planning layer, deals with everyday planning and contains a planner that can generate plans in order to achieve the agent's goals. The highest layer, called the cooperative planning layer, deals with social interactions and allows an agent to negotiate, reach agreements and form joint plans with other agents.

Each layer is associated with a knowledge base which is an appropriate representation of the world at the right abstraction level for that layer. The world model contains 'raw' information about the environment and is used by the behaviour layer. The mental or

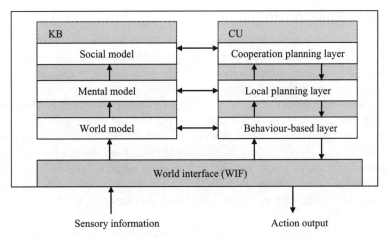

Figure 2.10: The architecture of InterRRaP

planning model contains hierarchically structured plans whose nodes are other plans or executable actions (patterns of behaviour). Finally, the social model represents the plans and actions of the other agents in the environment.

Although the functionality of the layers between TouringMachines and INTERRAP appears to be similar, the way in which the layers interact with each other is different. Each layer in INTERRAP consists of two subprocesses: the situation recognition and goal-activation process (SG), and the planning, scheduling and execution process (PS). Layers interact with each other through two main types of interaction: *activation requests* (bottom up) and *commitment postings* (top down). Activation requests are issued when a lower layer passes control to a higher one because it is not competent to deal with the current situation s. The activation requests are sent from the PS of layer i to the SG of layer $i + 1$. The situation s is enriched with additional knowledge from the respective knowledge base to produce an appropriate goal description which is then passed on to the PS of this layer. A layer i achieves its goals by sending commitment postings to layer $i - 1$. These commitment postings are communicated between the PSs of two layers.

2.7 AGENTS IN PERSPECTIVE

Agents and multi-agent systems are regarded by many as the new software engineering paradigm that will lead to the development of more complex and open systems capable of multiple dynamic interactions. At the same time, some fail to see their novelty in comparison to other approaches and do not consider them as comprising a distinct software engineering paradigm.

2.7.1 Agents and objects

There are three widely acceptable approaches to software development that evolved over the years in response to the need for more complex and larger programs: the procedural, modular and the object-oriented approach. In the procedural approach the problem is decomposed into a number of functions, procedures or subroutines that can be called from anywhere within the program. The focus is on algorithms as well as avoiding data repetition. The modular approach decomposes the problem into a number of modules that are usually stored in different files and are called from the main module. In this way, the effects of change in programs are minimized. Each module has its own data and internal state and can exist, at most, once within a program. The modular approach takes advantage of data hiding and data abstraction by concealing the design decisions in modules. Languages such as Ada and Modula-2 are based on a modular approach.

The object-oriented approach views a software system as a collection of interacting entities called *objects*. Each object has identity, state and behaviour. The state of an object is described by the member variables and its behaviour by a set of methods that can be invoked. Objects interact with each other by sending messages. If object i wants object j to execute one of j's methods, object i sends a message to j. In essence, a message is a procedure call which is executed in the context of the receiving object. Objects that share common characteristics are grouped into classes and are implemented as class objects. A number of different relations may hold among classes of objects: inheritance/classification, decomposition/aggregation, and 'InstanceOf' which relates a class to its instance objects or simply instances. Languages such as C++ and Java support object-oriented development.

In the agent-oriented approach, the system is viewed as a collection of loosely-coupled and interacting agents. In a similar way to objects, agents have an identity, a state and behaviour but these are much more complex than in simple objects. An agent's state may be described in terms of knowledge, beliefs, desires, intentions, design objectives or goals and obligations. Its behaviour may be described in terms of plans to achieve goals, actions, reactions to events and even roles. Consequently, the behaviour of an agent is not characterized by a direct mapping of input to output, i.e., of what the agent should do, but in terms of how to decide what to do.

Agents are different from objects in other ways (Wooldridge 2002, Odell 2002). First, agents exhibit autonomy, i.e., they have control over their state, execution and ultimately, behaviour. Whereas objects may be thought of as having control over their internal state, i.e., variables that have been declared private can only be manipulated by and are under the control of the object itself, they have no control over their execution and behaviour. If object i calls a method of object j which has been declared public, then object j has no choice on whether to allow its execution or not; the method will be executed. On the contrary, agents do not call methods of another agent, but request actions to be performed. If agent i requests an action to be performed by agent j, then j, having control over its execution and behaviour, may refuse to do so. The locus of control lies with agent *j*, whereas in object-oriented modelling the locus of control lies with the requesting object.

The second important difference between agents and objects is that agents exhibit goal-seeking, reactive and social behaviour. Agents communicate in complex conversational ways rather than simple message exchanges and they can assume different roles in different contexts. They may also be persistent, self-aware and able to learn and adapt to their environment. However, the object-oriented paradigm in itself has nothing to say about goal-seeking, reactive, social or adaptive behaviour; objects are not, *per se*, intelligent.

The third major distinction between objects and agents is that agents have their own thread of control within a multi-agent system, whereas in an object-based system there is a single thread of control. Of course, programming languages like Java offer the facilities for multi-threaded programming, but the object-oriented model in itself does not talk about multi-threaded control. Moreover, control in a multi-agent system is distributed. As there is no single agent that has control in a multi-agent system and agents can adopt different roles in different contexts as well as adapt their behaviour, the behaviour of the system as a whole cannot be strictly prescribed in advance.

Nevertheless, the most common way of building agents is through the use of object-oriented languages. What is important to understand is that, although we can build agents using objects, objects by themselves as defined in the object-oriented paradigm, are not agents. Active objects are closer to the concept of an agent. An active object has some degree of autonomy in that it can exhibit control over its behaviour without being operated upon by another object (Booch 1994). However, proactive, reactive and social behaviour are not part of the definition of an active object.

2.7.2 Agents and expert systems

When expert systems first appeared in the 1970s, they were heralded as the first intelligent pieces of software. Such systems were capable of solving problems or providing advice in a particular application domain (Jackson 1986). In this sense, they very much acted like experts providing recommendations in their field of expertise. One of the most well-known expert system is MYCIN whose purpose was to assist physicians in the treatment of blood conditions in humans (Shortliffe 1976). The user would interact with MYCIN through the use of a keyboard and input a number of symbolically represented facts. MYCIN would then use these facts along with the stored expertise in its knowledge base to come up with an appropriate diagnosis. MYCIN would act like an expert in its domain, i.e., a consultant.

But were MYCIN and other similar expert systems, agents? An expert system can be characterized as being intelligent, similar to an agent. However, expert systems have no control over their actions. They provide domain-specific information and usually do not adapt. Their ability to interact is rather limited: apart from an input/output direct interaction via the keyboard/screen, usually they do not interact with the environment or other expert systems and therefore they do not possess true social ability. Expert systems are decoupled from their environment, whereas agents live, act and interact in an environment with other agents. As a result, expert systems, in general, do not satisfy the criteria of agency, namely, they are not autonomous, they cannot exhibit reactive and proactive behaviour and they lack the ability to interact with other expert systems (Wooldridge 2002).

2.7.3 Agents, Web Services and the Semantic Web

By and large, today's Web consists of collections of web pages that are primarily to be viewed and operated on by people. The vision of the Semantic Web is to enrich web pages with meaning and enable automation so that information can be accessed programmatically (Berners-Lee et al. 2001). Thus, the idea is that the Web is gradually transformed from being simply a collection of web pages to a collection of programs that can offer combined functionality over standard protocols.

To facilitate automated processing on the Web and enable applications to communicate and work with each other, we need programmatic interfaces, namely web services. A web service is a collection of functions that are packaged as a single entity and published on the network to be used by other programs. Specifically, a web service is a software system identified by a Uniform Resource Identifier (URI), whose public interfaces and bindings are defined and described using the eXtended Markup Language (XML) (W3C 2006). Its definition can be discovered by other software systems. These systems may then interact with the web service as described in its definition, using XML-based messages over standard Internet protocols. The power of web services lies in that they can interact seamlessly and transparently to achieve combined functionality and produce the overall required result. In this way, programs providing simple services can be combined to deliver sophisticated value-added services. To put it another way, web services are building blocks for creating open distributed systems.

Given a request for a service from a user, web services need to be first located, matched against the particular request, and then executed. Ideally, to achieve the full potential of Web Services and the Semantic Web, users – individuals and organizations – should be able to identify their needs and delegate them to software agents who can then locate web services to bring about the users' goals as illustrated in Figure 2.11. Thus, agents can facilitate the seamless integration of web services so that the complexity of the execution of the request is transparent to the user – by hiding the underlying complexity of the execution of the request. Although web services and agents encapsulate functionality, they are different in that (Singh and Huhns 2005):

- A service is static and unable to adapt, and only knows about itself and its own functionality. On the other hand, agents can learn about the user, other agents and

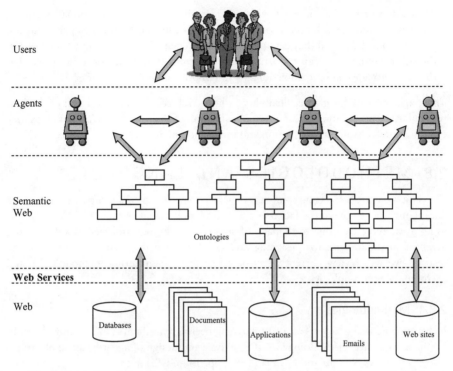

Figure 2.11: Working together: Agents and Web Services on the Semantic Web

services and may be able to adapt and offer personalized services according to the user's needs. Agents, can also take advantage of new information to best serve the user.

- Services are passive until they are invoked. Agents, on the other hand, are autonomous and proactive, and thus can actively seek to help the user, for instance, by checking periodically for new information on a topic that the user is interested in, or notifying her when a new product has arrived at a particular store. An agent may invoke a service at regular intervals to check the price of the stocks in the user's portfolio, but only alert the user when the price falls below a certain threshold. Once a service is invoked with the correct parameters, it will be executed, i.e., a service does not have control over its execution, whereas an agent can decide on its own whether to execute a request or not.

- The communication between services is at a low, syntactic level; services can exchange data, but they do not understand them. Thus, services are not designed to use and work with ontologies. If a requester and a service provider use different ontologies, the result of the web service invocation would be incomprehensible to the requester. Agents can take advantage of ontologies and the Semantic Web and resolve possible incompatibilities.

- Although a service can interact with other services, composed functionality among services can only be achieved if orchestrated by a third party; services *per se* do not have a social ability and they cannot coordinate to deliver composed functionality. On the other hand, agents can cooperate with one another and can form groups so that they can provide combined functionality and more comprehensive services.

Thus, agents allow for greater flexibility in how Web services are used and created. In particular, agents are fundamental to the realization of the Semantic Web vision, as they can facilitate the seamless interaction and integration of Semantic Web Services.

2.8 METHODOLOGIES AND LANGUAGES

The reluctance to accept agents and multi-agent systems as a distinct software engineering paradigm is partly due to the fact that agents and multi-agent systems are relatively new as an area, and partly due to the lack of standard definitions and well-established and accepted methodologies for designing and developing such systems. In the following sections we will review current agent-based software engineering methodologies and agent-enabling technologies.

2.8.1 Methodologies

If the full potential of agents as a software engineering paradigm is to be realized, establishing a systematic methodology for the analysis and design of agent-based applications is imperative. As Ndumu and Nwana (1997, pp. 14 and 15) put it:

> appropriate design methodologies for constructing the different types of agent systems for different application domains

are essential before

> the development of generic platforms for engineering agent-based applications.

The current methodologies for the analysis and design of agent-based and multi-agent systems can be divided into three categories:

- agent-oriented methodologies
- methodologies that directly extend or adapt object-oriented methodologies
- methodologies that adapt knowledge engineering models or other techniques.

2.8.2 Agent–oriented methodologies

In the first class of methodologies belong frameworks such as Gaia, Prometheus, Tropos, MaSE and ROADMAP.

Gaia

This is arguably the first agent-oriented methodology proposed (Wooldridge et al. 2000). Gaia is based on an organizational analysis to the design and development of multi-agent systems and deploys concepts such as roles, responsibilities and protocols. The methodology provides a set of agent-specific concepts, which are of two types: abstract (roles, permissions, responsibilities, protocols, activities, liveness properties and safety properties) and concrete (agent types, services, acquaintances). Abstract concepts are used to conceptualize the system during analysis, whereas concrete concepts are used within the design process. In the analysis phase, the system is viewed as an organization in terms of a collection of roles that stand in relation to each other and have interactions with one another. Once the roles in the system under consideration are identified a roles model is built. Then for each role, the required protocols need to be identified and the interaction model is developed. The roles and interaction models represent the system as interacting abstract roles. The roles model then is elaborated. In the next phase, which is the initial design, the agent, service and acquaintance models are created. These three models constitute the input of the detailed design phase. However, Gaia does not cover the detailed design phase. Instead it relies on standard methodologies for this aspect of the development cycle.

The advantages of Gaia are that it is independent of implementation language and agent architecture and can model both the macro (societal) aspects of multi-agent systems as well as the micro (individual agent's internal workings). On the other hand, Gaia does not cover the full cycle and was mainly designed for closed systems and thus the support for scalability is weak.

Prometheus

The Prometheus methodology (Dam and Winikoff 2003, Padgham and Winikoff 2002, 2004) is a detailed process for specifying, designing, and implementing agent-based and multi-agent systems, which can be used by nonexperts in agent systems. It has been developed by the Agent Oriented Software company which has also developed the JACK Intelligent Agents platform (see below). In particular, the Prometheus methodology supports the development of agents and multi-agent systems based on the BDI framework, i.e., agents are viewed as having beliefs, desires and intentions. The focus of the methodology is more on the functional aspects of the system, rather than on an organizational view.

Prometheus consists of three phases: system specification, architectural design, and detailed design. The system specification phase deals with first determining the system's environment and second its goals and functionality. The environment is defined in terms of percepts, actions, and external data, while the system's functionality is identified in terms of goals and subgoals. Use case scenarios are developed to provide a comprehensive view of the interaction between actions, percepts and functionalities.

The second phase, namely architectural design, focuses on defining agent types by grouping functionalities and deciding what agent types will be implemented. Agent messages, as well as possible interactions and protocols, are identified. One of the products of this stage is the system overview diagram which captures the system's overall structure and general functionality. It illustrates the system within its environment, the agents' types, and the communication links between agents, as well as data.

Finally, in the last stage the detailed design, the internal workings of the agents are specified in terms of capabilities, events, data and plans. Plans are introduced to handle events and the details of these as well as those of beliefs/data are defined. Agent overview diagrams are produced at this stage which provide an overview of the internal workings of the agents.

Prometheus is a very expressive methodology which provides comprehensive support for the entire development lifecycle. Also, it offers strong tool support and language integration. On the other hand, it is BDI-specific, which inevitably makes it less general and it is closely tied to the JACK platform.

Tropos

Tropos (Giunchiglia et al. 2002) is an agent-oriented methodology which deploys a set of knowledge-level concepts that are used uniformly throughout the software development process. Among the most important concepts in Tropos are those of actor, goal, dependency, plan, resource, capability and belief. Tropos includes five development stages. The first stage is called the early requirements stage. The main objective of this early requirements analysis is to identify the stakeholders in the target domain and their intentions. To this end, Tropos uses the concepts of actors and goals to model stakeholders and intentions, respectively. Goals are divided into hard-goals, which eventually lead to functional requirements, and soft-goals, which relate to nonfunctional requirements. Two types of models are produced at this stage: the Actor and Dependency models and the Goal and Plan models. The former ensue from the analysis of social and system actors, as well as their goals and dependencies for goal achievement. The latter show the analysis of goals and plans with regard to a specific actor, by using three suggested reasoning techniques: means-end analysis, contribution analysis, and AND/OR decomposition.

In the next stage, late requirements, the models that were previously created are extended so as to model the system-to-be as one or more actors within its environment. The dependencies between these actors are identified, and subsequently are translated into the system's functional and nonfunctional requirements.

The third stage is the architectural design. During this stage the actors and data-control flows are defined to form the system architecture. The first step in this process is to define the overall architectural organization of the system. The second step involves identifying the capabilities needed by the actors to accomplish their goals and plans. In the final step of the architectural design stage, agent types are defined and associated with capabilities.

In the detailed design stage that follows, the agents' details are further refined. Three types of diagrams facilitate this process: capability, plan, and agent-interaction diagrams, which represent the interaction between agents in the system.

In the final stage, which is implementation, Tropos chooses the JACK Intelligent Agents software platform for the development of the system. The Tropos concepts need to be mapped to JACK constructs, or alternatively first to BDI concepts and subsequently to JACK constructs during this stage. As the Tropos methodology is BDI specific, it is therefore less general.

ROADMAP

The ROADMAP methodology extends Gaia and focuses on developing open systems (Juan et al. 2002). As Gaia, ROADMAP views agent-based and multi-agent systems as organizations. In particular, there are four principal extensions to Gaia. First, use-cases are introduced to support the requirements gathering process. Second, explicit models of the agent environment and knowledge are introduced; these are derived from the use-cases and provide comprehensive views of the execution environment and the domain knowledge. Third, an interaction model is added, which is based on AUML diagrams. Finally, a dynamic role hierarchy model is introduced, which is carried into design and will have a run-time realization, allowing social aspects to be explicitly modelled, reasoned and modified at run-time.

ROADMAP consists of two phases: the specification and analysis phase, and the design phase. During the former, the following models are created sequentially: use-case, environment, knowledge, role, protocol and finally the interaction model. The development process of each one of these models takes all previous models as input. They then undergo a process of refinement until sufficient information about the system is captured.

All analysis models are carried into the design phase and they are updated to reflect the design decisions. Three design models: the agent, service and acquaintance models are created from the updated analysis models. Again these models go through a process of refinement until sufficient design information is captured. An approach to link the Prometheus with the ROADMAP methodology has also been proposed (Juan et al. 2003).

MaSE

The Multi-agent System Engineering (MaSE) (DeLoach et al. 2001) methodology takes an initial set of requirements and analyzes, designs, and implements a working multi-agent system. MaSE is architecture-independent and models a system in terms of goals, roles, agents, tasks and conversations. It involves two main phases: analysis and design. The analysis phase consists of three steps: capturing goals, creating use cases and refining roles. The goals of the system are first identified and structured as a goal hierarchy. Next, use cases are identified which are used to construct a set of sequence diagrams. Subsequently, roles are created and tasks are associated with each role. Every goal associated with a role can have a task that details how the goal is accomplished. The second part of the methodology essentially deals with the design of the system and consists of four steps. The first step: creation of agent classes, maps roles to agent classes in an agent-class diagram. In the next step: construction of conversations, the coordination protocols are defined. In the third step: assemblage of agent classes, the agent architecture and the components making up the architecture are defined. The final step: system design, creates actual agent instances based on the agent classes which are the output of the previous stage. MaSE is supported by the agentTool (agentTool 2006) for development which is a graphically based, fully interactive software engineering tool. This also serves as a validation platform and a proof of concept.

2.8.3 Object–oriented based methodologies

In the second class of methodologies belong works such as AAII and AUML.

AAII

The Agent Modelling Technique for Systems of BDI agents originated in the Australian Artificial Intelligence Institute (AAII) and was developed by Kinny et al. (1996). The methodology builds on and adapts existing object-oriented models. AAII is based on the BDI paradigm and provides an internal and external perspective of multi-agent systems. The internal model identifies the agents' beliefs, desires and intentions, whereas the external model provides a system-level view and identifies the agents in the system and their relationships. The external model consists of the agent model and the interaction model. The agent model itself comprises the agent-class model and the agent-instance model, which in combination identify the agent classes and agent instances that will be created at runtime as well as the inheritance relations between them.

AUML

A number of languages, notations and methodologies have been developed for the object-oriented paradigm in the past two decades. Despite sharing many similarities, there are nevertheless a number of differences among them. The Unified Modelling Language (UML) is a notation for modelling object-oriented systems which emanated from three of the founders of the object-oriented paradigm (Booch, Rumbaugh, and Jacobson) and has now become the standard in object-oriented analysis and design. Odell and colleagues (Odell et al. 2000, Odell 2000, Bergenti and Poggi 2002) explored UML extensions that can be used to model agents and agent-based systems. The result is a UML-based approach to building agent-based applications called Agent UML (AUML). AUML extends the UML notation by supporting concurrent threads of interaction and by extending the notion of role to allow an agent to have multiple roles.

2.8.4 Knowledge-engineering based and other methodologies

The final class of methodologies includes approaches such as DESIRE and MAS-CommonKADS.

MAS-CommonKADS

MAS-CommonKADS (Iglesias et al. 1998) extends the CommonKADS methodology for knowledge-based systems by employing techniques from object-oriented methodologies as well as protocol engineering. There are three main phases. The first phase, called conceptualization, deals with extracting the basic system requirements from the user. In the analysis phase a number of models are developed. The agent, task and expertise models specify the agent characteristics, the tasks that the agents can carry out and the knowledge that they require in order to achieve their goals. The coordination model describes the interactions among agents, while the organization model describes the social organization of the system, essentially as a society of agents. The communication model identifies the human-software agent interactions and the human factors for developing these user interfaces. In the third phase, called design, and based on the previously developed models, the architecture of the system and the individual agents are defined creating the design model.

DESIRE

The DEsign and Specification of Interacting REasoning components (DESIRE) framework (Brazier et al. 1997, 2001), supports the specification and implementation of compositional systems which consist of autonomous interacting agents. This high-level modelling framework can be used to model complex reasoning within agents, communication as well as interaction. DESIRE supports the conceptual design and specification of both dynamic and static aspects of agent behaviour.

Adapting knowledge engineering methodologies for the design of agent-based systems has certain advantages, as such methodologies provide techniques for modelling the agents' knowledge and knowledge acquisition processes. In addition, any existing tools, ontology libraries and problem-solving-method libraries can be reused. However, such methodologies fail to address the distributed or social aspects of agents, or their reflective and goal-oriented attitudes, since a knowledge-based system is conceived as a centralized one (Iglesias et al. 1999).

Other methodologies include, for instance, formal methods such as the use of Z language (Luck and d'Inverno 1995, Luck et al. 1997).

2.8.5 Programming languages and environments

As object-oriented programming is supported by a number of languages, similarly, one would expect that there would be languages supporting agent-oriented programming, allowing us to specify the agent's attributes as well as behaviour at a high level of abstraction.

One of the first attempts to create a pure agent-oriented language, based on a mentalistic view of agents, was Shoham's proposal on a new programming paradigm called agent-oriented programming (AOP) (Shoham 1993). The AOP promotes a societal view of computation and allows the direct programming of agents in terms of their mental state. Shoham developed the AGENT0 programming language as an implementation of the AOP paradigm. AGENT0 allows the specification of an agent in terms of a set of beliefs (as in the BDI architecture), capabilities (what the agent can do), initial commitments (similar to the BDI intentions) and a set of commitment rules which determine how the agent acts. Each commitment rule consists of a message condition, a mental condition and an action. The agent commits to the action if the message condition matches the messages received by the agent, and the mental condition matches its beliefs. However, the AGENT0 AOP language is only a prototype and not intended for building large-scale agent-based systems. It is also limited because the relationship between the logic and interpreted programming language is only loosely defined.

There have been a number of attempts to develop logic approaches to agent programming which have their roots in the logic-based architectures. Concurrent METATEM (Fisher 1994) is a multi-agent programming language based on linear temporal logic. A multi-agent system based on Concurrent METATEM consists of concurrently executing agents whose behaviour is implemented using executable temporal logic and which can communicate via asynchronous broadcast message passing.

Another example of a logic-based approach is AgentSpeak(L) (Rao 1996) which is a programming language that allows the specification of BDI agents. It is based on a restricted first order language with events and actions and consists of a set of base beliefs and a set of context-sensitive plans allowing for hierarchical decomposition of goals. Jason (2006) is a Java-based interpreter for an extended version of AgentSpeak. Jason implements the operational semantics of AgentSpeak and it is the first fully-fledged interpreter which also includes inter-agent communication based on speech acts.

APRIL (Skarmeas 1999) is a symbolic programming language that is designed for writing mobile, distributed and agent-based systems, particularly suited for the Internet. Its features include asynchronous message sending and receiving, code mobility, pattern matching, higher-order functions and strong typing. The language is compiled into byte-code which is then interpreted by the APRIL runtime-engine.

A number of toolkits and environments have been developed to support the agent developer over the last few years, mostly based on the Java programming language. ZEUS (Nwana et al. 1999) is a toolkit for constructing collaborative multi-agent applications. It is implemented in Java, and allows for the creation of agents by specifying their attributes and tasks. ZEUS supports both KQML and FIPA ACL agent communication languages, although initially it only supported the former.

Java Agent DEvelopment (JADE) (Bellifemine et al. 1999) is another framework, which is based on Java, that supports the development of multi-agent systems. JADE is compliant with the FIPA specifications and uses FIPA ACL messages for communication amongst agents. It makes use of Java's multi-threading mechanisms in order to support the coordination of behaviours. Furthermore, it provides a graphical user interface that allows for easy management and control of agents being created and executing on the platform.

JACK Intelligent Agents (Busetta et al. 1999, Howden et al. 2001) is also based on Java and enriches it with agent-oriented concepts, such as agents, capabilities, events and plans, among others. Although it supports the BDI architecture model, it can be extended to support different agent models. JACK is supported by methodologies such as Tropos and Prometheus.

Java Agent Template Lite (JATLite) (Jeon et al. 2000) is a collection of Java objects and class libraries that facilitates the creation of software agents for distributed problem-solving which can communicate over the Internet. The agent messages are based on the KQML language. In a similar way to JADE, JATLite makes use of Java's multi-threading mechanisms. Moreover, it includes a message router which is used for agent registration, connection, name and password services, and supports both stand-alone agents in Java and C++ as well as applet agents.

Other frameworks, toolkits and platforms for agent and multi-agent system development include the Open Agent Architecture (OAA) (Cheyer and Martin 2001) which is a domain-independent framework for constructing agent-based systems, FIPA-OS (Poslad et al. 2000) which is a platform designed to comply with the FIPA specifications, Grasshopper (Baumer et al. 2000), IBM's Agent Building and Learning Environment (ABLE) (Bigus et al. 2002) and AgentBuilder (AgentBuilder 2006) among others.

2.8.6 From legacy systems to agents

Agents are a relatively new software engineering paradigm in the short history of computer science and software engineering. Agents take advantage of a number of developments in computer science and artificial intelligence in particular, and offer us abstraction power that current methodologies and paradigms lack. However, there are numerous pieces of software out there which are not agents, namely *legacy systems*. In an increasingly interconnected world, how will agents and legacy systems be able to interface and work together? The process of transforming a piece of software into an agent or making it compatible so that it can interact in an agent-inhabited environment has been termed *agentification* (Shoham 1993). A legacy system can be transformed into an agent-compatible one in three ways (Genesereth and Ketchpel 1994):

- **Through a transducer**. A transducer is a piece of software that mediates between the legacy system and the environment and translates agent messages to input comprehensible by the legacy system and output produced by the legacy system into agent messages, Figure 2.12 (a). Using a transducer has certain advantages since one need only know the input required by and the output produced from, the legacy system and not the system's internal workings, data structures, etc.

- **Through a wrapper**. A wrapper is a piece of software that envelopes a legacy system, Figure 2.12 (b). The use of a wrapper does not simply involve translating messages to and from the legacy system into agent messages. A wrapper may also modify existing data structures, or even inject new code into the legacy system. Although this method is more efficient than using a transducer, the problem is that the source code of the legacy system needs to be accessible/available. The developer needs to understand the interworkings of the legacy system if new code is to be injected, or the data structures need to be modified. This is in addition to being able to read and comprehend programming languages that have long been out of use, such as COBOL.

- **By rewriting**. The most extreme method of agentification is simply to rewrite and redevelop the legacy system as an agent. This method is as efficient as one wants to pay for, Figure 2.12 (c).

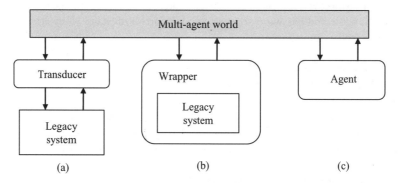

Figure 2.12: Agentification methods: (a) transducer; (b) wrapper; (c) rewrite

None of these methods is easy. Heterogeneity introduces problems since different developers may use different languages and different interfaces. There is always the possibility of incongruent writing of code when attempting to intervene with code written by someone else. One thing to bear in mind is that large investments were made on these systems and organizations may be reluctant to reinvest a huge amount of money to catch up with current technologies. Finally, as has always been the case with new technologies, they are not easily adopted and it takes time for people to get used to new ideas and accept new methodologies and paradigms.

2.9 Further Reading

There are a number of books providing thorough introductions to agents and multi-agent systems. The collection of papers by Huhns and Singh (1997) presents earlier research in agents, while Bradshaw (1997) presents topics on software agents. The most recent textbook by Wooldridge (2002) provides a thorough introduction into agents and various architectures for building them. The brief exposition of architectures here follows closely that of Wooldridge (1999, 2002) and in particular (Genesereth and Nilsson 1987) with regard to logic-based architectures. For the reader interested in BDI agents and, in particular, formal aspects of BDI agents, more details can be found in Rao and Georgeff (1991, 1998), Wooldridge (2000) and Fasli (2003). The paper by Wooldridge and Jennings (1995) provides a good overview of the theoretical issues on agents and multi-agent systems, albeit the section on languages and methodologies is now out of date. An excellent book on Artificial Intelligence is that of Russell and Norvig (2003) who use the concept of an agent throughout their exposition to discuss a number of issues in AI including search, planning, learning and decision-making under uncertainty. In particular, Chapter 2 as well as Chapters 16 and 17 describe how success can be measured and how agents can make simple as well as complex decisions. These are recommended to the reader along with Chapter 13 on utility theory. The discussion on environments as well as decision-making is based on Russell and Norvig (2003), while the formulation of the agent's decision-making problem and optimal policy follows (Vlassis 2003). A detailed introduction into Markov decision processes and stochastic models are found in Puterman (1994) and Tijms (2003). Other sources include Russell and Norvig (2003, Chapter 17) and Sutton and Barto (1998, Chapter 3), as well as Blythe (1999) and Kaelbling et al. (1998).

Planning and learning have a long tradition in AI. Russell and Norvig (2003) discuss planning in Chapters 11 and 12, and various mechanisms for learning are introduced in Chapters 18–21. A good collection of papers on planning can be found in Allen et al. (1990) and an introduction to multi-agent planning is provided in (Durfee 1999). The most well-known planning system STRIPS is discussed in detail in Fikes and Nilsson (1971). A thorough introduction into techniques for automated planning is given in Ghallab et al. (2004)

The discussion on why learning is important is based on the notes of Nilsson (1996). A comprehensive and technical introduction to machine learning and various algorithms is given in Mitchell (1997), while an excellent introduction to reinforcement learning is provided by Sutton and Barto (1998). Good references to multi-agent systems learning include Sen and Weiss (1999) and Stone (2000).

Dennett's book (Dennett 1987) on the intentional stance, describes folk psychology in detail and how it can aid in our understanding of complex systems. McCarthy's discussion on the merits of ascribing mental attitudes to machines and other artifacts is enlightening (McCarthy 1979).

The differences between agents and objects, and agents and expert systems are discussed in Wooldridge (2002), while an extended discussion on the former can be found in Odell (2002). Also, the papers by Farhoodi and Fingar (1997a,b) discuss how we can move from object-oriented to agent-oriented engineering for commerce and business applications. The discussion on agents, web services and the semantic web is based on Singh and Huhns (2005) which is a recent and thorough treatment of service-oriented computing and the underlying technologies and infrastructure.

There are a number of toolkits, languages and methodologies for developing agent-based and multi-agent systems. The interested reader can follow the references provided in the respective sections to learn more about specific methodologies and software platforms. Agent-based software development and a number of agent toolkits are discussed in Luck et al. (2004). A recent collection of papers which discusses a number of agent programming languages and platforms is Bordini et al. (2005).

2.10 Exercises and Topics for Discussion

1. Consider a software agent operating in the stock exchange market. What are the characteristics of this environment? What are the agent's perceptions and actions? Consider designing such an agent, what should be the agent's characteristics? What could be an acceptable performance measure? Which agent architecture would you use and why?

2. Design a solution to the Maze World using Brook's subsumption architecture. How does it compare to the logic-based solution?

3. Use your favourite programming language to code a solution to the basic Maze World problem as described in Section 2.6.1. How does it compare to the logic-based solution?

Exercises 2, 3, 5 and 8 have been adapted from (Wooldridge 1999).

4. Define the functions *old* and *new* as described in the logic-based architecture in Section 2.6.1. The former generates the predicates to be removed from the knowledge base, while the latter generates those to be added.

5. Extend the Maze World of Section 2.6.1 to include a 20×20 grid. How many rules would you need in order to encode this scaled-up world? Is there any way that these rules can be generalized? Use your favourite programming language to code a solution for this extended problem.

6. Use your favourite programming language to implement a performance measuring environment simulator for the Maze World. Suppose that the environment is fully-observable, i.e., the agent can perceive the entire grid, and thus can see exactly where there is gold. Also assume that, despite being able to perceive the environment, there is some uncertainty with regard to the outcomes of the agent's actions. The world is stochastic in the following sense: every action of the agent in the intended direction succeeds with probability 0.8, but with probability 0.2 the agent moves at right angles to the intended direction. Bumping on the walls leaves the position of the agent unchanged. Try to implement an optimal algorithm that will pick up all the gold in the shortest time possible. Make the environment more complicated by allowing gold to appear and disappear randomly, thus forcing the agent to 'rethink' the best solution to collect the gold.

7. You are asked to develop an agent system to control a nuclear reactor plant generating and distributing electricity to an area of the UK. Explain your design considerations for the development of such an agent, i.e., environment characteristics and performance measure, and suggest a suitable agent architecture.

8. Design a solution for the Luc Steels scenario based on the logic-based approach. How does it compare to the reactive approach?

9. Sketch the architecture of an INTERRAP agent for playing football. Indicate what form of processing is appropriate for each layer and what sort of knowledge is appropriate for each respective knowledge base. Give an example of a trace of execution for such an agent, starting with a percept – you can choose one – and ending with the resulting action, indicating how control passes between the different layers.

10. Sketch the architecture of a TouringMachines agent for playing football. Indicate what form of processing is appropriate for each layer. Suggest

appropriate control rules that the control subsystem could use to either suppress input to, or censor output from, each layer.

11. Sketch the architecture of an InteRRaP agent for driving to work. Indicate what form of processing is appropriate for each layer and what sort of knowledge is appropriate for each respective knowledge base. Give an example of a trace of execution for such an agent starting with the percept 'At home' and ending with the percept 'At work', indicating how control passes between the different layers.

12. Sketch a BDI agent whose goal is to get to work. The agent can drive to work, walk or use public transport. Recently the price of petrol has increased substantially, making the trip to work a bit expensive. However, the use of a car increases the chances that the agent will get to work on time – although there is always the risk of traffic jams. On the other hand, public transport is not very reliable as the buses may not necessarily adhere to the timetables. The agent prefers walking to work sometimes as this does not pollute the environment and it is cheaper; it takes the agent 40 minutes to get to work. It is raining heavily outside and the agent would rather get to work without getting wet or catching a cold. Also, it wants to be back home before 5:30 pm. The agent can obtain more information regarding the weather for the day as well as traffic information by listening to the radio. However, weather forecasting may be unreliable, and although traffic information is accurate at the time of broadcasting, the traffic conditions may change. (You can use the geographical and other details such as bus schedules of your own location to enrich this scenario.)

    (a) Specify (semi-formally) the initial beliefs (*Beliefs*), desires (*Desires*) or options and intentions (*Intentions*) of the agent.
    (b) Specify (semi-formally) functions *brf*, *options*, *filter* and *asf* for the agent.

CHAPTER 3

Multi-agent Systems

LEARNING OBJECTIVES

After reading and completing this chapter, you should be able to:

- Describe what a multi-agent system is and how it differs from a single agent-based system.
- Explain the different modes of interaction among agents and the role of interaction protocols.
- Describe the infrastructure requirements for agent communication.
- Describe and contrast the two main agent communication languages KQML and FIPA ACL.
- Construct and understand simple communication messages in KQML and FIPA ACL.
- Analyze the role of ontologies in agent communication.
- Discuss cooperative problem-solving, its applications and related issues.
- Explain how the ContractNet protocol works and its potential applications.

In an increasingly agent-inhabited world, it is very rare for an agent to act in isolation and it is even more rare for an agent to be useful on its own. Usually an agent will have to 'live' and act within an environment that involves other agents, be it software or human. A multi-agent system (MAS) can be seen as a loosely coupled network of autonomous agents that can work together on problems that may be beyond the scope, the resources and the capabilities of any of the agents individually. In this respect, an agent can be more useful in the context of others. Examples of MASs are a group of robots playing football (RoboCup), electronic marketplaces (e-commerce) and a number of distributed control processes in an intelligent building. However, a multi-agent system is not just a collection of agents; agents need ways to interact with one another in order to be truly useful. The key to realizing the huge potential and harnessing the power of the agent paradigm is efficient, effective, well-designed and implemented interaction protocols.

3.1 CHARACTERISTICS OF MULTI-AGENT SYSTEMS

Our world becomes increasingly interconnected, with computers spanning devices such as washing machines, mobile phones and even wearable devices. These devices may be fitted with embedded agents that could do things on our behalf. For instance, an intelligent fridge, sensing that you have run out of milk could notify your personal agent residing in your desktop at home which in turn could send you an email at work to remind you to buy some on your way home, or better still, update your shopping list on your PDA. This scenario presupposes the existence of a number of agents that have the ability to interact with each other. This leads us to the idea of a multi-agent system.

> **Definition 2** *A multi-agent system consists of a network of loosely-coupled computational autonomous agents who can perform actions, have resources at their disposal and possess knowledge, capabilities or skills. They are situated in a common environment and they can interact through a set of rules, namely an interaction protocol.*

Single agent-based systems differ from multi-agent systems along the following dimensions:

- **Environment.** In a multi-agent environment, individual agents need to take into account the other agents in their decision-making process. On the one hand, other agents may interfere with their actions and plans, and on the other, very often they may need to coordinate with them in order to achieve their goals or resolve conflicts. The presence of other autonomous agents inadvertently makes the environment dynamic and stochastic.

- **Knowledge/expertise/skills/design.** Whereas in a single agent-based system, the knowledge or expertise lies within a single agent, this is not the case in a multi-agent system. The knowledge/expertise/skills may be distributed to different agents. Moreover, the knowledge about the state of the world may differ from agent to agent. As the environment may be partially observable, an individual agent may not have a complete and accurate picture of the world's state. Agents need not be homogeneous: they may be designed and implemented in different ways by different developers using different languages.

- **Control**. The control in a multi-agent system is typically distributed. There is no single agent that has global control and is responsible for taking decisions. The data is decentralized and computation is inherently asynchronous. Each agent is responsible for its own decision-making, but agents need to coordinate their actions to achieve a common goal.

- **Interaction**. Agents live and interact in a common environment in which they engage with each other not randomly, but following rules of interaction that enable them to coordinate their actions in order to be able to cooperate or resolve conflicts.

Another related and essential concept in MASs is that of *coherence*, i.e., how well the system behaves as a unit (Bond and Gasser 1988). Coherence may be measured in various ways depending on the problem domain and can be, for instance, in terms of solution quality, effectiveness or efficiency. Coherence is usually measured from an external observer's perspective, who ascertains whether or not a system appears to be behaving in a coherent way, usually with respect to achieving a goal. Steels' example of robotic agents exploring a distant planet (described in the previous chapter) involves a multi-agent system whose objective is to gather rock and mineral samples and bring them back to Earth. As external observers, we say that the system is operating coherently if the objective is satisfied. If the agents were simply moving randomly around, unable to coordinate their actions and gather samples, then the system could not be said to behave in a coherent way. Coherence is therefore an external concept and not necessarily something that the agents themselves are aware of. In some cases, coherence can be designed into a multi-agent system if all the elements are known in advance (closed design). However, given autonomous multiple entities with different skills, expertise and goals, how global coherence can be achieved without imposing explicit global control on the system, is an open problem.

While the definition of a multi-agent system provided here refers explicitly to such systems being composed of computational agents, it is often the case that computational agents have to interact with human agents. Thus, the above definition can be extended to cover multi-agent systems consisting of both human and computational agents. In this book, the term multi-agent system will be used mostly to cover systems as described by the original definition. Occasionally, however, the term may be used to refer to the extended type of multi-agent system. This should be clear from the context.

3.1.1 Potential and challenges

There is a great potential for using MASs in a number of application domains, as the abstraction of MASs supports a modular, extensible approach to the design of complex systems. In particular, they are suitable for complex problems that cannot be solved by any one agent on its own. MASs are ideal for tackling problems that include many problem-solving methods, require different kinds of expertise and knowledge and for which there are multiple viewpoints. For instance, open systems may contain multiple autonomous agents acting on behalf of their users. Such systems can support distributed and concurrent problem-solving by agent collections that can dynamically organize themselves. Also, MASs are suitable for tasks in which the information resources are distributed, as in information gathering on the Internet.

The use of MASs technology offers a number of advantages (Sycara 1998):

1. Extensibility and flexibility, as the system comprises a number of agents with different expertise and capabilities. Inserting new capabilities into the system can be done relatively easily by adding new agents with the respective capabilities. Also, agents can adapt to new conditions in the environment.

2. Robustness and reliability as, when one agent fails, it does not cause the entire system to halt, but instead there is a 'graceful' performance degradation. Other agents can fill in the gaps and take over the tasks of the agent that failed.

3. Computational efficiency and speed, as computation is asynchronous and is performed in parallel.

4. Development and maintainability, as it is easier to develop and maintain a modular system rather than a monolithic one; individual developers may be responsible for the development and maintenance of different agents within the system.

5. Reusability, as agents developed for one MAS can be used in another one to solve a different problem.

6. Reduced cost, as agents are relatively low-cost units to develop and maintain, compared to the entire system.

Although MASs provide many potential advantages, they also raise many difficult challenges with regard to their design and implementation. Among these are (Weiss 1999):

- How to enable agents to interact with one another. What interaction protocols are required, i.e., communication, cooperation and negotiation protocols.
- How to formulate, describe and decompose a problem, allocate tasks to individual agents, and synthesize their partial results.
- How agents can find others in open environments, such as the Internet, where entities can appear and disappear for a number of reasons.
- How to ensure coherent and stable system behaviour and avoid harmful interactions.
- How to enable agents to represent knowledge about the state of the environment, as well as the other agents, their actions and their knowledge.

- How to enable agents to dynamically form structures such as teams and organizations in order to solve complex problems.
- How to develop efficient planning and learning algorithms for MASs.

3.1.2 Closed multi-agent systems

Closed MASs are based on a static design with predefined components and functionalities. This presupposes that the properties of the system are known in advance. In such systems, there is a common language for agent communication and agents are cooperative. Each agent can be developed as an expert in a particular area with specific problem-solving abilities, skills and knowledge. Multiple developers can work towards the development of the system at the same time. An example of a closed system is a MAS built for a particular organization in which there are agents representing different departments with different expertise and different roles.

One advantage of this type of MAS is that the load and expertise can be equally distributed amongst the agents. Moreover, the behaviour of the system is predictable since the components are known and the interaction language and protocols are designed well in advance in accordance with the needs of the system. The agents are usually cooperative and share a common goal. The architecture for building the individual agents is usually common, as well as the programming language for doing so. However, the cost of maintaining such a system can be high, as the entire system is under the control of one development team which has sole responsibility for maintaining it. In particular, adding new agents may require parts of the system to be redesigned including the communication language and other interaction protocols. As the expertise and problem domain capabilities are divided among the agents, such systems may be less fault-tolerant since, if one expert agent fails for some reason and there is no other agent to replace it or take over its tasks, the whole system may come to a halt. To avoid such situations, it is often the case that more than one agents share the same expertise. As these are closed systems, developed with specific objectives and communication and interaction protocols, it may be difficult to achieve interoperation with other systems.

3.1.3 Open multi-agent systems

In an open MAS, the system often has no prior static design, only single agents within. Agents are not necessarily aware of others or the expertise and services that they can offer. Therefore, a mechanism for locating other agents within the system is required. Agents may be non-cooperative, malicious or untrustworthy. An example of an open MAS is an electronic marketplace. Agents representing customers may not necessarily be aware of providers and to obtain services and products they need to be able to locate such agents. This is usually done through specially designed middle agents that act as a directory: yellow pages or broker agents (see chapter on Middle Agents).

One of the advantages of open MASs is that single agents or groups are designed separately. Such systems are more flexible and fault tolerant, since failure of one agent even if this agent is an expert in a particular area/task, does not mean failure of the entire system; another expert agent can be located and take on the task. Such a MAS is easier to maintain since no single individual/organization/team is responsible for the maintenance of the entire system. The system is dynamic like an open society, and may evolve according to the changing needs of the agents and the users they represent. The agents may adapt and evolve. However, since the individual entities within the system may be developed by different developers using different languages and frameworks, heterogeneity is inherent. As a result, communication protocols, languages and ontologies, may vary across agents. Agents and their interaction protocols need to be designed carefully in order to allow interoperation. Malicious behaviour is difficult to avoid and consequently the overall behaviour of the system is not predictable while at times, as there is no explicit global control, the behaviour may appear incoherent.

3.2 INTERACTION

One of the most important issues in MASs is that of interaction.

> *An interaction occurs when two or more agents are brought into a dynamic relationship through a set of reciprocal actions (Ferber 1999, p. 59).*

Therefore, interactions develop as a result of a series of actions, including communicative actions (messages), that transform the environment and thus inevitably affect the other agents within it. The consequences of these interactions influence the future behaviour of the agents. Interaction within a MAS is both unavoidable and necessary. Agents may interact with one another because they need to, or unintentionally. If a group of agents share the same resource and one of them decides to exceed its allowance, then this action will inherently affect the other agents in the system. Fundamentally, interaction assumes that agents are in an environment where situations arise that require and encourage interaction, e.g., need to share resources, or cooperate to solve a complex problem. Moreover, interaction presupposes that agents are capable of acting and/or communicating. Interaction may be direct or indirect, i.e., an agent may not interact directly with another one, but through a third agent. For instance, arranging car insurance through an insurance broker is a form of indirect interaction between the driver seeking insurance cover and the insurance company.

3.2.1 Elements of interactions

Agents in a complex and limited-resources environment need to interact in order to achieve a complex task, to share or allocate goods and resources, or to solve difficult problems. The interaction situation that agents can find themselves in can be characterized by three elements (Ferber 1999):

1. **Goals.** The agents' objectives or goals are obviously of fundamental importance in any interaction situation. Goals can be either compatible or incompatible. If the goals of two agents are compatible, it means that they can work with each other or in parallel towards the achievement of these goals and one goal does not obstruct, preclude or prevent the other from being achieved. On the contrary, if two goals are incompatible, it means that not both of them can be achieved at the same time, one prevents the other from being accomplished and as a result the agents are in conflict.

2. **Resources.** Resources is another factor that affects agent interaction. These may be any environmental, material or other elements that are required by an agent to achieve its goal. It may be financial resources, processor time, storage capacity, energy or any other resource needed to carry out an action. The availability of resources in the environment is critical for the kind of interactions that agents develop. If resources are not plentiful, then agents may have to compete against each other to secure access to them. In such situations, conflict is unavoidable and agents are antagonistic and see others as opponents who interfere with their own goals.

3. **Expertise/Skills/Capabilities.** Agents have their own goals which they try to achieve through actions. However, there are situations in which agents may simply lack the skills, expertise or other capabilities to bring about the desired goal on their own. The relation between expertise/skills/capabilities and the goal to be achieved is the third fundamental element that characterizes the type of interaction that agents have. There are goals that require the contribution of expertise/skills/capabilities of a number of agents in order to be accomplished. Building a house requires a number of different experts and technicians to bring their forces together. The architect is going to contribute his design expertise in order for a safe, ergonomic and long-lasting house to be designed, but he cannot carry out the construction of the house on his own; builders will have to be employed to undertake this. Electricians and plumbers will take care of the wiring and plumbing, respectively, and so on.

3.2.2 Modes of interaction

Agents may interact in different ways. The degree of interaction is the extent to which agents coordinate with each other, avoid conflicts, prevent livelock and deadlock within the system, and maintain applicable safety conditions (Huhns and Stephens 1999). Agents can be characterized as either self-interested/antagonistic, or cooperative/non-antagonistic. Self-interested agents have incompatible goals and are interested in maximizing their own personal utility (performance measure) and they do not necessarily care about the good of the society as a whole, (i.e., MAS). On the other hand, cooperative agents are agents with compatible goals that act in order to maximize their own utility

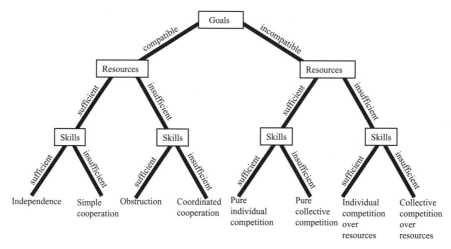

Figure 3.1: Elements and modes of interaction

in conjunction with that of the entire MAS. Thus, cooperation is coordination among cooperative agents, whereas competition is coordination among self-interested agents.

As agents may have different goals and skills and also depend on the resources available for the achievement of their goals, the following different modes of interaction ensue (Ferber 1999). These are graphically illustrated in Figure 3.1:

- **Independence**. The agents' goals are compatible, they have sufficient resources and skills and therefore no interaction among the agents takes place. Agents go about their own business without interfering with or needing one another.

- **Simple cooperation**. In simple cooperation, the agents' goals are compatible, they have sufficient resources, but insufficient skills or expertise. Interaction in this case consists of the simple addition of skills, capabilities or expertise. Such interactions occur, for instance, in problem-solving situations in which the agents are cooperating through knowledge sharing.

- **Obstruction**. Agents have incompatible goals, insufficient resources, but sufficient skills. Obstruction situations arise whenever an agent gets in another's way in accomplishing its objectives.

- **Coordinated cooperation**. The agents have compatible goals, insufficient resources, and insufficient skills. Such situations require that agents coordinate their actions to deal with the lack of resources, expertise and skills. These are the most complex interaction situations that agents have to deal with. Examples include distributed manufacturing and multi-agent robotic systems.

- **Pure individual competition.** In such situations the agents' goals are incompatible, but they have sufficient resources and sufficient skills. Due to goal incompatibility, agents have to compete against each other and, since there is no competition over resources, the best competitor wins. Sporting competitions come under this category of interaction: all agents have sufficient resources, skills and capabilities, but their goals are incompatible. Intuitively, one agent's goal to come first is incompatible with the others'; only one agent can have the first position in a sporting competition.

- **Pure collective competition.** This is different from pure individual competition. Although the agents' goals are still incompatible and they have sufficient resources, the agents lack the skills, expertise or capabilities to achieve their goals on their own. Therefore, they come together in teams or coalitions and compete against others. This process usually takes place in two phases: first the coalition or team is formed and then the teams are pitted against each other. In such situations, although teams compete against each other, they do not obstruct one another. Ferber (1999) gives the example of a relay race as a situation of pure collective competition: the different teams compete, but they do not obstruct one another, i.e., all teams can finish the race.

- **Individual competition over resources.** In this case the agents' goals are incompatible and they possess sufficient skills and expertise, but they lack the resources. Conflicts among individuals arise as resources are critical in achieving one's goals, for example, access to a processor or memory space.

- **Collective competition over resources.** The agents' goals are incompatible, they have insufficient resources and insufficient skills. The agents have to form teams or coalitions, as in pure collective competition, to achieve their goals. In contrast to pure collective competition, in this case the teams prevent one another from accomplishing their goals. Such situations include, for example, industrial competition and other kinds of collective conflict over resources such as territory or financial resources.

3.2.3 Interaction protocols

Multi-agent systems are becoming increasingly popular as a new software engineering paradigm that provides the right abstraction level and the right model to build a lot of distributed applications. The basic components, agents, interact with one another to achieve their individual design objectives. Interactions are the results of communicative actions or physical actions that transform the environment and are carried out by at least two agents. More often, we are not interested in random interactions, but in interactions that enable agents to coordinate themselves in achieving their tasks, either by cooperating or competing. Therefore, it is useful to have interaction protocols in place, that is, rules that guide the interaction that takes place between agents. These rules define the messages or actions that are possible for any particular interaction situation. This set of possible messages or actions that an agent can perform as part of an interaction protocol is finite. In agreeing to use a particular protocol, an agent agrees to conform to its rules and conventions.

Interaction protocols may be communication protocols, cooperation protocols or nego-tiation protocols. Cooperation protocols provide a framework within which agents can coordinate their actions to achieve a complex task or to solve a problem in a cooperative way. In cases of competition over resources or goal incompatibility, it is important to be able to limit and control the effects of the agents' antagonistic behaviour. Thus, situations of competition or conflicts can be resolved through mechanisms that enable the coordination of actions and facilitate conflict resolution. Negotiation protocols help the parties involved to reach a compromise and resolve the conflict by way of an agreement which can be reached after perhaps many stages of interaction and which moderates the satisfaction and the frustration of both sides. Communication protocols provide rules that structure message-passing and produce meaningful dialogues or con-versations. Alternatively, such protocols can be thought of as constraints on the possible valid exchanges of communication primitives, very much as in meaningful conversations among humans.

3.3 AGENT COMMUNICATION

It is only natural to assume that in environments where agents have to do things along with others, an effective means of communication is required. Communication is a key issue in multi-agent systems and in particular in e-commerce, where agents are required to enter into negotiations and transact with other agents. In a communication exchange an agent can have an active, passive or even both roles and therefore act as a master, a slave or a peer respectively (Huhns and Stephens 1999).

Communication among homogeneous agents in specific application domains is relatively straight-forward, as suitable communication protocols with precise syntax and semantics can be defined. However, in open multi-agent systems, diversity introduces heterogeneity and different developers may use different frameworks and programming languages for implementing agents. Nevertheless, we need some means by which heterogeneous agents can understand and be understood.

Communication has three aspects:

1. *syntax*: how the symbols of communication are structured;
2. *semantics*: what the symbols denote;
3. *pragmatics*: how the symbols are interpreted.

Meaning is then a combination of semantics and pragmatics.

The natural question that arises is what is an appropriate Agent Communication Language (ACL)? Is a natural human language such as English a candidate language for an ACL? Human languages are notoriously ambiguous and this is the case even for small fragments of human language unless the domain of discourse is very limited. So human languages as we know them do not appear to be appropriate candidates. Nevertheless, human communication languages have been the basis for drawing ideas and principles from to use in agent communication languages.

3.3.1 Speech Act theory

Perhaps the most influential theory in agent communication is that of *Speech Acts*. Speech Act theory was introduced by Austin (1962) and was extended by Searle (1969). The theory postulates that communication exchange is a form of action. Accordingly, what a speaker utters is not simply some true or false sentence, but a *speech act*. Speakers perform speech acts such as assertions, requests, suggestions, promises, etc., and such acts modify the mental state of the receiver or may even bring about a state of affairs. For example, consider the utterance "Close the door". Speech Act theory tells us that there are three aspects to this utterance. The *locution* is the physical utterance with context and reference, i.e., who is the speaker and the listener, which door, etc. The *illocution* is the act of conveying intentions, i.e., the speaker wants the listener to close the door. Finally, the *perlocution* is the action that occurs as a result of the illocution, i.e., the listener closes the door.

The intent, that is the illocutionary force of an utterance, is important as it constrains the semantics of the communication act itself. Therefore, identifying the intended illocutionary force is central to speech act theory. The term *performative* is often used to describe the illocutionary force. Speech acts can be categorized based on their illocutionary force as follows (Searle 1969):

- *Assertive*: statements of fact. These convey information from speaker to listener, as in "Maria is a lecturer".
- *Commissive*: commitments. These commit the speaker to bring about states of the world or perform actions in the future, as in "I will be in your office at 5:00 pm".
- *Directive*: commands in a master-slave structure. These are used to give directives or commands to the listener and, in essence, the speaker commits the listener to bring about a state or perform an action, as in "Close the door".
- *Declarative*: Using such speech acts, the speaker brings about a state of affairs by the mere performance of the utterance, as in "This lecture is now finished".
- *Expressive*: expressions of emotion. These express the speaker's mental state, as in "I am happy today".

3.3.2 Agent communication languages

An agent communication language is defined at three levels: the lower level, which specifies the method of interconnection; the middle level, which specifies the format or syntax; and the top level, which specifies the meaning or semantics.

An agent communication language has three components: the outer and inner languages and the vocabulary. The 'outer' language is the language that is used in order to express the primitives, i.e., the performatives that an agent is permitted to use in communicating with other agents. It defines an 'envelope' format for using messages and is used by the agent to explicitly state the intended illocutionary force of a message. The 'inner' or 'content' language (syntax) is the (logical or representation) language which is used to write the message itself. In other words, it is the syntax used for the message. This layer allows for knowledge sharing. The vocabulary describes the domain of discourse in terms of concepts and their relationships and prescribes meaning to the terms used, i.e., it is the semantics.

Labrou et al. (1997) identified a number of features as essential for a good ACL. First of all, a good ACL should be declarative and syntactically simple. Secondly, the ACL needs to have a well-defined set of primitives and also needs to distinguish between the communicative language which expresses the primitives, and the content language which expresses the message itself, although it should not commit to a content language. Thirdly, the semantics for the primitives should be clearly defined, preferably through a formal description, as in modal logic. Another desirable feature is that the implementation of the language should be efficient, both in terms of speed and bandwidth, with simple interfaces. Moreover, as networking is prevalent, a good ACL should support all of the basic connections, i.e., point-to-point, multicast and broadcast, and both synchronous and asynchronous communication. Given the heterogeneity of environments, programming languages and frameworks, a good ACL should provide tools for dealing with heterogeneity and support interoperability with other languages and protocols. Finally, an ACL should support reliable and secure communication among agents, including authentication facilities and error detection.

3.3.3 Knowledge and Query Manipulation Language (KQML)

The Knowledge and Query Manipulation Language (KQML), is a high-level, message-oriented, communication language and set of protocols for information exchange (Labrou et al. 1997, 1999). KQML emanated as the result of the DARPA-funded Knowledge Sharing Effort (KSE) in the early 1990s which concentrated on developing a methodology for distributing information among heterogeneous intelligent systems (Patil et al. 1997).

In essence, KQML is an 'outer' language and is based on speech act theory. It consists of three layers: the *content* layer, the *message* layer and the *communication* layer. The communication layer encodes a set of message features that describe the lower-level communication parameters, such as the identities of the sender and addressee(s) and a unique identifier associated with the message. The message layer is used to encode the message to be sent. This layer specifies the speech act or performative that the sender attaches to the content and sends to the addressee. It also includes optional features, such as the content language or the ontology used, among others. The content layer includes the content of the message itself. This can be in any representational language.

In KQML there is a separation of protocol semantics from content semantics. All the information required to understand the message is included in the message. The language is independent of the transport mechanism (TCP/IP, CORBA, etc.), the content language (KIF, SQL, etc.) or the ontology assumed by the content.

Each KQML message consists of the performative, i.e., speech act, and a list of attribute/value pairs:

```
(KQML-performative
    :sender <word>
    :receiver <word>
    :in-reply-to <word>
    :language <word>
    :ontology <word>
    :content <expression>
    ...)
```

KQML has its own keywords with reserved meaning, the most important of which are given in Table 3.1. An example of a KQML message using the **tell** performative is given below:

```
(tell
    :sender Agent435
    :receiver Agent450
    :in-reply-to id-msg-005
    :language KIF
    :ontology cycbase
    :content (salary 9876543 32765))
```

This message is sent by **Agent435** to **Agent450** in reply to a previous message **id-msg-005**. The language used to write the content of the message is KIF using the cycbase ontology. The message itself is **(salary 9876543 32765)** which represents the fact that the salary of employee with number 9876543 is £32765. The performative **tell** asserts what follows :**content**. The values in :**in-reply-to**, :**sender** and :**receiver** are the communication layer, the values in :**language** and :**ontology** comprise the message layer, and the value in :**content** is the content layer. The use of the :**in-reply-to** keyword indicates that this message is sent by **Agent435** to **Agent450** in response to a previous message which must have been a query.

The KQML performatives can be organized into the following categories:

1. Basic query: **evaluate, ask-if, ask-about, ask-one, ask-all, reply, sorry.**
2. Multi-response query: **stream-about, stream-all, eos.**
3. Basic response: **error.**

Keyword	Meaning
:sender	Indicates the sender of the performative.
:receiver	Indicates the receiver of the performative.
:from	The source of the performative in :content when :forward is used.
:to	The final destination of the performative in :content when :forward is used.
:in-reply-to	The expected label in response to a previous message.
:reply-with	The expected label in response to the current message.
:language	The name of the representation language of the :content.
:ontology	The name of the ontology assumed in the :content parameter.
:content	The information about which the performative expresses an attitude.

Table 3.1: Reserved keywords in KQML

4. Generator: **standby, ready, next, rest, discard, generator.**
5. Capability definition: **advertise.**
6. Networking: **register, unregister, forward, broadcast, pipe, break, transport-address.**
7. Facilitation: **broker-one, broker-all, recommend-one, recommend-all, recruit-one, recruit-all.**
8. Database: **insert, delete, delete-one, delete-all.**
9. Basic informative: **tell, deny.**
10. Basic effector: **achieve, unachieve.**
11. Notification: **subscribe, monitor.**

During the first years of its use, KQML lacked a rigorous definition of semantics and only a partial and informal description was provided (Labrou et al. 1997). This was identified as one of the shortcomings of the language and its designers tried to address it in later years (Labrou and Finin 1997, 1998).

Semantics to KQML performatives is given in terms of preconditions, postconditions and completion conditions. These are described in a language that includes operators for expressing the agents' mental attitudes, such as beliefs (BEL), knowledge ($KNOW$), desires ($WANT$) and intentions (INT) as well as action descriptors. Although no semantic models are provided for the mental attitudes, the language used to describe the agents' states restricts the ways in which the mental attitudes can be combined to compose these states.

If A and B are the sender and receiver respectively, $Pre(A)$ identifies the necessary state for the sender to send a performative and $Pre(B)$ the necessary state for the receiver to accept and process it. If the preconditions do not hold, then the most likely response is **error** or **sorry**. The postconditions *Post(A)* and *Post(B)* describe the states of agents *A* and *B* after the successful utterance of a performative by the former, and its receipt and processing by the latter, but before a response performative is sent back. The postconditions hold unless an **error** or **sorry** is sent as a response to indicate the unsuccessful processing of the message. A completion condition *Completion* for the performative describes the final state after the conversation has taken place and the original intention associated with the performative that started the conversation has been accomplished. Nonetheless, even if the preconditions for a performative hold, the successful execution of the performative is not guaranteed. The same applies to postconditions which simply describe the states of the agents assuming the successful execution of the performative. The semantics of the **tell** performative is given below (Labrou and Finin 1998):

> tell(A, B, X)
> $Pre(A)$: $BEL(A, X) \land KNOW(A, WANT(B, KNOW(B, S)))$
> $Pre(B)$: $INT(B, KNOW(B, S))$

where *S* may be any of $BEL(B, X)$ or $\neg(BEL(B, X))$

> $Post(A)$: $KNOW(A, KNOW(B, BEL(A, X)))$
> $Post(B)$: $KNOW(B, BEL(A, X))$
> $Completion$: $KNOW(B, BEL(A, X))$

Accordingly, the semantics of **tell** indicate that an agent cannot offer unsolicited information to another agent, that is without being asked first.

It goes without saying that, for two agents to be able to communicate in KQML, both of them need to be able to understand the 'inner' language being used as well as the ontology.

There are a number of exchange or conversation protocols supported by KQML. In the simplest form of communication one agent acts as the client and the other as the server. This exchange can be either synchronous (the sender awaits a reply) or asynchronous (the sender continues with its reasoning or acting after sending a message).

Being the first ACL to be developed, KQML has been criticized for a number of omissions and inconsistencies (Cohen and Levesque 1995). First, for the fact that some of its performatives such as **achieve**, **broker** and **stream-all** are not really speech acts. Nevertheless, such performatives are essential for agents to be able to interconnect with others. Second, for the total lack of commissive performatives, namely performatives that commit the speaker to accomplishing an action or bringing about a state of affairs. KQML has also been criticized for the lack of a security model; extensions that address this issue have been proposed in Thirunavukkarasu et al. (1995) and He et al. (1998). Despite these criticisms, variations of KQML have been implemented and used in a number of experimental systems and projects as the ACL of choice, including Infosleuth (Bayardo Jr. et al. 1997, Nodine and Unruh 1998), KAOS (Bradshaw et al. 1997), Infomaster (Genesereth et al. 1997), Jackal (Cost et al. 1998) and JATlite (Jeon et al. 2000).

3.3.4 FIPA ACL

As part of the standardization effort for agent interaction protocols, FIPA proposed the FIPA Agent Communication Language (FIPA 2002a), FIPA ACL for short.

Similar to KQML, FIPA ACL is based on speech acts, and messages are considered to be communicative acts (CAs). Communicative acts are described in both a narrative form and a formal semantics based on modal logic. The syntax of FIPA ACL is very similar to that of KQML. It contains a core of primitive communicative acts, and additional acts can be defined compositionally from the core ones. In fact, all performatives in FIPA ACL can be defined in terms of two core ones: **inform** and **request**. An example of the **inform** performative is given below:

```
(inform
    :sender Agent435
    :receiver Agent450
    :language Prolog
    :ontology companyx
    :content "salary(9876543,32765)")
```

In a similar way to KQML, FIPA ACL upkeeps the distinction between outer and inner languages and is independent of the content language. The communicative acts of FIPA ACL are listed in Table 3.2.

Semantics in FIPA ACL is defined through the *Semantic Language* (*SL*) which is a quantified multi-modal logic with operators for beliefs (*B*), uncertain beliefs (*U*), desires (*D*) and persistent goals or intentions (*PG*). *SL* is based on the theory of speech acts of Cohen and Levesque (1990) and, in particular, its extension by Sadek (Sadek 1992, Bretier and Sadek 1997). The semantics of each communicative act is defined in terms of two sets of *SL* formulas: *Feasibility Preconditions* and *Rational Effects*. For a communicative act *a*, the feasibility preconditions *FP*(*a*) describe the necessary conditions that need to hold true in order for the sender to send the act *a*. The feasibility precondition expresses a constraint which describes what the sender of the message must satisfy, if it is to be considered as conforming to FIPA ACL. Although the agent is not obliged to perform *a*, if *FP*(*a*) holds, it may choose to do so. The rational effect of a communicative act represents the effect that an agent can expect to occur as a result of it performing the act, and it may also specify conditions that should hold true for the receiver. In other words, the rational effect describes the purpose of the message, i.e., what it is that the sender attempts to achieve by sending it. However, as agents are autonomous, the rational effect

Communicative act	Meaning
accept-proposal	Accept a proposal made by another agent.
agree	Indicates that the receiver of a request act will carry out the intended action.
cancel	Follow up message of a request act; sender agent indicates that it no longer desires the action requested in **request** to be carried out.
cfp	A call for proposals (cfp) performative is used to initiate negotiation.
confirm	Allows the sender to confirm the truth of the content of the message to the receiver who, prior to the **confirm** message, believed that the sender was unsure about the truth or otherwise of the content.
disconfirm	Similar to **confirm**; indicates to the receiver that the sender believes the content is false.
failure	Indicates to the receiver that an attempt to perform (usually a previously) **request**ed action has failed.
inform	The sender communicates information to the receiver.
inform-if	A macro act for the sender agent to inform the receiver whether or not a proposition is true.
inform-ref	A macro act allowing the sender to inform the receiver of some object that the sender believes corresponds to a descriptor, such as a name or other identifying description.
not-understood	Indicates that an agent perceived that a communicative action took place by another agent, but did not understand why this action was performed.
propagate	Indicates that the sender wants the receiver to propagate the message to another agent(s) specified in the act.
propose	An agent submits a proposal to perform an action that could be in response to a previous **cfp**.
proxy	The sender wants the receiver to act as a proxy and forward the message to a set of agents denoted by a given description.
query-if	The sender asks the receiver whether or not a proposition is true.
query-ref	The sender asks the receiver for the value of a referential expression.

(continued overleaf)

Table 3.2: FIPA ACL Communicative Acts

Communicative act	Meaning
refuse	The sender indicates to the receiver that it will not perform some action and it also explains the reasons for the refusal.
reject-proposal	The sender rejects a proposal to perform some action during the process of a negotiation and it also includes the reasons for rejection.
request	The sender requests the receiver to perform some action.
request-when	The sender wants the receiver to perform some action when a condition becomes true.
request-whenever	The sender wants the receiver to perform some action when a condition becomes true and thereafter each time the condition becomes true again.
subscribe	The sender wants to be notified whenever there is a change in the object identified by the reference.

Table 3.2: (*continued*)

of a communicative action cannot be guaranteed. Therefore, the receiver of the message does not have to conform to the rational effect of the message. The semantics for **inform** is given below:

$$< i, \text{inform}(j, \phi) >$$
$$FP: B_i(\phi) \wedge \neg B_i(B_i f_j(\phi) \vee U_i f_j(\phi))$$
$$RE: B_j(\phi)$$

Accordingly, agent i informs agent j of the content ϕ where ϕ is a proposition. The sender i believes that the proposition ϕ is true $(B_i(\phi))$ and does not already believe that the receiver j has any knowledge about the truth or falsity of ϕ $(\neg B_i(B_i f_j(\phi) \vee U_i f_j(\phi)))$. The expected rational effect is that the receiver j will also come to believe that the proposition ϕ is true $((B_j(\phi))$.

FIPA provides the specification for a number of communication exchange protocols, such as the *Request*, *Query* and *Request When* interaction protocols, among others. Similar to KQML, the current FIPA specification does not provide any particular mechanism for secure agent communications. Although some preliminary suggestions have been made for secure agent communications in the FIPA Security Specification (FIPA 1998), there are no concrete mechanisms as yet. The implicit assumption is that agents are cooperative, reliable and trusted and that security is performed elsewhere in the infrastructure in which the agent is embedded. An approach to deal with security issues in FIPA agents including communication has been suggested in (Poslad et al. 2002). FIPA ACL compliant systems include JADE (Bellifemine et al. 1999), Agent Factory (Collier 2001, Collier et al. 2003), Grasshopper (Baumer et al. 2000) and JACK Intelligent Agents (Busetta et al. 1999).

3.3.5 Comparing KQML and FIPA ACL

Although KQML and FIPA ACL look syntactically similar and ascribe to the same theory, there are fundamental differences between them. The first and most prominent is that of semantics. In KQML, semantics is described in terms of pre, post and completion conditions, whereas FIPA ACL semantics is based on speech acts as rational actions (Cohen and Levesque 1990, Sadek 1992, Bretier and Sadek 1997) that have feasibility preconditions and rational effects. Each ACL uses different languages to describe the propositional mental attitudes, e.g., KQML's *BEL* operator is not the same as FIPA ACL's *B* operator. Although the FIPA ACL primitives can be approximated using the KQML performatives and vice versa, a direct transformation between the two languages is not possible. Both languages claim that they are independent of the use of content language. However, in order to be able to process some incoming communicative acts in FIPA ACL such as **request**, the agent needs to have a basic understanding of the *SL* language.

Other differences between the two languages include the use of different keywords, for instance, KQML uses **tell**, whereas FIPA ACL uses **inform** for the same communicative act. Even though the two performatives syntactically are almost identical, their semantics differ as well. A further difference has to do with the treatment of the 'administration' and 'facilitation' primitives. These are important as they allow an agent to register itself so that it can locate and be located in an open multi-agent system by other agents. In KQML such communicative acts are treated as first-class objects and constitute primitives. In FIPA ACL **register** and **unregister** are treated as requests for actions with reserved (natural language) meaning, while facilitation primitives such as **broker**, **recommend** and **recruit** are not part of the FIPA ACL specification.

3.3.6 Knowledge Interchange Format Language (KIF)

Agents need to be able to represent and reason about many things such as the world around them, the objects and their relations, their own beliefs, other agents, perceptions and tasks. Therefore, a common language for encoding and representing such things is required. Knowledge Interchange Format (KIF) is a content language based on first-order logic with extensions to support nonmonotonic reasoning and definitions (Genesereth and Fikes 1992). As KQML, KIF emanated from the KSE project.

KIF is a highly expressive language based on a prefix version of first-order predicate calculus. It can be used to represent knowledge in declarative form in knowledge bases and it is also human readable. For example, the following predicate describes that the salary of employee with number 013-87-8734 who works for the finance section is £35000:

(salary 013-87-8734 finance 35000)

More complicated relationships can be encoded in KIF using complex terms. The language also includes standard logical operators for expressing negation (**not**), disjunction (**or**), conjunction (**and**), quantification (**exists, forall**), etc. The following formula expresses that there is a bird perching on a tree:

(exists ((?x bird) (?y tree)) (on ?x ?y))

KIF can be used to define objects and relations between objects, as well as rules. For instance, the following formula describes the concept of a mother:

(defrelation mother(?x ?y):= (and (female ?x) (parent x? y?)))

The language also includes the quote (') and comma (,) operators that are used for encoding knowledge about knowledge. The comma operator indicates that the variables should not be taken literally. The formula below states that agent **agent435** is interested in receiving instances in the form of triplets in the **distance** relation which represents the distance in kilometres **z** between two cities **x** and **y**:

(interested agent435 '(distance ,?x ,?y ,?z))

KIF can also be used to write programs for agents to execute that resemble Lisp. The semantics of the core of the language (without definitions and rules) is very similar to first-order logic. KIF is probably the most widely used content language for knowledge bases. It is highly expressive, but this complicates the building of fully conforming systems, which also tend to be heavyweight. Moreover, its logic-oriented format may not be acceptable to a wider community.

3.3.7 Dialogues

Agents use communication to interact with one another in a variety of situations. In essence, a series of messages being exchanged comprise a dialogue or conversation. The purpose of engaging in a dialogue may vary. Dialogues can be distinguished into six types according to Walton and Krabbe (1995) which are illustrated in Table 3.3.

In the persuasion type of dialogue, agents will start with differing opinions and one attempts to convince the other about the truth or falsity of a position. In such dialogues, agents engage in persuasive argumentation with one another (see Section 9.6) and the purpose is to change each other's beliefs and ultimately influence each other's behaviour. Inquiry and information-seeking dialogues are related to verifying and gathering information, respectively. The former involves a group of agents, as in when an inquest is conducted, whereas the latter involves an individual finding out something on its own. Negotiation dialogues involve agents that attempt to maximize their utilities. In a deliberation dialogue, the agents communicate in order to decide on a course of action. An eristic dialogue involves agents who have a conflict and quarrel often in public in an attempt to reach a compromise. The mixed type of dialogue combines a number of dialogue types, and participants in this case may have multiple goals.

Type	Initial situation	Participant's goal	Main goal
Persuasion	conflict of opinions	persuade other agent	clarify/resolve issue
Inquiry	need for information	find evidence or proof	knowledge acquisition
Negotiation	conflict of interests	get best deal possible	reach a deal
Information seeking	personal ignorance	acquire or provide personal knowledge	distribute information
Deliberation	need to decide on action	influence outcome	reach a decision
Eristic	conflict	provoke other agent	reach a compromise
Mixed	various	various	various

Table 3.3: A classification of dialogues based on Walton and Krabbe (1995)

Protocols that govern the interactions of agents when participating in a dialogue are often called dialogue games. Thus, in dialogue games each agent 'makes a move' by making an utterance according to a set of rules. Dialogue game protocols that formalize the main types of dialogue as described by Walton and Krabbe (1995) have been proposed: persuasion dialogues (Amgoud et al. 2000a, Dignum et al. 2000); inquiry dialogues (McBurney and Parsons 2001); negotiation dialogues (Amgoud et al. 2000b, McBurney et al. 2003, Sadri et al. 2001) (also see Section 9.6.4); information-seeking dialogues (Walton and Krabbe 1995); and deliberation dialogues (Hitchcock et al. 2001).

3.3.8 A layered model of communication

Communication can take place among agents that reside in the same agent platform or among agents on different platforms. In the latter case, the message will have to be transported using the underlying network infrastructure. To enable effective agent communication among agent platforms, a layered approach is required. Figure 3.2 illustrates the different layers required for an agent to be able to send a message to another agent over the network (Helin and Laukkanen 2003). Some of the layers essential for communication have already been discussed.

The first layer, the transport and signalling layer, should provide an efficient and reliable data transport service. Examples of protocols used in this layer are the Transmission Control Protocol (TCP) and the User Datagram Protocol (UDP). This layer should be transparent to the agents.

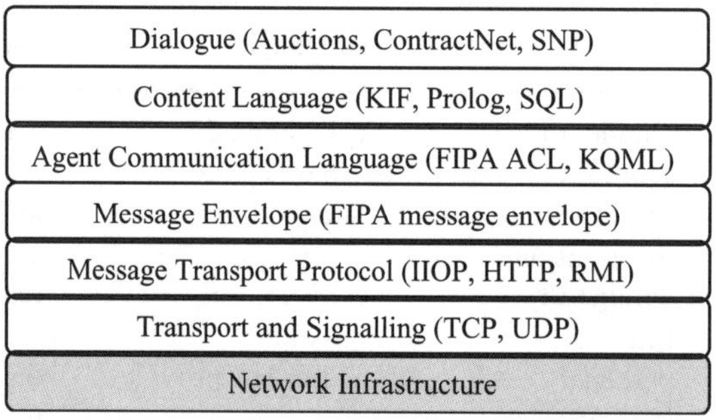

| Dialogue (Auctions, ContractNet, SNP) |
| Content Language (KIF, Prolog, SQL) |
| Agent Communication Language (FIPA ACL, KQML) |
| Message Envelope (FIPA message envelope) |
| Message Transport Protocol (IIOP, HTTP, RMI) |
| Transport and Signalling (TCP, UDP) |
| Network Infrastructure |

Figure 3.2: A layered model for agent communication

The message transport protocol (MTP) is used to carry out the physical transfer of messages between two agent platforms. This layer defines the structure of messages sent using a transport protocol. Consequently, the MTP may implicitly define the transport protocol to be used. In the FIPA specification two MTPs are defined, the Internet Inter-Orb Protocol (IIOP) and the HyperText Transport Protocol (HTTP). IIOP uses TCP as the underlying transport protocol.

The message envelope expresses transport information. All information in the message envelope is supporting information only. MTPs may use different internal representations to describe message envelopes, but must express the same terms, have the same semantics and perform the corresponding actions. The message envelope may be independent of the MTP, although in certain cases the envelope format is tightly coupled with a particular MTP. For instance, in the FIPA specification, the IIOP MTP protocol is tightly coupled with the message envelope. The message envelope is built into the protocol specification and thus the Interface Description Language (IDL) interface defines the message envelope structure. On the other hand, HTTP MTP is based on the transfer of data representing the entire agent message, including the message envelope in a HTTP request. The HTTP data transfer is a two-step process. First, the sender makes a HTTP request. After receiving the data the receiver sends an HTTP response. The receiver then parses the message envelope and the message is handled according to the instructions and information given in the message envelope. According to the FIPA specification, a message envelope consists of a collection of parameters, where a parameter is a name/value pair, and it contains at least the mandatory **to, from, date** and **acl-representation** parameters, and can also contain optional parameters. Each Agent Platform (in fact, the Agent Communication Channel (ACC)) handling a message may add new information to the message envelope, but it may never overwrite existing information. Agent Platforms (their corresponding ACCs) can add new parameters to a message envelope which override existing parameters; the mechanism for disambiguating message envelope entries is specified by each concrete message envelope syntax.

Above the message envelope there is the agent communication language layer which defines which agent communication language is used to write the message, i.e., FIPA ACL or KQML. The content language layer defines the inner language used to write the content of the message itself such as, for instance, KIF or Prolog. It goes without saying that ontologies need to be explicitly defined so that the message content can be understood by all participants in the communication exchange. Finally, the top layer is the dialogue or interaction protocol layer. The interaction protocol essentially identifies the sequence of messages that need to be exchanged, or in other words the structure of the conversation, for agents to have meaningful interactions. It is crucial that interaction protocols are well-designed and efficient while they minimize unnecessary message exchange. A badly designed interaction protocol means that the interaction will take longer to bring about a successful conclusion.

3.4 ONTOLOGIES

For agents to be able to communicate with and understand each other, a common language does not suffice, they also need to share the same terminology. Confusion and misunderstandings may arise if agents use the same language to communicate, but refer to the same concept employing different terms. For instance, agent i refers to anyone who buys products as a *client* whereas agent j refers to such an entity as a *customer*. Thus, the same thing can be portrayed in different ways, each representing different perspectives or ways of thinking. Confusion may also arise when agents refer to different concepts using the same term. For agent i an *employee* is anyone on the payroll system, whereas for agent j an *employee* is anyone receiving benefits. If agents are not aware of this distinction, they will not be able to enter into a meaningful dialogue. Consequently, a shared representation is essential for successful communication and interaction to take place between heterogeneous agents.

This common vocabulary or shared terminology can be captured and crystallized in an ontology. An ontology is a specification of the concepts, objects and their attributes, and relationships, in a specific knowledge domain. The subject of ontology is the study of the classes of things, their attributes and relationships that exist in some domain D. The product, an ontology, is a specification of the types of things that exist in D from a particular perspective, using a language L. As an ontology represents a domain from a particular perspective, conforming to an ontology means committing to seeing the world in a particular way as elegantly explained in (Davis et al. 1993, p. 19):

> ... representations are imperfect approximations to reality, each approximation attending to some things and ignoring others, then in selecting any representation we are in the very same act unavoidably making a set of decisions about how and what to see in the world. That is, selecting a representation means making a set of ontological commitments.

The commitments are in effect a strong pair of glasses that determine what we can see, bringing some part of the world into sharp focus, at the expense of blurring other parts.

An ontology defines a common vocabulary for those who need to share information in a domain. In other words, an ontology constitutes common ground for those wishing to engage in meaningful interactions. This is one of the primary reasons why we need to develop ontologies.

Ontologies are also important because they enable the reuse of domain knowledge (Noy and McGuinness 2001). For instance, models of many different domains need to represent the notion of time. If such an ontology is developed in sufficient detail once, then it can be deployed in many other domains. Existing ontologies that describe only parts of a domain and not its entirety, can also be integrated into one large domain ontology. Although this may not always be straightforward, it is still possible and allows for the reuse of domain knowledge.

Ontologies also allow us to encode assumptions about the domain explicitly. These encodings can be easily changed if our domain assumptions change. It is much easier to change domain assumptions when these are encoded in ontologies, rather than when they are hard-coded in a program. Consequently, it is also easier to share the changes in the domain assumptions.

Furthermore, ontologies allow us to separate domain from operational knowledge. For example, a program can be developed which configures a product from its parts according to a given specification. An ontology can then be developed describing the various components comprising a PC and fed into the program. The same program can be used with different ontologies describing different products, e.g., a car ontology. Finally, explicit specifications of domain knowledge are useful for new users who must learn the meanings of the terms in the domain.

Ontologies can be used by people, software agents, databases, and other applications that need to share information in a specific domain such as medicine, finance, web services, etc.

3.4.1 Explicit ontologies

Domain knowledge can be encoded in two ways: implicitly in procedures or explicitly in declarative statements. An explicit ontology is a formal explicit description of concepts in a domain of discourse, properties of each concept describing various features and attributes, and restrictions on the properties. The focus of ontologies is on classes. Classes describe concepts in the domain. Explicit ontologies are usually expressed in a logic-based language, so that precise, detailed, consistent, sound, and meaningful distinctions can be made among the classes, objects, attributes, and relationships. Explicit ontologies have three aspects: a conceptualization, a vocabulary and an axiomatization. The conceptualization describes the underlying model of the domain in terms of classes, objects, attributes and relations. The vocabulary assigns symbols or terms to refer to those classes, objects, attributes and relations. Finally, the axiomatization encodes rules and constraints, capturing significant aspects of the domain model.

For instance, the basic classes of objects and their relationships in a company ontology can be defined using KIF to encode concepts as unary predicates and relationships as higher-order predicates:

```
(Person x)
(Employee x)
∀x (Employee x) ⇒ (Person x)
(part-time x)
(full-time x)
∀x (Employee x) ⇒ (∧ (∨ (full-time x)(part-time x))(¬ (∧ (full-time x)(part-time x))))
```

Two explicit ontologies for the same domain can be based on different conceptualizations, which means that the relations and objects have been modelled in a different way. Two ontologies can be based on the same conceptualization, but use different vocabularies. Finally, two ontologies that attempt to capture and axiomatize the same domain may do so at a different level of detail.

3.4.2 Developing ontologies

A number of methodologies exist and tools have been built for developing ontologies. Although there is no 'correct' methodology, the development of ontologies is necessarily an iterative process (Uschold and Grüninger 1996, Noy and McGuinness 2001).

The first step in developing an ontology is to determine the domain and the scope of the ontology, as well as to clarify the purposes for using it. The next step is to acquire domain knowledge. This includes gathering appropriate information regarding the terms used formally to describe things and entities in the domain, so that they can be expressed in the language selected for the ontology. The following step is to organize the ontology and clearly design the overall conceptual structure of the domain. This involves identifying the domain's principal concepts and their properties, organizing concepts according to their features, and identifying their relationships. This means that the class hierarchy needs to be defined along with the various properties characterizing concepts. This is pivotal in ontology design and development. Typically, we create a few definitions of the concepts in the hierarchy and then continue by describing properties of these concepts and so on, in an iterative process. A class hierarchy can be developed using different approaches (Uschold and Grüninger 1996). A top-down approach starts with the definition of the most general concepts in the domain and proceeds by specializing the concepts. A bottom-up approach starts with the definition of the most specific classes, in other words, the leaves of the hierarchy. These are then grouped into more general concepts. Alternatively, a combination of the top-down and bottom-up approaches can be employed, in which the most significant concepts are usually defined first and then are generalized and specialized as required.

Concepts, relations and properties need to be added to the level of detail necessary to satisfy the purposes of the ontology. Individual instances of the classes in the hierarchy are then added.

Next, the ontology needs to be checked with regard to syntactic, logical, and semantic inconsistencies. Consistency checking may also involve automatic classification that defines new concepts based on individual properties and class relationships. Domain experts can be used to verify the accuracy of the ontology and the depicted concepts and their relations. It is often the case that ontologies undergo a series of versions before being committed to the public domain. Finally, the ontology is published and made available for use and it is deployed in the required domain of application. Ontologies, of course, need to be maintained, updated and perhaps linked with other ontologies.

In developing a new ontology, existing ontologies can be used and incorporated with newly developed in-house ontologies. Naturally in time, careful management of this collection of heterogeneous ontologies becomes necessary to keep track of them. Tools are needed to help map and link between them, compare them, reconcile and validate them, merge them, and convert them into other forms. One of the most well-known tools for developing ontologies is Ontolingua (Farquhar et al. 1997). Ontolingua is a language for building, publishing and sharing ontologies built at Stanford University. The ontology definition language, which is used for writing the ontologies themselves, is based on KIF. Ontolingua includes a web-based interface to a browser/editor server. Ontologies written in Ontolingua can be translated into other content languages like Prolog and LOOM. Many other languages and protocols have been used for writing ontologies such, as XML (XML 2006) and DARPA Agent Markup Language, DAML (DAML 2006), and more recently the Ontology Web Language, OWL (OWL 2006), which has been designed to serve as a Web ontology language. Several attempts have been made to build general ontologies for a number of domains. For instance, a number of ontologies have been built by Cycorp (Cycorp 2006). Another example is WordNet which is an on line lexical reference system (WordNet 2006).

3.4.3 OWL

OWL (2006) is an ontology language that can formally describe the meaning of terminology used in Web documents. OWL extends and is a revision of the DARPA Agent Markup Language+Ontology Inference Layer (DAML+OIL) web ontology language.

To understand the origins of OWL, we need to have a closer look at the Web. What makes the Web possible is two main elements: the HyperText Transport Protocol (HTTP) which provides a common set of rules enabling Web servers and clients to communicate with each other, and the HyperText Markup Language (HTML) format which essentially defines how documents should be displayed by a Web browser through the use of markup tags. These tags tell the browser which part of the document is a header, when some text should appear as bold and so on. But, although HTML contains tags that allow one to convey information about the layout of the document, it lacks tags that convey information about the meaning of data.

XML was developed in answer to this need, i.e., to be able to convey meaning about data. XML can represent semantic properties through its syntactic structure, via the nesting or sequentially ordering relationship among its elements, i.e., XML tags. This syntactic structure is in turn defined by a Document Type Definition (DTD). Thus, using XML, one can add information to a web page in such a way so as to allow not only its display, but also its processing and understanding by programs. This is the vision of the Semantic Web: the Web is not simply a collection of web pages, but web pages have a meaning and they can be understood and processed by programs or software agents. To develop a Web with semantics, the various resources need to be represented in or annotated with structured machine-understandable descriptions of their contents and relationships, using vocabularies and constructs that have been explicitly and formally defined through a domain ontology. XML provides a surface syntax for structured documents and, in essence, regularizes the syntax of HTML so that it is easier to parse and process. XML Schema is a language for restricting the structure of XML documents and also extends XML with datatypes. However, although XML provides a data format for documents and structured data, and thus one might derive some sort of semantics from the structure of the documents within the context of the document type, the semantics of each element (XML tag) is not defined, and its interpretation relies on the implicit knowledge hardcoded in application programs. Thus, despite XML being syntactically expressive, it is semantically rather limited.

The Resource Description Framework (RDF) is a datamodel for resource objects on the Web and the relations between them. It is mainly intended for representing metadata about resources such as the author, title and modification date, among others, but also in general about things that can be identified on the Web, even if they cannot be directly retrieved, such as product specifications and price information. RDF provides the means to represent graphs which express the structure of a given document as well as of the background knowledge or ontology with respect to which a given document may be understood. RDF documents are written in XML. But the RDF primitives themselves are rather sparse. RDF Schema is a basic vocabulary for describing properties and classes of RDF resources along with a semantics for generalization-hierarchies of such properties and classes. RDF Schema does not provide actual application-specific classes and properties, instead it provides the framework to describe them. Classes in RDF Schema are much like classes in object-oriented programming languages. This allows resources to be defined as instances of classes, and subclasses of classes.

OWL builds on RDF and proposes a specific vocabulary that provides selected frame and description logic primitives to capture ontologies. Thus, it has an enriched vocabulary which allows for describing classes and properties including relations between classes (e.g., disjointness), cardinality (e.g., 'exactly one'), equality, richer typing of properties, characteristics of properties (e.g., symmetry), and enumerated classes. OWL and RDF are much of the same thing, but OWL is a stronger language with greater machine interpretability than RDF. Similar to RDF, OWL is written in XML.

OWL provides three sublanguages with increasing expressiveness:

- OWL Lite is mainly intended for class hierarchies and limited constraints (cardinality 0 or 1, equality, etc.). OWL Lite has the lower formal complexity among the OWL sublanguages.

- OWL DL (includes OWL Lite) is intended in cases where completeness and decidability are important. In essence, the language constructs can only be used under certain conditions so that computational completeness (all conclusions are guaranteed to be computable) and decidability (all computations will finish in finite time) are retained. Such a restriction, for instance, is that while a class may be a subclass of many classes, it cannot be an instance of another class. OWL DL has the theoretical properties of Description Logic, hence the acronym.

- OWL Full (includes OWL DL) provides for maximum expressivity, but no computational guarantees. OWL Full allows an ontology to enhance the meaning of the pre-defined (RDF or OWL) vocabulary.

An OWL specification document which is an XML file has **rdf:RDF** as its top-level element. This element includes attributes declaring the key namespaces which would most certainly include the OWL, RDF and RDF Schema namespaces and often XML Schema, plus perhaps others that are specific to the domain. For instance, the following fragment would be part of a description of an OWL model for the domain of automobiles:

```
<rdf:RDF
  xmlns:rdf="http://www.w3.org/1999/02/22-rdf-syntax-ns#"
  xmlns:rdfs="http://www.w3.org/2000/01/rdf-schema#"
  xmlns:owl="http://www.w3.org/2002/07/owl#"
  xml:base="http://www.daml.org/2001/XMLSchema#">
  <rdfs:comment>The ontology is defined here</rdfs:comment>
</rdf:RDF>
```

Then the assertion **owl:Ontology** defines that the document is an ontology. Information about versions is usually included here.

```
<owl:Ontology rdf:about="Transportation">
  <owl:versionInfo>$Id: transportation.owl, v 1.0 2005/11/17 19:34:16 mfasli Exp$
```

```
</owl:versionInfo>
<rdfs:comment>An ontology for transportation</rdfs:comment>
</owl:Ontology>
```

An ontology defines classes, and relationships among those classes. For instance, the first definition asserts that there is a class named **Automobile** and the second that there is another class called **Truck** which is a subclass of **Automobile**.

```
<owl:Class rdf:ID="Automobile">
  <rdfs:label>Automobile </rdfs:label>
  <rdfs:comment>Automobile class</rdfs:comment>
</owl:Class>
<owl:Class rdf:ID="Truck">
  <rdfs:subClassOf rdf:resource="#Automobile"/ >
  <rdfs:comment>Class Truck is a subclass of Automobile</rdfs:comment>
</owl:Class>
```

A more detailed exposition of OWL is beyond the scope of this book, but see (Singh and Huhns 2005) for a thorough introduction with examples.

3.5 COOPERATIVE PROBLEM-SOLVING

As MASs can be seen as loosely coupled networks of problem solvers, they are well-suited for inherently distributed tasks and complex problems that may be beyond the scope and the capabilities of any one individual agent. In this respect, an agent can be more useful in the context of others since it can concentrate on tasks of its expertise and take advantage of its ability to intelligently communicate, coordinate, negotiate and delegate tasks to other agents. Expertise and load can be distributed among the agents within the system. Such agents are cooperative with compatible goals that act in order to maximize their own utility in conjunction with that of the MAS. Thus, cooperative problem-solving is the design of systems of agents that successfully cooperate to solve a difficult and large problem or perform a complex task.

Despite the immense potential of using MASs for cooperative problem-solving, there are a number of key questions in designing such systems (Sycara 1998, Huhns and Stephens 1999):

- How to determine shared goals and common tasks.
- How to decompose tasks, match subtasks to available agents and synthesize the partial results.
- How to reconcile different views and avoid unnecessary conflicts.
- Should the structure of the system be fixed, self-repairing or self-organizing?
- How to facilitate convergence on solutions despite incomplete or inconsistent knowledge or data.

3.5.1 Task decomposition and distribution

One of the central issues in cooperative problem-solving is that of task decomposition. In other words, given a complex task, how can this be divided into smaller, more manageable tasks.

Task decomposition and how it is accomplished depends on the particular domain and problem under consideration. A number of approaches can be used (Huhns and Stephens 1999). One approach is to deal with task decomposition at the implementation stage of the MAS, in which case it is programmed by the designer of the system. At runtime, agents can decompose complex tasks through hierarchical planning. Another approach is to decompose tasks according to the knowledge and capabilities of the agents within the system. Alternatively, task decomposition can be done taking into account the spatial distribution of data and information resources or decision nodes. For instance, tasks associated with a document repository can be assigned to the agent which is closer to that resource.

Once a complex task has been decomposed, the subtasks need to be distributed to agents for execution. In distributing tasks to agents, the following criteria should be considered (Durfee et al. 1987, Huhns and Stephens 1999):

- Avoid overloading critical and scarce resources.
- Assign tasks to agents with appropriate capabilities and expertise.
- Make agents with a wider view responsible for assigning tasks and subproblems to other agents.
- Assign tasks that overlap to some agents in order to achieve coherence.
- Assign closely-related tasks to agents that are in spatial or semantic proximity, to minimize the communication and synchronization costs.
- Reassign tasks if necessary for completing critical tasks, or when other agents fail.
- Allow agents to change or take on new roles in order to achieve better utilization of resources and distribution of load.

There are various task distribution mechanisms. For instance, market mechanisms or multi-agent planning can be used: planning agents have the responsibility for task assignment and distribution within a multi-agent system. Another alternative is to employ an organizational structure in which agents have fixed roles and responsibilities for particular tasks. One of the most well-known task distribution mechanisms for cooperative problem-solving is the ContractNet protocol, which is described next.

3.5.2 The ContractNet Protocol

The ContractNet is an interaction protocol for cooperative problem-solving among agents proposed by Reid Smith (Smith 1977, 1980a,b, Smith and Davis 1981). The protocol emulates the mechanism which is used in the business world for contracting and subcontracting. The ContractNet provides a solution to the *connection* problem, namely finding an appropriate agent to work on a given task.

There are two main roles that agents can play within the ContractNet protocol, the manager and the contractor. The manager agent has a task that wants to be performed, whereas the contractor agents have the capabilities to perform this task. The roles of the agents are not fixed and an agent may play a different role in different contracts and thus, contractors may themselves act as managers and delegate further. An implicit assumption in ContractNet is that the manager agent must be able to decompose tasks and problems and synthesize solutions out of sub-solutions as these are returned by the contractors. In essence, agents must be knowledgeable.

The general process is as follows. The manager announces the task that needs to be performed and sends out messages advertising the task to potential contractors. The contractors receive the message from the manager and evaluate the task according to the eligibility criteria and their personal capabilities. The contractors respond by offering bids. The manager receives the bids from the potential contractors and evaluates them. It then awards the contract/task to a suitable contractor and sends a message informing the agent. The contractor performs the task if its bid is accepted, and reports the results to the manager. The manager receives the results of the various tasks performed and synthesizes them. It then terminates the contracts. The series of messages being exchanged as part of the ContractNet protocol is illustrated in Figure 3.3.

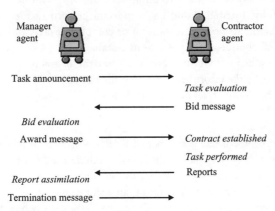

Figure 3.3: The exchange of messages between manager and contractor agents in the ContractNet protocol

The task announcement may be addressed to a number of potential contractors (general broadcast). If the manager agent has some knowledge about the contractors and their capabilities, then it can issue a limited broadcast. If it knows exactly which contractors would be suitable for a specific task, it can make a point-to-point announcement. The announcement includes fields for *addressee*, *eligibility specification*, *task abstraction*, *bid specification* and *expiration time*. For a contractor to be able to bid for a task, it must meet the eligibility criteria, as specified in the eligibility specification. The task abstraction, which is nothing more than a brief description of the task, is used by the contractors to rank tasks from different announcements. The bid specification indicates the information that needs to be provided as part of the bid to the manager, and which is subsequently used by the manager to rank all submitted bids for a specific task and decide to whom to award the contract. The expiration time specifies the deadline for receiving bids. If the manager does not receive any bids by the expiration time for a particular task, it can re-announce the task. The award message sent to the contractor by the manager includes the complete specification of the task to be executed, while the report returned by the contractor includes the result of the task execution.

A facility for direct contracts without negotiation is provided, if the manager knows exactly which contractor is suitable for the task. This seems to improve the efficiency for certain tasks. In this case, the selected contractor responds with a refusal or acceptance.

In the original ContractNet implementation, each node (agent) consisted of a communication processor, a task processor, a contract processor and a local database. A common internode language with a very simple grammar and a partly domain-independent vocabulary was used for communicating task specific information.

The ContractNet protocol is simple to implement, and it constitutes the basis for other protocols. It is fully distributed and has a graceful performance degradation since, if a contractor is unable to provide a solution or complete a task, the manager can seek out other potential contractors. Applications suitable for the ContractNet protocol are those that feature a hierarchy of tasks or levels of data abstraction, and relatively large subtasks which justify the effort being put into the agent-selection process. Examples of applications for the ContractNet protocol include manufacturing control and scheduling (Rabelo et al. 1999).

The ContractNet protocol has a number of limitations. First of all, an agent may bid on a task for which it is marginally suited, and preclude itself from bidding on a much more suitable task announced soon afterwards. Secondly, agents have knowledge only of contracts which they are part of. As a result, an agent cannot decide its bids in the light of other existing bids and contracts. Thirdly, agents do not know how busy other agents are. This is especially important for manager agents. A manager may not receive any bids because all potential contractors are engaged in other tasks; a potential contractor is idle, but may rank the proposed contract below other contracts being considered at that point in time; or no contractors, even if idle, meet the eligibility criteria for the contract. A remedy in this case would be for a manager to request immediate responses from the potential contractors with messages such as *eligible but busy*, *ineligible*, or *uninterested*.

Furthermore, managers are under no obligation to inform potential contractors that a contract has already been awarded. Thus, a contractor never knows whether or not at a given point in time after it has sent a bid, the contract has already been awarded to another agent, or the manager is still deliberating. Another potential problem is that the manager may not accept any of the bids submitted. Although managers are assumed to be knowledgeable and able to break down tasks and synthesize solutions, there is nothing in the ContractNet protocol which describes how tasks are to be decomposed into subtasks. This is inevitably a domain-specific matter.

3.6 VIRTUAL ORGANIZATIONS AS MULTI-AGENT SYSTEMS

In today's fast-evolving business world, organizations need to be agile and innovative to be able to withstand competition and respond to the changing needs of the customer force. A virtual organization (VO) often referred to as virtual enterprise (VE) or agile enterprise, comprises a number of partners that forge a consortium dynamically in order, for instance, to meet customer demand, offer new improved services or added value, or exploit a niche in the market.

MASs are ideal for tackling the problem of creating VOs as the constituent entities can be naturally viewed as agents (Petersen et al. 2001). These agents have an assortment of capabilities, resources and expertise and offer different services, so by pulling their forces together they can increase their gain.

Agents representing entities such as manufacturers, suppliers, service providers, brokers and other partners, can take advantage of new opportunities and changing circumstances in markets and organize themselves into VOs to achieve temporary objectives. Within a VO, agents join forces, coordinate and enact processes that span their constituent organizations. The creation of such VOs is dynamic and is driven by the market needs and conditions. Agents may join or leave the VO at different times depending on their own goals, but for an agent to join a VO it needs to be able to benefit from such membership. Hence, the focus is on the temporary objectives which essentially enable the various partners to accomplish their own goals. Although consisting of a number of autonomous partners, the VO acts and appears as a single conceptual entity to any other third party that will be dealing with it, therefore integration and coordination are fundamental issues. Agility and the ability to respond to constant change in an unpredictable environment is what characterizes VOs. Put simply, a VO is a MAS.

The lifecycle of a VO consists of four main phases: creation, operation, maintenance and disbanding. During the creation phase one or more agents become aware of the need for a VO. The initiator(s) will then contact other potential partners to determine their suitability and willingness to join the VO and through some selection process a group of agents will be established that are willing to work jointly in the context of the VO. The selection of partners with appropriate skills and resources is crucial in this stage as it determines the future success and effectiveness of the VO (Petersen and Greninger 2000,

Norman et al. 2004). Auction protocols can be used, for instance, in order to determine the most suitable partners in this phase. Once the VO has been created, the various tasks need to be distributed through some means among the partner agents. For instance, the ContractNet protocol has been used in this phase (Rabelo et al. 1999). Coalition formation techniques can also be applied in distributing tasks to the members of the VO (Shehory and Kraus 1998, Dang and Jennings 2004). The maintenance phase is essential in a dynamic environment. The VO may have to self-organize as partners may decide to leave the VO for a number of reasons; they may go out of business or change their business plans, and therefore may have to be replaced. Moreover, the VO itself may have to adapt to the changing market needs and conditions and, as a result, changes in its structure as well as objectives may be necessary in order to ensure its viability, effectiveness and continuing, successful operation. The final stage, disbanding, marks the end of the VO, and this may occur, for instance, if the VO is no longer profitable, the services provided are no longer needed or competitive, or the VO has served its purpose.

3.7 INFRASTRUCTURE REQUIREMENTS FOR OPEN MULTI-AGENT SYSTEMS

Despite the many challenges that open MASs raise, we envisage that they will become increasingly prevalent as they enable flexible, dynamic and fully distributed systems to be created on a 'per need' basis. Even though open MASs have no prior static design, such systems are not just simply collections of agents that are situated in a common environment. Fundamentally, agents in furthering their own objectives, come together in order to make use of the services of other agents, share resources, expertise and information, perform a complex task or solve a difficult problem. To facilitate the creation, operation and interaction of multiple agents, an underlying infrastructure is required. A MAS infrastructure consists of the set of services, conventions and knowledge that facilitate agent interactions (Sycara et al. 2003). The set of services that are considered essential for the enactment and support of an open MAS are illustrated in Figure 3.4.

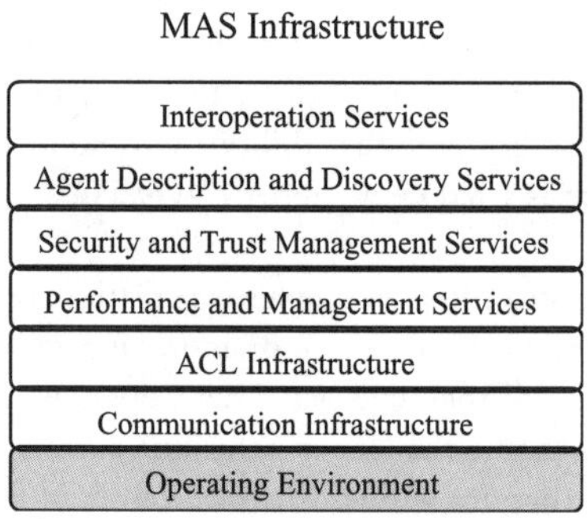

MAS Infrastructure

| Interoperation Services |
| Agent Description and Discovery Services |
| Security and Trust Management Services |
| Performance and Management Services |
| ACL Infrastructure |
| Communication Infrastructure |
| Operating Environment |

Figure 3.4: Infrastructure requirements for open MASs

At the most basic level a MAS relies on an operating environment which comprises the machines and their operating systems, the network infrastructure and the transport protocols such as TCP/IP, etc. Ideally, the operating environment should be totally transparent to the MAS and the agents, and both should be able to operate across different platforms.

A MAS also requires an underlying communication infrastructure. Messages between agents as well as between the agents and the MAS itself, need to be transferred through appropriate communication channels. The communication infrastructure should support different modes of communication, synchronous and asynchronous, point-to-point and multicast. Also the communication infrastructure should be independent of the Agent Communication Language (ACL) used by the MAS and the transport protocol. This means that systems that deploy different ACLs should be able to employ the same underlying communication infrastructure.

Agents need to be able to communicate with each other as well as with the system itself, through the exchange of messages. To this end a suitable ACL is required, which enables the agents to send different types of messages depending on the situation. An ACL should describe the syntax of the messages to be exchanged as well as their semantics. In addition to an ACL, a common terminology – an ontology – that enables the agents to understand and be understood is also essential. Conversational policies and protocols that govern the exchange of messages and facilitate meaningful interactions should also be defined at this level. For instance, a request should always be followed by a reply.

A MAS infrastructure should also provide performance and management services. These are services that enable one to monitor the system's activities as well as performance. Such services include, for instance, a logging module that records the communication exchanges between agents, and a visualizer that shows information about the system's activity. A performance module can monitor the performance of the system as a whole and that of individual agents. Such information could be used, for instance, to optimize the execution of a task and the allocation of resources, identify bottlenecks and take appropriate action such as assign more agents to a specific task.

As agents in open MASs will be inherently heterogeneously designed and developed by different individuals and organizations, they cannot be assumed to be benevolent. Security and trust management services are required in order to ensure that agents are who they claim to be and their behaviour is checked upon and regulated so as to avoid harmful interactions. Trusted third parties, such as certificate authorities and a set of protocols that guarantee privacy and secure communications, are crucial. Reputation systems that collect information about the different participants and their reliability and trustworthiness can also be used so as to enable agents to decide on potential partners and who to interact with.

In open MASs that allow agents to join and leave dynamically, the agents do not necessarily know others or their services, skills and capabilities. This is essentially the connection problem, i.e., finding an agent with appropriate capabilities to execute a task. Therefore a MAS infrastructure should offer appropriate description and discovery services. When agents enter a MAS they should be able to make themselves known through some process of registration with the system, and also describe their capabilities. Such services include, for instance, an Agent Name Server that maps the name of the agent to a physical location. Another important service that comes under this category is that of discovery and matching. Agents need to be able to advertise themselves and describe their capabilities or services to a middle agent who can then match them with incoming requests from requester agents.

Finally, a MAS infrastructure should allow for the interoperation between different MASs. For instance, as systems may be using different ACLs, translation services may be required in order to allow agents across different MASs to communicate and exchange services and information. Provisions for potential architectural mismatches also need to be made. For example, different systems may require different information from the individual agents at the time of registration, with respect to their capabilities and offered services, and may use different types of middle agents to perform the matching of requesters with potential providers. Reputation systems may use different means to indicate the trustworthiness of agents. In one system 10 may mean that the agent is reliable and trustworthy on a scale from 1 to 10, whereas in another, it may indicate that the agent came through with the goods in only 10% of the cases.

The MAS infrastructure views individual agents as black boxes, i.e., nothing is known about their internal workings, problem-solving abilities or components. It is the responsibility of the designer and developer to ensure that an agent has appropriate components that allow it to operate and interact within a MAS and use the services provided by the MAS infrastructure. For instance, although a MAS may offer description and discovery services, the designer and developer needs to implement the necessary methods that would enable an agent to register with these and advertise its capabilities and services. Failing to do so would result in an isolated and therefore not particularly useful agent.

Although defining a standard MAS infrastructure is crucial for the wide deployment of agent-based and multi-agent systems, at the time of writing there is no such standard. FIPA is developing standards for various aspects of the infrastructure required for MASs, such as communication and interaction protocols as well as directory description and naming services. In this context an abstract architecture for agents has also been proposed (FIPA 2002b), which clearly identifies the need for an agent to communicate via message exchange as well as to register and describe its services and capabilities with appropriate directory services.

3.8 Further Reading

A number of books provide more extensive introductions to multi-agent systems. The introductory text by (Ferber 1999) contains a good introduction on issues related to multi-agent systems, mainly from an organizational point of view. The discussion on the different modes of interaction among agents is based on Ferber's discussion. The volumes by Huhns (1987) Gasser and Huhns (1989), Bond and Gasser (1988) contain a number of papers that discuss issues related to multi-agent systems and interaction including communication, cooperation and negotiation.

The original papers on KQML (Labrou et al. 1997, 1999) provide many more details of the specifics of the language, while more information on FIPA ACL can be found at FIPA's website (FIPA 2006). An overview of dialogue games is given in (McBurney and Parsons 2003). The discussion on the layered model of communication presented here is based on (Helin and Laukkanen 2003).

The complex issue of developing ontologies is discussed in more detail in Uschold and Grüninger (1996) as well as in Noy and McGuinness (2001) where an example illustrating the development of a simple ontology is provided, using the Protege ontology development tool (Protege 2006). More information on OWL can be found in (OWL 2006) and a good introduction along with examples is provided in (Singh and Huhns 2005) who also discuss ontology management. An excellent paper discussing the applications and issues surrounding multi-agent systems is (Sycara 1998). Smith's original papers (Smith 1977, 1980a,b, Smith and Davis 1981) provide a thorough account of the principles and workings of the ContractNet protocol. The cooperative problem-solving process, in particular from a theoretical point of view, is discussed in (Wooldridge and Jennings 1999). Agent-based approaches to the formation and operation of virtual organizations and enterprises have been discussed in Petersen and Greninger (2000) Petersen et al. (2001) and Norman et al. (2004). A view of how agents and web services can facilitate the creation and seamless operation of virtual enterprises is given in Petrie and Bussler (2003).

Sycara et al. (2003) discuss the infrastructure requirements to support MASs and demonstrate how these are implemented in the RETSINA system.

3.9 Exercises and Topics for Discussion

1. The UK government has employed you as a specialist consultant in agent-based and multi-agent systems and has asked you to investigate the possibility

of interconnecting all the n power plants in the UK. There are three types of power plants: coal-fired, nuclear and wind-farm plants. The amount of electricity produced by each plant can vary. Some of the power plants are close to high-demand areas, whereas others are in low-demand areas. Occasionally the demand for energy in the high-demand areas exceeds the capacity of the local power plant and in this case, a manager responsible for energy distribution in that area will have to locate another plant that has extra capacity and negotiate for and 'borrow' extra power so as to cover the needs of that area. The government wants to replace this decision-making by humans with a system that will be flexible, intelligent and has the capability to reorganize the generation and allocation of electricity according to various conditions as these arise. They have asked you to consider the possibility of using agent technology to do so. Consider all relevant issues, i.e., environment, entities, possible interactions within the system (clearly identify what types of interactions can take place, conflict, cooperation, etc.).

(a) How would you design such a multi-agent system (open or closed)? How can you ensure fault-tolerant and robust behaviour in such a system? Would there be a central control point in the system or will control be distributed? What are the advantages and disadvantages of each approach?

(b) In Exercise 7 of Chapter 2 you were asked to suggest the architecture of an agent-based system to control a nuclear plant. Is this architecture suitable now for every agent in the MAS that you are proposing? If not, suggest an alternative architecture again by considering all the relevant issues.

(c) Discuss the communication issues involved in this multi-agent system. What would be an appropriate ACL for this system? Would it have to be as complicated as KQML or FIPA ACL or would a simpler language do? Is there a need for an ontology?

(d) Describe how the ContractNet protocol (or a suitable variation) could be used to automate the process of locating and 'borrowing' power from another plant.

2. List the sequence of KQML performatives that would be required to formalize the ContractNet protocol as described in Section 3.5.2.

3. List the sequence of FIPA ACL performatives that would be required to formalize the ContractNet protocol as described in Section 3.5.2.

4. Assume a 50×50 grid world in which there are gold gathering agents. The agents' objective is to collect all gold in the environment by moving around as in the original Maze world, i.e., the repertoire of actions is the same. Gold

appears randomly and in clusters occupying usually 4–5 grid positions. The agents can sense where they are in the grid, and whether or not there is gold in their current position. They can communicate with each other via message exchange. When an agent detects gold, then it has to notify the other agents so that they can cooperate with each other to collect all of it. If an agent is not busy, then it has to move towards the direction of the gold in order to help the other agent. If two agents are free, then the agent who is closest to the signalling agent should move towards that direction in order to help the first agent. Obviously, determining who is busy and who is the closest, needs to be communicated among the agents.

(a) Consider a suitable message-exchange mechanism for this scenario.

(b) Describe a protocol that would enable the agents to cooperate in order to collect all gold.

(c) Use your favourite programming language to encode this scenario.

5. Use your favourite programming language to implement a simulation of the Luc Steels scenario as described in Section 2.6.2. Assume a 500×500 dimensional environment in which agents can move around. Construct the simulation in such a way that you can vary the number of agents in the environment. Assume that the mothership is always in grid (0,0) and so the starting position of each agent is the same. Place random obstacles in the grid, such as hills, etc., and deposits of minerals. Assume that the agents have an unlimited power supply.

(a) Implement the basic rules that allow agents to move around, avoid obstacles, find and collect samples and return them to the mothership (ignore the use of vehicles). Run the simulation with five agents and observe the performance of the system. Try increasing and decreasing the number of agents and observe the difference on the system's performance. How coherent does the behaviour of the system appear to be?

(b) Incorporate rules such as those given in Section 2.6.2 and which facilitate cooperation among agents and modify the other rules as necessary. Run the simulation with varying numbers of agents and observe the performance of the system. How coherent does the behaviour of the system appear to be?

(c) Simulate the occurrence of 'accidents' in this world, for instance, agents can be destroyed if they are struck by small asteroids. Run the simulation with varying numbers of agents and vary the probability of agents having accidents. What is the effect on the performance of the system?

CHAPTER 4

Shopping Agents

LEARNING OBJECTIVES

After reading and completing this chapter, you should be able to:

- Describe the stages of the consumer buying behaviour model and discuss how agent technology could be potentially applied in each of them.
- Discuss how agent technology can be used to alleviate the problem of finding the right product or service.
- Explain the principles and techniques used in current shopping agents.
- Discuss the various limitations and issues surrounding the use of shopping agents.

Today's highly interconnected and borderless world has opened up new opportunities and markets for businesses as well as individuals. Electronic marketplaces are highly dynamic and complex environments. Unlike traditional software, agents are personalized, semi-autonomous and continuously running entities, and therefore particularly well-suited for electronic marketplaces. This chapter presents the starting point of our exploration into the use of agent technology in e-commerce applications.

4.1 CONSUMER BUYING BEHAVIOUR MODEL

When consumers engage in shopping activities, they usually go through a number of stages which enable them to ultimately decide what to buy and where from. Consumer Buying Behaviour (CBB) theory (Andreasen 1965, Nicosia 1966, Howard and Sheth 1969, Maes et al. 1999, Blackwell et al. 2006) provides a model that deals with the actions and decisions involved in buying and selling goods and services, mainly in retail markets, although most concepts are relevant in consumer-to-consumer (C2C), and business-to-business (B2B) markets as well. Such models involve a number of stages which represent an approximation and simplification of complex behaviours. The stages often overlap and transition from one to another can be nonsequential and iterative. Most CBB models describe the consumer decision-making process as involving the following six main stages:

1. **Need recognition.** In this stage the consumer becomes aware of an unfulfilled need which may involve a product or service. A need can arise as a result of external factors, such as advertising, or internal factors such as, for instance, an interest in science fiction books.

2. **Product brokering.** Having identified a need, this is the stage where the consumer searches for information on the options available in order to decide what to buy. The consumer typically evaluates different products according to her personal criteria. The result of this stage is a number of products that the consumer is considering which comprise the *consideration set*.

3. **Merchant brokering.** In this stage the consumer combines the consideration set formed in the previous stage with merchant-specific information in order to decide who to buy from. The evaluation of merchants is being done based on criteria such as price, warranty, availability and other value-added services, as well as the merchant's reputation.

4. **Negotiation.** This is the stage where the terms of the transaction are being determined. Negotiation depends on the kind of market. In some markets the price is fixed (supermarket goods) and there is no room for negotiation. In other types of markets, such as stocks, art and second-hand car markets, negotiation is an integral part of the whole process.

5. **Purchase and delivery.** This is the stage where the product or service is being paid for by the consumer and delivered by the merchant or provider. The available payment and delivery options offered can influence the product and merchant brokering stages.

6. **Service and evaluation.** This is a post-purchase stage and includes aspects such as product and customer servicing. Product or service evaluation, as well as evaluation of the whole buying experience, are part of this stage.

Agent technology can be potentially applied in every one of these stages. For instance, in the need recognition stage, agents can be used to stimulate the user through targeted and personalized advertising, which is achieved via creating detailed user profiles and attempting to identify products that may be of interest. Also, they can keep track of the user's interests and needs providing recommendations on new products, as well as alerting the user of new releases and product availability. Agents can be used in the next two stages, namely product and merchant brokering, to find and compare products, services and vendors based on the user's preferences. In the negotiation stage, agents acting on the user's behalf can negotiate the terms of a transaction or contract. Agents can also be used in the purchase and delivery stage to pay for goods and services. In addition, as agents can be service providers themselves, for instance they may offer information services, they can actually deliver such services. Even though agents cannot be involved in the delivery of material products such as books to customers, nevertheless they can be used to track orders and notify customers of status changes such as expected delivery date. Finally, in the service and evaluation stage, agents can be employed to keep records of customer satisfaction and recommendations by requesting feedback. They may also be able to assist the user with any queries and thus offer valuable customer services.

4.2 COMPARISON SHOPPING

E-commerce has changed the way organizations and individuals conduct business. Traditional brick-and-mortar companies have expanded to take advantage of the new opportunities offered by a global marketplace, while new companies have appeared that operate exclusively online. Inevitably, the Internet and the World Wide Web have also had a profound impact on the way individuals shop. Consumers can now shop from the privacy of their own homes for almost anything ranging from a house to flowers. Shopping malls have been replaced by e-commerce sites and the traditional shopping trip has been transformed into a virtual one which involves visiting the vendors' sites and viewing goods online.

A user looking for a particular product can currently visit various e-commerce sites that she has previously identified or use a standard search engine and keyword retrieval to identify potential vendors (Menczer et al. 2002a). In each site visited, the user has to search for the product and find out the price and other related information such as the product's specification or warranty. This simple approach has several shortcomings. First of all, there may be hundreds of vendors selling the same or very similar products. Unless the user is aware of particular vendors, she is faced with the problem of which of these to visit and, furthermore, when is it that *enough* vendors have been visited to acquire the necessary information. Visiting a number of sites requires considerable time, but not visiting enough may lead to a suboptimal decision. Moreover, identifying vendors using classical search engines and keywords, may not be the best way to go about it, as the returned set of vendors may be biased in favour of a few large sites, which may not necessarily offer the best prices. Secondly, if the user requires several items, there may be no single site that caters for all her shopping needs, which increases the search time for each new product category. Finally, every time that a new site or vendor is visited she has to get acquainted with new interfaces, which increases the search time and unavoidably hinders impulse shopping.

To help customers stay informed, vendors may allow them to sign up to receive alerts, for instance when the price of a product changes or falls below a specified amount, or when a product becomes available. Some vendors require lengthy surveys to be completed, although most such services tend to be impersonal. Another disadvantage of this approach is that the user may be required to provide personal data as part of the survey and, furthermore, to be able to receive email notifications she is also required to reveal part of her identity. Thus, the users' privacy is weakened.

As the amount of information and number of choices available to users have grown, so has the need for tools to help the users organize, manage and utilize this information for better decision-making. One of the ways in which intelligent agent technology can be used in e-commerce is in helping users search for products, services and vendors (Edwards 2000). In particular, shopping agents, also known as shopbots, can enhance the users' shopping experience by:

- helping them decide what to buy
- finding specifications and reviews for products
- comparing products, vendors and services according to user-defined criteria
- finding the best-value products or services
- monitoring online shops for product availability, special offers and discounts and sending alerts.

Delegating tasks such as those described above to shopping agents, which can scour the web on behalf of the user, has a number of benefits both for the individual user as well as the marketplace as a whole. For the individual user, the whole task can be done faster. There is no doubt that a shopping agent can search a number of vendors much faster than its human counterpart would. As a shopping agent can query many more vendors than a human could, it may also query vendors that the user may have no knowledge of and yet they may be offering better deals. In addition, shopping agents may be able to uncover special deals that the user would otherwise be unaware of. Thus, shopping agents can help users to manage information and make educated buying decisions without having to spend hours on end visiting vendors themselves. Another potential benefit of shopping agents to individual users is that of psychological burden-shifting (Rajiv and Aggarwal 2002). Users are often uncertain about buying a product. By employing a shopping agent to find the most appropriate product, they can shift some of the psychological cost of making a decision to the agent. If the decision turns out to be not a very good one, the shopping agent can be blamed, thereby minimizing the psychological risk in the purchase decision. On the other hand, by deploying shopping agents, consumers may not even be aware when the recommendations are only suboptimal.

Shopping agents can also benefit the marketplace as a whole. Online shopping is not without its risks: dubious vendors and online fraud are on the increase. Shopping agents may be able to steer users away from unreliable or dubious vendors by using reputation systems to filter out such vendors. Reputation systems collate information on vendors by aggregating feedback on past transactions from users (or agents) and then measuring the vendor's trustworthiness via some means (Resnick et al. 2000) (see Section 12.5). Thus, shopping agents may help tackle market fraud. Furthermore, the use of shopping agents can lead to more efficient marketplaces as users have access to a larger number of vendors. As shopping agents provide the means for individual users to compare the prices and services offered by a number of vendors, the competition in the marketplace increases. Smaller vendors offering competitive prices will be accessible to the user, thereby reducing the larger vendors' monopoly of the market.

Shopbots can benefit not only individual users in B2C markets but also organizations in business-to-business (B2B) markets. A shopping agent can perform searches and comparisons not for consumer goods and products, but for suppliers and components on behalf of an organization as in a supply chain. Shopbots can locate the cheapest suppliers, or suppliers that can satisfy certain conditions, i.e., delivery deadlines and shipping conditions.

4.3 WORKING FOR THE USER

Shopping agents that can collate information on products and services as well as vendors, can be a very valuable tool for users as they can help them to avoid drowning in choices. However, for the user to truly benefit from the deployment of such agents, the following important aspects need to be taken into account:

- **Impartiality**. To provide the best possible service to a user, a shopping agent needs to remain independent from vendors. Shopping agents need to be impartial and perform wide searches and take into account as many vendors as possible when, for instance, looking for a particular product, as opposed to only searching a small number of preferred vendors such as those sponsoring the agent.

- **Autonomy**. Autonomy means that a shopping agent proactively seeks to help the user, for instance, by checking periodically for new product information or availability or notifying her when a new product of potential interest has arrived in store.

- **Privacy**. Maintaining the user's privacy while searching for products is an important issue. Users may not want to reveal their identity or other information about their shopping patterns when searching for products. Thus, the privacy of the user needs to be protected by concealing her identity and behaviour. For instance, a shopping agent can conceal the IP address of the origin of the user's request when submitting queries to vendors. But, protecting one's privacy should only be conditional and should be selectively revoked if the user abuses it.

- **Personalization**. A shopping agent can offer personalized services to the user. The agent can learn the user preferences by observing her actions while shopping. When a user considers the items available at e-commerce sites, she indirectly provides relevant feedback, i.e., submitting queries for products or browsing catalogues will provide implicit information about the user's preferences[1]. The agent can utilize this feedback to infer the user's preferences and apply such learned knowledge in taking the initiative for future searches, as well as in predicting when a user might be interested in an item.

- **Flexibility**. Ideally, a shopping agent should be able to make comparisons which are not based on the attribute of price alone. Although price is often the most important factor in deciding where to shop from, other factors may affect the buying decision, such as extended warranties, delivery and payment options, possible extras, as well as the reputation of the vendor.

4.4 HOW SHOPPING AGENTS WORK

Current shopping agents operate in a similar way to meta search engines and they typically permit buyers to sort product and vendor information along some desired dimension, such as price. Agents are able to retrieve this information from different vendors by a form of 'screen-scraping'. In essence, shopbots interact with a vendor through HTML pages that are designed and generated to be read and understood by humans, not programs, Figure 4.1. They submit queries to vendors as a user would and then attempt to process the resulting HTTP pages by parsing them and searching for the name of the item of interest to the user and then the nearest set of characters that has a currency sign, which presumably is the item's price. To be able to retrieve information, agents rely on regularities in the layout of the vendor's web pages such as (Doorenbos et al. 1997):

- uniformity regularity: the web pages of a particular vendor are designed so that they have a similar look

---

[1] As opposed to explicit feedback which is obtained via completing surveys or rating items.

- navigation regularity: the pages of e-commerce sites are designed so that users can easily navigate through them and find what they need

- vertical separation regularity: white spaces are typically used to separate products and each new product description will start in a new line.

Shopping agents made their appearance in the mid 1990s and technology analysts at the time were predicting that they would make a huge impact on vendors and the way business is conducted (Edwards 2000). The first shopping agent for price comparisons was BargainFinder developed by Andersen Consulting (Krulwich 1996). BargainFinder allowed users to compare prices of music CDs from stores selling over the Internet. However, many retailers started blocking access to the agent as BargainFinder simply evaluated vendors based on the offered price and ignored all the other features that online music retailers had built into their sites. Inevitably, BargainFinder ceased operating.

PersonaLogic was a system that helped users make decisions on products and services that fit their needs and preferences by describing their tastes. The system created user profiles that allowed for the identification of products with features important to the users. For instance, if you wanted to buy a DVD player, you would have to tell the system how much you wanted to spend, what features were important to you, what you would use it mainly for, etc. PersonaLogic would then provide you with a list of models that best fitted the information submitted. However, the vendors had to provide an interface that explicitly disclosed the features of the products in a way that could be matched with the user profiles. PersonaLogic was acquired in 1998 by AOL and the system was withdrawn from the market.

ShopBot (Doorenbos et al. 1997) was an agent that could learn to submit queries to e-commerce sites and then parse results in order to extract information on products. ShopBot used an automatic process for building 'wrappers' to parse semi-structured HTML documents and extracted features, such as product description and price. The mechanism exploited the regularities present in e-commerce sites, i.e., navigation, uniformity and vertical separation regularities. ShopBot was later renamed Jango and was acquired and commercialized by Excite in 1997. Jango avoided the problem that Bargain-Finder faced as each product information request originated not from the agent's server, but from the user's browser. Consequently, a vendor could not distinguish between the requests sent by Jango via the user's web browser and those of a human user and, as a result, Jango's requests could not be blocked.

A more recent example of a shopping agent is IntelliShopper (Menczer et al. 2002b). IntelliShopper is a shopping assistant that observes the user's actions and unobtrusively attempts to learn the user's preferences and help her in her shopping. It also monitors various vendors for products that may match the user's needs and preferences or previously expressed interests. IntelliShopper consists of three different agents: the Learning, Monitor and Privacy agents. The Learning agent observes the user, learns her preferences and handles the user's requests for information on products. The Monitor agent monitors various vendors on behalf of the user and periodically checks for product availability or any other pending request. The Privacy agent provides privacy. In essence, the origin of the user, i.e., the IP address, is hidden by passing requests through one or more anonymizer servers. Moreover, IntelliShopper uses shopping personas to hide all information about a user from the IntelliShopper server. A persona reflects the mode of use of a particular user and its purpose is two-fold: to guarantee the user's privacy as no data about the user are revealed to the server and to allow the user to take on different personas, i.e., shopping characteristics, for different shopping needs. Logic about the different vendors that the IntelliShopper deals with is stored in the vendor modules, which specify how a vendor can be queried and how to interpret the results and extract the information required by the user from the returned HTML pages.

Currently, although a number of comparison shopping sites offer comparison services, these are not, strictly speaking, agents. Sites like MySimon (MySimon 2006), DealTime (DealTime 2006) and RoboShopper (RoboShopper 2006) collate catalogues of products which are provided by the vendors themselves who pay a commission to be listed on the site. Although they do allow comparisons among a number of vendors, they may not necessarily offer impartial advice and there may be better deals around offered by vendors who are not listed.

4.5 LIMITATIONS AND ISSUES

Despite the initial excitement and high expectations about the impact of shopping agents on retail markets, their true potential has not been realized. Shopping agents have a number of technical and business-imposed limitations.

The foremost problem is that current techniques for extracting information rely on syntax. Shopping agents can only retrieve limited information, such as price, which is relatively easy to identify from HTML pages, and ignore information such as shipping conditions, which are harder to retrieve. This is a severe limitation. Although price is often the most important factor in deciding what to buy and where from, other factors may affect the buying decision, such as the delivery and payment options, and even the vendor's reputation. In fact, these value-added services may be what differentiates vendors that otherwise may be offering the same price. In fact, the information that the shopping agent is after is stored in a machine-processable and well-structured format in the vendor's database. But the agent cannot interact with the database; it only has access to the web pages that are generated from it as illustrated in Figure 4.1. Consequently, developers have to implement clever heuristics that can extract the original well-structured data from the implicit information on the HTML pages. Such heuristics are inevitably ad-hoc, difficult and time-consuming to develop and prone to errors, while they are only able to retrieve limited information. Inevitably, they must be updated every time the layout of the

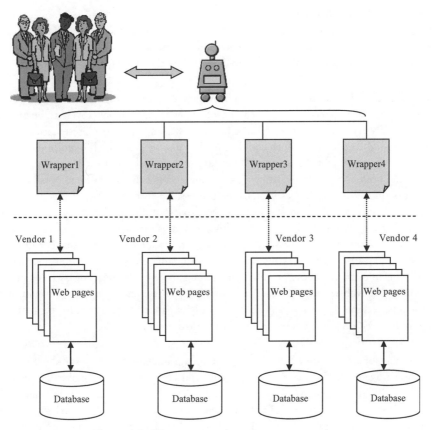

Figure 4.1: How current shopping agents work

vendor's site changes. This makes the development of shopping agents cumbersome and the resulting systems inflexible and vendor-specific. New vendors cannot be discovered and queried at runtime: they first have to be identified and then tailor-made methods for retrieving information from their web pages need to be developed.

This limitation has further consequences on the accuracy of the information that shopping agents can retrieve. Often there are discrepancies between the prices reported by shopping agents and those listed at the vendor's site. The price that the shopping agent returns may exclude taxes or shipping charges. As shopping agents do not understand the content of the retrieved web pages, they cannot distinguish between vendors that include shipping charges and taxes in their price, and those that do not.

As it is difficult to retrieve information on attributes such as warranty and shipping conditions, shopping agents can only make comparisons based on price. Naturally, vendors object to the idea of being compared on price alone as this does not necessarily reflect the full range of services and value for money that they offer. Many vendors block price requests from shopping agents thus further restricting their ability to make comparisons among multiple vendors and assist the user in finding the best deal around.

The problems that ensue from the way in which shopping agents retrieve information from vendors, i.e., screen-scraping, can be alleviated if the web pages were to be marked up not only with presentation details, but also with a separate representation of the meaning of their contents, which could be read by a program. The shopping agent would then be able to extract the required information on price even if the layout of the web page had been changed. Fully utilizing shopping agents can only become possible when vendors offer their catalogues in machine-processable formats which are coupled with explicit and shared ontologies, which can be processed directly by the agents. Another promising way forward with regard to this problem is through the use of web services. Web services can be used in essence as gateways to various vendors' sites. For instance, Amazon.com offers web services that allow programs to perform operations such as retrieving information about products and adding an item to a shopping cart. Agents can then employ web services in order to acquire, aggregate and compare information on products, services and vendors. This will greatly enhance the potential for comparisons not only based on price, but on various other attributes.

A number of other issues arise as a result of the underlying business model used in shopping agents. Typically, shopping agents and comparison sites make commissions in three different ways (Markopoulos and Kephart 2002): (i) for each hit made to a vendor's site as the result of a shopping agent recommendation; (ii) for sales that result from clickthrough purchases; or (iii) for a favourable placement on the shopping agent's generated recommended lists. The difference between the price reported by the shopping agent and the price listed at the vendor's site may be due to the commission that the shopping agents charge. If a vendor decides to collaborate with a particular shopping agent in order to gain more visibility and increase sales, then it incurs an additional expense which eats away its profit. Additionally, many vendors end up paying two or more services in order to obtain maximum exposure for their products. Buying directly from the vendor without the shopping agent's mediation may be cheaper, as the vendor is able to eliminate the shopping agent's fee and thus pass some or all of the savings along to the buyer. Such shopping agents or sites may often create the false impression that they have found the best deal when, in fact, much better deals exist. This is because they are biased and only search a limited number of vendors with whom they may be collaborating or are sponsored by.

From the vendor's perspective, although on the one hand shopping agents may improve their visibility and potential market share, on the other, they also put their products right next to identical or similar products from competitors. Whoever offers the best price will probably get the sale, which means that the profit margins can decrease substantially even below the point of profitability.

Shopping agents have the potential to have a major impact on both brick-and-mortar and Internet vendors and ultimately lead to more efficient marketplaces, as well as enhance the users' experience. Nevertheless, this is only possible if some of the aforementioned problems are adequately resolved and in particular the most important one, which is the inability of current shopping agents to retrieve semantic information on the services and products provided by vendors.

4.6 Further Reading

A number of consumer behaviour models have been proposed in the literature (Andreasen 1965, Nicosia 1966, Howard and Sheth 1969, Maes et al. 1999, Blackwell et al. 2006). A well-known paper on the use of agent technology in e-commerce applications is that of Maes et al. (1999) while a more recent account is provided in He et al. (2003). The discussion on the consumer buying behaviour model which was presented in this chapter is based on the former of these. The economic value of shopping agents is discussed in Markopoulos and Kephart (2002) and Kephart and Greenwald (2002).

A number of shopping agents have been developed and used in online shopping as described in Section 4.4. The most recent one is the IntelliShopper system (Menczer et al. 2002a,b). An alternative approach to searching for product information using web services is described in Kim et al. (2005). Web services, the Semantic Web and associate technologies as well as their integration with agents are discussed in Singh and Huhns (2005). An approach to alleviating the problems emanating from screen-scraping using Web services, is discussed in Fasli (2006).

4.7 Exercises and Topics for Discussion

1. Suppose you are interested in buying four different products. For each product:
   (a) First conduct a search via a traditional search engine to find potential vendors that are offering each one and note down the price.
   (b) Use at least two comparison shopping sites either from those listed in Section 4.4 or any others that you may know, to perform the equivalent search. Compare the results that these comparison shopping sites return.

How do these prices compare with the ones that you retrieved through the search engine?

2. Write a program which is able to extract the price of a book from the Amazon web site by screen-scrapping. The program needs to be able to parse the web page and look for identifiers such as the word 'price' or a currency sign. How easy it is to use the same program to extract price information from a different web site such as Computer Manuals[2]?

3. Study the Amazon e-commerce web service toolkit which can be downloaded from:
    http://www.amazon.com
    How could you use this toolkit to build a software agent that is able to obtain information on the price and other attributes of a product from Amazon?

4. Discuss the benefits of using shopping agents and their relative disadvantages.

5. Consider how the use of a shopping agent can protect the users' privacy and anonymity. Are there any risks to the users' privacy which emanate from the use of such agents?

---

[2] http://www.computermanuals.co.uk

CHAPTER 5

Middle Agents

LEARNING OBJECTIVES

After reading and completing this chapter, you should be able to:

- Discuss the implications of the connection problem.
- Explain the three phases of matchmaking and how end and middle agents interact during these phases.
- Describe the basic components of a middle agent and its principles of operation.
- Distinguish between different types of middle agents and the various privacy guarantees that they can provide.
- Describe the LARKS framework and distinguish among the different types of matches that can be performed and the techniques used to implement them.
- Describe the basic components of OWL-S.

Agents acting on behalf of their users, individuals or organizations, may need to locate and use the services of other agents in order to accomplish their objectives. In broad terms, this is known as the *connection* problem, namely finding an appropriate agent to do a given task or provide a service.

In the vast expanse of the Internet, agents do not necessarily know others and they need not be homogeneous. Software entities may come and go for a number of reasons: their users may take them off line, they may be malfunctioning or they may simply have crashed. The task of finding another agent is crucial, albeit nontrivial. Needless to say, broadcasting in order to find someone on a network of the scale of the Internet is inefficient. Consequently, agents need some means of locating other agents, such as service providers, manufacturers and suppliers in order to conduct business with them. Furthermore, agents may be looking for others in order to delegate a task, or join forces to accomplish a complex task or solve a problem and, as a result, they may be looking for agents with particular expertise or capabilities.

In everyday life, when one wants to locate a service provider or supplier there are several ways to go about it. If I need to find a plumber in my area, one of my options is to open a professional directory or the yellow pages and browse through the professionals that are listed. Yet another way is to ask for someone else's opinion or recommendation on a plumber, such as my friends, colleagues or neighbours. Analogous facilities and infrastructure need to be in place to enable software agents to locate and come into contact with others.

5.1 MATCHING

By and large, a multi-agent environment can be considered as being populated by two generic types of agents: *end* and *middle agents* (Wong and Sycara 2000). End agents can be service and information providers or suppliers of goods and products (from now on these are referred to simply as *providers*) or consumers that use services and acquire goods and products (referred to as *requesters*).

Middle agents stand in the middle, as their name suggests, and enable interactions between end agents. The task of a middle agent is to match the requester agent with one or more provider agents. This process is simply referred to as *matching*. Therefore, middle agents specialize in making connections between end agents and they store, maintain and provide connection information. They may also provide naming services and translation and interoperation services for agents speaking different communication languages.

There are two types of information communicated from end agents to a middle agent. Providers send advertisements which are, in essence, capability specifications and may also include additional information regarding conditions of service. Requesters send want-ads which are request specifications for required services and may also include preference parameters.

5.1.1 Middle agent architecture

Implicit, yet essential, in the matching process is the assumption that agents have the ability to communicate with each other. Communication as discussed in Chapter 3 has a number of facets and interrelated issues, such as the need to have a common communication language, but also the need for common ontologies so that the agents can understand each other.

In particular, two pivotal issues need to be addressed in matching. First, a common language is required for describing the capabilities and service parameters of providers and the needs and preferences of requesters. Second, efficient mechanisms for matching requests with advertisements are needed. This is complicated by the fact that, even if the agents use the same communication and content languages, they may be using a different ontology.

To be able to provide basic matching services a middle agent requires three essential components as illustrated in Figure 5.1. The database of advertisements contains all the advertisements and capability specifications that are received by the middle agent in a particular capability or service description language. The ontology of the middle agent consists of all the ontological descriptions of words in the capability specifications and advertisements stored in the database. The ontology may not be unique, but rather a collection of ontologies that the middle agent uses, in particular, if it has to provide service interoperation. The matching engine is the component which is responsible for matching advertisements with requests. A capability specification or advertisement matches a request when the specification describes a service that is *sufficiently similar* to the service requested.

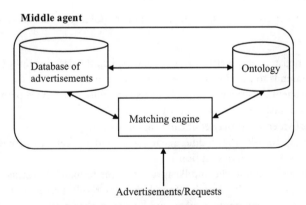

Figure 5.1: The components of a middle agent

Similarity can be defined at different levels. For instance, a capability specification and a request are sufficiently similar when they describe the same service. However, this definition is too restrictive as there is no prior agreement between different end agents on how a service or a capability is represented. Thus, this kind of matching is almost prohibitive. Matching engines should satisfy the following requirements (Sycara et al. 1998):

- They should allow a degree of flexibility and be able to recognize the degree of similarity between capability specifications and requests based on the accessible ontologies.

- They must have the means to minimize the *false negative* and *false positive* matches. A false positive results from the determination that there is a match between an advertisement and a request when, in fact, they are different. A false negative results from the determination that an advertisement and a request are different, when actually they match.

- They should encourage the providers and requesters to be honest regarding their capabilities and needs, respectively.

- They must operate on a nondiscriminatory basis and provide accurate information to all requesters.

- They should operate in an efficient way, i.e., unnecessary delays should be avoided.

In evaluating the effectiveness and efficiency of the matching process as performed by different middle agents, a number of criteria can be taken into consideration such as performance, robustness, scalability, load balancing, and privacy. Inevitably, there is a trade-off between the quality and efficiency of matching on the Internet (Decker et al. 1997).

5.1.2 Interacting through a middle agent

The interaction between requester, provider and middle agent can take the following forms:

1. A provider registers or advertises its capabilities, i.e., the descriptions of what services it can and intends to provide upon request, with a middle agent.
2. The middle agent asks the provider about its capabilities or service parameters, i.e., if it can perform tasks of a certain description.
3. A service provider agent may confirm a capability query.
4. A requester agent asks the middle agent for providers that can provide services or perform tasks of a given description.
5. Upon receiving a request, the middle agent attempts to match it against the advertisements of the providers. If a match is found, then the result is returned to the requester. The middle agent may contact other middle agents that may have a different set of providers registered with them, in order to find an appropriate match to a particular request.
6. The transaction between the provider and requester agents takes place, either directly or through the middle agent.

7. Once the transaction has taken place, the middle agent collects feedback from the requester regarding the quality of service received.

Taking into account these different forms of interaction, the matching process can be divided into three distinct phases, the *location*, *transaction* and *feedback* phases. In the location phase, providers advertise their capabilities to middle agents. On the other hand, requesters ask middle agents for services or service information regarding provider agents. Finally, middle agents match advertisements with requests. In the transaction phase the service is provided by the provider to the requester agent. This can be done in two ways:

1. Providers and requesters interact with each other directly. A negotiation may commence if the service parameters and preferences were not taken into account in the location phase.
2. Providers and requesters interact via a middle agent. This offers privacy through anonymity of providers and requesters, and truth through enforcement of honesty.

In the feedback phase the requester may provide feedback to the middle agent regarding the quality of service received and perhaps other aspects of its interaction with the provider.

Some middle agents are only involved in the location phase, others take part in the transaction phase as well, whereas some middle agents may take part in all three phases. It is also possible that a middle agent may take part in the location and feedback phases without mediating the transaction. For instance, after dealing with a provider directly, the requester may provide feedback to the middle agent regarding the quality of service received.

5.2 CLASSIFICATION OF MIDDLE AGENTS

The generic description of a middle agent is that of an agent who enables the connection between end agents. How this is done exactly may be different from middle agent to middle agent. In particular, different middle agents can provide different functionalities and privacy guarantees. A middle agent's functionality can be characterized along the following dimensions (Wong and Sycara 2000):

1. Who provides information to the middle agent. Information to the middle agent can be submitted by providers, requesters, or both. For instance, providers may advertise themselves, whereas requesters need not submit any information, but simply retrieve the contents of the middle agent's local database. When end agents send information about themselves to a middle agent this information becomes public, in that it will be known by the middle agent and potentially by those who obtain information through it.

2. How much and what sort of information is sent to the middle agent. The information sent to the middle agent can take two forms: it can be capabilities/requests only or capabilities/requests which include service parameters/preferences as well. A provider may send information about the types of requests that it can service along with parameters of service whereas the requester can send requests which may include service preferences. Depending on their privacy concerns, end agents may want to send limited information to the middle agent.

3. What happens to the information that the middle agent receives. The information can be broadcast and therefore is not stored locally, or can be stored in a local database for future use. This is an important issue from the point of view of privacy.

4. How is the information accessed. If the information sent by the end agents is kept in a database, this information can be browsed or queried. When browsed, the browsing agent has access to the entire content of the database. Otherwise the agent can only have access to a subset of the information in the database, based on the query submitted. Browsing and querying lead to different privacy guarantees. The agent who browses the database does not reveal information about itself to the middle agent. On the contrary, when the agent submits a query, then some information is revealed through the specified request.

5. How much information is specified in a query to the middle agent. One can include only essential information such as capability requests, or provide additional information in the form of service parameters or preferences as well. Obviously, depending on how much information is revealed in the query, more or less privacy is guaranteed.

6. Mediation in the end-agent transactions. There are a number of reasons for middle agents to mediate in transactions. For instance, they may do so to enforce anonymity of the parties involved in the transaction, to guarantee fairness, or to act like a trusted third party and collect evidence for possible future disputes.

7. Collection of feedback. The middle agent may optionally collect feedback from the requesters regarding the providers' provision of service. Whether this feedback is collected anonymously or not provides different assurances with regard to fairness and accuracy.

These seven dimensions give rise to different types of middle agent. Different middle agents provide different functionalities which entail different requirements in terms of the local processing that is undertaken by the middle agent. In deciding what type of middle agent is appropriate for a particular application domain, each of the issues above needs to be considered very carefully.

5.2.1 Matchmaker

The *matchmaker* is a middle agent that helps to make connections and serves as a liaison between requester and provider agents (Klusch and Sycara 2001). The matchmaker, as illustrated in Figure 5.2, receives advertisements from providers regarding the capabilities

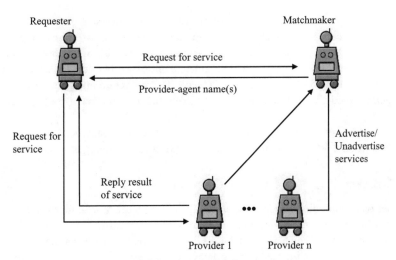

Figure 5.2: The matchmaker

and services they provide and stores them in its database. A provider may send an unadvertisement message in which case the middle agent removes it from its database. Requesters send requests for service to the matchmaker, which may include parameters and preferences. The matchmaker processes a received request as follows. First, it compares the request against all advertisements in the database and determines the provider agent(s) whose capabilities match best the request. It subsequently provides the resulting set of providers to the requester agent.

The matchmaker can operate in two modes. In the first mode, the matchmaker attempts to perform an exact matching of the request received with the advertised capabilities of different providers and returns to the requester the name and contact details of a unique service provider that best matches its request. In the second mode, the matchmaker returns to the requester not a unique provider, but a list of providers that match its request. This list can be sorted according to the degree of match, i.e., from most relevant matches to least. It is up to the requester then to select one of the available providers. In each of these modes, different levels of information are required. In the former, the matchmaker needs to have a detailed description of the requester's needs along with possible preferences or other restrictions, and the providers' advertisements need to include a detailed description of the services provided, along with parameters of service. In the latter mode, such detailed information is not necessary, although it can improve the matching process itself, i.e., requests and capabilities advertisements need to be descriptive, but need not include parameters of service and preferences.

Once information on provider(s) is passed on to the requester, it is the requester that contacts the appropriate provider and delegates the service. If more than one providers are returned to the requester, then some additional processing may be necessary. The requester could simply choose the top ranked provider to delegate the service. Alternatively, the requester could engage in negotiations with a number of potential providers and negotiate on additional parameters of service that perhaps were not taken into account during the matching phase. Hence, the transaction takes place between the end agents directly, without any involvement from the matchmaker.

Matchmakers have been used in the RETSINA (Sycara et al. 2003) and Infosleuth (Bayardo Jr. et al. 1997, Nodine and Unruh 1998) systems, among others.

5.2.2 Broker

Another type of middle agent is the *broker*, depicted in Figure 5.3. Similarly to the matchmaker, a broker receives advertisements from providers regarding their capabilities and provision of services, which are stored in its database. Again, a provider may request that its information is taken off the broker's database. Requesters send requests for service to the broker specifying the task that needs to be performed and its parameters. On receiving a request, the broker compares it against all advertisements in the database and determines the provider whose capabilities best match it. It then contacts the provider directly and asks for the service to be performed according to the preferences specified in the original request. If the provider decides to accept the request for service, it performs the task and returns the result to the broker. Next, the broker returns the result to the requester.

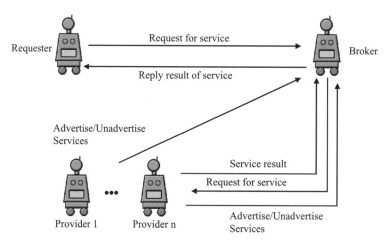

Figure 5.3: The broker

In contrast to the matchmaker, not only does the broker have the task of finding the most suitable provider for the requester's job, but critically also acts as a mediator between the two end agents and performs the transaction on behalf of the requester. This provides different security guarantees to end agents as it can ensure anonymity between providers and requesters. The broker may have to enquire of a number of providers and perhaps even negotiate the price or other aspects of the offered service with them before deciding who to delegate the task to.

5.2.3 Broadcaster

The *broadcaster*, shown in Figure 5.4, is another type of middle agent. The broadcaster receives advertisements/unadvertisements from service providers. Requester agents send requests for service to the broadcaster specifying the task that needs to be performed and its parameters. The middle agent then broadcasts the received request to the registered agents.

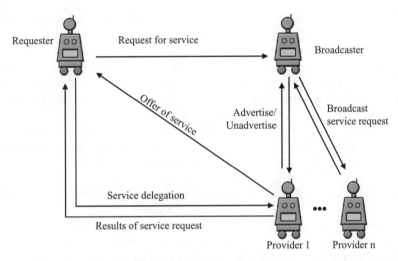

Figure 5.4: The broadcaster

The broadcaster can operate in two modes. In the first mode, the broadcaster maintains a database with registered providers, but only keeps information regarding contact details of agents and not their capabilities. When a new request arrives, the broadcaster's job is to simply forward, i.e., *broadcast*, the request to *all* agents registered with it. The addressees may or may not offer the requested service and in this case a provider may receive messages from the broadcaster about requests that are not of any interest to it. In the second mode, the broadcaster maintains a database of the providers' contact details, along with a description of the capabilities and services that they offer. Upon receiving a request, the broadcaster first attempts to match the request with a subset of the providers that offer the service and then forwards the request to those providers only, and not the entire set of registered agents. In this way, some local processing is required at the broadcaster, but on the other hand, there is less consumption of communication bandwidth and the registered agents are not inundated with irrelevant requests for service.

In either case, it is up to the individual providers to contact the requester agent and offer their services. At this stage the requester may negotiate with one or more providers. The chosen provider executes the task and returns the results of the service to the requester. As in the matchmaker's case, the broadcaster is not involved in the transaction phase.

5.2.4 FIPA Directory Facilitator

FIPA provides the specification of a Directory Facilitator (DF) agent as an essential component of an Agent Platform (AP) (FIPA 2006). A directory facilitator provides a yellow pages directory service to agents. At least one facilitator must be resident on each AP, which is the default facilitator. However, an AP may support any number of facilitators and facilitators may register with each other to form federations.

The facilitator is a trusted entity and its remit is to maintain an accurate and complete list of agents and provide the most current information about agents in its directory, on a nondiscriminatory basis, to requesters. Every agent that wants to publicize its services to other agents sends a request for registration including its description to a facilitator. The act of registering does not imply any future obligation or commitment for the registering agent: an agent can refuse a request for a service which is advertised through a facilitator, for instance, due to high load. A registered agent may request the facilitator to modify its registration information at any time, and for any reason. An agent may also request to unregister, which has as a consequence that there is no longer a commitment on behalf of the facilitator to broker information relating to that agent.

Agents can use the facilitator to locate other agents with which to communicate. Each facilitator must be able to perform the functions: *register*, *unregister*, *modify* and *search* on the agent descriptions and advertisements. The facilitator cannot guarantee the accuracy of the information provided in response to a search request, since it does not place any restrictions on the information that can be registered with it; the information is not checked. However, the facilitator may restrict access to information in its directory and will verify all access permissions for agents which attempt to inform it of state changes. A facilitator may also decide to restrict the visibility of the registered agent descriptions according to a certain policy.

5.3 DESCRIBING CAPABILITIES

Agent capability matching is the process of determining whether an advertisement registered with the middle agent matches a request. For agents to be able to describe their capabilities and requests, a language that enables them to do so is required, accompanied by the necessary ontologies. Although KQML and FIPA ACL allow the exchange of communicative acts, what is also required is a content language that allows the agents to express their capabilities to offer services along with service parameters, and their requests for services along with their preferences. A content language, such as KIF, may not be suitable for this task as it only describes knowledge and not the actions of a service. The problem of locating and matching agents is very closely related to that of locating and matching web services based on service advertisements and requests on the Web.

Among the desired properties for a capability description language are (Sycara et al. 2002, Paolucci et al. 2002):

- **Flexibility and expressiveness.** Descriptions of capabilities and requests may be quite complex. Some descriptions can be expressed simply in the form of attribute-value pairs whereas others may require more structure, such as nesting or iteration.

- **Ability to express semi-structured data.** Some capability specifications may include conditions of service whereas others may not. These may be open to subsequent negotiation between the provider and requester agents.

- **Ability for inferences and comparisons.** Inferences based on the descriptions should be allowed. For instance, comparisons based on types and subsumption are essential. As providers advertise their services, perhaps at different levels of abstraction, it is vital when retrieving providers through their advertisements to retrieve all provider agents that offer services that are subsumed by the requested type of service. Thus, if one requires all flower shops, the system should also be able to retrieve all those shops specializing in orchids.

- **Ability to express constraints.** In describing capabilities or requests, the agents may also need to express constraints. A capability description language should be able to express constraints either on the inputs and outputs or other parameters of service such as deadlines, price, etc.

- **Ease of use.** Users should be able to write capability descriptions and advertisements effortlessly. The language should also support the use of ontologies to aid common understanding and interoperability.

5.4 LARKS

An Agent Capability Description Language (ACDL) that enables agents to advertise, request, and match capabilities is the Language for Advertisement and Request for Knowledge Sharing (LARKS) (Sycara et al. 2002). A specification in LARKS is a frame which is wrapped up in a KQML performative that indicates whether the specification is a request or an advertisement.

A LARKS specification includes:

- the context (**Context**) of the advertisement or request specification, i.e., the semantic domain of the service

- the data types used in the specification (**Types**)
- the input and output parameters (**Input, Output**) as well as the constraints on these which take the form of Horn clauses (**InConstraints, OutConstraints**)
- a textual description of the specification of service or request (**TextDescription**)
- the concept descriptions (**ConcDescriptions**).

An example of a specification for finding information on laptops in LARKS is given in Table 5.1 (this example has been adapted from Sycara et al. (2002)).

FindLaptopInfo	
Context	Laptop*Laptop
Types	Infolist=**ListOf**(model:Model*LaptopModel,brand:Brand*Brand, price:Price*Money, colour:Colour*Colours);
Input	brands: **SetOf** Brand*Brand; processor: **SetOf** CPU*CPU; priceLow*LowPrice:**Integer**; priceHigh*HighPrice:**Integer**;
Output	Info:InfoList;
InConstraints	
OutConstraints	sorted(Info)
ConcDescriptions	Laptop=(**and** Product (**exists** has-processor CPU) (**all** has-memory Memory) (**all** is-model LaptopModel)); LowPrice=(**and** Price (**ge** 700) (**exists** in-currency **aset**(GBP))); HighPrice=(**and** Price (**le** 2500) (**exists** in-currency **aset**(GBP))); LaptopModel=**aset**(Dell,IBM,Samsung,Sony,Toshiba); CPU=**aset**(PentiumM,Centrino,AMDAthlon);
TextDescription	Find information about laptops.

Table 5.1: A LARKS specification for finding information on laptops

Given that agents may use different ontologies, one can describe the meaning of words, as these are used in the specification. Thus, a concept C can be attached to a word w, in the form w*C, while describing, for instance, a constraint, and then the meaning of the concept C can be clarified in the concept description. In other words, the concept C is the ontological description of the word w.

LARKS assumes that the domain ontologies are written in the Information Terminological Language (ITL), although potentially other languages can be used, such as KIF. ITL is a language that allows conceptual knowledge about a specific domain to be captured by a set of concepts and roles as terms. Each term as a definition of some concept C is a conjunction of logical constraints which must be satisfied for any object to be an instance of C. The set of definitions forms a *terminology*. For instance, the following fragment of a terminology defines concepts as used in the laptop domain of the specification of Table 5.1:

Product = (**and** (**all** is-manufactured-by Brand) (**atleast** 1 is-manufactured-by)
(**all** has-price Price))
Laptop = (**and** Product(**exists** has-processor CPU) (**all** has-memory Memory)
(**all** is-model LaptopModel))

A fundamental relation among concepts is that of subsumption. A concept C_1 subsumes another concept C_2, if the extension of C_2 is a subset of that of C_1. In other words, a concept C_1 is a more general concept than C_2 and the logical constraints defined in C_2 logically imply those of C_1. Computing all the subsumption relations among the concepts in a particular ontology yields the concept hierarchy of the domain. LARKS makes use both of subsumption relations as well as of the concept hierarchy in the matching process.

5.4.1 Matching in LARKS

The task of a middle agent is to take two specifications, an advertisement of capabilities and a request for service, and check whether they match. The issue is when we can say that two descriptions match each other, since matching may mean different things. For instance, it may mean that the two specifications have exactly the same text, although this is rarely the case. Matching may be considered to be the overlapping occurrence of the same words or keywords in the two descriptions. Nevertheless, it may be the case that two descriptions differ in their text – perhaps they use different ontologies – is it possible to match them in this case?

Three different types of match have been suggested in LARKS:

- **Exact match**. The most accurate match is when both descriptions are equivalent; either literally equal by virtue of their inputs and outputs being the same in terms of the variable names and the data types, equivalent by renaming the variables, or equivalent logically as obtained by logical inference. This type of matching is the most restrictive, but the most accurate one.

- **Plug-in match**. This is a less accurate, but more useful type of match. A plug-in match means that the agent whose capability description matches a given request can be 'plugged into the place' where that request was made. Given a pair of request and advertisement specifications, these can differ in the signatures of their input/output declarations, the number of constraints, or the constraints themselves. An example of a plug-in match is between the request to find flight tickets without any constraints on the output and an agent's advertisement which searches for flight tickets and returns a sorted list of them according to price. Exact match is a special case of plug-in match as, whenever two descriptions are an exact match, they are also a plug-in match.

- **Relaxed match**. This is the least accurate, but most useful match. A relaxed match has a much weaker semantic interpretation than the previous two types as it will not determine whether or not two descriptions semantically match. A relaxed match determines how close the advertisement and the request are by returning a numerical distance value: if the distance value is smaller than a preset threshold, then the two specifications match. An example of a relaxed match is that of the request to find the place (or address) of where to buy an Apple iBook and the capability specification of an agent that can provide the price and contact phone number for computer dealers. The plug-in and exact matches can be considered as special cases of the relaxed match, provided that the threshold value is not too small.

5.4.2 Matching methods

Ideally, matching capability with request specifications should not be based simply on keyword retrieval, as in the usual free text search engines. This is because descriptions of capabilities and requests have an underlying semantics and also a context.

In LARKS, five methods or *filters* have been used to provide for accurate, efficient and effective matching: context matching, profile comparison, similarity matching, signature matching, and constraint matching. These methods were proposed for a matchmaker agent (Section 5.2.1), but they can be applied to other types of middle agent as well. The filters are independent of each other and each one of them narrows the set of matching advertisements with respect to a given criterion. The first three methods are meant for relaxed matching, and the signature and constraint matching methods are meant for plug-in matching. All methods are used together in exact matching. Moreover, a user may select to perform any combination of these methods.

Context matching

The purpose of context matching is to filter out any capability specifications that are not relevant to the current request. Any capability or request specification has a particular context, namely a semantic domain which is indicated by a list of keywords. Context matching compares the similarity of the semantic domain of two specifications in two steps.

In the first step, for every pair of words u, v that are part of the **Context** slots in the specifications under consideration, the word distances $d_w(u, v) \in [0, 1]$ are computed as real values. Then the most similar matches for any word u are determined by selecting words v with the minimum distance value $d_w(u, v)$. These distances must not exceed a given threshold. The word distance is computed using the trigger-pair model (Rosenfield 1994), and so if two words are significantly correlated, then they are considered trigger-pairs. The value of the correlation depends on the particular domain. LARKS uses the Wall Street Journal corpus (Paul and Baker 1992) to compute the word distance.

In the second step, for every pair of most similar matching words, the semantic distance among the attached concepts, is checked so that it does not exceed a given threshold. To compute the semantic distance among concepts, a weighted associative network with directed edges between concepts as nodes is used. The edges denote the kind of binary relation (generalization, specialization and positive association) between two concepts, and also include a numerical weight which indicates the strength of belief in the relations.

Profile comparison

To carry out profile comparisons between specifications, advertisements and requests are considered to be documents. The profile comparison uses the term frequency-inverse document frequency weighting (TF-IDF) technique from Information Retrieval (Salton and McGill 1983, Salton et al. 1983). The collection of documents D is the database of advertisements. A word w in a specification $Request$ is weighted for that document as follows. The number of times w occurs throughout the collection of documents D is called the document frequency $df(w)$ of w. For a given document d, the relevance of d based on a word w is proportional to the number $wf(w, d)$ of times that word w occurs in d and is inversely proportional to $df(w)$. A weight $h(w, d)$ determines the significance of the classification of w for d and is defined as:

$$h(w,d) = wf(w,d) \cdot \log\left(\frac{|D|}{df(w)}\right)$$

The weighted keyword representation $wkv(d, Dictionary)$ of a document d contains, for every word w in a dictionary $Dictionary$, the weight $h(w, d)$ as an element. As most dictionaries provide a huge vocabulary, the dimension of the vector is cut down by using a fixed set of appropriate keywords determined by heuristics and the set of keywords in LARKS itself. The similarity between a request and an advertisement is calculated as:

$$dps(Request, Advertisement) = \frac{Request \cdot Advertisement}{|Request| \cdot |Advertisement|}$$

where $Request \cdot Advertisement$ is the inner product of the weighted keyword vectors. If the similarity value $dps(Request, Advertisement)$ exceeds a given threshold β, then the specifications are considered similar according to their profiles.

Similarity matching

Profile comparison may give some indication about the similarity of two specifications, but has two inherent limitations. First, it is not able to consider the structure of the specification itself and as a result it cannot distinguish, for instance, between the input and output declarations of the specification. Second, the semantics of the words is not taken into consideration in profile comparisons. Consequently, this method cannot recognize that the word pair (Computer, iBook), should have a closer distance than the pair (Computer, Book).

In order to establish similarity matching, a combination of distance values are calculated for pairs of input and output declarations, and input and output constraints. The distance values are computed in terms of the distance between concepts and words that occur in the particular parts of the specifications. In LARKS these values are computed when the advertisement is submitted and stored in the middle agent's database.

Let E_i, E_j be variable declarations or constraints, and $S(E)$ denote the set of words in E. The similarity between E_i and E_j is determined by pairwise computation of word distances:

$$Similarity(E_i, E_j) = 1 - \left(\left(\sum_{(u,v) \in S(E_i) \times S(E_j)} d_w(u,v) / |S(E_i) \times S(E_j)| \right) \right)$$

The similarity value $Similarity(S_a, S_b)$ between two specifications S_a and S_b is computed as the average of the sum of similarity computations among all pairs of declarations and constraints:

$$Similarity(S_a, S_b) = \frac{\displaystyle\sum_{(E_i,E_j) \in (D(S_a) \times D(S_b)) \cup (C(S_a) \times C(S_b))} Similarity(E_i, E_j)}{|(D(S_a) \times D(S_b)) \cup (C(S_a) \times C(S_b))|}$$

where $D(S)$ is the input/output declaration and $C(S)$ the input/output constraint parts of a specification S.

Signature matching

Although the similarity method takes into account the semantics of individual words in the description, it does not consider the meaning of the logical constraints in a specification. This is taken care of by the signature and constraint methods. The two methods work together to look for a semantic plug-in match. The signature method first considers the declaration parts of the request and the advertisement specifications and determines pairwise if their signatures of input and output variable types match. This is carried out by checking a set of subtype inference rules that determine when a type is a subtype of another, represented as $t_1 \preccurlyeq_{subtype} t_2$ (Sycara et al. 2002).

The matching of two signatures sig_1 and sig_2 is then defined by a binary string-valued function fsm:

$$fsm(sig_1, sig_2) = \begin{cases} sub & sig_2 \preccurlyeq_{subtype} sig_1 \\ Sub & sig_1 \preccurlyeq_{subtype} sig_2 \\ eq & sig_1 =_{subtype} sig_2 \\ disj & else \end{cases}$$

The syntactic similarity between two declarations or constraints is defined as follows. Given a threshold value γ, two declarations D_i and D_j syntactically match if they are sufficiently similar:

$$Similarity(D_i, D_j) \geq \gamma \wedge fsm(D_i, D_j) \neq disj$$

Two constraints C_i and C_j syntactically match if they are sufficiently similar:

$$Similarity(C_i, C_j) \geq \gamma$$

The profile comparison and similarity and signature matching methods contribute to determining the syntactical matching of two LARKS specifications. In the following, the syntactical match between two declarations or constraints is indicated by the boolean predicate *Syntactical*. Thus, two specifications S_a and S_b *syntactically match* if (Sycara et al. 2002):

1. Their profiles match, namely $dps(S_a, S_b)$ is greater than or equal to threshold β.

2. For each declaration (constraint) $E_i, i \in \{1, \ldots, n_a\}$ in the declaration (constraint) part of S_a there exists a most similar matching declaration (constraint) $E_j, j \in \{1, \ldots, n_b\}$ in the declaration (constraint) part of S_b such that:

$$Syntactical(E_i, E_j) \wedge Similarity(E_i, E_j)$$
$$= \max\{Similarity(E_i, E_k), k \in \{1, \ldots, n_b\}\}$$

And similarly for each declaration (constraint) in S_b.

3. For each pair of declarations (D_i, D_j) determined in (2) the matching of their signatures is of the same type, in other words the value of $fsm(D_i, D_j)$ is the same.

4. The similarity value $Similarity(S_a, S_b)$ exceeds a given threshold.

Constraint matching

Given that many matches can be found by applying the previous methods, some means of restricting the search is required. This is provided by the constraint matching method.

A specification S can be represented as a pair $(Pre_S, Post_S)$ where Pre_S and $Post_S$ are the pre and post-conditions respectively. Consider two specifications $S_a(Pre_{S_a}, Post_{S_a})$ and $S_b(Pre_{S_b}, Post_{S_b})$. S_a and S_b match in terms of constraints if:

$$(Pre_{S_a} \Rightarrow Pre_{S_b}) \wedge (Post_{S_b} \Rightarrow Post_{S_a})$$

In other words, the set of pre-conditions of S_a logically implies that of S_b, and the set of post-conditions of S_a is logically implied by that of S_b. As logical implication of clauses is undecidable (Schmidt-Schauß 1988), logical implication among constraints in LARKS is computed using polynomial-subsumption checking for Horn clauses.

A specification S_b *semantically plug-in* matches a specification S_a in LARKS if:

1. the signatures of their variable declaration parts match
2. the set of input constraints of S_a logically implies that of S_b
3. the set of output constraints of S_b logically implies that of S_a.

5.5 OWL-S

Advertising capabilities and matching them with requests is a related problem in the context of Web services. In particular, in the same way that agents need to be able to locate others, one needs to be able to locate web services based on the capabilities that they provide. Moreover, in order to achieve the full potential of web services and the Semantic Web, ideally users should be able to identify their needs and delegate them to software agents who can then locate web services in order to satisfy their users' goals. The location of web services should be based on the semantic match between a description of the service requested and the description of the service being advertised.

The problem with the current XML-based standards for describing web services such as the Simple Object Access Protocol (SOAP) (SOAP 2006) and Web Services Description Language (WSDL) (Christensen et al. 2006) is that they are designed to provide descriptions of transport formats and mechanisms, address binding, and the interface used by each service. As a result SOAP and WSDL cannot help with the automatic location of web services based on their capability specifications. Although Universal Description, Discovery and Integration protocol (UDDI) (UDDI 2006) which is another XML based standard, provides a registry of businesses and the web services that they provide, nevertheless it does not represent service capabilities. Another limitation shared by the aforementioned standards is that they lack an explicit semantics: although two XML descriptions of services may look exactly the same, they may mean different things in different contexts. However, one major issue in capability matching is that semantics is crucial and matching needs to be done in context.

A more suitable framework for describing the capabilities of services is that provided by the DAML effort (DAML 2006). The most recent reincarnation of DAML is the Ontology Web Language for Services (OWL-S) (OWL-S 2006) which is based on OWL (OWL 2006) discussed in Section 3.4.3.

OWL-S is organized around three interrelated sub-ontologies as illustrated in Figure 5.5:

- The *ServiceProfile* describes 'what the service does'. This description which can be regarded as the capability specification of a service, is essential if a requester agent, or a middle agent acting on behalf of a requester, is to determine whether or not the service meets its needs. This information is also essential for advertising purposes. This representation may, in addition, include limitations on service applicability and quality of service as well as any requirements that the requester must satisfy to use the service successfully, for example, authentication.

- The *ServiceModel* describes 'how a service works'. This is the process model which describes how a requester can use the service, how to ask for it and what happens when the service is carried out. This is used to enable invocation, enactment, composition, monitoring and recovery. In particular, for complex services that are composed of

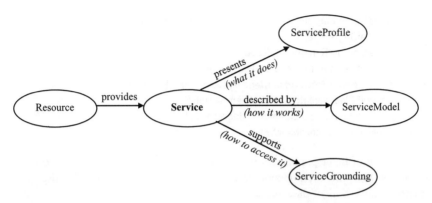

Figure 5.5: The OWL-S service description

several steps over time, the *ServiceModel* description may be used by a requester or middle agent in four different ways:

1. to examine in-depth whether the service meets its needs
2. to compose service descriptions from multiple services to perform a specific task
3. to coordinate the activities of the different participants during the course of the service enactment
4. to monitor the execution of the service.

- The *ServiceGrounding* or grounding for short, specifies the details of how a requester or middle agent can interact with or access a service. A grounding must specify a communication protocol, message formats and other service-specific details, such as port numbers used in contacting the service. This information can be expressed in WSDL. Furthermore, the grounding must specify for each semantic type of input or output specified in the ServiceModel, an unambiguous way of exchanging data elements of that type with the service, i.e., the serialization techniques employed.

Two constraints are imposed on the high-level ontology for services: a service can be described by, at most, one service model, and a grounding must be associated with exactly one service.

An advertisement specification matches a request when (i) all the outputs of the request are matched by the outputs of the advertisement, and (ii) all the inputs of the advertisement are matched by outputs of the request. A match between outputs is recognized if and only if, for each output **outputR** of the request, there is a matching one **outputA** in the advertisement, otherwise if there is no matching output in the advertisement, the match fails (Paolucci et al. 2002)[1]:

---

[1]Strictly speaking, the algorithms that follow were proposed in the context of DAML-S (Paolucci et al. 2002) which was the predecessor of OWL-S.

```
outputMatch(outputsRequest,outputsAdvertisement){
    globalDegreeMatch = exact
    forall outputR in outputsRequest do {
        find outputA in outputsAdvertisement such that
            degreeMatch = MaxDegreeMatch(outputR,outputA)
            if (degreeMatch<globalDegreeMatch)
                globalDegreeMatch = degreeMatch
    return sort(recordMatch);}
```

The matching of input parameters is computed in a similar way to that of the output parameters, but with the direction reversed, i.e., the inputs of the advertisement are matched against those of the request.

Matching requests with capability advertisements can be done by determining the minimal distance between the parameters that are used in the two specifications. Thus, the degree or level of a service match is determined by the degree of parameter matches. If **outputA** is one output of the advertisement and **outputR** is one output of the request, the degree of matching is decided as follows:

```
degreeOfMatch(outputR, outputA):
    if outputA = outputR then return exact
    if outputR subclassOf outputA then return exact
    if outputA subsumes outputR then return plugIn
    if outputR subsumes outputA then return subsumes
        else return fail
```

Accordingly, there are four levels of parameter match:

- *exact match*: **outputR** and **outputA** are an exact match when they are equivalent, or when **outputR** is a subclass of **outputA**, which means that by advertising **outputA** the provider commits to providing outputs consistent with every immediate subtype of **outputA**.

- *plug-in match*: if **outputA** subsumes **outputR**, then **outputA** includes **outputR** and therefore **outputA** could be plugged in place of **outputR**.

- *subsumes match*: if **outputR** subsumes **outputA**, then this means that the provider cannot fully fulfil the request. The requester may use this service for the partial achievement of its goals, but it will have to use additional services to fully accomplish them.

- *fail*: occurs when no subsumption relation exists between the advertisement and request specifications.

The degree of match of the input of an advertisement and the input of a request is decided in a similar way, but with the arguments reversed, that is **degreeOfMatch(inputA, inputR)**.

The ensuing degrees of match between a request and a set of advertisement specifications are organized from most to least preferable: exact matches are of course more preferable than plug-in matches, which are followed by subsumes matches in the scale. Needless to say, fail is the least desirable degree of match. The resulting matches are then sorted using as criterion the highest score in the outputs, as this indicates the extent to which the provider can carry out the requested service. The matching of input parameters is only taken into consideration for breaking up ties between equally scoring outputs.

5.6 Further Reading

A collection of papers by Katia Sycara and colleagues discuss matchmaking. Matching and a taxonomy of middle agents on the Internet are discussed in Wong and Sycara (2000) and Klusch and Sycara (2001). The need for an Agent Capability Description Language is discussed in Sycara et al. (2002) along with a more detailed discussion of the LARKS language and the different types of matching in this framework. An extended description of LARKS along with an example which uses the ITL language is provided in Sycara et al. (1998).

Matchmaking in the context of the Semantic Web is discussed in Paolucci et al. (2002) and Trastour et al. (2001). A thorough introduction to the OWL-S language can be found in Martin et al. (2004), whereas an extended description is available at (OWL-S 2006). An introduction into OWL-S is also presented in Singh and Huhns (2005, Section 15.5.2). The matching algorithms discussed here were originally described in the context of DAML-S in Paolucci et al. (2002), the predecessor of OWL-S. Matchmaking and workflow composition of services are discussed in Singh and Huhns (2005).

5.7 Exercises and Topics for Discussion

1. Consider the domain of mortgage lending. Individuals are interested in obtaining mortgages. Each individual has their own preferences regarding the amount that they would like to borrow and other terms such as repayment period, type of mortgage (repayment, interest only). How much an individual can borrow depends on their income. Matching requests from individuals and potential mortgage lenders is done through a middle agent. Suppose that the majority of requesters do not want to reveal their identity in the initial enquiry stage, as they do not want to be identified by the mortgage lenders (to avoid being inundated with mortgage advertisements).

(a) What privacy concerns does this scenario raise?

(b) What type of middle agent would be more appropriate for this domain and why?

(c) Describe how the services and requests could be specified.

(d) Sketch how the matching would take place given your recommended type of middle agent.

2. Consider the domain of currency exchange. Individuals are interested in the exchange rates of various currencies. A number of providers provide this service, but some providers specialize in particular currencies. Moreover, different providers offer different exchange rates and they operate either on a flat fee or on a commission base, which depends on the value of the transaction. Matching requests for service from requesters and potential providers is done through a middle agent.

(a) Suggest a type of middle agent that would be appropriate for this domain and explain why.

(b) Are there are any privacy-related concerns in this scenario?

(c) Sketch how the services, requests and potential constraints could be specified.

(d) Sketch how the matching would take place given your recommended type of middle agent.

CHAPTER 6

Recommender Systems

LEARNING OBJECTIVES

After reading and completing this chapter, you should be able to:

- Describe how recommender systems can be used in e-commerce applications and describe their potential benefits.
- Discuss how various types of information can be used to assist the user in her selections.
- Distinguish between the different technologies used to build recommender systems.
- Describe the principles underlying collaborative filtering techniques for recommender systems.
- Explain how neighbourhood algorithms work and apply them in simple problems.
- Discuss the problems associated with collaborative filtering technologies.
- Explain how user profiles can be used to provide for personalization of services to users, including dynamic pricing.

One of the most common problems users are faced with in today's information-rich world is that, in fact, there is too much information available. Consumers have to deal with an overwhelming number of alternatives, while information-seekers are inundated by the sheer volume of information. It would be helpful if there was some way in which we could narrow down our choices whilst looking, for instance, to buy a car or searching for news articles. It is often necessary to make choices without having sufficient personal experience or knowledge about all the possible alternatives. One of the most common means of obtaining information about possible alternatives in the absence of personal experience, is to rely on recommendations from other people, like our friends and colleagues or simply on *word of mouth*. More formal recommendations come in the form of movie and book reviews printed in newspapers and magazines, or general surveys such as hotel guides. Better still, we can enlist the help of experts in a particular area and trust them to provide us with good recommendations based on their expert knowledge. For instance, food critics may provide recommendations for restaurants.

To put it simply, a *recommender system* is a system which provides recommendations to a user (Resnick and Varian 1997). Such systems find application in web sites offering recommendations regarding books, music CDs, movies, documents, services and other products such as software games. For example, Amazon (Linden et al. 2003) makes use of a recommendation system. Every time that you select an item, Amazon provides you a with a list of items that have been purchased by other users who have also purchased the item that you are interested in. This is a form of recommendation based on what other users have bought.

Recommender systems are not limited to providing recommendations on consumer goods or services, but even on service providers and retailers. Such systems are often referred to as *reputation systems* (see Section 12.5). eBay (2006), for instance, allows you to rate a vendor or an individual that you have transacted with and these ratings are available to other users seeking information regarding the trustworthiness or quality of service provided by that vendor or individual.

When a recommender agent provides recommendations for services or providers, it can be viewed as a particular type of middle agent. As illustrated in Figure 6.1, a recommender system has the task of returning a set of recommendations to the requester agent. The providers may be registered with the recommender agent and, as time goes by, they are being rated by users or other end agents. The recommender collects and processes the ratings to provide accurate recommendations to the next requester. Therefore, recommender agents are also involved in the third phase of matching which includes collecting feedback as was discussed in the previous chapter. It is then up to the requester to decide to which of the providers it will delegate its request for service.

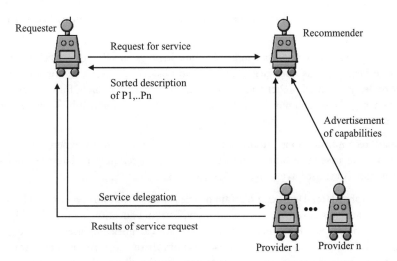

Figure 6.1: The recommender

6.1 INFORMATION NEEDED

In order to be able to provide recommendations for any product, commodity or service or even retailers and service providers, recommender systems require some form of input upon which to base their recommendations. Although typically this input is provided by the user(s), it may also come from different sources:

- **Purchase data.** This is data regarding the purchase history of users. For instance, one form of recommendation provided by Amazon is based on patterns of co-purchase between multiple customers.

- **Feedback provided by the users.** Feedback can be provided by the user implicitly or explicitly. Explicit ratings are entered by a user directly, i.e., the user ranks goods, products or services, whereas implicit feedback is inferred from the user's behaviour. For instance, a music recommender may use implicit data such as play lists, or it may use explicit rankings for songs or artists, or a combination of both, in providing a recommendation. Explicit ratings have a scale which represents the range and granularity of ratings. Some systems simply allow users to rate items as 'liked' or 'disliked', while others use 5-point, 7-point, or 100-point scales. Also, the presence of a timestamp on ratings is important, as in some cases the users' tastes and preferences may change over time.

- **Textual comments.** These are comments in free text form intended for other users to read. They are usually not interpreted by the recommender system, but provide additional information to the requester which cannot perhaps be described in terms of ratings.

- **Browsing and searching data.** Some recommender systems do not explicitly ask users to rate items such as documents, but instead observe the user's behaviour and infer her preferences based on her choices. For instance, when searching for news articles or documents, the system may infer if a particular item is of interest by keeping track of the time that the user has spent on it.

- **Expert recommendations.** Another form of input comes from experts. This is, for instance, the case in restaurant guides or sites recommending the latest technological innovations or must-have gadgets, PCs, cameras, etc.

- **Demographic data.** Demographic data profiles or data from surveys can also be used in recommender systems. Data such as age, sex, level of education, geographical location and income are used by such systems to create categories of users. The aggregate buying behaviour or preferences of users within these categories is then tracked and used to make recommendations to other demographically similar users.

6.2 PROVIDING RECOMMENDATIONS

The recommendations generated by a recommender system can take different forms (Schafer et al. 2001):

- **Attribute-based recommendations.** Such systems recommend items to users based on syntactic properties of the products. An example of an attribute-based recommendation is when a customer does a search for a science fiction book and the recommender system responds with a list of science fiction titles. Typically, attribute-based recommendations are offered when a user explicitly asks for them. Alternatively, the system can make such recommendations based on an 'understanding' of the user's preferences kept in profile. The recommendations can be generated on the fly or may be personal, depending on the existence of a profile.

- **Item-to-item correlation.** Systems can provide recommendations to users based on a small set of items in which they have already expressed interest. For instance, if a customer has placed a few products in her shopping basket, the system may recommend complementary products to increase the order size. The recommendation is usually based on information gathered by the system implicitly, but it may also be because the user explicitly asked for it. The recommendation produced is ephemeral as it is not based on the user's preferences or profile, but it is created on the fly based on the currently selected items.

- **User-to-user correlation.** User-to-user recommendations are provided by a recommender system based on the correlation between the active user seeking recommendation and other users who have expressed preferences, rated items or purchased them.

In such systems the users may have to rate the items explicitly or the system may collect information based on their buying patterns. The recommendations can be generated automatically or the user may ask for them.

- **Non-personalized recommendations.** Some systems recommend products or items to users based on what others, on average, have said about these. The recommendations are independent of the requester and as a result every user gets the same recommendations. As the system does not recognize the individual user from one session to the next, the recommendations are ephemeral. Such systems require little user effort to generate the recommendation. This form of non-personalized recommendation is very often used in traditional stores such as supermarkets, restaurants and bookshops: recommendations are set up on a display that is viewed without change by every customer, e.g., soup of the day.

6.3 RECOMMENDATION TECHNOLOGIES

A number of approaches have been developed to assist the user in search of recommendations. Information retrieval (IR) systems focus on allowing users to express queries to retrieve information relevant to a topic of interest or to fulfil a particular information need. IR systems may index a collection of documents using either the full text of the document or document abstracts. For nontextual items such as movies, IR systems index genres, keywords, actors, directors, etc. Such systems are generally optimized for ephemeral user queries, i.e., looking up a topic in a repository of documents. Internet search engines are popular IR systems. However, IR techniques are less valuable in the actual recommendation process, since they cannot capture any information about the user's preferences other than the specific query, and they cannot retrieve documents based on opinions or quality because their functionality is only based on text.

Two alternative key approaches have emerged to deal with these disadvantages: content-based filtering and collaborative-based filtering. The first technique views users as individuals: a user is characterized by the content of the items she shows interest in and any recommendations are guided by these pre-known interests. On the other hand, recommender systems employing the collaborative filtering approach view the user as part of a group. This view leads to recommendations based on other, similar users.

6.4 CONTENT–BASED FILTERING

In *content-based filtering* also known as *information filtering,* the system processes information from various sources and tries to extract useful elements about its content. This can be done either via the use of a keyword-based search (keywords sometimes in boolean form) or semantic-information extraction by using associative networks of keywords, weighted semantic networks or directed graphs of words.

In content-based filtering, each user is assumed to operate independently and the system requires a profile of the user's needs or preferences in order to be able to provide a recommendation. Thus, a user entering a site and seeking a recommendation would have to provide information on her personal preferences in order for the system to build a profile. The user profile includes information about the content of items of interest, namely web pages, movies, music, news items, or anything else. Using these items as a basis, the technique identifies similar items which are returned as recommendations. These techniques are particularly valuable to users who have specific interests and who are looking for related recommendations. For instance, a movie recommender based on (pure) content-based filtering will typically rely on information such as actors, director, genre and other keywords to describe different movies and match this against the learned user preferences to provide a recommendation. Thus, a Woody Allen fan will be recommended a new Woody Allen film. Content-based filtering techniques have the important property that they do not depend on having other users in the system and therefore they do not need a critical mass to be able to start providing recommendations.

One of the major limitations of pure content-based techniques for recommender systems is that they are not capable of exploring new items or topics. As the recommendations are only based on content information, only items or topics similar to those already in the user's profile can be suggested. For instance, the Woody Allen fan would probably never be recommended a non-Woody Allen film that just happens to be liked by most other Woody Allen fans. This, unfortunately, leads to over-specialization: one is restricted to seeing items similar to those that have already been rated highly. To alleviate this problem, some content-based recommender systems incorporate a degree of randomness (Sheth and Maes 1993).

To keep the user's profile up-to-date, content-based recommender systems require feedback about the relevance of their suggestions. Users are in general reluctant to provide feedback and tend to avoid it; this is a general problem in recommender systems and search engines. Furthermore, the user profile consists entirely of user ratings of items or topics of interest. As recommendations are based on these, the fewer the ratings, the more limited the set of possible recommendations. Thus, the performance of such systems depends critically on the number of ratings that the user has provided, i.e., how good the profile is. In some systems, machine-learning techniques have been employed to make recommendations using algorithms for learning user profiles to determine in which items the user is interested. Still, as the user preferences may change over time, the system needs to be able to keep an up-to-date profile in order to ensure that the user receives accurate and relevant recommendations. Another drawback is that such techniques are difficult to apply to situations where the desirability of an item, for example a web page, is determined in part by aesthetic qualities that are difficult to quantify. These types of materials are generally incompatible with the type of content analysis that these techniques require in order to make further recommendations, i.e., extraction of keywords.

Recommender systems using such techniques have been developed for e-mail and news filtering (Maes 1994, Lang 1995), and for recommending documents (Krulwich and Burkey 1996, 1997, Lieberman 1995).

6.5 COLLABORATIVE FILTERING

Collaborative-based filtering recommender systems can produce recommendations by identifying overlapping interests among users and computing the similarity between a user's preferences and those of other people. This technique is very similar to the way in which we ask friends or colleagues for recommendations. That is why it is often referred to as *social filtering* as it emulates the natural social process of seeking recommendations from like-minded people. For instance, when a new movie has just come out and a friend of yours has already seen it, it is only natural to ask them their opinion about it. When looking for a plumber, you may ask the opinion of colleagues or neighbours that have already used the services of a particular person before deciding whether or not to employ him. Once we have enough information, we can make a decision whether it is worth seeing the movie, or if a particular plumber is reliable and good at his trade.

Preferences are collected in the form of ratings which show how much people like or dislike a particular item or topic. Such systems do not attempt to analyze or understand the content of the items being recommended. Rather than treating each user as an individual and mapping users to items through content attributes or keywords, collaborative-based filtering treats users as belonging to a group. As a result, the main advantage of such systems is that the pool from which recommendations originate is not restricted to items for which the active user has indicated a preference. It therefore becomes possible to discover and explore new items of interest simply because other people liked them. It is also easier to provide good recommendations even when the attributes of great interest to users are unknown or hidden.

6.5.1 How collaborative filtering systems work

Recommender systems based on collaborative filtering need to know the preferences of the user in order to make personalized recommendations. These preferences are entered as ratings or votes which are numeric values representing how much a user likes or dislikes specific items. Once a user has registered her preferences and, provided that there is a database containing the preferences of other users, she can then ask the system for predictions or recommendations.

The users' preferences about different items create user-item matrices, such as the one illustrated in Table 6.1. Each of the cells in the matrix represents a user's rating for a specific item. The empty cells indicate that the user has not rated this item yet. The aim of a recommender system is to be able to fill in the empty cells in the user-item matrix in the most accurate way, as if the user herself had entered the rating in the matrix. Once

	Item1	Item2	Item3	Item4	Item5
User A	4	4	1	4	3
User B	2	1	4	2	5
User C	3	1	3	2	1
User D	5	4	2		3

Table 6.1: Example of user-item matrix

the matrix is filled in, the recommender is able to make a recommendation based on the results obtained. For instance, given the user-item matrix of Table 6.1, User D could ask for a recommendation on Item4.

In collaborative-based filtering, the recommendations produced depend on finding similar users to the active one, i.e., a user or a set of users that match closely the active user's preferences. The concept of 'similarity' needs to be defined in some way and this may differ from system to system. Specifying which users are to be considered similar has an impact on the performance of the system in terms of the accuracy of the recommendations. Recommender systems employing collaborative filtering have used different measures of similarity that are based on neighbourhood algorithms (Herlocker et al. 1999) such as the Pearson coefficients (Resnick et al. 1994) and mean-squared differences (Shardanand and Maes 1995), as well as other techniques, such as Bayes' rule (Pennock et al. 2000), probabilistic distance measures (Ha and Haddawy 1998) and vector similarity (Breese et al. 1998).

6.5.2 Neighbourhood–based algorithms

Among the most popular algorithms used to determine similarity in collaborative filtering systems are neighbourhood-based ones. Such algorithms attempt to identify a neighbourhood of like-minded users to the active one. The typical process involved in making a recommendation according to such algorithms involves three steps:

1. The degree of similarity between the active user and the other users in the database is computed, based on the ratings previously collected. This degree of similarity is positive if the current user tends to agree with another user, or negative if they disagree.

2. A set of users is chosen as the basis on which to make the prediction. This set is determined according to the degree of similarity with the active user. Some systems select a specific number of the most similar users, some others select only those that have a degree of similarity which is positive, and others select only those whose degree is over a threshold.

3. The system makes use of the set of users, selected in the previous step, to produce the recommendation. Many systems give weights to the ratings provided by users based on the degree of similarity they have with the active user. A user with a high degree of similarity with the active one will have more weight in the prediction than another with a low degree of similarity.

One of the most often-used similarity metrics in collaborative-based systems is Pearson's correlation coefficients. Pearson's correlation reflects the degree of linear relationship between two variables, i.e., the extent to which the variables are related, and ranges from $+1$ to -1. A correlation of $+1$ means that there is a perfect positive linear relationship between variables or, in other words, two users have very similar tastes, whereas a negative correlation indicates that the users have dissimilar tastes. The formula for Pearson's correlation takes on many forms, but a commonly used one to determine the degree of correlation between an active user a and another user u is:

$$w_{a,u} = \frac{\sum_{i=1}^{n}(r_{a,i} - \bar{r}_a)(r_{u,i} - \bar{r}_u)}{\sqrt{\sum_{i=1}^{n}(r_{a,i} - \bar{r}_a)^2}\sqrt{\sum_{i=1}^{n}(r_{u,i} - \bar{r}_u)^2}}$$

Consider the user-item matrix of Table 6.1. What should be the recommendation for user D for item $Item4$? $\bar{r}_a$ is the average of D's ratings, which is 3.5; $\bar{r}_u$ is the average of each of the other users' ratings, which is 3 for A, 3 for B and 2 for C. To obtain the average of each user we take into consideration $Item1$, $Item2$, $Item3$ and $Item5$ as these are the items that both recommender and active users have rated. Thus n, which indicates the number of items that both active and recommender users have rated, is 4. $r_{a,i}$ is the rating given by D to item i and $r_{u,i}$ is the rating given by the recommender users to item i. As a result we obtain the following regarding user D's correlation with the other three users:

$$w_{D,A} = 0.9, \; w_{D,B} = -0.7, \; w_{D,C} = 0$$

Accordingly, users A and D have a high correlation value, which implies that they have similar tastes. On the other hand, users B and D have a negative degree of correlation which means that their tastes are dissimilar, whereas C and D are not correlated.

The second step is to select the neighbourhood, which is the set of most similar users to the active one. Although in this example all users are taken into consideration, in some recommender systems only a subset of them (a fixed number or those whose correlation value is above a threshold) may be considered.

Finally, the weighted average of all the ratings given by the users on $Item4$ is calculated according to the formula:

$$p_{a,i} = \bar{r}_a + \frac{\sum_{u=1}^{m}(r_{u,i} - \bar{r}_u)w_{a,u}}{\sum_{u=1}^{m}|w_{a,u}|}$$

$p_{a,i}$ represents the prediction for user $a = D$ on item i which is *Item*4, m is the number of users, and $w_{a,u}$ is the degree of similarity between users a and u, which has been computed using the Pearson r correlation coefficients. The recommendation for user D for *Item*4 is:

$$p_{D,Item4} = 4.5$$

This prediction seems reasonable given that user D tends to agree with user A who rated the item high (4). The process defined above is carried out for every empty cell in the user-item matrix. In general terms, predictions are more accurate when the matrix has more ratings to be used in computing correlations.

6.5.3 Problems in collaborative filtering

The idea of using a pool of users to provide recommendations to others is very attractive, but it does come with its own set of problems. As such systems construct rating profiles of their users and provide recommendations by identifying other users with similar profiles, they rely heavily on their users providing these ratings or feedback. Indeed, a critical mass of users is needed to register their preferences and provide ratings in order for the system to start producing good recommendations. This limitation is often referred to as the *first-rater* or the *cold start problem* (Schein et al. 2002). These are situations where there are only a few ratings on which to base recommendations. New items cannot be recommended until some users have taken the time to rank them. This can cause problems for users seeking for instance recommendations on obscure items (e.g., obscure movies) since nobody may have rated them, or advice on new items (e.g., movies only just released) since nobody has had a chance to evaluate them. In addition, a user that is considered unusual based on her profile of interests will probably not be similar to any of the other users, which will lead to poor recommendations. Finally, since no information about the content of items is kept, even users with similar, but not identical interests, will not be considered similar *enough*.

The scarcity of ratings is another related issue. User profiles in this case are usually sparse vectors of ratings. A partial solution to this might be to use implicit feedback, or other methods, to increase the density of the dataset.

Recommendations are often based on the comparison between the models of the active user and the population of other users, where the user models are sets of votes. A common shortcoming of collaborative filtering algorithms is that the recommendations will only come from the users with which the active user shares votes. For example, Pearson's correlation coefficient finds the similarity between users a and u, but only takes into account the number of items for which both users have submitted ratings or votes. This can lead to problems when relatively few votes are available for either the active user or the users being used for comparisons. *Default voting* has been used to overcome this problem. With this method, default votes are assigned to unrated items so that there is more overlap between the two users to be compared, and votes may be assigned even to items that neither user has rated, in order to increase the total number of votes. Appropriate default votes might be a user's average vote or the average vote over all users for a particular item.

Another problem in recommender systems using collaborative filtering techniques is that of scalability: in systems with large numbers of users and items, computation grows linearly with the number of users and items and thus appropriate algorithms that scale up are needed. For instance, an approach using inverted files has been explored in Cöster and Svensson (2002).

There are also problems regarding the reliability of recommender systems based on collaborative filtering techniques and even more so in reputation systems. The ratings of items, sites, vendors and movies can be artificially inflated by phantom users registering and giving them high rankings. For instance, a game that has just been released can be given inflated ratings by people who would like to promote it. Vendors may rank themselves high in order to attract buyers. This can be done, for instance, quite easily if the users can vote using pseudonyms and the recommender system has no way of verifying who they are.

The lack of transparency is another issue. Collaborative systems are treated like oracles which give recommendations and advice, but on the other hand cannot be questioned (Herlocker et al. 2000). The user is given no indication whether to trust a recommendation or not. Building an explanation system into a recommender can help alleviate this problem as the user would be in a position to understand the reasoning behind a recommendation and decide on her own whether or not to trust it. Thus, the user's understanding of how the system works, as well as its strengths and limitations, would increase, which could improve the acceptance of recommender systems.

Recommender systems also raise concerns about the users' privacy since such systems may be collecting sensitive information about them. The more information a system has about a user's preferences and tastes, the better the recommendations it can provide. However, users may not want their habits or views widely known. Some recommender systems permit anonymous participation or participation under a pseudonym, but this only goes half-way in addressing the problem, as it leaves the system open to abuse. Trust and privacy-related problems have prevented wide acceptance of collaborative systems, especially in high-risk domains.

6.5.4 Collaborative filtering systems

A number of systems have been implemented using collaborative-based filtering techniques for recommending books, CDs, movies, etc. A few indicative systems will be briefly described in this section, but this represents a by no means exhaustive list.

Tapestry (Goldberg et al. 1992) was the earliest collaborative-based filtering system for retrieving documents from a growing repository. In fact, the term collaborative filtering itself was coined by Douglas Terry at Xerox PARC as part of the development of the Tapestry system. The system allows its users to annotate the documents they read. Other users can then retrieve documents to read, based not only on the content of the documents themselves, but also on what other users have said about them. Tapestry provides free text annotations as well as explicit 'likeit' and 'hateit' ones, so users can easily indicate which of the documents they have read, they liked the most or found relevant.

GroupLens is a Usenet news recommender system that helps people to find articles they like by combining collaboration with user profiles (Resnick et al. 1994, Konstan et al. 1997). In GroupLens, communities of users rank the articles they read on a numerical scale from 1 (lowest) to 5 (highest) based on how much they liked them. The underlying idea is that users who have agreed in their ratings of past articles are likely to agree again in future articles. The GroupLens system then finds correlations between the ratings that users have given the articles. Essentially, a user's profile consists of the ratings that she has given to the articles she has read. The similarity between users is measured using Pearson r correlation coefficients, as was described previously. Once the similarity between users has been computed, the system predicts the rating for every empty cell in the user-item matrix. The system takes into consideration all the users available as its neighbourhood to predict scores. The ratings from other users are then combined by weighting each user's rating in proportion to how well her profile correlates with that of the active user, to produce a recommendation. MovieLens (Miller et al. 2003, MovieLens 2006) is another web-based recommender system for movies based on the GroupLens technology.

Ringo (later renamed Firefly), developed at MIT, is a system which used the tastes of users to recommend music (Shardanand and Maes 1995). On using Ringo for the first time, users are given a list with artists and are asked to provide a rating to each of these using a scale from 1 (lowest) to 7 (highest). These ratings express how much a user likes to listen to a particular artist and are used to create profiles. Ringo compares these profiles to find similarities and make recommendations. In Ringo, four different algorithms were used: the mean-squared differences algorithm which measures the degree of dissimilarity between two user profiles; the Pearson correlation algorithm which works in a similar way to Pearson r correlation coefficients; the constrained Pearson r algorithm which measures the similarity between user profiles, but only uses positive correlations; and the artist-artist algorithm, which is an implementation of the constrained Pearson r correlation coefficient, which employs correlations between artists or albums. Once the system computes the degree of similarity according to the selected algorithm, it takes all the users with a degree of similarity greater than a threshold value. This set of users constitutes the neighbourhood. A prediction is then generated by taking a weighted average of the ratings given by the users for a specific item.

Alternative approaches to collaborative filtering include, for instance, the use of personality types to generate recommendations (Pennock et al. 2000). A user's personality type is described as a vector of ratings for all rated items. Then, given the ratings of the active user the system computes the probability that she is of the same personality type as another user. Subsequently, the system returns the most probable rating for the item as a recommendation.

Another method that originates from the information retrieval field and has been applied to collaborative filtering involves using frequency or similarity vectors (Salton and McGill 1983, Breese et al. 1998). Each user is characterized by a vector which contains the ratings for every item that she has rated. The vector of ratings contains positive values for preferred items and zero values for items that have not been rated. The similarity between two users is measured by computing the cosine of the angle formed by the two vectors. This method can be improved by reducing weights for commonly occurring items, i.e., items which are liked by most of the users are not considered in the prediction.

6.6 COMBINING CONTENT AND COLLABORATIVE FILTERING

Combining collaborative-based with content-based filtering techniques in one system, thereby creating hybrid systems, may bring together the strengths of the two approaches and alleviate some of the problems that these techniques suffer from individually (Good et al. 1999). The underlying idea of such systems is that the content of the items is also taken into consideration when identifying similar users for collaborative recommendations (Alspector et al. 1998).

Fab (Balabanovic and Shoham 1997), a recommender system developed at Stanford University, combines content and collaborative-based techniques. It has both a personal and a group filter, which are altered, based on the users' relevance feedback. Fab users receive recommendations both from collection agents that represent particular areas of interest and from a selection agent that operates exclusively on the particular user's interests.

The GroupLens group have suggested an approach termed item-based collaborative filtering, which first analyzes the user-item matrix to identify relationships between different items, and then uses these to indirectly compute recommendations (Sarwar et al. 2001).

The Tango system employs both content and collaborative filtering techniques, albeit the two filters are kept separate (Claypool et al. 1999). A prediction in Tango is based on a weighted average of the content-based prediction and the collaborative one. The weights are determined on a per-user and per-item basis: if the number of users and votes increases, then the corresponding predictions' weight (collaborative) will increase as well.

In the Recommender system (Basu et al. 1998) an inductive learning approach to making movie recommendations is used. The system employs both user votes and other forms of information about each item. What is returned as a recommendation is not a predicted vote as such, but a classification {liked, disliked} for a particular item.

6.7 RECOMMENDER SYSTEMS IN E-COMMERCE

Recommender systems can be seen as middle agents that can provide recommendations on items, products as well as merchants and retailers. When recommender systems are used in e-commerce sites to suggest products to their users, they can help boost sales. Products and items can be recommended based on the overall top-selling items on a site, the demographics of the user, the analysis of the past buying behaviour of the particular user or the tastes of other similar users. In particular, recommender systems can enhance e-commerce sites through (Schafer et al. 2001):

- **Turning browsers into customers**. Visitors to an e-commerce site very often browse for items and products without ever purchasing anything. Recommender systems can help customers find products they might be interested in purchasing through recommendations that, in essence, act as advertisements. In this sense, recommender systems are used in the need recognition stage and can stimulate customers through careful and, at times, tailor-made advertising.

- **Cross-selling**. Most often users who shop on the Internet engage in 'considered' shopping, i.e., they shop for specific products or services that they need and have decided on after careful consideration. Advertising usually leaves such users indifferent. But, recommender systems can improve cross-selling by suggesting additional products for the user to purchase. By allowing careful and targeted advertising the user may actually be enticed to purchase additional items. For instance, by analyzing the content of the user's shopping basket the system may recommend complementary products. If the recommendations are good, the average order size could potentially increase, thereby increasing the vendor's profit.

- **Personalization**. Having information on who is surfing one's web site enables vendors to offer personalized services and tailor-make their offers to individual customers (see Section 6.8). The web site itself can be personalized according to the user's preferences, thus offering a unique shopping experience.

- **Keeping customers informed**. Stores that know their customers interests can use this information to keep them up-to-date on current offers and the arrival of new products that may be of interest to them. Notification services offer personalized suggestions, facilitating stronger customer relationships. Such services may offer a great service to customers, but may also help bring back customers to the vendor's site on a regular basis.

- **Retaining customer loyalty.** Loyalty is a major issue when conducting business online. Users may be able to find a number of vendors selling the same item (Reichheld and Sasser Jr 1990, Reichheld 1993). By incorporating a recommender system into an e-commerce site, loyalty and customer retention may improve as the recommender system creates a value-added relationship between the site and the customer. Vendors invest in their customers: they learn about their preferences via recommender systems and provide them with the facilities to create custom interfaces which provides them with a unique shopping experience. As the customer invests effort and time in teaching the recommender system about her preferences, she has an incentive to return to the same site and not opt for another vendor. Even if a competitor were to build a similar recommender system, a customer would have to teach the new system from scratch what the old one already knows (Pine 1999, Pine et al. 1995). Finally, creating relationships between customers can also increase loyalty. Through the use of a recommender system users develop a sense of camaraderie and a community of users emerges naturally. Customers will return to the site which recommends people with whom they like to interact.

6.8 A NOTE ON PERSONALIZATION

E-commerce provides a unique opportunity when compared to traditional commerce. The use of the Internet enables merchants and vendors to know the identities of the users who enter their stores. The ability to know exactly who is surfing a vendor's site is invaluable. Having information on the individual users enables vendors to offer personalized services.

Agent technology can be used to gather information on the identity of a user and her characteristics in a number of ways: based on an acquired user profile, attributes can be inferred from observing the user, by monitoring her behaviour and learning her preferences, and through correlation with other users. Even the simple process of registering with a web site or vendor enables a vendor to start building a profile on the user. Every move that the user makes as she visits different pages can be recorded and be used to infer the user's potential interests.

Other forms of technology exist to enable vendors to monitor the users' behaviour. *Spyware* is the general term used for such software which was coined by American software writer Steve Gibson. Spyware describes software that is able to track the users' behaviour unbeknown to them and then transmit this information to the person who is gathering the data, be it a vendor, organization or even a government. Intrinsically, spyware breaches the rights of privacy of the individual user. Naturally, users object to this and there have been a number of instances of users suing organizations responsible for such breaches of privacy.

However, a vendor or organization does not necessarily need sophisticated spyware to be able to track the users' moves and build profiles; cookies can facilitate this. A cookie is nothing more than a string of information stored from a given website on the user's machine that enables the site to recognize the user. Cookies can be linked into an organization's or vendor's profiling system and used as a means to first identify the user, and then keep track of her movements, such as pages visited and duration, or purchases made. A lot of information can be mined out of user profiles, such as habits or even spending power. For instance, by tracking the number of holidays and the value of each, a system can infer information on the spending power of an individual. Holidays can be subsequently tailored, i.e., offer luxurious packages only, or only packages with five-star hotels. When the user has given an explicit permission for such data to be accumulated and subsequently used for marketing purposes, then there is no problem. The problem arises as users are often unaware that such data are stored and used in this way. In general, the problem with spyware and cookies is that of regulation. As the Internet has no governing or regulating body, breaches in privacy rights are difficult to regulate. Even if a vendor is not gathering consumer-related data on their own, it is very easy to purchase such data from other retailers and marketing companies.

Vendors can use such information to tailor their offerings to the requirements of the individual user: they can guess which goods or services the user is likely to want to purchase next and offer them in advance. This is one-to-one or push marketing. Thus, vendors have the opportunity to develop personal relationships so that they can better respond to their customers' needs and develop strong customer loyalty. In addition, information on users enables vendors to provide a unique experience to each user by creating a virtual store based on their preferences. This is one way of achieving mass customization (Pine 1999). In essence, information technology allows vendors to tailor-make the presentation of their stores to the users' requirements and present them only with products and services that may be of interest to them.

But, apart from tailoring their offers and services to customers, vendors can use the information held on individuals to measure their desire to acquire a particular product and use it to charge them different prices. The tactic of price discrimination that can be facilitated through user profiles is a particularly serious issue and may have a negative effect on consumer confidence. For instance, a case involving the online retailer Amazon came to light in September 2000 (Vulkan 2003). It appeared that Amazon was charging different prices for the same product to different customers. Those that the system could recognize as existing customers were considered as 'loyal' and were offered slightly higher prices than those that the system could not trace, or who were occasional buyers. The pricing variations were first noticed when members of the DVDTalk forum realized that they were being charged different prices for the same DVD. The story was reported in the Washington Post. Apparently, Amazon had been engaging in price discrimination tactics on various products such as MP3 players and DVDs since the spring of 2000. At the time, Amazon claimed that these price differentiations were part of a simple price test. This price discrimination tactic was subsequently discontinued.

6.9 Further Reading

An extensive review of recommender systems on the Internet is provided in Montaner et al. (2003), while an evaluation of recommender systems based on a number of collaborative filtering techniques is presented in Herlocker et al. (2004). How recommender systems can be used in e-commerce applications and a brief explanation of how some indicative sites offering recommendations work, can be found in Schafer et al. (2001). Apart from Pearson coefficients (Resnick et al. 1994), collaborative filtering systems have used other similarity measures that are based on neighbourhood algorithms, such as mean-squared differences (Shardanand and Maes 1995). Alternative techniques include Bayes' rule (Pennock et al. 2000), probabilistic distance measures (Ha and Haddawy 1998) and vector similarity (Breese et al. 1998). The workings of Amazon's recommendation system are described in Linden et al. (2003).

Vulkan (2003) discusses in more detail how personalization technology can be used by sellers, and the economics of dynamic pricing.

6.10 Exercises and Topics for Discussion

1. Assume the user-item matrix of Table 6.2. Fill in the recommendations for each one of the empty cells using Pearson's correlation coefficients as a similarity metric as described in Section 6.5.2. In particular, consider three variations of the algorithm in which:

   (a) All users are taken into account to provide a recommendation.
   (b) All users whose similarity degree is above 0.5 are used to provide a recommendation.
   (c) The three most relevant users are used to provide a recommendation.

   How different are the resulting recommendations?

	Movie1	Movie2	Movie3	Movie4	Movie5	Movie6	Movie7	Movie8
User A	3	3	3	4	2	4	1	2
User B	4		2	1	3	3	3	4
User C	3	4	4	3	2		4	1
User D	1	2	1	3		4	3	4
User E	3	2	4	1	4	3	2	
User F	4	1	3	2	4	2		3
User G		4	3	2	1	3	4	2
User H	2	3		4	4	2	3	3

Table 6.2: User-item matrix

2. Use your favourite programming language to write a program that would be able to read a user-item matrix, such as the one of Table 6.2, and then fill in the recommendations for every empty cell using Pearson's correlation coefficients for measuring similarity. As in the previous exercise, implement three variations of the algorithm and enable the user to choose which one to apply.

3. Discuss the issue of personalization and how it can be enhanced through the use of recommendation technologies and user profiling.

4. Discuss how personalization through user profiling, unbeknown to the user, and the use of spyware, breaches the user's right to privacy. What potential steps can you take as an individual to ensure your right to privacy when you are engaging in e-commerce related activities?

5. Identify three web sites that offer some form of recommendation. What sort of information is used to provide these recommendations (see Section 6.1)? Classify these recommendations according to Section 6.2. What technique is used to provide these recommendations?

CHAPTER 7

Elements of Strategic Interaction

LEARNING OBJECTIVES

After reading and completing this chapter, you should be able to:

- Explain how the basic forces of supply and demand shape the market.
- Explain how preference relations work, the principles by which they are governed and how they can be expressed as utilities.
- Describe the basic elements of strategic interaction situations as games.
- Describe and distinguish among different types of games.
- Explain various solution concepts in games.
- Apply various solution concepts to solve simple games.

Electronic markets are open, information-rich and process-rich environments. Agent technology is ideally suited for e-commerce since it offers personalized, continuously running, adaptable and autonomous software (Guttman et al. 1998).

The behaviour of agents (human or otherwise) in electronic markets, in a similar way to traditional markets, revolves around specific processes which have been customarily the subject of research and study in Economics and Game Theory. Economic agents can interact in a variety of ways, for instance, companies may negotiate trade deals and individuals may bargain. Such settings are characterized as situations of strategic interdependence. This is because an individual's welfare depends not only on her own decisions and actions, but crucially also on the other individuals' decisions and actions. In strategic situations, agents cannot afford to take decisions in isolation but, out of necessity, they have to take into account the decisions and actions of the other agents.

This chapter introduces some fundamental concepts and principles from Economics and Game Theory which will be used in the following chapters.

7.1 ELEMENTS OF ECONOMICS

Agents in financial markets have different and, most of the time, conflicting goals and may lack the resources even though they have sufficient skills. Accordingly, they are in situations of *individual competition over resources* as described in Chapter 3. Agents are antagonistic, i.e., self-interested, and each agent is trying to maximize its own payoff without necessarily being concerned about the welfare of the other agents. A market economy is a setting in which the goods and services that a consumer may acquire are available. In such an economy, the goods, initial endowments, and technological possibilities are owned by consumers. Their utility is derived from consuming (or owning) goods and services. Consumer agents are looking to buy commodities/goods/products or services whilst some of them, who own technological possibilities, can use some of the commodities to produce others through a process of transformation, i.e., manufacturing; and thus they become producers.

7.1.1 A simple market economy

To set this exposition into context, we will start by considering an example of a small market economy, along which certain basic principles will be introduced; these will be elaborated upon later in this chapter. The example is that of a market of flats in a small (or medium) sized UK university town such as Colchester (this example has been adapted from Varian (2006)). In this town there are two types of flats: those that are in close proximity to the university and the others that are further away. If a student lives in a flat close to the university, then she can reach the campus on foot. The flats that are a bit further away require the use of public transport or a bicycle, so naturally most students would prefer to live in a flat close to the university. However, this comes at a price, that is, flats closer to the university tend to be more expensive than those further away since students are prepared to pay more for them.

To simplify things, we assume that all flats have one bedroom and are identical in every aspect apart from the proximity to the university. Thus, we can concentrate on the price of the flats without worrying about the number of bedrooms or other particularities. Let us divide the flats as if they are located in two rings surrounding the university: the flats close to the university are in the inner ring, whereas the flats that are further away are in the outer-ring. We are interested in the inner ring market of flats and who manages to rent one. In particular, we are interested in the price of such flats which is called an *endogenous* variable. The outer ring flats are those flats that students, who cannot afford one close to the university, will rent. We assume that the price of the outer-ring flats is fixed at some particular level. Since we are not interested in this price, this is called an *exogenous* variable.

Generally speaking, the behaviour of human agents in an economic setting is governed by two principles (Varian 2006):

- **The optimization principle**. Agents try to choose the best patterns of consumption that they can afford. Intuitively, when agents are free to choose their actions, they try to choose goods or services that they want most, rather than those that they do not want.

- **The equilibrium principle**. The price of a good adjusts until the quantity demanded equals the quantity supplied. This process of adjustment may take some time to work out as the consumers' demand and the producers' supply may not be compatible.

In the example that we are considering, the rental price would be stable from month to month. It is this price, called the *equilibrium* price, that we are interested in. Notably, the concept of an equilibrium has different meaning in different situations or disciplines. But, for the simple market of flats, it suffices to say that in equilibrium, demand is met by supply and the price is stable.

Demand and supply

To determine the demand for flats we need to ask all potential student-tenants what is the maximum price that they would be willing to pay to rent one of the flats in the inner ring. The maximum price an agent is willing to pay for a good or service is called the *reservation price*. An agent's reservation price is the price at which she is just indifferent between purchasing and not purchasing the good. If a tenant has a reservation price p, it means that she would be just indifferent between renting in the inner ring and paying price p and renting in the outer ring.

One of these tenants will have the highest reservation price and hence be willing to pay the highest price for renting a flat close to the university. Perhaps this person is affluent, or not particularly inclined to use the local public transport – the reasons are irrelevant. Suppose that this highest price is £400 per month. If there is only one tenant who is willing to pay £400 for a flat, and the price for the flats were £400, then only one flat would be rented out – to the person who is willing to pay this price. Suppose that the next highest price that anyone is willing to pay is £390. If the rental price for the flats were £395, there would still be only one flat rented: the person willing to pay £400 would rent a flat, but the person only willing to pay £390 would not. If the market price were R, then M flats would be rented and so it goes on.

Given a price p^* the number of flats that will be rented at this price will be equal to the number of tenants whose reservation price is equal to or greater than p^*. Thus, anyone who is willing to pay p^* or more would get a flat close to the university, whereas everyone else would get a flat further away. The tenants' reservation prices can be plotted in a graph as illustrated in Figure 7.1 where the price is depicted on the vertical axis and the number of people who are willing to pay that price or more is depicted on the horizontal axis. The curve that results, although in this example with jumps, is called *demand curve* and relates the quantity demanded to a respective price. For instance, according to the demand curve, if the price is between £390 and £380, two flats will be rented, i.e., there are two persons whose reservation price is equal to or greater than £380. Intuitively, as the price decreases, more tenants can afford and are willing to rent flats at that price in the inner ring, in other words the demand curve slopes down. If there is a large number of tenants and the difference in their reservation price is small, the jumps would be so small in relation to the size of the market that they could be ignored altogether and the curve could be drawn as sloping downwards smoothly.

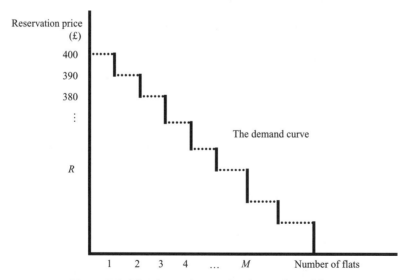

Figure 7.1: The demand curve for the market of flats

We assume that the market of flats is supplied by a number of landlords who operate independently and naturally would want to rent their flats at the highest possible price. This is then classified as a competitive market. Given that all landlords are trying to get the best price possible, and the tenants are fully informed about the prices that the landlords charge, the equilibrium price for all flats in the inner ring must be the same. To see why this must be the case, suppose that there is some high price p_{high} and some low price p_{low} being charged for the flats. The tenants who are renting their flats for a high price have an incentive to go to a landlord renting for a lower price and offer them a price somewhere between p_{high} and p_{low}. Such a price would be beneficial to both parties as the landlord would increase his profit while the student-tenant would be able to save some money. As both landlords and tenants are self-interested agents who seek to maximize their own gain, a situation with different prices for the flats cannot persist in the market.

Indeed, there can only be a single equilibrium price in such a market. What this price will be depends to some extent on the time frame that we are considering the market. If the market is considered in the short term, say a year, then the number of flats is more or less fixed. This is because the number of flats, N, available for rental is stable no matter what the rental price is. The supply curve in this case is illustrated in Figure 7.2 as a vertical line. But if a time frame of several years is considered, the number of flats will fluctuate (new flats may be built) so that it can respond to the price that is charged.

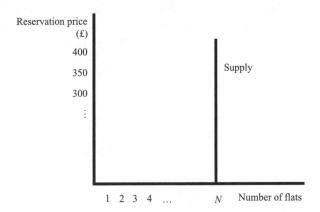

Figure 7.2: The supply curve in the short term for the market of flats

The market equilibrium

Intuitively, the equilibrium principle, as described earlier, states that prices will adjust until supply meets demand. Based on this simple principle and having already represented the demand and supply in the simplified market of flats, we are now in a position to identify the equilibrium price. The equilibrium price p^* is the price that is indicated by the intersection of the demand and supply curves as illustrated in Figure 7.3. In this situation, neither the tenants nor the landlords have any reason to deviate from this price.

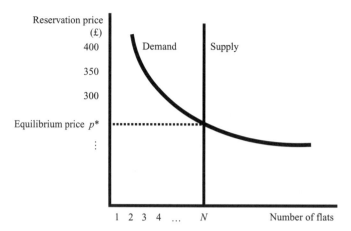

Figure 7.3: Equilibrium price in the market of flats: supply meets demand

But what makes price p^* the equilibrium price? Consider another price $p_{low} < p^*$ where demand is greater than supply. At this price and as there are inevitably more tenants who are willing to pay p_{low} than there are flats, at least a good number of landlords will have more tenants asking to rent a flat. Given that the landlords are self-interested and want to maximize their profit, certainly a good number of them would find it hard to resist not raising the price of their flats. Suppose that the price of flats is some price $p_{high} > p^*$. Then there will be less tenants who are able to afford p_{high} and some of the flats will inevitably remain vacant. The landlords of the vacant flats are now risking getting no revenue at all. Therefore, they will have an incentive to lower their price and fill their flats. Prices p_{low} and p_{high} lead to instability in the market and therefore such situations cannot persist. The price will keep adjusting until supply meets demand, i.e., until the price of flats stabilizes to p^*.

The question of who is going to get the flats in the inner ring is then straightforward as the assignment of flats to tenants is determined by how much one is willing to pay. Every tenant who is willing to pay p^* or more gets a flat in the inner ring, whereas tenants who are willing to pay less than p^* will get one in the outer ring.

The equilibrium price p^* that the landlords charge and the tenants pay in the simplified market of flats leads to an allocation, that is, a distribution of flats to tenants. An allocation assigns quantities of each resource to each agent. But what is a 'good' allocation? *Pareto*[1] *efficiency* is a useful criterion for checking if an economic system is producing an 'optimal' economic outcome. If there is a way to make an agent better off without making anyone else worse off, then this is a *Pareto improvement*. If an allocation allows for a Pareto improvement, it is called *Pareto inefficient*. A Pareto inefficient

---

[1]Italian economist Vilfredo Pareto (1848–1923).

allocation means that there is some way to make one agent better off without hurting another agent. So if there is such a way, why not do it? If an allocation has been found such that no Pareto improvements are possible, then this is a *Pareto efficient* allocation.

Returning to the example, the market of flats, the allocation that is the result of the equilibrium price p^* is a Pareto efficient allocation, as there is no other way that we can redistribute the flats which will make one agent better off without making another one worse off.

It is unavoidable that market conditions change with time: perhaps more flats are being built and therefore supply increases, or the university may start offering their own accommodation on campus and as a result the demand of flats may decrease. Such changes will nevertheless have an impact on the equilibrium price. As supply and demand change, the equilibrium price will have to reflect these changes. This movement from one equilibrium to another may take a considerable amount of time depending on the conditions in the market.

7.1.2 Consumption bundles and preferences

Acting as consumers in our everyday life we are faced with a number of choices. For instance, when I go to the supermarket to buy milk, there are different varieties to choose from: full fat, semi-skimmed, skimmed, organic, or (non-dairy) soya milk. This represents my *consumption, consideration* or *choice set*, that is, the set of all alternatives that I have at my disposal. Generally speaking, the objects of consumer choice are called *consumption bundles*.

Let each of the goods be measured in some way in units (kilos, packets, pints, etc.). We assume that only positive units of each of the goods are meaningful and that it is always possible to have zero quantity of a particular item. Further, we assume that there is a finite, fixed but arbitrary number n of different goods. Then a consumption bundle $x = (x_1, \ldots, x_n)$ is a vector containing different quantities of each of the available goods. For instance, if there are two goods available, say bread and butter, and there is x_1 quantity of bread and x_2 quantity of butter, then (x_1, x_2) represents a consumption bundle. Sometimes a consumption bundle (x_1, x_2) is written as x. Often only two goods are used; the one which is of interest and the other is called *all other goods* so that we can focus on the tradeoff between the former and everything else.

Preference relations

Given any two consumption bundles, agents have their own individual preferences over them. A preference relation typically reveals information about the agent's tastes for the different objects of choice. Formally, a preference relation is represented as a binary relation defined over the consumption set.

The symbol $\succeq$ indicates that the agent *weakly prefers* or simply *prefers* a consumption bundle to another one. An agent weakly prefers a consumption bundle (x_1, x_2) to another one (y_1, y_2), if the agent thinks that the first is at least as good as the second:

$$(x_1, x_2) \succeq (y_1, y_2)$$

The symbol $\succ$ indicates that a consumption bundle is *strictly preferred* to another one. For instance given two consumption bundles (x_1, x_2) and (y_1, y_2):

$$(x_1, x_2) \succ (y_1, y_2)$$

indicates that a consumer strictly desires bundle (x_1, x_2) over bundle (y_1, y_2) given the opportunity and choice. The symbol $\sim$ indicates that a consumer is *indifferent* to the choice between two consumption bundles. Given the two bundles as before:

$$(x_1, x_2) \sim (y_1, y_2)$$

indicates that the agent would be just as satisfied with consuming bundle (x_1, x_2) as it would be with consuming bundle (y_1, y_2). Quite often the symbols for strong preference, weak preference and indifference are indexed to indicate the particular agent whose preferences we talk about. These three concepts are interrelated; in fact, strong preference and indifference build on weak preference. If an agent i:

$$(x_1, x_2) \succeq_i (y_1, y_2) \text{ and } (y_1, y_2) \succeq_i (x_1, x_2), \text{ then } (x_1, x_2) \sim_i (y_1, y_2)$$

In words, if the agent thinks that (x_1, x_2) is at least as good as (y_1, y_2), and (y_1, y_2) is at least as good as (x_1, x_2), then the agent must be indifferent to the choice between the two bundles. Similarly, if the agent thinks that (x_1, x_2) is at least as good as (y_1, y_2), but it is not the case that the agent is indifferent to the choice between the two bundles, then it must be the case that the agent strictly prefers (x_1, x_2) to consumption bundle (y_1, y_2):

$$(x_1, x_2) \succeq_i (y_1, y_2) \text{ and not } (y_1, y_2) \sim_i (x_1, x_2), \text{ then } (x_1, x_2) \succ_i (y_1, y_2)$$

Building on the underlying preference relation, strict preference and indifference capture the usual sense in which the terms 'strict preference' and 'indifference' are used in everyday life.

The preferences which agents express over consumption bundles can be characterized axiomatically through the *axioms of consumer choice*. These refer to the 'consistency' of preference relations. Assume an agent i and consumption bundles x, y and z. Then:

Axiom 1 *Completeness: any two consumption bundles x and y are comparable, that is $x \succeq_i y$ or $y \succeq_i x$, or both, in which case the agent is indifferent to the choice between the two bundles.*

Axiom 2 *Reflexivity: any bundle is at least as good as an identical bundle, that is, $x \succeq_i x$.*

Axiom 3 *Transitivity: if $x \succeq_i y$ and $y \succeq_i z$, then it follows that $x \succeq_i z$.*

The first axiom suggests that the agent can make comparisons, i.e., that it has the ability to discriminate between different goods and the necessary knowledge to evaluate alternatives. The second axiom simply states that if two bundles are identical, then each of them is at least as good as the other. The third axiom requires that preferences are transitive. Although a consumer is asked to express a preference over two consumption bundles at a time, transitivity requires that these pairwise comparisons can be linked together in a consistent way. What would you think of an agent who said that it preferred a bundle x to y and preferred y to z, but then it also said that it preferred z to x? This would definitely be regarded as odd behaviour. Such an agent would have quite a problem deciding which bundle to choose if it were to be offered all three. Therefore, it is reasonable to accept transitivity as one of the properties of preferences.

The preference relation $\succeq$ is rational, if it is both complete and transitive. If $\succeq$ is rational then:

- $\succ$ is both irreflexive ($x \succ x$ never holds) and transitive
- $\sim$ is reflexive ($x \sim x$ for all x), transitive (if $x \sim y$ and $y \sim z$ then $x \sim z$) and symmetric (if $x \sim y$ then $y \sim x$)
- if $x \succ y \succeq z$, then $x \succ z$.

Agents can express preferences not only on consumption bundles, but in general whenever they are called upon to make a choice. This, for instance, includes vendors or services, the outcomes of games, or the outcomes of negotiation processes.

Well-behaved preferences

Preferences can be described by using a construction known as an *indifference curve*. In Figure 7.4 the two axes represent a consumer's consumption of products 1 and 2 respectively. Assume that we pick a consumption bundle (x_1, x_2) and shade in all of the consumption bundles that are weakly preferred to (x_1, x_2). This is called the *weakly preferred set* (Varian 2006). The bundles on the boundary of this set which represent the bundles for which the agent is just indifferent to (x_1, x_2), form the indifference curve. Indifference curves can be drawn for any consumption bundle. However, indifference curves representing distinct levels of preference cannot intersect.

An indifference curve only shows the bundles that the consumer perceives as being indifferent to each other, they do not show which bundles are better and which are worse. This can be done by drawing arrows on the indifference curves to indicate the direction of the preferred bundles as shown in Figure 7.5 (a).

Well-behaved preferences have the property of monotonicity. If (x_1, x_2) is a bundle of goods and (y_1, y_2) is another bundle of goods with at least as much of both goods and more of one, then the latter is preferred to the former $(y_1, y_2) \succeq (x_1, x_2)$. Accordingly, more is always preferred to less. In fact, *strict monotonicity* suggests that $(y_1, y_2) \succ (x_1, x_2)$.

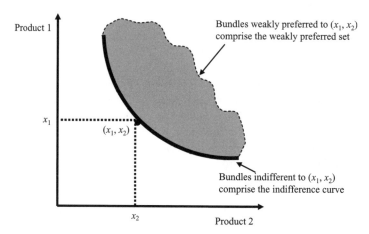

Figure 7.4: Indifference curve and weakly preferred set

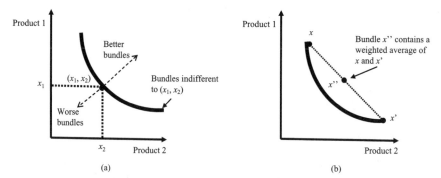

Figure 7.5: Properties of well-behaved preferences: (a) monotonicity: more is always preferred to less; (b) convexity: average bundles are preferred to extremes

Monotonicity implies that the indifference curve has a negative slope as in Figure 7.5 (a). This has further implications in that the preferred or better sets are always above the indifference curve, whereas the worse sets are below the indifference curve.

Another special feature of well-behaved preferences is convexity. If two consumption bundles x and x' are both elements of the consumption set, then the bundle $x'' = ax + (1-a)x'$ is also an element of the consumption set for any $a \in (0,1)$. Suppose that we take two bundles of goods (x_1, x_2) and (x_1', x_2') on the same indifference curve and the quantity of product 1 in (x_1, x_2) is extreme compared to the quantity of product 1 in (x_1', x_2') while the quantity of product 2 in (x_1', x_2') is extreme compared to the quantity of product 2 in (x_1, x_2). Although each contains a relatively high proportion of one of the goods in relation to the other, the agent is indifferent between the two bundles. Any bundle (x_1'', x_2'') that contains a weighted average of the two bundles, will be at least as good as each of the two extreme bundles:

$$(x_1'', x_2'') \succcurlyeq (x_1, x_2) \text{ and } (x_1'', x_2'') \succcurlyeq (x_1', x_2')$$

This balanced bundle contains a weighted average of the two bundles, if $a = 1/2$ then the balanced bundle has the average amount of product 1 and the average amount of product 2 that is present in the two bundles and, as a result, lies halfway along the straight line connecting the (x_1, x_2) and the (x_1', x_2') bundles as shown in Figure 7.5 (b). Any weighted average bundle where the weight $a \in (0, 1)$, is going to be preferred to the extreme bundles. Put simply, averages are preferred to extremes and essentially convexity restricts the agent from preferring extremes in consumption sets. A more strict requirement comes under the guise of strict convexity. This means that the weighted average of two indifferent bundles is strictly preferred to the extreme bundles.

7.1.3 Utilities

In Chapter 2, and in discussing performance measure, that is, how the performance of agents can be evaluated, we briefly discussed the concept of utility. In that context, utility is a function that maps each state of the environment onto a real number which represents how *good* that state is. The concept of a utility is relevant when we talk about preferences, as a utility function is simply a convenient device for summarizing the information contained in the agents' preference relations.

A *utility function* $u(x)$ assigns a numerical value to each element in the consumption set X, ranking the elements of X in accordance with the agent's preferences, and therefore more preferred bundles are assigned larger numbers than the less preferred ones. Thus, a bundle (x_1, x_2) is preferred to another one (y_1, y_2), if and only if the utility of (x_1, x_2) is larger than the utility of (y_1, y_2):

$$(x_1, x_2) \succ (y_1, y_2) \text{ if and only if } u(x_1, x_2) > u(y_1, y_2).$$

The fundamental feature of the utility assignment is that it orders the bundles of goods in the consumption set. The magnitude of the utility function is not important as long as it ranks the different consumption bundles. Consequently, the size of the utility difference between any two consumption bundles does not matter. As the emphasis is on ordering consumption bundles, this kind of utility is called *ordinal utility*. For instance, consider the example given in Table 7.1. The table illustrates three different ways that utilities can be assigned to consumption bundles x, y and z. All three utility functions rank the consumption bundles in exactly the same way, that is x has a higher utility than y and y has a higher utility than z, according to the agent's preferences, which are that it prefers x to y and also prefers y to z.

As the example of utility assignment illustrates, and since what is important is the ranking of the bundles, there is no unique way in which to assign utilities to bundles of goods. If one way to assign utilities to consumption bundles can be found, inevitably many more ways can be found. For instance, if $u(x_1, x_2)$ represents one way to assign

Bundle	u_1	u_2	u_3
x	10	3	2.4
y	5	2	0.8
z	1	1	0.2

Table 7.1: **Example of assigning utilities to consumption bundles**

utility numbers to bundle (x_1, x_2), then multiplying $u(x_1, x_2)$ by any positive number is just another way to assign a utility to that bundle. This is one form of transformation that can be performed on utilities and is called *monotonic transformation*. In essence, if there is a function u that represents the agent's preferences, then u can be transformed into some other, perhaps more convenient or easily manipulated form, as long as the transformation preserves the preference ordering.

When ordinal utilities are assigned, the magnitude between the utilities bears no significance. However, in some cases, the size of the utility difference between two bundles may be significant or may encode further information about the agent's preferences. For instance, it may be the case that I want to express the fact that I like vanilla ice-cream twice as much as I like chocolate ice-cream. How can utilities be assigned so that this type of preference, i.e., 'twice as much', can be expressed adequately? Perhaps, if I prefer an item twice as much as another, then I may be willing to pay twice as much, or wait for it twice as long (Varian 2006). Each one of these offers a possible interpretation, and would give rise to a way of assigning utilities to the bundles, the difference of which would indicate some significance. As the scale of the assignment matters, these are called *cardinal* utilities. However, none of the suggested approaches offers a universally accepted interpretation of what 'twice as much' means to different people.

7.1.4 Equilibrium

In the market of flats, we described the concept of an equilibrium as that point in the market where supply meets demand. In the following, a more formal description of the equilibrium in a marketplace will be given (Mas-Colell et al. 1995, Sandholm 1999).

Assume a market where $n > 0$ goods are present. These goods can be physical goods such as sugar, coffee, steel, or services. The market is characterised by a vector of prices $p = (p_1, p_2, \ldots, p_n)$ where $p_g \in \mathbb{R}$ is the price of good g.

There are two types of agents in the market: consumers i and producers (firms) j. Each consumer agent i has a utility function $u_i(x_i)$ which determines its preferences over the various consumption bundles $x_i = (x_{i1}, x_{i2}, \ldots, x_{in})$ in its consumption set $X_i \subset \mathbb{R}^n$. Thus, x_{ig} is consumer i's quantity or allocation of good g. Each consumer has an initial endowment of goods (or resources) $e_i = (e_{i1}, e_{i2}, \ldots, e_{in})$ where $e_{ig} \in \mathbb{R}$ is the agent's endowment of good g. The initial total endowment of good g available in the economy is $e_g = \sum_i e_{ig}$.

Producers can use some of the goods in order to produce others through some manufacturing or transformation process. Each producer agent j has a production vector $y_j = (y_{j1}, y_{j2}, \ldots, y_{jn})$ where y_{jg} is the amount of good g that producer j manufactures. A producer's capability of transforming one type of good into another is characterised by its production or technological possibilities $Y_j \subset \mathbb{R}^n$ which is the set of feasible production vectors. The total (net) amount of a good g available in the economy is therefore $e_g + \sum_j y_{jg}$. Furthermore, we assume that consumer i owns a share θ_{ij} of producer j (where $\sum_i \theta_{ij} = 1$), thus giving the consumer a claim to a fraction θ_{ij} of producer j's profits. The profit of producer j is py_j where $y_j \in Y_j$.

In a market economy each agent is competitive, rational and self-interested and wants to maximise its own utility irrespective of others. In essence, an agent wants to find a bundle that maximises its utility given the prices and subject to its budget. A market reaches an equilibrium state when there is no agent who wishes to deviate from that state.

Definition 3 (p^*, x^*, y^*) *constitutes a general market equilibrium (Walrasian or competitive) if:*

1. *Each consumer i maximises its preferences given the prices:*

$$x_i^* = \arg \max_{x_i \in X_i} u_i(x_i) \text{ such that } p^* x_i \leq p^* e_i + \sum_j \theta_{ij}(p^* y_j^*)$$

2. *Each producer j maximises its profits given the prices:*

$$y_j^* = \arg \max_{y_j \in Y_j} p^* y_j$$

3. *The market clears:*

$$\sum_i x_i^* = \sum_i e_i + \sum_j y_j^*$$

The general equilibrium solutions have some very attractive properties. First of all, each general equilibrium is Pareto efficient. This means that there is no other way to make an agent (consumer or producer) better off, without making another agent worse off. As a result, no agent has an incentive to deviate from the market equilibrium.

Although having a general equilibrium solution is a desirable state, there are domains or problems where no general equilibrium exists. For instance, a general equilibrium may not exist at all if:

- agents (consumers or producers) have market power (monopolists, oligopolists)
- the aggregate excess demand function is noncontinuous (small changes in price result in big jumps in the quantity demanded)

- the agents' preferences have: externalities (some agent's consumption or production directly influences another agent's utility), nonconvexities, or complementarities (one commodity complements another).

A general equilibrium does exist, if there is a positive endowment of all the goods and the agents' preferences are continuous, convex and monotone. In some cases, if a general equilibrium exists this may not be unique. A general equilibrium is unique if there is gross substitutability, i.e., if raising the price of one commodity, will not decrease the demand of another. Some of the most important properties of the general equilibrium are summarized by the First and Second Welfare theorems (Mas-Colell et al. 1995):

Theorem 1 *First Welfare Theorem: Any competitive equilibrium is Pareto efficient.*

Theorem 2 *Second Welfare Theorem: If the preferences and the technologies are convex, then any feasible Pareto optimal solution is a general equilibrium for some price vector and a set of endowments.*

Although general equilibrium theory provides the conditions under which a competitive market equilibrium exists, it does not describe how this is reached. Algorithms for finding equilibrium solutions should take into account the tradeoffs between agents and the fact that the values of different goods to a single agent may be interdependent in order to find efficient solutions without central information and control. The price tâtonnement process is such a distributed algorithm (Sandholm 1999). Proposed by Leon Walras[2] (Walras 1874), this is an iterative price adjustment scheme which uses a steepest-descent search method in order to find an efficient solution (equilibrium), provided, of course, that it exists.

7.2 ELEMENTS OF GAME THEORY

Agents interacting in a market setting are rational and self-interested, seeking to maximize their own profit without necessarily caring about the benefit of the other agents. But how do agents reach decisions, how do they choose which strategies to follow and what determines an outcome? In such a situation, the action of any one agent will have consequences on the others, so agents have to reason strategically. The essential difference between strategic and nonstrategic decisions is that the latter can be taken in isolation, that is, without taking into account the decisions of the other agents. Strategic situations can be perceived as games played by a number of agents with a number of strategies. Game Theory is concerned with the general analysis of strategic interaction and how rational agents behave in situations of strategic interdependence. Although game theory was originally designed for modelling economic interactions among agents, it has developed into an independent field and has found applications in other disciplines from artificial intelligence and multi-agent decision making, to biology. In the following

[2]French economist Leon Walras (1834–1910).

sections, I will introduce the basic concepts of game theory, but simplify the exposition by considering two-player games with a finite number of strategies.

7.2.1 Strategic games

A game is a formal representation of a situation in which a number of individuals interact in a setting of strategic interdependence. An agent's welfare depends not only on its own decisions and actions, but crucially also on the other agents' decisions and actions. A game involves the following elements:

1. *Players*: Who plays the game. Number of players.

2. *Rules*: What strategies or actions players can follow. Who plays when.

3. *Outcomes*: For each possible set of strategies/actions by the players, what is the outcome of the game.

4. *Payoffs*: What are the players' utilities over all the possible outcomes.

5. *Information*: What players know when they make decisions.

6. *Chance*: Probability distribution over chance events, if any.

A player is a decision-maker who is a participant in the game and whose goal is to choose the actions that produce the most preferred outcomes. Players are assumed to be rational: i.e., their preference orderings are complete and transitive and they always prefer a higher payoff. When playing a game, agents can choose among a set of actions or have to take decisions according to the rules of the game. A strategy is a complete contingent plan or decision rule that describes how the player will act in each possible and distinguishable situation in which it is called upon to play. Alternatively, a strategy can be thought of as a complete plan (recipe) that someone else could follow on the player's behalf. In a game with pure strategies, each agent will choose its strategy deterministically from its set of possible strategies. Formally:

> **Definition 4** *A strategic game is characterized by the following elements:*
> 1. *A finite set N of agents (the set of players) with $n > 1$[3].*
>
> 2. *Each agent $i \in N$ can choose a strategy s_i from a nonempty set S_i of strategies (or actions). The strategy space for each agent i is represented by a vector $S_i = (s_i^1, s_i^2, \ldots, s_i^m)$ where s_i^m is the m-th strategy chosen by agent i. In the following, the simple notation s_i will be used to indicate a particular strategy followed by agent i.*
>
> *The vector $(s_1, \ldots, s_n)$ of individual strategies is called a joint strategy or a strategy profile and is denoted by s or (s_i). The notation s_{-i} refers to the strategies of all agents except i, and (s_i, s_{-i}) refers to the joint strategy where agent i plays the particular strategy s_i. In a strategic game each agent chooses an action and then it receives a payoff that depends on the selected joint strategy. This joint strategy determines the outcome (o) of the game.*

[3]n denotes the number of agents, i.e., $n = |N|$.

3. *Each agent i has its own preference relation $\succeq_i$ over the different joint strategies s (or outcomes o). This preference relation $\succeq_i$ of player i in a strategic game can be represented by a payoff or utility function $u_i(s)$ which indicates the agent's utility at s. Thus $u_i(s) \geq u_i(s')$ whenever $s \succeq_i s'$.*

4. *All agents are self-interested and rational. Furthermore, all agents know each other, the strategy sets of each other, as well as the respective payoffs. Strictly speaking elements 1–3 are common knowledge among the agents.*

Let us consider a very simple game. There are two players creatively named A and B and the rules are as follows. Player A writes one of two words on a piece of paper 'Top' or 'Bottom'. At the same time player B independently writes 'Left' or 'Right' on a piece of paper. The actions {Top, Bottom} for A and {Left, Right} for B, constitute their respective strategies in this game. These strategies could represent economic choices or decisions on whether to enter into transactions or cooperate with other agents. So, for instance, A's possible strategies may be 'raise price' and 'decrease price', or 'cooperate' and 'defect' respectively. Each player submits their piece of paper simultaneously. Crucial in the description of this game is the fact that the players do not have information about each other's chosen strategies, they cannot see what the other has written down, until both choices are revealed simultaneously. The outcomes and payoffs are described in the *payoff matrix* in Table 7.2. This is also called the *normal form representation* of a game and it captures the agent's possible strategies and the resulting outcomes and payoffs for the players in the form of a matrix, where each grid represents the result of a pair of strategies played.

		Player B	
		Left	Right
Player A	Top	1,3	1,1
	Bottom	3,1	1,0

Table 7.2: **Normal form representation of the simple game**

The different strategy profiles (i.e., pairs of strategies) result in the following outcomes:

$s = $ (Top,Left): outcome o_1;

$s' = $ (Top,Right): outcome o_2;

$s'' = $ (Bottom, Left): outcome o_3;

$s''' = $ (Bottom, Right): outcome o_4.

Agents can then express preferences over the joint strategies or the resulting outcomes. Player A's preferences are as follows:

$s'' \succeq_A s''' \succeq_A s \succeq_A s'$ (or alternatively $o_3 \succeq_A o_4 \succeq_A o_1 \succeq_A o_2$),

since the utility gained from each respective joint strategy is:

$$u_A(s'') \geq u_A(s''') \geq u_A(s) \geq u_A(s').$$

Player B's preferences are:

$$s \succeq_B s'' \succeq_B s' \succeq_B s''' \text{ (or alternatively } o_1 \succeq_B o_3 \succeq_B o_2 \succeq_B o_4),$$

since the utility gained from each respective joint strategy is:

$$u_B(s') \geq u_B(s'') \geq u_B(s') \geq u_B(s''').$$

7.2.2 Extensive form representation

An alternative way to represent a game is to use what is called the *extensive form representation*, according to which a game is represented by a tree, as shown in Figure 7.6. The extensive form representation of a game consists of:

- the initial node (root)
- branches
- decision nodes
- terminal nodes.

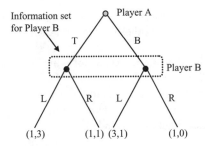

Figure 7.6: **Extensive form representation of the simple game**

The extensive form captures who moves when, what actions each player can take, what players know when they move, what the outcome is as a function of the actions taken by the players and finally, the players' payoffs from each possible outcome.

In the simple game used here, both players play simultaneously, so the root node can be any of the two players – I could have drawn the tree starting from player B instead of A. However, in games where players play sequentially and there are rules regarding who moves when, the root node needs to be the player who moves first. The branches of the tree are labelled with the actions, decisions or moves that the players can take at that stage in the game. So in Figure 7.6, the first two branches are labelled with the two moves that player A can follow; either to write 'Top' or 'Bottom' on a piece of paper. Decision nodes are those nodes in which players have to make a decision, such as the two dark-coloured nodes in Figure 7.6, which are the two decision nodes for player B. Furthermore, we need a way to represent what each player knows when it is their turn to make a move. The *information set* for some player i summarizes what the player knows when they get to move. Player B's information when they are about to make their move consists of the two decisions nodes as shown in Figure 7.6, i.e., in other words B does not know in which decision node it really is as it does not know what player A intends to play. Finally, terminal nodes are the final nodes in a game and they indicate the possible outcomes and payoffs for the players.

7.2.3 Information

One of the most important elements in a game is the information that the agents have at their disposal when they are about to make a decision. A player has *perfect information* if it can observe the other players' moves and thus can distinguish in which decision node it is at a particular moment in time in a game. In this case, the *information set*, as captured in the extensive form representation of a game, for a particular agent, contains one single node. However, if an agent cannot observe the other players' moves and thus cannot distinguish in which decision node it is, it has *imperfect information*. The agent's information set contains more than one decision node, as in the game of Figure 7.6, where the information set for player B contains two decision nodes. The same applies to player A; if we were to draw the tree starting from agent B instead, A's information set would contain two decision nodes. Therefore, both players have imperfect information since they do not know about each other's move until each submits its piece of paper.

If a player does not forget what it once knew, including its own decisions and actions, then it has *perfect recall* or perfect memory. In real life, human players do not have perfect recall; our physical memory has limitations. The same applies to a certain extent to computational agents as their memory, although potentially large given the current technological advances, nevertheless is bounded.

A fundamental assumption in game theory is that all players know the structure of the game, (i.e., the rules, the respective outcomes and payoffs), they know that the other players know it, and know that the other players know that they know it and so on. This form of iterative and reflective knowledge is captured by the concept of *common knowledge*.

A game is one of *certainty* if there are no chance events, otherwise it is characterized as a game of *uncertainty*. Chance events that may take place during a game are represented as random moves of Nature[4]. Nature, denoted by **N**, is a pseudo-player whose actions are purely mechanical and probabilistic, that is, they determine the probability distribution over the chance events. For instance, in a game of cards between two players in which each draws a random card from a deck, Nature 'chooses' the colour of the card. Since the number of red cards equals the number of black cards and the deck is shuffled, the probability of the randomly chosen card being red is 0.5.

If agents have common knowledge of all other agents' payoff functions, then the game is one of *complete* information, otherwise it is a game of *incomplete* information. A game

---

[4]The first formulation of playing against Nature is due to Milnor (1954).

is one of *symmetric* information if no player has information that is different from that of the other players when it moves or at the terminal nodes, otherwise it is a game of *asymmetric* information.

7.2.4 Categories of games

Games can be categorized depending on the problem that they are describing:

- **Cooperative games.** In cooperative games the issue at hand is to develop mechanisms that enable cooperation. The payoffs in such games are always higher for both players for cooperation than those for noncooperation.

- **Competition games.** In competition games, otherwise known as zero-sum games, the total benefit of all players in the game for every combination of strategies, always adds up to zero. In other words, the payoff of one player is equal to the losses of the other. As one can only benefit at the expense of the other, in such games there can only be one winner. Games like chess, poker and most sport games are zero-sum games, as the players' interests are diametrically opposed and one wins exactly the amount that one's opponents lose.

- **Coexistence games.** Game theory has been recently used by biologists as a tool to study animal interaction. The underlying idea is that various kinds of behaviour are genetically programmed and that evolution selects the mixture of population that is stable with respect to evolutionary forces. Thus, the question to be answered is what is the right (equilibrium) mixture of behaviours (strategies) among a population of a particular species.

- **Commitment games.** These are games that involve sequential moves in which case a player knows or can see the previous player's move. The critical issue that arises in such games is that of commitment. If player *A* makes a move first, player *B* has the opportunity to make a move that will ultimately benefit itself rather than player *A*. However, if player *A* has made a choice in such a way that both players can benefit, it needs to ensure that player *B* recognizes this and plays such a move that will not harm *A*, but lead to an outcome that is beneficial for both.

A more detailed discussion and examples can be found in Varian (2006, Chapter 29) and Osborne and Rubinstein (1994).

7.2.5 Solution concepts

In simultaneous games, although the payoff functions of the agents are considered to be common knowledge, the agents' information sets contain more than one decision node, i.e., the agents do not know the other agents' choices. The best that they can do is to decide on their own actions taking into account the known payoffs, as well as the fact that the other agents are rational and will behave strategically. An agent in game theory is considered to be an expected utility maximizer, and therefore will select a strategy that maximizes its expected utility or payoff, given its preferences over the outcomes, its knowledge about the utilities (payoffs) of the other agents and the structure of the game. In the following sections a number of solution concepts, to compute the outcome of a game, are discussed.

Dominant strategy equilibrium

What will be the outcome of the game depicted in Table 7.3? From player A's perspective, it is always better to choose to play 'Bottom', as the corresponding payoffs by playing this move are always better than their counterparts by playing 'Top'. From player B's perspective, it is always better to choose 'Left', as the corresponding payoffs by playing this move are always better than their counterparts by playing 'Right'. A's and B's choices are irrespective of each other's choice in this case.

		Player B	
		Left	Right
Player A	Top	1,3	1,1
	Bottom	**3,1**	1,0

Table 7.3: Game with a dominant strategy equilibrium

Definition 5   *A strategy s_i^* is player i's strictly dominant strategy, if it maximizes the agent's expected utility for all possible strategies of other agents, $u_i(s_i^*, s_{-i}) > u_i(s_i', s_{-i})$ for all $s_i^* \neq s_i'$ and $s_{-i} \in S_{-i}$.*

A strategy for a player i is called *dominated* if there exists some alternative strategy that yields a greater payoff. Thus, a strategy s_i^* is strictly dominant if it dominates every other strategy in S_i.

Agents are self-interested and rational and therefore they will always choose to play the strategy that maximizes their payoff, if there is such a strategy. Consequently, if both players have a strictly dominant strategy, it is easy to predict the outcome of the game. In the simple game, the outcome will be o_3 as shown in Table 7.3. The outcome o_3 that emanates from the pair of strategies (Bottom, Left) is called a *dominant strategy equilibrium*.

Definition 6   *A dominant strategy equilibrium of a strategic game is a strategy profile $s^* \in S$ with the property that for every player $i \in N$ we have $(s_i^*, s_{-i}) \succeq_i (s_i, s_{-i})$ for all $s \in S$.*

Thus, a dominant strategy equilibrium is an outcome that the players arrive at by playing their dominant strategies. The dominant strategy equilibrium makes no assumptions about the information available to agents about each other, and does not require an agent to believe that other agents will behave rationally in order to select its own optimal strategy. As such, it is a very strong and robust solution concept.

However, there may be games in which not all players, or none of them, have strictly dominant strategies. As a result, a game may not have a dominant strategy equilibrium, but if there is one, then this is a unique outcome.

The concept of a Pareto efficient solution is applicable in game theory, namely a solution is Pareto efficient if there is no other solution in which a player is strictly better off and no other player is worse off:

Definition 7 *A joint strategy s is Pareto optimal if there is no other joint strategy s' for which $u_i(s') > u_i(s)$ for all $i \in N$.*

A Pareto efficient solution is the socially optimal solution. A dominant strategy for one agent may not be Pareto efficient, in other words, it may not lead to the best and socially optimal result for all players.

		Kevin Shopping	Basketball
Sally	Shopping	2,1	0,0
	Basketball	0,0	1,2

Table 7.4: The battle of the sexes (BoS) game

Nash equilibrium

Dominant strategies and dominant strategy equilibria are desirable features in games, but not every game has a strictly dominant strategy for each player, or a dominant strategy equilibrium. For instance, consider the game known as 'Battle of the Sexes' (BoS) illustrated in Table 7.4. In this game two players, Sally and Kevin, need to decide whether to go shopping or to a basketball game. They need to make their decisions independently and simultaneously. In this game there is no unique strategy for Sally that she can play, which guarantees the best payoff, irrespective of what Kevin does. Similarly, there is no unique strategy for Kevin that he can play, which guarantees the best payoff for him, irrespective of what Sally does. However, not all is lost. Sally can reason strategically: knowing Kevin's possible strategies, outcomes and payoffs, she can attempt to maximize her own payoff by taking into consideration Kevin's possible move. Sally thinks that since Kevin is a self-interested, rational player and wants to maximize his payoff, he would play 'Basketball' as this move would give him the maximum payoff (2). In this case, Sally is better off by playing 'Basketball' since that would give her 1 instead of 0 if she plays 'Shopping'. The pair of strategies (Basketball, Basketball) is another form of equilibrium called *Nash equilibrium*[5]. An outcome (a strategy profile) is a Nash equilibrium if each player's strategy is an optimal choice given the other

[5] American mathematician John Forbes Nash.

players' strategies. Although each player cannot know what the others are going to do, nevertheless each can form a reasonable expectation about the other players' choices, given that players are symmetric and rational. Formally:

> **Definition 8**   *A Nash equilibrium of a strategic game is a joint strategy s* with the property that for all agents i ∈ N it is the case that $u_i(s_i^*, s_{-i}^*) \geq u_i(s_i, s_{-i}^*)$ for all strategies $s_i \in S_i$.*

Now if we examine the game from Kevin's perspective, then taking into consideration Sally's possible outcomes and strategies, he knows that Sally obtains the maximum payoff by playing 'Shopping' since that will give her 2, which is the best that she can get. Kevin is best off by playing 'Shopping' taking into consideration Sally's actions. So the outcome (Shopping, Shopping) is another Nash equilibrium. Therefore, although it is desirable to have a Nash equilibrium in the absence of a dominant strategy equilibrium in a game, it turns out that a game can have more than one Nash equilibria. On the other hand, there are games that do not have a Nash equilibrium.

The Nash equilibrium can also be defined in terms of the so-called *best-response function*. The best-response function of agent i to the strategies of the other agents denoted by $B_i(s_{-i})$ is defined as:

$$B_i(s_{-i}) = \{s_i \in S_i : u_i(s_i, s_{-i}) \geq u_i(s_i', s_{-i}) \text{ for all } s_i' \in S_i\}$$

$B_i(s_{-i})$ can be a set containing many strategies.

> **Definition 9**   *A Nash equilibrium is a joint strategy s* for which $s^* \in B_i(s_{-i}^*)$ for all i ∈ N.*

In other words, at a Nash Equilibrium, each agent's strategy is an optimal response to the other agents' strategies.

Although the Nash solution concept is fundamental to game theory, it is underpinned by very strong assumptions about the agents' information and beliefs about the other agents. To play a Nash equilibrium in a single-shot game, every agent must have complete information about the others' payoffs and preferences over outcomes, i.e., these must be common knowledge, and rationality must also be common knowledge. Finally, all agents must select the same Nash equilibrium.

7.2.6 Mixed strategies

In the discussion above, the concept of an equilibrium has been examined in the context of games with pure strategies (deterministic), which means that agents in such games choose their strategy once and stick to it. However, players do not always make their choices with certainty. A player can randomize when faced with a choice.

> **Definition 10**   *A mixed strategy for player i denoted σ_i is a probability distribution over i's pure set of strategies S_i. If $\sigma_i(s_i)$ is the probability that σ_i assigns to the*

pure strategy $s_i \in S_i$, the mixed strategy space for player i is denoted Σ_i and the space of mixed strategy profiles is $\Sigma = \Delta\Sigma_i$.

If player i has m pure strategies: $S_i = (s_i^1, s_i^2, \ldots, s_i^m)$, then a mixed strategy for the player is a probability distribution, $\sigma_i = \{\sigma_i(s_i^1), \sigma_i(s_i^2), \ldots, \sigma_i(s_i^m)\}$ where $\sigma_i(s_i^m)$ is the probability that player i will choose strategy s_i^m. Since σ_i is a probability distribution we require that $\sigma_i(s_i^m) \in [0, 1]$ and $\sum_{i=1}^{m} \sigma_i(s_i^m) = 1$. That is, the probabilities must be non-negative and they should sum up to 1.

In a game with mixed strategies, players randomize their choices, they assign a probability to each choice and play their choices according to those probabilities. A Nash equilibrium in mixed strategies, is an equilibrium in which each player chooses the optimal frequency with which to play its strategies given the frequency of choices of the other players.

Definition 11 *A mixed strategy profile σ^* is a mixed strategy Nash equilibrium if, for all players $i \in N$, $u_i(\sigma_i^*, \sigma_{-i}^*) \geq u_i(\sigma_i, \sigma_{-i}^*)$ for all $\sigma_i \in \Sigma_i$.*

As in the Nash equilibrium for pure strategies, an alternative definition can be provided in terms of the best-response function. The best-response function $B_i(\sigma_{-i})$ denotes agent i's best-response correspondence when the other agents play σ_{-i}.

Definition 12 *A mixed strategy profile σ^* is a mixed strategy Nash Equilibrium if and only if $\sigma^* \in B_i(\sigma_{-i}^*)$ for all $i \in N$.*

Once the concept of mixed strategies is introduced into a game, it follows that every finite strategic-form game has a mixed strategy equilibrium (Osborne and Rubinstein 1994).

Consider the battle of the sexes game that we examined in the previous section. This game possesses two pure strategy Nash equilibria, namely (Basketball, Basketball) and (Shopping, Shopping). Now, are there any equilibria in mixed strategies?

It is easy to see that both players must choose each of their pure strategies with strictly positive probability. Let $p > 0$ denote the probability that Sally chooses Basketball, and let $q > 0$ denote the probability that Kevin chooses Shopping. Then each player must be indifferent between each of their pure strategies. For Sally this means:

$$q(2) + (1 - q)(0) = q(0) + (1 - q)(1)$$

while for Kevin:

$$(1 - p)(1) + p(0) = (1 - p)(0) + p(2)$$

Solving these yields $p = q = 1/3$. Thus the mixed strategy in which each player chooses the other's favourite event with probability 1/3 and their own with probability 2/3 is a mixed strategy equilibrium. Thus, the strategy profile $\sigma^* = (\sigma_1^*, \sigma_2^*) = ((2/3, 1/3), (1/3, 2/3))$ is the third equilibrium in the battle of the sexes game. However, this mixed strategy Nash equilibrium is inefficient. As each player's expected payoff is 2/3, each would be strictly better off if either of the pure strategy equilibria were to be played.

There are a number of interpretations for mixed strategies (Osborne and Rubinstein 1994). One way to think of a mixed strategy for player *A* is as an attempt to behave unpredictably, i.e., as a deliberate attempt on *A*'s part to randomize. There are certain situations in which agents wish to introduce an element of randomness into their behaviour, for instance, players 'bluff' in card games.

The other way to think of a mixed strategy for *A* is as an expression of *B*'s beliefs regarding the pure strategy that *A* itself will choose. Consider the battle of the sexes game. According to this second view, Sally's equilibrium strategy of placing probability 2/3 on 'Shopping' and 1/3 on 'Basketball' can be thought of us reflecting Kevin's uncertainty regarding the pure strategy that Sally herself will follow. Kevin believes that Sally will choose 'Shopping' with probability 2/3 and 'Basketball' with probability 1/3. Similarly, Kevin's mixed strategy can be interpreted as Sally's belief about the probability that Kevin will choose one pure strategy or the other. So, an agent's mixed strategy can be understood as simply representing the beliefs that the others hold about the pure strategy which the agent itself is going to choose.

The concept of Nash equilibrium can be interpreted as a steady state in an environment in which players act repeatedly, and disregard any strategic link that may exist between successive interactions (Osborne and Rubinstein 1994). In this case, a third way to interpret mixed strategies is to think about them as representing information that players have about past interactions. For example, if 80% of past play by player *A* involved choosing strategy *s* and 20% involved choosing strategy *s'*, then these frequencies form the beliefs each player can form about the future behaviour of other players when they are in the role of player *A*. Thus, the corresponding belief will be that player *A* plays *s* with probability 0.8 and *s'* with probability 0.2. In equilibrium, the frequencies will remain constant over time, and each player's strategy is optimal given the steady-state beliefs.

Another way to interpret mixed strategies is as if, before a player makes a decision, it receives a private signal on which it can base the decision. Most importantly, the player may not consciously link the signal with this decision (e.g., a player may be in a particular mood which made them choose one strategy over another). This behaviour will appear as random to the other players if they perceive the factors affecting the choice as irrelevant, or find it too difficult or costly to determine any relationship. The problem with this interpretation is that it is hard to accept the idea that rational players deliberately make choices depending on factors (e.g., mood) that do not affect the payoffs.

Finally, Harsanyi (1973) introduced another interpretation of mixed strategies, according to which a game is a frequently occurring situation, in which the players' preferences are subject to small random variations. As in the previous interpretation, random factors are introduced, but now they affect the payoffs. Each player observes its own preferences, but not that of other players. In this sense, the mixed strategy equilibrium is a summary of the frequencies with which the players choose their actions over time.

In extensive form games, there is another way that players can randomize. A *behaviour strategy* σ_i in an extensive form game specifies the probability with which each action will be chosen, conditional on reaching that information set. In other words, a behaviour strategy specifies at each information set, a conditional probability distribution over the actions available at that information set. In the remainder of the text, the term 'mixed' will be used to refer in general to randomized strategies, regardless of the form of the game.

7.2.7 The prisoner's dilemma

Games can represent strategic situations in which the players are called upon to take an action and thus they can describe a variety of situations from economic decisions to decisions on whether to cooperate with other agents or even to declare war. Let us consider the infamous prisoner's dilemma game. The story goes as follows. There are two small-time crooks who are being arrested for a minor crime. They were not exactly caught in the act. The crooks are best friends, but after being arrested they are kept in different rooms while they are being interrogated. Crook A is offered the following deal: if she confesses the crime, then she will receive a warning while her partner will receive ten months imprisonment. B is offered the same deal. Both A and B know that if both do not confess, and because they have not been caught red-handed, they will both have to pay a minor fine. However, if both of them confess, then they will both receive five months imprisonment. The situation is described using the normal form representation in Table 7.5. We will refer to confessing as *defection* (D) and not confessing as *cooperation* (C).

		Player B	
		Cooperate	Defect
Player A	Cooperate	−1,−1	−10,0
	Defect	0,−10	−5,−5

Table 7.5: The prisoner's dilemma game

The outcomes that ensue are:

$$o_1 = (C, C), o_2 = (C, D), o_3 = (D, C), o_1 = (D, D)$$

For player A the utilities over the possible outcomes are as follows:

$$u_A(o_1) = -1, u_A(o_2) = -10, u_A(o_3) = 0, u_A(o_4) = -5$$

A's preferences over the possible outcomes are then:

$$o_3 \succ_A o_1 \succ_A o_4 \succ_A o_2$$

For player B the utilities and preferences over the respective outcomes are as follows:

$$u_B(o_1) = -1, u_B(o_2) = 0, u_B(o_3) = -10, u_B(o_4) = -5$$

$$o_2 \succ_B o_1 \succ_B o_4 \succ_B o_3$$

The Pareto efficient solution in this game is for both players not to confess, that is to cooperate with each other, and as a result they will both have to pay a small fine. This is the best solution for both players and constitutes the socially optimal outcome. Both players know this. However, as is evident from the utility and preference analysis above, it is not the case that the players prefer all the outcomes in which they cooperate over all the outcomes in which they defect. This is rather counterintuitive. Given the choice to cooperate or defect, and knowing the possible outcomes and utilities, as well as what is the socially optimal outcome, the agents seem to prefer outcomes in which they are better off and the other party gets all the blame. Let us consider the prisoners' reasoning for a minute. Suppose I am prisoner A. If B decides not to confess, then strictly speaking I am better off by confessing since I will not be punished in any way. If B confesses, then I am better off confessing myself as I will only get 5 months in prison and not the 10 month sentence if I do not confess. Therefore, whatever B does I am better off confessing, i.e., defecting. Since the players' reasoning is symmetric, B will think in exactly the same way as A and will conclude that for her the best strategy, no matter what A does, is to confess. As a result, for each player, the strictly dominant strategy – the *rational* thing to do – is to defect.

The problem lies in the uncertainty that each player faces about the other's move. Each player speculates about what the other one is going to do and, as a result, they both confess. It seems that the mistrustful human nature gets the better of our players in this case. So, even though there is a Pareto efficient solution, there is a dominant strategy equilibrium that is not Pareto efficient. The two agents cannot really coordinate their actions in order to cooperate. In certain interaction situations, such as cooperation, trust is essential as we depend on the other party to either do something on our behalf or to carry out their part of a previously-reached agreement.

The prisoner's dilemma has generated a lot of controversy, in particular around the issue of cooperation. The conclusion reached, based on the analysis of the prisoner's dilemma game, seems to suggest that cooperation among agents arises as the result of *irrational* behaviour. Individuals who decide to cooperate in strategic situations, such as the one described by the prisoner's dilemma game, will be exploited by those who behave rationally. Binmore (1992) discusses ways in which cooperation can be salvaged in prisoner's dilemma situations. Another issue of debate is what is a reasonable way to play the game. The answer to this question seems to depend upon whether the game is a one-off or if it is to be repeated a finite or infinite number of times.

7.2.8 Repeated games

The discussion of the prisoner's dilemma in the previous section was in the context of single-shot games in which agents come together and only play a game once. The situation may be different if the game is to be played a number of times by the same agents. In this case, a new set of possibilities open up to the agents. If one agent chooses to defect in one round and the other has cooperated, then in the next round the second agent can *punish* the first agent by defecting as well. In a repeated game, each agent has the opportunity to establish a reputation for cooperation. Whether this is an efficient and viable strategy for the agent, depends on whether the game will be played a fixed or infinite number of times.

Consider the case when A and B play the prisoner's dilemma game 10 times. What is going to happen in the last game? Well, since it is the last one and no other game will be played, cooperation is not really essential. A can choose to defect as this will no longer affect her reputation – the rounds will have finished by then. As the agents are symmetric, B will think in exactly the same way and defect as well. So, playing the last game is like playing the game only once. What is going to happen in game nine? If A cooperates, then B might as well defect now and exploit A's cooperative behaviour as the last game does not matter anyway. Due to symmetry, A will reason in exactly the same way and thus both agents will choose to defect in game nine. Using the same principle of backward induction, both agents will defect in game eight, and so on. If the number of rounds is known, then in each round both agents will choose to defect.

It appears that, if there is no way to enforce cooperation in the last round, there is no way cooperation can be enforced in the previous rounds. Players only have an incentive to cooperate as they expect that this will induce further cooperation in the future, and potentially better payoffs. But this requires that there is always the possibility to play more games. Since there is no possibility of future play in the last round, no-one will cooperate in that round. But then why would one want to cooperate in the round before that one and the one before?

The situation changes when the game is to be played an infinite number of times. The agents then do have an incentive to cooperate in each round because, if one does not, then she may as well get punished in the next one. As long as both agents care about the future payoffs, the threat of noncooperation on behalf of the other party – *the shadow of the future* – may be enough to induce cooperation and lead both agents to a Pareto efficient outcome (Axelrod 1984).

The agent's behaviour in a prisoner's dilemma situation has been the focus of a series of experiments in the form of a competition run by Axelrod (1984). Robert Axelrod is a political scientist working in the University of Michigan and is interested in how cooperation can arise in a society of self-interested, rational agents. In 1980, he invited political scientists, psychologists, economists and game theoreticians to encode their favourite strategy for the prisoner's dilemma in a computer program and play the iterated version of the game. Each program-player had at their disposal the previous choice made by the opponent and simply had to select whether to cooperate or defect in the current round. Each player played against all the others for five games, each game consisting of 200 rounds. The winner of the tournament was the player who did best overall. The winner of this competition turned out to be a very simple strategy called tit-for-tat, created by psychologist and game theorist Anatol Rappaport. Tit-for-tat was encoded in two lines of Fortran code and works as follows:

- in the first round cooperate
- in round $r > 1$, do whatever your opponent did in round $r - 1$.

Thus, you start by cooperating and encouraging the other player to do so as well. However, if the other player does not cooperate, then you punish them by defecting, whereas if they have cooperated you keep cooperating with them. Tit-for-tat is easy to comprehend and it is computationally efficient as one need only remember the opponent's previous move to decide what to do next. This simple strategy won Axelrod's tournament in 1980. At first sight, this result seems extraordinary as it appears that cooperation prevails even in strategic situations among rational, self-interested agents after all. However, a careful post-tournament analysis reveals that tit-for-tat only came up as the top-winning strategy because the overall score was calculated taking into consideration all the strategies that it played against. In fact, pitting tit-for-tat against the dominant strategy which is to defect in all rounds, the dominant strategy came up top. The only reason that tit-for-tat won the tournament was because it had the opportunity to play against other strategies that also encouraged cooperation.

Axelrod tried to interpret the success of the tit-for-tat strategy and he suggested that:

- tit-for-tat does very well because it offers an immediate punishment for the other agent's defection
- it is a forgiving strategy, it only punishes the other agent once for each defection
- it is a rewarding strategy, if the other agent cooperates, it rewards this by continuing to cooperate.

7.2.9 Dynamic games

As not all strategic interactions occur simultaneously, there is often some element of sequentiality in the order of moves by different agents. Moreover, when the timing is sequential, the agent moving later has an obvious advantage as it has information about what has happened in the game before its move. Timing and information relating to sequentiality is much better captured in the extensive form representation of a game (tree). Games involving a sequential structure are called *dynamic* games. A subgame in an extensive form game is a sub-tree which:

- starts at a single node (a singleton information set)

- includes all decision nodes and terminal payoffs of the original tree following this node, and
- does not cut any information set of the extensive form representation of the original game.

Consider a variation of the prisoner's dilemma game which is played sequentially (strictly speaking this is no longer a prisoner's dilemma game) that is, agent *A* moves first and then agent *B* is in a position to observe *A*'s move and make its choice accordingly. The extensive form of the game is illustrated in Figure 7.7.

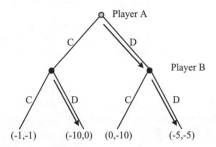

Figure 7.7: The sequential version of the prisoner's dilemma game

As one can observe, agent *B*'s information set contains one node; playing second, it can distinguish between the two decision nodes it is at. According to the definition of a subgame, the game that starts with the decision node of agent *B* after *A* has cooperated, is a subgame. The same applies to the subgame that starts with the decision node where player *A* has defected.

Since agents think ahead rationally before playing the game, agent *B* would play D if it is ever to move in its left node (and get 0 instead of −1). Similarly, agent *B* would play D if ever it had to move in its right node (and get −5 instead of −10). Both these choices are indicated by arrows. DD appears to be the logical strategy for agent *B*. Since agent *A* is also rational, it can think ahead and decide what is best for itself. If it plays C, it gets −10 (as this would be followed by D by agent *B*) while if it plays D, it gets −5 (this would also be followed by D by agent *B*). Agent *A* should choose D. The strategy combination (D, DD) is the *subgame perfect equilibrium* of the game, which is also the backward induction outcome.

Definition 13 *A strategy profile s constitutes a subgame perfect Nash equilibrium if it constitutes a Nash equilibrium of all subgames of the game (including the game itself).*

Consider the entrant-incumbent game illustrated in Figure 7.8 in its extensive form. In this game two firms are interested in a particular market. One is currently producing

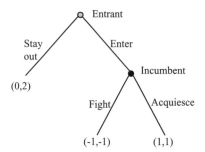

Figure 7.8: The entrant-incumbent game

(incumbent) and the other is not (entrant). The entrant must now decide whether to enter into the market or stay out. If the entrant stays out, the status quo prevails, the incumbent does not have to take any action and the game ends. If the entrant decides to enter, then the incumbent needs to decide whether to fight it by flooding the market with products to drive the price down, or to acquiesce by not doing anything. In the status quo the entrant's payoff is 0, whereas the incumbent's is 2. If the entrant enters and the incumbent fights, then they both get −1, whereas if the incumbent acquiesces, both firms get 1.

Obviously, the incumbent would like the entrant to stay out of the market and let it continue with its monopoly. Will the entrant decide to enter the market? This depends on how the incumbent is going to react to the entrant's entry. If the incumbent reacts by fighting then the entrant is going to get −1 as a payoff, so it prefers to stay out. On the other hand, if the incumbent acquiesces, then the entrant should enter.

Assume that the entrant has entered the market. What is the best thing for the incumbent to do? Clearly from the payoffs it is best for it to acquiesce as, by doing so, it will get a payoff of 1, whereas if it fights, it is going to get −1. The entrant will choose to enter as this yields it a payoff of 1 rather than 0. Since all agents behave rationally, the incumbent's threat to fight does not make sense at all. Once a new firm enters (the subgame starts), the best strategy for the incumbent would be to acquiesce, since it would get 1 if it does, while it would have a loss of −1 if it fights. Knowing that the incumbent is rational, and thus would acquiesce if it enters, the new firm will enter the market. Therefore, (Enter, Acquiesce) would be the subgame perfect Nash equilibrium in this game.

7.2.10 Bayesian Nash games

So far, we have assumed that all players have complete information regarding all elements of a game and the other players' payoffs. However, in many real-life situations players do not have complete information about all aspects of a game. For instance, if there are two firms competing for the same market, it is highly unlikely that each firm has precise information about the other's production costs. Inevitably, any uncertainty about the other agents' payoffs has a bearing on how individual agents analyze the strategic situation at hand and decide on their strategies.

How can we model such contexts where information is not commonly shared by all the agents? A game with incomplete information tries to model situations in which at least one player has uncertainty about the other players' payoff functions. Following the seminal work of Harsanyi (1967, 1968a,b), a game of incomplete information can be modelled by introducing Nature as a player. Nature chooses stochastically, in the beginning of the game, all those aspects that are not common knowledge. More specifically, Nature assigns a type to each agent from a set of types which determines that player's payoff function. Players have initial beliefs about the type of each other, where a belief is a probability distribution over the possible types for a player, and can update their beliefs according to Bayes' rule.

A Bayesian game of incomplete information is characterized by the following elements:

- a finite set N of agents (the set of players) with $n > 1$
- each agent $i \in N$ can choose a strategy s_i from a nonempty set S_i of strategies
- each agent i has some private information $\theta_i \in \Theta_i$, called the type of the agent
- a probability function $p_i : \Theta_i \to \Delta(\Theta_{-i})$ which specifies i's belief about the type of the other agents given its own type
- a payoff or utility function, $u_i : S \times \Theta \to \mathbb{R}$.

The introduction of types enables us to model the fact that an agent knows its own payoff function, but it is incompletely informed about the types of the other agents. Let $\theta_i \in \Theta_i$ represent the type of player i and so Θ_i is simply the set of all player i's types. We assume that Θ_i has a finite number of elements. An agent's type determines its preferences. For example, types could be the privately known valuations of an object in an auction. In other words, each type corresponds to a different payoff function that player i might have. Since each player's choice of strategy depends on its type, we let $s_i(\theta_i) \in S_i$ denote the pure strategy which player i chooses when its type is θ_i ($\sigma_i(\theta_i)$ is the mixed strategy).

If player i has k possible payoff functions, then the type space has k elements, $\#(\Theta_i) = k$, and we say that player i has k possible types. Thus, to say that a player i knows its own payoff function, is equivalent to saying that it knows its type. Similarly, saying that player i may be uncertain about the other players' payoff functions is equivalent to saying that it may be uncertain about their types, denoted by Θ_{-i} (Θ_{-i} denotes the set of all possible types of all players apart from player i). The probability distribution $p_i(\theta_{-i}|\theta_i)$ denotes player i's belief about the other players types θ_{-i}, given its knowledge of its own type θ_i. The probability distribution p is often referred to as the *common prior* because it is the common probability distribution that all agents use to assess the probability that the agents' types have any particular value. In essence, the probability distribution p_i summarizes what player i believes about the types of the other players, given its type. If player i knew the strategies of the other players as a function of their type, that is, it knew $\{\sigma_j(\cdot)\}_{j\neq i}$, it could use its beliefs $p_i(\theta_{-i}|\theta_i)$ to compute the expected utility for each choice and thus find its optimal response $\sigma_i(\theta_i)$.

Following Harsanyi, the timing of the static Bayesian game is as follows:

- Nature draws a type vector $\theta = (\theta_1, \ldots, \theta_n)$, where θ_i is drawn from the set of possible types Θ_i using some objective distribution p that is common knowledge
- Nature reveals θ_i to player i but not to any other player
- the players simultaneously choose their actions depending on the assigned type
- payoffs $u_i(s_1, \ldots, s_n|\theta)$ are received.

Since we assumed, in step (1) above, that it is common knowledge that Nature draws the vector θ from the prior distribution $p(\theta)$, player i can use Bayes' rule to compute its posterior belief $p_i(\theta_{-i}|\theta_i)$:

$$p_i(\theta_{-i}|\theta_i) = p_i(\theta_{-i}|\theta_i)/ \sum_{\theta_{-i} \in \Theta_{-i}} p_i(\theta_{-i}, \theta_i)$$

In the same way, the other players can compute the various beliefs that player i might hold, depending on i's type.

Given the description of a static Bayesian game, the concept of a Nash equilibrium for such a game is defined as the strategy profile in which each player's (type-contingent) strategy must be the best response to the other players strategies. That is, a Bayesian Nash equilibrium is simply a Nash equilibrium in a Bayesian game.

Given a strategy profile $s(\cdot)$ and a strategy $s'(\cdot) \in S_i$, let $(s_i'(\cdot), s_{-i}(\cdot))$ denote the profile where player i plays $s_i'(\cdot)$ and the other players play $s_{-i}(\cdot)$, and let

$$(s_i'(\theta_i), s_{-i}(\theta_{-i})) = (s_1(\theta_1), \ldots, s_{i-1}(\theta_{i-1}), s_i'(\theta_i), s_{i+1}(\theta_{i+1}), \ldots, s_n(\theta_n))$$

denote the value of this profile at $\theta = (\theta_i, \theta_{-i})$.

Definition 14 *Let G be a Bayesian game with a finite number of types Θ_i for each player i, a prior distribution p, and strategy spaces S_i. The profile $s(\cdot)$ is a (pure strategy) Bayesian equilibrium of G if for each player i and every $\theta_i \in \Theta_i$,*

$$s_i(\theta_i) \in \arg\max_{s_i' \in S_i} \sum_{\theta_{-i}} u_i(s_i', s_{-i}(\theta_{-i})|\theta_i, \theta_{-i})p(\theta_{-i}|\theta_i).$$

Simply stated, each type-contingent strategy is a best response to the type-contingent strategies of the other players. Player i calculates the expected utility of playing every possible type-contingent strategy $s_i(\theta_i)$ given its type θ_i. To do this, it sums over all possible combinations of types for its opponents, θ_{-i}, and, for each combination, it calculates the expected utility of playing against this particular set of opponents. The utility, $u_i(s_i', s_{-i}(\theta_{-i})|\theta_i, \theta_{-i})$, is multiplied by the probability that this set of opponents

θ_{-i} is selected by Nature, i.e., $p(\theta_{-i}|\theta_i)$. This yields the optimal behaviour of player i when it is of type θ_i. This process is then repeated for all possible $\theta_i \in \Theta_i$ and all players.

In equilibrium, every agent chooses a strategy to maximize expected utility in equilibrium with expected-utility maximizing strategies of other agents. The main difference between the Nash equilibrium and the Bayesian Nash, is that i's strategy $s_i(\theta_i)$ must be a best response to the distribution over strategies of other agents, given distributional information about the preferences of the other agents. In this sense, agent i does not necessarily play a best response to the actual strategies of the other agents. Consequently, the Bayesian Nash equilibrium makes more reasonable assumptions about the agents' information than Nash, but it is a weaker solution concept than dominant strategy equilibrium. As with Nash, there may be multiple Bayesian Nash equilibria in a game.

Consider a variation of the battle of the sexes game that we examined in Section 7.2.5. Suppose again that Kevin and Sally need to decide whether to go shopping or to the basketball game. Kevin's payoffs are as described in Table 7.6 (a) (the payoffs for Kevin are the same in both tables (a) and (b)). However, Sally's payoffs depend on whether she is a shopping fan or a basketball fan. If she is the former, she always prefers to go shopping no matter what Kevin does; if she is the latter, she always prefers going to the basketball game, again irrespective of what Kevin decides. Nevertheless, for any of the two possibilities, she always prefers to be joined by Kevin, rather than be on her own. The payoffs for Kevin do not change, but Sally's payoffs depend on what type of fan she is.

		Kevin Basketball	Shopping				Kevin Basketball	Shopping
Sally	Basketball	3,2	2,1		Sally	Basketball	1,2	0,1
	Shopping	0,0	1,3			Shopping	2,0	3,3
		(a)					(b)	

Table 7.6: The battle of the sexes game: (a) Sally is a basketball fan; (b) Sally is a shopping fan

Assume that Sally knows her preferences, i.e., her type, as well as Kevin's, but Kevin only knows his own. That is, Kevin is uncertain as to what type of fan Sally really is. The only information that *a priori* Kevin has, is the payoffs based on the two different types. Suppose Kevin attributes the subjective probability p to Sally being a basketball fan, and the probability $1 - p$ to her being a shopping fan.

Formalizing this situation as a Bayesian game, the type spaces of the two players are as follows:

$$\Theta_1 = \{\theta_{11}, \theta_{12}\}, \Theta_2 = \{\theta_2\}$$

Let θ_{11}, θ_{12} indicate that Sally is a basketball and a shopping fan, respectively. Then to model the situation as a Bayesian game, Nature is postulated to select the profiles $\theta \in \Theta \equiv \Theta_1 \times \Theta_2$ with respective probabilities:

$$P(\theta_{11}, \theta_2) = p, P(\theta_{12}, \theta_2) = 1 - p$$

The strategy spaces are $S_i = \{Basketball, Shopping\}$. The payoff function is $u_i : \Theta \times S_1 \times S_2 \to \mathbb{R}$.

In this case, Sally's decision problem is straightforward: she should play *Basketball* or *Shopping* as these are dominant strategies when she is of the basketball and shopping-fan type, respectively. On the other hand, for Kevin, who should anticipate Sally's contingent behaviour, what is optimal depends on the value p. If $p > 3/4$, then

$$2p + 0(1 - p) > 1p + 3(1 - p)$$

and he must play *Basketball*, which yields a higher expected payoff than *Shopping*. Otherwise, if $p < 3/4$, the highest expected payoff is obtained by playing *Shopping*, which is then the optimal strategy. Of course in the exact case where $p = 3/4$ Kevin is indifferent to playing *Baskeball* or *Shopping*.

The computation of the Bayesian Nash equilibrium follows from the fact that Sally, who has complete information in this game, has a dominant strategy in either case: strategy *Basketball* if her type is θ_{11} (basketball fan), and strategy *Shopping* if her type is θ_{12} (shopping fan). This leads to the equilibrium strategy:

$$s_1^*(\theta_{11}) = Basketball; s_1^*(\theta_{12}) = Shopping$$

Then Kevin's optimal response depends on p:

$$s_2^*(\theta_2) = \left\{ \begin{array}{ll} Basketball & \text{if } p > 3/4 \\ (q, 1-q), q \in [0, 1] & \text{if } p = 3/4 \\ Shopping & \text{if } p < 3/4 \end{array} \right\}$$

The above jointly characterize the strategy profile s^*, which defines the Bayesian Nash equilibrium of the game as a function of $p \equiv P(\theta_{11}, \theta_2)$. If $p \neq 3/4$, then the Bayesian Nash equilibrium is unique.

7.2.11 Beliefs and sequential rationality

It is often the case that agents may have to make moves, while being uncertain about the history of prior play, i.e., what moves the other agents played. Consider the dynamic game illustrated in Figure 7.9. Player A chooses first among three actions L, M and N. If it chooses N, the game ends without player B having to move. If A chooses either actions L or M, then player B realizes that N was not chosen by A. B has to choose between two actions L' and M' and subsequently the game ends with the players receiving their respective payoffs, according to the outcome that ensues.

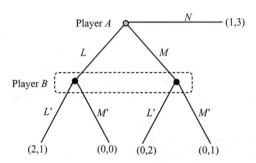

Figure 7.9: Example game

As we can see from the normal form representation of the game given in Table 7.7, there are two pure strategy Nash equilibria. These are (L, L') and (N, M'). But are these equilibria subgame perfect, as defined in Section 7.2.9? As a subgame is defined to begin at a decision node that includes only one node in the information set, other than the game's first decision node, this game has no subgames. Consequently, the requirement for subgame perfection, namely that the players' strategies constitute a Nash equilibrium at every subgame, is satisfied. Intuitively, in any game that has no subgames, the definition of subgame perfect Nash equilibrium is equivalent to the Nash equilibrium. However, the strategy profile (N, M') depends on a noncredible threat: if player B gets to move, then playing L' dominates playing M', so player A should not be induced to play N by B's threat to play M', if given the move.

		Player	B
		L'	M'
Player A	L	2,1	0,0
	M	0,2	0,1
	N	1,3	1,3

Table 7.7: The normal form representation of the example game

In order to rule out the unreasonable subgame perfect Nash equilibrium, we need to strengthen the equilibrium concept. First, we need to endow agents with beliefs at each of their information sets. If the information set includes more than one node, a belief is a probability distribution over the nodes. If the information set is a singleton, the player's belief assigns probability 1 to the node. This is formalized as follows:

Definition 15 *A system of beliefs μ in an extensive form game G is a specification of a probability $\mu(x) \in [0, 1]$ for each decision node x in G such that:*

$$\sum_{x \in H} \mu(x) = 1 \text{ for all information sets } H.$$

Given their beliefs, the players' strategies must be sequentially rational. This means that, at each information set, the strategy followed by the player who has to move (and the player's subsequent strategy) must be optimal, given the player's belief at that information set and the other players' subsequent strategies. To define sequential rationality formally, let $EU[u_i|H, \mu, \sigma_i, \sigma_{-i}]$ denote the expected utility of player i starting at its information set H, given the system of beliefs μ, if it follows strategy[6] σ_i and the other agents follow strategies σ_{-i}.

> **Definition 16** *A strategy profile σ in extensive form game G is sequentially rational at information set H given a system of beliefs μ if we have:*
>
> $$EU[u_{i(H)}|H, \mu, \sigma_{i(H)}, \sigma_{-i(H)}] \geq EU[u_{i(H)}|H, \mu, \sigma'_{i(H)}, \sigma'_{-i(H)}]$$
>
> *for all $\sigma'_{i(H)} \in \Delta(S_{i(H)})$ and where $i(H)$ denotes the player who makes a move at information set H. If the strategy profile satisfies this condition for all information sets H, then the profile is sequentially rational, given the system of beliefs μ.*

We also need to distinguish between the information sets that are on the equilibrium path and those that are off. For a given equilibrium in a given extensive form game G, an information set H is on the equilibrium path if it will be reached with positive probability if the game is played according to the equilibrium strategies, and off the equilibrium path if it is certain that it will not be reached if the game is played according to the equilibrium strategies. On the equilibrium path, all that the players need to update their beliefs are their prior probabilities and Bayes' rule. More formally:

> **Definition 17** *For any information set H such that $P(H|\sigma) > 0$, i.e., the probability of reaching information set H is positive under strategies σ, we must have:*
>
> $$\mu(x) = \frac{P(x|\sigma)}{P(H|\sigma)} \text{ for all } x \in H.$$

A natural way to define an equilibrium is as a strategy combination consisting of best responses, given that equilibrium beliefs follow Bayes' rule.

> **Definition 18** *A profile of strategies and a system of beliefs (σ, μ) is a perfect Bayesian Nash equilibrium in an extensive form game G if it has the following properties:*
>
> *(i) the strategy profile σ is sequentially rational, given the system of beliefs μ;*
>
> *(ii) at information sets on the equilibrium path beliefs are determined by Bayes' rule and the players' equilibrium strategies, and at information sets off the equilibrium path beliefs are determined by Bayes' rule and the players' equilibrium strategies whenever possible.*

Returning to our example game, if the play in the game reaches B's information set which contains two nodes, then B must have a belief about which node has been reached, i.e.,

---

[6] Strategy σ_i is a behaviour strategy as was discussed in Section 7.2.6.

whether A has played L or M. This belief is represented by probabilities p and $1 - p$, respectively. Given B's belief, the expected payoff from playing M' is $p(0) + (1 - p)(1) = 1 - p$, whereas the expected payoff from playing L' is $p(1) + (1 - p)(2) = 2 - p$. Since $2 - p > 1 - p$ for any value of p, sequential rationality prevents B from choosing M'. Thus, requiring that each player has a belief and acts optimally given this belief, the unreasonable equilibrium (N, M') can be eliminated.

Another related concept is that of sequential equilibrium which was developed by Kreps and Wilson (1982). The concept of sequential equilibrium imposes additional consistency constraints on beliefs. In particular, it is required that the strategies are totally or fully mixed. A totally mixed strategy in an extensive form game assigns strictly positive probabilities to every action at every information set. As a result, Bayes' rule alone uniquely determines the players' beliefs in this case.

Definition 19   *A strategy profile and a system of beliefs (σ, μ) for an extensive form game G is consistent if there is a sequence of totally mixed strategies σ^n converging to σ, such that the associated sequence systems of beliefs μ^n which are derived via Bayes' rule converges to μ.*

Kreps and Wilson (1982) refer to the combination of a strategy profile and a system of beliefs (σ, μ) as an assessment. A sequential equilibrium is defined as follows:

Definition 20   *A strategy profile and a system of beliefs (σ, μ) is a sequential equilibrium if it is both consistent and sequentially rational.*

7.3 Further Reading

The introduction to basic concepts of Economics and Game Theory presented here is somewhat elemental, but a more in-depth exposition of these topics is beyond the scope of this book. There are numerous textbooks on microeconomics and game theory that provide much more comprehensive and technical coverage of these two subjects.

Varian (2006) provides an excellent introduction to microeconomics for undergraduate students. The discussion here draws heavily on this work. Other good texts include Jehle and Reny (2001) and Bergin (2005). A more advanced and technical coverage is provided in Mas-Colell et al. (1995) where the concept of equilibrium is examined in more detail. A brief description of general equilibrium theory is also provided in Sandholm (1999).

The book by von Neumann and Morgenstern (1964) and the article by Nash (1950b) are classics in game theory. Osborne and Rubinstein (1994) provide an excellent introduction to game theory, albeit quite technical. A comprehensive introduction is also provided by Binmore (1992) and other good texts include Gibbons (1992), Fudenberg and Tirole (1998), Dutta (1999) and Rasmusen (2001). Dixit and Skeath (1999) provide an informal but very good introduction to the basic ideas of game theory. Varian (2006, Chapters 28–29) also includes an introduction to game theory, as well as Russell and Norvig (2003, Chapter 17). Another very good text which introduces game theory and economics with a number of examples is Vega-Rodondo (2003). The perfect Bayesian Nash equilibrium and the, closely related, concept of sequential equilibrium in dynamic games of incomplete information are discussed in more detail in Mas-Colell et al. (1995, Chapter 9), Jehle and Reny (2001, Chapter 7) and Fudenberg and Tirole (1998, Chapter 8).

7.4 Exercises and Topics for Discussion

1. A consumer B would like to acquire a bundle of goods $(p1, p2)$, where $p1$ is butter and $p2$ is potatoes. The following bundles are available:

   $$x = (4, 3)$$
   $$y = (3, 3)$$
   $$z = (5, 1)$$
   $$n = (2, 4)$$

   (a) Express the following preferences between bundles:
   x is strictly preferred to y;
   y is weakly preferred to n;
   n is strongly preferred to z.
   (b) what other relations between the four different bundles can you derive, assuming that the axioms of consumer preference hold, and that $\succeq$ is rational?
   (c) Explain what convexity entails for the above bundles.
   (d) Assign utilities to the four bundles according to the consumer's preferences.

2. In Matching Pennies there are two agents A, B. Each agent has a penny and both agents have to put their pennies down simultaneously. If both pennies match, then agent A gets £2 and agent B gets £1. If the pennies do not match, then agent A gets £0 and agent B gets £3.

(a) Represent the game in normal form (payoff matrix).
(b) Represent the game in extensive form.
(c) What are the information sets for the two agents A and B?
(d) What are the dominant strategies for the two agents (if any)?
(e) Is there a dominant strategy equilibrium?
(f) Is there a Nash equilibrium in this game? Is it unique?

3. Consider the game illustrated in Table 7.8.

		Player B	
		Left	Right
Player A	Up	0,3	3,0
	Down	4,0	0,4

Table 7.8: The game for Exercise 3

(a) What is the dominant strategy for B (if any)?
(b) Is there a dominant strategy equilibrium?
(c) Is there a Nash equilibrium in this game? Is it unique?

4. Consider the game illustrated in Table 7.9.
(a) What are the dominant strategies for A and B (if any)?
(b) Is there a dominant strategy equilibrium?
(c) Is there a Nash equilibrium? Is it unique?

		Player B	
		Left	Right
Player A	Up	−1,−1	−10,0
	Down	0,−10	−8,−8

Table 7.9: The game for Exercise 4

5. Consider the game illustrated in Table 7.10.

		Player B	
		Left	Right
Player A	Up	3,1	0,0
	Down	0,0	1,2

Table 7.10: The game for Exercise 5

(a) What are the dominant strategies for A and B (if any)?

(b) Is there a dominant strategy equilibrium?

(c) Is there a Nash equilibrium? Is it unique?

(d) Compute all the mixed strategy Nash equilibria in this game.

6. Consider the extensive form game illustrated in Figure 7.10.

(a) Find the subgame perfect Nash equilibrium of this game. Is it unique? Are there any other Nash equilibria?

(b) Suppose that player B cannot observe A's moves. Represent the game in normal form. What are the equilibria in this game?

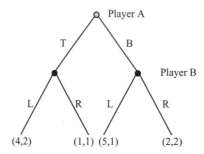

Figure 7.10: Dynamic game for Exercise 6

7. Consider the modified version of the battle of sexes game provided in Table 7.11 in which Sally's payoffs are as given, whereas Kevin's payoffs depend on his type, i.e., whether he is a basketball fan or a shopping fan. If he is the former, he always prefers to go to basketball no matter what Sally does; if he is the latter, he always prefers going shopping, again irrespective of what Sally decides. Nevertheless, for any of the two possibilities he always prefers to be joined by Sally, rather than to be on his own. Calculate the Bayesian Nash equilibrium of this game.

		Kevin				Kevin	
		Basketball	Shopping			Basketball	Shopping
Sally	Basketball	1,3	1,1	Sally	Basketball	1,2	1,1
	Shopping	2,1	3,1		Shopping	2,2	3,3
	(a)				(b)		

Table 7.11: The battle of the sexes game for Exercise 7: (a) Kevin is a basketball fan; (b) Kevin is a shopping fan

8. Consider another modified version of the battle of sexes game provided in Table 7.12, in which Sally's payoffs are as given, whereas Kevin's payoffs depend on his type. Sally does not know which type Kevin is, i.e., basketball or shopping, and consequently does not know which payoff matrix applies, but assigns probability 1/2 to each. Kevin knows his type. Calculate the Bayesian Nash equilibrium of this game.

		Kevin Basketball	Shopping			Kevin Basketball	Shopping
Sally	Basketball	4,3	1,1	Sally	Basketball	4,0	1,4
	Shopping	0,0	3,4		Shopping	0,3	3,1
	(a)				(b)		

Table 7.12: The battle of the sexes game for Exercise 8: (a) Kevin is a basketball fan; (b) Kevin is a shopping fan

CHAPTER 8

Negotiation I

LEARNING OBJECTIVES

After reading and completing this chapter, you should be able to:

- Discuss the role of negotiation protocols in electronic marketplaces.
- Describe the desired properties for negotiation protocols.
- Describe how auctions can be classified.
- Describe and distinguish among the four basic single-side auction formats, their characteristics, differences and advantages and disadvantages.
- Explain the Mth and $(M + 1)$st price rules and how they apply in double and single-side auctions.
- Apply the Mth and $(M + 1)$st price rules on sets of bids to determine the clearing price and the transaction set.
- Analyze simple scenarios and propose suitable auction protocols.
- Explain the basic principles and modes of operation of multi-attribute and combinatorial auctions.

The previous chapter introduced basic concepts of Economics and in particular the notion of an equilibrium, which is that state in a market when supply meets demand. Equilibrium theory explains very elegantly the conditions that are necessary for reaching that state in a market and what it means for the individual agents. What equilibrium theory is not concerned with is *how* this market equilibrium is reached: *how* we move from one state of the market in which agents own some goods and have some initial endowments, but do not derive their full utility, and therefore wish to deviate and reach another state in which they own different goods. Such a situation is illustrated in Figure 8.1, where agents are initially in a particular state, owning a set of goods and end up being in a another state, owning a different set of goods. The arrow indicates that some kind of process is used to enable agents to move from one state into another. This process is the main subject of this and the next chapter. Namely, *negotiation*. A negotiation mechanism is a coordination device which brings together participants, buyers and sellers, and facilitates trading or exchange.

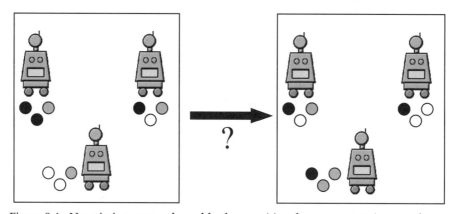

Figure 8.1: **Negotiation protocols enable the transition from one state in a market to another**

Negotiation is one of the stages in the Consumer Buying Behaviour model which we discussed in Chapter 4. This is the stage in which the terms of the transaction are being negotiated, and agreed upon in markets. Agent technology can be used in this stage in the form of trading agents. A trading agent is an agent that lives, acts, and interacts in an electronic market. It represents a user, knows her preferences, respects the set budget, and acts in the market by negotiating and performing transactions on behalf of the user.

Negotiation is, however, important in more general settings, beyond that of markets. We use negotiation in our everyday life to reach agreements on different issues. In cases of competition over resources or goal incompatibility among self-interested agents, it is important to be able to limit and control the effects of the agents' antagonistic behaviour. Such situations of competition or conflict can be resolved through mechanisms of coordination of actions and conflict resolution. Negotiation protocols help the parties involved to reach a compromise and, in some cases, a mutually beneficial, agreement. This agreement may be reached after perhaps many rounds of interaction.

8.1 NEGOTIATION PROTOCOLS

When agents are in competition or have conflicting goals and attempt to resolve these, they do not interact randomly, but their interaction is governed by a set of rules, namely an interaction protocol. In particular, a negotiation situation is characterized by three elements: the negotiation set, which represents the space of possible offers or proposals that agents can make; the protocol, which defines the rules that govern the agents' interactions; and finally, the set of strategies that the agents can use to participate in the negotiation. The agents' strategies are private, they are not dictated by the protocol itself and may take into consideration the possible strategies of other agents.

A negotiation or market protocol provides a set of rules and behaviours to be followed by agents that will interact in it. *Mechanism design* is the design of protocols governing strategic interaction among self-interested agents. The protocol determines, at each stage of the negotiation, who is allowed to send what messages and to whom. Thus, protocols facilitate structured interaction. In particular, a protocol may include the following types of rules (Jennings et al. 2001, Rahwan et al. 2003):

- Admission rules determine when an agent can participate in a negotiation and under what conditions. Such rules may state, for example, eligibility criteria.

- Interaction rules specify the structure of the interaction. Such rules indicate the sequence of admissible or valid actions in a particular situation, for instance, an auctioneer submits a reserve price first, and then the bidders are allowed to submit bids.

- Validity rules state what constitutes a legal offer or proposal. For example, a new bid needs to be higher than the last submitted bid.

- Outcome determination rules specify when an agreement has been reached or a solution has been found and what this is. Such rules also specify the winner(s) in a negotiation situation, e.g., who is allocated what and at what price.

- Withdrawal rules indicate when an agent can withdraw from the negotiation.

- Termination rules specify the conditions under which an encounter is terminated.

- Commitment rules determine how the commitments that agents make during the negotiation are managed. Such rules specify whether an agent can withdraw a previously made commitment and under what conditions.

There are a number of factors that determine the type of mechanism or negotiation protocol that is suitable for a particular situation:

- **Number of attributes**. Negotiation can take place over one attribute or many. Negotiating for a commodity with regard to price is single-attribute negotiation, but when more attributes are taken into consideration it is multiple-attribute negotiation. Buying a car may involve negotiating not only the price, but additional features such as the warranty, a CD player, leather seats, etc. The number of attributes to be considered inherently complicates the negotiation process.

- **Number of agents**. The number of agents involved in the negotiation process also affects mechanism design. There are three distinct cases:

  1. *One-to-one*: an agent negotiates with just one other.
  2. *One-to-many*: an agent negotiates with a number of other agents.
  3. *Many-to-many*: many agents negotiate with many other agents. If there are n agents, there are potentially $n(n-1)/2$ negotiation threads among them, taking place simultaneously.

- **Number of units**. The number of items that are available also plays a role in determining the best protocol to use. The price of multiple units may differ from protocol to protocol.

- **Interrelated goods**. In certain cases, negotiation is not taking place over one of the goods, but over a number of goods that are interrelated. The goods are only of value to agents when they are in combinations, so agents negotiate over *packages* or *bundles*, rather than individual goods. The complexity of the mechanisms for dealing with such negotiations is an open problem.

8.2 DESIRED PROPERTIES OF NEGOTIATION PROTOCOLS

Agents have their individual preferences and evaluations of goods and services that are available in the market and they are seeking to maximize their utilities by exchanging goods and services with others. When designing mechanisms for strategic interactions, we are particularly interested in those mechanisms that enjoy certain game-theoretic and computational properties (Rosenchein and Zlotkin 1994, Sandholm 1999):

- **Pareto efficiency**. Pareto efficiency has already been examined in the context of allocations and game theory. Pareto or economic efficiency is a useful criterion for comparing the outcomes of different protocols, as it measures global good. A solution x is Pareto efficient if there is no other solution x' such that at least one agent is better off in x' than in x and no agent is worse off in x' than in x.

- **Social welfare**. In contrast to Pareto efficiency, social welfare measures the distribution of wealth across agents. Social welfare is measured by a *social welfare function* which provides a way of adding together the different agents' utilities. In essence, a welfare function provides a way to rank different distributions of utility among agents.

However, in order to measure social welfare, inter-agent utility comparisons are required which may involve utility transformations.

- **Individual rationality**. Individual rationality dictates that an agent should participate in a protocol if its payoff from the negotiated solution is no less than the payoff that the agent would have by not participating. In other words, an agent should not lose out by participating in a mechanism. A protocol is individual rational, if it is individual rational for each agent.

- **Stability**. A negotiation protocol is stable if it is designed so that it motivates the agents to behave in the desired way. Protocol mechanisms can be designed with dominant strategies: specific strategies that an agent can use which guarantee maximization of payoffs without taking into account the other agents' strategies.

- **Budget balance**. In strict budget balance, the total payment that agents make must be equal to zero, in other words, money is not injected into or removed from a mechanism. Alternatively, in weak budget balance the total payment is non-negative, which ensures that the mechanism does not run at a loss. In *ex ante* budget balance the mechanism is balanced on average, while in *ex post* the mechanism is balanced at all times and for all instances.

- **Computational efficiency**. The negotiation protocol should be computationally efficient. As little computation as possible should be required on behalf of the agents.

- **Distribution and communication efficiency**. Distributed protocols are preferred to protocols with a central control point, since they avoid failure and performance bottleneck. The protocol should be communication efficient by requiring as little communication as possible in order to reach the desired outcome.

8.3 ABSTRACT ARCHITECTURE FOR NEGOTIATING AGENTS

In Chapter 2 we discussed a number of proposed architectures for building agents. As we are interested in software agents for electronic commerce applications and, in particular, in agents that are capable of negotiating using appropriate protocols, at this point it will be useful to look at the particular architectural requirements for negotiating agents.

Figure 8.2 illustrates the basic components that are required in order for an agent to be capable of negotiating. Accordingly, a negotiating agent consists of three main components: the communication, decision-making and knowledge-base components. As this is an abstract view of a negotiating agent, developers may choose to develop their agents in different ways and the complexity of the components may inevitably differ from agent to agent (Ashri et al. 2003, Rahwan et al. 2003). For simplicity, this abstract architecture does not explicitly show, for instance, ontologies or other components that can facilitate learning.

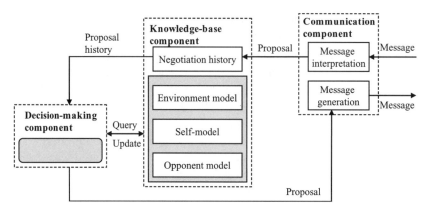

Figure 8.2: Abstract architecture for negotiating agents

Agents communicate with each other by exchanging messages, i.e., communicative acts or performatives. Consequently, a negotiating agent needs to have a communication component which is responsible for receiving and interpreting the incoming messages and extracting the proposals. Each proposal may be an offer, an acceptance or rejection of a previous proposal or a termination message. It goes without saying that for two agents to be able to communicate they need to be able to understand the communication and content languages used as well as the terminology, i.e., ontology or vocabulary. The communication component is also responsible for generating the necessary messages for communicating the agent's proposals to others once these have been decided upon.

The second major component is the internal knowledge base of the agent. Intuitively, the internal knowledge base represents the information that the agent has about itself and its environment. The agent's knowledge base may consist of a number of knowledge bases as illustrated in Figure 8.2. In more sophisticated and deliberative agents, the knowledge base may comprise: the environment model, which represents information about the agent's environment; the self-model, which contains the agent's preferences and objectives; and the opponent model, which models the other agents in the environment. The agent's self-model may be represented in terms of beliefs, intentions, preferences or other mental attitudes. Simpler agents may not have such a complex self-model, or an explicit model of the other agents. A separate knowledge base may be used for recording the negotiation history for future reference. This history may also be used for learning purposes or updating the opponents' models. In addition, the rules for the various protocols that the agent can use in negotiation can be stored in a separate knowledge base (Ashri et al. 2003) – although this is not shown in the abstract architecture presented here. Separating the rules of the protocol from reasoning about the protocol, allows an agent to handle a number of different protocols. The various knowledge bases may also be updated, based on information received from the environment, such as the content of messages (e.g., proposals, bids) or other events as they take place (e.g., another agent dropping out of the negotiation).

Once a message has been parsed and the proposal has been extracted, it is stored in the negotiation history and then also passed on to the decision-making component. The decision-making component of an agent is obviously critical to its success. This component is responsible for the evaluation of a current proposal and the generation of a new proposal, which may take the form of an acceptance, rejection, counter-offer or a termination message. The decision-making component considers the currently received proposal and, along with the agent's objectives and information about the world, as well as negotiation history, it decides what action to take next and generates the appropriate proposal. In processing a proposal, additional useful information may be inferred, which can be used to update aspects of the knowledge base. For instance, a significant concession made by an agent on a particular issue under negotiation may indicate that the agent has a deadline and thus wishes the negotiation process to complete swiftly. The decision-making component has been deliberatively left empty as its internal workings depend on a number of factors, including the particular negotiation situation and protocol used.

8.4 AUCTIONS

Auctions are one of the oldest forms of market and some pinpoint their origin to Babylon in 500 BC. The term auction comes from the Latin root 'auctio' which means 'increase'. In essence, auctions constitute a method of allocating goods based upon competition among the interested parties. Goods of undetermined quality can be traded and the price is set by the bidders, not the auctioneer.

Nowadays, all sorts of goods and services are being traded in auctions ranging from paintings to spectrum licences. With the advent of the World Wide Web, auctions have become extremely popular as the negotiation protocol of choice for conducting consumer-to-consumer (C2C) negotiations. Auction sites such as eBay (eBay 2006) have been reporting millions of dollars in transactions from auction sales. Governments have used auctions to sell spectrum and TV licences, rights to drill for oil and for privatizing government-owned companies (Klemperer 2004). Another potential application of auctions, which has received increasing attention recently, is in Grid computing environments (Foster and Kesselman 2004) for the allocation of computational resources (Gomoluch and Schroeder 2004).

There are two main self-interested parties in an auction:

- **The auctioneer.** The auctioneer can be a seller who wants to sell goods at the highest possible price (or subcontract-out tasks at the lowest possible price) who may be the owner of the goods or services, or a representative of the actual seller. An auctioneer can also be a buyer who is looking to buy an item from a number of sellers at the lowest possible price.

- **The bidders.** The bidders can be buyers who want to buy goods at the lowest possible price (or get awarded contracts at the highest possible price), or sellers who compete for sales.

Agents that participate in auctions are self-interested and rational, seeking to maximize their own profit. They can have different attitudes towards risk: they can be *risk-prone* or *risk-neutral*. The former are likely to raise their bids so that they are more likely to win, whereas the latter will never exceed their true valuations.

A typical auction proceeds as follows. First, buyers and sellers register with the auction house. The auction event is set up and scheduled, and it is advertised in the local press or via other means (Internet, mailing lists, etc.). The actual bidding takes place: bidders offer their bids according to the rules of the particular auction protocol used. During the bidding phase and depending on the auction format used, some information may be revealed to participants such as the bid and ask quotes. The bids are evaluated and the auction closes with a winner being determined if any of the bids is successful. Finally, the transaction takes place: the buyer pays for the goods and the seller ships them.

Some common terminology used in auctions is described in Table 8.1.

Term	Meaning
Bid	Bids are offered by the bidders to buy or sell the auctioned item.
Buy bid	The price that a bidder is willing to pay to own an item.
Sell bid	The price a bidder is willing to accept to sell an item.
Reservation price	The maximum (minimum) price a buyer (seller) is willing to pay (accept) for an item. This is usually private information.
Process bid	The auctioneer checks the validity of a bid according to the rules of the auction protocol and updates its database (manual or electronic).
Price quote generation	The auction house via the auctioneer or by other means may provide information about the status of the bids.
Bid quote	The amount a seller would have to offer to sell an item.
Ask quote	The amount a buyer would have to offer to buy an item.
Clearance	Through clearance buyers and sellers are matched and the transaction price is set.
Clearing price	The final transaction price that the buyer pays and the seller receives.

Table 8.1: Common auction terminology

Auctions are very versatile protocols and a number of mechanisms have been designed to deal with different situations and requirements. Due to their variety and flexibility they deserve special attention and therefore the rest of this chapter will be devoted to them.

8.5 CLASSIFICATION OF AUCTIONS

Auctions can be characterized along three main dimensions (Wurman et al. 2001): the *bidding rules*, the *information revelation policy* and the *clearing policy* used.

The bidding rules specify how the auction is to be conducted and what type of bids the participants are allowed to submit:

- **Single-object or multiple-object.** In single-object auctions, bidders can bid for one object only, whereas in multiple-object auctions, bidders are interested in multiple objects. Multiple-object auctions can be further divided into auctions for homogeneous and heterogeneous objects. In the former, the goods are identical, whereas in the latter the objects differ. Heterogeneous objects can be auctioned in sequential, simultaneous or combinatorial auctions. In such auctions, it is often the case that goods are only of value to bidders in combination and not separately. In sequential auctions, the various items are auctioned one after the other in separate auctions. In simultaneous auctions, the items are auctioned in auctions which run in parallel. Finally, in combinatorial auctions, the bidders are allowed to submit bids in bundles or combinations of items. Auctions for multiple homogeneous objects can also be divided in sequential, simultaneous and multi-unit auctions. As before, in sequential auctions, single items are auctioned in one auction after the other, whereas in simultaneous auctions, the items are auctioned in a number of auctions which run in parallel. In multi-unit auctions, a number of items are offered in one auction and bidders can submit bids for any number of them.

- **Single-attribute or multi-attribute.** In single-attribute auctions the negotiation takes place over one dimension or attribute of the item, namely price. In multi-attribute auctions more than one attributes of the good are being negotiated upon, i.e. warranty, delivery day etc.

- **Single or double.** In single-side auctions, there is a single seller (or buyer) who negotiates with multiple buyers (or sellers), whereas in double auctions there are multiple buyers who negotiate with multiple sellers.

- **Open (outcry) or sealed-bid (SB).** In open auctions the bidders bid openly and thus the other participants know theirs bids. In contrast, in sealed-bid auctions, the bidders offer their bids in secret (on a piece of paper, via a handshake, or electronically), thus not revealing any information to the other participants.

- **Ascending or descending price**. In ascending-price auctions, the bids start at a low price and then progressively increase. The highest bidder gets the item. In descending-price auctions, the commodities start at a high price, which is then lowered by the auctioneer until a buyer decides to bid and obtain the item.

- **First-price or second-price (Mth)**. In first-price auctions, the highest bidder wins and pays the value of their bid, whereas in second-price (Mth) auctions, the highest bidder wins but only pays the amount designated by the second-highest (Mth) bid.

- **Uniform or discriminatory**. In uniform auctions, all winning bidders pay the same price, whereas in discriminatory auctions, the bidders pay their bids.

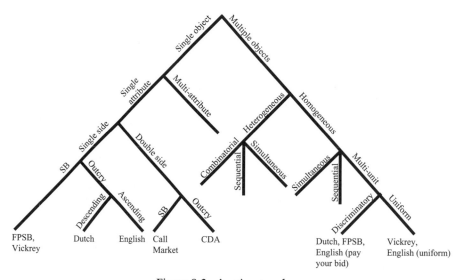

Figure 8.3: Auction typology

A typology of auctions based on the above distinctions is illustrated in Figure 8.3. However, this typology is not an exhaustive representation of all different varieties of auction formats. For instance, multiple-object auctions can be open or sealed-bid. Moreover, although multi-dimensional auctions, such as combinatorial and multi-attribute auctions are included, more complicated formats such as multi-attribute combinatorial auctions have been left out. Multi-dimensional auctions are, in general, highly complicated auction formats and are currently the subject of research with somewhat restricted use in practice.

The information revelation policy specifies what information, if any, is revealed to the participants of the auction. The information revelation policy determines three aspects:

- When to reveal information: on arrival of each bid, periodically, on inactivity or on market clearance.

- What information is to be revealed: if the participants are to obtain information that helps them revise their bids, then the ask and bid quotes need to be made available. Auction closure is another piece of information that can be revealed to the agents as it may be useful in formulating their strategy.

- Who obtains the information: participants only, or everyone.

The clearing policy specifies when the market clears, i.e., when buyers and sellers are matched, and consists of decisions for the following:

- When to clear the market: on arrival of each bid, on closure, periodically, after a period of activity/inactivity.

- Who gets what: who is allocated the goods, how are the winners determined.

- At what prices: what price buyers pay and sellers receive and how this is determined. They may pay the first, second or some other price. Finally, when there are multiple units being auctioned, buyers may all pay the same price (uniform) or a different one (discriminatory).

Auctions can be distinguished into *private value*, *common value* and *correlated value*, according to the bidders' valuation of the commodity.

In private value auctions, the value of the good depends only on the bidders' own preferences and usually the bidder wants to acquire an item for its own use and consumption. For instance, a bidder may wish to acquire a painting for their own home. How much the painting is worth in this case depends on the bidder's own valuation of the painting and personal taste.

In common value auctions, a bidder's value of an item depends entirely on the others' value of it, which in turn, by symmetry, is identical to the bidder's, i.e., the item is worth essentially the same to every bidder, but the bidders may have different estimations of this value. In such auctions the bidders want to acquire the commodities for resale or commercial use. For instance, in auctions of works of art, bidders may participate to acquire items for resale, as for sale in a gallery. The items, paintings, sculptures, etc., are worth the same to every bidder, but each may have a different estimation of this value. In essence, the bidders have to think of how much their potential clients would be willing to pay for a particular item.

In correlated value auctions, a bidder's value depends partly on its own preferences and partly on what it thinks the other agents' valuations are. For instance, an art collector may decide to acquire a painting partly because they like it personally, but also as a potential investment with a view to selling it later for a higher price. In this case, the bidder's valuation depends on their own tastes as well as on beliefs and expectations about the likely increase in value of the item in the coming years.

8.6 BASIC AUCTION FORMATS

In single-good, single-attribute, single-side auctions, agents are negotiating over one item which is available on its own (not in combinations), the negotiation has one dimension – usually price – and there is one seller (or buyer) and multiple buyers (or sellers).

8.6.1 English auction

The English auction is an open-outcry and ascending-price auction. It has been commonly used for selling works of art, antiques, cars and other commodities. The general process is as follows:

- The auction begins with the auctioneer announcing the lowest possible price, which often constitutes the reservation price, or inviting bidders to bid.
- Bidders submit bids and the auction proceeds to successively higher bids.
- When there are no more raises, the winner of the auction is the bidder of the highest bid and pays the amount of the bid.

The distinct characteristic of the English auction is that bidders gain information by observing what the other participants bid. This may be invaluable in forming their own strategy and, in some cases, even revising their valuation of the auctioned item. There are several variations on the English auction basic format. A bidder may exit the auction by publicly announcing so, with or without a re-entering option. This provides additional information to the remaining bidders about the valuation of the one who exits the auction.

In traditional auctions, the submission of bids may be made by shouting, a signal – such as tugging the ear, or raising a bidding paddle. The English auction tends to generate enthusiasm among bidders and due to its fast pace, risk-prone bidders get excited and tend to overbid, acquiring the item at higher prices than their true valuation.

The bidder's strategy is a series of bids as a function of the private value, the prior estimates of the other bidders' valuations, and the past bids of others. The bidder's best strategy (dominant) is to bid a small amount more than the previous highest bid until it reaches its private value and then stop. In this way a bidder may acquire an object for considerably less than its maximum valuation, simply because they need only increase each bid by a small increment. This, on the other hand, means that the seller does not necessarily receive the maximum value for the auctioned item.

English auctions have certain disadvantages. For instance, the reservation price may not be met and thus the item may remain unsold. The auctioneer may cheat by overstating the reservation price or present a reservation price that does not exist in order to increase its profit. This type of auction is susceptible to rings (collusions). Also due to its fast pace, some bidders may get carried away and overbid. Finally, as already pointed out, the seller may not necessarily receive the maximum value for an item.

Multi-unit English auctions are not straightforward as different pricing policies can be used, i.e., uniform or discriminatory. In uniform-price auctions, the winners may pay the highest losing ($(M + 1)$st price) or lowest winning price (Mth price), whereas in discriminatory auctions, the bidders pay their bids. Different tie-breaking rules can be used, based on price or quantity.

8.6.2 Dutch auction

The Dutch auction is an open and descending-price auction. It has taken its name from its very common use in The Netherlands for selling fresh flowers. The general process is as follows:

- The auctioneer announces a very high opening price.
- The price is subsequently lowered until a bidder accepts it.
- The winner pays the price of the bid.

In non-electronic auctions, the auctioneer may be a mechanical device which lowers the price until a bidder presses a button. The Dutch auction is very efficient in real time, since the auctioneer can decrease the price at a brisk pace. Each bidder needs to decide in advance the maximum amount that they will bid. Bidders must decide when to stop the auction, i.e., to submit a bid, based upon their own valuation of the commodity and prior beliefs about the valuations of the other bidders. No relevant information on the valuation of the other bidders is disclosed during the process of the auction, until it is too late. Generally speaking, there is no dominant strategy in the Dutch auction.

Due to its format, the effect of competition on the potential buyers in the Dutch auction sometimes may be stronger than in the English auction. In the English auction, a bidder forces the bid up only by a small increment at a time, therefore the winner may end up paying well under its valuation and thus the seller does not receive the maximum price. However, in the Dutch auction, if the bidder really wants an item, they need to bid at or near their valuation. Not knowing the other bidders' valuations, a bidder cannot afford to wait too long to enter their bid, because if they wait for the price to drop well below their valuation, they risk loosing the auction; by the time they have information about the other bidders' valuations it is too late.

Dutch auctions can be used for selling multiple units and in this case, as the price gets lowered, more bidders may respond. Each winner will have to pay a different price, i.e., the price that they bid. Hence, the multi-unit Dutch auction is discriminatory. The bidding is over when the goods are exhausted.

8.6.3 First-price sealed-bid auction

In the first-price sealed-bid auction (FPSB), the bid that each bidder submits is sealed. Consequently, each bidder submits their own bid (usually in writing) without knowledge of the bids of others. The name *first-price* stems from the fact that the highest bidder wins and pays the amount of their bid. There are two distinctive phases:

- The bidding phase, in which participants submit their bids.
- The resolution phase, in which the bids are opened and the winner is determined.

An agent's strategy is their bid as a function of their own private value and prior beliefs about the other bidders' valuations. There is no dominant strategy in the first-price sealed-bid auction. A high bid raises the probability of winning, but lowers the profit if the bidder is actually awarded the item. Assume that an agent bids its true valuation and this turns out to be the highest bid, b_h, and wins the auction. Now consider the second-highest bid offered, b_{h-1}. The winner could have offered just a small increment on that price and still be the winner. Thus, the difference between b_h and b_{h-1} represents a loss for the winner. Therefore, agents are better off not bidding their true valuations, but a small amount below it.

The winner pays the highest price if it is a single-unit auction. When multiple units are being auctioned, not all winning bidders pay the same amount, the first-price sealed-bid auction is discriminatory. In a multiple-unit auction, sealed bids are sorted from high to low, and the items are awarded at highest bid price until the supply is exhausted.

8.6.4 Vickrey auction

The Vickrey auction is also known as the uniform second-price sealed-bid or the philatelist auction. This form of auction was originally used by collectors to buy and sell stamps. William Vickrey[1] who won the Nobel prize in 1996 for his work on analyzing auctions, was the first who studied and analyzed the formal properties of this format. As in its counterpart, the first-price sealed-bid auction, there are two phases, the bidding and the resolution:

- Each bidder submits their bid without knowledge of the others' bids.
- The bids are opened and the winner is determined – the highest bid wins. But, the winner pays the amount specified by the second-highest bid.

The Vickrey auction sounds a bit peculiar at best, or counterintuitive at worst. At first sight one may think that no auctioneer would be willing to use it as it provides a lower profit. But, in reality, it works very well. Why does it work? Although it seems that the auctioneer would make more money out of a first-price sealed-bid auction, this is not the case. In the first-price sealed-bid auction, the bidders do not have an incentive to

---

[1] American economist William S. Vickrey (1914–1996).

bid their true valuations. In fact, quite the opposite, they tend to underbid in order to cut their losses in case they are awarded the item. In contrast, in the Vickrey auction, bidders adjust their bids upwards since they are not deterred by fear that they will have to pay too much. Even if a bidder bids exactly their true valuation and wins the auction, one thing is certain, they will pay less than their bid. Even aggressive bidders pay a price closer to the market consensus. The price that the winning bidder pays depends on the others' bids alone and not on any action that the bidder undertakes.

The agent's strategy is a function of its private value and prior beliefs of the others' valuations, but the best strategy for a bidder, which constitutes a dominant one, is to bid the true valuation, i.e., $b_i = v_i$. It then accepts all offers that are below this valuation and none that are above. Truth-telling in the Vickrey auction ensures that globally efficient decisions are being made; bidders do not waste time in counterspeculating what the other bidders will do. Let us see why this is the case:

- Consider bidding $v - x$ when your true valuation is v.
- Suppose the next highest bid other than yours is y.
- If $v - x > y$ you win the auction and pay y, just as if you had bid v.
- If $y > v$ you lose the auction and get nothing, just as if you had bid v.
- But if $v > y > v - x$, bidding $v - x$ causes you to lose the auction, whereas if you had bid v, you would have won the auction and paid y for a net surplus of $v - y$.
- Therefore you can only lose, and never gain, by bidding $v - x$.

What if you consider bidding $v + x$ and the highest bid other than yours is w? This is left as an exercise for the reader.

The multi-unit Vickrey auction is uniform, in other words, when multiple units are being auctioned, the bidders pay the same price for the commodities, which is the highest losing price.

8.6.5 Allocation and revenue comparisons

An auction is *incentive compatible* if the agents optimize their expected utilities by bidding their true valuations for the item. An auction is *individual rational* if its allocation does not make any agent worse off than had the agent not participated. An allocation of goods is *efficient* if there can be no more gains from trade. A Pareto efficient allocation in the context of auctions, means that the item is awarded to the bidder with the highest valuation. It turns out that no auction mechanism is individual rational, efficient and incentive compatible for *both* sellers and buyers. Incentive compatibility, for both parties, means that some party is willing to subsidize the auction.

In private value auctions in which a bidder's valuation of the item depends only on their own preferences, all four basic auction formats lead to Pareto efficient allocations.

When agents are risk-neutral

- *The Dutch and FPSB auctions are strategically equivalent.* In the FPSB auction, each bidder decides how much they should bid and submits their bid. In the Dutch auction, each bidder must choose a price at which they will call out 'Mine', conditional on no other bidder having yet called out. The situation facing the bidder is the same, as they must decide how high to bid, based on their own private valuation. The bidder bids some amount less than their true valuation. The strategy space is the same for the two auctions, i.e., the Dutch auction is strategically equivalent to the first-price sealed-bid auction[2]. Therefore, the payoff functions, and hence the equilibrium outcomes, are the same. What are the equilibrium strategies in the Dutch and FPSB auctions? If there are two bidders, each bidder submits a bid equal to half of their true valuation $b_i(v_i) = v_i/2$. This reflects the inherent tradeoff between a high bid which increases the likelihood of winning the auction, and a low bid which increases the bidder's gain if indeed it wins. Thus, if there are $N \geq 2$ bidders, and each bidder's value is seen as uniformly distributed, the Bayesian Nash equilibrium is for a bidder to bid: $b_i(v_i) = v_i(N-1)/N$. The term $(N-1)/N$ indicates how much the bidder shades its bid below its true valuation depending on the number of participants in the auction.

- *The English and Vickrey auctions are equivalent.* In the English auction, the dominant strategy for an agent is to keep bidding until the price reaches its true valuation and it is indifferent between winning and not winning. The next-to-last agent will drop out when its valuation is reached. Therefore, the agent with the highest valuation will win at a price equal to the value of the second-highest bid (plus a small amount to break the tie). In the Vickrey auction, the dominant strategy is for a bidder to bid its true valuation. It then accepts all prices that are below this, and none that are above. Thus, in both auctions, a truth-revealing strategy where one always bids one's true valuation, is a dominant strategy. One important thing to note is that, unlike the Vickrey auction, in an English auction bidders can respond to rivals' bids. Therefore, the two auctions are not strategically equivalent, but bidders still have the dominant strategy to bid an amount equal to their own true valuation.

- As the English and the Vickrey auctions have dominant strategies, they are more efficient than the FPSB and the Dutch auctions. A bidder need not waste time counterspeculating what the other bidders will do, or engage in opponent modelling; bidders can simply play the dominant strategy.

- Assuming valuations are drawn independently, all four mechanisms yield the same revenue, on average, for the auctioneer. This is known as the *revenue equivalence* theorem. In the FPSB and Dutch auctions, each bidder estimates how far below their own valuation the next highest valuation is, on average, and then submits a bid that is this amount below its own valuation. Thus bidders tend to underbid. In the English

---

[2]Two games with the same set of players and strategy space are strategically equivalent if they have the same normal form. In other words, each player's expected payoffs in the first game are the same as in the second one.

and the Vickrey auctions, it is the second-highest price that wins. Hence, on average, the price reached in all four auctions is the same.

When agents are risk-prone

- If the bidders are risk-prone, then the Dutch and the FPSB auctions yield higher revenue than the English and the Vickrey.
- If the auctioneer is risk-prone, then the English and the Vickrey yield higher revenue than the Dutch and the FPSB.

In non-private value auctions

- The Dutch auction is strategically equivalent to the FPSB.
- The Vickrey is not equivalent to the English auction. In an English auction a bidder can learn about the evaluations of the other participants by observing their bidding behaviour.
- All four protocols allocate items efficiently.
- With more than two bidders, the expected revenues are not the same: English $\geq$ Vickrey $\geq$ Dutch $=$ FPSB. This is known as the *revenue nonequivalence* theorem.

So which auction is better? Auctions with dominant strategies like the English and the Vickrey are more efficient as the bidders need not speculate. From the auctioneer's perspective, in second-price auctions, the revenue is less than the true price. However, in first-price auctions the bidders tend to underbid.

8.6.6 Disadvantages of auctions

Auctions as negotiation protocols offer certain advantages. First of all, flexibility. A traditional auction protocol, such as the English, can be modified according to the requirements of a particular situation. Secondly, they are less time consuming and expensive than negotiating a price via some other means and they offer simplicity in determining market-based prices. On the other hand, auctions have several disadvantages. In traditional auction settings, a bidder can use various ways to deceive an auction house and other bidders. Some protocols need not commit a winner to pay. Some of the most common problems arising in auctions are discussed next.

Winner's curse

Winners in auctions are often plagued by the *winner's curse*. This is what bidders suffer when they win an auction by overestimating how much something is worth and therefore bidding too much. Thus, a win may actually mean loss for the winner agent. Suppose you bid in an auction and you are actually awarded the item. Winning means that your valuation was the highest one among those of all the other bidders. Suppose that there were only two bidders, then your valuation was higher that the other person's. However, once you win, you start considering the possibility that you may have actually overestimated the value of the item. The more bidders participating along in an auction with you, the more optimistic you are, as you have managed to be awarded the item and in essence beaten all the other bidders' valuations. Should you be happy about this?

The winner's curse is more severe in common and correlated value auctions as one's valuation depends on the others. Consider the following example. Four firms are considering bidding for the drilling rights to a piece of land. Suppose there is £10M worth of oil in the ground. Oil firms are not sure about the value of the oil, but they conduct independent geological surveys to get estimates which are as follows: Firm A: £5M, Firm B: £10M, Firm C: £12M and Firm D: £15M. When the bidding commences the chances are that since Firm D has a higher valuation for the oil in the ground than the other firms, it will outbid them and win. But the consequences of such a win may actually be that the company loses out significantly.

So what can a bidder do in the face of the winner's curse? In general, the possibility of the winner's curse must be taken into account at the bidding stage by shading the bid down. Failing to do so might result in winning bids that earn less than average profits, or even losses. A bidder should therefore anticipate the effects of the winner's curse before bidding:

- Assume that you have the highest estimate and therefore you are going to win.
- When incorrect, this assumption is costless because someone else wins and you pay nothing.
- Bid more cautiously than the estimate in itself would indicate, i.e., correct downwards or discount your own bid.

Any piece of information that can be obtained should be used to adjust the bidder's bid. Such information includes how aggressively others bid, how many bidders remain in the auction and when others apparently drop out of the bidding.

The more information the bidder has, the less it rationally distrusts its own information, and so the smaller the correction that is to be applied to the bid.

Lying auctioneer

In any auction the auctioneer's objective is to maximize the revenue. Certain auctions are vulnerable to a number of tricks that the auctioneer can use in an attempt to maximize the expected revenue. This sort of behaviour is known as the *lying auctioneer* problem. For instance, in the English auction, auctioneers may overstate the reservation price or may even state a nonexistent reservation price in order to increase their own profit. *Shills* may be used, that is, people working for the auctioneer who constantly raise the bids in order to prompt real bidders to bid higher and thus again increase the revenue for the auctioneer. In addition, the English auction is also prone to *phantom bidders*: in traditional settings the auctioneer may pretend that he has received a new bid from someone at the back of the room by simply nodding his head, again in order to stimulate bidders to bid higher.

In the Vickrey auction the auctioneer may overstate the second-highest bid to the winner, since the bids are not revealed to the participants even after they are opened. This can be alleviated by modifying the protocol and revealing the bids after the winner has been declared. Another way is to sign bids using digital signatures so that the winner can verify the value of the second-highest bid, or alternatively use trusted third parties to handle the bids.

Rings

All auction formats described are susceptible to rings or collusion to a different extent. A ring is formed by a subset of the bidders that come together and agree not to outbid each other. In essence, they coordinate their actions to keep their bids artificially low and then one of them bids slightly higher and wins the item. The item is then re-auctioned among the members of the ring or is sold and the profit is divided among them. In its extreme, the ring can be the entire group of bidders who meet and agree in advance to keep their bids low. One way to counteract rings is to modify the protocol in such a way so that bidders cannot identify each other, for instance, the English auction is conducted online. However, bidders in open auctions would want to make sure that they have accurate information about the bids submitted by others.

In the English and Vickrey auctions, collusion among the bidders is a dominant strategy as there is no incentive to betray the ring. Let bidder A have a valuation 100 and every other bidder have a valuation 90 for the auctioned item. Assume that the bidders come together and agree to coordinate their bids. A will bid 50 and everyone else will bid 40. In an English auction, if someone decides to deviate from this agreement and bid more than 40, A is in a position to observe this and it would then be willing to go up to its true valuation (100) in order to win the item. The deviating agent has nothing to win by exceeding the agreed bid of 40. Consider the Vickrey auction now. The agreement among the ring may be that A will bid 100 and everyone else will bid 40 or below. Bidding 100 removes the incentive from any bidder to deviate from the agreement reached by the ring, since even bidding at a price between 40 and 90 will not win the auction. Thus, the agreement within the ring is self-enforcing.

In contrast, in the FPSB and Dutch auctions, the agreement is not self-enforcing. Assume such an auction and the agreement among the ring that the designated 'winner' will place a bid equal (or very close) to the seller's minimum price, while the other ring members will refrain from bidding. Albeit, each of those other bidders can gain by placing a slightly higher bid violating the ring's agreement. In the FPSB, the bids submitted are sealed so the deviating agent can safely place such a bid. On the other hand, in the Dutch auction the deviating agent can shout 'Mine' before the auctioneer reaches the agreed minimum price and win the item.

Finally, sealed-bid auctions are vulnerable to collusion between the auctioneer and one or more bidders. Ranking the four basic auction formats from most prone to collusion to least, the order is as follows:

English > Vickrey > First-price sealed-bid > Dutch.

Sniping

A particular issue that is more severe in online auctions is that of sniping. More specifically, in auctions with pre-determined duration, i.e., the closing time is known, sniping is bidding very late in the auction in the hope that other bidders do not have time to respond and you can snatch a bargain (Roth and Ockenfels 2002). Bidders may resort to sniping in order to avoid:

- increasing the price of the item early on in the auction
- revealing their preferences early in the auction (especially experts)
- bidding wars with other like-minded agents.

Sniping in online auctions can be the result of human agents bidding late on purpose, or due to the use of software agents that automatically bid on behalf of their users. For instance, eBay offer a proxy agent (eBay 2006) which places bids on behalf of the user. As long as the user's valuation hasn't been reached, the agent will keep incrementing its bid (by a very small amount) in response to the other bidders' in order to ensure a win for its user.

8.7 DOUBLE AUCTIONS

In double or two-side auctions, multiple sellers and multiple buyers participate in order to trade a commodity. These types of auction are more often used in exchanges and financial markets for trading stocks, bonds, securities, etc. The general process is as follows:

- Both buyers and sellers submit their bids.
- The bids are then ranked from highest to lowest to generate demand and supply profiles.
- From the profiles the maximum quantity exchanged can be determined by matching selling offers with demand bids.
- The transaction price is set and the market clears.

Double auctions may clear either continuously or periodically. In continuous double auctions, the buyers and sellers are matched immediately on detection of compatible bids, while in periodic ones, also known as call markets or clearing houses, bids are collected over specified intervals of time and then the market clears at the expiration of the bidding interval.

Two issues arise in double auctions: how to determine the transaction or clearing price, and the winners, i.e., the buyers and sellers who are going to transact. For instance, given the buy and sell bids of Figure 8.4, which of these are going to transact and what will be the clearing price?

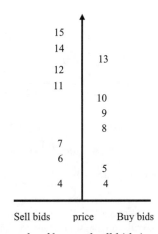

Figure 8.4: **Example of buy and sell bids in a double auction**

8.7.1 *M*th and (*M* + 1)st price rules

Consider a set of single unit bids L. M of these bids are sell offers and the remaining $N = L - M$ are buy offers. The Mth price rule sets the clearing price at the Mth highest price among all L bids. The $(M + 1)$st price rule sets the clearing price at the $(M + 1)$st highest price among all L bids. Determining the bids that are going to transact, the transaction set, proceeds as follows: while the highest remaining buy bid is greater than or equal to the lowest sell bid, remove these from the set of outstanding bids (breaking the ties arbitrarily) and add them to the set of matched bids (transaction set) (Wurman et al. 1998a).

For instance, consider the set of bids in the double auction of Figure 8.5. The number of total bids L is 13, the number of sell bids M is 7 and the number of buy bids N is 6. The Mth clearing price is the Mth bid among all submitted bids while the $(M + 1)$st price is the $(M + 1)$st bid among all bids L. In order to determine the transaction set, we successively match the highest buy bid with the lowest sell bid until we reach a state in which the buy bid is lower than the sell bid. The transaction set in the example consists of the bids $\{(13, 4), (10, 6), (9, 7)\}$. The buy bid 8 cannot transact with the sell bid 11. Why this is the case should be fairly obvious: a sell bid indicates the lowest price that

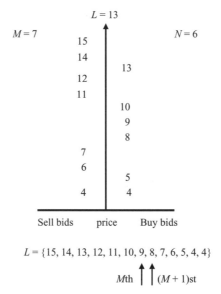

$$L = \{15, 14, 13, 12, 11, 10, 9, 8, 7, 6, 5, 4, 4\}$$

$Mth \uparrow \uparrow (M + 1)st$

Figure 8.5: Determining the Mth and $(M + 1)$st clearing prices

a seller is willing to accept in order to sell the item, whereas a buy bid indicates the maximum price that a buyer is willing to pay in order to acquire an item. Therefore, the two bids are incompatible. As a buyer is only willing to pay 8 or less and the seller is only willing to sell for 11 or more, the two bids cannot transact. The transaction price can be set either as the Mth or the $(M + 1)$st price. For instance, take the first set of bids in the transaction set (13, 4). If the Mth price ($(M + 1)$st price) is used, then the buyer will pay 9 (8) and the seller will receive 9 (8).

It turns out that the Mth and $(M + 1)$st price rules are generic rules that apply not only in double auctions, but in single auctions as well. In the English auction there is one seller and multiple buyers. The seller (auctioneer) may submit a reservation price or a bid of 0 which indicates that it is willing to sell for whatever is the highest price and, according to the rules of the auction, the bidders will start submitting successively higher bids. The Mth price in the English auction is going to be the highest bid submitted, which determines the winner. In the Dutch auction the seller starts by announcing a high price and then successively lowers it until a bidder agrees to pay that price. In this respect, as the auctioneer successively lowers the price, it essentially withdraws the old bid and submits a new one. M is 1, and this is the Mth price which is the clearing price that the bidder is willing to pay when they announce that they accept the auctioneer's bid, it is as if the bidder submits a buy bid which is equal to that of the auctioneer. In the FPSB auction, the Mth price works in exactly the same way as the English auction. The auctioneer has a reservation price, which can be 0, and the Mth price is the highest bid in the auction. In the Vickrey auction, the clearing price is defined as the $(M + 1)$st bid among all bids. Again the auctioneer can be perceived as having a bid which is the reservation price or 0, and the bidders submit bids. The winner is the bidder with the highest bid (Mth bid) but it only pays the $(M + 1)$st highest bid among all bids.

The Mth price is undefined if there are no sellers and the $(M + 1)$st price is undefined if there are no buyers. In double auctions and as there are multiple buyers and sellers, there are mechanisms that allow the agents to obtain information about the current state of the auction in terms of the submitted buy and sell bids. The price quote reveals information to the agents as to whether their bids would be in the transaction set. The bid quote is the price that a seller must offer in order to trade, that is the $(M + 1)$st price. The ask quote is the price that the buyer must offer in order to trade, that is the Mth price.

The Mth and $(M + 1)$st prices can also be used for clearing multi-unit auctions. In this case, multi-unit bids are broken down to single-unit bids and the Mth and $(M + 1)$st prices are determined as usual. Multi-unit bids can transact fully or partially, i.e., a partially transacted bid means that the quantity of the original bid could not be satisfied and the remainder of the bid (quantity that has not been matched) remains as a standing bid in the auction. The multi-unit Vickrey auction uses the Mth and $(M + 1)$st prices: the clearing price is determined as the highest losing price, in other words the $(M + 1)$st price.

8.7.2 Implementation of the Mth and $(M + 1)$st price rules

The Mth and $(M + 1)$st clearing price rules can be implemented using ordered lists. An alternative implementation based on heaps, the four-heap algorithm (Wurman et al. 1998a), was used in the AuctionBot system (Wurman et al. 1998b, see Section 8.10.1)).

The organization of the bids is based on four ordered lists (McCabe and Smith 1993). Bids are distinguished by whether they represent sell or buy bids and whether or not they are in the current transaction set:

- B_{in}: An ascending ordered list which contains all the buy bids that are in the current transaction set.
- B_{out}: A descending ordered list which contains all the buy bids that are not in the current transaction set.
- S_{in}: A descending ordered list which contains all the sell bids that are in the current transaction set.
- S_{out}: An ascending ordered list which contains all the sell bids that are not in the current transaction set.

The following constraints are also imposed (Wurman et al. 1998a):

- The number of bids in B_{in} must be equal to the number of bids in S_{in}.
- If b_{in}, b_{out}, s_{in} and s_{out} are the heads of each list, then:

— $value(b_{in}) \geq value(b_{out})$
— $value(s_{out}) \geq value(s_{in})$
— $value(s_{out}) \geq value(b_{out})$
— $value(b_{in}) \geq value(s_{in})$

The Mth price is then defined as $\min(value(s_{out}), value(b_{in}))$ and the $(M+1)$st price is defined as $\max(value(s_{in}), value(b_{out}))$. A price quote is then generated by just looking at the heads of the lists. A bid quote is just the $(M+1)$st price and an ask quote is the Mth price.

Figure 8.6 illustrates the organization of the bids in the four lists. The sell bids are on the left and the buy bids on the right. The dotted horizontal line separates the buy and sell bids into the four lists according to the Mth and $(M+1)$st prices.

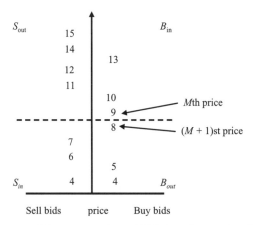

Figure 8.6: The organization of bids into four ordered lists

Insertion of a new bid

Assume that a new sell bid 5 has been submitted. The insertion of a new bid will affect the four lists and may affect the transaction set and the clearing price. The four lists now need to be adjusted as shown in Figure 8.7 (a). The pseudocode for the insertion of a new sell bid s_{new} is given below (and is similar to Wurman et al. (1998a)):

```
If ((value(s_new) <= (value(b_out)) and (value(s_in) <= (value(b_out))) then
    put(s_new, S_in);
    b_temp :=(get(B_out));
    put(b_temp, B_in);
else if (value(s_new) < value(s_in)) then
    s_temp :=(get(S_in));
    put(s_temp, S_out);
```

```
        put(s_new, S_in);
    else
        put(s_new, S_out);
```

The algorithm needs to consider three distinct cases:

1. The transaction set changes: the s_{new} bid is in the S_{in} list, but another buy bid needs to be transferred to the B_{in} list as well, as the total number of bids in S_{in} and B_{in} need to be equal.
2. The transaction set changes in that the s_{new} bid replaces one of the bids in the S_{in} list which now needs to be moved into the S_{out} list.
3. The transaction set does not change, the s_{new} bid is not in the transaction set and is placed in S_{out}.

A similar algorithm can be given for the insertion of a buy bid – this is left as an exercise to the reader.

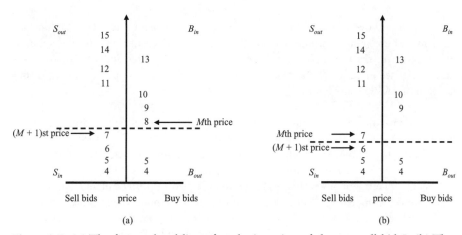

Figure 8.7: (a) The four ordered lists after the insertion of the new sell bid 5. (b) The four ordered lists after the removal of buy bid 8

Removal of a bid

Assume that the buy bid 8 is withdrawn. The four lists need to be adjusted again as shown in Figure 8.7 (b).

The process of removing a bid is, in general, as follows. The bid is located in one of the lists. If the bid is in one of the *out* lists, it is simply removed. If it is in S_{in} or B_{in}, then the top bid from the other *in* list is transferred to the corresponding *out* list. The pseudocode for the removal of a buy bid b_{old} is as follows:

If $((value(b_{old}) >= (value(b_{in}))$ **then**
 get(b_{old});
 $s_{temp} :=($**get**$(S_{in}))$;
 put(s_{temp}, S_{out});
else
 get(b_{old});

8.8 MULTI-ATTRIBUTE AUCTIONS

The auctions that were described in the previous sections enable negotiation between sellers and buyers along a single dimension, usually price. However, often buyers and sellers are interested in other attributes of an item, apart from its price. For instance, when you negotiate the purchase of a car with your local dealer, you negotiate not only the price, but other attributes too, such as the warranty, any extras such a CD player and leather seats, or perhaps free insurance cover for a year.

Auctions that allow bidders to submit bids on more than one attributes or dimensions of an item are called multi-attribute auctions (Bichler 2001). Such auctions are very common in procurement situations (Sun and Sadeh 2004). The attributes under negotiation are usually defined in advance, and bidders can compete either in an open-cry or sealed-bid auction on multiple attributes.

Consider the following example. A manufacturer assembles PCs by putting together motherboards, CPUs, hard disks, etc., which it purchases from a number of suppliers. There may be a number of suppliers that supply motherboards, for instance. The manufacturer sends a request for quote (RFQ) to the suppliers asking them to submit offers on a quantity of motherboards that it requires, say 1000. The manufacturer is not only interested in getting a good deal from one of the suppliers, but is also interested in the delivery date offered by the supplier. The delivery date may be crucial to the manufacturer, as if it does not have the right components on time, it will not be in a position to manufacture PCs to cover an existing order from a customer. If the production is delayed, the order to the customer may not be ready on time which may mean a loss in revenue as the manufacturer may be penalized for delaying delivery, or loss in reputation. So both price and delivery date matter to the manufacturer when it makes a decision who to buy from. Each of these attributes will have a weight connected to it that indicates the significance of the attribute that the manufacturer assigns and then uses in making a decision. If the suppliers return offers (bids) in response to the manufacturer's RFQs which include the full quantity that it has requested, then the manufacturer only has to take into consideration the values of the attributes in the suppliers' offers and make a decision which maximizes its profit (in this case minimizing costs which include production costs, penalties, loss of reputation). If the manufacturer buys from only one supplier, this is called *sole sourcing*. However, it may be the case that no single supplier can cover the entire quantity requested by the manufacturer. As a result, an additional attribute will be returned, namely quantity, as part of the suppliers' bids. This further complicates things as now the manufacturer cannot consider the suppliers' bids (offers) on their own, but has to do so in combination in order to cover its demand. This is called *multiple sourcing*.

Mechanism designers for multi-attribute auctions are faced with a number of problems in determining the winner for such auctions, also known as the *winner determination problem*. First of all, eliciting the buyer preferences, in our case the manufacturer's, and consequently the construction of an appropriate *scoring function* is of pivotal importance. If there are I bids offered by suppliers involving J attributes, each attribute $j \in J$ can take values from an attribute space K_j. A multi-attribute offer received by the buyer can then be described as an n-dimensional vector $\mathbf{v}_i = (v_{i1} \ldots v_{ij})$ where v_{ij} is the level of attribute j. The buyer evaluates each relevant attribute v_{ij} through a scoring function $S_j(v_{ij})$. The overall value $S(\mathbf{v}_i)$ for a bid $\mathbf{v}_i$ is given by the sum of all individual scorings of the attributes, that is $S(\mathbf{v}_i)$ is an additive scoring function. Most of the times $S(\mathbf{v}_i)$ and each of the single-attribute utility functions are scaled from zero to one. Thus:

$$s_i = S(\mathbf{v}_i) = \sum_{j \in J} w_j S_j(v_{ij}) \text{ and } \sum_{j \in J} w_j = 1$$

The problem a buyer faces is to determine appropriate scoring functions and weights. The scoring function serves as a guideline for the bidders-suppliers. The winning bid or bids are the ones with the highest score. An optimal auction allocates the deal to the suppliers in a way that maximizes the utility for the buyer-manufacturer, i.e., the supplier providing the bid with the highest overall utility score for the buyer. The fact that attributes may be complementary or substitutable, further complicates preference elicitation. In such cases, an additive utility function does not suffice to express attribute interdependencies and alternatively the scoring function can be expressed via a multi-linear expression. For two attributes x and y the multi-linear expression would take the form:

$$S(x, y) = w_x S_x(x) + w_y S_y(y) + (1 - w_x - w_y)S_x(x)S_y(y)$$

According to Keeney and Raiffa (1993) the sign of the coefficient $(1 - w_x - w_y)$ indicates the relationship between the two attributes x and y. A positive coefficient means that the two attributes complement each other and therefore the overall utility for the pair increases, while a negative coefficient means that the two attributes are substitutes.

Another factor that complicates the winner determination problem is allowing for multiple winners, namely multiple sourcing (Bichler and Kalagnanam 2005). Clearly, buyers would like to minimize the risk emanating from sourcing from too few suppliers, since some of them may not be able to deliver on time due to unexpected difficulties, thus leaving them exposed. However, sourcing from too many suppliers requires managing a large number of supplier relationships, which results in high overhead costs. Consequently, the issue of multiple sourcing requires careful consideration. Constraints on the minimum N_{min}, and maximum N_{max}, number of winning suppliers in the solution to the winner determination problem can be introduced.

Multi-attribute auctions have been envisioned to extend the scope of auctions beyond the dimension of price to take into account additional qualitative attributes. This process allows more degrees of freedom for bidders in specifying their bids, while at the same time it allows for an efficient information exchange among the market participants. Such auction formats are currently the subject of research and experimentation.

8.9 COMBINATORIAL AUCTIONS

The auction formats described so far allow a bidder to express preferences and submit a bid with respect to one item. But it is often the case that goods are only of value to bidders in combination and not when sold separately. So buyers and sellers may have preferences not only for a particular commodity, but for packages or bundles of commodities. By allowing bidders to bid on combinations of different commodities, the efficiency of the negotiation process can be enhanced. Such auctions are called combinatorial or combinational auctions.

Consider the following example. Suppose agent A is interested in auctioning off one three-seater sofa, one two-seater sofa, two armchairs and a coffee table. Is it better to auction the entire set as one commodity, or run individual auctions for every item – five auctions in total. Of course, in answering this question, one has to think of what the bidders – the potential buyers – are interested in. If the bidders are interested in acquiring the entire set, then grouping together all items and auctioning the set as one item is the most preferred option. However, there may be buyers that are not interested in buying both sofas or the armchairs. Some of them would like to have the three-seater sofa and the armchairs, others the table and both sofas, and a few the two-seater sofa, the armchairs and the table. Yet there are other bidders who do not like the table at all, but would like to buy the sofas and the armchairs. In this case it is not obvious what to do. Clearly, as a rational agent, A would like to maximize the revenue from the set of goods. The issue in this situation is that bidders have preferences over combinations of goods and goods may be complementary or substitutable.

A could run sequential auctions whereby one item is auctioned after the other. From the bidder's perspective, it is extremely difficult to determine the best strategy as the game tree is huge. Moreover, in such auctions, inefficiencies can result from future uncertainties as the bidders have to guess what the prices will be in future auctions. Also, it is impossible for bidders to switch back to an earlier item, if the prices increase in a subsequent auction. Bidders may regret buying either too early or too late, depending on the price fluctuations. Thus, speculating about future auction prices results in complex strategies, while the ensuing outcomes may not be efficient.

A could run simultaneous auctions, i.e., all goods are auctioned in auctions which run in parallel. But it is very difficult to keep track of several simultaneous auctions with substitutable and complementary goods. Although bidders obtain more information about the prices of the goods as the auctions proceed, inefficiencies can still result from future uncertainties.

To resolve the issues that arise in sequential and simultaneous auctions, an alternative solution is to allow bidders to bid on combinations of goods instead of bidding on individual items. Designers of combinatorial auction mechanisms are faced with a number of choices:

- Should the combinations of commodities on which bids are allowed be restricted? If so, to what?
- How many rounds of bidding should the auction involve, one or multiple?
- In single-round auctions how should the bundles be allocated as a function of the bids and what should the payment rules be?
- If multiple rounds are to be conducted, namely iterative combinatorial auctions (Parkes and Ungar 2000, Parkes 2006), what information should be made available to bidders from round to round?

In particular, iterative auctions can be distinguished into *quantity setting* and *price setting* (de Vries and Vohra 2003). In quantity-setting iterative auctions, the bidders submit their prices on various bundles on each round. On receiving the bids, the auctioneer makes a provisional allocation based on the submitted prices. Subsequently, bidders are allowed to adjust their bids and the auction continues. In such auctions, the auctioneer sets the allocation or quantity in response to the prices submitted by the bidders. However, quantity-setting auctions are harder to analyze as they offer more freedom to the bidders in terms of the bids that they can submit.

In price-setting iterative auctions, the auctioneer sets the price and the bidders announce which bundles they want at the posted prices. The auctioneer receives the bids and adjusts the prices. This price adjustment is therefore driven by the need to balance supply and demand. These auctions are easier to analyze than the first class, as the bidders are restricted to announcing which bundles meet their needs at the posted prices.

Iterative auctions have certain advantages over single-shot auctions. First, the bidders do not have to specify their bids for every possible combination in advance. Second, such methods are suited to dynamic environments where bidders and goods arrive and depart at different times. Third, in certain settings some bidders may have private information, albeit relevant to other bidders, and iterative auctions with appropriate feedback mechanisms allow that information to be disclosed to other bidders.

A fundamental role on deciding these aspects of the protocol is played by the auctioneer. What is the auctioneer's objective: to maximize revenue from the auction or economic efficiency? Furthermore, speed, practicality, effectiveness, the cost of communicating bids, the bidders' preferences, the need to encourage competition among bidders and discourage collusion, also play important roles.

The auction designer is faced with three crucial problems which are difficult to solve in the context of combinatorial auctions. The first fundamental problem has to do with the complexity of communicating bids (Andersson et al. 2000). As bidders are allowed to submit bids on combinations of goods, each bidder may have to determine a bid for every bundle in which they are interested. In theory, a bidder may be interested in every possible combination of goods. But, in practice, they will only submit bids on a limited number of combinations (bundles) due to resource and computational restrictions in calculating bids for every possible combination. Having decided the bundles to bid on, the next related issue to bid expression is to communicate this, which is essentially a list of bids, to the auctioneer, in such a way that it is actually useful to the auctioneer from a computational point of view. The auctioneer may specify the language that the bidders need to use in order to express their bids. There are different ways in which bids can be restricted (Nisan 1999). One such method is to restrict the bundles, i.e., combinations of goods, on which the bidders can bid (Rothkopf et al. 1998, Pekec and Rothkopf 2003).

Assuming that a satisfactory solution has been found to the first problem, and the bidders managed to communicate their bids to the auctioneer, the second fundamental problem a designer has to solve is that of identifying which collection of bids to accept so as to optimize a criterion, i.e. revenue maximization or economic efficiency. The winner determination problem for combinatorial auctions is usually referred to as the Combinatorial Auction Problem (CAP). How to resolve this problem efficiently and effectively is still an open issue (Parkes 2001). The formalization of CAP is usually in terms of an integer program. One of the difficulties in determining the winners in a combinatorial auction is that there is no guarantee that the winning bids for such an auction can be found in a 'reasonable' amount of time, especially when the number of bidders and goods increases.

The third problem is inherently related to the solutions provided to the first two problems; namely, what are their incentive implications. For instance, assume that the criterion used for allocating the goods to bidders is to maximize the seller's revenue. This revenue depends on the bids submitted, but there is no guarantee that the submitted bids represent or approximate the bidders true valuations of the goods. Thus, the solutions and choices made for the first two problems need to provide an incentive to the bidders to reveal their true valuations.

Although combinatorial auctions are the focus of intense research (de Vries and Vohra 2003, Nisan 1999, 2000, Nisan and Ronen 2001, Pekec and Rothkopf 2003), they are not very common in practice. This has partly to do with the aforementioned problems regarding efficient and computationally tractable mechanism design for such auctions, and partly with the fact that such auctions are cognitively complex and therefore difficult to comprehend.

8.10 AUCTION PLATFORMS

The following sections briefly present two experimental online auction platforms, introduce the Trading Agent Competition and discuss the use of online auctions today.

8.10.1 AuctionBot

The AuctionBot system was implemented by researchers at the University of Michigan as a tool to support research into auctions and mechanism design (Wurman et al. 1998b). AuctionBot was a flexible, scalable, robust auction server capable of supporting both human and software agents. Its architecture is illustrated in Figure 8.8.

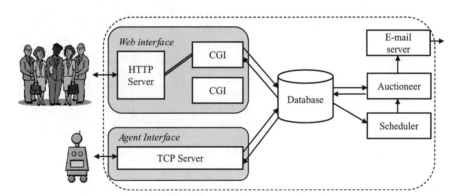

Figure 8.8: The architecture of AuctionBot

The AuctionBot system included a Web interface that allowed human agents to create, monitor and participate in auctions via web forms. The second component was a TCP/IP interface that allowed artificial software agents to connect and participate in auctions. The database was used to store the bids submitted by both human and artificial agents. The scheduler which was a daemon process was used to continually monitor the database for auctions that had events to process or bids to verify. An auctioneer process would load the auction parameters and the set of current bids from the database and would then validate bids as necessary and could do one clear and/or one price quote each time it run.

A number of auctions were implemented and the system was capable of running many auctions simultaneously. These auctions could be parameterized, offering great flexibility. Participation in auctions for trading discrete goods could be on the following basis: {1 seller: many buyers}, {many sellers :1 buyer}, {many buyers: many sellers}. The system would reveal information by providing a price quote which could be a either a bid or an ask quote. There was the option of revealing the transaction history and auctions could publish information about past transactions. The auctions' closing time and the timing of clear and/or quote events were among the parameters that could be determined.

The Mth and $(M + 1)$st price rules were used as the basis for all auctions. In particular, the implementation of the Mth and $(M + 1)$st rules was based on the four-heap algorithm (Wurman et al. 1998a). AuctionBot was used as the underlying platform for the design and implementation of the travelling agent scenario game that was used for the first three years of the Trading Agent Competition (TAC) event (TAC 2006).

8.10.2 e-Game

The *electronic Generic auction marketplace* (e-Game) is a configurable auction server that supports the design and development of auction-based market simulations and trading games (Fasli and Michalakopoulos 2004).

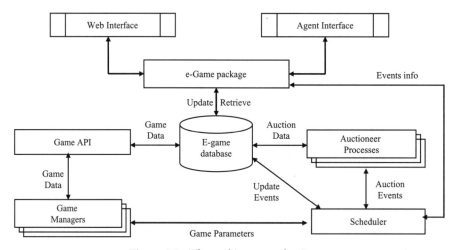

Figure 8.9: The architecture of e-Game

e-Game is based on a modular architecture separating the interface layer from the data processing modules and the database (Figure 8.9). It is designed to allow for both web users and software agents to participate and, as such, has two interfaces to the outer world: the *Web* and the *Agent* interfaces similarly to AuctionBot. The *Agent* interface provides agent developers the same functionality with the *Web* interface with respect to auctions, plus an additional set of commands for participating in market games. Agents connect to the *Agent* Interface using the TCP protocol and submit their commands using a simple string format which complies with the syntax of the HTTP query string: (command: parameter1 = value1\&..parameterN = valueN). This facilitates participation in individual auctions as well as auction-based market scenarios. Such commands allow agents for instance, to retrieve information about an auction such as startup and closing time to submit bids to auctions or to obtain information about the state of a submitted bid.

The database is used to model the auction space (parameters such as auction type, startup, closing time, clearing rules), as well as the user data (registration, user bids, auctions the user created). It also stores information regarding games (which game started which auctions, ids of players, scores).

The *Scheduler* runs in parallel with the *Web* and the *Agent* interfaces and is responsible for starting up auctions, games and passing bids to the appropriate *Auctioneer* processes which implement the various auction protocols. The auctions can be scheduled by web users or by a specific *GameManager* handler according to a market scenario's rules, while games are scheduled by web users. The *Scheduler* provides a fault-tolerant behaviour, since if it is brought off-line for some reason, when it is restarted it can reconstruct its lists of events by looking into the database for pending events.

Currently e-Game supports the English, Vickrey, FPSB, Dutch, Continuous Single Seller, and Double auction formats. These basic formats can be further refined by allowing the user to define additional parameters that include the price quote calculation, intermediate clearings and the information revelation policy. Such a parameterization can have an effect on the users' or agents' behaviour, since they modify the basic functionality of an auction as well as change the amount of information being revealed regarding bids and closing time. For instance, to achieve a chronological order clearing in an auction, one can set the intermediate clearing periods to be as soon as a bid is received and thus the parameterized auctioneer will attempt to perform intermediate clearings upon the arrival of a new bid. As in classical chronological matching, if a portion of the bid cannot transact, then it remains as a standing offer to buy (or sell).

The implementation of all auctions is based on the Mth and $(M + 1)$st price-clearing rules and uses ordered lists.

Apart from the support for agents and web users regarding auction operations, e-Game's main feature is that it supports the design and development of auction-based market simulations and trading games analogous to those of the Trading Agent Competition (TAC 2006). The need to build simulated marketplaces is two-fold. First, testing trading agents and strategies in real-life complex marketplaces is difficult, impractical and carries high risks. One approach to this problem is to run simulated market scenarios and test one's bidding strategies. Second, designing and implementing electronic markets is a complex and intricate process (Neumann and Weinhardt 2002). Not all negotiation protocols may be appropriate for a given situation. Again, simulated marketplaces may offer the only way to actually approach this problem in a systematic way. Guided first by theory and following a detailed analysis of a given domain, one can proceed to choose appropriate negotiation protocols and then design and implement a marketplace and finally experiment to verify the appropriateness of the protocols used.

Arguably, one of the first attempts to construct and experiment with an agent-based financial market framework is the Santa Fe Artificial Stock Market Model (Arthur et al. 1997, LeBaron et al. 1999). Other approaches to electronic marketplaces and financial exchange systems include Kasbah (Chavez and Maes 1996), MAGMA (Tsvetovatyy et al. 1997) the Agent Trade Server (Lybäck and Boman 2004), the Fishmarket (Rodríguez et al. 1997) and MASFIT (Cuní et al. 2004).

8.10.3 Trading agent competition

The Trading Agent Competition is a non-profitable organization the aim of which is to promote research into trading agents and electronic markets. The purpose of the competition is to stimulate research in trading agents and market mechanisms by providing a platform for agents competing in well-defined market games with an emphasis on developing successful strategies for maximizing profit in constrained environments. The competition has been running since 2000 and for the first three years it was based on the AuctionBot infrastructure. Since 2003, the underlying infrastructure for the games and the competition has been provided by a team of researchers at the Swedish Institute of Computer Science (SICS). Currently, there are two games that are part of the competition: the travelling agent game and the more recent (introduced in 2003) supply chain management game[3].

The market-based scenario featured in TAC travel is that of a travel agent who has to assemble travel packages for a number of clients. Although constructing an agent to take part in an auction for a single item is relatively simple, developing an agent to participate in simultaneous auctions offering complementary and substitutable goods, is a complex task. This is the form of the problem that agents face in the TAC travelling game.

The second game simulates a supply chain management (SCM) environment. Traditional SCM deals with the activities within an organization that range from procuring raw materials and manufacturing, to negotiating with customers and acquiring orders from them, and then delivering finished products. In today's highly interconnected and networked world, more and more businesses and organizations choose to do business online. This is a dynamic environment where manufacturers may negotiate with suppliers on the one hand, and at the same time compete for customer orders and have to arrange their production schedule and delivery so that customer orders are delivered on time.

---

[3] At the time of writing a new game was being developed.

The ability to respond to changes as they occur and adapt to variations in customer demand and the restrictions as imposed by procurement, is of paramount importance. This is the kind of environment to which agent technology is best suited. The TAC supply chain management game was designed to capture many of the dynamics of such an environment. The interested reader can find more details about TAC and the market games in (TAC 2006).

8.10.4 Online auctions

Several auction sites have sprung up in the last decade such as eBay (eBay 2006) and onSale (onSale 2006) among others. Such sites allow for consumer-to-consumer (C2C) and business-to-consumer (B2C) interactions respectively, in which the negotiation protocols used are auctions. A wide range of products can be purchased in such auction sites, ranging from holidays to computer spare parts. On the other hand, auctions are being used in business-to-business (B2B) commerce too. For instance, Ariba with its FreeMarkets (FreeMarkets 2006) provides the underlying technology for running auctions for its members.

By far the most successful application of auctions online has been in C2C negotiations. With the advent of the World Wide Web and the wider accessibility to the Internet, C2C auction sites have been very successful, allowing the trading of thousands of items every day and reporting multi-billion dollars worth of transactions every year. Their success is due to the simplicity of the rules that they employ and the fact that they allow fairly secure trading among participants through a variety of mechanisms, for instance eBay offers the PayPal and the standard purchase-protection program, as well as a reputation system to guide the participants in choosing their trading partners (eBay 2006). However, the popularity and success of these sites can be mainly attributed to the fact that they have allowed millions of people with no specialist knowledge of negotiation protocols and strategies to exchange both ordinary goods and more exclusive ones, on a scale never before possible or imaginable.

Attempts to automate the bidding process in auctions so far have been quite limited. Auctions running on eBay can last several days and it is rather inconvenient for users to monitor their bids twenty four hours a day, and let us not forget the time difference involved in some cases, which further complicates things for users. eBay have introduced proxy bidding to make this process more convenient and less time-consuming for buyers. The user enters the maximum amount she would be willing to pay for an item, which is kept confidential from the other bidders and the seller. The eBay system then compares that maximum bid to those of the other bidders. The system places bids on behalf of the bidder by proxy by using only as much of their bid as is necessary to maintain their high bid position (or to meet the reservation price). The system will only bid up to the maximum amount entered by a bidder. Obviously, if another bidder has a higher maximum, then the bidder by proxy would be outbid. But if no other bidder submits a higher bid, then the proxy bidder will win the item. Although simple, this is an attempt to use an agent to bid on behalf of the user. The advantages are that the user does not have to constantly be online checking the status of the auction and her bid. The way that the proxy agent works is an example of a Vickrey auction: each user reveals to her bidding agent the maximum price she is willing to pay. In theory, the participant who enters the highest bid will win, but she will only have to pay the second-highest price plus a minimal bid increment to break the tie. In this case, each bidder has an incentive to enter her true valuation as the maximum bid.

In online auctions, however, it is quite often the case that bidders may wait until the auction is about to close in order to submit their bids, this is known as sniping. Buyers do not want to reveal interest too early in the auction process as they do not want to drive prices high too quickly and hope to get a bargain in an auction with few participants. Sniping can also be the result of the use of a proxy agent: if other bidders raise their bids, the proxy agent will keep up with these by slightly increasing its bid until the user's reservation price is reached.

8.11 ISSUES IN PRACTICAL AUCTION DESIGN

Apart from their use in C2C, B2B and B2B commerce, auctions have been used in other situations such, for instance, for privatizing government-owned companies or other goods and services, such as 3G mobile phone licences. In all these cases auction protocols were used, as they were deemed appropriate for generating interest and competition among participants and they were expected to yield an efficient outcome. But, in practice, there were occasions where auctions were not used successfully and this was down to flawed design (Klemperer 2004).

Mechanism design is the development of protocols governing strategic interaction among self-interested agents. Negotiation protocols need to be stable and individual rational as well as to satisfy a number of other criteria, as we saw in Section 8.2. The problem that a mechanism designer faces is to design protocols that will enable the privately-known preferences of a set of self-interested agents to be aggregated towards an efficient outcome. This is a nontrivial problem as individual agents need to be provided with incentives to reveal their true preferences. Otherwise, if they can benefit from lying, they will do so. The issue of mechanism design will be considered and analyzed from a theoretical perspective in Chapter 10, but in this section, some of the potential pitfalls of practical auction design will be considered.

As a general rule, the choice of an auction protocol depends on the underlying circumstances in which it will be deployed. The details of a particular situation, the number of goods, bidders, the nature of the goods, the structure of the market and a number of other factors can affect the outcome of an auction, so the choice of protocol must be considered very carefully.

There are a number of issues in practical auction design (Klemperer 2004):

- **Collusive behaviour.** Participants in an auction may explicitly or implicitly collude and keep prices artificially low, thus leading to a less than efficient outcome. Bidders can collude and form an auction ring, as we saw previously. But collusion may consist not only of explicit agreements among participants, but also implicit ones. For instance, in multi-unit auctions, collusion may consist of implicit understanding about which bidder is allowed to win any particular auction. One bidder may signal to another their intentions, for instance, by changing the last digit of their price offer to the auctioneer. In 1996–97 in a multi-licence spectrum auction in the US, two companies, US West and McLeod, were competing fiercely for a licence with lot number 378 in Rochester, Minnesota. Most bids in the auction were in exact thousands of dollars. Then US West bid $313378 and $62378 for two licences in Iowa in which it had shown no prior interest, overbidding McLeod who until that point seemed to be the highest bidder for both of these licences. McLeod understood the implicit message that it was being punished for competing for the Rochester licence and as a result it dropped out of that auction. Thus, the two firms arrived at a tacit agreement on who was going to get which licence. Such behaviour cannot be easily challenged legally because it may be difficult to prove collusion, but also due to the legal costs involved. Nevertheless, agreement among the ring has to be self-enforcing. As we have seen, the Vickrey and the English auctions are more prone to rings than the FPSB and Dutch auctions.

- **Entry deterrence and predatory behaviour.** An auction needs to attract bidders, as an auction with too few bidders risks being unprofitable for the auctioneer. Aggressive bidders may actively drive weaker bidders out of the auction. Strong competitors may be known in advance or bidders may drive prices high quickly in order to establish a reputation for being aggressive and deter other potential participants from entering the auction. This effect is more serious in open ascending auctions as each bidder can observe the other's bids. In sealed-bid auctions, weaker bidders have at least some chance of winning and so potential participants are more likely to enter. In some cases, bidders have been known to openly declare their willingness to win an auction at all costs or even threaten weaker participants to stay out of the market. When the pharmaceutical giant Glaxo was bidding to take over another firm Wellcome, they made it clear that they would almost certainly outbid any other rival (Klemperer 2004). Nevertheless, precautions need to be taken at the design stage in order to facilitate and encourage new participants to enter and, thus, increase competition which will potentially lead to more efficient outcomes.

- **Reservation prices.** Failure to set a proper reservation price, i.e., a minimum amount which the winner is required to pay, can be catastrophic. Inadequate reserves may even encourage collusion among participants. In particular, a strong bidder in an English auction can either implicitly collude to end the auction at a low price, or force the price up to drive out weaker bidders. The lower the reservation price at which the auction can be concluded, the more attractive collusion will be. When the Swiss government auctioned four 3G licences, they set the reservation price at only one-thirtieth of the per capita revenue that was raised by similar auctions in Germany and the UK. In combination with the auction format used, which deterred weaker bidders from entering, only four participants entered the competition for the four licences. As a bidder was only allowed to acquire one licence, the sale price was determined by the reservation price, which had been set too low.

- **Political problems**. The setting of adequate reservation prices is often opposed by government officials for whom the worst outcome is that the reservation price is not met and therefore the object is not sold. As this is regarded as failure, sometimes officials would rather sell off the commodity under auction, even below its market price.

- **Loopholes**. The terms and conditions that apply to a negotiation situation need to be carefully scrutinized for possible loopholes that could lead to potentially undesirable outcomes. For instance, in an Australian auction for satellite-television licences, two bidders submitted considerably high sealed bids. But subsequently the bidders defaulted on their bids. The problem in this case was that the terms and conditions of participation in the auction did not include a clause regarding defaulting and any penalties for doing so.

- **Credibility of rules**. Whatever rules, terms and conditions one sets out to impose regarding the conduct of the negotiations, they need to be credible. There is no point in threatening that action will be taken against participants deviating from the prescribed rules, if one has no intention of upholding them in the end. This can only damage the reputation of the auction and the institution (government, organization, business, etc.) conducting the auction.

The dilemma in which designers often find themselves is which auction to use: an English or a sealed-bid one. An ascending-price auction allows for collusion, entry deterrence, and predation, but it is likely to achieve an efficient outcome as it encourages more competition. It is also likely that the bidder who has the highest valuation of the item will win the auction, although they will not necessarily pay their true valuation. A sealed-bid auction may prevent collusion and it allows entry of weaker bidders, but leaves open the possibility of an inefficient outcome as bidders tend to underbid.

One potential solution to this problem that has been proposed is to combine the two into what is known as the Anglo-Dutch auction (Klemperer 1998). The Anglo-Dutch auction works as follows. The auctioneer first runs an English auction in which the price is raised continuously until all but two (or n) bidders have dropped out. The remaining bidders are then required to make a final sealed-bid offer that is no lower than the current asking price, and the winner pays their bid. The advantages of this modified format are that, in the first stage of the auction (English), there is less loss of efficiency than might result from running a pure sealed-bid auction. The use of a sealed-bid process at the final stage induces some uncertainty about which of the finalists will win. As a result, weaker entrants may be attracted by the possibility of making it to the final stage.

Other concerns have been raised with regard to using auctions as the protocol of choice for conducting negotiations. One of the most commonly voiced objections has to do with the price effects that auctions may generate. In particular, it is a common fear that a firm's costs of participating in an auction will be passed on to consumers in the form of higher prices. But the prices that firms charge are dictated by the market and they aim at maximizing their profits, which is independent of the auction fees that they incurred at the time of an auction. Moreover, firms usually make lump-sum payments and not royalties. But firms may convince regulators into believing that an auction is a reason for allowing artificially high prices. The second major objection to auctions concerns the potential investment effects. The argument is that large auction fees may slow investment because of capital constraints. This is theoretically possible, as a firm's cash flow can be significantly affected by upfront payments to the auctioneer, government or other organization. But practically, it is unlikely that many profitable investments are being delayed or missed because of cash being put aside for auction payments. For instance, within one year, four of the five winners of the UK 3G licences had arranged the necessary funding for their new networks (Klemperer 2004).

8.12 Further Reading

The abstract architecture for negotiating agents is based on Ashri et al. (2003) and Rahwan et al. (2003), though the architecture presented here also identifies the major components of negotiating agents.

There are a number of technical and nontechnical readings on auctions. A brief introduction is given in Varian (2006, Chapter 17), while Agorics (2006) provides an informal introduction to the basic auction formats and their advantages and disadvantages. More advanced and technical expositions include Krishna (2002), Menezes and Monteiro (2005) and Milgrom (2002). These texts also describe the strategic equivalence between the FPSB and the Dutch auctions, as well as the revenue equivalence and nonequivalence theorems for single-side auctions in more technical terms. For the reader interested in auctions, the seminal work of Myerson (1981), on the design of optimal auctions, is recommended. Other essential references on optimal auction design are: Riley and Samuelson (1981) and Bulow and Roberts (1989). A good collection of papers which includes a survey on auction theory and a discussion of auctions in practice is Klemperer (2004). The discussion on the issues in practical auction design draws heavily on Klemperer (2004). An interesting discussion on the design of the UK 3G mobile phone licence auctions is found in Binmore and Klemperer (2002). Another good article on auctions is McAfee and McMillan (1987). An approach to formalizing auctions as trading institutions is described in Esteva et al. (2001b).

The parameterization of the auction design space is discussed in detail in Wurman et al. (2001). Double auctions and the Mth and $(M + 1)$st clearing prices along with an incentive analysis and the four-heap algorithm are described in Wurman et al. (1998a). Advanced readings in double auctions can be found in Friedman and Rust (1993).

A good book on multi-attribute auctions and related issues is Bichler (2001), while the winner determination problem in such auctions is discussed in Bichler and Kalagnanam (2005). Issues around suitable bidding languages for multi-attribute auctions are discussed in Bichler and Kalagnanam (2006). The recently published volume of papers edited by Crampton et al. (2006) contains a discussion of current topics in combinatorial auctions. Iterative combinatorial auctions are discussed in detail in Parkes (2001) and an algorithm for single-side ascending combinatorial auctions is provided in Parkes (1999).

More information on the Trading Agent Competition and the market games can be found at the official site (TAC 2006), while a collection of papers describing various approaches to designing and implementing trading agents and strategies is available at the TAC Reports site (TAC Reports 2006).

8.13 Exercises and Topics for Discussion

1. Prove that the Bayesian Nash equilibrium in the Dutch auction is for the bidder to bid: $b_i(v_i) = v_i(N - 1)/N$, when there are $N \geq 2$ bidders, and each bidder's value is seen as uniformly distributed.

2. Prove that the Bayesian Nash equilibrium in the First-Price Sealed-Bid (FPSB) auction is for the bidder to bid: $b_i(v_i) = v_i(N - 1)/N$, when there are $N \geq 2$ bidders, and each bidder's value is seen as uniformly distributed.

3. Assume the sell bids $M = \{14, 13, 11, 10, 6, 4, 3\}$ and the buy bids $N = \{12, 9, 8, 4, 3, 2\}$.
   (a) What are the Mth and $(M + 1)$st clearing prices?
   (b) What is the transaction set?
   (c) Identify the content of the four lists $(B_{in}, B_{out}, S_{in}, S_{out})$.
   (d) A sell bid of 7 is inserted. Identify the new Mth clearing price and the new transaction set. Adjust the four lists.
   (e) The sell bid 5 is inserted. Identify the new Mth clearing price and the new transaction set. Adjust the four lists.

(f) The buy bid 11 is inserted. Identify the new Mth clearing price and the new transaction set. Adjust the four lists.

(g) The sell bid 6 is withdrawn. Identify the new Mth clearing price and the new transaction set. Adjust the four lists.

4. In village A the main occupation of the residents is cultivating the land and producing vegetables and fruits. In an attempt to boost the farmers' income and streamline the distribution of the produce to potential buyers, the local union is considering creating a local marketplace where the farmers could sell their produce. The idea is that local restaurants, shops, supermarkets, etc., would be able to visit the marketplace and buy produce directly from the farmers. Describe an auction protocol, that would help individual farmers to achieve the best prices and that takes into consideration the following restrictions: each farmer may have more than one variety of vegetables to sell, the vegetables are in different quantities and, finally, vegetables need to be sold as soon as possible. What are the possible risks (if any), if the protocol you have suggested is adopted?

5. As part of their final-year project, the students in the Art Department of College A have to create a work of art which can be a painting or a sculpture. These works are stored in the College's storerooms. The College has decided to sell these works, and all proceedings of the sale will go to charity. The students have already been contacted and consented to this. The College has employed you as a consultant and they have asked you to suggest a negotiation protocol that will first maximize revenue from the sales, and second will sell all the works of art. Describe a negotiation protocol that would help the College in this situation. What are the possible risks and problems (if any), if the protocol you have suggested is to be adopted?

6. Assume the sell bids $M = \{15, 14, 13, 12, 11, 10, 9, 8, 4, 3\}$ and the buy bids $N = \{12, 11, 10, 7, 6, 5, 3, 2, 1\}$.

(a) Indicate the Mth price and the transaction set for this set of bids.

(b) Identify the content of the four lists.

(c) Remove the buy bid 3. Adjust the four lists and indicate the Mth price.

(d) Insert the sell bid 7. Adjust the four lists and indicate the Mth price.

7. Describe using pseudo-code, as in Section 8.7.2, the part of the algorithm for the insertion of a new buy bid. Identify the individual cases that the algorithm needs to consider.

8. Write a program in your favourite programming language that takes as input a list of buy bids and a list of sell bids and returns the Mth and $(M + 1)$st prices, the transaction set, as well as the contents of the four lists $(B_{in}, B_{out}, S_{in}, S_{out})$.

9. Based on the previous exercise, write a program which can take as input any number of bids. Buy bids should be indicated as positive numbers, whereas sell bids should be indicated as negative numbers. On receipt of a new bid, the program should return the current Mth and $(M + 1)$st prices, the transaction set, as well as the contents of the four lists $(B_{in}, B_{out}, S_{in}, S_{out})$.

10. Modify the program developed in the previous exercise, so that it now displays a menu and allows the user to choose the type of auction in which to submit bids (English, Dutch, FPSB, Vickrey, Double). Upon selection, the user should be allowed to enter a number of bids for the chosen auction. On receipt of a new bid, the program should return the current Mth and $(M + 1)$st prices, the transaction set, and also the contents of the four lists $(B_{in}, B_{out}, S_{in}, S_{out})$.

11. Project idea: develop a trading agent for the Trading Agent Competition Travel game (TAC 2006). You can find out about agents that have been developed for this game at the TAC Reports site (TAC Reports 2006).

12. Project idea: develop a trading agent for the TAC Supply Chain Management Game (TAC 2006) This project can also be undertaken by a small group of students (2–4). You can find out about agents that have been developed for this game at the TAC Reports site (TAC Reports 2006).

CHAPTER 9

Negotiation II

LEARNING OBJECTIVES

After reading and completing this chapter, you should be able to:

- Describe the elements of a bargaining situation and the key factors that determine one's bargaining power.
- Discuss the two different approaches to solving bargaining problems, their underlying principles and differences.
- Explain how the strategic negotiation protocol works and its potential applications.
- Describe the characteristics of task-oriented environments and the monotonic concession protocol for such environments.
- Describe the underlying principles of coalition formation, the issue of stability and how it relates to the division of payoffs.
- Compare and contrast the different protocols that can be used for the formation of customer and supplier coalitions.
- Analyze simple scenarios and propose suitable negotiation protocols.
- Describe a social choice problem and explain the difficulties in reaching a socially acceptable outcome.
- Discuss the need for systems to be able to offer arguments and justify negotiation positions, proposals and offers.

Continuing our exploration on the use of agent technology for e-commerce, in this chapter we will discuss a number of other approaches to negotiation and reaching agreements in strategic interaction situations, including bargaining, voting and coalition formation protocols, as well as argumentation-based negotiation.

9.1 BARGAINING

When agents are in conflict over some issue, they may try to resolve this by committing themselves to a course of action that is beneficial to all of them. However, if there is more than one course of action which is more desirable than disagreement for all agents, and there is conflict over which course of action to pursue, then some form of negotiation over how to resolve the conflict is necessary. A *bargaining situation* is a situation in which two or more agents have a common interest and could reach a mutually beneficial agreement, but have a conflict of interest about which one to reach. To put it simply, the agents would like to cooperate to reach an outcome, but they have conflicting interests.

Many situations that we encounter in our everyday lives are bargaining situations. For instance, exchange situations, such as agreements on wages are often the outcome of negotiations amongst the concerned parties, i.e., employers and unions (or employees). Mergers and acquisitions require negotiations over the price at which such transactions will take place. Government policy is often a bargaining situation: whether or not a piece of legislation is passed may depend on the outcome of negotiations amongst the various political parties and the government may have to make concessions. Countries negotiate through their governments on matters ranging from trade deals to environmental issues, such as carbon emissions and the control of nuclear weapons. But even within marriage, spouses often 'bargain' over a variety of matters, e.g., who will do what in the house, who will take the children to school or do the shopping.

The essence of bargaining is that two or more agents will try to reach an agreement on a set of possible outcomes which will leave them both at least as well off as they could be if they reached no agreement. But they need to bargain because they have conflicting interests over the set of outcomes. The bargaining process is typically time consuming and involves the players making offers and counteroffers. The main focus of any theory of bargaining is on the efficiency and distribution properties of the outcome reached. Efficiency relates to the possibility that the outcome reached is not Pareto efficient, i.e., the players fail to reach an agreement, or they reach an agreement after some costly delay. For instance, an agreement over wages is reached between a union and the employer, but only after two weeks' lost production due to a strike. Distribution relates to how the gains from cooperation are divided amongst the agents.

Consider the following example. Agent A would like to sell a house and the minimum acceptable value, i.e., the reservation price, p_s is £70 000. Clearly A would like to sell

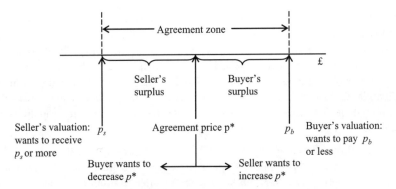

Figure 9.1: A typical bargaining situation

the house for as much as possible. On the other hand, agent B would like to buy A's house and values it at p_b £90 000. Although B values the house at that price, B would like to pay as little as possible for it. Both agents would like to reach an agreement on the transaction price of the house, rather than disagree, as A wants to sell the house, and B wants to buy it. But each agent would like the deal reached to be as favourable as possible to themselves. The situation is depicted in Figure 9.1. The two agents could settle for some price within their agreement zone, but the seller would like to move the agreement price p^* to the right, i.e., increase it, whereas the buyer would like to move p^* to the left, i.e., decrease it. The agents' reservation prices are private information. What will be the final price agreed and whether it lies on the right or left of the agreement zone depends on the agents' bargaining power.

9.1.1 Bargaining power

There are a number of key factors that determine the agents' *bargaining power* in a bargaining situation which, as a result, have an impact on the efficiency and distribution of the outcome reached (Muthoo 1999, 2000):

- **Impatience.** If the bargaining process is frictionless, that is, no agent incurs any cost from haggling, then negotiations are likely to end up in a deadlock; the outcome of a frictionless bargaining process is indeterminate. However, in real life, bargaining situations are not frictionless. At the most basic level, any bargaining process takes time and time is valuable to an agent, therefore each agent prefers to reach agreement on any particular issue sooner rather than later (i.e., today rather than tomorrow). An agent's value of time can depend on various factors such as income, wealth, or the market interest rate. For instance, a poor agent is typically more impatient than a rich one, since they are more eager to reach an agreement in order to obtain the gains from trade as soon as possible. An agent's bargaining power, namely the share of the gains from trade, is greater the more patient the agent is, relative to the other party.

- **Risk of breakdown.** In bargaining situations there is always the possibility that the negotiations might break down into disagreement because of factors out of the agent's control. A risk-neutral agent would like to minimize the risk of breakdown and is therefore more eager to make a deal. This may be exploited by the other party, if they are a less risk-neutral agent and may demand a larger share of the gains from trade. When players have the same attitude towards risk, they are both equally risk-neutral and equally patient, then they are likely to split the gains from trade equally between themselves.

- **Outside options.** When agents are bargaining, they may have outside options. In the example given earlier, if agent A is negotiating with a potential buyer B over the price of the house and already has had another offer from another buyer C, then A can use this to their own advantage and force buyer B to up their price. Thus, the more attractive are an agent's alternative outside options to a bargain, the better the negotiated outcome will be for that agent. What is referred to as the *Outside Options Principle* (OOPS) states that an outside option increases an agent's bargaining power, provided of course that it is sufficiently attractive (Muthoo 2000).

- **Inside options.** During the bargaining process, agents may derive additional utilities while they are in temporary disagreement. While A is negotiating over the price of the house, they derive an extra utility per day – inside option – from renting the house. When both agents' outside options are sufficiently unattractive, then an agent's bargaining power is higher the more attractive the inside option is for that agent, relative to that of the other agent.

- **Commitment tactics.** Often, the agents take some form of action prior to the bargaining process which commits them to some strategically chosen bargaining position. The committed agent thereby attempts to manipulate the opponent's expectations, and, inadvertently, to restrict their options. For example, in negotiations over wages between unions and employers, it is very often the case that one of the two sides will commit not to accept a deal that has certain properties, i.e., the unions will not accept a deal that is less than %x. The ability of an agent to make credible commitments – commitments that can be carried out – while the opponent cannot, means that the former has much of the bargaining power. In essence, the power to constrain an opponent depends upon the power to commit oneself (Schelling 1960).

- **Asymmetric information.** Agents may not have symmetric information when they bargain. That is, they may not have the same kind of information in order to be able to estimate the value of a deal. In negotiating with a dealer for a second-hand car, the dealer has more information than the buyer. If the car is of low quality, the dealer would have an incentive to pretend that it is of high quality and try to sell it as such. Since the buyer is aware of that incentive, the maximum price that they would be willing to pay for the car may be less than the value that the seller would place on the car if it is actually of high quality. In general, the presence of asymmetric information will lead to inefficient bargaining outcomes; either failure to reach an agreement at all, or an agreement which will be reached after some costly delay.

A bargaining solution may be interpreted as a formula which determines an outcome for a bargaining situation. There are two branches of bargaining theory: the axiomatic and the strategic. John Nash laid the foundations for both related approaches in two seminal papers (Nash 1950a, 1953).

9.1.2 Axiomatic bargaining

Axiomatic bargaining theory assumes no equilibrium. Instead, axiomatic models of bargaining yield solutions that satisfy a set of desired properties – the *axioms* of the bargaining solution.

Consider two agents, A and B, who need to divide a cake of size π. The set of possible agreements that they can reach is:

$$\mathcal{O} = \{(o_A, o_B) : 0 \leq o_A \leq \pi \text{ and } o_B = \pi - o_A\}$$

where o_i is the share of the cake for each agent $i \in [A, B]$. Their utilities from obtaining their shares o_A and o_B respectively are:

$$U_A(o_A) = u_A \text{ and } U_B(o_B) = u_B$$

If the agents fail to reach a deal, then a default solution is implemented and the agents obtain utilities (d_A, d_B). This utility pair is also called the *disagreement point*. The *Nash bargaining solution* (NBS) of this bargaining situation is the allocation of utilities (u_A, u_B) which solves the following maximization problem:

$$o^* = \max(u_A - d_A)(u_B - d_B) \text{ subject to } u_A \geq d_A \text{ and } u_B \geq d_B$$

The NBS is the only bargaining solution which satisfies the following four axioms:

1. *Pareto efficiency*: it is not feasible to give both players more utility in a solution other than the NBS.

2. *Symmetry*: if the players are identical in every respect, then the Nash-bargained utility payoffs to the players are the same.

3. *Invariance*: The agents' numeric utility functions represent ordinal preferences over outcomes, the cardinalities of the utilities do not matter. As a result, the NBS is invariant to positive affine transformations of the agents' utility functions.

4. *Independence of irrelevant alternatives*: If some outcome is removed, but o^* is not, then o^* still remains the solution. Suppose that the agents agree on the element o^* when the set $\mathcal{O}$ of possible agreements consists of o^*, o' and o'', and the disagreement outcome is d. Now consider another bargaining situation in which the agents have to agree on an element from a subset $\mathcal{O}'$ of this set $\mathcal{O}$. For example, the set of possible agreements $\mathcal{O}'$ consists of o^* and o'. Moreover, suppose the disagreement outcome is still the same, namely d. Since o^* was agreed to in the initial bargaining situation over o' and o'', and since the disagreement outcome is the same in the new bargaining situation, o^* should be agreed to over o', despite the fact that o'' is no longer available.

Outcome o'' is irrelevant. However, in some negotiation processes the outcome may be influenced by such apparently irrelevant alternatives.

Returning to the example, assume that $u_A = o_A\pi$ and $u_B = o_B\pi = (1 - o_A)\pi$. The NBS is the sharing rule (o_A, o_B) that maximizes the Nash product:

$$(o_A\pi - d_A)(o_A\pi - d_B)$$
$$\text{subject to } o_B = 1 - o_A$$

The NBS is at:

$$u_A = [\pi + d_A - d_B]/2 \text{ and } u_B = [\pi + d_B - d_A]/2$$
$$u_A = d_A + [\pi - d_A - d_B]/2 \text{ and } u_B = d_B + [\pi - d_B - d_A]/2$$

As a result, the two agents split the difference: the agents first agree to take a part of the cake equal to their d_i and then they split the remaining cake equally between themselves.

The Nash bargaining solution can be extended to more than two agents as long as the disagreement point occurs, if at least one agent disagrees.

9.1.3 Strategic bargaining

In contrast to axiomatic bargaining theory, in game-theoretic (strategic) models of bargaining, the bargaining solution emerges as the equilibrium of a sequential game in which the parties take turns in making offers and counteroffers. It follows that, for some games, the solution is not unique. Strategic bargaining theory explains the behaviour of rational utility maximizing agents better than axiomatic approaches. The latter are not based on what the agents can choose for strategies, but instead, rely on the agents pertaining to axiomatic, imposed notions of fairness.

Strategic bargaining theory usually analyzes sequential bargaining where agents make alternating offers to each other in a pre-specified order. This is intuitive, since making offers and counteroffers is what we do in a number of situations in everyday life.

Consider two agents, A and B who bargain about the partition of a cake of size π. Offers are made at discrete points in time $T = \{0, 1, 2, \ldots\}$. An offer is a number greater than or equal to zero and less than or equal to π. As the offer is made by the proposer, this intuitively describes a share of the cake for the proposer, and therefore, π minus the offer goes to the responder. At time 0, A makes an offer o_A representing their proposed share of the cake. If B accepts, the game ends. If B rejects A's offer, he gets to make a counteroffer at time Δ. This offer will specify the share o_B that B proposes to keep. If A accepts this offer, the game ends. If A rejects B's counteroffer, he can make another offer at time 2Δ and so on.

The bargaining process is not frictionless. The players are impatient in the sense that they would agree on the same deal today rather than tomorrow. Impatience is expressed

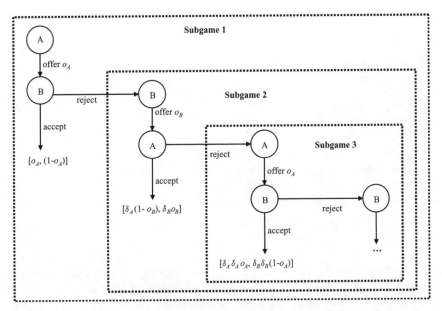

Figure 9.2: The alternating offers bargaining situation as an extensive form game

as a discount factor $\delta = \exp(-r_i\Delta)$. If the players reach agreement at time $t\Delta$ on a partition that gives $i \in [A, B]$ a share o_i $(0 \leq o_i \leq \pi)$ of the cake, then agent i's payoff is $o_i \exp(-r_i t\Delta)$ where $r_i > 0$ is agent i's discount rate. If the agents disagree, then each agent's payoff is zero. The bargaining situation can be depicted as a sequential game with subgames in extensive form as illustrated in Figure 9.2.

Theorem 3 *Rubinstein's bargaining solution. The basic alternating offers game described above has a subgame perfect Nash equilibrium outcome. Agent A gets $(1 - \delta_B)/(1 - \delta_A\delta_B)$ where δ_A is A's discount factor and δ_B is B's. Agent B gets 1 minus this. Agreement is reached in the first round.*

This unique subgame perfect Nash equilibrium satisfies two properties:

- *No delay*: whenever a player has to make an offer, the equilibrium offer is accepted by the other player.

- *Stationarity*: in equilibrium, a player makes the same offer whenever they have to make an offer.

Specifically, the following strategies define the unique subgame perfect equilibrium:

Player *A* always offers:

$$o_A^* = \frac{1 - \delta_B}{1 - \delta_A\delta_B},$$

and always accepts an offer:

$$o_B^* <= \frac{1 - \delta_A}{1 - \delta_A \delta_B}.$$

Player B always offers:

$$o_B^* = \frac{1 - \delta_A}{1 - \delta_A \delta_B},$$

and always accepts an offer:

$$o_A^* <= \frac{1 - \delta_B}{1 - \delta_A \delta_B}.$$

A detailed analysis of the proof can be found in Muthoo (1999).

9.1.4 The Strategic Negotiation Protocol

The Strategic Negotiation Protocol (SNP) (Kraus 2001) is an extension of Rubinstein's (Osborne and Rubinstein 1990) protocol of alternating offers. Assume a set of agents $A = \{a_1, \ldots, a_n\}$ who need to reach an agreement on a particular issue. They can take actions at discrete points in time $T = \{0, 1, \ldots\}$ which are determined in advance and are known to the agents. In each period $t \in T$ of the negotiation, if an agreement has not been reached in the previous stage, the agent whose turn it is to make an offer at time t suggests a potential solution. Each of the other agents responds to the offer by accepting (*Yes*), refusing (*No*), or opting out of the negotiation (*Opt*).

The SNP provides a framework for the negotiation process and specifies the termination condition, although there is no limit to the number of negotiating rounds. Moreover, the protocol does not dictate any specific strategy to the agents.

The set of possible agreements is S and an outcome which represents an agreement reached at time $t \in T$ is denoted by (s, t). *Disagreement* denotes a perpetual disagreement, that is the agents cannot agree on a solution and the negotiation continues for ever, without any of the agents opting out. If all the agents choose *Yes*, then the negotiation ends and the agreed solution is implemented. If at least one of the agents opts out, then the negotiation ends and a default conflictual solution is implemented. If no agent has opted out, but at least one has refused the offer, the negotiation proceeds to round $t + 1$ and the next agent makes a counteroffer. It is important to note that an agent who responds to an offer is not aware of the other agents' responses in the current negotiation round. This ensures that no agent has additional information when considering their own response. The agents are not bound to any previous offer that has been made. In particular, after an offer has been rejected, the agent next in line to make a counteroffer may decide to make the same offer as before or propose an entirely new one.

The SNP is underpinned by the following assumptions:

1. Rationality. The agents are self-interested and rational; they try to maximize their utilities according to their preferences.

2. Agents avoid opting out. When an agent's utility from opting out is the same as accepting an offer, then they will accept the offer.

3. Commitments are upheld. If an agreement is reached, all sides will honour it.

4. No long-term commitments. Negotiations over different issues are independent of each other. An agent cannot commit themselves to any future outcome, apart from those already agreed upon.

5. Assumptions 1–4 are common knowledge among the agents.

Agents care about possible outcomes and the utilities that they can derive from these. As in the bargaining situations described earlier, time is of the essence as *when* a deal is reached is important to the agents. The exact order of offers and counteroffers is not of importance.

Each agent $a_i \in A$ has a preference relation over all possible outcomes, which is expressed via a utility function $u_i : \{S \cup \{Opt\} \times T\} \cup \{Disagreement\} \to \mathbb{R}$. The exact nature of the utility function obviously depends on the particular domain of application. The time and other resources such as, for instance, computation for deciding on an offer or communication costs, also affect the utility of an agent. The utility functions can be divided into the following categories (Kraus 2001):

- Fixed losses/gains per time unit: $u_i(o, t) = u_i(o, 0) + tc_i$.

  The agent has a utility function with a constant cost ($c_i < 0$) or gain ($c_i > 0$) for each round. This fixed cost can represent the computation cost for computing a counteroffer, or communication costs. The fixed gain can be obtained, for instance, by consuming or using the resource under negotiation.

- Time constant discount rate: $u_i(o, t) = \delta_i^t u_i(o, 0)$ where $0 < \delta_i^t < 1$.

  Every agent i has a fixed discount rate δ_i^t.

- Financial systems with an interest rate r: $u_i(o, t) = \left(\frac{1}{1+r}\right)^t u_i(o, 0) + c \frac{1}{1+r}\left(1 - \frac{1}{1+r}^t\right)$.

  In this model a monetary system exists in which an agent is able to borrow or lend money at interest rate r. Thus, $u_i(o, t)$ is evaluated as the net present value (NPV) of the future utility of the solution computed given the interest rate r. The NPV is used in financial systems to assess the profitability of an investment or project and plan for long-term investments. The value of an investment is calculated as the difference between the present value of cash inflows and the present value of cash outflows. The interest rate r is used to discount future cash flows to their present values. The utility of agent i when outcome o is reached at time t is $u_i(o, t) = \left(\frac{1}{1+r}\right)^t u_i(o, 0)$ and the agent also bears a constant gain or loss over the course of the negotiation process determined by $c \frac{1}{1+r}\left(1 - \frac{1}{1+r}^t\right)$.

- Finite-horizon models with fixed losses per time unit: $u_i(o, t) = u_i(o, 0)(1 - t/k) - tc$ for $t \leq k$.

This utility function can be applied if it is known in advance that the outcome of the negotiation is valid for k periods and that, in the first round of the negotiation, the agent can obtain utility $u_i(o, 0)$. In addition, the agent also bears a constant loss or gain over the course of the negotiation process.

An agent's negotiation strategy specifies what the agent should do next, for each sequence of offers $s_0, s_1, \ldots s_t$. Such a strategy specifies for an agent what counteroffer to make at time t if no agreement has been reached at that point and there has been a series of offers, and also whether to choose *Yes*, *No*, or *Opt* out of the negotiation, in response to another agent's counteroffer.

To determine an agent's strategy and since the SNP protocol is based on Rubinstein's alternating offers protocol, the concept of subgame perfect Nash equilibrium applies. A strategy profile, i.e., a collection of strategies, one for each agent, is a subgame perfect equilibrium of a model of alternating offers if the strategy profile induced at every subgame is a Nash equilibrium of that subgame. Thus, at any point during the negotiation process, no agent has an incentive to deviate from the strategy described in the strategy profile.

The SNP protocol is particularly useful in situations where:

- the agents cannot agree on any entity-oracle to provide a centralized solution
- the system is dynamic and therefore a predefined solution cannot be imposed
- attempting to provide a centralized solution may cause a performance bottleneck
- there is incomplete information and no entity-oracle has all the necessary information to calculate a solution.

The application of SNP has been demonstrated in a number of domains including data and task allocation, negotiation over pollution issues, and hostage-crisis situations (Kraus 2001).

9.2 NEGOTIATION IN DIFFERENT DOMAINS

Rosenchein and Zlotkin (1994) studied negotiation protocols from the point of view of the environment or domain. As agents may be operating in different environments, Rosenchein and Zlotkin (1994) postulated that not all protocols may be suitable for all environments. In particular, they distinguish environments into two broad categories: task-oriented and worth-oriented.

9.2.1 Task-oriented domains

In task-oriented domains, an agent's activity can be defined in terms of a set of tasks where a task is a nondivisible job which the agent needs to perform. For instance, consider the following situation. Two agents A and B both have a list of chores to do. A's list has two tasks: post the letters at the post office, and return the books to the library. Agent B's to-do list includes posting a package at the post office and visiting the library to borrow this month's issue of National Geographic. An agent's objective is to minimize the overall cost of accomplishing these tasks. Thus, agents can reach agreements and exchange tasks or share in their execution. In this scenario, the agents could reach such an agreement and A, for instance, could go to the library to return their own books and borrow the National Geographic issue for B, while B could go to the post office, post A's letters and send their own package. Thus, both agents would benefit from this agreement as each one would only have to make a single trip, either to the post office or the library, thus minimizing the cost of petrol and/or the time spent to achieve their tasks. The agents would nevertheless have to negotiate such a beneficial deal between themselves.

Such a domain, is called a Task-Oriented Domain (TOD) and can be formalized as a tuple $\langle T, A, c \rangle$ where:

- T is a finite set of tasks.

- $A = \{a_1, \ldots, a_n\}$ is the set of agents and any agent is capable of carrying out any combination set of tasks.

- c is the cost function which is defined as $c : \mathcal{P}(T) \to \mathbb{R}$. Thus, for any finite set of tasks $T' \subseteq T$, $c(T')$ represents the cost of executing all the tasks in T' by any single agent a_i. The cost function takes no other parameters apart from the list of tasks and therefore the cost of a set of tasks is independent of the agent who carries it out. c is monotonic, i.e., if $T'' \subseteq T' \subseteq T$, then $c(T'') \leq c(T')$. In words, adding tasks never decreases the cost. The cost of the empty set of tasks is 0.

An encounter within a TOD is an ordered list of tasks $\langle T_1, \ldots, T_n \rangle$ such that T_i is the list of tasks allocated to agent a_i. In the following, we will restrict our attention to the two-agent case. Given an encounter $\langle T_1, T_2 \rangle$, a deal $\delta = \langle D_1, D_2 \rangle$ will be an allocation of tasks $T_1 \cup T_2$ to agents a_1 and a_2. Intuitively, when agents reach a particular deal, they commit to executing the tasks in D_i. The cost of deal $\delta = \langle D_1, D_2 \rangle$ to agent a_i is $c(D_i)$ and will be denoted by $cost_i(\delta)$.

The utility of δ to agent a_i is the cost of accomplishing its tasks on its own minus the cost of its part of the deal:

$$u_i(\delta) = c(T_i) - cost_i(\delta)$$

If the agents fail to agree on a deal, then the default conflict deal Ξ is for each agent to execute the originally allocated tasks. The conflict deal has utility 0, i.e., $u_i(\Xi) = 0$ for all agents. As agents are self-interested utility maximizers, they will never agree to any deal that gives them negative utility, but will opt for the conflict deal instead.

Given two deals δ and δ' and depending on the utility derived from these, agents will have preferences over them. We say that deal δ dominates another one δ' written $\delta \succ \delta'$

if and only if, for all $a_i \in A$, $u_i(\delta) > u_i(\delta')$. Weak dominance is then defined as follows. We say that deal δ weakly dominates another deal δ' written $\delta \succcurlyeq \delta'$ if an only if, for all $a_i \in A$, $u_i(\delta) \geq u_i(\delta')$. Similarly, we can define equivalence among deals. A deal is then individual rational if $\delta \succcurlyeq \Xi$, in other words, if it gives the agent at least as much utility as the conflict deal. The concept of Pareto optimality finds application here as well. We say that a deal is Pareto optimal if there exists no other deal that dominates it. As before, a Pareto efficient allocation or deal cannot be improved upon for any of the agents without making any other agent worse off. The negotiation set (NS) in TODs consists of all the deals that are Pareto optimal and individual rational.

Monotonic Concession Protocol

We now need to define a protocol that the agents can use in such situations in order to reach a deal. The Monotonic Concession Protocol is a bargaining protocol which proceeds in rounds and works as follows (Rosenchein and Zlotkin 1994). In the first round $t = 0$, agents simultaneously propose a deal from the negotiation set. An agreement is reached and the protocol terminates, if one agent finds that the deal proposed by the other is at least as good or better than its own proposal. If no agreement is reached, the negotiation proceeds to the next round, $t + 1$. In round $t + 1$ the agents again make simultaneous proposals. These proposals are, however, restricted as follows: a new proposal can be the previously made proposal by the agent (the agent stands still), or a new proposal which gives the other agent more utility than the proposal made in the previous round t (the agent concedes). Put simply, in any round t the agent cannot make a proposal which is less preferred by the other agent than the deal proposed in round $t - 1$. If none of the agents make a concession in some round, then the negotiation terminates and the conflict deal is implemented.

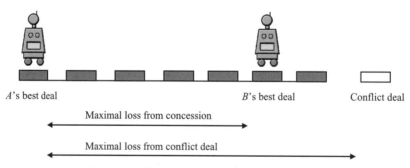

Figure 9.3: The Monotonic Concession Protocol

The situation is illustrated in Figure 9.3. As the negotiation proceeds, agents take steps, i.e., propose deals that bring them closer to each other. Agents cannot backtrack in this protocol. Although they can stand still, they cannot do so simultaneously more than once during the negotiation process – the first time this occurs the conflict deal ensues.

These conditions guarantee that the negotiation process will end after a finite number of rounds.

The Zeuthian strategy

Given this situation, what should be an agent's negotiation strategy? In fact, there are three interrelated questions that need to be answered in the context of the Monotonic Concession Protocol. First of all, what should an agent's first proposal be? Secondly, on any given round, who should concede? Finally, if an agent decides to concede, how much should they concede?

Naturally, we would like to endow agents with stable strategies that will help them reach an efficient outcome. The answer to the first question is fairly obvious: an agent should start by making a proposal which is best for that agent. In this case, if the other agent finds this a good deal, the first agent can benefit the most. At the same time, if the second agent accepts this deal, then this means that this offer either has the same or higher utility than its own best proposal.

The answers to the other two questions depend on how much an agent has to lose by running into conflict at any given round of the negotiation process. Suppose that the agent has conceded a lot. Then this means that the proposal is now near the conflict deal and if conflict indeed occurs this agent does not have much to lose and therefore is more willing to risk conflict. On the contrary, an agent who has not made many concessions has more to lose if conflict occurs. Thus, if the agent's willingness to risk conflict could be measured, then the agent with less willingness to risk could be the one who makes the concession. An agent would be more willing to risk conflict if the difference in utility between the current proposal and the conflict deal is low. The extent to which an agent is more willing to risk a conflict, or the degree of willingness to take a risk of agent a_i in round t, is denoted by $dwrisk_{i,t}$ and is defined as follows:

$$dwrisk_{i,t} = \begin{cases} 1 & \text{if } u_i(\delta_{i,t}) = 0 \\ \frac{u_i(\delta_{i,t}) - u_i(\delta_{j,t})}{u_i(\delta_{i,t})} & \text{otherwise} \end{cases}$$

In words, an agent's degree of willingness to risk is the result of the utility that the agent loses by conceding and accepting the other agent's proposal, divided by the utility the agent loses by not conceding and causing a conflict. For any round other than the last one, the risk is always between 0 and 1 for both agents. Otherwise, at least one of them has a negative willingness to risk, i.e., it has been offered more than it asked for. As $dwrisk_{i,t}$ increases, the agent has less to lose if a conflict occurs, and as a result, will not be willing to concede. Thus, the agent with the lowest $dwrisk_{i,t}$ should make a concession, as this is the agent who has more to lose if a conflict occurs.

The final question is then, once an agent has decided to concede, how much they should concede. The agent should concede by the amount required so that the balance of risk is changed between itself and its opponent. If a sufficient concession is made, then the opponent's risk is less than the agent's, which means that it will be the opponent that will have to concede in the next round. The minimal sufficient concession offered by an agent gives the opponent the least utility.

This strategy is called the Zeuthian strategy and, in summary, it works as follows. An agent starts by proposing to its opponent the deal that is best for itself among all possible deals in the negotiation set. In every round t, the agent calculates its own degree of willingness to risk $dwrisk_{i,t}$ as well as that of the opponent $dwrisk_{j,t}$. If the agent's willingness to risk is smaller or equal to that of its opponent, then the agent makes a proposal that involves the minimal sufficient concession so that the balance changes. Otherwise, it stands still, i.e., offers the same deal as in the round before.

The Zeuthian strategy guarantees that the agents will not run into conflict as, in each round, at least one of them will make a concession. Therefore, the outcome that will be reached will be efficient, i.e., Pareto efficient. But the Zeuthian strategy is not in Nash equilibrium. To see why this is the case, suppose that, in the final round, both agents have an equal degree of willingness to risk. According to the Zeuthian strategy, both of them should concede, although it is sufficient if at least one of them does. But a self-interested agent who knows that the opponent is using the Zeuthian strategy, may decide to exploit this and deviate from the strategy by not making a concession, thereby benefiting from the other agent's concession. As agents are symmetric, they will think in exactly the same way and both of them may deviate from the prescribed behaviour and therefore conflict will occur.

In this case, the remedy is to decide which of the agents will have to concede on a flip of a fair coin. In game theoretic terms, this resembles the use of mixed strategies. As every noncooperative game has at least one mixed strategy equilibrium, this extended Zeuthian strategy is in equilibrium. Thus, stability has been achieved. Nevertheless, since in the last round the agents are playing with mixed strategies, there is some positive probability that the conflict deal will be reached. Inevitably, although the extended Zeuthian strategy is stable, it may result in an inefficient outcome, i.e., not a Pareto efficient outcome.

Computational and communication efficiency are two other desirable features for negotiation protocols. Intuitively, we would like the protocol to require as little computation as possible on behalf of the agents who are computing their strategies and also as little communication as possible should be required to reach the desired outcome. This, however, is no simple matter in the Monotonic Concession Protocol with agents who use the extended Zeuthian strategy. In order for the agents to decide on their strategies they need to compute the entire negotiation set. This requires that agents have full information on the allocated tasks. The space of possible deals may be exponential in the number of tasks and as a result an agent may have to perform ($O(2^{|T|})$) calculations of the cost function c. Moreover, the negotiation process may involve a large number of steps before the agents reach a mutually acceptable deal or resort to conflict. A large number of messages may have to be exchanged between the agents and hence the protocol may not be communication efficient.

Deception

So far we have assumed that agents have complete information regarding the problem domain. This inherently means that agents know each other's original task allocations and therefore they can calculate their opponent's degree of willingness to risk during the negotiation phase and make appropriate concessions, if necessary. This assumption may not be realistic for all problems. Typically, agents will have to declare their tasks before the negotiation process begins. In this case, we have to rely on the agents to reveal information truthfully (this is discussed in more detail in Chapter 10). But being utility maximizers, agents may decide to declare their tasks insincerely in order to take advantage of the other agents. In TODs there are two ways in which deception can benefit the agents.

An agent can declare *phantom* or *decoy* tasks. The agent pretends that they have been allocated more tasks than they have in an attempt to influence the outcome of the negotiation process. Consider the example of the agents trying to reach a deal on which one is going to the post office and the library. Suppose that the post office is a greater distance away from the two agents' location than the library. If one of them is a penny-pincher, they may want to avoid going to the post office. They could then declare that they also have to make a cash withdrawal from a bank which just happens to be in the same direction as the library. This additional task will obviously affect the negotiation process and the outcome reached and the penny-pincher agent will end up going to the library. The issue here is whether or not tasks can be publicly verified. If an agent can produce a phantom task on request, then this is called a decoy task and, in such cases, detecting deception is almost impossible. For instance, the task of having to withdraw cash is such a decoy task. When agents declare phantom tasks that they cannot easily produce, then it is easier to detect deception. Whether or not phantom tasks can be produced within a domain provides the agents with different deception power (Rosenchein and Zlotkin 1994).

Apart from declaring phantom tasks, an agent could also hide tasks in order to benefit. Although this may sound a bit counter-intuitive, there are circumstances where the agents can indeed benefit by hiding tasks. Consider a modified version of the example. Agent A has to go both to the library and the post-office, whereas agent B only has to go to the post office. It takes an agent 40 minutes to go both to the library and the post office, but only 30 minutes to go to one of them. A can hide the fact that it has to go to the library and thus, perhaps, get B to go to the post-office for both of them, thereby increasing its overall utility by simply having to perform the task that takes the least time on its own.

9.2.2 Worth-oriented domains

As we saw in Chapter 2, rational agents are interested in reaching states of the world in which their goals are satisfied. As different environment states have different values, one natural way to guide the agent's behaviour is to equip it with a strategy that allows it to bring about the state of the world that has the greatest value. Agents can transform one state of the environment to another and thus bring about desired or goal states by executing individual plans. If there are a number of agents present in an environment then they can interfere with each other's goals. This interference can be positive, or negative (Castelfranchi 2003). If interference is negative, then an agent's goals may obstruct or hinder the achievement of another agent's goals. If interference is positive, one agent's goals can support or facilitate another agent's goal achievement. A joint plan is a plan that can be carried out by a number of agents.

In worth-oriented domains (WOD) a worth function assigns to every state some worth value. More formally, a WOD is a tuple $\langle S, A, J, c \rangle$ where:

- S is the set of all possible world states
- $A = \{a_1, \ldots, a_n\}$ is the set of agents
- J is the set of all possible joint plans
- c is the cost function which is defined as $c : J \times A \to \mathbb{R}$. Thus, for every plan $j \in J$ and every agent $a_i \in A$ the cost function assigns a real number which represents the cost $c(i, j)$ of agent a_i executing the plan j.

An encounter within a WOD is a tuple $\langle s, W \rangle$ where $s \in S$ is the initial state of the world and $W : S \times A \to \mathbb{R}$ is a worth function which assigns to each state of the environment and each agent, a real number $W(i, s)$ which represents the value or worth of state s to agent a_i.

$j : s_1 \mapsto s_2$ will be used to denote that the execution of plan j in state s_1 leads to state s_2. The utility of an agent u_i in a WOD is defined as the difference between the worth of a final state and the cost that the agent has to pay in order to bring about this final state. In an environment where the agent operates on their own, it can bring the world to its own 'stand-alone optimal' using its own plan (Rosenchein and Zlotkin 1994):

$$u_i(s) = \arg \max_{j : s_0 \mapsto s} W(i, s) - c(i, j)$$

Thus, $u_i(s)$ is agent a_i's maximum utility if it were alone in the world. But, in most applications, agents will have to share the environment with other agents. If the interference is negative, it may be impossible for each of the agents to perform the best single-agent plan and bring the world to a desirable state. This may be due to resource constraints, conflicting goals or interfering actions. On the other hand, interference may be positive in the sense that agents may be able to benefit from each other's presence in the environment, if their actions can be chosen and coordinated properly. To this end, agents can coordinate and execute joint plans that would enable them to bring about states of the world that they would be unable to bring about on their own. Consider, for instance, a couple who own one car. The husband wants to go fishing, whereas the wife wants to go shopping and of course both need to use the car. In this case, it is not possible for both agents to bring about their individual goals, which can be achieved by individual plans to use the same car for different purposes and destinations on the very same day, i.e., there is a conflict over resources. But there may be joint plans that move the world from its initial state to a mutually desired state. The couple may decide that the husband will take the car for the day, drive the wife to the shopping mall and then leave for his fishing trip, while the wife gets a taxi back home once she finishes her shopping. Alternatively, the wife can keep the car for the day, drive the husband to a friend's house where he can get a lift if he contributes to the cost of the petrol.

Agents in WODs can reach a compromize by negotiating not only over what parts of their goals will be achieved, but also over the means, i.e., the joint plan that will be used to achieve these parts. There is a tradeoff between these two elements. An agent might be willing to accept a state with a lower worth, if they end up doing less of the work to bring about this state. In such domains agents can negotiate over joint plans which allow them to reach any final state, but not necessarily one that fully satisfies both agents' goals. In other words, in WODs, an agent may achieve only some of their sub-goals and not all of them. Rosenchein and Zlotkin (1994) examine how agents can negotiate over joint plans in this case and they also consider a special case of worth-oriented domains called state-oriented domains (SOD) in which the worth value is associated only with the achievement of an agent's full goal.

9.3 COALITIONS

Agents negotiate in a great number of economic situations on issues of common interest. This leads to the formation of coalitions, which often interact with other coalitions. Several reasons explain the formation of these coalitions such as, for instance, economies of scale, reduced competition, costs or risk. Self-interested agents may form coalitions either because they cannot perform a task alone or because they can reduce their costs by working together. In a market setting the risk or costs for buyers or sellers can be reduced, if they take joint action.

9.3.1 Coalition formation

The problem of coalition formation can be studied in the context of cooperative games and, in particular, characteristic function games (CFG) (Osborne and Rubinstein 1994, Sandholm et al. 1999). In such games there is a set N of agents in which each subset of N is called a coalition and the value of a coalition S is given by a characteristic function v_S. The value v_S does not depend on the actions of nonmember agents of the coalition, i.e., agents outside the coalition. The coalition structure CS is the set of all coalitions such that all agents belong to one. The set of all possible coalition structures will be denoted by M. Any coalition forms by a binding agreement on the distribution of its coalition value v_S among its members. The solution of a game with side payments is a coalition configuration which consists of a partition S of N, the coalition structure CS, and an n-dimensional payoff distribution vector in which components are computed by a utility function u. The payoff distribution assigns each agent $i \in N$ its utility u_i out of the value v_S of the coalition S in a given coalition structure CS.

Coalition formation in CFG games includes two main activities:

- Coalition structure generation: the agents form coalitions such that they can coordinate their activities within these coalitions, but agents do not coordinate between coalitions. Thus, the set of agents is partitioned into exhaustive and disjoint coalitions. This partition is called a *coalition structure*.

- Division of the value of the generated coalition structure among the agents. As agents will have used their resources and have incurred a cost, this value may be negative.

The two activities are intertwined. On the one hand, the division of payoffs to the agents depends on the coalitions that finally form while on the other, the coalitions that actually form, depend on the payoffs available to each agent in each of these coalitions. Intuitively, the payoffs influence the coalition structure generation and vice versa. A self-interested agent would want to join a coalition that will provide it with the highest possible payoff and therefore before it joins, it needs to search all the possible coalitions and find the one that maximizes its utility.

9.3.2 Coalition structure generation

The formation of an optimal, maximum welfare, coalition structure is trivial when the coalition values are either super or sub-additive. Super and sub-additivity indicate the relations between coalition values:

Definition 21 *The coalition values are super-additive if and only if for every pair of disjoint coalitions $S, T \subseteq N : v_{S \cup T} \geq v_S + v_T$.*

Definition 22 *The coalition values are sub-additive if and only if for every pair of disjoint coalitions $S, T \subseteq N : v_{S \cup T} < v_S + v_T$.*

In the first case, super-additivity means that any pair of coalitions is best off by merging into one. If the coalition values are super-additive, there is at least one optimal coalition structure: the coalition structure that contains one coalition, the *grand coalition N* containing all agents. The second special case arises when the costs of a larger coalition outweigh the potential benefits, i.e., the coalition values are sub-additive. In this case, the optimal coalition structure is the one in which every agent acts on their own.

Most of the time there will be some cost involved in the formation of a coalition. Examples of such costs are negotiation and communication costs, or penalties against cartel formation. As coalition values are usually neither super-additive nor sub-additive, this makes the coalition formation process very hard: determining the optimal coalition structure given the coalition values v_S is an NP-hard problem.

When games are not super-additive, some coalitions are best off merging, whereas others are not. In such games, the coalition structure that maximizes social welfare, varies and thus the process of coalition structure generation is typically nontrivial. The objective is to maximize the social welfare of the agents by finding an optimal coalition structure CS^* such that (Sandholm et al. 1999):

$$CS^* = \arg \max_{CS \in M} V(CS)$$

where $V(CS)$ is the value of a coalition structure:

$$V(CS) = \sum_{S \in CS} v_S$$

The number of coalition structures CS is exponential in the number of coalitions S. Since there are $2^n - 1$ possible coalitions given the set of agents n, the complexity of the coalition formation process is even worse with respect to the number of agents. The number of possible coalition structures, amongst which the agent must find the optimal one, is $O(n^n)$. The number of coalitions is:

$$\sum_{i=1}^{n} = Z(n,j)$$

where $Z(k,j)$[1] is the number of coalition structures with j coalitions if the total number of agents is k. So, in practice, not all coalition structures can be enumerated unless the number of agents is small (typically less than 15).

As a consequence, in general, agents will not be able to determine the optimal coalition structure for carrying out a task. The question is: can the agents approximate the optimal coalition structure? In other words, can they search through a subset $L \subset M$ and pick the best coalition structure seen so far, CS_L^* such that:

$$CS_L^* = \arg \max_{CS \in L} V(CS)$$

In attempting to approximate the optimal coalition structure, the agents should examine several of them before they can establish that the best coalition structure found so far is a sufficiently good approximation. This begs the question of how many coalition structures the agents should examine in order to guarantee an approximation quality, that is, a worst-case bound. So, which coalition structures should the agents at least examine?

---

[1] The quantity $Z(n,j)$ is also known as the Stirling number of the second kind.

j	Coalition Structures			
[4]	{{1}, {2}, {3}, {4}}			
[3]	{{1}, {2}, {3, 4}}	{{1}, {3}, {2, 4}}	{{2}, {3}, {1, 4}}	
	{{1}, {4}, {2, 3}}	{{2 }, {4}, {1, 3}}	{{3}, {4}, {1, 2}}	
[2]	{{1, 2 }, {3, 4}}	{{1, 3}, {2, 4}}	{{1, 4}, {2, 3}}	
	{{1}, {2, 3, 4}}	{{2}, {1, 3, 4}}	{{3}, {1, 2, 4 }}	{{4}, {1, 2, 3}}
[1]	{{1, 2, 3, 4}}			

Table 9.1: Coalition structures for four agents

Consider the case of four agents. There are 15 possible coalition structures. If these are ordered with respect to the number of coalitions which they contain from highest to lowest, where j is the number of coalitions in the coalition structures, the result is illustrated in Table 9.1.

Starting with the coalition structures that contain the $j = 1$ coalition, there is a unique such coalition structure containing the grand coalition of all agents N. This coalition structure contains no other coalitions and is the last case indicated in Table 9.1. Continuing with the coalition structures which contain $j = 2$ coalitions, such coalition structures include either:

- one coalition of size $n - 1$ and one coalition of size 1 as in the coalition structure {{4}, {1, 2, 3}}; or
- two coalitions of size $n - 2$ as in the coalition structure {{1, 3}, {2, 4}}.

However, these two classes of coalition structures together, i.e., coalition structures that include coalitions of size 1 and 2, comprise the set of all possible coalitions. Thus, if the coalition structures are ordered in terms of the number of coalitions they contain, the agents must inspect the lowest two levels of the ordering. If the agents inspect all coalition structures with 1 and 2 coalitions, they have seen every possible coalition. We can therefore conclude that the agents must at least inspect 2^{n-1} different coalition structures in order to determine a worse-case bound for the quality of the best coalition structure CS_L^* inspected so far. This bound is also tight, that is, if we assign every coalition of one agent the value 1 and every other coalition the value 0, then the value of the optimal coalition structure is a factor n higher than the value of the best coalition structure in the first two levels of the coalition structure ordering of Table 9.1.

If more time for computation is available, tighter bounds can be defined by inspecting more coalitions structures (Sandholm et al. 1999). By inspecting the top level, the bound surprisingly drops in half to $\frac{n}{2}$. If $h = \lfloor \frac{n-l}{2} \rfloor + 2$, then after searching level l, the bound is $\lceil \frac{n}{h} \rceil$ if $n \equiv h - 1 \pmod{h}$ and $n \equiv l \pmod 2$; otherwise the bound is $\lfloor \frac{n}{h} \rfloor$. The interested reader is referred to Sandholm et al. (1999) for the full details of the algorithm and the proof, while an improved algorithm is discussed in Dang and Jennings (2004). An alternative distributed approach to coalition formation is described in Shehory and Kraus (1998).

9.3.3 Division of payoffs

Self-interested agents join coalitions in order to maximize their utility. Payoff division is concerned with dividing the value of the chosen coalition structure among agents in a fair and stable way so that agents are motivated to remain with the coalition structure rather than opt out. Even if an optimal coalition structure CS is identified, it might not be worth much if it is not stable. The interpretation of coalition stability depends on the considered discipline and application domain. Many coalition formation algorithms rely on game-theory concepts for stable payoff division within coalitions such as, for instance, the Core (Gillies 1959), the Shapley value (Shapley 1953), the bargaining set (Aumann and Maschler 1964), or the kernel (Davis and Maschler 1965).

The idea behind the Core is analogous to that behind the Nash equilibrium of a noncooperative game. According to the Core, an outcome is stable if no coalition can deviate and obtain a better outcome for all its members. For a coalition game with transferable payoffs, the stability condition is that no coalition can obtain a payoff that exceeds the sum of its current members' payoffs. More formally, the core of a CFG game with transferable payoffs is a set of payoff configurations $(\overrightarrow{p}, CS)$ where each $\overrightarrow{p}$ is a vector of payoffs to agents such that no subgroup is motivated to deviate from the given CS:

$$Core = \{(\overrightarrow{p}, CS)| \text{ for all } S \subseteq N : \sum_{i \in S} p_i \geq v_S \text{ and } \sum_{i \in N} p_i = \sum_{S \in CS} v_S\}$$

There are a number of problems related to the Core. Firstly, the Core is the strongest of the solution concepts in coalition formation and, as a result, it may be empty. This implies that in such games there is no way to divide the payoffs so that the coalition structure remains stable. Consequently, agents may switch between coalitions indefinitely during the negotiations as they have an incentive to deviate from the current coalition structure. This resembles the absence of a Nash equilibrium: agents are free to choose among different strategies. In the context of coalitions, a strategy comprises joining another coalition. Solutions to the problem might be to limit the number of negotiation rounds allowed to establish a coalition or introduce a cost for the negotiation time. Secondly, the Core may contain multiple solutions and the agents have to agree on one of them. To resolve this issue, quite often the *nucleolus* is chosen, which is the payoff vector that is in the centre of the set of payoff vectors in the Core. Finally, calculating the Core is an NP-hard problem.

The Shapley value is another possible way of dividing payoffs among the members of a coalition. This is determined as follows:

- agent i is a dummy if $v_{S \cup i} - v_S = v_i$ for every coalition S that does not include i

- agents i and j are interchangeable if for all S with either i or j, v_S remains the same if i is replaced by j, in other words $v_{(S \setminus \{i\} \cup \{j\})} = v_S$.

We now require a set of payoffs that satisfy:

- Symmetry: If i and j are interchangeable, then $p_i = p_j$ (where p is the set of payoffs).

- Dummies: If i is a dummy, then $p_i = v_{\{i\}}$.

- Additivity: For any two games v and w, p_i in $v + w$ equals p_i in v plus p_i in w, where $v + w$ is the game defined by $(v + w)_S = v_S + w_S$.

The Shapley value satisfies all these conditions and sets the payoff of an agent to:

$$p_i = \sum_{S \subseteq N} \frac{(n - |S|)!(|S| - 1)!}{n!}(v_S - v_{S - \{i\}})$$

p_i is called the Shapley value of agent i and it can be regarded as the marginal contribution of the agent to the coalition structure, averaged over all possible joining orders. The joining order is significant, since the contribution of agent i varies depending on which other agents have joined before.

Among the properties of the Shapley value p_i is that it always exists and is unique. It is also Pareto efficient as all the value is distributed among the agents. The Shapley value guarantees that individual agents and the grand coalition, have an incentive to stay with the coalition structure. Nevertheless, there is no guarantee that all subgroups of agents are better off in the coalition structure than by splitting out into a coalition of their own. Finally, as p_i has to be computed over all joining orders and since there are $n!$ such orders, inevitably this takes a long time to compute.

9.4 APPLICATIONS OF COALITION FORMATION

Generally speaking, a coalition is a set of agents who agree to cooperate in order to achieve a common objective. In the context of markets, agents may decide to join forces if this will enable them to maximize their utility. There are several reasons for creating/joining a coalition:

- monetary, such as in the reduction of cost or increased profit
- risk reduction or allowing someone else to assume risk
- increase in market size or share
- take advantage of new opportunities or exploit a niche in the market that otherwise is not possible on one's own.

9.4.1 Customer coalitions

Suppose you want to buy a personal computer (PC). You may visit several stores in your area and check the prices offered by them, but the prices offered to you are *retail* prices. The retail price is the total price charged for a product sold to an individual customer, which includes the manufacturing and other costs, plus a retail markup, i.e., the vendor's profit. This retail price is charged for individual items and has been calculated by the vendor in such a way as to make enough profit to cover expenses like the advertisement and storage costs, plus the cost of manufacturing or acquiring the item from a producer. As an individual customer, you do not have much bargaining or market power, that, is you cannot negotiate a better deal with the vendor if you are only interested in one PC. The vendor would like to receive a healthy profit from every purchase made and its profit margins may be quite narrow. Now, suppose that nine of your friends are also interested in buying a PC with the same configuration as you require. If you could somehow join forces with them and buy the 10 PCs together, you could ask one, or a number, of vendors to offer you a better price for the PCs, given that you are now buying in bulk. In this case, and given the number of PCs involved, the vendor has an incentive to offer you a better deal. This is because, if she does not reduce the price, the chances are that another vendor in your area would be willing to do so and thus she is going to lose a sale. From the vendor's perspective, even though her profit margin for each individual PC will be lower, she actually increases her utility as she is now selling in bulk, and not individual items. Therefore, if a sufficient number of items are to be sold together, then the vendor has an incentive to lower the price and sell *wholesale*.

As a result, individual customers may join their forces and take advantage of the fact that power lies in numbers and negotiate better deals with suppliers. This is a particular application of coalition formation in electronic commerce where in essence *buying clubs* are created (Tsvetovat et al. 2000).

Let us look at the customers' and suppliers' incentives in more detail. All participants in electronic (or traditional) marketplaces are self-interested agents who are trying to maximize their utility: the sellers by selling goods at the highest possible price and the buyers by acquiring goods at the lowest possible price.

Suppose, for the sake of simplicity, that the manufacturing cost of one item is constant and above some threshold and that it is independent of the amount of units sold. Assume that the supplier agent is selling its goods retail. Let u_{item} be the profit or utility of the supplier from selling one item at retail price and c_{item} the cost of manufacturing one item (or obtaining it from a producer). p_{item} is the sale price of the item or reservation price. The cost of retail marketing per item which includes costs, such as advertising, is indicated by $c_{retail-mkt}$. The utility an agent receives from selling one item is therefore:

$$u_{item} = p_{item} - c_{retail-mkt} - c_{item}$$

The utility of selling n items retail would then be:

$$u_n^{retail} = np_{item} - nc_{retail-mkt} - nc_{item}$$

The utility for selling n items wholesale, that is to one buyer in bulk instead of many, would be:

$$u_n^{wholesale} = np_{item} - c_{wholesale-mkt} - nc_{item}$$

Consequently, an agent would be willing to sell wholesale, if she receives higher utility from such a sale. In essence, the supplier has an incentive to sell wholesale if the cost of wholesale marketing is lower than the cost of retail marketing for n items. The assumption is that marketing to one buyer is usually less expensive than marketing to multiple buyers, and so there is an incentive to sell wholesale. Nevertheless, wholesale marketing to one customer will be more expensive than retail marketing to one customer, usually due to prolonged negotiation. Up to some number n_{retail}, the supplier does not have an incentive to sell at wholesale price as marketing costs will be almost identical to retail costs and decreasing the price to wholesale level is not reasonable. As the size of the lot increases past the n_{retail} point, selling goods wholesale becomes more profitable for the agent. Therefore, the number of items n is crucial.

On the other hand, an individual customer also has an incentive to buy wholesale. A customer's utility from an item is the value of the item minus the price paid to acquire it, minus any storage or management costs:

$$u_{customer} = v_{item} - p_{item} - c_{storage}$$

As the number of items that the customer purchases increases, they can negotiate a better deal with the supplier. Let us define the customer's maximum utility range (MUR) as:

$$MUR(n_{min}, n_{max})$$

This is the range of items (minimum and maximum) in which the utility is high while the management or storage costs remain low. If the supplier's optimal size of wholesale lot $n_{wholesale} \in MUR$, then the customer can purchase the items at wholesale price. In other words, the supplier's profit is enough for her to lower the price, and as a result the customer can buy at wholesale price. But unless the wholesale price of goods in larger lots is below the retail price, the customer has no incentive to buy such lots wholesale and might as well consider buying them from other retailers. Consequently, if a supplier has an incentive to sell wholesale lots, she must give the customer an incentive to buy wholesale. This is commonly done by providing a discount on the price of the item which may depend on the quantity that the buyer is buying. Thus, the larger the quantity, the larger the discount. Therefore, the customer's utility of an item is higher if the price of the item is lower, while all other factors (Ω) remain constant, that is $\Delta u_{customer} = \Omega(\Delta p)$.

But in practice, an individual customer very rarely wants to buy large enough quantities of goods so as to be offered wholesale prices. This is the case with individual customers, and not organizations which act like single customers. In order to lower the price of an item, agents can join forces and create coalitions so that the number of goods purchased through the coalition is large. The utility of the coalition is now $MUR_{coalition} = \sum MUR_i$ where MUR_i is the MUR of each member i of the coalition. If $n_{wholesale} \in MUR_{coalition}$ then the coalition can make a purchase in bulk at wholesale price from the supplier and subsequently break it into lots and distribute them to the members. This raises the utility of each member who can benefit from the lower price which the coalition can achieve. However, the formation of the coalition itself, the negotiation between the coalition and the supplier agent(s), the administration of the coalition as well as the distribution of goods have a cost, $c_{coalition}$. In some cases, such as distributing copies of music, movies or software, some of the costs can be very small, and in other cases they may be exceptionally high. For a coalition to be stable and therefore viable, the increase in the group's total utility from wholesale purchases must be greater than the cost of creating and running the coalition, i.e., $\Delta u_{coalition} > c_{coalition}$. The larger the difference, the stronger the incentive to remain in the coalition.

9.4.2 Coalition Protocols

The general stages involved in a coalition protocol for creating buyer coalitions are as follows (Tsvetovat et al. 2000):

- **Negotiation.** The initiator, or *coalition leader* negotiates with one or more suppliers or service providers. The protocol used can be any of the protocols that we discussed in the previous sections, though the choice of protocol obviously depends on the particular situation.

- **Coalition formation.** The initiator or coalition leader invites new members to join the coalition. Some admission constraints may be imposed such as, for instance, geographical proximity. In other cases, credit status checks may be carried out at this stage to ensure that the prospective coalition member can pay for the goods.

- **Leader election.** The members elect a leader or a representative. This agent is then responsible for administering the coalition and negotiating with the suppliers. Not all protocols have this stage, as the leader may be the agent who initiated the coalition.

- **Payment collection.** The coalition leader or another designated representative collects the payments from the members of the coalition.

- **Execution/distribution.** The transaction between the leader and the supplier is executed and the purchased goods arrive. The leader must distribute the goods to the members of the coalition.

Several issues need to be taken into consideration in designing a coalition protocol. A major issue in coalition formation, in general, as was discussed previously, is that of stability. The agents should have an incentive to stay within the coalition and not opt out as this has consequences for the utility of the coalition. For instance, one way of providing an incentive to remain within the coalition is by requiring agents to pay a membership fee or a deposit, which is then deducted from future payments that the members have to make. This fee or deposit may not be returned if the agent decides to leave the coalition and can be used for covering part of the cost of the coalition, or the cost of that agent leaving the coalition. If there is no such fee or deposit to cover for the cost of the leaving agent, this cost needs to be absorbed by the coalition as a whole or passed on in some way to the supplier.

Dividing the potential gains from the difference between retail and wholesale prices of an item to the members of the coalition, is another issue. Forming a coalition and administering it involves a cost. Who bears this cost along with the cost of the distribution of goods and the logistics involved needs to be taken into account.

Moreover, in forming a coalition, the members bear financial risks and experience uncertainty. For instance, there is a risk as the transaction is executed. How large the various risks are and what sort of action can be taken in order to minimize such risks is crucial for the stability of the coalition. The risks associated with coalitions are:

- Risk of transaction failure is the probable cost of recovery from a transaction failure such as when the supplier chosen decides not to honour the agreement reached.

- Risk of coalition failure is the probable cost of recovery from one or more members leaving the coalition.

- Price uncertainty is a measure of the price fluctuation due to the possible variation in the size of the coalition. This affects the utilities of both the coalition and the supplier.

Finally, trust is fundamental in conducting business through a coalition. In particular, trust needs to be placed in the coalition leader in three stages:

- Negotiation stage: the members of the coalition need to have trust in the leader when it conducts the negotiations with the suppliers. For instance, leaders may collude with the suppliers and secure a better deal for themselves while passing on a higher price to the rest of the coalition members.

- Payment collection: members need to place enormous trust in the leader at this stage as the leader may collect payments from the members without having the intention to pay the supplier.

- Distribution stage: even if the leader does pay the supplier for the goods, it may decide to sell the items and keep all the profit himself.

In designing a coalition formation protocol, the issue of trust needs to be carefully considered. Protocols that would not require such trust or minimize the number of stages where trust is required would be preferable. A related issue is how the coalition can deal with a breach of trust.

Depending on when the negotiation between the coalition and the supplier(s) and the coalition formation itself takes place, coalition protocols can be divided into post-negotiation and pre-negotiation protocols (Tsvetovat et al. 2000).

9.4.3 Post-negotiation protocol

Assume a coalition leader (L), a set of suppliers $S = \{s_1, s_2, \ldots, s_k\}$ and a set of potential coalition members $M = \{m_1, m_2, \ldots, m_n\}$. The post-negotiation coalition formation protocol works as follows:

- The leader L advertises the creation of a coalition with certain parameters. The coalition opens to members for a limited period of time or until a specified group size is reached. The invitation to join the coalition is advertised via some means, electronic or otherwise.

- Each potential coalition member m_i considers whether to join the coalition and sends the necessary message to the leader if it decides to join, i.e., 'Join the coalition'.

- At the expiration of the coalition deadline or when a sufficient or minimum size has been reached, the leader closes the coalition and enters into negotiations with the suppliers $s_i \in S$ using its private strategy and decides on a deal.

- L collects the payments from the coalition members, executes the transaction with the chosen supplier and arranges for the shipping and distribution of goods.

The major issue in this protocol is the level of trust that is required in the coalition leader. This protocol is open to manipulation as the initiator can be the representative of a particular supplier, i.e., a shill. In other words, an agent working for a supplier and pretending to be a customer itself can initiate a coalition with the purpose of attracting customers for the particular supplier. This has as a result that the supplier's share of the market increases and consequently revenue increases as well. In addition, trust in the payment collection and goods distribution stages is also required. If the potential members of the coalition do not know the leader through a previous business relationship, or by reputation, mechanisms that help the coalition members to establish this trust or conduct transactions without having to trust the leader, are required.

Trust in the coalition leader can be established in different ways. Instead of the initiator taking on the role of the leader by default, the leader can be elected from among the group before the negotiation phase. As the coalition leader is the one who conducts the negotiation with the suppliers it does so using its own strategy as well as its own reservation price, which may be very different from that of the rest of the coalition members. The leader could be required to reveal information at every step of the negotiation process to the members, in order to ensure transparency and fairness. Alternatively, the negotiation can be conducted by having the members vote on the offers (bids) submitted by the different suppliers and the offer with the majority of votes is accepted. A large number of (supplier) shills would be required to manipulate the result in this case. However, utilizing voting is time consuming. Another solution is for the group to appoint a trusted third party to conduct the negotiations on their behalf.

The protocol which is used by the leader in the negotiation stage can be one of the protocols that we have examined so far. For instance, an auction protocol can be used if the leader has to negotiate with multiple suppliers, or a bargaining protocol if it negotiates with one supplier. This depends on the particular situation.

9.4.4 Pre-negotiation protocol

As in the post-negotiation protocol, assume a coalition leader (L), a set of suppliers $S = \{s_1, s_2, \ldots, s_k\}$ and a set of potential coalition members $M = \{m_1, m_2, \ldots, m_n\}$. The pre-negotiation protocol proceeds as follows:

- The initiator or leader L enters into negotiations with a set of suppliers S, using its private strategy and other parameters such as reservation price.

- Once an agreement has been reached with a supplier, the leader L opens the coalition to new members, revealing the details of the deal. The invitation to join the coalition is distributed to potential members via electronic or other means.

- Each potential member m_i considers whether to join the coalition and sends the necessary message 'Join the coalition' to the leader.

- After the closing deadline, or when the coalition reaches some minimum size, L closes the coalition to new members, then collects the payments from the members and executes the transaction with the chosen supplier and also arranges for the shipping and distribution of goods.

Although L uses a private reservation price and negotiation strategy when dealing with the suppliers, this is not a major issue in this protocol as the details of the deal and the discounts are revealed before the agents decide whether to join the coalition. Therefore, in this protocol the coalition members do not have to trust the leader in the negotiation stage, but trust in the payment collection and distribution stages is required.

The major issue in this protocol is the risk that L assumes in attempting to estimate the size of the coalition in negotiating a deal with the suppliers. To be able to provide volume discounts, suppliers need to have an idea of the number of members expected to join the coalition or, alternatively, the approximate number of goods to be sold. Although this number can be estimated, L carries the risk of not being able to find enough members to join the coalition. If the estimate is wrong, the coalition leader must also absorb the loss or distribute it to the members of the coalition. Alternatively, the deal must be re-negotiated, resulting in a higher price and, possibly, some members leaving the coalition. As more members leave, this leads to even higher prices for the remaining members. This vicious cycle can completely destroy the coalition.

A variation of this protocol can be adopted in the negotiation stage in order to deal with this problem. When L negotiates with the suppliers, it presents not the estimated coalition size, but a range of possible sizes. The suppliers bid with a step function $p = f_{bid}(quantity)$. The details of the deal can then be revealed to the coalition members when advertising the coalition. For instance, a supplier may offer the goods for the price of £10 if the quantity to be sold is between 10 and 20, £9 if the quantity is 21–50 and £7.50 if there are more than 51 items to be purchased.

As a result of this modification, the risk in the transaction is shifted onto the coalition members due to the price uncertainty. Hence, prior to joining a coalition a potential member needs to ascertain if participation will be to its benefit. If a potential buyer has a reservation price $p_{reserve}$, then the decision whether to join the coalition depends on the buyer's estimate of the probability that the final price will be lower than its reservation price, i.e., if $p_{max-coalition} > p_{reserve} > p_{min-coalition}$, then the buyer may decide to join the coalition. This is essentially an estimate of the final size of the coalition. In this case, the dominant strategy for a buyer would be to wait until the coalition is almost closed for new members, which would provide them with more accurate information regarding the final coalition size. However, if a large number of buyers use this strategy, there is the risk that the coalition will not attract a sufficient number of members as every agent will be waiting for the others to join first.

9.4.5 Distribution of costs and utility

The coalition leader can be either the initiator or an elected member from the general membership of the coalition. Obviously, as agents operating in markets are self-interested, the leader needs to have an incentive for taking on this role, and any potential risks. A leader can operate either on a non-profit or a for-profit basis. When the leader operates on a non-profit basis, they do not gain anything from assuming this role, apart from the usual gains as a coalition member, i.e., the difference between retail and wholesale price. The cost of the coalition $c_{coalition}$ is distributed either equally among all participants, or on the sub-lot size basis which each buyer purchases. Such coalitions can be formed on the fly for negotiating one particular deal, or can be stable *buyers' clubs* that operate over a period of time. A leader who operates on a for-profit basis receives a profit. Such agents can operate in two ways:

- **Consolidator.** If the coalition leader acts as a consolidator, it negotiates a deal with the supplier given an estimated group size and then re-sells the items individually, keeping enough of the savings to cover the cost of the coalition and make a profit. This is the model used by travel consolidators and show or concert ticket distributors. Such agents can usually fairly accurately estimate the demand for tickets, based on data on the popularity of certain routes, bands, or shows. Any losses from unsold tickets are absorbed by the consolidator.

- **Rebater**. When the coalition leader operates as a rebater, it obtains the items at wholesale price and sells them at retail price, minus a small rebate, and keeps the rest of the savings.

9.4.6 Other applications

Individual customers manage to exercise market power by joining a coalition. In particular, this is the case when customers have to negotiate with big conglomerates or suppliers.

However, small suppliers can also benefit from coalition formation. Small suppliers may have limited market power in relation to a big buyer, but by joining forces they can increase their market share and perhaps demand better prices. For example, if small-scale fishermen sell their catch of the day individually, they may not be in a position to negotiate better prices, in particular if they are dealing with a buyer which has market power, such as a supermarket chain. Individuals may perhaps have a large variety of fish, but small quantities, and therefore a big supermarket has an advantage over the individual fishermen and puts pressure on them in the sense of low market prices. Besides, individual fishermen need to make sure that they *do* sell their catch of the day, as otherwise it will be worthless. But if all or a number of individual fishermen decide to join their forces (perhaps through a union) they have the opportunity to be more in control of the prices that they demand and can achieve. The same kind of pre and post-negotiation coalition formation protocols could be used in this case as well.

Coalition formation has also found applications in the context of virtual organizations. In essence, the purpose is to partition the members of the VO into coalitions that maximize the social payoff of the groups by pulling the resources and capabilities of the members of the groups to perform the required tasks. Such an approach has been explored in (Dang and Jennings 2004). A decentralized approach for the allocation of tasks to groups of cooperative agents is presented in Shehory and Kraus (1998). Agents may have different capabilities and the tasks to be executed may be dependent on various resources or require a particular execution order. The agents decide on the coalitions to be formed using any-time algorithms, that is, algorithms that provide a solution even if they are stopped before they finish executing.

9.5 SOCIAL CHOICE PROBLEMS

There are certain situations in which agents have their own preferences over a set of outcomes, but nevertheless they need to reach a joint outcome. This set of outcomes can be, for instance, different ways in which profits can be divided among the shareholders of a company or different ways to divide a box of sweets among a set of people, etc. Such problems have a common characteristic, they are *social choice* problems. A social choice problem arises whenever a group of agents must make a collective choice from among a set of alternatives. Each agent has their own preferences over these alternatives and clearly one agent's preferences may be incompatible with those of the others. The problem is then to decide, given the agents' individual preferences, which possible alternative is the best for the society.

9.5.1 Making a social choice

Given a society of agents N and their preferences, we would like to have a way to 'aggregate' them into one *social preference*. That is, if we know how all the agents rank various allocations or outcomes, we would like to be able to use this information to develop a social ranking of the various allocations and thus allow the socially preferred outcome to be imposed. The ranking of alternative outcomes from the society's point of view should obviously depend on the individual agents' rankings. The issue in broad terms is this: how can we go from often divergent and incompatible, but individually consistent views on what is the socially best outcome, to a single and *socially consistent* view.

Assume that there is a set of mutually exclusive social states, or feasible outcomes $\mathcal{O}$ for the society. The society comprises a set of agents N, and each individual $i \in N$ has its own preference relation $\succ_i$ over the set of possible outcomes $\mathcal{O}$. The preference relations $\succ_i$ are complete and transitive. Intuitively, we require that agents are able to make comparisons between any two elements of $\mathcal{O}$ and those comparisons are consistent in the sense that they are transitive. When preferences are transitive and complete, an agent can completely rank all the elements in $\mathcal{O}$ from best to worst. The preference relation $\succ_i$ conveys all the information that is needed to determine the individual's choice from among all the alternatives in $\mathcal{O}$. To move from the individual choices to the society's choice, we need a mechanism that will produce a ranking of the outcomes in $\mathcal{O}$ that reflects the society's preferences. Ideally, we would like to be able to compare any two alternatives from the society's point of view and we would like those binary comparisons to be consistent in the same way that they are for individual agents.

A *social choice rule* takes as input the agents' preference relations $(\succ_1, \ldots, \succ_n)$ and produces as output the social preferences denoted by a relation $\succ^*$. It seems reasonable to require the following conditions to be satisfied from the application of a social choice rule:

1. A social preference ordering $\succ^*$ should exist for all possible inputs, and should be complete and transitive over $\mathcal{O}$.

2. The outcome of the social choice rule should be Pareto efficient: if for all $i \in N, o \succ_i o'$, then $o \succ^* o'$.

3. The scheme should be independent of irrelevant alternatives. Specifically, if $\succ^*$ and $\succ_*$ are two social preference orderings and $o, o' \in \mathcal{O}$, if each individual agent i ranks o versus o' under $\succ_i$ the same way that it does under $\succ_i'$, then the social ranking of o versus o' is the same under $\succ^*$ and $\succ_*$.

4. No agent should be a dictator: there is no individual agent i such that for all $o, o' \in \mathcal{O}$, $o \succ_i o'$ implies $o \succ^* o'$ regardless of the preferences of all the other agents.

The first condition states that the social choice rule should be able to generate a social preference that is defined over all the feasible outcomes and has the same properties as the individual agents' preference relations. Condition (2) requires that society should prefer o to o' if every single member of the society prefers o to o'. The third condition describes that the social ranking of o and o' should only depend on the individual rankings of o and o'. Two social preference orderings $\succ^*$ and $\succ_*$ may be different in their rankings of other pairs over the set of alternatives $\mathcal{O}$, but their rankings regarding o and o' should be the same. Finally, condition (4) requires that there should be no single individual who 'gets their way' on every single social choice regardless of everyone else's view in the society. Unfortunately, as Arrow (1951)[2] informs us:

> **Theorem 4** *Arrow's Impossibility Theorem. There is no social choice rule that satisfies all four conditions.*

This theorem is quite surprising as it unequivocally states that there is no perfect way to aggregate and reconcile the different views represented by the agents' preferences into a single, socially consistent, preference relation. If we want to find a rule or a function capable of aggregating individual preferences to form social preferences, one of the four conditions needs to be abandoned.

9.5.2 Voting protocols

Despite the negative implications of Arrow's theorem, we require mechanisms in which agents provide, as input, their preferences over a set of outcomes, and an outcome based on these inputs is chosen which is the solution imposed upon all participating agents. As we need to drop one of the conditions above, the third one can be relaxed. Such a class of social choice rules, in which the third condition is relaxed, comprise voting protocols. We assume a set of agents N who need to make a social choice among a set of possible outcomes $\mathcal{O}$. Each agent i has their own preferences over the set of possible outcomes which they (truthfully) declare to the mechanism. Voting protocols can be classified according to the number of alternatives or outcomes that the voters are asked to consider at a time.

Binary protocols

In *binary* protocols, agents are asked to choose between two alternatives at a time. If there are only two alternatives to choose from, then the majority rule can be used, namely, the alternative with the majority of votes wins. If there are more than two alternatives, these are compared pairwise and the winner challenges further alternatives. In the *Condorcet*[3]

---

[2] American economist Kenneth J. Arrow.
[3] French theorist Jean Antoine Nicholas Caritat, Marquis de Condorcet (1743–1794).

Agent A	Agent B	Agent C
a	b	c
b	c	a
c	a	b

Table 9.2: Example preferences

protocol each alternative is pitted against all the others and the alternative that defeats all others wins. If the number of alternatives is large, then binary protocols can become time-consuming.

Binary protocols have a number of problems. For instance, in the Condorcet protocol there may not be a unique winner that defeats all other alternatives. Consider the following example. We could agree that a is 'socially preferred' to b if a majority of agents prefer a to b. However, there is a problem with this method as it may not generate a transitive social preference ordering. Assume that a, b and c denote particular outcomes and Table 9.2 lists the rankings of the three alternatives for three different agents. A majority of the agents prefer a to b, a majority prefer b to c, and a majority prefer c to a, thus the group's social preferences are cyclical. In general, the social preferences resulting from majority voting are not well-behaved preferences, if they are not transitive. But if the preferences are not transitive, consequently there is no 'best' alternative from the set of possible outcomes (a, b, c). Which outcome society chooses will depend on the order in which the vote is taken.

As the overall winner depends crucially on the order in which the alternatives are offered to the voters, the order of pairings (agenda) may totally change the socially chosen outcome. Consider the example of Figure 9.4. Here there are four alternatives a, b, c and d. The agents have the following preferences:

28% prefer $c \succ d \succ b \succ a$

25% prefer $a \succ c \succ d \succ b$

24% prefer $b \succ a \succ c \succ d$

23% prefer $a \succ d \succ c \succ b$

Suppose the agents are asked to vote on the different alternatives given in the order a, b, c, d. The result from binary voting is c. If the agents are given the agenda b, d, c, a instead, the outcome is a. Yet again, if the agents are given a third agenda c, a, d, b the outcome is b. Finally, if the agents are given the agenda c, a, b, d the outcome is d. All four different agendas lead to different social choice outcomes, albeit the preferences of the agents are the same.

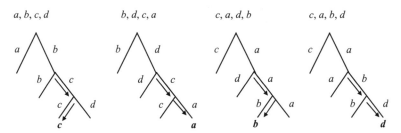

Figure 9.4: Binary voting protocols: different agendas may lead to different outcomes

Plurality protocols

A *plurality* voting protocol is a majority protocol where all alternatives are compared simultaneously and the one with the highest number of votes wins. Such protocols are used in political elections, for instance.

One well known plurality voting mechanism is the *rank order* or Borda[4] protocol. In rank-order protocols each agent ranks the alternatives according to their own preferences and assigns a number that indicates the rank in its ordering. The Borda count assigns an alternative $|\mathcal{O}|$ points whenever it is highest in some agent's preference list, $|\mathcal{O}| - 1$ whenever it is second, and so on. The alternative with the highest count becomes the social choice. For instance, in the example of Table 9.3, there are seven agents that need

	Preferences				Preferences $(-d)$		
Agent	4	3	2	1	3	2	1
A	$a \succ c \succ d \succ b$				$a \succ c \succ b$		
B	$b \succ d \succ c \succ a$				$b \succ c \succ a$		
C	$c \succ d \succ a \succ b$				$c \succ a \succ b$		
D	$a \succ b \succ c \succ d$				$a \succ b \succ c$		
E	$b \succ c \succ d \succ a$				$b \succ c \succ a$		
F	$c \succ d \succ a \succ b$				$c \succ a \succ b$		
G	$a \succ b \succ c \succ d$				$a \succ b \succ c$		
Borda Count	$a = 18, b = 17, c = 21, d = 15$						
Borda Count $(-d)$					$a = 15, b = 12, c = 14$		

Table 9.3: Borda voting protocol example

---

[4]French mathematician Jean-Charles de Borda (1733–1799).

to decide among four possible outcomes, a, b, c and d. The Borda count in this case will assign numbers to each of the outcomes according to the agents' preferences. According to agent A's preferences, a will get 4, b will get 3, c will get 2 and finally d will get 1 count. In the same way, the rest of the agents' preferences will be given counts and, in the end, the scores for each alternative will be summed up to determine an aggregate score. The alternative with the highest score is the socially preferred outcome. In this example, c is the socially preferred alternative as it has the highest Borda count among all others.

In plurality protocols, the introduction of an irrelevant alternative may split the majority. Some agents may still prefer the old most-favoured alternative, while some agents may now prefer the newly introduced one. Yet another problem is that both the old favourite and the newly introduced alternative may drop below one of the previously least preferred alternatives, which could then become the new socially preferred outcome.

The Borda protocol can be manipulated and can lead to paradoxical results if an irrelevant alternative is removed or introduced. Consider the example of Table 9.3 again, where now d has been removed since it has the fewest votes. Going through the same process described above and assigning Borda counts to every alternative according to the agents' preferences, the protocol now leads to a different result than before. Alternative a is the socially preferred outcome with the highest count.

Mixed protocols

Some protocols involve stages which combine plurality and binary protocols. The *majority runoff* protocol is conducted in two stages. In the first stage, voters indicate their preferences among a set of alternatives by casting one vote. If one alternative receives the majority of votes, then this is declared the winner. Otherwise, the protocol proceeds to the second stage in which the two most preferred alternatives run against each other, and the alternative with the most votes wins.

Another mixed protocol is the *proportional representation* in which the full preference rankings of the voters are taken into account and provide for a proportional representation. Such schemes are often used in political elections. For instance, if in a country X the electorate consists of 45% Yellow, 32% Brown and 23% Grey, these preferences would yield a body of representatives which reflects the aforementioned party preferences of the electorate. A variation of proportional representation is the *single transferable vote* or *Hare* [5] protocol. In this protocol the agents consider the various alternatives and cast one vote, but indicate their preference rankings over all alternatives. Typically, alternatives which obtain a certain percentage of votes are elected and those that fail to obtain that percentage, or in some cases the alternative(s) with the fewer votes, are eliminated. The votes from the eliminated alternatives are transferred to the next highest ranking

[5] British barrister Thomas Hare (1806–1891).

alternative according to the agents' preference rankings. This process is repeated until an appropriate number of alternatives are elected.

In general, although agents are required to reveal their preferences over alternatives truthfully to the mechanism, they may lie, declare their preferences insincerely or vote strategically in order to increase their own gain. Those responsible for setting up the process can also attempt to manipulate the proceedings for their own benefit. For instance, in the binary protocol, the agenda of alternatives can be manipulated so that a particular outcome ensues.

Moreover, the application of different protocols to the same situation may lead to different outcomes. A typical example is the election held for the Olympic site for the 1996 Summer games (Dixit and Skeath 1999). The protocol used for the selection of the Olympic site involves multiple plurality rounds in which the alternative with the fewest votes is eliminated, and a final stage in which the last two alternatives are pitted against each other and the one with the majority wins. Athens was one of the candidate cities and in the initial rounds it was in the lead. As 1996 marked the centenary of the games and Greece is the birthplace of the Olympic ideal, Athens was considered by a number of members of the International Olympic Committee as the natural candidate. If a single plurality protocol had been used, Athens would have been selected. However, as a mixed protocol was used, Athens gained few additional votes as other cities got eliminated. In the penultimate round the three contenders were Athens, Atlanta (US) and Sydney (Australia). Sydney was eliminated in that round and most votes went to Atlanta and thus Athens missed the opportunity to host the centenary games.

9.5.3 Maximizing social welfare

Given a set of outcomes $\mathcal{O}$ and a set of agents N, a utility function $u_i(o)$ summarizes the agent's preferences: agent i prefers o to o' if and only if $u_i(o) > u_i(o')$. One possible way to obtain social preferences from the agents' preferences is to add up their utilities and use the resulting number to represent the social utility (Varian 2006). Thus, the allocation o is socially preferred to allocation o' if:

$$\sum_{i=1}^{n} u_i(o) > \sum_{i=1}^{n} u_i(o')$$

Although this may seem a reasonable way to aggregate preferences, it is totally arbitrary. Indeed, instead of the sum, one could have used the squares of all utilities or the product as the aggregating function. But one reasonable requirement on the aggregating function, is that it should be increasing in each agent's utility. In this way, if everybody prefers o to o', the social preference will prefer o to o'. Such an aggregating function is called a *social welfare function*. This is just a function of the agent utility functions $W(u_1(o), \ldots, u_n(o))$ which gives a way to rank different allocations that depends only on the agents' preferences, and is an increasing function of each individual agent's utility.

The sum of all utilities above, is just an example of such a social welfare function. Another example is the weighted sum of utilities:

$$W(u_1, \ldots, u_n) = \sum_{i=1}^{n} v_i u_i$$

Where each v_i is positive and indicates the weight associated with agent i which represents how important that agent's utility is to the overall social welfare of the society.

Given a welfare function, we can now look into the problem of welfare maximization. Let o_i^j indicate how much individual i has of item j and suppose that there are n agents and k goods. Then the allocation o consists of the list of how much each of the agents has of each of the goods. If $X^1, \ldots, X^k$ represent the quantities of goods $1, \ldots, k$ to distribute among the agents, the social welfare maximization problem takes the form (Varian 2006):

$$\arg\max_{o \in \mathcal{O}} W(u_1(o), \ldots, u_n(o))$$

such that $\sum_{i=1}^{n} o_i^1 = X^1$

$$\vdots$$

$$\sum_{i=1}^{n} o_i^k = X^k$$

Such a maximal welfare allocation must be Pareto efficient. This is fairly straightforward, as if it is not Pareto efficient, then there should be some other feasible allocation that gives everyone at least as large a utility, and someone strictly a greater utility. But, as the welfare function is an increasing function of each agent's utility, the new allocation would have a higher welfare utility which contradicts the assumption that the allocation, which we had originally, constitutes a welfare maximum. In a similar way, every Pareto efficient allocation is a welfare maximum, this follows in a similar way.

9.6 ARGUMENTATION

Agents using the various negotiation protocols that have been described thus far are able to make an offer/proposal within the space of acceptable offers/proposals, and accept or decline a previously made offer/proposal. This process of negotiation as purported by game theory, although it does allow agents to make offers and counter-offers, has the following two inherent limitations (Jennings et al. 2001):

1. Proposals/offers and negotiation positions are not justified. Often when humans negotiate, not only do they make proposals and counter-proposals, but they also use arguments to justify these proposals and convince the other participants of their

proposals' merits. Consider a situation where two companies, A and B, are negotiating on a number of issues to reach an agreement and sign a contract. If company A simply states that it can offer 10 000 components of x on a specific day at 50 monetary units per item, when the usual market price is 40 units, company B may turn down this offer altogether without giving it much consideration. However, if A is able to offer a justification for the higher price – it can only produce the required number of components if additional workers are hired, or overtime is paid to workers as the order's deadline is too close to be produced within normal production – then B may come to realize that A's position is not unreasonable. B may even accept the fact that, due to the close proximity of the order's delivery date, an additional cost has to be incurred. The ability to explain and justify one's position in negotiation situations is also invaluable when we consider the kind of tasks that we would ideally like to delegate to software agents. For instance, if the task of booking a flight is delegated to an agent, the user may want to know why the agent booked a particular flight, i.e., the user may ask the agent to justify its choice. Such a facility increases transparency in decision-making and also aids the building of trust between human and software agents.

2. Proposals/offers and negotiation positions cannot be modified. So far we have implicitly assumed that an agent's utility function is fixed and does not change while the agent engages in the negotiation process. However, this may not necessarily be the case. In the contract negotiation example above, when B hears A's argument and justification for the increased cost, it may be able to modify its position (and in a way its utility function). Agent B accepting A's argument may then offer a modified proposal that splits the initial order in two, i.e., 5000 components for the original delivery date and 5000 components for a later day for 45 and 42 monetary units, respectively. Agent A may then be able to agree with this modified position.

One way to overcome these limitations is through argumentation-based negotiation (Sycara 1990, Parsons et al. 1998, Kraus et al. 1998). The underlying idea of argumentation is to allow additional information to be exchanged on top of one's negotiation position, offer or proposal. In essence, agents enter into a dialogue and use arguments and counter-arguments to advance and impose their own views, and ultimately to promote their own interests. Thus, agents attempt to convince one another about the value of their own position or the lack of merit of another party's position. This is the persuasion type of dialogue as we briefly discussed in Section 3.3.7.

Argumentation amongst humans takes the following form (Gilbert 1994):

- **Logical mode.** This form of argumentation resembles logical or mathematical proofs. It is usually deductive in nature, i.e., if you accept x and x implies y, then you accept y. This is customarily the form of argumentation used in courts of law.

- **Emotional mode.** This mode of argumentation makes use of one's feelings, emotions and other attitudes. A characteristic example of an argument in this mode is that of 'how would you feel, if this happened to you'.

- **Visceral mode.** Arguments in this mode involve physical and social aspects. For instance, in labour negotiations, when the union's representative bangs her hand on the table declaring that the union will not accept any agreement which involves laying off personnel, this shows determination.

- **Kisceral mode.** The kisceral mode of argumentation makes appeals to the religious, mystical or intuitive side of human nature.

In agent-based negotiation, the visceral, emotional or kisceral modes of argumentation are not applicable, at least in the foreseeable future.

9.6.1 Generating arguments

The underlying idea in argumentation-based negotiation is to allow for additional information to be exchanged during the negotiation process; information which is over and above the proposals. This additional information consists of arguments, which explain explicitly the opinion of the agent on a particular proposal or other issue pertinent to the negotiation situation. Hence, when an agent j rejects a proposal or offer by agent i, it also offers a critique which explains the reasons why it is unacceptable. The effect of such a statement is that it clarifies the negotiation space of agent j, and in particular, it identifies an area as not being of interest to the agent.

An agent can accompany a proposal with an argument which gives reasons why the other agent should accept it. This type of argument makes it possible to influence the other agent's beliefs and ultimately its decision on whether to accept the proposal or not. But, as agents are self-interested and they attempt to maximize their own utility, they may not necessarily be truthful and, as a consequence, their arguments may not be valid. Agents need to be able to evaluate and assess the validity and merits of the other agents' arguments in a particular situation and decide on a response.

There are two parties involved in argumentation: the persuader and the persuadee. The former wishes to convince the latter of the value, or not, of a proposition or proposal. Persuasive arguments are used in order to change the behaviour of the persuadee. This can occur in two ways, either the argument will lead the persuadee to change its behaviour, or its beliefs which will subsequently lead to a change in behaviour. What is of importance, for the persuader, however, is that the behaviour changes, not necessarily the beliefs. In persuasive argumentation, arguments that are based on threats of punishment, or promises of reward, can effectively lead to changes in behaviour without necessarily changing beliefs. The following issues need to be taken into account in persuasive argumentation (Sycara 1990):

- **Representing and maintaining belief models of others.** As the ultimate goal of argumentation is to affect behaviour and perhaps influence another agent's beliefs, to be able to argue effectively and convince one's opponent of one's position, an agent must be able to represent and maintain belief models of the other agents. Such models are inherently incomplete and, perhaps, inaccurate.

- **Selecting which beliefs to change.** For effective argumentation, an agent needs to be in a position to discern which of the persuadee's beliefs need to be influenced and in what way.

- **Connecting beliefs with behaviour.** To produce effective arguments that will change the persuadee's behaviour, the persuader needs to be in a position to make a connection between beliefs and behaviour, i.e., to predict which beliefs directly affect specific behaviours in other agents.

- **Choosing an appropriate argument.** Potentially, a number of arguments can be generated depending on a particular situation. The persuader needs to be able to evaluate different arguments and then choose the most effective one.

- **Offering counter-arguments.** Once a persuader has explained a particular argument on a negotiation position, the persuadee will offer a response on the argument in the form of acceptance, rejection or a counter-argument in an attempt to refute the persuader's position. The persuader needs to be able to reason about this counter-argument and offer another argument or modify its original negotiation position. In addition, based on the persuadee's response, the persuader needs to modify its model of the persuadee.

- **Modifying one's position.** As negotiation or argumentation takes place, the environment may change and the same applies to the agents' goals. Agents need to be flexible and take into account new conditions and situations as they arise and modify their positions accordingly. This includes modifying one's position in view of a counter-argument, or proposal offered by another agent.

Inevitably, generating convincing arguments is a cognitively complex task. Agents that negotiate via argumentation-based negotiation are able to participate in negotiation dialogues in which they can offer, not only proposals, counterproposals and accept and reject the proposals of others, but most importantly they can generate and exchange meta-level information. To be able to generate and exchange such meta-level information, the agent's decision-making process needs to be augmented with the capability to evaluate the arguments of others and also generate arguments to support one's own positions. In this respect, the abstract architecture of a negotiating agent which was described in Section 8.3 needs to be extended by an argumentation component as is illustrated in Figure 9.5 (Ashri et al. 2003, Rahwan et al. 2003).

When an argumentation-based negotiating agent receives a message, the communication component and, in particular, the message interpretation process needs to break it down into its constituent proposal and supporting argument – if such an argument is included in the message. Although the proposal part is treated as before, the argument forms the input in the argument evaluation process which, as the name suggests, evaluates the newly received argument and also updates the agent's model of the world. For

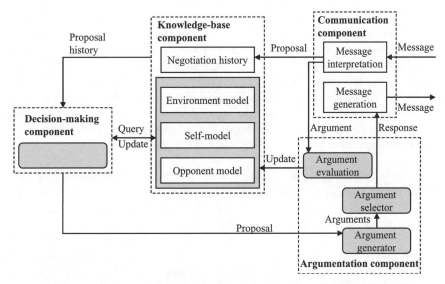

Figure 9.5: Abstract architecture for argumentation-based negotiating agents

instance, it may be the case that the argument offered by another agent may modify the agent's beliefs, or convince it about the value of the other agent's proposal. The new proposal is evaluated by the decision-making component and a response is generated, taking into account the updated model of the world and the updated negotiation history. The generated proposal forms the input of the argument generation process, which is responsible for generating arguments for supporting the proposal, if this is required. For example, no argument needs to be generated if the response is simply to accept the other agent's proposal. For other types of proposals, a number of supportive arguments may be generated. The purpose of the argument selection process is then to select the most appropriate one, i.e., the strongest supportive argument. The proposal, along with the supportive argument, are subsequently passed on to the message generation process and the appropriate message is generated and sent to the other participant(s).

9.6.2 The PERSUADER system

Being able to provide arguments and counter-arguments in a negotiation situation can be very useful and enhance the negotiation process, enabling agents to reach an agreement satisfying all negotiating parties, to a certain extent.

One of the first systems which made use of argumentation was the PERSUADER for negotiating labour contracts among employees and employers (Sycara 1990). The PERSUADER system makes use of a mediator agent who mediates between the employer and the employees who are represented by their union and allows participants to negotiate on various issues including wages, pensions and seniority. The participants exchange proposals and counter-proposals and argue the merits of these in order to convince the other party. The negotiation process in the PERSUADER system consists of three main tasks that are repeated until an agreement is found: proposal generation, counter-proposal generation based on response from the disagreeing participant, and persuasive argumentation. The agents have a representation of the others' beliefs which they update, based on the proposals and arguments that are being generated during the negotiation process. Beliefs also reflect the agent's goals and the interrelationships among them. An example of a goal for the company may be to increase profit, which can be achieved through the reduction of production costs, or an increase in sales.

When a conflict arises between the parties, the PERSUADER system takes into account the beliefs and goals of the participants and attempts to generate a compromise. For example, if the union demands higher wages, the system will attempt to generate an argument to convince the union to accept the current offer on the table, as a further increase in wages may force the company to lay off personnel, in order to afford it. To generate this argument, PERSUADER determines which goals are violated by the union's refusal, and then looks for actions to compensate these.

The system can generate more than one possible argument for a particular negotiation position. The types of argument that are considered, in order of increasing convincing power, are as follows:

1. Appeal to universal principle: the persuader appeals to some universal principal or some core belief of the persuadee.

2. Appeal to a theme or a package of goals: the persuader attempts to convince the persuadee that the former has the latter's interests at heart.

3. Appeal to authority: the persuader may present arguments supported by a third party which is seen as having some authority.

4. Appeal to status quo: a justification is provided based on current conditions which are extrapolated in the future.

5. Appeal to 'minor standard': arguments based on 'minor standards' can be used as a basis for refutation anchored in prevailing practice.

6. Appeal to prevailing practice: the persuader appeals to standards in the community.

7. Appeal to precedents as counterexamples: the persuader uses precedents as counterexamples to convince the persuadee of the attainability of their position.

8. Appeal to self-interest: the persuader makes an argument based on the importance of the goal being promoted.

9. Threats and promises: the persuader can use threats to punish, or promises to reward a persuadee. Such arguments are effective when one party is in a relative position of power with respect to the other.

9.6.3 Logic-based argumentation

We have already discussed logic-based agents in the context of agent architectures in chapter 2. Such agents represent the world around them, including themselves and other agents via a set of logical formulas. An agent attempts to satisfy its own goals by proving that a sequence of actions will lead to the achievement of the goals. In this context, it is natural to see argumentation as the process of generating a series of logical arguments for and against propositions, negotiation positions, offers or proposals.

In classical logic, an argument comprises a series of logical steps which lead to a conclusion. Assume a knowledge base $\mathcal{KB}$ which describes the world. We write:

$$\mathcal{KB} \vdash \langle \phi, KB \rangle$$

to indicate that ϕ can be established through a sequence of inferences from the set of formulas $KB \subseteq \mathcal{KB}$. In essence, the series of steps which consists of applying the rules of inference on KB provides the justification, i.e., can prove, the conclusion ϕ. Formally, an argument is a pair $\langle \phi, KB \rangle$. For instance, consider a knowledge base containing facts about the world, $\mathcal{KB}$, among which we have:

bird(*Crow*)

bird(X) $\Rightarrow$ *flies*(X)

The conclusion *flies*(*Crow*) can be correctly inferred, based on the logical axioms and rules of inference of classical logic. In words, if the agent knows that anything that is a bird flies and crows are birds, then it can correctly infer that crows fly.

When agents are negotiating via argumentation and in order to be able to understand each other, $\mathcal{KB}$ needs to be common knowledge, i.e., it represents the common ground or information that all agents have which facilitates argumentation. This relates to the point that was raised earlier with regard to agents having a model of the other agents in order to be able to reason about them, and also their knowledge about the world, so that they are in a position to offer arguments that the other agents can understand and lead them to change their behaviour.

The knowledge base $\mathcal{KB}$ may not be consistent, and thus several arguments of varying degrees of strength can be build. This degree of strength needs to be quantified in some way to enable agents to rate different arguments. Arguments can be distinguished into tautological and nontrivial. The former follow from the rules of inference and do not rely on formulas from the agent's theories. An argument is nontrivial if it is consistent, i.e., if there are no KB_1, KB_2 such that $\mathcal{KB} \vdash \langle \phi, KB_1 \rangle$ and $\mathcal{KB} \vdash \langle \neg\phi, KB_2 \rangle$ at the same time.

Given an argument $\langle \phi, KB \rangle$, there are two types of argument against it: those that *rebut* it and those that *undercut* it. The argument $\langle \phi_1, KB_1 \rangle$ rebuts $\langle \phi_2, KB_2 \rangle$ if ϕ_1 attacks ϕ_2, whereas $\langle \phi_1, KB_1 \rangle$ undercuts $\langle \phi_2, KB_2 \rangle$ if ϕ_1 attacks ψ for some $\psi \in KB_2$. An attack is then defined as follows: for any propositions ϕ and ψ, ϕ attacks ψ, if and only if $\phi \equiv \neg \psi$.

Taking into consideration the concepts of rebutting and undercutting, arguments can be classified in order of increasing acceptability of power as follows (Krause et al. 1995, Parsons et al. 1998):

Class A1: All arguments that can be made from KB.

Class A2: All nontrivial arguments that may be made from KB.

Class A3: All arguments that may be made from KB for propositions for which there are no rebutting arguments.

Class A4: All arguments that may be made from KB for propositions, for which there are no undercutting arguments.

Class A5: All tautological arguments.

The arguments in higher classes are more acceptable as they are less questionable. Intrinsically, an undercutting attack is less damaging than a rebutting attack as an undercut allows for another, undefeated, supporting argument for the same conclusion.

Consider the following set of formulas as comprising the knowledge base KB (this example has been adapted from Wooldridge (2002)):

$human(Heracles)$

$father(Heracles, Zeus)$

$father(Athena, Zeus)$

$immortal(X) \Rightarrow \neg mortal(X)$

$father(X, Zeus) \Rightarrow immortal(X)$

$\neg(father(X, Zeus) \Rightarrow immortal(X))$

From these we can build the following argument Arg_1 about $Heracles$:

$\langle mortal(Heracles), \{human(Heracles, human(X) \Rightarrow mortal(X)\} \rangle$

And the rebutting argument Arg_2:

$\langle \neg mortal(Heracles),$

$\{father(Heracles, Zeus), father(X, Zeus) \Rightarrow immortal(X), immortal(X) \Rightarrow \neg mortal(X)\} \rangle$

which is undercut by Arg_3:

$\langle \neg(father(X, Zeus) \Rightarrow immortal(X)), \{\neg father(X, Zeus) \Rightarrow immortal(X))\} \rangle$

The argument Arg_4:

$$\langle immortal(Heracles) \vee \neg immortal(Heracles), \emptyset \rangle$$

is a tautology, therefore it is in the A5 class of arguments, whereas Arg_1 and Arg_2 are in class A2 and finally Arg_5 below belongs to class A4:

$$\langle \neg mortal(Athena),$$

$$\{father(Athena,Zeus), father(X,Zeus) \Rightarrow immortal(X), immortal \Rightarrow \neg mortal(X)\} \rangle$$

9.6.4 Negotiation as dialogue games

One recent approach to argumentation-based negotiation in multi-agent systems is to use dialogue game frameworks (Amgoud et al. 2000a,b, McBurney et al. 2003). In such frameworks, the interactions of the negotiating agents are modelled as dialogue games which have their roots in the philosophical literature of argumentation (Hamblin 1970, MacKenzie 1979). Dialogue games describe interactions between two or more agents where each agent 'makes a move' by making an utterance according to a set of rules. The specification of a dialogue game consists of the following types of rules (McBurney et al. 2003):

- Commencement rules determine the conditions under which dialogues are initiated.

- Locution rules specify the utterances that are allowed as part of a dialogue game, i.e., assert or justify propositions, or question or challenge previously uttered propositions. The locution rules may also allow the negotiating agents to utter propositions to which they assign differing degrees of commitment. For example, proposing a proposition commits the agent less than if asserting the proposition.

- Combination rules determine the dialogical contexts in which particular utterances are permitted or not, or are obligatory or not. As an example, participants may not be allowed to assert a proposition and subsequently assert its negation in the same dialogue, without first retracting the former.

- Commitment rules identify the circumstances under which the negotiating agents make dialogical commitment to a proposition. For instance, asserting a proposition indicates such a commitment to the proposition. The agent who made the assertion is expected to defend the proposition and offer arguments to its support, if challenged by other participants. An agent's expressed commitments form its *commitment store* which may not necessarily be monotonic; in other words, the agent is allowed to retract previously made commitments. In the context of dialogue games, it is usually the case that commitments have no psychological or other meaning outside of the particular dialogue context (Hamblin 1970).

- Termination rules specify the conditions under which the dialogue comes to an end.

A dialogue game for modelling the interactions among buyers and sellers in a purchase transaction situation has been proposed by McBurney et al. (2003). There are three types of agents in this framework: buyers, sellers and advisors. A buyer is interested in purchasing goods and goods are supplied by sellers. The role of the advisor is to provide information when asked by a buyer agent, for instance, when a buyer does not have a clear idea of what is available in the market. The buyer may have a number of candidate items that it can choose from, i.e., its consideration set. It can then use its selection criteria to decide which item(s) to purchase. Once the buyer has decided which item(s) to purchase, it may engage in negotiations with one or more sellers. This dialogue game includes the following stages:

1. *Open dialogue*. The dialogue between buyer and seller or advisor commences.

2. *Inform*. The buyer seeks information from the seller and/or advisor agents regarding the various options available and their attributes. The information is provided by the other participants.

3. *Consideration set formation*. The buyer considers the information provided in stage (2) on the available options along with its inclusion criteria and decides on the elements of the consideration set.

4. *Option selection*. The buyer applies its selection criteria on the consideration set, and the output of this process is a list of purchase options in order of preference.

5. *Negotiation*. Negotiations between the buyer and one or more sellers commence over the buyer's purchase options in order of preference. During this stage, the buyer and seller(s) may interact in a number of ways. A buyer may simply request a particular option from a particular seller. The buyer may also request an option which had not been presented by the seller, but which the buyer is interested in and, for instance, may combine a number of attributes not present in any of the current purchase options. Sellers may not necessarily accommodate such requests. If no purchase option meets the buyer's criteria, no request is submitted to the seller. Depending on the particular situation, more than one of these sequences of interactions may take place and often repeatedly.

6. *Confirmation*. In this stage the participants confirm any agreements on purchases reached.

7. *Dialogue termination*. The dialogue ends normally.

Strictly speaking stages (3) and (4) are not part of the dialogue between participant agents, but refer to calculations done internally by the buyer agent. These decision-making processes may differ from agent to agent; some algorithms are suggested in McBurney et al. (2003).

Although we assumed that the buyers have their own inclusion and evaluation criteria which they apply to form the consideration set and select their options respectively, this may not always be the case. A buyer may not have a clear idea of how to evaluate the different products available. In this case, the buyer may seek the advice of a seller or an advisor agent. A more complex form of dialogue that would allow a buyer to enquire about criteria and assess them would involve the following two stages between stages (2) and (3):

- *Request criteria.* The buyer requests information from seller(s) and/or advisor(s) regarding what criteria are appropriate for including goods in its consideration set. The buyer may also request information on criteria for assessing the different options and their associated importance weightings. The other participants provide the requested information. In both cases, the buyer may also request justifications or reasons for the provided suggestions and engage in a debate with the agent(s) providing the suggestions.

- *Assess criteria.* Having been provided with a set of criteria, the buyer now assesses these and through some means generates a list of inclusion criteria and a list of selection criteria that will be used in subsequent stages. Such criteria may also determine appropriate thresholds.

Again the *Assess criteria* stage would not be part of the dialogue protocol, but indicates calculations done internally by the buyer agent.

The simplest form of dialogue follows the sequence of stages (1–7) as described above. But more complex dialogues can have loops, and participants are also allowed to enter stages multiple times in any combination and order, subject to the following constraints:

- The first stage in every dialogue game is the *Open dialogue* stage. This stage may occur only once.

- The last stage in every dialogue game that ends normally is the *Dialogue termination* stage. This stage may occur only once.

- The only stages which must occur in every dialogue that terminates normally are the *Open dialogue* and *Dialogue termination* stages.

- The first instance of every stage apart from the *Open dialogue* and *Dialogue termination* stages must be preceded by an instance of the *Inform* stage.

- The *Confirmation* stage may only be entered following an instance of the *Negotiation* stage.

To automate such dialogues, appropriate locutions are required to enable the agents to request information, negotiate, etc. The set of locutions along with their intended meaning required to facilitate dialogues that involve stages (1–7) as described above, are briefly described in Table 9.4 (McBurney et al. 2003). Each locution includes a set of pre and post-conditions which determine the effects on the agents' commitment and information stores (the latter stores information about dialogues). For example, the full definition of the locution **willing_to_sell(.)** is as follows:

Locution	Meaning
open_dialogue(.)	Suggests the opening of a purchase dialogue to other participants.
enter_dialogue(.)	Indicates the willingness of the participant to enter a dialogue.
seek_info(.)	Requests information from one or more other participants.
willing_to_sell(.)	The participant (seller or advisor) returns a set of sale options that a seller is willing to sell. This is in answer to a previously submitted seek_info(.) locution.
desire_to_buy(.)	The participant is interested in purchasing a set of options from a set of sellers.
prefer(.)	The participant prefers one options set over another.
refuse_to_buy(.)	The participant refuses to purchase any option from an options set from a set of sellers.
refuse_to_sell(.)	The participant refuses to sell to a set of buyers any option from a particular options set.
agree_to_buy(.)	The buyer commits to purchasing one item of each commodity in its options set from a particular seller.
agree_to_sell(.)	The seller commits to selling each of the options in an options set to a particular buyer.
withdraw_dialogue(.)	Announces that the participant withdraws from the dialogue.

Table 9.4: Locutions in the dialogue game protocol of McBurney et al. (2003)

Locution: willing_to_sell(P_i, T, P_j, V) where P_i is either the seller or advisor agent, T is the set of participants, P_j is a seller and V is the set of sale options.

Preconditions: Some participant P_x must have previously uttered a locution seek_info (P_x, S, p) where $P_i \in S$ (S the set of sellers), and the set of sales options V satisfy constraint p.

Meaning: Participant P_i indicates to audience T that agent P_j is willing to supply the finite set of sale options $V = \{\widehat{a}, \widehat{b}, \ldots\}$ to any buyer in set T. Each of the options in V must satisfy constraint p which was previously uttered as part of the seek_info(.) locution.

Response: None required.

Information store: For each $\widehat{a} \in V$, the three-tuple $(T, P_j, \widehat{a})$ is inserted into the information store of participant P_i, $IS(P_i)$.

Commitment store: No effects.

Agents can engage in dialogues where each of the dialogue stages consists of a number of locutions. The *Open dialogue* stage commences with the **open_dialogue(.)** locution and is followed by at least one **enter_dialogue**(.) locution. The *Inform* stage consists of the utterances **seek_info**(.) and **willing_to_sell**(.). The *Negotiation* stage is facilitated through the locutions **desire_to_buy**(.), **prefer**(.), **refuse_to_buy**(.), and **refuse_to_sell**(.). The **seek_info**(.) and **willing_to_sell**(.) locutions can also be used in this stage. The *Confirmation* stage includes the locutions **agree_to_sell**(.) and **agree_to_buy**(.). Finally, the *Dialogue termination* stage involves the utterance **withdraw_dialogue**(.).

Negotiation conducted in the context of dialogue games enables a richer exchange between participants, rather than simple offers and counter-offers. One of the main advantages of dialogue games such as the one described here is that is easy to verify whether or not agents conform to the underlying protocol. This is due to the fact that such approaches refer only to pre and post-conditions which are described in terms of observable linguistic behaviour, rather than the agents' mental attitudes. Such semantics is termed *public* axiomatic semantics, in contrast to *private* axiomatic semantics where the pre and post-conditions are defined in terms of the participants' mental states (McBurney and Parsons 2003).

9.7 Further Reading

The seminal papers by John Nash laid the foundations for both approaches to bargaining (Nash 1950a, 1953). A thorough introduction into bargaining and an extended discussion of Rubinstein's bargaining solution can be found in Osborne and Rubinstein (1990). An interesting reading in bargaining theory and its applications is Muthoo (1999). Axiomatic bargaining is also introduced in Mas-Colell et al. (1995, Chapter 22). Kraus (2001) extensively discusses the principles of the Strategic Negotiation Protocol, and its applications are demonstrated in a number of domains. The discussion on task and worth-oriented domains draws on Rosenchein and Zlotkin (1994), where the two topics are covered in depth.

The problem of coalition formation can be studied in the context of cooperative games and, in particular, characteristic function games (CFG). A succinct introduction to coalition formation is provided in Sandholm (1999), whereas a detailed discussion of the game-theoretic solution concepts to coalition games can be found in Osborne and Rubinstein (1994). The problem of coalition formation, from a computational point of view, is examined in Sandholm et al. (1999) while an improved algorithm is presented in Dang and Jennings (2004). An alternative decentralized approach to coalition formation for the allocation of tasks to groups of cooperative agents is presented in Shehory and Kraus (1998).

The original papers describing the Core (Gillies 1959), the Shapley value (Shapley 1953), the bargaining set (Aumann and Maschler 1964) and the kernel (Davis and Maschler 1965) provide a more thorough explanation of these solutions. The discussion on customer coalitions and the pre and post-negotiation protocols presented here, is based on Tsvetovat et al. (2000).

Social choice problems are described in detail in Mas-Colell et al. (1995, Chapters 21 and 22) and Varian (2006, Chapter 33), the former being a more technical exposition. Voting protocols are discussed in Dixit and Skeath (1999, Chapter 14), Sandholm (1999) and briefly in Varian (2006, Chapter 36).

Argumentation has been traditionally the subject of study in philosophy and logic (Barth and Krabbe 1982, Walton 1989, Walton and Krabbe 1995). Good starting points in argumentation in multi-agent systems and, in particular, argumentation-based negotiation, are Sycara (1990), Parsons et al. (1998) and Kraus et al. (1998). The discussion here is based mainly on the first two works. A survey of work in argumentation-based negotiation in multi-agent systems, as well as current research challenges, are presented in Rahwan et al. (2003). Dialogue game protocols are reviewed in McBurney and Parsons (2003), while the details of the dialogue game protocol discussed here can be found in McBurney et al. (2003). The abstract architecture for argumentation-based negotiating agents presented here is based on Ashri et al. (2003) and Rahwan et al. (2003).

9.8 Exercises and Topics for Discussion

1. An agent A decides on whether or not to steal an amount of money $\pi > 0$. If she steals the money, then with some probability p she is caught by a police officer P. However, the police officer is corruptible and can let go of A provided that she is bribed. A and P bargain over the amount of bribery b that A will have to pay to P in return for not reporting the crime. P reports A if and only if they fail to reach an agreement, and in this case A pays a fine. The set of possible agreements is the set of possible divisions of the stolen money (money is perfectly divisible) which is: $\{(\pi - b, b) : 0 \leq b \leq \pi\}$. The disagreement point $(d_A, d_P) = (\pi(1 - v), 0)$ where $v \in (0, 1]$ is the penalty rate. The utility of obtaining x units of money is x. What is the Nash bargaining solution in this case? Given that A will be caught with probability p, will she decide to commit the crime?

2. Consider the bargaining problem of splitting a pie of size 1 with utility $u(x_1) = x_1$ for player A and $v(x_2) = 2x_2 - (x_2)^2$ for player B, where x_1 and x_2 are taken from the interval [0,1]. Suppose the players are bargaining over how to split the pie according to an alternating offers procedure.

   (a) What are the key properties of the basic alternating offers bargaining model? Depict the game-tree for the first three rounds of negotiations.

   (b) What are the equilibrium offers for players A and B respectively? What are the utilities for the two players when player A moves first?

3. There are n servers dispersed around your country which provide information services. The servers are connected via a communication network. Each server stores data which are accessible not only to its own clients, but to other servers as well. Each server specializes and stores documents in specific topics which are indicated by keywords. When a server receives a query for a document, it retrieves this document either from its own repository or from another server. The cost to retrieve information from another server depends on the virtual distance between the servers. As new documents arrive, the servers need to agree on which server is going to store the document – only one server can store a document. The longer the servers take to agree on where the document will be stored, the higher the cost for temporarily storing the document, which all servers have to share. Sketch a negotiation protocol that would enable the servers to reach an agreement in this situation.

4. In village K, the farmers get water to irrigate their fields from the local water company. The farmers have plots of different size and they produce a variety of vegetables. The price of water per gallon is not fixed and the farmers are free to negotiate a price with the company. The problem is that farmers with small plots of land do not have much negotiation power, whereas farmers with bigger sized plots can negotiate better prices, since they require larger quantities of water. The local farmers' union has employed you as a consultant. Describe a negotiation protocol that would help the farmers in this situation. What are the possible risks (if any) if the protocol you have suggested is adopted?

5. In an attempt to boost the income of small-scale fishermen, the government is providing incentives for the creation of local marketplaces where the fishermen could sell their catch of the day. The idea is that local restaurants, shops, etc., would be able to visit the marketplace and buy fish directly from the producers. In area A there are fifteen villages that participate in this initiative. The fishermen form a local union in order to go ahead with the

project. They have decided to call their local marketplace Fresh Fish and have employed you as a consultant.

(a) Describe a negotiation protocol, that would help individual fishermen to achieve the best prices, which takes into consideration the following restrictions: each fisherman may have several different varieties of fish to sell (or even only one) and at different quantities and, finally, the fish need to be sold as soon as possible. What are the possible risks (if any) if the protocol you have suggested is adopted?

(b) A big supermarket firm decides to buy its fish supply in bulk from the Fresh Fish marketplace. Describe a negotiation protocol for this situation. What are the potential risks of the protocol you are suggesting?

6. Given a binary voting protocol, five possible alternatives a, b, c, d, e and the following preferences:

20% prefer $e \succ d \succ b \succ a \succ c$

15% prefer $b \succ e \succ a \succ c \succ d$

23% prefer $c \succ d \succ a \succ b \succ e$

18% prefer $b \succ e \succ d \succ c \succ a$

24% prefer $d \succ a \succ c \succ e \succ b$

what will be the outcome of the protocol according to the following agendas?
(a) e, a, b, c, d
(b) a, c, e, d, b
(c) b, e, d, c, a
(d) d, e, c, b, a

7. Given the following agent preferences over five alternatives a, b, c, d, e, what will be the outcome according to the Borda protocol?

User1 $a \succ e \succ c \succ b \succ d$

User2 $c \succ b \succ d \succ a \succ e$

User3 $e \succ a \succ b \succ d \succ c$

User4 $d \succ a \succ e \succ c \succ b$

User5 $e \succ c \succ b \succ a \succ d$

User6 $b \succ d \succ e \succ a \succ c$

User7 $a \succ b \succ c \succ d \succ e$

User8 $c \succ a \succ e \succ d \succ b$

8. Assume a set of buyers B, sellers S, and advisor agents A. Suppose a buyer i is interested in purchasing a car. Using the locutions described in Section 9.6.4, and observing the rules, sketch a dialogue in which the buyer first asks for information from a number of sellers/advisors about cars. Subsequently the buyer negotiates with a couple of sellers and eventually reaches an agreement with one of them. You can enrich this scenario with other details. For instance, you can consider that the buyer asks for additional information from sellers/advisors while negotiating, or expresses preferences. For the full details of the dialogue game protocol the reader is referred to McBurney et al. (2003).

CHAPTER 10

Mechanism Design

LEARNING OBJECTIVES

After reading and completing this chapter, you should be able to:

- Explain the aims, objectives and limitations of mechanism design.
- Describe the problem of incentive compatible mechanisms and preference elicitation.
- Apply the Generalized Vickrey Auction mechanism to simple problems.
- Discuss the computational issues surrounding mechanism design.

In the previous chapters, after introducing some basic concepts of Economics and Game theory, we saw a number of negotiation protocols including auctions, bargaining, coalition formation and also voting protocols. We looked into how individual preferences might be aggregated into social preferences and, ultimately, into a collective or social decision. However, an important feature of many practical situations in which collective decisions must be made is that individual agents are self-interested and their actual preferences are private information. Consequently, agents must be trusted to reveal these preferences. But as agents are self-interested and rational, if they can benefit from being insincere, they will not declare their preferences truthfully.

Thus, when designing a negotiation protocol or any other mechanism for social or collective decision-making, we want these to lead to socially desirable outcomes. In general, this requires considering incentives so that the agents choose to reveal appropriate information about their preferences. Suppose we want a set of trading agents, representing their users, to participate in an online auction. Clearly, first we have to motivate the agents to participate in the auction. Second, we have to consider the possibility that the agents may try to manipulate the protocol or lie about their true preferences to maximize their own utility.

The development of protocols that are stable and individual rational for the agents is the subject of mechanism design, a subclass of implementation theory. Mechanism design studies how privately known preferences of a set of self-interested agents can be aggregated towards a social choice. In particular, in this chapter we consider the problem of information revelation, i.e., how information about the individual agents' preferences can be elicited and, moreover, how the privacy of this information constrains the ways in which social choice problems can be resolved in an optimal way. Mechanism design has many important applications, ranging from voting and auction protocols to decisions regarding the construction of public projects and, more recently, the design of electronic markets and resource allocation problems.

10.1 THE MECHANISM DESIGN PROBLEM

Consider a situation with a set of agents N. These agents must make a collective choice from a set $\mathcal{O}$ of possible alternatives. Each agent i has some private information $\theta_i \in \Theta_i$, called the type of the agent, which is not revealed to the other agents or to the mechanism designer[1]. The type of an agent determines its preferences over outcomes $o \in \mathcal{O}$. An agent is an expected utility maximizer and its utility function is parameterized on the type θ_i. Thus $u_i(o, \theta_i)$ denotes the utility of agent i for outcome $o \in \mathcal{O}$ given type θ_i. An agent i prefers outcome o over o' when $u_i(o, \theta_i) > u_i(o', \theta_i)$. An outcome can be practically anything, for example, the assignment of an item or a resource to a set of agents, or the construction of a public project. An outcome may also involve payments between the agents and to some third party.

[1] In this chapter we build on the notation that was introduced in Section 7.2.10 for formalizing Bayesian games.

Agents can reach an outcome by interacting through an *institution* or *mechanism* in which there are rules governing the actions which the agents may take and how these actions translate to an outcome. Examples of very commonly used institutions, through which agents interact and make collective choices, are those of auctions and voting protocols. Obviously, the outcome that the society of agents chooses depends on the individual agents' types θ_i. The mechanism design problem is to implement an optimal outcome given that the agents have private information about their types. Alternatively, the problem can be seen as implementing an optimal overall system solution to a decentralized optimization problem with self-interested agents, with private preferences over the different outcomes. This goal can be defined by a social choice function. A social choice function selects the optimal outcome given the agent types.

Definition 23 *A social choice function* $f : \Theta_1 \times \cdots \times \Theta_n \to \mathcal{O}$ *chooses an outcome* $f(\theta_1, \ldots, \theta_n) \in \mathcal{O}$, *given the agents' types* $\theta = (\theta_1, \ldots, \theta_n)$.

The social choice function encapsulates the designer's objectives, i.e., the properties that the designer would like the outcome to possess. One of the desiderata for social choice functions is that of Pareto optimality:

Definition 24 *The social choice function* $f : \Theta_1 \times \cdots \times \Theta_n \to \mathcal{O}$ *is Pareto optimal if for no profile* $\theta = (\theta_1, \ldots, \theta_n)$ *is there an* $o \in \mathcal{O}$, *such that* $u_i(o, \theta_i) \geq u_i(f(\theta), \theta_i)$ *for every i, and* $u_i(o, \theta_i) > u_i(f(\theta), \theta_i)$ *for some i.*

Another desired property is to maximize the total utility across all agents:

$$f(\theta) = \arg \max_{o \in \mathcal{O}} \sum_{i=1}^{n} u_i(o, \theta_i)$$

A social choice function could be *indirectly* implemented by having agents interact through an institution or mechanism. In other words, the mechanism design problem can be viewed as providing the 'rules of a game' to implement the solution to the social choice function when agents are self-interested and their preferences are private information. More formally, a mechanism is defined as follows:

Definition 25 *The mechanism* $\mathcal{M} = (S_1, \ldots, S_n, g(\cdot))$ *defines the set of strategies* S_i *available to each agent, and an outcome rule* $g : S_1 \times \cdots \times S_n \to \mathcal{O}$, *such that* $g(s)$ *is the outcome implemented by the mechanism for the strategy profile* $s = (s_1, \ldots, s_n)$.

A mechanism defines the strategies available S_i (e.g., bid at least the ask price) and the rule of how the agent actions are turned into a social choice is given by the outcome function $g(\cdot)$ (e.g., the item is allocated to the agent with the highest bid). The mechanism and the agent types together define a game. We can then use the tools of game theory to analyze the outcome of a mechanism. Given a mechanism $\mathcal{M}$ with outcome function $g(\cdot)$, we say that the mechanism implements social choice function $f(\cdot)$, if the outcome computed with equilibrium agent strategies is a solution to the social choice function for all possible profiles of types $\theta = (\theta_1, \ldots, \theta_n)$:

Definition 26 *The mechanism* $\mathcal{M} = (S_1, \ldots, S_n, g(\cdot))$ *implements social choice function* $f(\theta)$ *if* $g(s_1^*(\theta_1), \ldots, s_n^*(\theta_n)) = f(\theta)$, *for all* $(\theta_1, \ldots, \theta_n) \in \Theta_1 \times \cdots \times \Theta_n$, *where strategy profile* $s = (s_1^*, \ldots, s_n^*)$ *is an equilibrium solution to the game induced by* $\mathcal{M}$.

From a computational point of view, mechanism design is the development of efficient algorithms for optimization problems in which some of the parameters of the objective function are in the control of the agents who have private preferences over different outcomes (Parkes 2001).

To summarize, the mechanism design problem involves designing a mechanism which consists of a set of possible agent strategies and an outcome rule, to implement a social choice function with desirable properties in a solution concept. The equilibrium concept is left undefined at this stage. Recall from Chapter 7 that there are different solution concepts, i.e., dominant strategy, Bayesian Nash, Nash, etc. A number of solution concepts have been considered in the mechanism design literature. We will focus on the dominant strategy equilibrium solution in the following sections.

10.2 DOMINANT STRATEGY IMPLEMENTATION

Implementing a social choice function would be easy if information on θ was available. The problem is that the agents' preferences are private information and so, for the social choice function $f(\theta_1, \ldots, \theta_n)$ to be chosen when the agents' types are $(\theta_1, \ldots, \theta_n)$, each agent must be relied upon to reveal their type θ_i. However, for a given social choice function $f(\cdot)$, an agent may not find it in their best interest to disclose their real preferences. As each agent i forms their own preferences over outcomes given by the utility function $u_i(o, \theta_i)$ with θ_i being the true type, if by reporting a false type $\widehat{\theta}_i \neq \theta_i$ an agent i expects to receive a higher payoff than by reporting θ_i, then this agent has an incentive to lie. For example, if a social choice function chooses the outcome that is last in the reported preferences of, say agent j, then this agent will report its preferences inverted to take advantage of the mechanism.

Hence, when the agents' preferences are private information, the information revelation problem, i.e., the fact that agents may not reveal truthful information about their preferences, may constrain the set of social choice functions that can be successfully implemented. This now begs the question: what social choice functions can be implemented when the agents' types are private information?

The identification of all the social choice functions that can be implemented seems an extremely difficult task: searching the entire space of possible mechanisms, which is a very large set, would be infeasible. Fortunately, an important result, known as the *revelation principle*, tells us that we need not search the entire space of mechanisms, but we can restrict our attention to the very simple type of mechanisms in which each agent is asked to reveal their type, and given the type announcements $(\widehat{\theta}_1, \ldots, \widehat{\theta}_n)$ the alternative chosen is $f(\widehat{\theta}_1, \ldots, \widehat{\theta}_n) \in \mathcal{O}$. These are known as direct revelation mechanisms:

Definition 27 *A direct revelation mechanism $\mathcal{M} = (\Theta_1, \ldots, \Theta_n, g(\cdot))$ is a mechanism in which the strategy set is $S_i = \Theta_i$ for all i and the outcome rule $g : \Theta_1 \times \cdots \times \Theta_n \to \mathcal{O}$ selects an outcome $g(\widehat{\theta})$ based on the reported preferences $\widehat{\theta} = (\widehat{\theta}_1, \ldots, \widehat{\theta}_n)$.*

In a direct revelation mechanism, the strategy of agent i is to report type $\widehat{\theta}_i = s_i(\theta_i)$, based on their true type θ_i. A strategy s_i is *truth-revealing* if it reports true information about types, that is $s_i(\theta_i) = \theta_i$ for all $\theta_i \in \Theta_i$. In an *incentive compatible mechanism*, the agents report truthful information about their types in equilibrium. Incentive compatibility is a very important concept in mechanism design: if a mechanism is incentive compatible, then the agents will choose to report their true preferences (or types) out of their own self-interest. A direct revelation mechanism, where agents have a dominant strategy that involves revealing their true types, is called *strategy-proof* or *dominant strategy incentive compatible*. We start by defining the concept of a dominant strategy equilibrium for a mechanism:

Definition 28 *The strategy profile $s_i^*(\cdot) = (s_1^*(\cdot), \ldots, s_n^*(\cdot))$ is a dominant strategy equilibrium of mechanism $\mathcal{M} = (S_1, \ldots, S_n, g(\cdot))$ if for all $i \in N$ and all $\theta_i \in \Theta_i$, $u_i(g(s_i^*(\theta_i), s_{-i}), \theta_i) \geq u_i(g(s_i', s_{-i}), \theta_i)$ for all $s_i' \in S_i$ and all $s_{-i} \in S_{-i}$.*

Thus, the definition of implementation of a social choice function by a mechanism can be specialized to the case of dominant strategies. The mechanism $\mathcal{M} = (S_1, \ldots, S_n, g(\cdot))$ implements the social choice function $f(\cdot)$ in dominant strategies, if there exists a dominant strategy equilibrium of $\mathcal{M}, s_i^*(\cdot) = (s_1^*(\cdot), \ldots, s_n^*(\cdot))$ such that $g(s^*(\theta)) = f(\theta)$ for all $\theta \in \Theta$.

The concept of dominant strategy implementation is of special interest: if we can find a mechanism $\mathcal{M} = (S_1, \ldots, S_n, g(\cdot))$ that implements $f(\cdot)$ in dominant strategies, then this mechanism implements $f(\cdot)$ in a very strong and robust way. If a rational agent has a dominant strategy, then it will indeed choose to play it. From a computational point of view, an agent can compute its optimal strategy without modelling the strategies and preferences of the other agents, i.e., without counter-speculating or having to do any opponent modelling.

The revelation principle asserts that, under quite weak conditions, any mechanism can be transformed into an equivalent strategy-proof (i.e., incentive compatible) direct revelation mechanism, such that it implements the same social choice function.

Definition 29 *A direct revelation mechanism $\mathcal{M}$ is strategy-proof or incentive compatible if truth-revelation is a dominant strategy equilibrium.*

A simple equivalence exists between the outcome of function $g(\widehat{\theta})$ of a direct revelation mechanism which selects the outcome based on the reported types $\widehat{\theta}$, and the social choice function $f(\theta)$ implemented by the mechanism, i.e., computed in equilibrium. We say that an incentive compatible direct revelation mechanism $\mathcal{M}$ implements social choice function $f(\theta) = g(\theta)$, where $g(\theta)$ is the outcome rule of the mechanism. In other words, in an incentive compatible mechanism, the outcome rule is the social choice function implemented by the mechanism:

Definition 30 *The social choice function $f(\cdot)$ is truthfully implementable in dominant strategies (or dominant strategy incentive compatible, or strategy-proof or straightforward) if $s_i^*(\theta_i) = \theta_i$ for all $\theta_i \in \Theta_i$ and $i \in N$ is a dominant strategy equilibrium of the direct revelation mechanism $\mathcal{M} = (\Theta_1, \ldots, \Theta_n, f(\cdot))$. That is, if for all i and all $\theta_i \in \Theta_i$, $u_i(f(\theta_i, \theta_{-i}), \theta_i) \geq u_i(f(\widehat{\theta}_i, \theta_{-i}), \theta_i)$ for all $\widehat{\theta}_i \in \Theta_i$ and all $\theta_{-i} \in \Theta_{-i}$.*

The revelation principle for dominant strategy implementation asserts that any social choice function that is implementable in dominant strategy is also implementable in a strategy-proof mechanism. In essence, this principle allows us to restrict our attention without loss of generality to the question of whether $f(\cdot)$ is truthfully implementable.

Proposition 1 *The Revelation Principle for Dominant Strategies. Suppose that there exists a mechanism $\mathcal{M} = (S_1, \ldots, S_n, g(\cdot))$ that implements the social choice function $f(\cdot)$ in dominant strategies. Then $f(\cdot)$ is truthfully implementable in dominant strategies.*

Proof *(Mas-Colell et al. (1995)) If $\mathcal{M} = (S_1, \ldots, S_n, g(\cdot))$ implements $f(\cdot)$ in dominant strategies, then there exists a profile of strategies $s^*(\cdot) = (s_1^*(\cdot), \ldots, s_n^*(\cdot))$ such that $g(s^*(\theta)) = f(\theta)$ for all θ and for all i and all $\theta_i \in \Theta_i$,*

$$u_i(g(s_i^*(\theta_i), s_{-i}^*), \theta_i) \geq u_i(g(\widehat{s}_i, s_{-i}^*), \theta_i)$$

for all $\widehat{s}_i \in S_i$ and all $s_{-i} \in S_{-i}$ by definition of dominant strategy implementation. Substituting $s_{-i}^*(\theta_{-i})$ for s_{-i} and $s_i^*(\widehat{\theta}_i)$ for $\widehat{s}_i$ we have:

$$u_i(g(s_i^*(\theta_i), s_{-i}^*(\theta_{-i})), \theta_i) \geq u_i(g(s_i^*(\widehat{\theta}_i), s_{-i}^*(\widehat{\theta}_{-i})), \theta_i)$$

for all $\widehat{\theta}_i \in \Theta_i$ and all $\theta_{-i} \in \Theta_{-i}$. Finally since $g(s^*(\theta)) = f(\theta)$ for all θ, we have:

$$u_i(f(\theta_i, \theta_{-i}), \theta_i) \geq u_i(f(\widehat{\theta}_i, \theta_{-i}), \theta_i)$$

for all $\widehat{\theta}_i \in \Theta_i$ and all $\theta_{-i} \in \Theta_{-i}$. In fact, this is the condition required for $f(\cdot)$ to be truthfully implementable in dominant strategies in a direct revelation mechanism. The outcome rule in the strategy-proof mechanism $g : \theta_1 \times \cdots \times \theta_n \to \mathcal{O}$, is simply equal to the social choice function $f(\cdot)$. ∎

The intuitive idea behind the revelation principle for dominant strategies can be put as follows: suppose that the indirect mechanism $\mathcal{M} = (S_1, \ldots, S_n, g(\cdot))$ implements $f(\cdot)$ in dominant strategies, and that, in this indirect mechanism, each agent i finds playing $s_i^*(\theta_i)$ when its type is θ_i better than playing any other $s_i \in S_i$ for any choices $s_{-i} \in S_{-i}$ by agents

$j \neq i$. Suppose that a mediator agent is introduced who says to each agent i: "tell me your type, and when you say your type is θ_i, I will play $s_i^*(\theta_i)$ for you". Clearly if $s_i^*(\theta_i)$ is agent i's optimal choice for each $\theta_i \in \Theta_i$ in the initial mechanism $\mathcal{M}$, for any strategies chosen by the other agents, then agent i will find telling the truth to be a dominant strategy in this new setting. However, this also means that we can truthfully implement $f(\cdot)$.

The dominant strategy revelation principle is quite remarkable. Its implication is that, to identify which social choice functions are implementable in dominant strategies, we need only identify those functions $f(\cdot)$ for which truth-revelation is a dominant strategy for all agents in a direct revelation mechanism with outcome rule $g(\cdot) = f(\cdot)$. The notation $\mathcal{M}(\Theta, f)$ can be adopted for dominant strategy incentive compatible direct revelation mechanisms because of this equivalence between the outcome rule and the social choice function.

10.3 THE GIBBARD–SATTERTHWAITE IMPOSSIBILITY THEOREM

The Gibbard–Satterthwaite impossibility theorem was discovered independently by the two economists in the early 1970s and is similar in spirit to Arrow's impossibility theorem, which was discussed in Section 9.5.1. This result shows that, for a very general class of problems in a sufficiently rich environment, there is no hope of implementing satisfactory social choice functions in dominant strategies.

Recall from Section 7.1.2 that an ordering of preferences over outcomes is complete if for $o_1, o_2 \in \mathcal{O}$ we have $o_1 \succ o_2$ or $o_2 \succ o_1$. An ordering is transitive if for all $o_1, o_2, o_3 \in \mathcal{O}$ if $o_1 \succ o_2$ and $o_2 \succ o_3$ then it is the case that $o_1 \succ o_3$. Preferences θ_i are *general* when they provide a complete and transitive preference ordering $\succ$ on outcomes.

A social choice function is dictatorial if one (or more) agent(s) always receives one of its most-preferred alternatives. Formally, the social choice function $f(\cdot)$ is dictatorial if there is an agent i such that for all $\theta = (\theta_1, \ldots, \theta_n) \in \Theta$, $f(\theta) \in \{o \in \mathcal{O} : u_i(o, \theta_i) \geq u_i(o', \theta_i)$ for all $o' \in \mathcal{O}\}$.

The negative result of Gibbard and Satterthwaite states that it is impossible, in a sufficiently rich environment, to implement a nondictatorial social choice function in dominant strategy equilibrium.

> **Theorem 5   (Gibbard-Satterthwaite Impossibility Theorem)**   *If agents have general preferences and there are at least two agents, and at least three different optimal outcomes over the set of all agent preferences, then a social choice function is dominant strategy implementable if and only if it is dictatorial.*

Clearly, all dictatorial social choice functions must be strategy-proof. This is simple to show because the outcome that is selected is the most preferred or the optimal outcome for the reported preferences of one (or more) of the agents – so an agent has the incentive to report their true preferences. For a proof in the other direction, that any strategy-proof social choice function must be dictatorial, see Mas-Colell et al. (1995).

This impossibility result must be interpreted with caution. In particular, the results do not necessarily continue to hold in restricted environments. For instance, although no dictatorial social choice function can be Pareto optimal or efficient, this impossibility result does not apply directly to markets. The market environment naturally imposes additional structure on preferences. In particular, the Gibbard–Satterthwaite theorem may not hold when additional constraints are imposed on preferences, or weaker implementation concepts are considered.

Given this negative conclusion, if we are to implement desirable social choice functions, we must either weaken the demands of our implementation concept by accepting implementation by means of less robust equilibrium notions (such as the Bayesian Nash equilibrium) or we must focus on more restricted environments. In fact, market environments have been shown to make implementation easier. We will see examples in the following sections.

10.4 THE GROVES–CLARKE MECHANISMS

In this section, we consider environments in which the preferences of the agents take a quasilinear form, that is, we restrict the form that the agents' payoffs may take.

10.4.1 Quasilinear environments

The utility $u_i(\cdot)$ of agent i encapsulates its preferences over its own strategy and the strategies of the other agents, given its type θ_i. In a quasilinear environment, the agents' preferences take the form:

$$u_i(k, t_i, \theta_i) = v_i(k, \theta_i) + t_i$$

The outcome rule, $g(s)$ in a mechanism with quasilinear preferences is decomposed into a choice rule $k(s)$ which selects a choice from the choice set, given strategy profile s, and a payment rule $t_i(s)$ which selects a payment to agent i, based on strategy profile s.

A mechanism for quasilinear environments $\mathcal{M} = (S_1, \ldots, S_n, k(\cdot), t_1(\cdot), \ldots, t_n(\cdot))$ defines the set of strategies S_i available to each agent; a choice rule $k : S_1 \times \cdots \times S_n \to K$ such that $k(s)$ is the choice implemented for strategy profile $s = (s_1, \ldots, s_n)$, and transfer rules $t_i : S_1 \times \cdots \times S_n \to \mathbb{R}$, one for each agent i to compute the payment $t_i(s)$ made to the agent.

A quasilinear environment has certain properties that make it convenient for analysis. In particular, there are no income effects that influence the demand for the various goods. If the agents' preferences are quasilinear, then an agent should not care how others divide payoffs among themselves. Moreover, an agent's valuation function should not depend on the amount of money that the agent will have.

Given that the agents' preferences are quasilinear, the following properties can be defined.

Definition 31   *A mechanism $\mathcal{M}$ is allocatively efficient if it selects the choice k that maximizes the total value for all preferences $\theta = (\theta_1, \ldots, \theta_n)$:*

$$\sum_{i=1}^{n} v_i(k, \theta_i) \geq \sum_{i=1}^{n} v_i(k', \theta_i), \text{ for all } k' \in K$$

Such a social rule maximizes the sum of the agents' valuations given their preferences (types).

Definition 32   *A mechanism $\mathcal{M}$ is (ex post) budget-balanced if the equilibrium net transfers to the mechanism are balanced for all agent preferences, i.e., $\sum_{i=1}^{n} t_i(\theta) = 0$ for all preferences $\theta = (\theta_1, \ldots, \theta_n)$.*

In other words, there are no net transfers out of the system or into the system.

Definition 33   *A mechanism $\mathcal{M}$ is (ex post) weak budget-balanced if the equilibrium net transfers to the mechanism are non-negative for all agent preferences, i.e., $\sum_{i=1}^{n} t_i(\theta) \geqslant 0$ for all preferences $\theta = (\theta_1, \ldots, \theta_n)$.*

This means that there can be a net payment made from the agents to the mechanism, but not from the mechanism to the agents.

10.4.2 The Groves mechanism

Consider a set of possible alternatives K, and agents with quasilinear utility functions such that:

$$u_i(k, t_i, \theta_i) = v_i(k, \theta_i) + t_i$$

where $v_i(k, \theta_i)$ is the agent's value for alternative k, and t_i is a payment to the agent. In a direct revelation mechanism for quasilinear preferences, we write the outcome of the $g(\widehat{\theta})$ rule in terms of a choice rule $k : \Theta_1 \times \cdots \times \Theta_n \to K$ and a payment rule $t_i : \Theta_1 \times \cdots \times \Theta_n \to \mathbb{R}$, for each agent i.

In a Groves mechanism, agent i reports type $\widehat{\theta}_i = s_i(\theta_i)$, which may not be their true type. Given the reported types $\widehat{\theta} = (\widehat{\theta}_1, \ldots, \widehat{\theta}_n)$, the choice rule in the Groves mechanism computes an optimal outcome $k^*(\widehat{\theta})$:

$$k^*(\widehat{\theta}) = \arg \max_{k \in K} \sum_{i=1}^{n} v_i(k, \widehat{\theta}_i)$$

Choice k^* maximizes the total reported value over all agents, i.e., it is ex post efficient.

The payment rule in the Groves mechanism is then defined as:

$$t_i(\widehat{\theta}) = \left[\sum_{j \neq i} v_j(k^*(\widehat{\theta}), \theta_j) \right] + h_i(\widehat{\theta}_{-i})$$

where $h_i : \Theta_{-i} \to \mathbb{R}$ is an arbitrary function on the reported types of every agent except i. The Groves mechanism pays the agent when h_i is zero. The class of social choice functions that are characterized by the above, are truthfully implementable in dominant strategies, i.e., the agents report their true preferences to the mechanism and thus $\widehat{\theta}_i = \theta_i$.

Theorem 6 *Let $k^*(\cdot)$ be ex post efficient. The social choice function $f(\cdot) = (k^*(\cdot), t_1(\cdot), \ldots, t_n(\cdot))$ is truthfully implementable in dominant strategies if for all $i = 1, \ldots, n$:*

$$t_i(\theta) = \left[\sum_{j \neq i} v_j(k^*(\theta), \theta_j) \right] + h_i(\theta_{-i}) \ (i)$$

Proof *If truth is not a dominant strategy for some agent i, then there exist $\theta_i, \widehat{\theta}_i$, and θ_{-i} such that*

$$v_i(k^*(\widehat{\theta}_i, \theta_{-i}), \theta_i) + t_i(\widehat{\theta}_i, \theta_{-i}) > v_i(k^*(\theta_i, \theta_{-i}), \theta_i) + t_i(\theta_i, \theta_{-i}).$$

Substituting from (i) for $t_i(\widehat{\theta}_i, \theta_{-i})$ and $t_i(\theta_i, \theta_{-i})$, this implies that

$$\sum_{j=1}^{n} v_j(k^*(\widehat{\theta}_i, \theta_{-i}), \theta_j) > \sum_{j=1}^{n} v_j(k^*(\theta), \theta_j)$$

which contradicts $k^*(\cdot)$ being ex post efficient. Thus $f(\cdot)$ must be truthfully implementable in dominant strategies. ∎

In the Groves mechanism, given the announcements θ_{-i} of agents $j \neq i$, agent i's payment depends on reported preferences only through the effect of preferences on the alternative $k^*(\theta)$. Moreover, the change in agent i's payment which results when its reported preferences change the alternative choice k, is exactly equal to the effect of this change in k on agents $j \neq i$.

As a result, agent i has an incentive to truthfully report its preferences, which leads to a level of k that maximizes the n agents' joint payoff from the alternative $\sum_{i=1}^{n} v_i(k, \theta_i)$.

10.4.3 The Clarke mechanism

The Clarke, otherwise known as the Pivotal or VCG mechanism, is a special case of the Groves mechanism which was discovered by Clarke (1971). The Clarke mechanism uses a specific taxing scheme. How much an agent i pays depends on how much i influences the outcome chosen. An agent pays nothing if its reported preferences do not change the outcome, but it does pay if its influence is pivotal. In the Clarke mechanism:

$$h_i(\theta_{-i}) = - \sum_{j \neq i} v_j(k^*_{-i}(\theta_{-i}), \theta_j)$$

where $k^*_{-i}(\theta_{-i})$ is the optimal collective choice (i.e., ex post efficient) with agent i taken out of the system:

$$k^*_{-i}(\theta_{-i}) = \arg \max_{k \in K} \sum_{j \neq i} v_j(k, \theta_j)$$

or alternatively:

$$\sum_{j \neq i} v_j(k^*_{-i}(\theta_{-i}), \theta_j) \geq \sum_{j \neq i} v_j(k, \theta_j) \text{ for all } k \in K$$

Then agent i's transfer is given by:

$$t_i(\theta) = \left[\sum_{j \neq i} v_j(k^*(\theta), \theta_j) \right] - \left[\sum_{j \neq i} v_j(k^*_{-i}(\theta_{-i}), \theta_j) \right]$$

If i's reported preferences do not change the decision, then $k^*(\theta) = k^*_{-i}(\theta_{-i})$ and therefore the transfer $t_i = 0$. However, if $k^*(\theta) \neq k^*_{-i}(\theta_{-i})$ then the agent's reported preferences are pivotal in determining the outcome, and t_i is negative, in other words, the agent has to pay tax.

In the Clarke mechanism, the payment rule $h_i(\theta_{-i})$ is carefully set to achieve individual rationality, while also maximizing the payments made by the agents to the mechanism. In particular, the Clarke mechanism is individual rational in some settings. Suppose that the agent's utility from not participating in the mechanism is $\overline{u}_i(\theta_i) = 0$. The Clarke mechanism is individual rational when the following conditions are satisfied:

- **Choice set monotonicity.** The feasible choice set K available to the mechanism (weakly) increases as additional agents are introduced into the system. In other words, an agent cannot 'block' a selection.

- **Normalization.** Agent i has non-negative value, i.e., $v_i(k^*_{-i}, \theta_i) \geq 0$, for any optimal solution choice, $k^*_{-i}(\theta_{-i})$ without agent i, for all i and all θ_i. That is to say, any choice not involving the agent has a neutral (or positive) effect on that agent.

The Clarke mechanism is ex post weak budget-balanced when there are *no positive externalities,* which means that the presence of an agent i does not introduce choices that are more valuable to other agents. This is the case in auctions with multiple buyers and a single seller who is known to have no intrinsic value for the items, and in social choice problems, such as public projects. On the other hand, this is not true for markets in which both buyers and sellers have private information on the values of the items.

10.4.4 The Generalized Vickrey Auction

The Generalized Vickrey Auction (GVA) is an application of the Clarke mechanism, described in the previous section, to resource allocation problems. Suppose that an auctioneer wants to allocate a set of items X to a set of agents N. The vector of goods

$\bar{x}$ has the form $\bar{x} = \{(x_1, \ldots, x_n) : x_i \subseteq X\}$ where x_i is an allocation of goods to agent i. Each agent has a valuation $v_i(x_i)$. The valuation depends on the type θ_i of an agent i, but we drop the type here for simplicity. We would like the goods to be allocated among agents in such a way so that the sum of their valuations is maximized:

$$\arg\max_{x_i} \sum_{i=1}^{n} v_i(x_i)$$

subject to the constraint:

$$\sum_{i=1}^{n} x_i = \bar{x}$$

However, the participants of this resource allocation problem may not want to reveal their true preferences. The problem then is to design a mechanism that will induce the participants to truthfully reveal their private preferences:

1. Each agent i reports a valuation function $\hat{v}_i$ which may not be truthful to the mechanism.

2. The mechanism calculates the allocation (x_i^*) that maximizes the sum of the reported values, subject to the resource constraint.

3. The mechanism also calculates the allocation (x_{-i}^*) that maximizes the sum of the values, other than that of agent i.

4. Agent i receives the bundle x_i^* and receives a payment from the centre (which can be negative) which is calculated as:

$$\sum_{j \neq i} [\hat{v}_j(x_j^*) - \hat{v}_j(x_{-i,j}^*)]$$

The final payoff to agent i in the GVA takes the form:

$$v_i(x_i^*) + \sum_{j \neq i} \hat{v}_j(x_j^*) - \sum_{j \neq i} \hat{v}_j(x_{-i,j}^*)$$

The GVA is efficient, strategy-proof, individual rational, and weak budget-balanced for agents with quasilinear preferences in the resource allocation problem.

The third term in the above sum, which is denoted simply by Q, is irrelevant to agent i's decision since it is totally outside their control. Although Q is useful in reducing the magnitude of the side payment to agent i, it has no impact on the strategy of agent i.

The mechanism will choose x_i^* so as to maximize:

$$\hat{v}_i(x_i^*) + \sum_{j \neq i} \hat{v}_j(x_j^*)$$

subject to the resource constraint. Agent i then wants to maximize its payoff:

$$v_i(x_i^*) + \sum_{j \neq i} \hat{v}_j(x_j^*) - Q$$

Thus, the optimal choice for the agent is to report $\hat{v} = v$, so that its true valuation function is actually the one that is being maximized.

Consider the standard Vickrey auction. In this case, the valuation function of agent i is $v_i - p$ where v_i is agent i's true valuation and p is the price it pays. Let $x_i = 1$ if agent i gets the item and $x_i = 0$ if it does not. Then the sum of the valuations is:

$$\sum_{i=1}^{n} v_i(x_i)$$

and the resource constraint is

$$\sum_{i=1}^{n} x_i = 1$$

Let m be the index of the agent with the maximum value of v_i. To maximize the sum of valuations, the mechanism will allocate $x_m^* = 1$ and $x_j = 0$ for all $j \neq m$. Suppose agent l has the second-highest value. Then if agent m is eliminated, the maximum sum of the remaining valuations will be v_l. The net payoff to agent m in the GVA will be $v_m - v_l$, which is the result of the Vickrey auction, i.e., the winner pays the second-highest price.

Consider now the situation where multiple units of a commodity need to be allocated. Suppose that there is one commodity but there are $\bar{x}$ units of it to sell. Agents may want to obtain multiple units. Let (x_i^*) be the allocation that maximizes the sum of all agents' valuations and let $x_{-i,j}^*$ be the amount allocated to agent j if the sum of all agents' valuations, but agent i, is maximized. Then agent i's payoff in the GVA is:

$$v_i(x_i^*) + \sum_{j \neq i} v_j(x_j^*) - \sum_{j \neq i} v_j(x_{-i,j}^*)$$

Assume that there are two agents and three units of a commodity to allocate. Agent A values the first unit of the commodity at 10, the second unit at 8 and the third one at 5. Agent B values the commodities at (9, 7, 6), respectively. The optimal allocation of the commodity is to give agent A two units of the commodity and B one unit of the commodity. Thus, A receives a total value of 18 and B receives a total value of 9.

Using the GVA, the problem is solved as follows. If A is not present, all the goods go to agent B who receives a total value $9 + 7 + 6 = 22$. In the GVA, A's net payoff is $18 + [9-22] = 5$. So agent A pays 13 for the 2 units of the commodity that it receives.

Similarly if agent B is not present, all the goods go to agent A who receives a total value $10 + 8 + 5 = 23$. B's net payoff is then $9 + [18-23] = 4$. Hence, agent B pays 5 for one unit of the commodity that it receives. The seller receives $13 + 5 = 18$ for the three units sold.

10.4.5 Inducing truth–telling in voting mechanisms

A social choice rule, such as a voting mechanism, takes the agents' preferences as input and attempts to find the socially optimal allocation or outcome. The implicit assumption in the previous chapter has been that the agents' preferences are truthful. However, an agents' preferences are not known in advance, they have to reveal them to the mechanism or declare them through some other means. Since they are self-interested and not necessarily cooperative, if they can gain from lying, they will lie.

Suppose a community of residents is deliberating on whether to build a community gym that everyone could use. They have adopted a binary voting protocol in order to decide what the majority prefers. Suppose that the agents have to pay for the gym via some form of tax, which depends on what they reveal about their preferences. For instance, it may be the case that only the pro-gym voters would have to pay. Consequently, the residents would have an incentive to vote insincerely and free-ride the gym that might be built anyway due to the other agents' votes. So how can we ensure that the agents reveal their true preferences to the mechanism?

Let the outcome be of the form $o = (g, \pi_1, \ldots, \pi_n)$, where π_i is the numeraire or monetary transfer that agent i receives in the outcome (which can be negative), and g encodes the other features of the outcome. In voting whether to build a joint gym, $g = 1$ if the gym is built, and $g = 0$ if it is not. An agent's utility consists of the utility from g plus the numeraire and takes the form $u_i(o) = v_i(g) + \pi_i$. Since the agents' preferences are quasilinear, then this also implies that no agent should care how others divide payoffs amongst themselves. This might be violated if, for instance, an agent wants her group of close friends to pay less than the rest of the residents. Moreover, an agent's valuation function of the gym should not depend on the amount of money that she will have. This might be violated, for example, if rich agents have more time to enjoy the gym, as perhaps they do not have to work long hours.

Let $v_i(g)$ denote an agent i's true valuation and $\widehat{v}_i(g)$ denote what she reveals about her valuation. The solution to providing incentives to agents, to reveal their true preferences in this case is to make those agents, whose vote changes the outcome, pay a tax. The tax is proportional to how much the agent's vote lowers the other agents' utilities. Agents that do not end up changing the outcome do not have to pay any tax. The Clarke tax mechanism can be used in this case. The social choice, according to the Clarke mechanism, is defined as:

$$g^* = \arg\max_g \sum_{i=1}^n \widehat{v}_i(g)$$

Every agent i has to pay a tax which is calculated as:

$$tax_i(g^*) = \sum_{j \neq i} \widehat{v}_j \left(\arg\max_g \sum_{k \neq i} \widehat{v}_k(g) \right) - \sum_{j \neq i} \widehat{v}_j(g^*)$$

The above equation evaluates the sum of individual valuations (i.e., social welfare function) for all the agents in the community, but agent i, at the outcome that would have been chosen if agent i's valuation had been ignored. Intuitively, if agent i had not been part of the community, then the community's chosen outcome would be the one that maximized the social welfare function of the subgroup. The tax is then defined as the difference between the subgroup social welfare function evaluated at the subgroup's choice, $\arg\max_g \sum_{k \neq i} \widehat{v}_k(g)$, and the subgroup social welfare function evaluated at the entire community's choice, g^*. Alternatively, agent i can be thought of as having to pay a tax equal to the amount that the community lost because she participated. Thus, if agent i's valuation caused the community's welfare to decrease, then she should pay a tax proportional to this decrease. Each agent's dominant strategy is then to reveal her true preferences, and thus $\widehat{v}_i(g) = v_i(g)$ for all g. The monetary transfer then for agent i is $\pi_i = -tax_i(g)$.

The mechanism provides an incentive to the agents to reveal their true preferences and it therefore leads to the socially most preferred g to be chosen. As truthtelling is every agents' dominant strategy, the agents need not waste effort in counter-speculating each other's preference declarations. Furthermore, participation in the mechanism can only increase an agent's utility and therefore the mechanism is individual rational.

Unfortunately, the mechanism does not maintain budget balance as too much tax is collected (Sandholm 1999). There are other truth-dominant algorithms for this problem where too little tax is collected, but none that guarantees that the sum of the taxes is zero. The schemes where too little is collected require an external benefactor to operate, whereas the schemes that collect too much, are not Pareto efficient because the extra tax revenue has to be used in some way. The extra tax collected cannot be given back to the agents or used in any other project that any of them are interested in. Such redistribution would thereby affect the agents' utilities and truth-telling would no longer be a dominant strategy. Another problem of the Clarke tax algorithm is that it is not collusion proof. Some group of voters might coordinate their insincere preference revelations and achieve higher utilities.

10.5 MECHANISM DESIGN AND COMPUTATIONAL ISSUES

From the multi-agent systems point of view, mechanism design is the design of protocols governing multi-agent strategic interactions. Agents have their individual preferences and evaluations of goods and services that are available in the market and they seek to maximize their utilities by exchanging goods and services with the other participants. The aim of traditional mechanism design is to design a system in which rational agents interact in such a way that desirable social outcomes follow. The desired properties of the social outcomes are encapsulated in the social choice function, which ultimately describes what is to be achieved by the use of the mechanism, i.e., utility maximization across all agents, efficient allocation of goods and resources, etc.

In the previous sections we discussed mechanisms that have certain game-theoretic properties. Much of traditional mechanism design is driven by the revelation principle which allows us to restrict attention to direct revelation mechanisms. In a direct revelation mechanism, each agent is required to send a single message which contains its preferences over possible outcomes to the mechanism. The transformation assumed in the revelation principle from indirect mechanisms (e.g., an iterative auction) to direct ones (e.g., a sealed-bid auction) entails unlimited computational resources, both for the agents in submitting their complete preferences, and for the auctioneer in computing the outcome of the mechanism. Hence, although the revelation principle provides a very important theoretical tool, it is not very useful when one wants to use mechanism design in difficult domains, such as distributed optimization problems, e.g., supply chain procurement.

In particular, traditional mechanism design is underpinned by a set of assumptions that may not be realistic for computational agents in complex environments[2] (Dash et al. 2003). The most crucial assumption is that agents are rational and therefore can compute their complete preferences with respect to all possible outcomes. Agents are also assumed to know and understand the protocols and abide by them. In addition, the society of agents participating in the mechanism is closed, i.e., the agent population is static. Most attention in mechanism design has focused on centralized mechanisms; agents reveal their preferences to a central mechanism which then computes the optimal solution, given these preferences. Furthermore, communication costs are irrelevant in traditional mechanism design and the communication channels are assumed to be faultless. These assumptions are problematic, in particular in the context of electronic commerce being conducted by software agents, for several reasons. First, agents do not have unbounded memory and computational power. Second, electronic marketplaces are open and dynamic environments in which agents may appear or disappear for a number of reasons. In such open systems with heterogeneous agents, a machine-understandable specification of all the associated interaction protocols and their elements cannot be guaranteed and neither can semantic interoperation between all agents. Another reason is that centralized mechanisms may be unable to compute the outcome because the problem might simply be intractable. Finally, communication does not come for free and may not be faultless in a computational setting.

Computation in mechanism design can be considered at two distinct levels (Parkes 2001). At the agent level we can distinguish between:

- **Valuation complexity.** How much computation is required to provide information about preferences within a mechanism?

---

[2] These assumptions are often also unreasonable for human agents.

- **Strategic complexity**. Are there dominant strategies? Do agents have to counter-speculate or do any opponent modelling when computing an optimal strategy?

At the infrastructure/mechanism level we can distinguish between:

- **Solution complexity**. How much computation is required of the mechanism to compute an optimal outcome, given the agents' preferences?

- **Communication complexity**. How much communication is required between the agents and the mechanism, in order for the mechanism to obtain preference information and compute an outcome?

Mechanisms that have dominant strategies, such as the Groves, are efficient, giving them excellent strategic complexity. As such mechanisms entail dominant strategies, an agent can compute its strategy without resulting to counter-speculation or having to do opponent modelling. Nonetheless, the direct revelation property of Groves mechanisms provides very bad agent valuation complexity. For an agent to compute its optimal bidding strategy, first it has to determine its complete preferences over all possible outcomes. The winner determination complexity of Groves mechanisms, in particular in combinatorial domains, limits their applicability – winner determination in the combinatorial allocation problem (CAP) is NP-hard.

A number of approaches have been proposed to resolve this tension between game-theoretic and computational properties (Parkes 2001) including:

- using approximation methods
- identifying tractable special cases within more general problems
- providing compact and expressive representation languages for agents to express their preferences
- employing dynamic instead of single-shot direct revelation mechanisms which enable agents to provide incremental information about their preferences for different outcomes
- using decentralized mechanisms to compute the outcome instead of centralized ones.

There are certain advantages in moving away from a centralized mechanism and opting for a decentralized one (Dash et al. 2003). First of all, in terms of tractability. A distributed mechanism transfers the burden of computing a solution from a central agent to the system as a whole, in effect transforming the problem into a distributed optimization one that uses the computational resources of multiple agents. Second, in terms of robustness. In a centralized system, the communication links connecting the multiple agents with the centre are critical for the system's operation and failure might disable the system altogether. But, in a decentralized mechanism, such failure will not disable the entire system, although it might lead to a suboptimal solution. Third, in a centralized mechanism the agents need to place their trust in the centre which decides on the outcome or solution. But, in a distributed mechanism, the solution develops as a result of the agents' interactions and thus no such trust in a single entity is required. Finally, as there is no central agent which has to communicate with all other agents and is responsible for the overall solution, bottlenecks can be avoided.

Mechanism design has a fundamental role to play in devising protocols for complex distributed systems consisting of self-interested interacting agents. The challenge is to design computationally efficient mechanisms for electronic markets without sacrificing useful game-theoretic properties, such as efficiency and stability.

10.6 Further Reading

A number of advanced texts provide extended coverage of mechanism design. A good starting point is Parkes (2001). Osborne and Rubinstein (1994), (Chapter 10) also cover mechanism design. For a very thorough and technical description of mechanism design, which includes results regarding other equilibrium concepts see Mas-Colell et al. (1995), Chapter 23. The papers by Vickrey (1961), Clarke (1971), Groves (1973) and the paper on the revelation principle by Gibbard (1973) are seminal. Another good book on mechanism design is Bergin (2005). A related issue on mechanism design is that of designing optimal auctions. The seminal work of Myerson (1981) is recommended, and other good articles include Riley and Samuelson (1981) and Bulow and Roberts (1989).

Computational issues in mechanism design are discussed in Nisan (1999), Nisan and Ronen (2001), Parkes (2001) and Papadimitriou (2001). Our discussion on computational issues on mechanism design is mainly based on Parkes (2001), Chapter 3, and Dash et al. (2003). For an approach to decentralized mechanism design see Parkes and Shneidman (2004).

10.7 Exercises and Topics for Discussion

1. Assume that there are two agents and five units of a commodity to allocate. Agent A values the first unit of the commodity at 15, the second one at 13, the third at 10 and the fourth and fifth at 9 and 6, respectively. Agent B values the commodities at (14, 12, 11, 5, 3), respectively. What is the optimal allocation of the commodities? Use the Generalized Vickrey Auction (GVA) to solve this problem.

2. Show that if $f : \Theta \to \mathcal{O}$ is truthfully implementable in dominant strategies when the set of possible types is Θ_i (for $i = 1, \ldots, n$), i.e., the direct revelation mechanism $M = (\Theta, f)$ is strategy-proof, then when each agent i's set of possible types is $\widehat{\Theta}_i \subset \Theta_i$ (for $i = 1, \ldots, n$) the social choice function $\widehat{f} : \widehat{\Theta} \to \mathcal{O}$ which satisfies $\widehat{f}(\theta) = f(\theta)$ for all $\theta \in \widehat{\Theta}$, is truthfully implementable in dominant strategies.[3]

---

[3] Adopted from Mas-Colell et al. (1995).

CHAPTER 11

Mobile Agents

LEARNING OBJECTIVES

After reading and completing this chapter, you should be able to:

- Explain the distinguishing characteristics of mobile agents.
- Describe the infrastructure requirements for mobile agents.
- Describe the Aglets mobile agent framework.
- Discuss the security issues around mobile agents and how these can be addressed.
- Discuss the advantages and disadvantages of using mobile agents and assess their applicability in e-commerce applications.

The agents that we have been discussing in previous chapters may have a number of different attributes, but they nevertheless share one common characteristic: they are stationary (static). This means that they are created and executed in an environment on a host which may be connected on a network, but they are unable to navigate of their own volition through an arbitrary number of hosts. An agent may be able to communicate and interact with other agents and software entities and use their services, but it does so using some mechanism, such as remote procedure calls.

When discussing mobility we can distinguish between physical mobility and logical mobility. Physical mobility means that physical entities like laptops, PDAs and other mobile devices are being moved around a network, thus their actual location changes. Logical mobility means that logical entities, like a running user application, or an agent, move or migrate around a network. In this chapter we are interested in logical mobility.

The underlying idea and driving force of mobile agents is that agents themselves, as software entities, are able to move around a network when they deem it necessary and appropriate. This is a particularly compelling concept as mobile agents can move to places and hosts where they are required to perform tasks or computations locally on a per need basis and avoid communication overheads and consuming network bandwidth. This is an attractive idea, especially in the area of e-commerce, as agents representing individual users or organizations can come together and conduct business in virtual marketplaces as their physical counterparts would do (Kowalczyk et al. 2003a,b). So instead of an agent submitting perhaps thousands of bids in an electronic auction over the Internet, using an unreliable connection at times, it can simply transport itself to the electronic marketplace and participate in negotiations locally. Thus, it can always have up-to-date and accurate information about the conditions in the market without having to account for possible network delays or disruptions.

In this chapter we will discuss the main ideas behind and technologies for mobile agents as well as their relative advantages, challenges and issues.

11.1 INTRODUCING MOBILITY

The concept of a mobile agent offers an alternative and very powerful paradigm for network and distributed computing which comes in sharp contrast to the predominant methodologies currently around: the client-server model, code-on-demand and the more recent web-services approach.

In the client-server paradigm, the server advertises a set of services that it provides access to or methods for. If clients are interested in accessing some of the server's methods or services, then they have to call them remotely through remote procedure calls (RPC), remote method invocation (RMI) or object request brokers (ORB). The main advantage of this model is enhanced security as the client only sends requests for execution and has no access to either the data or the code of the server. However, as there can be exceptionally high network traffic, this can cause a bottleneck which contributes to network latency as well as overloading of resources.

In the code-on-demand approach, the client owns the resources needed for the execution of a service or task, but lacks the know-how needed to perform the task or execute the service. The code is available in remote servers that act as repositories of code and can be downloaded on a per need basis to the client and then the computation can be carried out locally. Java applets and servlets are examples of this paradigm. Applets get downloaded and executed in web browsers, whereas servlets get uploaded and executed in remote web servers. This approach offers more flexibility as the behaviour of the client can change dynamically, based on the code downloaded from the server.

Another approach that has recently emerged and is gaining momentum is that of web services. Web services have been heralded by some as the next big thing in distributed computing. We are currently moving from an environment where applications are deployed on individual machines and web servers to one where applications are composed of a number of software components called services, which are distributed across many different machines and are programmatically accessible over standard Internet protocols. The power of web services is that they can interact seamlessly and transparently to achieve combined functionality and produce the overall required result. In this way, programs providing simple services can interact with each other in order to deliver sophisticated added-value services.

In contrast to these three approaches, a mobile agent is an autonomous executing entity that has the ability to navigate through a heterogeneous network and resume its execution. Mobile agents have a number of advantages when compared with current approaches to distributed computing (Lange and Oshima 1999). First of all, they reduce network traffic. Interactions in distributed systems rely on communication protocols and involve the exchange of messages to accomplish a task, which may lead to an excessive number of messages being exchanged. Transferring the mobile agents to the sources of data creates less traffic than transferring the data itself. For instance, when an agent is required to process a set of documents that reside in a remote document repository, it is more efficient to transfer the agent to the repository so that the documents can be processed locally, rather than to retrieve every document needed and perform the operations required. Thus, mobile agents can also make better use of resources. Secondly, they overcome network latency. In some critical systems, in which a real-time and effective response is of paramount importance, control through a network may introduce unacceptable latencies. For instance, in many online auctions most of the bidding takes place just before the auction closes. A user can dispatch a mobile agent to the auction house that can then carry out the bidding locally, having instant and accurate up-to-date information from the auctioneer without running the risk of being affected by a slow or down network connection. Thirdly, when mobile agents are dispatched to perform certain tasks by a delegating entity, they become self-governing and execute asynchronously and independently of the creating entity. Even if the creating entity ceases to exist or the connection is severed, as in the case of a mobile agent being dispatched from a mobile phone, the agent will continue its execution until it achieves its objective or completes the task that has been delegated to it. Another advantage is that they can sense and adapt to the changing conditions in the environment in which they operate. For example, they may decide which hosts to occupy to make better use of resources or clone themselves to perform the required task more efficiently and effectively. Finally, they are robust and fault tolerant. For instance, if a host is about to shut down, mobile agents can move to another host and resume their execution.

11.2 FACILITATING MOBILITY

Although the idea of mobile agents which are created in one host and then roam the Internet, performing computations and complex tasks on the spot where they are required, is appealing, building a mobile agent is nontrivial with regard to the environment that is required. In particular, in order to navigate from machine to machine, mobile agents depend on an underlying mobile agent system which consists of three components (Cockayne and Zyda 1998).

The first component is a suitable and transportable language in which the agent's code will be written. The second component is the engine or interpreter for that language. The engine is a software program that implements the language for writing mobile agents and serves as the virtual machine for agents, where they are maintained and executed. A machine can run one or more engines, and engines accept mobile agents who can dispatch themselves and start, or resume, execution on these engines. For that matter, engines do not accept mobile agents directly, but implement one or more *places* or *contexts* and agents execute within these. A place or context is a virtual location in which an agent can execute and perform tasks. Each host has at least one place in order to be able to accept mobile agents. Servers provide some places and user computers provide others. For instance, the home place on a user's personal computer serves as the departure and return place of a mobile agent, whereas a server may provide a ticket place and a used-car auction place. When an agent is accepted, the appropriate execution environment is started, the agent's state information is loaded, and the execution of the agent is resumed. These four basic elements: hosts, engines, places and agents give rise to a hierarchical structure, which is essential for the creation, execution and migration of mobile agents as illustrated in Figure 11.1.

Finally, to facilitate migration, engines need to be able to exchange agents. Thus, the third component required is a set of protocols that enable two engines to communicate. The protocol suite should be able to operate over a variety of transport networks

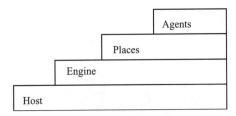

Figure 11.1: Hierarchical structure for mobile agent creation and execution

such as TCP/IP or even SMTP. The protocols operate at two levels. The lower level is responsible for the transport of agents, while the higher is responsible for their encoding and decoding. The encoding rules determine how an engine encodes an agent as binary data. The platform interconnect protocol determines how two engines can authenticate each other using, for instance, public key cryptography, and then exchange agents.

11.2.1 Migration

The actual process of migrating to another host involves a number of steps as is illustrated in Figure 11.2. First of all, an agent needs to identify its destination. If the place is not specified, then the agent will run in the default place provided by the destination host engine. Once the location of the destination is established, the agent informs the local mobile system that it wants to transfer itself to the destination. This is usually done through an appropriate migration primitive. On receiving a request for transfer, the mobile agent system goes through the following steps:

- *Suspension.* The agent is notified of the imminent transfer and is allowed to complete any current tasks and prepare for departure. Its execution thread is then halted.

- *Serialization.* The mobile agent system serializes the agent, i.e., it creates a persistent representation of the agent suitable for transport over the network.

- *Encoding.* The engine encodes the serialized agent for the chosen transport protocol.

- *Dispatch.* The engine establishes a connection with the destination host and dispatches the now encoded and serialized agent.

Before the destination host receives an agent, the engine needs to verify whether it can accept an agent from the sender host. If the sender host successfully authenticates itself, the agent transfer takes place and follows the steps as illustrated in Figure 11.2:

- *Receipt.* The encoded and serialized agent is received by the destination host.

- *Decoding.* The engine decodes the incoming agent.

- *Deserialization.* The agent is deserialized, its class is instantiated and its state is restored.

- *Execution resumption.* The instantiated agent is notified of arrival, it is given a new thread of execution and finally it prepares to resume its execution.

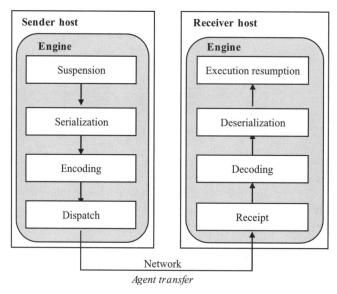

Figure 11.2: The process of migration

11.2.2 Modes of migration

To be able to migrate and recommence execution on different hosts, the underlying mobile agent system needs to be able to capture an agent and transport it over the network. Serialization has to do with what it is that is being transported, i.e., what aspects of the agent have to be captured. There are two approaches to migration. In the *statefull* or *strong mobility (go model)*, when a migration primitive is executed, an agent's object state, code, and control state are captured. Execution is allowed to continue from the instruction following the migration primitive. This is obviously more convenient for the end programmer, but it requires far more work for the system developer. This is because routines to capture state and execution control are required on top of the interpreters of the language used for writing the mobile agent code. However, the fact that the mobile agent system has access to an agent's execution stack raises some security issues. Figure 11.3 illustrates an example of statefull migration. When the **dispatch** primitive is executed, the agent's execution state is captured and transported along with its code to host2. When execution resumes, the next primitive to be executed in host2 is the one right after the **dispatch** primitive.

In the *stateless* or *weak mobility (known entry point model)*, the agent's object state and code are captured. The execution in the new host is continued from a known entry point. Most commercial Java-based systems use this model as the Java standard virtual machine does not allow one to have access to the execution stack. Figure 11.4 illustrates an example of stateless migration. When the **dispatch** primitive is executed, only the

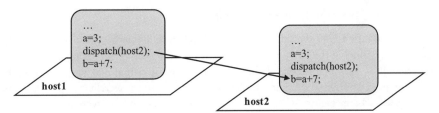

Figure 11.3: Statefull migration

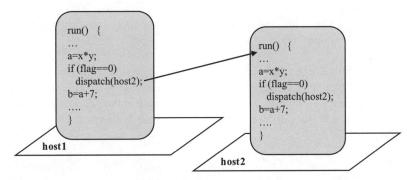

Figure 11.4: Stateless migration

agent's code is captured and transported to host2. Execution is resumed from a known entry point which is the **run()** method.

An agent's code may also include the code from all of its inherited and/or referenced types. There are three approaches to code migration:

1. The code does not migrate. The agent's code needs to be pre-loaded by all the hosts that the agent might visit and only the current state, that is data and execution stack, migrates.

2. All code migrates. In this case, all of the agent's code including the code of inherited and referenced objects migrates.

3. Code migrates on a per need basis. Initially only the basic code of the agent migrates. The remaining code migrates and loads dynamically on a per need basis at runtime.

11.3 MOBILE AGENT SYSTEMS

A number of mobile agent systems have emerged in the last decade. The rapid development of mobile agents has been, to an extent, facilitated by the development and adoption of the Java language. However, not all mobile agent systems use Java as their underlying platform.

11.3.1 Non-Java mobile agent systems

Telescript (White 1994) was the first commercial mobile agent system developed by General Magic Inc. in the early 1990s. Telescript is an object-oriented language, similar to Java and C++, which is compiled into bytecodes for a virtual machine which is part of the server. The original domain of inspiration for Telescript was that of an electronic marketplace where agents are producers offering goods and services, or consumers seeking to obtain goods and services. Telescript supported strong mobility. It was rapidly overtaken by Java and is not currently in use, but it has been the basis for many of the recent mobile agent systems. After its demise, and given the popularity of the Java language, General Magic Inc. re-implemented its mobile agent framework in Java. The result was the Odyssey system.

A number of mobile agent systems have been based on the Tool control language (Tcl) which is a high-level scripting language (Ousterhout 1994). Tcl is an interpreted language, and therefore portable. It can be embedded in other applications and can also be extended with user-defined commands which are built based on a core set of primitives.

Agent Tcl later renamed to D'Agents has been developed at Dartmouth University and supports multiple languages (Tcl, Java, Scheme) (Gray 1995, 1996, Kotz et al. 1997, Gray et al. 2002). It has a simple architecture, a robust security mechanism and comprehensive communication services. The architecture of D'Agents is based on four levels: transport mechanisms, server, language interpreter and agents. At the lowest level, there is an interface to each available transport mechanism. The next level is the server that runs on each machine. The server is responsible for:

1. keeping track of the agents running on the machine
2. providing low level communication services through message passing and streams
3. receiving and authenticating agents from other machines
4. starting agents in the appropriate execution environment.

The next level comprises the execution environments, one for each language supported by D'Agents, while the final level encompasses the agents themselves, which execute in the appropriate execution environment.

Other languages can be supported by D'Agents by extending the interpreter to provide state-capture routines that capture and restore the agent states and an interface to the agent servers.

Agents communicate with low-level mechanisms, such as message passing and byte streams or high-level mechanisms, such as AgentRPC, which is similar to the traditional RPC and is implemented at the agent level on top of the lower level mechanisms.

D'Agents also provides a docking system which allows an agent to jump off partially connected computers by waiting by a docking machine, which is responsible for transporting the agent when the connection is re-established.

Individual machines are protected against ill-programmed and malicious agents that attempt to access too many resources or corrupt restricted information. D'Agents also protects groups of machines controlled by a single organization. Agents are cryptographically signed using Pretty Good Privacy (PGP), while access restrictions are enforced with Safe Tcl, Java security managers, and Scheme 48 modules respectively, combined with security policies for access control.

Agents for Remote Action (Ara), is another Tcl-based framework for the portable and secure execution of mobile agents in heterogeneous networks (Peine and Stolpmann 1997, Peine 2002). Ara's specific aim, in comparison with similar platforms, is to provide full mobile agent functionality while retaining as much as possible of the established programming models and languages.

TACOMA is a mobile-agent framework that emanated from the joint efforts of the Universities of Tromso and Cornell (Johansen et al. 2002). TACOMA focuses on operating system support for agents and how agents can be used to solve problems which are traditionally addressed by other distributed computing paradigms, e.g., the client/server model. TACOMA can support agents that can be built in Tcl-Tk, C, Perl, Python, and Scheme.

11.3.2 Java–based mobile agent systems

Java is perhaps the most popular language for building agents and multi-agent systems. Arguably it is also the most mobility-enabling language, since it has a number of desirable features that make it the ideal candidate as the underlying platform for mobile-agent systems (Lange and Oshima 1998). For instance, Java is designed to operate in heterogeneous environments and gives simple access to network communication. It also enables multi-threaded programming as well as synchronization between threads, which can be used to facilitate interaction among autonomously executing agents. Object serialization, dynamic class loading and reflection, are also powerful features of Java. Finally, the security architecture of Java makes it reasonably safe to host an untrusted mobile agent, as the agent is not allowed to tamper with the host or access private information.

Java-based mobile agent systems have a lot in common. In addition to the programming language, most of them depend on a standard version of the Java virtual machine and Java's object serialization mechanism. Java-based systems have multi-threaded servers and usually run each agent in a thread of the server process itself.

ObjectSpace's Voyager provides an extensive set of object messaging capabilities, in addition to allowing objects to move as agents around a network (Voyager 2006). Voyager combines the properties of a Java-based object broker with those of a mobile-agent system. Thus, developers can create network applications using both traditional and agent-enhanced distributed programming techniques. It includes a flexible security framework which supports secure network communication through SSL adapters, and firewall tunnelling using HTTP, or the SOCKS protocol.

Concordia is a mobile agent system by Mitsubishi (Kiniry and Zimmerman 1997). Concordia consists of multiple components, all written in Java, which are combined to provide a complete environment for distributed applications. In its simplest form, a Concordia system is made up of a standard Java virtual machine, a server and a set of agents.

NOMADS is a Java-based mobile agent system (Suri et al. 2000a,b) which supports strong mobility by enabling the full execution state of an agent to be captured and transferred. Hence, mobile agents in NOMADS can move any time and their execution in the new host commences from the instruction following the migration primitive. Migration can be initiated either by the agent itself or externally by the host (forced mobility) as, for instance, when there are limited resources or the host is about to shut down. Additionally, NOMADS offers increased security and resource-control facilities in terms of disk and network limits. The limits can be divided into three categories: rate limits which allow the read and write rates of any program to be limited; quantity limits which allow the total bytes read or written to be limited; and space limits which apply to disk-space usage. CPU and memory-resource control are also feasible. NOMADS consists of two components:

- Aroma is a Java-compatible Virtual Machine (VM) capable of capturing the execution state of all running agents/threads (Suri 2001). Each Java thread is mapped onto a native operating system thread. To facilitate portability, the Aroma VM assumes that the word size is always 32 bits and the floating-point representations are the same. Moreover, to solve any incompatibility issues between little-endian and big-endian systems[1], Aroma writes a parameter as part of the state information which indicates the type of the source platform. The destination platform is then responsible for any necessary byte-swapping. Users can use a standard Java compiler to compile Java source code to run on Aroma.

- Oasis is the execution environment that embeds the Aroma VM. Oasis is divided into two independent systems: the Console, which is a front-end interaction and administration program, and the Process, which is a back-end execution environment (Figure 11.5). The Console is used to perform administrative tasks such as creating

---

[1] In a big-endian system, the most significant byte is stored at the memory location with the lowest address (i.e., first). In a little-endian system, the least significant byte in the sequence is stored first.

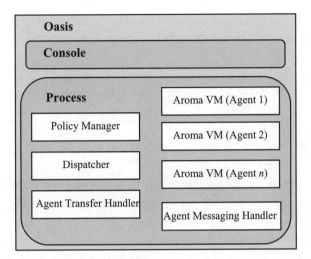

Figure 11.5: The Oasis execution environment

accounts, establishing resource limits and may be also used to interact with agents running within the Process environment. The Process is the execution environment for agents each of which is running on a separate instance of the Aroma VM. The Process environment contains also a Policy Manager and a Dispatcher. The Policy Manager is responsible for establishing security policies for all agents. These policies may be established on an individual or group basis. Upon startup, the Policy Manager reads a policies file which specifies resource limits that need to be applied to accounts. However, the Policy Manager is not responsible for enforcing the policies. Enforcement of the security policies is carried out by the Agent Transfer Protocol handler for authentication and agent transfer control, the Dispatcher for execution control, the Java security manager for access control, the Aroma execution environment for messaging control, and the Aroma VM for the resource usage control. The Dispatcher is responsible for executing an agent once its state information has been received. Agents communicate through message exchange which is implemented by a simple API. The messages themselves can contain any serializable Java object. Agents are addressed via Universally Unique Identifiers (UUIDs).

Other current Java-based mobile agent systems include Agentspace (Silva et al. 1998), Jumping Beans (JumpingBeans 1999) and Grasshopper (Baumer et al. 2000).

11.4 AGLETS

Perhaps the most well known Java-based mobile agent system is Aglets which stands for 'agent app*lets*' and was developed at the IBM Tokyo Research Laboratory (Aglets 2006, Lange and Oshima 1998). The key elements in the Aglets framework are:

- An *aglet* is a mobile Java object that visits aglet-enabled hosts in a network. It is autonomous, as it runs in its own thread of execution and reactive, as it responds to messages and events.

- A *proxy* is a representative of an aglet. It serves as a shield to protect the aglet from direct access to its public methods and it also hides its true location. Thus, a proxy provides location transparency.

- A *context* is an aglet's workplace and provides the means for managing and maintaining running aglets. Multiple contexts may reside on the same engine on one machine and they are distinguished by their name and address.

- Each aglet is assigned a globally unique and permanent *identifier* on initialization.

- A *message* is an object exchanged between aglets. It allows for synchronous as well as asynchronous communication between aglets. A *message manager* allows for concurrency control of incoming messages.

- An *itinerary* is an aglet's travel plan and provides a convenient abstraction for routing and complex travel patterns.

There are two ways in which an aglet can be created: from scratch or through cloning from another aglet. The creation of an aglet takes place in a context. The new aglet is assigned a unique identifier, inserted into the context and initialized. After initialization execution starts. Creation through cloning produces an almost identical aglet to the initial one. The differences are that another identifier is assigned to the clone, and execution restarts in the new aglet.

Aglets can move around a network of aglet-enabled hosts in two ways, actively or passively. In the former case, an aglet decides to move to another host and dispatches itself of its own volition. Dispatching an aglet from one context to another will remove it from its current context and insert it into the destination context where it will restart execution. In the latter case, a remote host can retract a mobile agent from another host or context.

Naturally, when aglets are running, they take up resources. If it is necessary to release essential resources, an aglet can go to sleep temporarily (deactivate), i.e., halt its execution and store its state in secondary storage (disk), and later it can be re-activated to continue with its task. Aglets interact through messaging. Finally, an aglet can be disposed of, i.e., destroyed, when it has achieved its goals. The disposal of an aglet will halt its execution and remove it from its context.

11.4.1 Programming model

The **Aglet** abstract class defines the fundamental methods that can be used to write personalized mobile agents and to control their mobility and lifecycle. Only classes extending the **Aglet** class can be moved across the network.

A mobile agent that wants to migrate, calls the **dispatch()** method. The new location is specified by the destination argument in the method and the address is given in the form of a URL which, apart from the host and domain names, also includes information about the protocol to be used for communicating with the remote host. The URL may also include the name of the context in which the aglet is to be inserted on arrival. For instance, the following dispatch call specifies the host as well as the context:

```
dispatch(new URL("atp://myhost.host.com/emarket"));
```

The Aglets system calls the agent's **onDispatching()** method, which performs application specific cleanup, kills the agent's threads, serializes the agent's code and object state, and sends the agent's code and object state to the new machine and context which are specified in the argument of the **dispatch()** method. On the new machine the system calls the agent's **onArrival()** method which performs application-specific initialization. Finally, the agent's **run()** method is called in order to start the agent's execution. Unlike normal Java objects, aglets are never garbage-collected automatically, because an aglet is active and has its own thread of control. The programmer needs to explicitly dispose of an aglet using the **dispose()** method which removes the aglet from its current context and essentially destroys it.

The programming model is based on a number of different events during the life-cycle of an aglet. There are three types of listener that can be customized and used to catch particular events:

1. Clone listeners listen for cloning events.
2. Mobility listeners listen for mobility events, such as the dispatching, retraction or the arrival of an aglet.
3. Persistence listeners listen for deactivation and activation events.

The behaviour of the aglet in response to different events can be specified by overriding a number of methods, the most important of which are summarized in Table 11.1.

11.4.2 Communication

Communication in Aglets can be distinguished into communication between aglets and communication between engines. When an aglet wants to communicate with other aglets, it has to first obtain the proxy to the object. This proxy is an interface that acts as a handle of an aglet and provides a common way of accessing the aglet behind it. Public aglet methods cannot be accessed directly from other aglets for security reasons. When the **AgletProxy** is invoked, it consults the Security Manager to determine whether the current execution context is permitted to perform the method. Aglet objects communicate by exchanging objects of the **Message** class. There are three different types of message:

- *Now-type*. A now-type message is synchronous and blocks current execution until the receiver has completed the handling of the message.

Event	As it takes place	After
Creation		onCreation()
Cloning	onCloning()	onClone()
Dispatching	onDispatching()	onArrival()
Retraction	onReverting()	onArrival()
Disposal	onDisposing()	
Deactivation	onDeactivating()	
Activation		onActivation()
Messaging	handleMessage()	

Table 11.1: Aglet events

- *Future-type.* A future-type message is asynchronous and does not block the current execution.

- *Oneway-type.* This type of message is asynchronous and does not block the current execution. It is different from a future-type message in that it does not have a return value and it is placed at the tail of the queue, even if it is sent by the aglet to itself.

As the Aglets runtime itself has no communication mechanism for transferring the serialized agents to destination hosts, it uses the communication layer that defines and implements a set of generic methods that support interagent messaging and agent transportation. This application program interface (API) abstracts the communication between agent systems and defines methods for creating, transferring, tracking, and managing agents. The communication API is based on the OMG standard Mobile Agent System Interoperability Facility (MASIF) (OMG 2006, Milojicic et al. 1998), which enables different agent systems to interoperate. The Aglets framework uses the Agent Transfer Protocol (ATP) as the default implementation of the communication layer. ATP is a platform-independent protocol for transferring agents between networked computers (Lange and Aridor 1997). ATP also enables remote communication between agents through message passing.

11.4.3 Security

The Aglets framework comes with its own configurable Security Manager as part of the Tahiti visual agent manager. The Security Manager provides a reasonable degree of security for the hosting computer system and its owner. The default security configuration is very restrictive. Any attempt by an agent to access a file to which access has not been granted will be regarded as security violation, and the agent will not be allowed that specific access. The Security Manager supports the definition of policies and describes how and where a secure aglet system enforces these policies. These policies are enforced by the principals, namely the authenticated entities which can be the aglet, the context or the network domain.

All the principals may define security policies which are formulated as sets of rules denoted by principals and privileges. It is the policy authority that defines these policies, i.e., the person or organization responsible for resources consumed by other entities. There are three authorities in the Aglets model. The owner of an aglet may want to enforce certain security policies to protect the aglet from attacks. The context authority is responsible for keeping the server and the underlying system safe from attacks from aglets. The context owner's security policy defines the actions that the aglet can take in a given context. Finally, the network domain authority is responsible for keeping its network secure, so that the servers within the domain provide their services safely, and all incoming aglets can complete their tasks. The domain authority defines the security policy for the domain.

The following security features are supported in Aglets:

- **Domain and user authentication.** Aglet servers are able to authenticate each other within a certain domain. All servers within a particular domain share a secret key, and can authenticate the contacting server by means of that key using Message Authentication Code (MAC) which is a secure hash value computed from a content and nonce value. Once the authentication between servers has been established, the credentials of the aglet are sent along with the aglet itself. Based on the authentication information, the receiver server will decide how much it trusts the credentials sent by the sender. If the credentials were sent by a server within the same domain, the receiver server simply trusts the sender.

- **Communication integrity within a domain.** Communication integrity can be checked in a similar way to that described in domain authentication. The sender computes the Message Integrity Code (MIC) value of the content and the shared secret, in a similar way to MAC, and sends it along with the nonce and the content. The receiver can then verify the message.

- **Authorization.** When an aglet accesses any security-sensitive information and resources such as Java properties, threads, and/or any other external resources such as files, it must be controlled under the permissions given to the aglet as described earlier.

11.5 MOBILE AGENT SECURITY

The characteristics of mobile agents make them appealing for electronic commerce applications in open networks. A mobile agent can hop to different marketplaces in search of products and services and negotiate, on behalf of its owner, with other entities. Furthermore, mobile agents can be used to search for and take advantage of new opportunities and markets. However, one of the most crucial issues in mobile agents is that of security.

Security is of paramount importance for any system and even more so in an open environment such as the Internet. Security is also essential to any mobile agent system, because accepting a hostile agent may lead to your computer being damaged or your privacy intruded upon (Tschudin 1999). Mobile agents can be created and dispatched by unknown individuals with unknown or dubious credentials. Thus, accepting a mobile agent and allowing access to resources such as CPU time, or disk space may have irreparable consequences for the host machine. It opens the gates for abuse of resources which may emanate from denial of service attacks, or accessing sensitive data at the host, or even through corrupting, or deleting, data. At the same time, a mobile agent depends for execution on the underlying execution environment and thus the server has access to the mobile agent's code as well as data which may include sensitive data such as credit card numbers, keys and other confidential information. Again the potential for abuse is there.

Mobile agent security has two main aspects: protecting the host machine and protecting the mobile agent. Attacks that can be launched against mobile agents and hosts can be divided into two broad categories: passive and active. Passive attacks do not modify the agent's or host's code or other information, whereas active attacks have direct consequences on the agent's or host's code.

11.5.1 Threats

Mobile agents and hosts are vulnerable to a number of threats. One possible way to categorize these is according to the source and target of the attack. In view of this, three general categories can be identified: agent to host, agent to agent, and host to agent (Jansen and Karygiannis 1999).

Agent to host

This category represents the set of threats in which agents may take advantage of security weaknesses at the host and abuse its services and resources.

- **Masquerade.** It is important that an agent presents its true identity when visiting a host. If an agent assumes the identity of another agent, it is said to be masquerading. The masquerading agent may pose as a trusted agent and do whatever that agent can do, which includes gaining access to services and resources. The masquerading agent could also falsify its identity in order to shift the blame for any actions for which it does not want to be held accountable. A masquerading agent may damage the host, as well as the reputation of the agent whose identity it has assumed. Therefore agents need to be properly authenticated.

- **Unauthorised access.** A mobile agent operating on a foreign host may attempt to access information, services or resources that it has not been granted permission to access.

- **Tampering.** Even though every precaution can be taken to authenticate an incoming agent and restrict access to services or resources, mobile agents may still be able to tamper with the host. A mobile agent's code may violate its boundaries and in this way delete or overwrite the host's data, or the data of another mobile agent. This may be intentional or by accident.

- **Denial of service.** Mobile agents may deliberately attempt to consume an excessive amount of the host's computational resources or services, so that service to other agents is disrupted. This is known as a denial of service attack (DoS). The resources can be disk space, network bandwidth, memory, or any other service that the host provides. Ill-programmed or malicious agents may launch denial of service attacks and disrupt the services offered by the server and degrade its performance as well as affecting other co-located mobile agents. One form of denial of service attack can be brought about through agent cloning. An ill-programmed or malicious mobile agent may keep cloning itself, clogging up the host's services and consuming all resources. In extreme cases, a mobile agent may be able to completely shut down the host.

Agent to agent

This category represents the set of threats in which agents may take advantage of security weaknesses of other agents or actively launch attacks against them.

- **Masquerade.** A masquerading agent may assume the identity of a trusted agent and attempt to deceive others. For instance, an agent can pose as a trusted vendor and attempt to extract information such as credit card details from other agents. Masquerading as another agent harms both the agent that is being deceived, but also the agent whose identity has been assumed and abused. In particular, the reputation of the latter could be severely damaged.

- **Tampering.** If there are no adequate control mechanisms in place at the host, a mobile agent may interfere with another agent by accessing or even altering the agent's code or data or by invoking its public methods. Tampering with an agent's code is a particularly serious form of attack and the consequences may be of varying degrees of severity. It can result in modifying the agent's behaviour and transforming a benevolent agent into a malicious one; modifying the agent's behaviour in such a way that the attacker can take advantage of it, or by gaining information about the agent's activities or strategies. For example, if a mobile agent, acting as a seller in a marketplace, gains access to the reservation price of one of the buyer agents, then it can take advantage of this when making its offer, or even alter the buyer's reservation price for its own benefit.

- **Denial of service.** Agents can launch denial of service attacks on other agents, for instance, by inundating them with repeated messages. The recipient may block the messages coming from an unauthorised agent, but this requires processing either by the agent itself or its proxy. A malicious or ill-programmed agent may also attempt to use heavily the services offered by an agent so that service to others is disrupted. If an agent is charged by the number of CPU cycles it consumes on a host, inundating it with messages or requesting the same service again and again will cause the affected agent to have to pay an extra cost.

- **Repudiation.** Repudiation occurs when an agent who participated in a communication or transaction with another agent, later denies that the exchange ever took place. For instance, an auctioneer agent may deny ever receiving a bid from a bidder. The cause for repudiation can be deliberate or accidental, but nevertheless repudiation can lead to disputes between the parties involved, which may be difficult to resolve. Disputes may also arise because of different views on what has been agreed through a contract or the outcome of a transaction. Although hosts cannot prevent an agent from repudiating a transaction, they can ensure that there are mechanisms to keep evidence of communication exchanges and transactions between agents to support the resolution of disputes.

Host to agent

The host to agent category represents the set of threats in which hosts compromise the integrity of agents.

- **Masquerade.** A host may attempt to falsify its identity and present itself to the agent as a trusted host in order to trick the agent into disclosing sensitive information. For instance, a host may masquerade as a bank and attempt to obtain, through the agent, the user's bank account details and password. As a result of such an attack, both the agent as well as the host whose identity is assumed and abused are harmed.

- **Tampering.** Even though a host may reveal its true identity to the agent, it does not necessarily mean that the agent's integrity is guaranteed. The host may still attempt to tamper with the agent's code or data in an attempt to take advantage of the agent. Crucially, a mobile agent depends on the host for its correct execution. This inadvertently means that the host has access to the agent's code, state and data and other sensitive information, such as proprietary algorithms, trade secrets, or negotiation strategies. A mobile agent visiting an auction house may have its reservation price altered by the host. A host can also modify the agent's code, essentially changing the agent's behaviour, and then dispatch it to a competitive host where the agent can cause damage.

  Hosts may also interfere with the agent's communication exchanges, both outgoing and incoming. This includes alteration of data fields, as in financial transactions, or modification of the content of messages. For example, the host may intercept the communication of an agent who is asking for confirmation from a user to purchase a flight, and may alter the user's reply from 'abort transaction' to 'confirm transaction'.

  The risk of tampering increases when a mobile agent performs multiple hops, i.e., visits several hosts on its itinerary. The host responsible for the alteration of an agent's code, state, or data needs to be detected immediately, otherwise it may be impossible to track down after the agent has visited other hosts and its state and data have undergone many more changes.

- **Eavesdropping and traffic analysis.** A mobile agent not only depends on a host for its correct execution, but also for its communication. Eavesdropping involves intercepting and monitoring an agent's communications with other agents, hosts or the user. A host can monitor the messages being exchanged which may contain useful information. A more sophisticated variant of eavesdropping is traffic analysis which involves monitoring and analysing the pattern of message exchanges between agents or hosts. Even if the message itself cannot be accessed because it is encrypted, still the attacker may be able to infer useful information from the pattern of messages.

- **Denial of service.** As agents move to hosts to perform computations locally, they rely on the hosts for their execution and a fair allocation of resources. However, a malicious host may deliberately ignore an agent's service requests, deprive it of the necessary resources to execute efficiently, introduce unacceptable delays in dealing with its requests, or the execution of critical tasks, or even dispose of the agent without notification. If other agents or users are waiting for the results of the agent's computations, this creates further problems and may even lead to deadlocks. A malicious host can also cause an agent to livelock by constantly assigning to it tasks to execute, thereby preventing it from achieving its goal.

11.5.2 Security services

If mobile agents and hosts are to be protected against attacks, appropriate security services need to be available. These include (Jansen and Karygiannis 1999):

- **Authentication.** Before accepting an agent on a host, the sender needs to be verified. The process of verifying an incoming agent includes verifying the agent creator, owner, or user, as well as the sender of the agent. The owner or user of an agent may be its creator, but not necessarily. Also the sender may be the owner or possibly another host. Specifically, authentication involves:
  - User authentication. The user needs to authenticate herself to a host. Public key encryption or passwords can be used for this purpose.
  - Host authentication. Before a host starts communicating with another host, it needs to verify this entity.
  - Agent authentication. Before executing an incoming agent, a host needs to verify the identity of the owner, i.e., who is responsible for the agent.
  - Code authentication. Before instantiating and starting the execution of a mobile agent, a host needs to verify the agent's creator or who is responsible for its development. Digital signatures is the standard for this purpose.

- **Access control.** An incoming agent should be given access rights to information and resources according to the entity, i.e., the individual or organization, that it represents. For instance, an agent representing a user may have access to the user's bank account, but a third agent should not be granted access.

- **Integrity.** It is vital to ensure that an agent's code cannot be tampered with and the same applies to the host. In particular, checking the integrity of the agent's code is crucial before allowing it to start execution on a host machine. Checking that no illegal alterations have been performed to the agent's state is more difficult.

- **Confidentiality**. An agent may be carrying private and sensitive information while in transit from host to host. Such information should be kept confidential and protected from malicious hosts or other agents.

- **Nonrepudiation**. An agent or host cannot deny that a communication exchange or transaction has taken place.

- **Auditing**. Logging and auditing services must be provided and records of security related activities including communication exchanges, transactions, as well as information on accessing data or resources need to be maintained for future reference.

11.5.3 Protecting the host

One of the main concerns with a mobile agent system is ensuring that the agents cannot interfere or tamper with the host. A number of techniques have been devised to protect the host machine (Jansen and Karygiannis 1999, Tschudin 1999).

Safe code interpretation

An agent that is accepted at a host machine is executed in an execution environment (EE), which is often an interpreter that executes the agent's high-level instructions. The use of an interpreter ensures portability, but it is also a security measure as the interpreter can act as a so-called sandbox and check memory bounds, verify parameters for system-service requests and maintain access-control lists. Agents have their own address space from where they have no direct access to a host's or another agent's data. Java-based mobile agents adhere to this principle, as well as those based on Tcl.

Authentication

Authentication techniques, such as digital signatures can be used for authenticating a mobile agent (author, sender, previous EE). A digital signature serves as a means of verifying the authenticity of an agent, its origin, and its integrity. Usually, the signer of the code is either the creator of the agent, the user (individual or organization), or some other entity, such as a trusted third party that has reviewed the agent. As an agent represents an entity, such as an end-user or organization, mobile agent systems often use the signature of the represented entity as an indication of the authority under which an agent can operate.

Authorisation

The host can decide on the capabilities or access rights to be granted to different agents. A host can either decide on each access individually, or give an agent a resource 'capability', which the agent has to present every time that it requires access to the specific resource. In some cases the authorization decision can be far from simple. For instance, although the agent's sender may be known, the agent may have arrived from an untrusted host. Whether or not to grant authorization in this case depends on the security policy that the host or the owner of the host would like to enforce. A common formalization of a security policy is through an access-control list which associates principles, i.e., authenticated entities, with their rights. However, if an agent abuses its rights, it is essential that appropriate mechanisms are in place to counteract this and also to inform future policy.

Resource allocation

The allocation of resources in the presence of denial of service threats, must be considered very carefully. In some cases, it may be possible to schedule the agents' requests for a particular resource so that all of them are satisfied. However, there may be occasions when resource requests among agents are conflicting and may even result in deadlocks. Techniques to address the resource allocation problem have been developed in the context of distributed operating systems. A recent approach involves using market-based mechanisms (Clearwater 1996, Lai et al. 2004), that is, agents have to pay for the use of resources and services at a host.

Path histories

Agents are more prone to tampering when they make multiple hops, i.e., they visit several hosts in their itinerary. If a record of all the hosts that the agent has visited is maintained, the decision of whether to accept an incoming agent, or execute it, can be based on this path history. Maintaining a path history requires each host to add a signed entry to the path, indicating its identity and the identity of the next host to be visited, and to provide the complete path history to the next host. When a mobile agent arrives at a host, the host can then decide whether or not to trust it by reviewing the list of previously visited hosts and checking their credentials. In addition, reputation systems can be used to check the reputation ratings of hosts, agents and users/authors.

11.5.4 Protecting the mobile agent

Mobile agents are far more susceptible to attacks than hosts. The problem stems from the fact that a mobile agent depends on the host for its execution and communication exchanges. As a result, it is impossible to guarantee a trusted execution environment once the agent leaves its home environment. Although the user may digitally sign an agent on its home machine before it moves onto a second host, that protection is limited. The second host can determine whether or not the agent can be trusted by checking the signatures. But, on any subsequent hosts, there is a problem: the initial signature only verifies the source and integrity of the agent's original code, data and state information, but not any data, state or code modifications that were generated while at other hosts. While in transit, intermediate hosts can also tamper with the mobile agent.

One of the ways in which malicious attacks on mobile agents can be prevented is by placing a security perimeter over a number of hosts wherein one can trust all entities, which in essence creates a fortress model (Tschudin 1999). The mobile agent can only move within this closed environment and all communications between hosts are encrypted and signed by the sending host. Thus, the mobile agent can be protected from external attacks. In principle, hosts within this environment are trusted, even though nothing prevents a host from tampering with an agent. Due care needs to be taken so that untrusted or malicious hosts, or agents, are not allowed to join the system. This form of security measure seriously compromises the advantages of mobile agents, such as migration, and weakens their usefulness as well as restricting their application.

Although we may not be able to prevent an agent from being tampered with, it may be possible to take measures to detect this, which in itself may act as a deterrent.

Sealing and signing intermediate results

In order to keep information collected or computed thus far confidential, mobile agents can encrypt the data immediately after being acquired at each host visited. The agent encrypts the information using the owner's public key. This, in essence, seals the information and prevents it from being tampered with for the rest of the journey, as only the agent's owner will be able to decrypt it, being the only one knowing the private key. This method depends on the host's compliance as the host can delete or modify data and, knowing the public key, can apply the same encryption function.

Shared secrets and interlocking

One way to avoid agent tampering is by having two or more agents being responsible for a task, while none of them has enough information to carry it out on its own. Thus, no agent alone would possess all the elements required to complete a transaction. For instance, one agent could be carrying the credit card details, whereas a second one might carry the authorization code, then a third one would keep track of the communication exchanges and securely log the intended transaction before agreeing to it.

Execution tracing

Another technique for detecting agent tampering, which can act as a deterrent for malicious hosts, is called execution tracing. The agent's behaviour during its execution on each host is recorded. Each host creates and maintains a nonrepudiatable trace of the operations performed by the agent whilst executing on that host. Once the agent completes its execution, the host submits a cryptographic hash of the trace as a trace summary or fingerprint. In the event of problems arising, or suspicious results, the traces and trace summaries can be obtained and verified and the malicious host(s) can be tracked. This technique has the inherent disadvantage that a significant number of logs have to be maintained on each host.

Executable encrypted functions

Another way to prevent agent tampering is through a technique called Computing with Encrypted Functions (CEF) (Sander and Tschudin 1998). This technique consists of having the host execute a program embodying an enciphered function, without being able to discern the original function. This approach requires distinguishing between a function and a program that implements the function.

Suppose that a user A has a function f and the untrusted host B has data x. A wants to send a mobile agent to B to compute $f(x)$, but A does not want to reveal f to B. If f can be encrypted in a way that results in another function $E(f)$, then A can create a program $P(E(f))$, which implements $E(f)$, and send it to B embedded within the mobile agent. B then runs the agent, which executes $P(E(f))$ on x, and returns the result to A who decrypts it to obtain $f(x)$. If f is a signature algorithm with an embedded key, the agent has an effective means of signing information without the host knowing the key. Similarly, if it is an encryption algorithm containing an embedded key, the agent has an effective means of encrypting information at the host. The security of this method relies on the difficulty of decomposing the encrypted function.

11.5.5 Dealing with the perpetrators

One issue that arises is what we do with malicious hosts or agents once these have been identified. It is important that some sort of infrastructure is in place so that appropriate measures can be taken against the perpetrators. The consequences of malicious behaviour can be of varying degrees of severity. For instance, a mobile agent may be destroyed, or prevented from accessing certain hosts. In extreme cases, an agent's or a host's authority, i.e., the entity that it represents, may have to incur financial sanctions in order to recover the cost of damages to host(s) or mobile agent(s).

Another means of dealing with the perpetrators is to use reputation systems (Resnick et al. 2000) and publish ratings on the trustworthiness of mobile agents and hosts. Thus, agents and hosts could check the reputations ratings of other entities in order to decide whether or not to hop to a host, or accept a mobile agent. Untrustworthy agents, hosts and users would therefore get increasingly isolated as other entities would not be willing to interact with them. Such a social system is prone to attacks from competitors who can pose as victims with the purpose of lowering the reputation of a particular host or mobile-agent, or even the represented authority (individual or organization), for their own benefit. For example, an auctioneer agent may give a very low rating to another auctioneer, in an attempt to lower its reputation so as to attract more buyers itself. One way to protect a reputation system of this sort is to use cryptographic techniques that allow all parties involved in a dispute to prove whether they behaved correctly or not. To enable this, hosts would have to maintain records of all security-relevant information, including agent reception, access to resources, transactions and communication exchanges and also would have to digitally sign the validity of these traces. An arbitrator could then look at the evidence and decide whether or not an attack of some sort had taken place. Another way would be to require an entity to authenticate itself in order to submit a rating for another entity in the reputation system.

11.6 ISSUES ON MOBILE AGENTS

Although mobile agents offer a powerful alternative to current approaches to distributed computing, the take-up of the technology has been limited. The reasons for this are manifold and can be attributed to both technical and nontechnical issues surrounding mobile agents (Milojicic et al. 1999, Kotz and Gray 1999, Schoder and Eymann 2000).

From the technical point of view, mobile agents have been criticized on a number of fronts. One criticism is that current mobile agent systems do not bring about any significant benefits with regard to efficiency. As mobile agents are often written in an interpreted language for portability and security reasons, they are relatively slow. Moreover, there is an overhead, as the agents need to be inserted into the right execution environment upon arrival, which often needs to be started on a per need basis. Thus, although mobile agents seem to be able to save network latency and bandwidth, currently this comes at the expense of higher loads in transporting them and executing them locally.

One of the main benefits of using mobile agents, is that they can move to the place where the data are and thus perform the computation locally without being affected by slow or down connections. Nevertheless, mobility requires additional support in order to recover from failure during migration, as well as to support agents while they are trying to migrate to partially connected machines. As an agent moves around a network, there is also the need for appropriate naming and locating services. When a mobile agent hops from host to host, the communication channels must be reconstructed so that it can keep in touch and continue working with other agents as well as its owner-user.

Security is one of the most crucial issues in mobile agents and is perhaps the most important reason for the limited take-up. Despite the significant steps that have been taken to protect both the host machine and the mobile agent, there are still issues to be resolved such as for instance, adequately protecting hosts without artificially limiting the agents' access rights, providing effective resource management, and protecting agents from malicious hosts, among others. As long as no effective solution is found to these and other security-related problems, the use of mobile agents in a truly open environment, such as the Internet, will be severely limited.

The field also suffers from a lack of standardization. Mobile agent systems allow an agent to move freely among heterogeneous machines, but this is only possible as long as the hosts are running the 'right' mobile agent system. Thus, code is not portable across mobile agent systems. Although it is unrealistic to expect that the mobile agent community will be able to agree on a single framework, nevertheless, allowing for portability across mobile agent platforms is one essential step if mobile agents are to be widely accepted and deployed. Some efforts towards this direction include the OMG MASIF standard, albeit this only addresses cross-system communication and administration.

On the nontechnical front, one important handicap of mobile agents is the lack of a killer application. Most proposed applications for mobile agents can be implemented just as well and efficiently with another approach, although different approaches would be suitable for different applications. Consequently, one can purport that the advantages of mobile agents are modest when any particular application is considered in isolation. It is therefore fundamental that a killer application, or a set of applications, can be shown to be implemented with much less effort and more efficiently with mobile agents, rather than with any other approach on its own. One potential such application domain is e-commerce where electronic marketplaces are created dynamically and on a per need basis. Given the agility of mobile agents, they are well-suited for taking advantage of opportunities as they appear and adapting in highly competitive, dynamic and constrained environments. For instance, the Nomad system enables the creation and management of mobile agents that can participate in online auctions in the eAuctionHouse system (Sandholm and Huai 2000). Another potential application for mobile agents is with regards to devices such as mobile phones and PDAs. As network connectivity may not be continuous and the computational resources of such devices are rather limited, mobile agents offer a realistic and attractive solution. They can be dispatched from the user's mobile phone when computationally intensive tasks need to be performed, or large amounts of information need to be processed, or when uninterrupted connectivity is required for a particular task. The mobile agent can perform the tasks required and return with the results. Even if there is a network disruption, the mobile agent could wait by an appropriate docking platform until connection with the user is re-established. Another potential application of mobile agents is in Grid (Foster and Kesselman 2004) environments to discover and access resources and services (Aversa et al. 2004, Di Martino and Rana 2004).

Having such clear-cut cases will help much in the take-up and wider acceptance of the technology. In combination with solving the technical issues mentioned above, this could convince conventional Internet service providers to open their sites and allow mobile agents to dock and operate on their systems. In particular, service providers and web sites must have a strong motivation to adopt a new technology that involves upgrading, or adapting their current systems. This is only possible if the new technology offers substantial benefits in terms of faster and more efficient access to information and services, more useful applications, and better overall user experience.

11.7 Further Reading

The collection of papers by Milojicic et al. (1999), although now dated, provides a thorough introduction to different aspects of mobile computing including processes, computers, and agents. An overview of contemporary mobile agent systems is given in da Silva et al. (2001). The book by Cockayne and Zyda (1998) describes a number of mobile agent systems such as Ara and Aglets. The most thorough account of Aglets, along with examples of code, is in Lange and Oshima (1998) and security issues are discussed in Karjoth et al. (1997). The reader interested in other mobile agent systems, Java and non-Java, should follow the references in Sections 11.3.2 and 11.3.1.

The discussion on mobile agent security is based mainly on Jansen and Kary-giannis (1999) and Tschudin (1999). Mobile agents and their use in e-commerce are discussed in Kowalczyk et al. (2003a,b) and Sandholm and Huai (2000). Particular issues with regard to mobile agent security in electronic marketplaces are discussed in Claessens et al. (2003).

11.8 Exercises and Topics for Discussion

1. Discuss the advantages and disadvantages of using mobile agents, in general, and in particular in e-commerce applications. Do you think that the disadvantages outweigh the potential benefits?

2. If you are familiar with the Java programming language, download the Aglets Software Development Kit from http://www.trl.ibm.com/aglets/. Install it on your machine and create a simple agent that can migrate from one context to another (on the same machine). If you have access to a network of machines, you can create contexts on different machines and program your aglet to migrate to different contexts.

3. Consider a marketplace that enables mobile agents, buyers and sellers, to meet, negotiate and perform transactions on behalf of their users. The marketplace (host) operates on a commission fee, which is determined as a percentage of the value of each successful transaction. Consider the potential ways in which the host, i.e., the marketplace, can interfere with the agents for its own benefit (code, data, transactions, communications, etc.). Sketch how individual agents could be potentially protected against such attacks.

CHAPTER 12

Trust, Security and Legal Issues

LEARNING OBJECTIVES

After reading and completing this chapter, you should be able to:

- Explain the risks involved by the use of agent technology in e-commerce.
- Discuss the concept of trust in agent technology and electronic marketplaces.
- Explain the role of institutions in regulating the agents' behaviour in electronic marketplaces.
- Describe the basic principles of cryptography.
- Compare and contrast the two main types of cryptographic system.
- Discuss how cryptography can be used to enhance and enforce security and trust in agent-mediated e-commerce.
- Illustrate how agent technology can hinder as well as help to preserve an individual's privacy.
- Discuss the legal issues surrounding the use of agents in e-commerce and their wider implications on society.
- Assess the advantages and disadvantages of agent technology for e-commerce.

The vision of future electronic marketplaces is that of being populated by autonomous intelligent entities – software, trading, e-agents – representing their users or owners and conducting business on their behalf. E-markets are fully automated from end-to-end: finding potential business partners, negotiating terms and conditions of transactions and contracts, signing and monitoring contracts, payment, and even dispute resolution will all be done automatically by software agents. In theory, the only time humans become involved is in specifying their portfolios or preferences.

For this vision to materialize, one crucial issue that needs to be addressed is that of trust. Trust becomes a fundamental requirement, in particular, if an agent's actions can cause its user physical, financial, or even psychological harm. The prospect of disclosing personal and financial information to an agent and delegating to it the task of conducting business on one's behalf does involves a number of risks. Hence, trust is essential to the uptake and deployment of agent technology.

Concomitant to trust is security, in fact, trust can derive from security. Central to e-commerce is the ability to perform transactions over the Internet which involve the exchange of private and sensitive information. There are inherent risks in the transmission of information over the Internet which need to be managed and guarantees need to be provided that transactions and exchanges are secure.

Moreover, agents engage in a number of activities which are significant from a legal perspective: they access computer systems, networks and data, they retrieve and distribute information, they mediate personal and business relations, they negotiate for and buy and sell goods and services. Autonomy implies that agents act without the constant and direct intervention of their users or owners. The introduction of electronic agents which conduct business on behalf of natural or legal persons, inevitably raises issues with regard to accountability and liability. The traditional paradigms have all developed along the lines of physical and geographical bounds of space and time. The Internet society, however, is not confined by geographical, legal, or corporate boundaries. Policy makers need to consider the repercussions of this new technology and provide safeguards and appropriate legislation that covers their operation.

Despite the excitement about agents and their immense potential, there are serious concerns about the associated trust, security and legal issues. We cannot simply assume that agents will be well-designed and implemented and behave correctly and thus provide for security and protect the users' privacy; explicit assurances and guarantees must be provided to this effect. For agent technology to fulfil its true potential and for users to be willing to engage with and delegate tasks to agents, a number of challenges need to be overcome. In particular, users need to:

- trust that agents do what they say they do
- be confident that their privacy is protected and that the security risks involved in entrusting agents to perform transactions on their behalf are minimized

- be assured that any legal issues relating to agents trading electronically are fully covered, as they are in traditional trading practices.

In the next sections of this final chapter of the book we will discuss in more detail some of the issues raised by the introduction of software agents in electronic markets.

12.1 PERCEIVED RISKS

As has often been remarked, there is a close connection between trust and risk (Luhmann 1979, 1990). To put it simply, if there is no risk, the question of trust does not arise. The absence of risk regarding future outcomes implies confidence and certainty. In the presence of risk, trust is required to overcome the inherent uncertainty involved.

Deploying agent technology in e-commerce is certainly not without risk (Brazier et al. 2004a). Agents run on an agent platform, they communicate and interact with other agents, objects and web services on the Internet and they function autonomously without the user's constant control and intervention. Undoubtedly, mobility increases the risks an agent faces as agents may be hosted by a potentially malicious agent platform, outside the control of their user, and thus they are even more vulnerable, as discussed in the previous chapter.

Most of the time users are unaware of which other agents, objects or web services with which agents are involved or interacting. In an open environment, an agent runs the risk that agent platforms, other agents, humans, viruses, etc., can access, copy or even modify its code or data either by design, or by mistake. These attacks can take place while an agent operates, lies in storage, or is being transmitted. The risks for the users are considerable and the potential consequences are indeed serious. For instance, an unauthorized modification of an agent's code or data may influence the agent's behaviour and result, for example, in buying goods for inflated prices, making faulty flight reservations or engaging in malicious behaviour. Even accessing data, especially confidential and sensitive information such as bank accounts, credit card numbers, reservation prices, may be sufficient to cause significant damage. As an example, while interacting in a marketplace, a buyer agent's reservation price may be modified, thus increasing the likelihood of the agent purchasing goods and at higher prices than originally intended. Even if the reservation price is simply accessed without permission by a seller agent, which gives the latter an advantage during negotiation, as knowing this information, it can adjust its counter-offer in such a way as to achieve maximum profit. In a similar way, a seller's reservation price may be increased by another seller so as to steal its potential share of the market, or decreased by a buyer to obtain a better deal.

Significant risks emanate from stealing information, including private information such as addresses, bank accounts, credit card numbers, and an agent's goals and instructions.

Such information can be stolen while in transit or in storage. Information on bank accounts and credit card numbers can be misappropriated: money can be transferred out of the user's account or used to purchase goods and services. The agent's identity, and as a consequence that of the user as well as her authority, can be hijacked by a malicious agent who can then use it and cause damage. Agents or users may be banned from a marketplace if they are found to have acted maliciously, even though a user may not be directly responsible for the agent's behaviour – the misbehaviour may have been the result of the agent's code being tampered with by another entity. Depending on the severity of the damages caused by a misbehaving agent, the user or owner may even have to face litigation. The issue is whether such policies constitute viable business practices and are perceived as fair by users. Apart from the potential financial losses, a user risks her reputation being damaged irreparably. Reputation is, in fact, an asset which both individuals and companies value as much as any other asset and it has a replacement cost. Reputation is difficult to built, but very easy to tear down.

Risks from nonrepudiation are also considerable. An agent or host can deny that a communication exchange or transaction has taken place, thus leaving another agent exposed. For instance, an agent responsible for procurement in a supply chain may order components essential for manufacturing a particular product. However, a supplier may deny ever receiving an order or agreeing on a contract. If such a situation arises, even the mere delay involved in investigating and resolving the dispute may mean significant losses. The buyer agent may not be able to receive the necessary components for manufacturing on time, and as a result it may not be able to satisfy a customer order with subsequent monetary losses, as well as damages to its reputation. Logging and auditing of communications and transactions need to be systematic in order to avoid such problems, and also to be able to trace what has happened in case of possible dispute or litigation.

Another potential risk is that an agent may disappear temporarily or permanently, representing a possible loss of investment in training and acquisition to the user/owner. More significantly, valuable results, trading data or records of transactions can be lost altogether, along with the agent. Depending on the situation, tracing and reconstructing transactions may be extremely difficult if not impossible, as an agent may have interacted with numerous other entities.

Electronic markets are real-time, dynamic and nondeterministic environments. Exceptional situations that are usually characterized by higher risk cannot be ruled out. Users are uncomfortable with the idea of software agents dealing with nonroutine or exceptional situations that perhaps the latter are facing for the first time and which they may not necessarily have been designed for, or have not learnt how to deal with. It is a widely held belief that automation is not in a position to deal with exceptional situations – the 'irony of automation' (Norman 1990).

Using agent platforms is also not without risk (Tschudin 1999). As discussed in the previous chapter in detail, an agent platform hosts an agent and provides services to it. The validity, reliability and trustworthiness of an agent's code and data cannot be easily determined automatically. Agents compete for resources such as processor cycles, bandwidth, storage space, and services such as communication and mobility. Malicious agents may succeed in migrating to a trustworthy platform, and code or data of the system can be modified or stolen, by accident or intentionally. Information on management or access policies can be altered. The platform may exhibit undesirable behaviour, e.g., by allowing unknown agents to enter, assign to or remove resources from agents, kill agents, or allow third parties to have access to the agents' code and private information; or it may simply crash. The platform could also be inundated with 'denial of service' attacks. If an agent platform ceases to function, this means possible financial losses to the agent platform owner as well as to the owners and users of the other agents operating on the platform. The reputation of the agent platform and its owners can be irreparably damaged, and depending on the severity of the misbehaviour, the owner may have to face litigation.

12.2 TRUST

Trust is a fundamental concept in our everyday lives and to a great extent guides our decision-making process. Without trust, virtually all of our social relationships would break down, and it would be impossible to function normally in our every day lives. If we cannot trust other drivers to stop at a red light, it would become impossible to drive. We depend on others every day, but we are usually comfortable in doing so because we trust that their actions will not be detrimental to us (Rotter 1980).

Trust can be considered as the generalized expectation that an individual, a group or an artifact (i.e., technology) can be relied upon. Trust is associated with risk and could be viewed as confidence in the face of risk. There are two parties in a trusting relationship: the principal who trusts, and the trustee who is the one who is entrusted. In trusting someone, one depends on this person and accepts vulnerability based upon positive expectations of the intentions or behaviour of this person, which are not under one's control. The need to trust, stems from this vulnerability and dependency on others and the need to delegate tasks to others. Delegation, in particular, presupposes trust, as it inevitably means loss of control. The process of delegation allows for passing responsibility for a task to another person and equipping them with the necessary authority and access to the resources needed to fulfil that task. However, task accountability remains with the principal (Oates 1993). This means that the principal assumes a risk in that the task may not be completed according to their standards and they will be personally accountable for the outcome. As a result, it is in the principal's best interest to choose the person who they believe to be more capable of accomplishing the task with great care.

Trust can be divided into: personal and impersonal. Personal trust is subjective and is formed by an individual based on beliefs, observations, reasoning, social stereotypes, communication, past experiences, etc. (Marsh 1994, Falcone and Castelfranchi 2004). The interaction between principal and trustee constitutes the basis for the development of trust between the two parties. Thus, trust is built by updating a priori expectations about another party by interacting with it. Trust develops, following a positive experience from the interaction, even when the initial expectations about the other party's behaviour were negative, and conversely, trust is reduced following a negative experience. People have different propensities or dispositions towards trust, in other words different baseline levels of trust; some people are more willing to trust than others. This baseline trust depends on an individual's personality and affects decision-making, as well as how new experiences are taken into account in updating one's trust (Marsh 1994).

Nevertheless, developing personal trust is not always possible due to situational constraints (Shapiro 1987). In the absence of personal trust, impersonal trust mechanisms can act as a substitute. Intuitively, impersonal trust is trust which can be derived from information or experiences as reported by third parties. There are a number of trust-inducing mechanisms that fall under this category such as trusted third parties, rule-based trust and word of mouth or reputation mechanisms. In the absence of any personal experience regarding the trustworthiness of someone, third-party intermediaries can be used to mediate between the principal and the trustee. Thus, the principal may not interact directly with the trustee, but through a third party which is mutually trusted by both of them. Alternatively, a principal can adopt the trust of a trusted third party as one's own. Trusted third parties are, for instance, banks, consumer institutes and governments. Another form of impersonal trust is rule-based trust. Trust can be induced by the knowledge that there are certain performance criteria and sanctions for nonconformance in place, which all members agree to abide by when they first join the marketplace, i.e., institutions. Finally, another form of impersonal trust is word of mouth or reputation. In the absence of personal experience with a person, a principal may seek information from third parties regarding past interactions. The outcomes of these past experiences are aggregated and make up reputation (Resnick et al. 2000). Relying on word of mouth or someone's reputation is, in essence, reliance on the aggregated experiences of third parties which are then used to inform one's decision-making. Such third parties can be a community, one's circle of friends, colleagues or the society. This sharing of past interaction histories can take many forms: informal gossip networks or institutionalized review or reputation systems.

12.3 TRUST IN E-COMMERCE

Typically, trading in markets involves trusting that the other participants are going to comply with the rules of the protocol and carry out their part of the transaction or honour the terms of the contract agreed, as well as the marketplace as an institution itself. In delegating such tasks to software agents, the need to trust the agents themselves also arises. Thus, trust in electronic marketplaces populated by software agents who act on behalf of their users/owners takes two forms: trust in the software agent as one's representative; and trust in the marketplace infrastructure (that it is fair, nonmanipulable, and rules and safeguards are in place) and the other participants (that they will act according to the rules of the protocol, honour contracts and agreements).

12.3.1 Trust in agent technology

Without doubt a trusting relationship must develop between the user and the agent. There are many valid reasons why users might hesitate to trust personal software agents, in particular in electronic markets. Generally speaking, there is always reluctance to trust and adopt new technology, and especially technology that one does not understand or comprehend the workings of, or technology that has not been tested extensively. In particular, trust becomes very important if the use of technology is perceived to carry high risks, i.e., can cause its user physical, financial, or psychological harm (Bickmore and Cassell 2001).

In fact, users need to place enormous trust on the agent that represents them and acts on their behalf in a marketplace, so they must be confident that agents will do what they ask, and only what they ask. Users also have to entrust agents with private and sensitive information, and agents will have to handle that information in a secure way (Patrick 2002). Such a software agent needs to have built-in mechanisms to ensure reliability, transparency and to make sure than no one can tamper with or manipulate it while it is operating in the market.

The distrust in agents and the reluctance to delegate tasks to them may be attributed to the fact that software agents are perceived as 'faceless strangers' (Shapiro 1987). Users may often limit their relationships and entrust parties with whom they have previous experience or, have an ongoing relation with, or with those whose performance and reliability has already been established. Moreover, it is often the case that users, whether individuals or organizations, consider familiarizing themselves and developing relations with their customer base and suppliers to be important in order to improve the level of service provided/received (Child and Linketscher 2001).

Another contributing factor to the users' tendency to distrust agents is that of the nature of the tasks being delegated to them. Such tasks are 'twice removed from the interface' (Patrick 2002). Consider a buyer who is interested in purchasing a particular item. In a traditional shopping trip, the buyer interacts with vendors directly by visiting their shops. A shopping trip nowadays may take place through a computer, where the buyer interacts with a Web browser to view information provided by the vendors. The buyer, having information from a number of vendors, is then in a position to compare prices and subsequently make a decision. Hence, the interaction between the buyer and the potential vendor is *once-removed* from the interface or a *disembedded* transaction (Riegelsberger and Sasse 2001). When the shopping task is delegated to a software agent, the buyer interacts with it in order to provide instructions and preferences through some sort of interface. The agent would then search the Internet, gather information provided by one or more vendors, and perform comparisons according to the buyer's criteria. As a result, there is no direct connection between the buyer and the search or comparison activities. The interaction between the buyer and the potential vendor is *twice-removed* (or *dis-disembedded*). Developing trust can be difficult during once-removed interactions, but even more so in twice-removed interactions. At the same time, as agents facilitate twice-removed interactions between users and other parties, they are ideal for tasks that require high degrees of privacy or anonymity (see discussion below).

Finally, the user must also be confident that the agent has the mechanisms itself to cope in an uncertain environment where it will have to make decisions concerning which other agent or service provider to trust, in looking after its user's interests. With all of these concerns, developing a trusting relationship between users and their agents is nontrivial.

Allowing agents to act autonomously may be too much to ask from the user right from the start. The user must come to develop faith in the agent's sense of obligation, that is, that it can be trusted to act in the user's best interests to achieve optimal performance (Lee and Moray 1992). In the beginning of the interaction, the agent can perhaps have more of an advisory role, and as trust builds up, this leads to a more active role in the transactions being carried out, ultimately allowing it to act autonomously in the user's interests. As trust is built gradually through positive experiences, one way forward may be to allow greater degrees of control to users. Control and trust seem to be two opposite sides of the same coin. In essence, a user needs to have high levels of control when she has low levels of trust, whereas when trust is high, the level of control can be low (Child and Linketscher 2001). In the early stages of interaction with a principal, the agent needs to have more built-in mechanisms of control to compensate for the lack of trust. These relate to input, choice and ultimately decision control.

An agent's behaviour can be controlled in three stages: (i) pre-activity; (ii) real-time, (iii) post-activity (Jenks and Kelly 1985). In the first stage, the principal sets and communicates to the agent, the criteria for evaluating performance as well as any specific instructions for accomplishing tasks. Obviously a user should give clear instructions to the agent on the task to be performed and the various parameters such as budget and other preferences. But this instructing phase could potentially fail if (Youll 2001):

1. the user does not convey her intentions clearly
2. the agent does not fully comprehend the instructions
3. the user and the agent interpret the instructions provided differently.

If the agent understands the instructions, the user must be confident that it will execute the instructions correctly, and will only perform the tasks the user intended.

In the second stage, in real-time, the principal controls the agent by monitoring its performance. The principal may also choose to intervene if necessary to guide the agent, correct or even override the agent's decisions. To be able to evaluate whether an agent's behaviour is consistent, the user needs to have a clear picture of what the agent does. Reporting to the user regularly or providing periodic progress reports can facilitate observability and a better understanding of what goes on in the 'black box'. Providing an explanation or justification on decisions and actions reduces the user's uncertainty about what happens inside the agent and provides system process and benchmarking information. Provided that the agent's behaviour is consistent and stable over time, the principal is likely to deem the agent as dependable and eventually as trustworthy of future delegation.

On task completion, the principal reviews the agent's performance and task achievement and may reward good performance or mark and even punish deviation from the user's goals.

As the level of trust increases, the user may relinquish some of the control, thus the agent needs to be able to adapt to the user's ever-changing needs. Hence, in the absence of initial trust, high levels of control and transparency of operation can aid towards the gradual building of it.

12.3.2 Trust in the marketplace

In traditional, as well as electronic marketplaces, exchanges are often carried out among participants who have never met before and may have little or no idea about each other's reliability and trustworthiness. Trust in the marketplace is an essential ingredient if participants are to keep negotiating with each other in order to reach a deal, and for transactions to go through. This trust reflects the risk that a person undertakes towards the protocol, the marketplace and also the other participants. One needs to trust that the protocol and the market infrastructure is fair and nonmanipulable. Electronic markets provide a fertile ground for deceitful participants to engage in old as well as new types of fraud. For instance, items may not be delivered at all or may be of different quality than that agreed, the prices charged may be higher than the ones appearing on electronic catalogues or originally agreed, refunds may not be given despite being advertised differently, buyers may delay payments, or not pay at all, or post cheques that are not valid.

To minimize risk in electronic marketplaces, the issues of trust management and security need to be addressed. In particular, electronic marketplaces must address how they intend to provide trust, security, enforce contracts and establish a legal framework. The marketplace itself may provide safeguards and guarantees against fraud and breaches of the protocol, as well as impose sanctions on those who have deviated from the prescribed rules. This can be facilitated through the use of institutions.

In addition, apart from making sure that transactions are secure, there is the need to equip software agents with mechanisms that allow them to reason about, and assess trust towards, other market participants much in the same way their users would do in traditional market settings. Consequently, we need built-in mechanisms for evaluating the outcomes of interactions with other agents as positive or negative experiences and building a notion of trust through them (Michalakopoulos and Fasli 2005).

12.4 ELECTRONIC INSTITUTIONS

The main strength of the agent paradigm is that it allows us to build inherently complex and distributed systems which are composed of simpler entities – agents. Within such systems, agents representing individuals and organizations operate in a common environment attempting to achieve their design objectives. Such environments are inherently heterogeneous, dynamic and open. 'Interference' is inevitable (Castelfranchi 2003); the actions of one agent can support or facilitate the goals of another (positive interference) or obstruct them (negative interference). As a result, some means of regulating the behaviour of individuals and groups of agents is needed to minimize disruption and ensure smooth performance, and promote fairness and stability.

Designing efficient and robust open electronic marketplaces in which heterogeneous self-interested agents engage in interactions, attempting to further their own objectives, is an open problem. Traditional mechanism design is concerned with the development of protocols that are stable and individual rational and which lead to socially desirable outcomes. However, as we saw in Chapter 10, some of the underlying assumptions of mechanism design are not realistic in the context of heterogeneous software agents in complex environments with limited computational resources and reasoning power. In particular, guiding and regulating the behaviour of the agents in such systems to discourage malicious behaviour, harmful interactions and enhance trust, is a difficult problem. Given the inherent heterogeneity, agents cannot be expected to have the same level of sophistication or necessarily to follow the rules prescribed by the interaction protocols. Moreover, their interactions may lead to unexpected, dysfunctional behaviour and inadvertently trigger systemic failures (Dellarocas and Klein 1999).

The counterpart of artificial societies and electronic markets, human societies and traditional markets, have dealt with the above issues by developing norms which guide, monitor and regulate the agents' behaviour (Dellarocas and Klein 1999, Dignum 2001, 2002, Sierra and Noriega 2002). Norms or social constraints are the essence of *institutions* (North 1990). In a similar fashion, the behaviour of agents within electronic marketplaces, virtual organizations or enterprises and, in general, within multi-agent systems, can be regulated via appropriate electronic social institutions. Electronic institutions identify a set of norms that the agents should adhere to when they participate in a particular institution. To this end, interaction protocols (auctions, ContractNet, SNP, etc.) can be augmented with norms to improve their stability, robustness and performance in the presence of heterogeneity, potential malicious behaviour, and systemic failures.

12.4.1 Norms, institutions and organizations

Norms are rules, constraints or standards of behaviour which are shared by a group of agents or societies. In general, norms encapsulate abstract values or principles such as 'fairness', 'justice' or 'equality' which may be encoded as specific rules or policies, or conventions. In this respect, norms simplify the interactions among agents and enhance trust. Institutions are amalgamations of interdependent conventions or norms.

Institutions can be formal or informal. The former consist of norms which are encoded as explicit rules or regulations and are enforced within the group or society and prescribe sanctions for deviating from these norms. For instance, a formal norm, which is usually explicitly encoded as a statute, is that stealing is not permitted behaviour within a society. Any agent deviating from this norm will have to suffer the consequences in the form of sanctions (i.e., prison sentence, or fine). Informal institutions are characterized by norms which are not enforced by regulations, but still guide the agents' behaviour, such as taboos, customs, conventions or codes of behaviour. For instance, giving up one's seat on a bus to an older person is an informal norm, but an agent will not be punished for violating this.

Thus, institutions determine what individual agents are allowed to do or are prohibited from doing, they ascertain deviations from the prescribed behaviour and violation of rules and determine the sanctions to be imposed on the deviating agents. North (1990) studied institutions and their effect on human organizations and postulated that the fundamental role of institutions is to provide a stable framework for interaction, guide the behaviour of human agents and reduce uncertainty. Within an institutional framework, the interaction costs can be potentially reduced, while the interactions can grow in complexity and their outcomes can largely be anticipated as participants adhere to the prescribed norms.

At this point we need to clarify the relationship between institutions and organizations. Organizations are groups of agents united by some common purpose to achieve a set of objectives. They constitute social entities with structure, resources and authority. They are created with the purpose of taking advantage of opportunities that arise, for example, in markets or societies within the existing institutional frameworks. Organizations such as, for instance, corporate organizations and other types of (formal and informal) groups become instances of specific institutions or a combination of a set of norms (Vázquez-Salceda et al. 2003), i.e., institutions manifest themselves in organizations. Organizations require norms to support their objectives, enhance their functionality and instill confidence and thus, inherently, are governed by institutions. The relationships between norms, institutions and organizations are illustrated in Figure 12.1. For example, the English auction is a trade institution that prescribes how negotiations can be conducted. A particular auction house X can be an instantiation of the English auction and can conduct auctions using the specific rules as described by the protocol. The auction house may include additional norms that further restrict the behaviour of the agents and which may not typically be part of the English auction protocol[1]. For instance, bidders who wish to participate in an auction may be required to pay a registration fee. The auction house X is an organization – it has structure, members and resources – which instantiates a trade institution and may also impose additional norms.

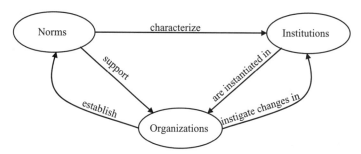

Figure 12.1: The relationships between norms, institutions and organizations

To summarize, the need for norms stems from the fact that uncertainty is endemic in environments with heterogeneous agents and their interactions need to be structured to promote stability, fairness and trust and to avoid harmful interactions. Norms characterize institutions. Organizations can be created as instances of specific institutions or a combination of norms. Norms support organizations, and thus organizations establish norms to improve their functionality and interactions. As organizations are not static entities, their norms evolve according to the needs of the constituent agents and the environment in which they operate, and as a consequence, this may also instigate changes in the institutions. In the following, the terms institution and organization will be used interchangeably, where no confusion can arise.

12.4.2 From norms to institutions

Norms that govern electronic institutions can be distinguished into three categories according to Sierra and Noriega (2002): ontological and communication norms, social interaction norms, and norms that impose restrictions on the behaviour of individual agents.

Ontological and communication norms intuitively enable clear and unambiguous communication among the various participants. Such norms make explicit various aspects that affect communication such as, for instance, the communication language to be used, the performatives that can be exchanged and their meaning, the content language, any underlying ontologies, as well as the roles of the participants themselves and other conventions for exchanging messages. Ontological and communication norms are essential

---

[1] McAfee and McMillan (1987) refer to auctions as institutions that include normative aspects.

in a system where agents will almost certainly be heterogeneous and they need to be able to communicate with each other in clear unambiguous terms.

Social interaction norms essentially dictate the protocols to be used within the institution and enable the participants to interact with each other. For instance, in an electronic marketplace the Dutch auction is such an interaction protocol which describes how participants can engage in negotiation via this particular protocol. Such norms may also describe the correct sequence of activities within an institution, e.g., first an agent needs to register with the auction house, then it can bid in various auctions; payment follows if the agent wins an auction, and finally an agent can exit the auction house after successful payment has been completed. These distinct but, in some cases, interdependent activities are usually referred to as *scenes* (Sierra and Noriega 2002).

The third class of norms, behaviour norms, are normative rules that dictate permissible and acceptable behaviour as well as prohibitions within the institution, i.e., such norms describe an agent's obligations and rights.

The aim of imposing norms is that they act as deterrents, disincentives, and fundamentally are preventative measures against unwanted behaviour (Dignum 2002). The designer of an auction house, for instance, would like to make it impossible or extremely difficult for the agents to violate any of the prescribed norms. Norms are therefore translated into rules that impose restrictions on the agents' behaviour or sanctions on deviant behaviour. These rules form the *policy* of a particular organization.

Norms that indicate prohibitions can be translated into regulations. For instance, to prohibit unregistered agents from bidding in auctions, the auction house may require that agents register first. Norms that indicate desirable behaviour are, whenever possible, translated into restrictions on unwanted behaviour. The issue here is that the institution cannot really enforce such behaviour. For instance, the desired behaviour that we would like the winner of an auction to exhibit, i.e., to pay for the item won, cannot easily be enforced. Alternatively, other rules can be put in place to act as incentives to adhere to the norm or act as deterrents to unwanted behaviour. For example, an auction house may withhold an agent's deposit or entry fee paid, if the agent refuses to pay for an item won in an auction. Furthermore, the auction house can prevent the agent from participating and bidding in any subsequent auctions. Norms that indicate that certain actions are permitted only under specific conditions, can be translated into checking that the conditions are satisfied before the agent is allowed to execute the action. As an example, agents may be permitted to pay by credit card, provided that the credit card is valid and their credit limit is not violated. Thus, unless these two conditions are fulfilled the agent is prevented from performing the action of paying by credit card.

Nevertheless, there are other kinds of unwanted behaviour that cannot be translated from norms into explicit rules which can easily be enforced. For instance, in auctions we would like to prevent participants from colluding and forming rings. Such a norm cannot be easily enforced, as the agents may decide to act outside the institution and thus the institution has no way of checking their behaviour. In this case, the mechanism or protocol designer might try to deter such behaviour by designing the rules of the game, i.e., the rules of the interaction protocol (e.g. Dutch auction), in such a way that the agents have little incentive to collude. As we saw in Chapter 8, the agreement within the ring needs to be self-enforcing'.

Alternatively, instead of attempting to enforce a norm by restricting the agents' behaviour, it may be more efficient to react to violations of norms (Dignum 2002). For instance, agents that are caught attempting to manipulate the auction can be banned from the auction house, or have their registration fees or deposits withheld as a form of fine. For each norm that the institution would like to enforce, a rule is required that specifies either:

- the procedure within the institution that enforces the norm; or

- the conditions that constitute violations of the norm and the consequences, or sanctions imposed by the institution.

12.4.3 Formalizing norms

Deontics is the study of norms and associated concepts, such as obligations and permissions for human agents. The study and modelling of norms has also been undertaken within multi-agent systems and, in particular, agent theories which serve as specification and validation tools to the designers and developers of multi-agent systems (Esteva et al. 2001b). Such theories describe what a system, i.e., agent, or multi-agent system, is supposed to do. To this end, regulation of behaviour, stable group activity and elements that contribute to social order in multi-agent systems need to be considered (Castelfranchi 2000). A plethora of approaches have been proposed to capture social order in MAS including social and collective attitudes (Castelfranchi 1995, Dunin-Keplicz and Verbrugge 2003), normative concepts (Dignum 2002, van der Torre and Tan 1999, Broersen et al. 2002) as well as organizational ones (Ferber and Gutknecht 1998, Wooldridge et al. 2000, Zambonelli et al. 2000, Cavedon and Sonenberg 1998).

Obligations and other normative concepts are typically formalized within deontic modal logic (Åqvist 1984, Hilpinen 1971, von Wright 1951). Obligations seem to be external to agents, they are usually imposed by another agent or perhaps a larger body, such as a group, an organization or society, and intuitively express what ought to be the case. We can distinguish between two broad categories of obligations: general and relativized. General obligations express normative sentences for all agents and can be seen as rules that provide the minimal means for social interaction, i.e., what all agents are obliged to do. In standard propositional deontic logic (SDL), a modal obligation operator O prefixes propositions $\phi, \psi, \ldots$ to create formulas of the form $O(\phi)$. Such a formula is read 'it is obligatory that ϕ'. Agents may also hold obligations towards specific agents or groups. Deontic logic can be extended so that relativized obligations can be expressed with another modal operator $O(i, j, \phi)$ which is read as 'agent i is obligated to j to bring about ϕ' (Fasli 2002).

But the concept of obligation, as explained above, lacks the characteristic notion of commitment on behalf of the agent. In other words, an agent who is obligated to bring about a state of affairs does not necessarily mean that it is itself committed to do so. Another concept is required to capture this, namely social commitment. Social commitments can be expressed via a modal operator $SCom(i, j, \phi)$ which is read 'agent i is committed to agent j to bring about ϕ'. For instance, the formula $SCom(seller, buyer, ship-ordered-goods)$ expresses the commitment of a seller to the buyer to ship the ordered goods. At the same time of course, the buyer needs to commit to pay the seller for the ordered goods.

Organizations which are supported by norms, provide the necessary context for making such commitments. For instance, the aforementioned commitments can be made in the context of an auction house. The role of the auction house is to witness the agents' commitments and monitor that the agents honour their commitments and that transactions are executed smoothly. If there are deviations from the prescribed behaviour, then the role of the institution is to intervene and take appropriate measures.

Organizations are characterized by a formal structure, which is defined in terms of roles and authority relations, among other things, and have an objective which is supported by the individual agents and subgroups within the organization. Roles are, in effect, standardized patterns of behaviour (Esteva et al. 2001a). Within organizations agents enact roles: agents assume at least one role, although they can have multiple roles. Institutions prescribe a set of norms that the agents have to adhere to when they operate within such a system. In essence, institutions provide the infrastructure which is required to ensure smooth operation, stability and fairness within the system, as well as to reduce uncertainty and enhance trust. Each role can be regarded as being associated with a set of normative positions such as commitments, obligations, permissions and rights (Fasli 2004). A role specifies the position of the agent in the organization as well as its commitments towards other agents, the group as whole, as well as other groups. Each member of the organization knows its place and acts accordingly, and furthermore, each knows the implications of exercising rights and breaking commitments.

12.4.4 Agents in electronic institutions

Agents join electronic marketplaces in order to interact with other agents and further their own objectives. Marketplaces can be regarded as electronic institutions which are underpinned by a set of norms. By entering a marketplace, an agent assumes a role and commits to adhere to the institution's norms, namely its policy. Every participating agent in such a marketplace should act, and also expect others to act, according to the institution's policy.

Commitments may take the shape of formal contracts between the institution and the agent. Contracts can be private or social (Dellarocas and Klein 1999). Private contracts are drawn between two or more agents who want to engage in interaction and execute a transaction. The institution's role in this case is to protect the agents, throughout the duration of the contract, from any potential exceptions, including exceptions that arise as a result of nonconformance or malicious behaviour on behalf of the other agents. A social contract is a commitment on behalf of an agent towards the institution, to adhere to its norms. The institution, on the other hand, commits to enforce the agent's private contracts as well as protect the agent from the unsolicited behaviour of any other agents or any systemic failures.

Within the context of electronic institutions, agent designers and developers can develop their agents so that they behave according to norms (Dignum 2001). Agents need not necessarily be aware of the norms that different institutions impose, as long as they are designed to conform to a wide range of principles and do not exhibit malicious behaviour. However, although some generic norms may be hardcoded into the agent, such agents cannot adapt to different institutions. Alternatively, agents can be designed so that they are able to reason about norms and make decisions accordingly. In this case, norms need to be represented explicitly alongside the rules for different interaction protocols. For instance, alongside the rules of various auction protocols, an auction house should also include a list of rules which describe desirable behaviour, while operating within the auction house. One of these rules can be, for instance, that only registered agents are allowed to place bids in an auction.

In a similar way to traditional institutions, which facilitate interactions among human participants and regulate and enforce desirable behaviour, electronic institutions can be created to regulate the behaviour of agents within marketplaces and promote fairness and stability and also to minimize harmful interactions. Inevitably, institutions restrict the agents' autonomy. Agents that want to participate in electronic institutions of any form, will lose some of their autonomy, as they have to adhere to the institution's norms. This is the price that agents have to pay in order to be able to interact with others within the context of an institution that provides safeguards against breaches of protocol. But agents exercise their autonomy in entering into those institutions and committing to comply with their policies in the first place. Nevertheless, an agent being autonomous may decide to violate the rules if it perceives that it can benefit from this, but risks being ostracized and becoming isolated, and therefore unable to further its objectives.

12.5 REPUTATION SYSTEMS

Trust is an essential prerequisite for establishing and developing open, but stable, online trading communities. In seeking out and engaging with new partners and in the absence of past interactions with them that would provide an indication of their trustworthiness, one has to resort to alternative means to trust management. One such alternative is the use of reputation reporting systems to encourage trustworthiness and good behaviour in exchanges.

Reputation encapsulates the distributed knowledge of a set of entities about another and is used to predict future behaviour based on past behaviour (Bromley 1993). When people interact with one another over time, the history of past interactions informs them about each other's dispositions and traits. An interaction, such as an economic transaction, can be viewed in very simple terms as a prisoners' dilemma situation. The buyer and the seller are faced with the following dilemma: to cooperate with each other, i.e., the buyer pays what is due to the seller and the seller ships the goods as agreed, or to defect, i.e., the buyer does not pay for the goods, and the seller does not ship them or they are of lower quality than that agreed. The socially acceptable outcome of this interaction, which constitutes the Pareto optimal solution, is for both of them to cooperate. But, each has the incentive to defect in order to maximize their own temporary gain. The reason participants fail to cooperate when they do not know each other is the lack of a shadow of the future (Axelrod 1984). The lack of a common interaction history and the relative ease with which buyers and sellers can change partners from one transaction to the next, gives incentives to both parties to provide inferior quality of service or to deviate from the original agreement. Mechanisms for establishing trust attempt to create this shadow of the future. Of course, trust among unknown parties is much more difficult to build. By keeping track of one's past interactions and making the results available to others, reputation systems establish this shadow of the future by creating an expectation that others will consult the aggregated past history. This fear of retaliation in future interactions, if one has not behaved well, creates a powerful incentive to cooperate. For any party deciding whether to initiate a transaction, reputation is a source of information that can reduce uncertainty and guide the decision of whether to trust, or not to trust, a potential partner.

12.5.1 Reputation systems in practice

Generally, a reputation system collects, aggregates and distributes feedback about participants' past behaviour (Kollock 1999, Resnick et al. 2000). Such systems help interested parties to decide whom to trust, encourage trustworthy behaviour and aim to deter deceitful participants. Reputation systems work in a similar way to recommender systems, which were discussed in Chapter 6. Each participant provides feedback and rates the interaction experience with another participant once a transaction has been completed successfully, or otherwise. As in recommender systems, there are different ways of providing feedback, such as rating in terms of a scale, for instance, from 1 to 5 and/or providing textual comments. Reputation systems can be used to rate individual traders, vendors, sites, software agents or products and services.

An indicative example of a successful reputation system being used in a large-scale system is that of the Feedback Forum as deployed by eBay. eBay is the largest person-to-person online auction site, with more than four million auctions active at any time. At first glance, the exchanges on eBay may appear highly problematic: the insurance provided is limited and both buyers and sellers accept the associated risks of transacting with unknown parties, which can be significant. Despite this, however, the overall rate of successful transactions on eBay remains remarkably high for a market that opens the possibility of large-scale fraud and deceit. The high rate of successful transactions is attributed by eBay and its users to its reputation system. After a transaction is complete, the buyer and seller have the opportunity to rate each other using 1, 0 and −1 to indicate a positive, neutral and a negative experience, respectively. Participants have running totals of feedback points attached to their user names, which might be pseudonyms. When one is considering whether or not to enter into a transaction with another participant, the reputation rating provides clear guidance as to the participant's trustworthiness in the past. Among the most useful features of the Feedback Forum is that it allows participants to leave textual comments describing in detail their experiences with other buyers and sellers. With such clear reputation indicators, low-quality or unreliable sellers get lower prices and eventually they become isolated or are banned from transacting, leaving the reliable participants to enjoy a healthier market with prices that correspond to the quality of service that they offer. It is very often the case that sellers with excellent reputations may enjoy a premium for their services, as some users may be willing to pay more for the additional security, reliability and higher quality of service. Other auction sites such as Yahoo! Auction and Amazon, feature similar reputation systems with variations on the rating scale (5 or 15), several measures (friendliness, prompt response, quality of service) and different ways of aggregating feedback (averaging instead of total feedback score).

Ratings are, of course, not the only indicators of reputation. Agreeing to be rated when rating is optional is possibly an indication of higher-quality services even before ratings are available. Other ways of promoting one's reputation would be to use one's real name, rather than a pseudonym, and disclose other information such as a physical store's address or phone number.

There are a number of prerequisites that must be in place in order for an online reputation system to operate effectively and to provide incentives for honest and trustworthy behaviour:

- participants must be long-lived entities, human or artificial, that have the potential for future interaction

- the costs for submitting and distributing feedback must be very low

- feedback information must be aggregated and presented in a way that enables and guides trusting decisions

- clear guidelines on how the rating system operates and how potential conflicts can be resolved

- the reputation server itself must be reputable and trustworthy.

12.5.2 Issues and problems

Although reputation systems offer a viable trust-management method that emerges from a community which will use it, there are significant issues to be addressed with regard to eliciting, aggregating, and distributing feedback information (Resnick et al. 2000).

Obtaining feedback from users presents three main problems. First, as in recommender systems, users may be reluctant to provide feedback. For instance, after a transaction has been completed, there is little incentive to spend time filling out a form. Nevertheless, a significant number of users choose to do so, at least on eBay, which perhaps is an indication of the participants' willingness to engage with the community, their gratitude, or their desire to air their frustration. Although some form of economic incentive can be offered for providing feedback, such a scheme introduces additional problems regarding the feedback's reliability and credibility. Second, it is difficult to ensure honest reporting and that the system is nonmanipulable. In particular, this relates to two issues: unfair ratings and discriminatory seller behaviour (Dellarocas 2000a,b). Unfair ratings can be divided into:

- **Unfairly high ratings (ballot stuffing).** A seller can collude with a group of buyers in order to obtain unfairly high ratings. As a consequence the seller's reputation will be inflated, thus allowing the seller to have a bigger share of the market and perhaps at higher prices than deserved.

- **Unfairly low ratings (bad-mouthing).** Sellers can collude with buyers in order to bad-mouth other sellers whom they want to drive out of the market. Sellers can also masquerade as buyers and provide negative ratings to other sellers. Either of these has as the effect that the reputation of the seller being bad-mouthed becomes lower and this may potentially lead to the seller being banned from the marketplace.

A seller's behaviour can be discriminatory towards different buyers:

- **Negative discrimination.** A seller may provide good service to everyone except a few specific buyers that it does not like. If the number of buyers being discriminated upon is relatively small, the cumulative reputation of the seller will remain good, but an externality will be created against the discriminated buyers.

- **Positive discrimination.** A seller may provide exceptionally good service to a few individuals and average service to the others. This resembles the effects of ballot stuffing. If the number of buyers being favoured is sufficiently large, their high ratings will inflate the reputation of the seller and will create an externality against the rest of the buyers.

Third, it may be particularly difficult to elicit negative feedback. Some users may be afraid of further unpleasant interactions with the other party and so they may keep quiet.

The next phase, aggregating feedback, poses its own problems. How is feedback aggregated so that it can be useful to participants in their trusting decisions? Are ratings being weighted in some way, depending on how recent they are? For instance, eBay displays net feedback which is positives minus negatives, whereas others such as Amazon, display an average. But these simple numerical ratings may fail to convey important information about online interactions. For instance, did the feedback come from low or high-value transactions? What were the reputation ratings of the evaluators?

The distributing phase raises additional issues. Who has access to the reputation ratings? Everyone? Only registered users? As each site uses its own way of representing ratings there is a problem with the portability of one's ratings from one system to another. Ideally one would, for instance, like to be able to import one's ratings from eBay into another system, to establish a good name quickly, rather than to start from scratch. However, for the time being this is beyond the capabilities of current reputation systems. Finally, name changes present a problem in reputation systems. Users may register with a number of pseudonyms, essentially erasing the effects of prior feedback. One solution might be to assume that new users, i.e., those with no feedback, should always be distrusted until they have somehow proven themselves, either through paying an entry fee (deposit or insurance) or by accepting more risk or worse prices while building their reputations. An alternative is to prevent name changes either by using real names or through forcing users to acquire unique pseudonyms, namely once-in-a-lifetime pseudonyms. Another problem of centralized reputation systems is that of vulnerability to falsified information. In such systems, ratings and reports can be easily falsified. For instance, a seller can easily rate itself several times highly in order to increase its reputation rating and attract more buyers. One solution that has been proposed is the use of decentralized reputation systems (Schneider et al. 2000, Yu and Singh 2002). In such systems, participants keep their own database of reputation ratings about others with whom they have interacted or they have been told about. Participants can exchange and update their reputation databases when they meet with others and, in this way, information about interactions is propagated out to the rest of the participants.

As electronic marketplaces on the Internet flourish, reputation systems may constitute a viable solution to the problem of trust management, in particular in short-term relationships. Their power stems from their ability to facilitate and induce cooperation in uncertain and often precarious environments without the need for costly and complex enforcement institutions. Reputation systems are being powered by the participants themselves – the community – and work to create a safer community. Nevertheless, there are many challenges that need to be addressed, in particular with regard to fairness and nonmanipulation.

12.6 SECURITY

Security is essential in any computer system and even more so in an open network such as the Internet in which agents, hosts and other entities may be of unknown origin, or may not be benevolent. Hosts, agents and other entities are vulnerable to a number of attacks ranging from eavesdropping communications to stealing sensitive and private data and inflicting damage, by design, through viruses. It is essential that hosts, agents and their exchanges are appropriately safeguarded against these attacks. Security encompasses mechanisms to ensure (Stallings 2003, Rhee 2003, Jansen and Karygiannis 1999):

- confidentiality
- integrity
- authentication
- access control
- availability
- nonrepudiation
- logging and auditing.

The discussion that follows is more oriented towards agents, rather than general computer security.

Confidentiality

Typically, confidentiality is the assurance that information about identifiable persons will not be disclosed without consent from those persons, except as allowed and required by law. Identifiable information is any information which will identify or may reasonably lead to the identification of individuals, such as personal, medical, finance information, data on shopping patterns and demographic information. The release of such information would constitute an invasion of privacy for any individual. Hence, confidentiality is closely related to privacy, but the two are not identical. Confidentiality refers to the obligations of individuals and institutions to use information that has been disclosed to them and is under their control, appropriately. Thus, rules of confidentiality are observed out of respect for, and to protect and preserve, the privacy of others.

Confidentiality in our specific context is about ensuring that information is only accessible to those who have authorized access. Confidentiality extends to the agent's code as well as data.

As an inevitable consequence of the nature of tasks being delegated to software agents, namely to conduct business on behalf of their users, they have to carry or exchange data that enable them to do so. Such data can be sensitive financial data, such as credit card numbers or bank account numbers and passwords or pin numbers, or private data that enable the identification of a user such as her name, home address or security number. Protecting these data is of paramount importance in an electronic marketplace. Other types of data may also have to be kept confidential. For example, the terms of a contract with a company may need to be held confidential and protected from competitors. An agent's code may be encoding trading and negotiation strategies and proprietary algorithms, therefore it is important that these remain confidential as well. Finally, communications among agents, users and hosts that are designated as confidential need to be so, i.e., only an authorized recipient should have access to the contents of the message, otherwise, it should not be possible to obtain any significant information about the message contents. Besides, messages exchanged between hosts may actually involve the exchange of mobile agents.

Authentication

Authentication is the process of determining whether an agent, a host or a user is, in fact, who or what it claims to be. Thus a host, an agent, or a user attempts to establish that a communication received from another entity is authentic, i.e., it does indeed originate from the latter.

Authentication is closely related to authorization. Authorization is the process of giving someone permission to have access to something. A computer system is supposed to be accessed only by those who are authorized. Thus, it must attempt to detect and exclude any unauthorized parties. Access to a system is usually controlled by putting in place an authentication procedure to establish with some degree of confidence the identity of the entity requesting access.

Access control

Access control is about limiting and controlling access to host systems and their resources, applications, agents and data. Thus, each entity trying to gain access must be first identified or authenticated. An agent should be given access rights to information and resources according to the entity that it represents, i.e., user or organization. For instance, an agent representing a user may have access to the user's bank account, but a third agent should not be granted access to this information. Access control is especially important in mobile agent systems as the accessing of resources by mobile agents must be strictly controlled and monitored.

Integrity

Integrity is the assurance that information can only be accessed or modified by those authorized to do so. Integrity has to do with making sure that the agent's code, data or communication exchanges have not been tampered with, altered or destroyed either intentionally or by accident. Messages should not be duplicated, reordered or replayed. In mobile agents it is vital to ensure that an agent's code cannot be tampered with and the same applies to the host. In particular, checking the integrity of the agent's code is crucial before allowing it to start execution on a host machine. Checking that no illegal alterations have been performed to the agent's state is more difficult.

Availability

Availability refers to the system being able to provide the prescribed services according to its design specification to authorized parties. Denial of service attacks, for instance, can reduce or interrupt a system's availability or even shut it down altogether.

Nonrepudiation

Mechanisms to ensure nonrepudiation are vital if electronic marketplaces are to be trusted. As software agents close deals and agree on contracts, some means of ensuring that either party cannot deny that a deal or communication has ever taken place is becoming extremely important. Electronic transactions are also potentially subject to fraud. Participants may attempt to use various pretexts to repudiate a transaction. For instance, they may claim that their system has been broken into or has been infected with Trojan horses or viruses, to repudiate a transaction. In essence, nonrepudiation prevents either sender or receiver of a communication from denying that communication. Nonrepudiation of origin proves that data has been sent by a particular sender, while nonrepudiation of delivery proves it has been received by the receiver.

Auditing

Some form of logging and auditing must be provided. Records of security-related activities, including communication exchanges and transactions among agents, users and hosts, as well as information on accessing data, or resources by agents and hosts need to be maintained for future reference. In case of damage caused to a host, agent or data, or a potential dispute, the audit trail can be checked and actions by individual entities can be verified. Logging transactions and communication exchanges also aids nonrepudiation.

12.7 CRYPTOGRAPHY

Modern day cryptography is considered the science of information security (Rhee 2003, Stallings 2003). Cryptography uses linguistic and mathematical techniques for securing information, in particular, communication exchanges. The term is derived from the Greek 'kryptos' which means hidden and 'graphe' which means writing. Traditionally, cryptography was concerned with encryption, that is converting a plaintext message from its normal comprehensible form into an incomprehensible format, a ciphertext, rendering it unreadable and as a result useless to opponents or enemies. Encryption was used primarily to ensure the secrecy and security of important and confidential communications, such as those of spies, military leaders and diplomats. The information could only be decrypted if one had prior knowledge of the technique or algorithm used for encrypting it. Without having access to the secret knowledge which was used to convert the information into the ciphertext, one could not easily obtain the original plaintext.

Cryptography encompasses two strands: *cryptology* which is the discipline concerned with finding ways to encrypt a piece of information into a ciphertext in a secure way, and *cryptanalysis* which is concerned with attempting to discover either the plaintext, the secret algorithm, or the secret key from the ciphertext.

In today's Internet-centred world, the field of cryptography has expanded its remit: modern cryptography provides mechanisms for more than just keeping communication exchanges secure and has a variety of applications including authentication, digital signatures, electronic voting and digital cash. Even in our everyday transactions, cryptographic technology is frequently present, often built transparently into much of the computing and telecommunications infrastructure. For instance, when we pay online by credit card, this information is transmitted by means of the Secure Socket Layer (SSL) protocol which uses an asymmetric cryptographic system.

The term *cryptosystem* refers to a package of protocols and cryptographic algorithms, including the instructions for encoding and decoding messages. There are two kinds of modern cryptosystems: symmetric and asymmetric.

12.7.1 Symmetric cryptosystems

Symmetric encryption, also known as conventional, or secret key, or single-key encryption, is perhaps the most widely known type of encryption. Symmetric cryptosystems use the same key (the secret key) to encrypt and decrypt a message. The principles are simple. Assume that agent A needs to send a message to B which only B will be able to read, i.e., the message should be incomprehensible to everyone else but B. A symmetric encryption algorithm takes as input the plaintext message and, by applying a secret key, produces a scrambled message, the ciphertext. The ciphertext is then transmitted over the network and on receipt, B decrypts it by applying the algorithm in reverse using the same key to extract the original message. The key is usually a set of bits.

A symmetric cryptosystem is secure provided that two conditions are satisfied. First, the encryption algorithm should be hard to break. The minimum requirement is that an opponent who knows the algorithm and has access to the ciphertext would be unable to decipher it or discover the secret key. A stronger requirement is that an opponent should be unable to decrypt the ciphertext or discover the key, even if it is in possession of a number of ciphertexts together with the original plaintexts which produced them. Second, both sender and receiver must have obtained copies of the secret key in a secure way and the key must be kept secret at all times during its use by both parties. If an opponent finds out the key and also knows the algorithm, then all communications using this key are compromised.

The security of symmetric cryptosystems depends on the secrecy of the key and not the algorithm. An encryption scheme is said to be computationally secure if the ciphertext generated by the scheme meets one or both of the following criteria (Stallings 2003):

- The cost of breaking the cipher exceeds the value of the encrypted information.
- The time required to break the cipher exceeds the useful lifetime of the information.

Provided that an algorithm is strong, the ability of an encryption algorithm to withstand an exhaustion attack, increases with respect to the length of the key. Assuming that the key is of sufficient length, usually above 56 bits, the time that it would take to generate all keys and discover the correct one and thus break the algorithm, may be prohibitive even for the fastest computers.

But symmetric cryptosystems present a problem: how do you transport the secret key from the sender to the recipient securely and in a tamper-proof way? If one could send the secret key via some secure channel, then, in theory, one would not need the symmetric cryptosystem in the first place – the secure channel could be used for communication. The strength of any cryptographic system lies with the key distribution technique used, that is, in how a key is delivered to two parties who wish to exchange information without allowing third parties to see or intercept the key. There are several methods for key distribution:

1. A key could be selected by one party and then delivered to the other physically.

2. A third party could select the key and physically deliver it to the two interested parties.

3. If the two parties have recently used a particular key, then they can use the old key to encrypt the new one and communicate it to each other.

4. If the two parties have an encrypted connection to a trusted third party, then this party could deliver a key on the encrypted links to either of the two parties.

5. Another, more efficient and reliable solution is to use a public key cryptosystem (see following section).

The most commonly used symmetric encryption algorithms are block ciphers. A block cipher takes as input the plaintext in fixed-size blocks and produces a block or cipher of equal size for each plaintext block. The most widely known block encryption algorithms are the Data Encryption Standard (DES), the triple DES (3DES) and the advanced encryption standard (AES). DES is not considered computationally secure nowadays as its key is only 56 bits long and, with the current performance of computers systems and parallel processing, the key can be potentially discovered within a reasonable amount of time.

12.7.2 Asymmetric cryptosystems

Another form of encryption is achieved through asymmetric cryptosystems otherwise known as public key cryptography. Public key cryptography is a form of cryptography which generally allows users to communicate securely without having prior access to a shared secret key. This type of encryption was proposed by Diffie and Hellman (1976) and constitutes a significant landmark in cryptography.

Public key cryptography depends on the use of mathematical one-way functions, that is computations that are easy to do, but hard to reverse. Factoring is one of the most commonly used one-way functions. Multiplying two big prime numbers to produce another big number is easy, but factoring this really big number into its two components is very hard. Of course if one of the big numbers is already known, then factoring is easy.

Security in public key encryption is derived from the difficulty in computing the factors p, q if pq is large.

Public key cryptography is asymmetric: it involves the use of two separate keys which are related mathematically, designated as public and private keys. The private key is kept secret, while the public key may be widely distributed. In a sense, one key is used to 'lock' a lock, while the other one is required to 'unlock' it (Stallings 2003). It should not be possible to deduce the private key of a pair, given the public key. Larger key sizes provide for more security. Provided that the keys are sufficiently large, an exhaustive attack would take the world's fastest computers hundreds or thousands of years to obtain the private key from the public key.

Public key cryptography works in the following way. Each entity (user, host, agent) generates a pair of keys to be used for the encryption and decryption of communications. Each entity places one of the two keys in a public register or another publicly accessible file, or communicates the key directly to the other party. This now becomes the public key. The second key is kept private. Thus, each entity may maintain a collection of public keys as published by others. If B wants to communicate a message to A, B uses A's public key to encrypt the message and subsequently sends it. When A receives the message, it decrypts it using the private key. If the message is intercepted by a third party, it cannot be deciphered. Only A can decrypt the message, as only A is in possession of the private key which can decrypt it.

Depending on the application, the sender uses either its own private key, or the receiver's public key, or both, to perform some type of cryptographic function.

With this approach all entities have public and private keys, but there is no need to distribute private keys – only public keys. As long as an entity protects its private key, all incoming communications are secure. Thus, it is imperative that private keys are kept secure. At any time, an entity can change the private key and publish a new public key to replace the old one.

Typically, public key techniques are much more computationally intensive than symmetric algorithms. The two most widely used public key algorithms are the RSA and the Diffie–Hellman.

12.7.3 Applications of public key cryptography

The most obvious and common application of cryptography is for securing communications, thus ensuring confidentiality and privacy. However, cryptography can also be used to provide for authentication and integrity as well as nonrepudiation.

In particular, the use of public key cryptography systems can be classified into three categories (Stallings 2003):

1. **Encryption/decryption.** The sender encrypts the message with the recipient's public key, the recipient decrypts it with its private key.

2. **Digital signatures.** The sender encrypts a message with its private key, effectively signing it.

3. **Key exchange.** Two entities cooperate to exchange a session key, i.e., a key to be used as part of symmetric encryption.

Some public key algorithms are suitable for all three types of application, whereas others are only used for one or two of these. For instance, the RSA algorithm can be used in all three applications, whereas the Diffie–Hellman algorithm is mostly used for key exchange.

Cryptography for confidentiality and privacy

Encryption can provide for confidentiality – the assurance that no one else can read a message unless they have been entrusted with a private or secret key.

When using an asymmetric system, both agents generate their public and private keys, and make available to each other their respective public keys. If agent A wants to send a confidential communication to agent B, then it uses B's public key to encrypt the message, and sends the ciphertext to B. B then uses its private key to decrypt the ciphertext and obtain the original message. What is crucial is that the secret or private keys are secure and remain secret.

A symmetric cryptosystem could be used instead. But the main advantages of using an asymmetric cryptosystem over a symmetric one are that the two parties can be total strangers with no prior relationship, and that no key needs to be agreed upon or securely exchanged.

Cryptography for authentication, data integrity and nonrepudiation

Although confidentiality is fundamental to security, another issue that is really important is that of authentication, i.e., being confident that the sender of a communication really is who it claims to be. Suppose that an agent A wants to send a message to B. The content of the message may not be that important, but what is really important is that B is in a position to verify that the message has indeed come from A. In this case, A uses its own private key to encrypt the message and sends it to B. When B receives the ciphertext, it can decrypt it using A's public key, thus proving that the message was indeed sent by A as this is the only agent that has access to the private key and can encrypt a message which can only be decrypted with A's public key. Thus, authenticity of the message is verified and the source is established and the entire encrypted message serves as a 'digital signature'. Even if the message is intercepted by third parties, all they would be able to do is read the message by using A's public key to decrypt it. But the message content is not intended to be confidential in the first place. Nevertheless, it is impossible to alter the message without access to A's private key. As a matter of fact, a third party could change the content of the message, but without knowing A's private key, it cannot encrypt it and send it to B as if it was A's original communication. Hence, the content of the message cannot be changed without B realising it. Thus, data integrity is also ensured. In addition, authentication using public key encryption limits message repudiation: if a message is confirmed as authentic, the sender cannot easily deny sending that message. In essence, public key cryptography enables an entity to authenticate messages from complete strangers.

Distribution of secret keys

With conventional encryption, a fundamental requirement is that two parties must share the same secret key in order to be able to communicate securely and authenticate one another. The issue in symmetric cryptographic systems is the secure exchange of the secret keys used. One way that this can be achieved is through the use of public key encryption.

Suppose two agents A and B would like to exchange secure communications by conventional encryption means. However, they need to find a secure way of exchanging the secret key to be used in the conventional cryptographic system. First, the agents generate private and public keys to be used as part of an asymmetric cryptosystem. Assume that A has generated the secret key to be used in the conventional cryptographic system. A can encrypt the key using B's public key and send it to B. B being the only one in possession of the private key that can decrypt the message, uses it to obtain the original message which includes the secret key. A and B are now in a position to communicate with each other securely using a conventional cryptographic algorithm.

12.7.4 Digital signatures

Electronic signatures are different from digital signatures. An electronic signature is any electronic analogue to a written signature; for instance, as used for signing one's email messages from a scanned signature. Although, electronic signatures can serve as a means of identification, they are not tamper-proof as they need not rely on cryptographic methods. In contrast, the term digital signature has come to be limited only to technology that relies on public key cryptography to authenticate information (Rhee 2003, Stallings 2003, Baker and Hurst 1998).

Public key encryption can be used to provide 'digital signatures' to uniquely identify entities. The way digital signatures work is as follows. The sender encrypts the message using their private key, in effect 'signing' it, and subsequently sends it to the recipient. On receipt, the recipient decrypts the message using the sender's public key, thereby verifying that the message indeed originated from the sender and not from another entity.

But public key cryptography is computationally demanding and it takes too long to 'sign', i.e., encrypt, large documents or communications. Moreover, as the entire message is encrypted, thus validating both source and contents, it requires a lot of storage space, especially if the message or document is large. Each communication must be kept in plaintext in order to be used for practical purposes, but also a copy must be kept in ciphertext so that the source and contents can be verified in case of a potential future dispute.

To avoid this, special functions can be used to reduce the amount of information that must be encrypted in order to sign the message, and decrypted in order to verify one's signature. An authenticator can be attached to a document to effectively sign it. The authenticator is produced by encrypting a small block of bits which is a function of the original document and has the property that it is impossible to change the document without changing the authenticator. This process works as follows. Prior to being digitally signed, a message is hashed. Hashing is the process of applying a hashing algorithm or function to a message to obtain a condensed message digest of fixed length, otherwise known as a hash. Hashing functions are mathematical functions with two important properties. First, the hash must be almost unique and consequently if the original message is altered, the resulting hash must be different. Second, hashing functions are one-way functions, and therefore it is practically impossible to determine the original message from which the hash was computed. The sender signs the hash with their private key and this now becomes the authenticator, which is attached to the plaintext message and sent to another entity.

On receipt, the recipient reads the message. In order to verify that the communication did indeed come from the sender as purported, the recipient applies the original hash function to the plaintext message. It then applies the sender's public key to the authenticator, namely the signed hash that it received. If the communication was indeed from the sender and has not been altered in any way, then the two hashes must be identical. This is because the sender's public key can only decrypt messages encrypted by the sender with their private key, and in theory it is only the sender who has access to the private key. Consequently, the recipient is assured of the origin, content and sequencing of the message sent by the sender. The process described enables authentication, but does not ensure confidentiality. Although the message is safe from alteration, it is not safe from eavesdropping. An example of a commonly used hashing algorithm is SHA-1.

Despite the fact that digital signatures allow for authentication, in practice, applying the sender's public key is not enough to ensure that a digitally signed document originated from a particular entity (Baker and Hurst 1998). The recipient must also have confidence that the sender's private key is indeed private and that it actually belongs to the sender. The problem is that any entity X can pretend to be another entity A, and send or broadcast a public key to a number of other entities, who may not necessarily have the means to verify that X is indeed who they claim to be. When there is no prior relationship between sender and recipient, how does the latter ensure that a particular entity is associated with a particular public–private key pair?

12.7.5 Digital certificates

To address the problem of trusting the link between the sender and a specific public key, several approaches have been devised (Baker and Hurst 1998). One such approach is based on the X.500 telecommunications standard for directory services. In essence, a trusted directory of individuals and public keys is created. When a digitally signed document is received, the recipient can verify the public key of the signer by simply looking it up in the trusted directory. This is possible when the trusted directory is available at all times, and recipients have constant access to it. But if the recipient does not want to go online to verify every signature every time a communication is received, this presents a problem.

To address this, another approach has been developed which relies on public key or *digital certificates*. A digital certificate associates a public key with an entity's identity. In practical terms, a digital certificate is a simple electronic document containing information about an entity including the entity's public key which is digitally signed by some trusted party. A sender can subsequently attach a copy of their digital certificate, which has been issued by a trusted third party, to any of its messages. On receiving a message accompanied by a digital certificate, the recipient can rely on the public key of the issuing trusted third party to authenticate the message. As a result, a recipient can now link the message to a particular entity. Intuitively, digital certificates are a source of trust: they confirm that a trusted party vouches for the link between an entity and a public key (Baker and Hurst 1998). The question that arises now is, who are the trusted parties and how do we know we can trust them?

A certificate or certification authority (CA) is an entity which issues, publishes, revokes and archives digital certificates which link an entity's identity to its public key. CAs are considered to be trustworthy. Governments, financial and other credible institutions may act as CAs and there are also commercial CAs. A CA will issue a public key certificate, confirming that the public key contained in the certificate belongs to the user, organization, agent, or other entity noted in it. Intuitively, if one trusts the CA and can verify its signature, then one is also assured that a certain public key does indeed belong to the entity identified in the certificate. The role of the CA is to verify the credentials submitted by applicants, so that the relying parties can trust the information contained in the certificates. To verify the credentials of various entities, CAs often use a combination of procedures and information, including enquiring government bureaus, the payment infrastructure, databases and other services.

One of the most common implementations of digital certificates employs the X.509 standard which defines a framework for the provision of authentication services (Rhee 2003, Stallings 2003). X.509 is sometimes referred to as the *credit card* model, as it allows a hierarchy of trusted parties to authenticate other entities in very much the same way as in the credit card industry (Baker and Hurst 1998). When a consumer purchases goods and pays by credit card, the vendor does not necessarily know the consumer. But the vendor is willing to accept the credit card as payment. This is because the vendor trusts the credit card, which is a form of digital certificate. The credit card was issued to the consumer by a trusted financial institution, i.e., a bank, whose name is on the card. The vendor may know and trust this bank. But even if the vendor does not know the bank – it may be a foreign bank – it knows that the bank has been authenticated by the credit card company, i.e. Visa or Mastercard. Hence, if the vendor knows and trusts the credit card company, it can trust the issuing bank and the consumer.

In a similar way, X.509 allows a hierarchical chain of CAs to issue digital certificates that the recipient of the certificate can verify. The original certificate authority in this trust tree is called a root. X.509 has two main advantages. First, many certificates can be related back to a trusted root. Thus, when an entity digitally signs a document, it sends its digital certificate along with all the supported digital certificates associated with its trust hierarchy. Second, it facilitates trusted communication among entities who may not necessarily know each other or have had any prior exchange. The main disadvantage of X.509 is that, if the CA root or any member is compromised, the rest of the tree becomes unreliable and inevitably the security of the system breaks down.

An alternative approach is termed the *web of trust* model. In a similar way to X.509, a web of trust uses digital certificates to link a public–private key pair to an individual. But in contrast to X.509, the web of trust model is not hierarchical: there are no CAs or trusted third parties. Instead, individuals sign each other's keys, forming a web of intertwined signatures. An entity can subsequently decide who to trust and how much, based on the confidence in the keys as well as the entities introducing and vouching for a particular participant. This model is better suited for small communities of users who perhaps have regular contact, but it is difficult to implement on a large scale. Pretty Good Privacy (PGP) one of the best known applications, primarily for encrypting email communications and data files, is based on the web of trust model (Rhee 2003).

12.8 PRIVACY, ANONYMITY AND AGENTS

The digital world has made individuals both stronger and weaker: stronger as a result of abundant choice, democratizing access to information, new forms of social interaction and opportunities, and weaker in terms of threats to one's privacy, new forms of electronic fraud, and also lack of safeguards, clear rules, laws and jurisdiction in a networked borderless world.

12.8.1 Agents and privacy

Privacy denotes a condition or state in which a natural or legal person (organization or corporation) is more or less inaccessible to others, on the physical, psychological or informational plane (Bygrave 2001). The ability of natural and legal persons to have control over the release and distribution of information about themselves is crucial to informational privacy. For our discussion, privacy denotes a state of limited accessibility on the informational plane. A breach of privacy may have serious consequences for the user, with regard to autonomy, security, integrity, and dignity. Agent technology plays a mixed role in relation to one's privacy. On the one hand, agents can render their users and owners more vulnerable to loss of privacy. On the other, they can be used as a means to safeguard and preserve privacy.

As we have seen repeatedly in the course of this book, in order for agents to be able to perform transactions on behalf of their owners/users they may have to carry or exchange sensitive and private information such as personal or financial data. If intercepted by a third party, such data render the user/owner of the agent identifiable, thus breaching their privacy.

An agent encapsulates part of its user's traits and needs by encoding their preferences and other information; in other words an agent may embody the profile of its user. Data on a user can be collected as an agent performs seemingly innocuous tasks, such as searching for information or articles in a repository, searching for a product or comparing prices. For instance, an interest in anarchism may be inferred if a user's agent is searching for articles on anarchist theories, perhaps as part of their research into political science and the relationship, if any, between anarchist movements and women. But, one can imagine situations where this is taken one step further, and the user may be suspected of conspiring to overthrow one's government, based on the articles searched. Although this may seem extreme, in the current climate of continuous alert and fear from terrorism, anything can be taken out of context, sometimes with irreparable consequences.

The monitoring and tapping of agent operations might reveal a considerable amount of information about their users. This information can be used for building or augmenting user profiles which can be subsequently used by third parties in various ways, such as direct marketing, further exacerbating the initial loss of privacy. Of course, the collection of such information and the building of profiles can be facilitated by other agents. Even more worryingly, agent operations can be covert or nontransparent. For instance, an agent can be instructed to monitor someone without the knowledge of the subject. This would compromise the privacy and related interests of the latter, though not those of the agent's owner. Moreover, an agent could pass on information about its user to third parties without the user being aware of the information transfer. For instance, an Agent Provider (AP) that hires or sells agents to users may collect information on the users and their activities through the agents (Bygrave 2001). An agent may be recording and reporting transactions, sites visited, searches performed and other information back to the AP unbeknown to the user. In effect, such an agent would be acting in a similar way to a Trojan horse.

12.8.2 Anonymity

Despite having the potential to compromise the user's privacy, agent technology can also be used to preserve it. For instance, the very nature of the tasks being delegated to agents, i.e., being twice removed from the interface, enables a user to maintain their privacy to some extent. Nonetheless, a third party may actively seek to identify a user.

Another way to safeguard privacy is through anonymity (Brazier et al. 2004b). Anonymity offers a form of privacy and is characterized by the fact that other parties do not know one's identity. There are occasions when anonymity is desirable, for example, to report a crime, search for information, or compare vendors or products. Individuals may not wish to have their searches or purchases recorded because they would want to avoid the junk mail that may result from being identified as the likely purchaser of a particular kind of commodity. Others may be embarrassed to be identified, due to the nature of the material or product. In some cases, having been identified weakens one's negotiation position and bargaining power. If a vendor knows that a user has an interest in science fiction books, because the user has been profiled, the vendor may decide not to offer the user a discount on the next purchase of a science fiction book. To make matters worse, if the vendor practices perfect price discrimination, it may even try to charge the user extra knowing their interests on the subject (Vulkan 2003).

In electronic communications, it may often be the case that individuals do not want to reveal their identity. Not revealing one's identity includes concealing one's identity as well as using a pseudonym instead of one's real name. Froomkin (1995, 1996) identified four types of anonymity and pseudoanonymity in electronic communication:

1. **Traceable anonymity**. The receiver does not have any indication of the sender's identity. Information linking the communication with the sender is in the hands of an intermediary; usually an anonymous remailer.

2. **Untraceable anonymity**. The sender of an electronic message cannot be identified.

3. **Untraceable pseudonymity**. This is similar to untraceable anonymity, but instead, the sender uses a pseudonym to sign a message which cannot be traced back to them. A pseudonym can be used consistently over a period of time to establish a personality and a reputation, just like any other online personality.

4. **Traceable pseudonymity**. The user signs messages with a pseudonym which can be traced back to them, although not necessarily by the receiver. Traceable pseudonyms can be distinguished into those that have been assigned formally to someone by a third party, and those that have been chosen by the user themself.

Successful anonymization is technically complex to achieve. Most often users rely on third parties who supply them with the software or the services to facilitate anonymization. Current services facilitating anonymity and pseudonymity that have been designed for human users enable anonymous email and surfing (Martin 1998). Anonymity in electronic communications can be achieved through anonymizer remailer servers. In searching for and comparing the prices of products, the user's anonymity can be protected by passing the requests through one or more anonymizer servers that hide all information about the user's identity. Personas may also be used to protect anonymity as in the IntelliShopper system (Menczer et al. 2002b).

However, anonymity is a double-edged sword (Froomkin 1996). Techniques that facilitate anonymity may incidentally facilitate and support illegal and criminal activities and even encourage dishonest and anti-social behaviour. One can hide behind anonymity to commit online fraud or spread disinformation and hate mail, among other things. Anonymity is not prevented by law, but it is not explicitly protected as is the right to one's privacy. The issue is that of finding a balance.

12.8.3 Protecting privacy

Protecting confidential, sensitive and private information is imperative. An agent carrying or exchanging such information needs to be safeguarded against both passive and active attacks which are aimed at compromising a user's privacy. This can be achieved in a number of ways (Brazier et al. 2004b) by:

- placing only minimal confidential information in a software agent
- using cryptographic techniques to conceal confidential information
- using secure protocols when interacting with other agents and entities
- providing the agent with appropriate protective strategies
- using access control policies to restrict an agent's access to resources and information while at a host.

Alternatively, one could avoid entrusting a software agent with confidential information altogether. For instance, agents without any confidential information which simply collect information and report back to the user can be used; upon receipt of the information the user can take action. Digital cash as a means of payment which does not require information about the user could also be used (Chaum 1982).

However, an individual or an organization trying to trace the identity of the user could also perform traffic analysis, i.e., track which sites an agent visits or its requests. Traffic analysis could shed light on who the user of the software agent might be. The simplest approach to counter the risk that traffic analysis poses to the user's privacy is by an anonymizer server. An anonymizer server could, for instance, receive requests for information or services from agents and then submit them to third parties after stripping them of all possible identifying information. Provided that there is a high level of traffic, it is difficult for any observer to match agents with specific requests for information or services to third parties. If the requests are sent encrypted with the server's public key, the observer has no way of knowing what the request is all about, and likewise, if the answer or result of a service is sent back encrypted (using public key or symmetric encryption), the observer has no way of matching the result or request for a service to a specific user. This preserves the user's privacy to some extent, as it prevents any possible intruder from identifying the activities of a particular user and building a profile for them through these activities. The volume of requests should be hindering the development of a profile for a particular user.

The traceability of a mobile agent could also be counteracted to some degree if the agent is anonymized, i.e., all identification information is concealed or removed. An anonymizer server would have the task of complicating and, ideally, blocking any attempt to perform traffic analysis (Brazier et al. 2004b). The server could work by transforming an incoming mobile agent and its identity in such a way that it would be difficult for an observer to relate a software agent that departs from the server to an agent that had entered it earlier. Again, this solution could work if the volume of incoming and outgoing traffic were sufficiently large. For the destination host, the agent would appear as if it had originated from the anonymizer server and thus, the new host would not be able to determine where the agent had been before. Of course, the anonymizer server will have to be regarded as a trusted party in order for a host to accept an incoming agent. An alternative measure would be for the agent to work from varying IP-addresses and not visit its home place too often. The advantage of using an anonymizer server is that such an infrastructure makes it much harder and, ideally impossible, to trace a user by way of traffic analysis: although the agent is known to be affiliated with the server, its real user remains unknown. However, the success of this approach depends on volumes of traffic: too little traffic and it is easy to relate outgoing agents to incoming ones, too much traffic and the server becomes a bottleneck.

Another approach to protecting the user's privacy without using an anonymizer server is by using a new agent for each new task. A user can have a personal agent who generates task-specific agents which are subsequently destroyed once they have accomplished their tasks. The experiences and information gathered by the task-specific agents can be incorporated into the personal agent. Alternatively, agents can be rented or hired from agent providers to perform specific tasks. Although the agent can be traced, the user-client cannot be easily traced, in particular when secure communications are used. It goes without saying that the user needs to trust the agent provider offering this service.

Another alternative is to consider fitting agents with a kind of privacy-enhancing technology (PET) such as an identity protector (IP) (Senicar et al. 2003). An IP can be used in two ways: it can be placed between the user and the agent, or between the agent and the environment. In the former case, the agent cannot collect or exchange any personal data about the user without the prior and explicit approval of the user. Hence, the user has total control of the amount of personal data that is being passed on to the agent. The latter approach gives the agent complete power to obtain and record personal data from its user. The IP in this case prevents the agent from distributing the user's personal information unless it is essential to execute a transaction, for instance.

12.9 AGENTS AND THE LAW

As agents interact on the Internet and participate in electronic marketplaces, they engage in a number of activities which are significant from a legal perspective: they access computer systems, networks and data, they retrieve and distribute information, they mediate personal and business relations, they negotiate for and buy and sell goods and services. Autonomy implies that agents act without the constant and direct intervention of their users/owners.

Naturally, the introduction of electronic agents that conduct business on behalf of natural or legal persons raises issues with regard to accountability and liability (Andrade et al. 2004, Apistola et al. 2002). An agent could perform transactions that are very difficult to undo or correct, i.e., buying goods at exorbitant prices or buying multiple items. Depending on the particular situation and the agent's complexity, it might be difficult to determine what exactly went wrong. Thus, through their activities, agents may trigger off consequences for relevant parties relating to different areas of the law, such as contract, tort, intellectual property, data protection and even criminal responsibility. The traditional paradigms have all developed along the lines of physical and geographical bounds of space and time. However, the Internet society is not confined to geographical, legal, or corporate boundaries. Inevitably, new technologies such as the Internet and, in particular software agents, have an impact on society and consequently also on the law. Policy makers need to consider the repercussions of this new technology and provide safeguards and appropriate legislation that covers their operation.

There are four parties that are involved in the use of agents and whose interests are affected by any legal considerations (Geurts 2002):

1. **Agent designer/developer**. The agent designer/developer is the person or organization who designs and develops the agent. The designer/developer determines the agent's functionality and sophistication. This is also the person that puts the user manual of the agent together.

2. **Agent supplier or provider**. The supplier is the person or organization who sells the agent to the user. The agent designer/developer and supplier may be the same person. The supplier may be able to customize the agent according to the user's preferences. An agent provider is a person or organization that leases the agent to the user, in this case the agent is not sold to the user, instead it is rented.

3. **Agent user**. The person or organization who uses the agent. If the agent has been bought from a supplier, then the user is also the legal owner of the agent. The user may configure and customize the agent according to personal preferences.

4. **Third parties**. Third parties are all entities other than the user with whom the agent interacts, i.e., other agents, users, organizations, hosts. A third party can also be an entity who tampers with the agent.

Providing a framework for guiding and regulating agent-based interactions and exchanges is an interesting problem for lawyers and legal theorists, but also a fundamental issue for the success of agent technology in e-commerce (Sartor 2002). The question that then arises is who can be held liable and on what grounds for infringements made or for damages caused by a software agent:

- **Tort or wrongful acts.** The use of an agent can result in damages which can lead to an action by the counterparty who has suffered the damages, in order to obtain compensation. But who is to be held liable for an agent's misbehaviour? The designer/developer, who perhaps did not test the agent extensively and did not verify its behaviour? What if an agent has been customized by a supplier or provider? Maybe the customization had an adverse effect on the agent's behaviour – it may have been impossible for designers/developers to test all possible configurations. Did the user of the agent do something wrong which caused the agent to misbehave? Or was it a third party interfering accidentally or by design with the agent, which caused this undesirable behaviour? To make matters worse, agents may have the ability to learn and adapt to their environment. As agents learn, their behaviour becomes less predictable, in the sense that the exhibited behaviour is different from the original designed behaviour. Is it the learning process that is at fault? Was the misbehaviour as a result of an exceptional situation that perhaps the agent did not know how to deal with?

- **Privacy and data protection.** Agents may be used to collect information about other users (or even one's own user) unbeknown to the subjects. These data can be personal or financial data which characterize persons and can be used for identifying them, profiling them and subsequently using these profiles for direct marketing and other purposes. Such a collection of data is regarded as unlawful and the persons' right to privacy has been breached. Is it the agent's user who is liable or the designer/developer who has actually developed a product that infringes individual rights?

- **Intellectual property rights.** Information and search agents can collect and aggregate information from various sources. For instance, articles or other scientific data can be downloaded from repositories. However, information or data may be copyrighted and thus an agent may be infringing copyright laws by downloading information on behalf of the user. So far there is no standard way of indicating that a piece of information is copyrighted on the Internet. But this may change in the near future. Nevertheless, this is an important issue, as an agent and its user may find themselves accused of breaking copyright laws.

- **Product liability.** Assuming that an agent is a product, then the liability for a defective agent could potentially be shifted to the designer/developer. The designer/developer may be held responsible for any damages caused by the agent if the exhibited behaviour does not conform to the design specification. But what if the agent has been customized or configured by the user or another party? Who is liable then? What if the agent learns and adapts to the environment?

- **Contractual liabilities.** Who is to blame if a software agent that has been contracted to provide a service to another agent or user, does not provide the agreed quality of service or does not provide the service at all? Is it the software agent that is held accountable and, if so what sort of sanctions can be imposed on a software agent? Or is it the legal owner or user who bears the responsibility of ensuring that the agent's behaviour is correct, that it abides by the necessary protocols and honours commitments and contracts? The former hinges on the possibility of software agents being regarded as legal persons in the eyes of the law. Is the user bound to the terms and conditions of a contract that an agent signed? Are there any situations in which the user is not bound to the terms and conditions?

- **Criminal responsibility.** There may be cases when agents inflict financial losses on their users or other parties. Such agents may act very much like viruses and Trojan horses by stealing private and sensitive information and using it by design to cause damage. Who is then to be held responsible?

Another interesting issue that arises, is with regard to the international nature of the transactions that agents may be carrying out on behalf of their users. The physical location of information, processes, services and agents is no longer necessarily the same as the perceived location. This then raises questions regarding which laws apply to a particular situation, such as a transaction that has been conducted by agents that may reside or represent users/owners who reside in different countries governed by different laws. Under which jurisdiction does a transaction fall when it involves a bidding agent based in Sweden and an auction house based in the US?

There have been some limited regulatory initiatives with regard to software agents. For instance, the UCITA (UCITA 2006), UETA (UETA 2006), and E-Sign (E-Sign 2006) statutes in the United States, and the UECA (UECA 2006) in Canada, provide the means to regulate electronic transactions and contracts. The UCITA and the UECA refer to electronic agents and provide a legal basis for using agents in electronic commerce and some limited provisions on what to do in case something goes wrong. Accordingly, the actions of an agent are attributed to the human who uses the agent. Hence, a person assents to a declaration or a contract of their agent, although they may not be aware of the agent's actions at the time, i.e., responsibility lies with the agent's user or owner. Even so, these statutes leave many unanswered questions.

Agents do not feature in any European initiatives or current legislation. The European Union Directive on E-commerce (EC-Directive 2006) does not include legislation on software agents. The critical question is now whether the current legislation offers protection for all parties involved when agents are used in electronic commerce transactions. For the time being, perhaps the answer is yes, as the use of agent technology is neither widespread nor sophisticated. But in the long run, the issues surrounding software agents in e-commerce will have to be carefully considered by policy makers. Intelligent agents that act proactively and autonomously in order to accomplish their design objectives exhibit qualities that are not covered in the current legislation.

12.10 AGENTS AS LEGAL PERSONS

Legal systems recognize two kinds of legal persons as having will, intention, obligations, rights and contractual capability: natural persons and legal entities. Natural persons are human beings, whereas legal entities can be associations, organizations, companies, governments, etc. A contract is a legal transaction comprising declarations of intention of at least two persons, one stated relative to the other (Weitzenböck 2001). Contracts are usually enforceable by law. A contract consists of the main obligations of the two (or more) parties coming into an agreement and the terms and conditions of the contract. Contractual capability is the ability to perform legal transactions effectively, i.e., actions that imply legal consequences. Having contractual capability involves declaring intentions, but this is only meaningful if the acting persons can understand the consequences of their declarations.

For the time being, computer systems and software applications are not attributed any legal status; they are deemed tools to be used by legal or natural persons. However, an agent's nature may be very different to that of a software application. Intelligent software agents are attributed exceptional characteristics such as autonomy, goal-directness and sociality. They become capable of learning from experience and adapting to their environment according to cognitive, reactive and proactive processes, quite similar to the ones used by humans. They are also ascribed mental attitudes such as beliefs, desires, intentions and commitments. These characteristics set agents apart from other pieces of software, rendering them unique.

Agents used in e-commerce applications may negotiate contracts or bid in auctions on behalf of their users. But such actions imply that a legal transaction takes place between the agent and the other party, which can be another agent, natural person or legal entity (Weitzenböck 2001, Brazier et al. 2003). For instance, when an agent bids in an electronic auction, it declares its intention to acquire an item for the price of the bid submitted. If it wins the auction, then it has the obligation to provide payment equal to the value of its bid, or as otherwise dictated by the rules of the auction. However, this raises some questions with regard to the legal status of agents. In essence, the fundamental question is, can software agents be considered as legal personas? One could argue that agents do not currently have the ability to understand their declarations and their implications, and therefore they cannot engage in any legal transactions – any such transaction is void. Thus, in the eyes of the law, agents do not have a contractual capability and this presents a problem. If they lack such a capability, then they cannot perform legal transactions such as closing contracts and bidding in auctions. If the agents are to be considered acting as the representatives of users, they still need to have some contractual capability.

Unless the will or intention to perform an action is distinguished from the action itself. The will or intention is attributed to the natural or legal person, whereas the action is the one attributed to the agent. In this case, responsibility lies with the principal, i.e., the agent user. Thus, if the agent were to sign an unauthorized contract, the responsibility would still lie with the user, as it would be assumed that the user has the intention or will and that the agent carries out the action. Hence, the risk of transactions would be put entirely on those persons who program, control or otherwise use a software agent. Alternatively, a user could be required to explicitly authorize an agent to sign a contract on their behalf, before it is actually finalized. But still this limits the applicability of agent technology; one of the main advantages of using software agents is that certain processes can be automated as agents can act autonomously in order to further their users' goals.

An alternative and radical proposal is that agents could potentially be attributed a legal persona or they could be granted a special status, that of an *e-person* (Andrade et al. 2004, Wettig and Zehender 2004). Such a provision would solve a number of problems. First, the issue regarding the validity of the declarations and contracts being negotiated and concluded by software agents would be resolved. As agents would have some form of legal status, they would be considered as being able to express will and intention. This does not necessarily have an impact on legal theories about consent and declaration, contractual freedom and conclusion of contracts, as legal systems already consider the declarations of other non-natural persons, i.e., legal entities such as organizations. Second, it could limit the owner's liability and responsibility for the agent's behaviour.

Although convenient in some respects, this solution presents a number of difficulties. First of all, the question of what constitutes an agent would have to be answered: is it the software, the hardware, both? What about mobile agents? More fundamentally, the essential attributes or characteristics that an agent needs to possess or exhibit in order to be granted the status of a legal person or e-person would have to be clearly defined. As natural or legal persons are identified uniquely, the same requirement applies to agents; they would need to have unique identities. Another requirement for an agent to be rendered a legal person is that it must have a residence or domicile (Andrade et al. 2004). But mobile agents do not have an established physical location, although in this case the domicile of the agent could be considered to be that of its user.

Agent registers could be set up in a similar fashion to company registers. Such registers could be maintained by trusted third parties, such as governments or Certification Authorities. Through this registration procedure, an agent could be attributed a unique identity and a domicile. The owner could also grant the agent with a minimum amount of capital which would act as the agent's patrimony (Sartor 2002). This fund would be deposited in order to ensure that an agent could fulfil its financial obligations and liabilities and it would represent a warranty for the counterparties. Since liability safeguarding is very important, this fund could back-up claims of the contracting parties in case of problems. Another measure to protect users and other counterparties against possible liabilities would be to establish a compulsory insurance regime for agent-related activities. Hence, a kind of agent with limited liability is indeed possible.

When agents are involved in the negotiation of contracts, each contracting party, agent or nonagent, can use the agent register to check the soundness of the agents with whom negotiations are being conducted, before deciding on the conclusion of the contract. Reputation systems could also be employed to augment this process. However, sometimes negotiations fail. Most often, parties go their separate ways without further obligations. But in some cases, the negotiations are not fully noncommittal (Weitzenböck 2002). Costs may have been incurred or expectations may have been raised that have led to the breaking-off of negotiations with other parties, for instance. From a legal point of view, this is the domain of precontractual liability. The agent's patrimony or insurance policy can be used to cover any costs incurred as a result of negotiations being abandoned.

The concept of an agent register raises some privacy issues with regard to the information that would be included in such a register. For instance, would the register contain information connecting the agent to a unique user? Would access to the register be open to everyone? If a user can be identified through its agent, then the user could be profiled through the agent's actions. Access could be limited to only checking that an agent is actually registered with a particular authority as it claims. Access to information regarding the user's identification could be restricted and only granted in exceptional circumstances, i.e., in case of litigation. Moreover, along with the agent's identification, its public key could also be included that would allow any other entity to communicate and transact with the agent in a secure way.

Of course the crucial question still remains: who is liable? If business is done without any problems or complications, then the legal concerns are irrelevant. But if problems emerge, legal concerns are of the essence. If the agent is regarded as a legal person or an e-person, then in principle *it* is liable. But since claims practically cannot be realized against the agent, liability falls back again on the owner of the agent. The agent's patrimony as well as the insurance covering its activities could be used to cover any liabilities. Of course, an agent should be attributed a way of being represented in case of legal actions against it, as a claim may well be unfounded or malicious.

12.11 CLOSING REMARKS

Agent technology for e-commerce is a fascinating area of research and development, with the potential to bring about significant benefits both to individuals as well as businesses and organizations. But it also has the potential to bring about significant benefits to society as a whole.

The Internet and, in particular, the use of agent technology to automate financial transactions and other tasks, challenges our traditional views of regulation and responsibility. We may have to rethink and re-evaluate the way that agents, operating autonomously, can be regulated. Eventually, such smart pieces of software may have to be granted the status of a legal person in order to overcome problems with legal responsibilities in contracting or executing financial transactions. Punishment may involve restricting the agent's rights and access to resources, platforms and marketplaces, or even termination.

Agent developers need to know how to design and develop software agents that comply with known legal requirements and the policies of institutions. They also need to adhere to good practice and ethical considerations. Thus, it is crucial that the legal and technical communities embark on interdisciplinary research to deal with these issues. Ultimately such considerations and provisions could help promote trust and confidence in agent technology.

In time, we may have to rethink certain issues such as, for instance, the law and how it applies on the Internet. A possible scenario involves the Internet being considered as a virtual environment which will be governed by its own laws, regulations and in which different norms may apply. Inevitably, the Internet may be subject to international law, and not that of any single country. How such regulations can be enforced, while at the same time the users' rights and privacy are preserved and protected, needs to be very carefully considered.

12.12 Further Reading

Traditionally, trust has been studied within a sociological context. Nowadays trust is the subject of research in computer science as well (Falcone et al. 2001). There is a very rich bibliography on trust, some indicative texts are Gambetta (1988) and Sztompka (1999). Patrick (2002) discusses the reasons underlying the lack of trust of users in agents and the perceived risks. The complex issue of users trusting technology in e-commerce is discussed in Linketscher and Child (2001). Others exploring the issue of trust online include Shneiderman (2000) Rosenbloom (2000) and Friedman et al. (2000). Prins et al. (2002) contains an interesting collection of papers introducing issues related to trust in electronic commerce from a legal, organizational and technical point of view.

Institutions have been the subject of study in Economic and Political Sciences as well as Sociology. North (1990) discusses institutions and institutional change within the context of economies, while Harré and Secord (1972) analyze how human behaviour can be restricted in social settings, from a sociological point of view. Ostrom (1990) uses institutions to explore solutions to Common-Pool Resource (CPR) problems. In CPR problems, self-interested agents have to use common resources such as oceans, fresh water, pastures, etc. Each agent wants to maximize its own use of the resource. However, the unrestricted use will eventually lead to the depletion of the resource. This has been termed the *Tragedy of the Commons* (Hardin 1968).

The use of electronic institutions and norms for the establishment of multi-agent systems and for regulating the behaviour of agents, has been discussed in Dellarocas and Klein (1999), Dignum (2001, 2002) and Sierra and Noriega (2002). The particular role that institutions can play in multi-agent systems is explained in Dignum (2001). An approach to the formal specification of electronic institutions is described in Esteva et al. (2001b,a, 2002). The work of Castelfranchi has been influential in the area of social order in multi-agent systems (Castelfranchi 2000). A plethora of approaches have been proposed to capture social order in multi-agent systems, including social and collective attitudes (Castelfranchi 1995, Dunin-Keplicz and Verbrugge 2003) and normative concepts (van der Torre and Tan 1999, Broersen et al. 2002). Other approaches attempt to capture social order by employing organizational concepts, such as roles and power (Ferber and Gutknecht 1998, Zambonelli et al. 2000, Cavedon and Sonenberg 1998, Dignum et al. 2002, Fasli 2004, 2005, Boella and van der Torre 2005). The role of commitments and conventions in multi-agent systems is discussed in Jennings (1993). Deontic logic is described in Åqvist (1984) and Hilpinen (1971), although to be able to follow those texts, readers need to be familiar with modal logic. Recommended texts in modal logic include Hughes and Cresswell (1996) and Chellas (1996). An excellent introduction to modal logic and, in particular, its applications to reasoning about knowledge is the book by Fagin et al. (1995).

Bromley (1993) discusses reputation, and reputation systems and their problems and limitations are described in Resnick et al. (2000), while Dellarocas (2000a,b) explores the issues of unfair ratings in such systems.

There are a number of introductory and advanced texts in security and cryptography. The discussion here is based on Stallings (2003) and Rhee (2003) who discuss Internet security in general and cryptography in particular, including specific algorithms for symmetric and asymmetric cryptosystems such as DES, 3DES, AES, RSA, and Diffie-Hellman, as well as hashing algorithms such as SHA-1. Cryptography has raised some issues with respect to its uses and government control. Some governments feel that the use of cryptography must be regulated because they do not trust all users of cryptography. For an extended and interesting discussion which covers legal points of view from a number of countries see Baker and Hurst (1998). Mobile agents are associated with additional risks as was extensively discussed in the previous chapter. A discussion on the issue of secure transactions and mobile agents can be found in Claessens et al. (2003).

The impact of agent technology on privacy and the implications of their use in e-commerce on legal systems are complex issues. Some of these issues are discussed in Bygrave (2001) and Higgins (1998). The issue of agents acting as representatives and the potential implications are discussed in Andrade et al. (2004). Legal aspects of agent technology are considered in Apistola et al. (2002) and Geurts (2002). Potential risks as they arise from the use of agents on the Internet and also potential preventative measures are described in Brazier et al. (2004a). The issues surrounding anonymity and agents are discussed in Brazier et al. (2004b) whereas agents closing contracts are described in Brazier et al. (2003) and Weitzenböck (2001). In Wettig and Zehender (2004) the issue of attributing agents with legal status is considered, in particular, from the point of view of German law.

12.13 Exercises and Topics for Discussion

1. Discuss the issue of user profiling. Identify two sites that you often visit and which may have been building profiles of you. How do you think these profiles are used? What is the organization's privacy policy?

2. Discuss the issue of loyalty-card schemes as they are used by a variety of vendors including retail shops, supermarkets, etc. How do they affect a user's privacy?

3. Examine the laws regarding the conduct of electronic commerce and contracting of your own country. Do they explicitly mention electronic agents? What is an electronic agent in the eyes of the law? Who is responsible if something goes wrong? If electronic agents are not covered by legislation, do you think that the current legislation sufficiently protects and can resolve any potential complications which arise from using electronic agents?

Appendix A

Introduction to Decision Theory

Decision theory is the study of making decisions, in particular good decisions (French 1988). Although we make decisions all the time as part of our everyday lives, decision theory is not concerned with those minor everyday decisions, but with decisions which may have a significant impact. For instance, although which cereal to choose for breakfast is a decision, its consequences are minor in comparison to, say, the decision of which car to purchase. The cost involved in the latter is much higher.

Modern decision theory has developed since the middle of the 20th century through contributions from several other disciplines. Nowadays, decision theory is studied by economists, computer scientists, statisticians, and operational research and political scientists, amongst others.

Decision-making is usually divided into *decision-making under certainty* and *decision-making under noncertainty*. In the former, the state of the world when making a decision is known. The latter type of decision-making is often distinguished into: *decision-making under risk* and *decision-making under uncertainty*. Luce and Raiffa (1957) consider the first to be decision-making when the state of the world is not known, but probabilities for the various possible states are known, whereas the second is decision-making when the state of the world is not known and probabilities for the various possible states are not known. However, under the subjective interpretation of probability, it is always possible to assign probabilities to events or various states of the world. In the following, we consider decision-making under uncertainty to be decision-making when the states of the world are not known, but probabilities are either known or can be assigned. Risk will be discussed in the context of utility, instead.

Before introducing the basic principles and concepts underlying decision theory, we will briefly review the most fundamental principles of probability theory.

A.1 PROBABILITY THEORY

Most of the time we are called upon to make decisions in the presence of uncertainty. To use a tired example, suppose that I need to decide whether to take my umbrella on my way out in case it rains. However, I do not know for sure if it is going to rain. I may listen to the weather forecast or look outside the window to obtain more information. If it is sunny, I may infer that rain is not very likely. This observation can only provide me with a degree of belief as to whether it is going to rain.

The main tool to deal with situations which are characterized by the absence of certain knowledge is probability theory. Probability theory assigns to propositions that express states of the world or events a numerical value between 1 and 0. Assigning to a proposition the value 1 means that we are certain of the truth of this proposition, whereas assigning it the value 0 means that we believe it to be false. Any value in between expresses uncertainty, and the closer the value to 1, the higher our degree of belief that the proposition is true.

Thus, probability theory, which is often described as the language of uncertainty, quantifies uncertainty regarding the occurrence of events or states of the world. The basic element in probability theory is the random variable which can be thought of as describing a part of the world whose state is initially unknown. Random variables can be thought of as proposition symbols in propositional logic. Each random variable has a domain of values that it can take on. For instance, the random variable of *Weather* can take on the discrete values of {*sunny, cloudy, rain, snow*}. The simplest kind of proposition asserts that a random variable has a particular value, i.e., *Weather = sunny*. Random variables can also be boolean or continuous. An atomic event is a complete specification of the state of the world about which the agent is uncertain. Alternatively, an atomic event can be thought of as an assignment of values to all variables of which the world is composed. Atomic events have some important properties. First, they are mutually exclusive, i.e., at most one can true. Second, the set of all possible atomic events is exhaustive, that is at least one must be true. In other words, the disjunction of all atomic events is logically equivalent to true.

More formally, a probability space represents our uncertainty regarding a situation or an experiment and it consists of two parts:

1. The sample space $S = \{e_1, e_2, \ldots, e_n\}$, which is a set of atomic events.
2. The probability measure P which assigns a real number between 0 and 1 to the members of the sample space.

Probability theory is governed by a set of axioms[1]:

Axiom 4   *All probabilities are between 0 and 1. For any event e, $0 \leq P(e) \leq 1$.*

[1] These are a popular version of the Kolmogorov axioms.

Axiom 5 *The sum of probabilities for the atomic events of a probability space must sum to 1:*

$$\sum_{i=1}^{n} P(e_i) = 1$$

Axiom 6 *The certain event S, namely the sample space itself, has probability 1 and the impossible event Ø which never occurs, has probability 0.*

A.1.1 Prior probability

In the absence of any other information, a proposition *a* is ascribed a degree of belief, which is called *unconditional* or *prior* probability. If X is the random variable *Weather* = {*sunny, cloudy, rain, snow*}, the probabilities may be as follows:

$$P(sunny) = 0.2$$
$$P(cloudy) = 0.25$$
$$P(rain) = 0.5$$
$$P(snow) = 0.05$$

The notation $\mathbf{P}(X)$ denotes the vector consisting of the probabilities of all possible values that a random variable may take. Accordingly, the prior probability distribution for the random variable *Weather* is written $\mathbf{P}(Weather) = \langle 0.2, 0.5, 0.25, 0.05 \rangle$. If more than one random variable is considered, then we have *joint probability* distributions. Often we may want to reason about the probabilities of all variables in the probability space S. If the probability space consists of the random variables of *Weather* and *Entertainment* which takes the values {*cinema, theatre, restaurant, stay home*}, then $\mathbf{P}(Weather, Entertainment)$ is the *full joint probability distribution*.

Typically, the term *lottery* is used to describe a probability distribution over a set of outcomes. A lottery L with possible outcomes $o_1, \ldots, o_n$ that can occur with probabilities $p_1, \ldots, p_n$ is written in the form $L = [p_1, o_1; p_2, o_2; \ldots; p_n, o_n]$.

A.1.2 Conditional probability

It may be possible to obtain some information concerning the previously unknown random variables making up the domain. In this case, we use posterior or conditional probabilities. If a and b are propositions then $P(a|b)$ is read as 'the probability of a given that all we know is b'. For instance, $P(rain|high - precipitation) = 0.8$ indicates that the probability of raining given that there is high precipitation – the agent has listened to the weather forecast and got this information – is 0.8. The prior probability $P(rain)$ can be regarded as a special case of $P(rain|)$ where the probability is conditioned on no evidence.

Conditional probabilities can be defined in terms of unconditional probabilities as follows:

$$P(a|b) = \frac{P(a \wedge b)}{P(b)}$$

which holds whenever $P(b) > 0$. Alternatively, this equation can be written as:

$$P(a \wedge b) = P(a|b)P(b)$$

which is known as the *product rule*. Intuitively, the product rule says that for a and b to be true, we need b to be true, but also a to be true given b. The rule can also be written the other way round:

$$P(a \wedge b) = P(b|a)P(a)$$

The notation $\mathbf{P}$ can be used for conditional distributions, thus $\mathbf{P}(X|Y)$ gives the values of $P(X = x_m | Y = y_n)$ for each possible m and n.

A.1.3 Independence

In the previous section we briefly explained the important concept of conditional probabilities. Quite often, events may be independent of each other and in this sense they do not influence each other's probabilities. For instance, the weather is independent of a country's interest rate, i.e., the weather is not influenced by the interest rate or the other way round. In this case, the independence of two propositions or events is indicated as:

$$P(a|b) = P(a) \text{ or } P(b|a) = P(b) \text{ or } P(a \wedge b) = P(a)P(b)$$

Independence between variables X and Y is then written as:

$$\mathbf{P}(X|Y) = \mathbf{P}(X) \text{ or } \mathbf{P}(Y|X) = \mathbf{P}(Y) \text{ or } \mathbf{P}(X, Y) = \mathbf{P}(X)\mathbf{P}(Y).$$

A.1.4 Bayes' rule

The product rule that emanates from conditional probabilities can be written in two different forms as:

$$P(a \wedge b) = P(a|b)P(b)$$
$$P(a \wedge b) = P(b|a)P(a)$$

By simply equating the two right-hand sides and dividing by $P(a)$ we get:

$$P(b|a) = \frac{P(a|b)P(b)}{P(a)}$$

This is known as Bayes' rule or Bayes' law or theorem. Bayes' rule is useful in answering probabilistic queries conditioned on one or more pieces of evidence and has been used extensively in modern Artificial Intelligence systems for probabilistic inference.

The rule for multi-valued variables takes the form:

$$\mathbf{P}(Y|X) = \frac{\mathbf{P}(X|Y)\mathbf{P}(Y)}{\mathbf{P}(X)}$$

Finally, a more general version conditionalised on some background evidence $\mathbf{e}$ is written as:

$$\mathbf{P}(Y|X, \mathbf{e}) = \frac{\mathbf{P}(X|Y, \mathbf{e})\mathbf{P}(Y|\mathbf{e})}{\mathbf{P}(X|\mathbf{e})}$$

A.2 MAKING DECISIONS

When we are called upon to make a decision, we have a set of actions available to us and we need to choose one of them. This set of actions is usually mutually exclusive, i.e., we can only choose one. In the umbrella example, there are two actions available to me: carry the umbrella or not. My decision to carry the umbrella has to do with the state of the world. I need to carry my umbrella in case it rains. However, the problem is that I am not certain about the state of the world, but my decisions have consequences that depend on the state of the world. If I take the umbrella and it does not rain, then I have to carry it around, which I consider to be inconvenient. If I carry the umbrella and it does rain, it has fulfilled its purpose, which is to protect me from getting soaked and potentially catching a cold, although I still consider it an inconvenience to carry it around. If I do not carry the umbrella and it does not rain, everything is fine, but if it does rain, then my expensive coat may be ruined. The consequences of decisions can be expressed in terms of payoffs. A *payoff* or reward can be interpreted in monetary terms and it represents the net change in an agent's total wealth as a result of a decision and the actual state of the world which, however, is not known in advance. The payoff can be either positive or negative. In the umbrella example, the various payoffs are given in Table A.1.

		World state	
		Rain	No rain
Action	Carry umbrella	−£1	−£1
	Not carry umbrella	−£50	£0

Table A.1: Payoff table for the umbrella example

A payoff table consists of a set of payoffs for all possible combinations of actions and states of the world. If there are m actions and n states of the world, then there are $m \times n$ entries. Payoffs will be denoted by R as P is reserved for probabilities. The payoff of carrying the umbrella when it rains is $R(\text{carry umbrella, rain}) = -£1$. Carrying the umbrella has a cost, say the inconvenience of carrying it around, which has been converted into money. The other possible consequences have been converted into monetary equivalents as well.

Instead of measuring consequences in terms of payoffs, one can use the alternative concept of losses. Loss is interpreted here as *opportunity loss* (Winkler 1972). Essentially, for any combination of action and state of the world the question is: could one have obtained a higher payoff, given that particular state of the world? If the answer is no, then loss is zero, if the answer is yes then the loss is calculated as the positive difference between the highest payoff given that state of the world, and that payoff. To convert a payoff table to a loss table, we work with every column of the payoff table separately. In each column, we find the highest payoff. The opportunity loss corresponding to this payoff is zero. The opportunity loss for every other cell in the same column is obtained by subtracting that payoff from the highest payoff in the column. The loss table for the umbrella example is given in Table A.2. Loss tables are sometimes called regret tables, as the various entries reflect the agent's regret at not having made the decision that turns out to be the optimal for the actual state of the world.

		World state	
		Rain	No rain
Action	Carry umbrella	£0	£1
	Not carry umbrella	£49	£0

Table A.2: Loss table for the umbrella example

An alternative way to represent payoffs and losses in a decision-making problem is via a tree diagram, such as the one illustrated in Figure A.1. Tree diagrams are particularly useful in representing complex decision-making problems with sequences of actions and events over time. Representing such problems in tabular form is much more difficult.

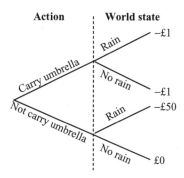

Figure A.1: Tree diagram for the umbrella example

An important concept in decision theory is that of admissibility: *admissible* actions or decisions. An action is said to dominate a second action if for each possible state of the world the first action leads to at least as high a payoff (or at least as small a loss) as the second one, and if for at least one state of the world the first action leads to a higher payoff (or smaller loss) than the second one. If one action dominates another, then the latter should never be selected and it is called *inadmissible*. This is because an agent will always prefer a higher payoff to a lower one (or a smaller loss to a higher one). For an action to be inadmissible, it needs to be dominated by another single action, not just by a combination of other actions. By eliminating inadmissible actions, a decision-making problem can be simplified and thus its complexity can be reduced.

Consider the following problem (this example is adapted from Winkler (1972)). An agent wants to invest £1000 in a stock and has the choice to buy among stocks x, y or z, each of which currently costs £50 a share. It intends to keep the stock for a year, and then sell it at the going price. Naturally, it would like to make a profit from this investment. The selection of the stock constitutes the decision or action in this decision-making problem. The prices of the stocks one year from now constitute the possible states of the world that the agent is uncertain about. For simplicity, assume that there are only four possible states. In state (i), the prices of the stocks in a year's time are (60, 60, 40). In state (ii), the prices are (70, 60, 40) and in states (iii) and (iv), they are (20, 40, 20) and (60, 60, 60) respectively. The payoffs are given in Table A.3.

		World	state		
		(i)	(ii)	(iii)	(iv)
Action	Buy x	£200	£400	−£600	£200
	Buy y	£200	£200	−£200	£200
	Buy z	−£200	−£200	−£600	£200

Table A.3: Payoff table for the stocks example

The third action (Buy z) is dominated by both of the other two actions. The first action is better than the third for states (i) and (ii) and it is just as good as the third action for states (iii) and (iv). The second action is better than the third for states (i), (ii) and (iii) and it is just as good as the third action for state (iv). Hence, the third action is inadmissible and the agent does not need to consider it any further.

A.2.1 Non-probabilistic decision-making under uncertainty

When the state of the world is known, then making a decision is fairly easy. We simply choose the action that provides the highest payoff given the state of the world. However, if there is uncertainty about the state of the world, then making a decision is not straightforward. The only way to introduce the nature of the uncertainty about the state of the world in the decision-making problem, is to consider a probability distribution. The probability distribution can be interpreted in terms of degrees of belief that a particular state of the world will occur. To avoid assessing probabilities, a number of decision-making rules have been developed.

Let us consider the stocks example of the previous section, but with the following modification. We assume that in state (ii) the price of z is £30 instead of £40, and in state (iii) the price of z is £50 instead of £20. The new payoff and losses are given in Tables A.4 and A.5 respectively.

One decision rule is called the *maximin* rule and uses the payoff table to choose an action. The rule is as follows: for each action, we find the smallest possible payoff and

		World	state	
		(i)	(ii)	(iii)	(iv)
Action	Buy x	£200	£400	−£600	£200
	Buy y	£200	£200	−£200	£200
	Buy z	−£200	−£400	£0	£200

Table A.4: Payoff table for the modified stocks example

		World	state	
		(i)	(ii)	(iii)	(iv)
Action	Buy x	£0	£0	£600	£0
	Buy y	£0	£200	£200	£0
	Buy z	£400	£800	£0	£0

Table A.5: Loss table for the modified stocks example

then we choose the action for which this smallest payoff is largest. According to this rule, an agent should choose the second action in the example. This rule tells the agent to assume that, for each action, the worst possible state of the world will occur. This is an extremely conservative and pessimistic approach since it considers the lowest payoff in each row, and completely ignores the magnitudes of the other payoffs. It is easy to think of situations in which this rule gives counter-intuitive results. This is left as an exercise to the reader.

The second-decision rule is called the *maximax* rule. In contrast to the maximin rule, this rule assumes that the best, not the worst state of the world will happen. The agent should find the largest possible payoff for each possible action, and choose the action for which this largest payoff is largest. This rule attempts to maximize the maximum payoff. In the stock example, the agent should choose the first action, if it follows this rule. But the maximax rule ignores the low payoffs and, as in the previous rule, one can think of circumstances in which the rule gives counter-intuitive results.

One more rule can be applied if the loss table is used instead. The *minimax loss* rule dictates that, for each action, an agent needs to find the largest possible loss, and then choose an action for which this largest loss is the smallest. In the example, the second action would be chosen according to this rule. As the name implies, this rule attempts to minimize the maximum loss.

Other nonprobabilistic rules have also been suggested such as, for instance, a combination of the maximin and the maximax rules. Nevertheless, these rules fail to take into account the probabilistic nature of uncertainty, and in some cases, they yield counter-intuitive results.

A.2.2 Probabilistic decision-making under uncertainty

Information regarding the possible state of the world can be expressed in terms of a probability distribution and taken into account in an agent's decision making. These probabilities can be used to calculate the expected payoffs and the expected losses. But how are the probabilities of the state of the world determined? Such probabilities are usually posterior probabilities. If no information is available, then prior probabilities can be used instead.

The *Expected Payoff* (ER) rule dictates that the action with the highest expected payoff should be chosen, whereas the *Expected Loss* (EL) rule dictates that the action with the smallest expected loss should be chosen.

Going back to the original umbrella example, if I assess that $P(\text{rain}) = 0.7$ and $P(\text{no rain}) = 0.3$, then the expected payoffs of the two actions are as follows:

$$ER(\text{carry umbrella}) \quad = 0.7(-£1) + 0.3(-£1) = -£1$$
$$ER(\text{not carry umbrella}) = 0.7(-£50) + 0.3(-£0) = -£35$$

According to the loss table and using the *EL* rule:

$$EL(\text{carry umbrella}) \quad = 0.7(£0) + 0.3(£1) = £0.3$$
$$EL(\text{not carry umbrella}) = 0.7(£49) + 0.3(£0) = £34.3$$

The act to carry the umbrella has the highest expected payoff and the lowest expected loss. Furthermore, its ER is £34 higher than the ER of the other action and its EL is £34 lower than the EL of the other action. Thus, there is a relation between expected payoffs and expected losses: the action with the highest ER will always have the lowest EL and vice versa. Moreover, if the ER of one action is x units higher than the ER of a second action, then the EL of the first action will be x units lower than the EL of the second action.

Assuming some probability distribution, the ER and EL rules can be used to calculate the maximum expected payoff and the minimum expected loss in the stocks example.

A.3 UTILITIES

In the two examples used in the previous sections, the consequences of the various actions were considered in terms of money. Although in most cases it is possible to describe the consequences of decisions in monetary terms, there may be additional factors such as time spent, reputation and so on. Often these too can be translated into money. In the umbrella example, the inconvenience of having to carry the umbrella around was expressed as a value of $-£1$, whereas the consequence of not carrying the umbrella and being caught in the rain was expressed as the cost of a ruined coat. Other factors, such as the possibility of getting ill were simply not taken into account to simplify the problem.

Besides, such factors may be valued differently by various individuals. Nevertheless, it may not always be possible to express the consequences of actions in terms of money.

Furthermore, there is a problem with regard to the use of money to describe the consequences of actions. Assume the following bet or lottery on one toss of a fair coin: you win £1 if the coin comes up heads, and you lose £0.75 if the coin comes up tails. As the coin is fair, $P(heads) = P(tails) = 0.5$, the expected payoffs are $0.5(£1) + 0.5(-£0.75) = £0.125$ if you decide to take the bet, and £0 if you do not take the bet. According to the ER rule, you should take the bet and most people would take such a bet.

Now suppose that the amounts involved are £1000 and $-£750$ rather than £1 and $-£0.75$. The expected payoffs are £125 if you take the bet, and £0 if you do not. Most people would seriously think about this, and probably decide not to take the bet. Losing £750 is a considerable amount of money, for most people. If you would still take this bet, consider larger amounts of money such as £10 000 and £7500, respectively. In this case, you would not take this bet, unless you were a millionaire and losing £7500 did not mean much to you. But, according to the ER rule you should take the bet. So what is going on? Although the monetary gains are clear and the bet is fair, there are other factors involved. If you are a student and you lose £750, this will represent a sharp reduction in your savings account, which unavoidably has further consequences for you, apart from the monetary loss. For instance, you may have to abandon plans to buy a new computer or you will be unable to pay the rent for two months. If, on the other hand, you are a millionaire, you would take this bet as losing £750 does not represent a significant loss to you.

As this example illustrates, the value of a currency such as the pound or the dollar, or money in general, may differ from person to person. Thus, the ER rule may not always give satisfactory results if the consequences are described in terms of money. If there was another way in which the value of a consequence of a decision could be measured, relative to a particular person, then this value instead could be taken into account instead of the monetary payoff. This alternative is provided by utility theory. Simply put, a utility function provides a mapping from states to real numbers. Then instead of payoffs we use utilities, and we can apply the rule of maximum expected utility (MEU) which is very similar to ER, but instead of payoffs we consider utilities and their respective distributions.

A.3.1 Preferences

Before we discuss in more detail what utility functions are and how they can be assessed, it is important to explain the concept of a preference which so far has been implicitly used. When we make decisions, or choose between options, we try to obtain as good an outcome as possible, according to some standard of what is good or bad. In our everyday lives we use the concept of *preferences* to designate that we prefer one thing over another. In the same way, in making decisions, an agent can express preferences regarding the various outcomes of a set of possible actions in different states of the world. So, for instance, I would prefer to carry an umbrella if it rains, rather than not.

Formally, we write $o \succ o'$ to indicate that o is preferred to o' and we write $o \sim o'$ to indicate that an agent is indifferent between o and o'. Preferences are governed by a set of principles or axioms:

- Given any two outcomes o and o' (these may be payoffs expressed in terms of money or utilities) an agent must either prefer one to the other, or be indifferent between the two: $o \succ o'$ or $o' \succ o$ or $o \sim o'$.

- Given any three outcomes o, o' and o'', if an agent prefers o to o' and also prefers o' to o'', then it must also prefer o to o'': if $o \succ o'$ and $o' \succ o''$, then it must be the case that $o \succ o''$.

- If some state o' is between o and o'' in preference, then there is some probability p for which the agent will be indifferent between getting o' for sure, and the lottery that yields o with probability p and o'' with probability $1 - p$: if $o \succ o' \succ o''$, then there is a p such that $[p, o; 1 - p, o''] \sim o'$.

- If an agent is indifferent between two lotteries o and o', then the agent is indifferent between two more complex lotteries that are the same, except that o' is substituted for o in one of them. This holds irrespective of the probabilities and the other outcomes in the lotteries: if $o \sim o'$, then $[p, o; 1 - p, o''] \sim [p, o'; 1 - p, o'']$.

- If there are two lotteries that have the same outcomes o and o', and if the agent prefers o to o', then the agent must prefer the lottery that has a higher probability for o: if $o \succ o'$, then $(p \geq q \Leftrightarrow [p, o; 1 - p, o'] \succeq [q, o; 1 - q, o'])$.

An agent whose preferences obey the above principles, will always prefer outcomes that have higher utilities than lower. In other words, such an agent is a rational decision-maker or a utility maximizer.

A.3.2 Utility functions

A utility function essentially provides another way of conveying information about an agent's preferences. The two basic axioms of utility are as follows:

1. If an outcome o is preferred to o', then $u(o) > u(o')$; if o' is preferred to o, then $u(o') > u(o)$; and if an agent is indifferent between the two, then $u(o) = u(o')$.

2. If an agent is indifferent between (a) outcome o for certain and (b) taking a bet or lottery in which it receives outcome o' with probability p and outcome o'' with probability $(1 - p)$ then:

$$u(o) = pU(o') + (1 - p)u(o'')$$

The latter axiom effectively describes the principle of maximum expected utility (MEU). In other words, the agent will prefer an action that maximizes on average its maximum expected utility over a set of possible states. The utility of a lottery is the sum of the probability of each outcome multiplied by the utility of the outcome. In essence, it is the ER rule, but now instead of payoffs, we consider utilities.

A utility function is not unique, in fact it is said that a utility function is only unique up to a positive linear transformation.

But how can an agent assess a utility function? Assume a decision-making problem with a number of possible payoffs or outcomes. An agent first needs to decide what are the most and least preferable payoffs or outcomes. Suppose that the most preferable payoff is R^+ and the least R_-. As a utility function is unique only up to a positive linear transformation, we can arbitrarily assign values to $u(R^+)$ and $u(R_-)$, provided that the preference ordering is maintained. In other words, we can assign any real numbers to $u(R^+)$ and $u(R_-)$, provided that the preference ordering $R^+ \succ R_-$ is preserved. Suppose that we let $u(R^+) = 1$ and $u(R_-) = 0$.

Consider any payoff R. Based on the first axiom, it must be the case that:

$$u(R^+) \geq u(R) \geq u(R_-) \text{ or } 1 \geq u(R) \geq 0$$

To determine the value of $u(R)$ consider the following choice of lotteries:

L_1: Receive R for certain.
L_2: Receive R^+ with probability p and R_- with probability $(1 - p)$.

How would an agent choose between these two lotteries? According to the second axiom, i.e., the MEU rule, the lottery with the higher expected utility should be chosen. The expected utilities of the two lotteries are as follows:

$$EU(L_1) = u(R)$$
$$EU(L_2) = (p)u(R^+) + (1 - p)u(R_-) = (p)(1) + (1 - p)(0) = p$$

As a result, if $u(R) > p$, L_1 should be selected, whereas if $u(R) < p$, L_2 should be selected, and if $u(R) = p$, then the agent is indifferent between the two lotteries. In other words, the relationship between $u(R)$ and p can be used to determine the utility of R. If a probability p can be determined that makes an agent indifferent between the two lotteries, then the utility of R must be equal to this value p. Once the most and least preferable outcomes or payoffs are determined in terms of 1 and 0 respectively, the utility of any other outcome can be determined. Due to the choice of utilities for the most and least preferable outcomes, the utility of any other payoff can be regarded as an indifference probability.

Consider the umbrella example. The three possible outcomes expressed in terms of money are £0, −£1 and −£50. Accordingly, R^+ is £0, and R_- is −£50. To find the utility of −£1, $u(-£1)$ assume $u(R^+) = 1$ and $u(R_-) = 0$ and the lotteries:

L_1: Receive −£1 for certain.
L_2: Receive 0 with probability p and −£50 with probability $(1 − p)$.

What is the value of p that makes me indifferent between L_1 and L_2? Suppose that $p = 0.9$. Then $u(-£1) = 0.9$ and the utilities for the umbrella example are illustrated in Table A.6.

| | | World state | |
		Rain	No rain
Action	Carry umbrella	0.9	0.9
	Not carry umbrella	0	1

Table A.6: Utilities for the umbrella example

If $P(rain) = 0.6$ and $P(no\ rain) = 0.4$, the expected utilities are as follows:

EU(carry umbrella) $= 0.6(0.9) + 0.4(0.9) = 0.9$
EU(not carry umbrella) $= 0.6(0) + 0.4(1) = 0.4$

The MEU rule tells me to carry an umbrella.

A.3.3 Utility and money

There are many situations in which utilities can be directly expressed in terms of monetary gain. In this case, the MEU rule is equivalent to the ER rule. But as we saw in an earlier example, the *value*, i.e., the utility, of money may differ from person to person. To determine the relationship between utility and money over a given interval of monetary values for an agent, the same procedure as above can be used.

Assume an agent is offered the following two lotteries:

L_1: Receive £0 for certain.
L_2: Receive £100 with probability p and −£100 with probability $(1 − p)$.

Suppose the agent decides that 0.75 makes it indifferent between these two lotteries: for $p < 0.75$ it prefers L_1, whereas for $p > 0.75$ it prefers L_2, otherwise it is indifferent. Even though $p = 0.5$ would make the expected payoffs of the two lotteries equal in terms of money, the agent feels that the probability of winning L_2 has to be 0.75 before it is indifferent between the certain outcome of receiving nothing, and the risky one of having to pay £100. Similarly, the agent assesses $u(-£50)$ to be 0.4 and $u(£50)$ to be 0.9. These values can be plotted onto a graph and a curve can be drawn connecting them as illustrated in Figure A.2. This curve comprises the utility function for money of this particular agent.

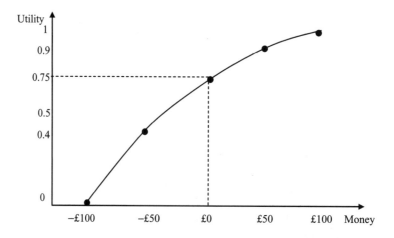

Figure A.2: Utility function for money

Alternatively, if the probability p is fixed, then the amount of money that an agent would need to receive for certain in L_1 to make it indifferent between two lotteries can be determined. Consider $p = 0.5$ and the following two lotteries:

L_1: Receive £x for certain.
L_2: Receive £100 with probability 0.5 and −£100 with probability 0.5.

Suppose that $x = -£30$ makes the agent indifferent between the two lotteries. Then $u(-£30) = 0.5$ and −£30 is considered to be the cash equivalent for the gamble that is involved in L_2. The amount of £30 is called a *risk premium* and represents the largest amount of money that an agent would be willing to pay to avoid the inherent risk in L_2. Although the bet is perfectly fair in terms of monetary returns, L_2 involves the risk of having to pay £100. Consequently, the agent would be willing to pay a risk premium (£30) to avoid the bet and the risk of possibly having to pay a considerably larger amount (£100).

Consider the following bet: on the toss of a coin an agent wins £100 if it comes up heads with probability 0.5, and it loses £100 if it comes up tails with probability 0.5, i.e., the coin is fair. An agent should be indifferent between betting and not betting as the expected payoff is zero. But in terms of expected utility, whether an agent should accept

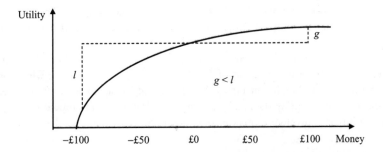

Figure A.3: The utility function of a risk-averse agent

the bet or not depends on the shape of its utility function. As illustrated in Figure A.3, the gain in utility if such a bet is won is:

$$g = u(\pounds100) - u(0) \text{ (i)}$$

while the loss in utility is:

$$l = u(0) - u(-\pounds100) \text{ (ii)}$$

The expected utility of the bet $EU(\text{bet}) = 0.5u(\pounds100) + 0.5u(-\pounds100)$. The expected utility of not betting is $EU(\text{not bet}) = u(\pounds0)$. When would an agent accept such a bet? Using the MEU rule, the agent would only accept the bet if $EU(\text{bet}) > EU(\text{not bet})$, or alternatively, if $EU(\text{bet}) - EU(\text{not bet}) > 0$. But from the above we have:

$$EU(\text{bet}) - EU(\text{not bet}) = 0.5u(\pounds100) + 0.5u(-\pounds100) - u(\pounds0).$$

The right-hand side is equivalent to:

$$0.5u(\pounds100) + 0.5u(-\pounds100) - 0.5u(\pounds0) - 0.5u(\pounds0) =$$
$$[0.5u(\pounds100) - 0.5u(\pounds0)] - [0.5u(\pounds0) - 0.5u(-\pounds100)]$$

or alternatively using (i) and (ii):

$$0.5g - 0.5l = 0.5(g - l)$$

Thus, the rule that determines whether or not to take the bet is: take the bet if $0.5(g - l) > 0$, but do not take the bet if $0.5(g - l) < 0$.

As the decision whether to accept a bet depends on the shape of the utility function, an agent can simply make that decision by looking at g and l. In Figure A.3, g is smaller than l, so $(g - l)$ is negative and thus the agent should not take the bet. The curve in Figure A.3 represents the utility function of a *risk-averse* agent. When an agent is risk-averse, it does not like taking bets that are risky as the ones described above, even though the expected payoff is zero. Risk aversion is the basis for the insurance industry. People would rather pay a relatively small amount than gamble the price of their car against the chance of theft, fire or other forms of damage. From the insurance company's perspective, the price of the car is very small compared to the total reserves of the company. The gamble costs are negligible as the insurance company's utility curve is linear over such a small region.

In Figure A.4, g is greater than l and, as a result, the agent should accept the bet. This curve represents the utility function of a *risk-prone* agent, i.e., an agent who is willing to assume more risk. Finally, in Figure A.5, $g = l$ and the agent is indifferent between accepting and not accepting the bet. For an agent with linear utility function maximizing expected utility is equivalent to maximizing payoff. Such an agent is called *risk-neutral*.

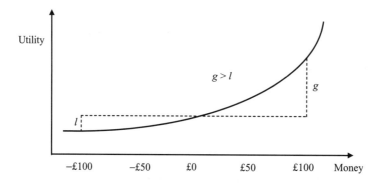

Figure A.4: The utility function of a risk-prone agent

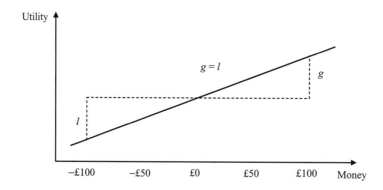

Figure A.5: The utility function of a risk-neutral agent

In the case considered above, the probabilities of winning and losing are equal and therefore the decision on whether to place the bet, or not, simply depends on the sign of $g - l$. If the probabilities are not equal, the difference in expected utilities of the two actions and as a result the decision, will not just depend on the sign of $g - l$, but also on their relative magnitudes. Nevertheless, the shapes of the curves do not change.

A.3.4 Multi-attribute utility functions

Often we are faced with situations in which determining utilities is no easy task as the utility may depend on a number of factors. Consider evaluating a set of job offers that you have been made. If these job offers involve different salaries, career opportunities, pension packages and they are in different cities, then determining the utility of each of the proposals is nontrivial. This is the problem of multi-dimensional or multi-attribute utility theory. One possible way to determine the utility in this decision-making problem is to add up the utilities of each individual contributing factor as below:

$$u(\text{job-offer}) = u(\text{salary}) + u(\text{location}) + u(\text{pension package}) \\ + u(\text{career opportunities}).$$

Such a utility function is called *additive*. One potential problem is that such a utility function assigns equal weight to each contributing factor, which may not necessarily be the case. Perhaps salary is the most important factor, the pension package and career opportunities come next, while location is the least important factor for an agent. Alternatively, weights can be assigned to each contributing factor to indicate its significance. Typically, weights are normalized, i.e., they sum up to 1. Such a utility function is called *weighted additive* multi-attribute function. An example of how job offers could be evaluated is given below:

$$u(\text{job-offer}) = 0.4u(\text{salary}) + 0.1u(\text{location}) + 0.3u(\text{pension package}) \\ + 0.2u(\text{career opportunities})$$

Another potential problem with additive utility functions is that they assume that the various contributing factors are independent of each other. This may not necessarily be so. For instance, the salary may not be independent of location. Attributes may also be complementary or substitutable. In such cases, an additive utility function does not suffice to express attribute interdependencies and alternatively the utility function can be expressed via a multi-linear expression. For two attributes x and y and corresponding weights w_x and w_y respectively, the multi-linear expression would take the form:

$$u(x, y) = w_x u(x) + w_y u(y) + (1 - w_x - w_y)u(x)u(y)$$

According to Keeney and Raiffa (1993) the sign of the coefficient $(1 - w_x - w_y)$ indicates the relationship between the two attributes x and y. A positive coefficient means that the two attributes complement each other and therefore the overall utility for the pair increases, while a negative coefficient means that the two attributes are substitutes.

A.4 Further Reading

The introduction to probability and decision theory provided here is basic. The discussion and examples used here draw on Winkler (1972). There are a number of texts that provide a thorough introduction into decision theory. Clemen (1996) provides an introduction to normative decision theory while in the more recent book by Clemen and Reilly (2000) decision theory is illustrated via the Decision Tools Suite toolkit. Keeney and Raiffa (1993) cover utility theory including multi-attribute utility theory. Other useful texts include French (1988), Luce and Raiffa (1957), Lindley (1971), Shafer and Pearl (1990), Raiffa (1997) and Winkler (1972). Probability and utility theory in the context of artificial intelligence are also covered in Russell and Norvig (2003).

Bibliography

ACM Portal (2006). The ACM Portal to Computing Literature. See http://portal.acm.org/.

AgentBuilder (2006). See http://www.agentbuilder.com.

AgentLink (2006a). See http://www.agentlink.org/.

AgentLink (2006b). Agent-based factory modelling: Eurobios and SCA packaging. A case study. Technical report, AgentLink. Available at http://www.agentlink.org/resources/webCS/AL3_CS_002_EUROBIOS.pdf.

agentTool (2006). See http://macr.cis.ksu.edu/projects/agentTool/agentool.htm.

Aglets (2006). See http://www.trl.ibm.com/aglets/.

Agorics (2006). See http://www.agorics.com/Library/auctions.html.

Allen, J., Hendler, J., and Tate, A., editors (1990). *Readings in Planning*. Morgan Kaufmann, San Mateo, CA.

Alspector, J., Kolcz, A., and Karunanithi, N. (1998). Comparing feature-based and clique-based user models for movie selection. In *Proceedings of the Third International ACM Conference on Digital Libraries*, pages 11–18, Pittsburgh, PA.

Amazon (2006). See http://www.amazon.com.

Amgoud, L., Maudet, N., and Parsons, S. (2000a). Modelling dialogues using argumentation. In *Proceedings of the Fourth International Conference on Multi-Agent Systems (ICMAS-00)*, pages 31–38, Boston, MA.

Amgoud, L., Parsons, S., and Maudet, N. (2000b). Arguments, dialogue and negotiation. In *Proceedings of the 14th European Conference on Artificial Intelligence (ECAI-00)*, pages 338–342, Berlin, Germany.

Andersson, A., Tenhunen, M., and Ygge, F. (2000). Integer programming for combinatorial auction winner determination. In *Proceedings of the Fourth International Conference on Multi-Agent Systems (ICMAS-00)*, pages 39–46, Boston, MA.

Andrade, F., Novais, P., and Neves, J. (2004). Issues on intelligent electronic agents and legal relations. In *Proceedings of the Law of Electronic Agents Workshop (LEA-04)*, pages 81–94.

Andreasen, A. (1965). Attitudes and customer behavior: A decision model. In Preston, L., editor, *New Research in Marketing*. California Institute of Business and Economics Research, University of California.

Apistola, M., Brazier, F. M. T., Kubbe, O., Oskamp, A., Schellekens, M. H. M., and Voulon, M. (2002). Legal aspects of agent technology. In *Proceedings of the 17th British and Irish Legal Education Technology Association (BILETA) Conference*.

Åqvist, L. (1984). Deontic logics. In Gabbay, D. and Guenthner, F., editors, *Handbook of Philosophical Logic Vol. II*, pages 605–714. Reidel Publishing Company, Dordrecht.

Arrow, K. (1951). *Social choice and individual values*. Cowles Foundation, New Haven.

Arthur, W. B., Holland, J., LeBaron, B., Palmer, R., and Tayler, P. (1997). Asset pricing under endogenous expectations in an artificial stock market. In Arthur, W. B., Durlauf, S., and Lane, D., editors, *The Economy as an Evolving Complex System II*, pages 15–44. Addison-Wesley Longman, Reading, MA.

Ashri, R., Rahwan, I., and Luck, M. (2003). Architectures for negotiating agents. In Marik, V., Müller, J. P., and Pechoucek, M., editors, *Multi-Agent Systems and Applications III: Proceedings of the Third Central and Eastern European Conference on Multi-agent Systems (CEEMAS-03)*, LNAI Volume 2691, pages 133–146. Springer, Berlin.

Aumann, R. J. and Maschler, M. (1964). The bargaining set for cooperative games. In Dresher, M., Shapley, L. S., and Tucker, A. W., editors, *Advances in Game Theory*, volume 52 of *Annals of Mathematical Studies*, pages 443–476. Princeton University Press, Princeton, NJ.

Austin, J. L. (1962). *How to Do Things with Words*. Clarendon Press, Oxford.

Aversa, R., Di Martino, B., Mazzocca, N., and Venticinque, S. (2004). A resource discovery service for a mobile agents based Grid infrastructure. In *High performance scientific and engineering computing: hardware/software support*, pages 189–200. Kluwer Academic Publishers, Norwell, MA.

Axelrod, R. M. (1984). *The Evolution of Cooperation*. Basic Books, New York, NY.

Baker, S. A. and Hurst, P. R. (1998). *The limits of trust: Cryptography, governments and electronic commerce*. Kluwer Law International, The Hague.

Balabanovic, M. and Shoham, Y. (1997). Fab: content-based, collaborative recommendation. *Communications of the ACM*, 40(3):66–72.

Barth, E. M. and Krabbe, E. C. W. (1982). *From axiom to dialogue: a philosophical study of logics and argumentation*. W. de Gruyter, Berlin.

Basu, C., Hirsh, H., and Cohen, W. W. (1998). Recommendation as classification: Using social and content-based information in recommendation. In *Proceedings of the 15th National Conference on Artificial Intelligence and 10th Innovative Applications of Artificial Intelligence Conference AAAI/IAAI*, pages 714–720, Madison, WI.

Bates, J. (1992). Virtual reality, art, and entertainment. *Presence: Teleoperators and Virtual Environments*, 1(1):133–138.

Baumer, C., Breugst, M., Choy, S., and Magedanz, T. (2000). Grasshopper: a universal agent platform based on OMG MASIF and FIPA standards. Technical report, IKV++ GmbH.

Bayardo Jr., R. J., Bohrer, W., Brice, R. S., Cichocki, A., Fowler, J., Helal, A., Kashyap, V., Ksiezyk, T., Martin, G., Nodine, M. H., Rashid, M., Rusinkiewicz, M., Shea, R., Unnikrishnan, C., Unruh, A., and Woelk, D. (1997). InfoSleuth: Semantic integration of information in open and dynamic environments. In *Proceedings of the ACM SIGMOD International Conference on Management of Data*, pages 195–206, Tucson, AZ.

Bellifemine, F., Poggi, A., and Rimassa, G. (1999). JADE: A FIPA-compliant agent framework. In *Proceedings of the Fourth International Conference and Exhibition on the Practical Application of Intelligent Agents and Multi-Agent Technology (PAAM-99)*, pages 97–108, London, UK.

Bellman, R. E. (1957). *Dynamic Programming*. Princeton University Press, Princeton, NJ.

Bergenti, F. and Poggi, A. (2002). Supporting agent-oriented modelling with UML. *International Journal of Software Engineering and Knowledge Engineering*, 12(6): 605–618.

Bergin, J. (2005). *Microeconomic Theory a Concise Course*. Oxford University Press, Oxford.

Berners-Lee, T., Hendler, J., and Lassila, O. (2001). The Semantic Web. *Scientific American*, pages 34–43.

Bichler, M. (2001). *The future of e-markets: Multidimensional Market Mechanisms*. Cambridge University Press, Cambridge.

Bichler, M. and Kalagnanam, J. (2005). Configurable offers and winner determination in multi-attribute auctions. *European Journal of Operational Research*, 160(2): 380–394.

Bichler, M. and Kalagnanam, J. (2006). Bidding languages and winner determination in multi-attribute auctions. Technical Report RC 22478, IBM T. J. Watson Research Center.

Bickmore, T. W. and Cassell, J. (2001). Relational agents: a model and implementation of building user trust. In *Proceedings of the SIGCHI Conference on Human Factors in Computing Systems (CHI 2001)*, pages 396–403, Seattle, WA.

Bigus, J. P., Schlosnagle, D. A., Pilgrim, J. R., Mills III, W. N., and Diao, Y. (2002). ABLE: A toolkit for building multiagent autonomic systems. *IBM Systems Journal*, 41(3).

Binmore, K. (1992). *Fun and Games: A Text on Game Theory*. D. C. Heath and Company, Lexington, MA.

Binmore, K. and Klemperer, P. (2002). The biggest auction ever: The sale of the British 3G Telecom Licences. *The Economic Journal*, 112:74–96.

Blackwell, R. D., Miniard, P. W., and Engel, J. F. (2006). *Consumer Behavior*. Thomson/South-Western, Mason, OH.

Blythe, J. (1999). An overview of planning under uncertainty. In Wooldridge, M. and Veloso, M., editors, *Artificial Intelligence Today*, LNAI Volume 1600, pages 85–110. Springer, Berlin.

Boella, G. and van der Torre, L. W. N. (2005). Enforceable social laws. In Dignum, F., Dignum, V., Koenig, S., Kraus, S., Singh, M. P., and Wooldridge, M., editors, *Proceedings of the Fourth International Joint Conference on Autonomous Agents and Multiagent Systems (AAMAS'05)*, pages 682–689, Utrecht, The Netherlands.

Bond, A. H. and Gasser, L., editors (1988). *Readings in Distributed Artificial Intelligence*. Morgan Kaufmann, San Mateo, CA.

Booch, G., editor (1994). *Object – Oriented Analysis and Design with Applications*. Addison-Wesley Longman, Reading, MA.

Bordini, R. H., Dastani, M., Dix, J., and El Fallah Seghrouchni, A., editors (2005). *Multi-Agent Programming: Languages, Platforms and Applications.* Springer, Berlin.

Bradshaw, J. M., editor (1997). *Software Agents.* MIT Press, Cambridge, MA.

Bradshaw, J. M., Dutfield, S., Benoit, P., and Woolley, J. D. (1997). KAoS: Toward an industrial-strength generic agent architecture. In Bradshaw, J. M., editor, *Software Agents*, pages 375–418. MIT Press, Cambridge, MA.

Bratman, M. E. (1987). *Intentions, Plans, and Practical Reason.* Harvard University Press, Cambridge, MA.

Brazier, F. M. T., Dunin-Keplicz, B., Jennings, N. R., and Treur, J. (1997). DESIRE: Modelling multi-agent systems in a compositional formal framework. *International Journal of Cooperative Information Systems*, 6(1):67–94.

Brazier, F. M. T., Oskamp, A., Prins, J. E. J., Schellekens, M. H. M., and Wijngaards, N. J. E. (2004b). Anonymity and software agents: An interdisciplinary challenge. *Artificial Intelligence and Law*, 12(1-2):137–157.

Brazier, F. M. T., Oskamp, A., Prins, J. E. J., Schellekens, M. H. M., and Wijngaards, N. J. E. (2004a). Law-abiding & integrity on the Internet: a case for agents. *Artificial Intelligence and Law*, 12(1-2):5–37.

Brazier, F. M. T., Oskamp, A., Schellekens, M. H. M., and Wijngaards, N. J. E. (2003). Can agents close contracts? In Oskamp, A. and Weitzenboeck, E., editors, *Proceedings of the Law of Electronic Agents Workshop (LEA-03)*, pages 9–20.

Brazier, F. M. T., van Eck, P. A. T., and Treur, J. (2001). Modelling a society of simple agents: From conceptual specification to experimentation. *Journal of Applied Intelligence*, 14(2):161–178.

Breese, J. S., Heckerman, D., and Kadie, C. M. (1998). Empirical analysis of predictive algorithms for collaborative filtering. In *Proceedings of the 14th Conference on Uncertainty in Artificial Intelligence (UAI-98)*, pages 43–52, Madison, WI.

Bretier, P. and Sadek, D. (1997). A rational agent as the kernel of a cooperative spoken dialogue system: implementing a logical theory of interaction. In Müller, J., Wooldridge, M., and Jennings, N., editors, *Intelligent Agents III: Agent Theories, Architectures, and Languages (ATAL)*, LNAI Volume 1193, pages 189–203. Springer, Berlin.

Broersen, J., Dastani, M., Hulstijn, J., and van der Torre, L. (2002). Goal generation in the BOID architecture. *Cognitive Science Quarterly*, 2(3-4):428–447.

Bromley, D. B. (1993). *Reputation, Image and Impression Management.* John Wiley and Sons, Chichester.

Brooks, R. (1986). A robust layered control system for a mobile robot. *IEEE Journal of Robotics and Automation*, 2(1):14–23.

Brooks, R. A. (1990). Elephants don't play chess. In Maes, P., editor, *Designing Autonomous Agents*, pages 3–15. The MIT Press, Cambridge, MA.

Brooks, R. A. (1991a). Intelligence without reason. In *Proceedings of the 12th International Joint Conference on Artificial Intelligence (IJCAI-91)*, pages 569–595, Sydney, Australia.

Brooks, R. A. (1991b). Intelligence without representation. *Artificial Intelligence*, 47:139–159.

Bulow, J. and Roberts, J. (1989). The simple economics of optimal auctions. *The Journal of Political Economy*, 97(5):1060–1090.

Busetta, P., Rönnquist, R., Hodgson, A., and Lucas, A. (1999). JACK Intelligent Agents: Components for intelligent agents in Java. *AgentLink Newsletter*, (2):2–5.

Bygrave, L. A. (2001). Electronic agents and privacy: A Cyberspace Odyssey 2001. *International Journal of Law and Information Technology*, 9(3):275–294.

Castelfranchi, C. (1995). Commitments: From individual intentions to groups and organisations. In Lesser, V. and Gasser, L., editors, *Proceedings of the First International Conference on Multi-Agent Systems (ICMAS-95)*, pages 41–48, San Francisco, CA.

Castelfranchi, C. (2000). Engineering social order. In Omicini, A., Tolksdorf, R., and Zambonelli, F., editors, *Proceedings of the First International Workshop on Engineering Societies in the Agent World, (ESAW 2000)*, pages 1–18. Springer, Berlin.

Castelfranchi, C. (2003). The micro-macro constitution of power. *ProtoSociology*, 18-19:208–268.

Cavedon, L. and Sonenberg, L. (1998). On social commitments, roles and preferred goals. In *Proceedings of the Third International Conference on Multi-Agent Systems (ICMAS-98)*, pages 80–87, Paris, France.

Chan, T.-W. (1996). Learning companion systems, learning social systems, and the global social learning club. *Journal of Artificial Intelligence in Education*, 7(2):125–159.

Chaum, D. (1982). Blind signatures for untraceable payments. In Chaum, D., Rivest, R. L., and Sherman, A. T., editors, *Advances in Cryptology: Proceedings of the CRYPTO'82 Conference*, pages 199–203, Santa Barbara, CA.

Chavez, A. and Maes, P. (1996). Kasbah: An agent marketplace for buying and selling goods. In *Proceedings of the First International Conference on the Practical Application of Intelligent Agents and Multi-Agent Technology (PAAM-96)*, pages 75–90, London, UK.

Chellas, B. F. (1996). *Modal Logic: An Introduction*. Cambridge University Press, Cambridge.

Cheyer, A. and Martin, D. L. (2001). The Open Agent Architecture. *Autonomous Agents and Multi-Agent Systems*, 4(1/2):143–148.

Child, M. and Linketscher, N. (2001). Trust issues and user reactions to e-services and electronic marketplaces: A customer survey. Technical Report HPL-2001-32, Hewlett Packard, Trusted E-Services Laboratory, HP Laboratories Bristol.

Christensen, E., Curbera, F., Meredith, G., and Weerawarana, S. (2006). WSDL: Web Services Description Language. See http://www.w3.org/TR/wsdl.

CiteSeer (2006). CiteSeer: The NECI Scientific Literature Digital Library. See http://citeseer.ist.psu.edu/.

Claessens, J., Preneel, B., and Vandewalle, J. (2003). (How) can mobile agents do secure electronic transactions on untrusted hosts? A survey of the security issues and the current solutions. *ACM Transactions on Internet Technology*, 3(1):28–48.

Clarke, H. E. (1971). Multipart pricing of public goods. *Public Choice*, 11:17–33.

Claypool, M., Gokhale, A., Miranda, T., Murnikov, P., Netes, D., and Sartin, M. (1999). Combining content-based and collaborative filters in an online newspaper. In *Proceedings of the ACM SIGIR Workshop on Recommender Systems*, Berkeley, CA.

Clearwater, S. H., editor (1996). *Market-based control: a paradigm for distributed resource allocation*. World Scientific Publishing Co., Inc., River Edge, NJ.

Clemen, R. T. (1996). *Making Hard Decisions: Introduction to Decision Analysis*. Duxbury Press, Belmont, CA.

Clemen, R. T. and Reilly, T. (2000). *Making Hard Decisions with Decision Tools Suite*. Duxbury Press, Belmont, CA.

Cockayne, W. R. and Zyda, M. (1998). *Mobile agents*. Manning Press, Greenwich.

Cohen, P. R. and Levesque, H. J. (1990). Rational interaction as the basis for communication. In Cohen, P. R., Morgan, J., and Pollack, M. E., editors, *Intentions in Communication*, pages 221–256. Cambridge, MA.

Cohen, P. R. and Levesque, H. J. (1995). Communicative actions for artificial intelligence. In Lesser, V. and Gasser, L., editors, *Proceedings of the First International Conference on Multi-Agent Systems (ICMAS-95)*, pages 65–72, San Francisco, CA.

Collier, R. W. (2001). *Agent Factory: A Framework for the Engineering of Agent-Oriented Applications*. PhD thesis, University College Dublin.

Collier, R. W., O'Hare, G. M. P., Lowen, T., and Rooney, C. (2003). Beyond prototyping in the Factory of the Agents. In Marik, V., Müller, J. P., and Pechoucek, M., editors, *Multi-Agent Systems and Applications III: Proceedings of the Third Central and Eastern European Conference on Multi-agent Systems (CEEMAS-03)*, LNAI Volume 2691, pages 383–393. Springer, Berlin.

Cost, R. S., Finin, T., Labrou, Y., Luan, X., Peng, Y., Soboroff, I., Mayfield, J., and Boughannam, A. (1998). Jackal: A Java-based Tool for Agent Development. In *Proceedings of the AAAI-98, Workshop on Tools for Agent Development*, Madison, WI.

Cöster, R. and Svensson, M. (2002). Inverted file search algorithms for collaborative filtering. In *Proceedings of the 25th Annual International ACM SIGIR Conference on Research and Development in Information Retrieval (SIGIR 2002)*, pages 246–252, Tampere, Finland.

Crampton, P., Shoham, Y., and Steinberg, R., editors (2006). *Combinatorial Auctions*. The MIT Press, Cambridge, MA.

Cuni, G., Esteva, M., Garcia, P., Puertas, E., Sierra, C., and Solchaga, T. (2004). MASFIT: Multi-Agent System for FIsh Trading. In *Proceedings of the 16th European Conference on Artificial Intelligence (ECAI-04) including Prestigious Applications of Intelligent Systems (PAIS-04)*, pages 710–714, Valencia, Spain.

Cycorp (2006). See http://www.cyc.com.

da Silva, A. R., Romao, A., Deugo, D., and da Silva, M. M. (2001). Towards a reference model for surveying mobile agent systems. *Autonomous Agents and Multi-Agent Systems*, 4(3):187–231.

Dam, K. H. and Winikoff, M. (2003). Comparing agent-oriented methodologies. In *Agent-Oriented Information Systems, Proceedings of the Fifth International Bi-Conference Workshop (AOIS-03), Revised Selected Papers*, LNCS Volume 3030, pages 78–93. Springer, Berlin.

DAML (2006). The DARPA Agent Markup Language. See **http://www.daml.org**.

Dang, V. D. and Jennings, N. R. (2004). Generating coalition structures with finite bound from the optimal guarantees. In *Proceedings of the Third International Joint Conference on Autonomous Agents and Multiagent Systems (AAMAS'04)*, pages 564–571, New York, NY.

Dash, R. K., Jennings, N. R., and Parkes, D. C. (2003). Computational-mechanism design: A call to arms. *IEEE Intelligent Systems*, 18(6):40–47.

Davis, M. and Maschler, M. (1965). The kernel of a cooperative game. *Naval Research Logistics Quarterly*, 12:223–259.

Davis, R., Shrobe, H., and Szolovits, P. (1993). What is a knowledge representation? *AI Magazine*, 14(1):17–33.

DBLP (2006). The DBLP Computer Science Bibliography. See **http://dblp.uni-trier.de/**.

de Vries, S. and Vohra, R. (2003). Combinatorial auctions: A survey. *INFORMS Journal on Computing*, 15(3):284–309.

DealTime (2006). See **http://www.dealtime.com/**.

Decker, K., Sycara, K. P., and Williamson, M. (1997). Middle agents for the Internet. In *Proceedings of the 15th International Joint Conference on Artificial Intelligence (IJCAI-97)*, pages 578–583, Nagoya, Japan.

Dellarocas, C. (2000a). Immunizing online reputation reporting systems against unfair ratings and discriminatory behavior. In *Proceedings of the Second ACM Conference on Electronic Commerce (EC-00)*, pages 150–157, Minneapolis, MN.

Dellarocas, C. (2000b). Mechanisms for coping with unfair ratings and discriminatory behavior in online reputation reporting systems. In *Proceedings of the 21st International Conference on Information Systems (ICIS-00)*, pages 520–525, Atlanta, GA.

Dellarocas, C. and Klein, M. (1999). Civil agent societies: Tools for inventing open agent-mediated electronic marketplaces. In Moukas, A., Sierra, C., and Ygge, F., editors, *Agent Mediated Electronic Commerce II, Towards Next-Generation Agent-Based Electronic Commerce Systems, IJCAI 1999 Workshop*, LNAI Volume 1788, pages 24–39. Springer, Berlin.

DeLoach, S. A., Wood, M. F., and Sparkman, C. H. (2001). Multiagent systems engineering. *International Journal of Software Engineering and Knowledge Engineering*, 11(3):231–258.

Dennett, D. C. (1987). *The Intentional Stance*. The MIT Press, Cambridge, MA.

Denning, P. J. and Metcalfe, R. M., editors (1997). *Beyond calculation: The next fifty years*. Copernicus, New York, NY.

Di Martino, B. and Rana, O. F. (2004). Grid performance and resource management using mobile agents. In Getov, V., Gerndt, M., Hoisie, A., Malony, A., and Miller, B., editors, *Performance analysis and grid computing*, pages 251–263. Kluwer Academic Publishers, Norwell, MA.

Diffie, W. and Hellman, M. (1976). Multiuser cryptographic techniques. In *Proceedings of the AFIPS National Computer Conference*, pages 109–112, New York, NY.

Dignum, F. (2001). Agents, markets, institutions, and protocols. In Dignum, F. and Sierra, C., editors, *Agent Mediated Electronic Commerce, The European AgentLink Perspective*, LNAI Volume 1991, pages 98–114. Springer, Berlin.

Dignum, F. (2002). Abstract norms and electronic institutions. In Lindemann, G., Moldt, D., Paolucci, M., and Yu, B., editors, *Proceedings of the Regulated Agent-based Social Systems: Theory and Applications Workshop (RASTA'02)*, pages 93–103, Bologna, Italy.

Dignum, F., Dunin-Keplicz, B., and Verbrugge, R. (2000). Agent theory for team formation by dialogue. In Castelfranchi, C. and Lespérance, Y., editors, *Intelligent Agents VII: Agent Theories, Architectures, and Languages (ATAL)*, LNAI Volume 1986, pages 150–166. Springer, Berlin.

Dignum, V., Meyer, J.-J. C., and Weigand, H. (2002). Towards an organizational model for agent societies using contracts. In *Proceedings of the First International Joint Conference on Autonomous Agents and Multiagent Systems (AAMAS'02)*, pages 694–695, Bologna, Italy.

d'Inverno, M., Luck, M., Georgeff, M. P., Kinny, D., and Wooldridge, M. (2004). The dMARS architecture: A specification of the distributed Multi-Agent Reasoning System. *Autonomous Agents and Multi-Agent Systems*, 9(1-2):5–53.

Dixit, A. and Skeath, S. (1999). *Games of Strategy*. W. W. Norton & Company, New York, NY.

Doorenbos, R. B., Etzioni, O., and Weld, D. S. (1997). A scalable comparison-shopping agent for the World-Wide Web. In *Proceedings of the First International Conference on Autonomous Agents (Agents 97)*, pages 39–48, Marina del Rey, CA.

Dunin-Keplicz, B. and Verbrugge, R. (2003). Calibrating collective commitments. In Mauk, V., Müller, J. P., and Pechoucek, M., editors, *Multi-agent Systems and Applications III: Proceedings of the Third International Central and Eastern European Conference on Multi-agent Systems (CEEMAS-03)*, LNAI Volume 2691, pages 73–83. Springer, Berlin.

Durfee, E. H. (1999). Distributed problem solving and planning. In Weiss, G., editor, *Multiagent Systems: A Modern Approach to Distributed Artificial Intelligence*, pages 121–164. The MIT Press, Cambridge, MA.

Durfee, E. H., Lesser, V. R., and Corkill, D. D. (1987). Coherent cooperation among communicating problem solvers. *IEEE Transactions on Computers*, 36(11):1275–1291.

Dutta, P. K. (1999). *Strategies and Games: Theory and Practice*. The MIT Press, Cambridge, MA.

E-Sign (2006). Federal electronic signatures on global and national commerce act. See http://www.cio.noaa.gov/itmanagement/pl106229.pdf.

eBay (2006). See http://www.ebay.com/.

EC-Directive (2006). The Electronic Commerce Directive. See **http://www.dti.gov.uk/
sectors/ictpolicy/ecommsdirective/page10133.html**.

Edwards, J. (2000). Is that your best offer? shopbots search the Web for bargains. *CIO
Magazine*. Available at **http://www.cio.com/archive/110100/et.html**.

Esteva, M., de la Cruz, D., and Sierra, C. (2002). ISLANDER: An electronic institutions
editor. In *Proceedings of the First International Joint Conference on Autonomous
Agents and Multiagent Systems (AAMAS'02)*, pages 1045–1052, Bologna, Italy.

Esteva, M., Padget, J. A., and Sierra, C. (2001a). Formalizing a language for institutions
and norms. In Meyer, J.-J. C. and Tambe, M., editors, *Intelligent Agents VIII: Agent
Theories, Architectures, and Languages (ATAL)*, LNAI Volume 2333, pages 348–366.
Springer, Berlin.

Esteva, M., Rodríguez-Aguilar, J. A., Sierra, C., Garcia, P., and Arcos, J. L. (2001b).
On the formal specification of electronic institutions. In Dignum, F. and Sierra, C.,
editors, *Agent Mediated Electronic Commerce, The European AgentLink Perspective*,
LNAI Volume 1991, pages 126–147. Springer, Berlin.

Fagin, R., Halpern, J., Moses, Y., and Vardi, M. (1995). *Reasoning about Knowledge*.
The MIT Press, Cambridge, MA.

Falcone, R. and Castelfranchi, C. (2004). Trust dynamics: How trust is influenced
by direct experiences and by trust itself. In *Proceedings of the Third International
Joint Conference on Autonomous Agents and Multiagent Systems (AAMAS'04)*, pages
740–747, New York, NY.

Falcone, R., Singh, M. P., and Tan, Y.-H., editors (2001). *Trust in cyber-societies:
Integrating the human and artificial perspectives*. Springer, Berlin.

Farhoodi, F. and Fingar, P. (1997a). Competing for the future with intelligent
agent technology. *Distributed Object Computing (DOC) Magazine*. Available at
http://home1.gte.net/pfingar/agents_doc_rev4.htm.

Farhoodi, F. and Fingar, P. (1997b). Developing enterprise systems with intelligent
agent technology. *Distributed Object Computing (DOC) Magazine*. Available at
http://home1.gte.net/pfingar/docmag_part2.htm.

Farquhar, A., Fikes, R., and Rice, J. (1997). The Ontolingua server: a tool for collaborative ontology construction. *International Journal of Human-Computer Studies*,
46(6):707–727.

Fasli, M. (2002). On commitments, roles and obligations. In *From Theory to Practice in
Multi-Agent Systems, Proceedings of the Second International Workshop of Central
and Eastern Europe on Multi-agent Systems (CEEMAS-01), Revised Papers*, LNAI
Volume 2296, pages 93–102. Springer, Berlin.

Fasli, M. (2003). Heterogeneous BDI agents. *Cognitive Systems Research*, 4(1):1–22.

Fasli, M. (2004). Accounting for social order in multi-agent systems: preliminary report.
In *Proceedings of the IEEE/WIC/ACM Intelligent Agent Technology Conference (IAT
2004)*, pages 204–210, Beijing, China.

Fasli, M. (2005). On the interplay of roles and power. In Skowron, A., Barthes, J.-
P. A., Jain, L. C., Sun, R., Morizet-Mahoudeaux, P., Liu, J., and Zhong, N., editors,

Proceedings of the IEEE/WIC/ACM Intelligent Agent Technology Conference (IAT 2005), pages 499–502, Compiegne, France.

Fasli, M. (2006). Shopbots: A syntactic present, a semantic future. *IEEE Internet Computing*, 10(6):69–75.

Fasli, M. and Michalakopoulos, M. (2004). e-Game: A generic auction platform supporting customizable market games. In *Proceedings of the IEEE/WIC/ACM Intelligent Agent Technology Conference (IAT 2004)*, pages 190–196, Beijing, China.

Ferber, J. (1996). Reactive distributed artificial intelligence. In O'Hare, G. M. P. and Jennings, N. R., editors, *Foundations of Distributed Artificial Intelligence*, pages 287–317. John Wiley and Sons, Chichester.

Ferber, J. (1999). *Multi-Agent Systems: An Introduction to Distributed Artificial Intelligence*. Addison-Wesley Longman, Reading, MA.

Ferber, J. and Gutknecht, O. (1998). A meta-model for the analysis and design of organizations in multi-agent systems. In *Proceedings of the Third International Conference on Multi-Agent Systems (ICMAS-98)*, pages 128–135, Paris, France.

Ferguson, I. A. (1992a). Touring Machines: Autonomous agents with attitudes. *IEEE Computer*, 25(5):51–55.

Ferguson, I. A. (1992b). *TOURINGMACHINES: An Architecture for Dynamic, Rational, Mobile Agents*. PhD thesis, Clare Hall, University of Cambridge, UK. Also available as Technical Report UCAM-CL-TR-273, University of Cambridge Computer Laboratory, see **http://www.cl.cam.ac.uk/TechReports/UCAM-CL-TR-273.html**.

Fikes, R. and Nilsson, N. J. (1971). STRIPS: A new approach to the application of theorem proving to problem solving. *Artificial Intelligence*, 2(3/4):189–208.

FIPA (1998). Security Management Specification. See **http://www.fipa.org/specs/fipa00020/**.

FIPA (2002a). Communicative Act Library Specification. See **http://www.fipa.org/specs/fipa00037/**.

FIPA (2002b). FIPA Abstract Architecture Specification. See **http://www.fipa.org/specs/fipa00001/SC00001.html**.

FIPA (2006). The Foundation for Intelligent Physical Agents. See **http://www.fipa.org**.

Fischer, K., Müller, J. P., and Pischel, M. (1994). Unifying control in a layered agent architecture. Technical Report TM-94-05, German Research Center for AI, DFKI GmbH.

Fisher, M. (1994). A survey of Concurrent METATEM – the language and its applications. In Gabbay, D. M. and Ohlbach, H. J., editors, *Proceedings of the First International Conference on Temporal Logic (ICTL)*, LNAI Volume 827, pages 480–505. Springer, Berlin.

Foster, I. T. and Kesselman, C., editors (2004). *The Grid: Blueprint for a New Computing Infrastructure*. Morgan Kaufmann, San Mateo, CA.

FreeMarkets (2006). See **http://www.freemarkets.com/**.

French, S. (1988). *Decision Theory: An Introduction to the Mathematics of Rationality*. Ellis Horwood, Chichester.

Friedman, B., Khan Jr., P. H., and Howe, D. C. (2000). Trust online. *Communications of the ACM*, 43(12):34–40.

Friedman, D. and Rust, J., editors (1993). SFI Studies in the Sciences of Complexity. Addison-Wesley Longman, Reading, MA.

Froomkin, A. M. (1995). Anonymity and its enmities. *Journal of Online Law*. art. 4.

Froomkin, A. M. (1996). Flood control on the information ocean: Living with anonymity, digital cash, and distributed databases. *Journal of Law and Commerce*, 15: 395–479.

Fudenberg, D. and Tirole, J., editors (1998). *Game Theory*. The MIT Press, Cambridge, MA.

Gambetta, D. (1988). Can we trust trust? In Gambetta, D., editor, *Trust: Making and Breaking Cooperative Relations*, pages 213–238. Basil-Blackwell, Oxford.

Gasser, L. (1995). Computational organization research. In Gasser, L., editor, *Proceedings of the First International Conference on Multi-Agent Systems (ICMAS-95)*, pages 414–415, San Francisco, CA.

Gasser, L. and Huhns, M., editors (1989). *Distributed Artificial Intelligence*, volume II. Morgan Kaufmann, San Mateo, CA.

Genesereth, M. R. and Fikes, R. E. (1992). Knowledge Interchange Format, Version 3.0, Reference Manual. Technical Report logic-92-1, Stanford University, Computer Science Department.

Genesereth, M. R., Keller, A. M., and Duschka, O. M. (1997). Infomaster: an information integration system. In *Proceedings of the ACM SIGMOD International Conference on Management of Data*, pages 539–542, Tucson, AZ.

Genesereth, M. R. and Ketchpel, S. P. (1994). Software agents. *Communications of the ACM*, 37(7):48–53.

Genesereth, M. R. and Nilsson, N. J. (1987). *Logical foundations of artificial intelligence*. Morgan Kaufmann, San Mateo, CA.

Georgeff, M. P. and Ingrand, F. F. (1989). Decision-making in an embedded reasoning system. In *Proceedings of the 11th International Joint Conference on Artificial Intelligence (IJCAI-89)*, pages 972–978, Detroit, MI.

Georgeff, M. P. and Lansky, A. L. (1987). Reactive reasoning and planning. In *Proceedings of the Sixth National Conference on Artificial Intelligence (AAAI-87)*, pages 677–682, Seattle, WA.

Geurts, R. (2002). Legal aspects of software agents. In Prins, J. E. J., Ribbers, P. M. A., van Tilborg, H. C. A., Veth, A. F. L., and van der Wees, J. G. L., editors, *Trust in electronic commerce: The role of trust from a legal, an organizational and a technical point of view*, pages 231–270. Kluwer Law International, The Hague.

Ghallab, M., Nau, D., and Traverso, P., editors (2004). *Automated Planning: Theory and Practice*. Morgan Kaufmann, San Mateo, CA.

Gibbard, A. (1973). Manipulation of voting schemes: a general result. *Econometrica*, 41:587–601.

Gibbons, R. (1992). *Game theory for applied economists*. Princeton University Press, Princeton, NJ.

Gilbert, M. A. (1994). Multi-modal argumentation. *Philosophy of the Social Sciences*, 24(2):159–177.

Gillies, D. B. (1959). Solutions to general non zero sum games. In Tucker, A. W. and Luce, R. D., editors, *Contributions to the Theory of Games IV*, volume 40 of *Annals of Mathematical Studies*, pages 47–85. Princeton University Press, Princeton, NJ.

Giunchiglia, F., Mylopoulos, J., and Perini, A. (2002). The Tropos software development methodology: processes, models and diagrams. In *Proceedings of the First International Joint Conference on Autonomous Agents and Multiagent Systems (AAMAS'02)*, pages 35–36, Bologna, Italy.

Goldberg, D., Nichols, D., Oki, B. M., and Terry, D. (1992). Using collaborative filtering to weave an information tapestry. *Communications of the ACM*, 35(12):61–70.

Gomoluch, J. and Schroeder, M. (2004). Performance evaluation of market-based resource allocation for grid computing. *Concurrency and Computation: Practice and Experience*, 16(5):469–475.

Good, N., Schafer, J. B., Konstan, J. A., Borchers, A., Sarwar, B. M., Herlocker, J. L., and Riedl, J. (1999). Combining collaborative filtering with personal agents for better recommendations. In *Proceedings of the 16th National Conference on Artificial Intelligence and 11th Conference on Innovative Applications of Artificial Intelligence (AAAI/IAAI)*, pages 439–446, Orlando, Florida.

Grand, S. and Cliff, D. (1998). Creatures: Entertainment software agents with artificial life. *Autonomous Agents and Multi-Agent Systems*, 1(1):39–57.

Gray, R. S. (1995). Agent Tcl: A transportable agent system. In *Proceedings of the CIKM Workshop on Intelligent Information Agents, Fourth International Conference on Information and Knowledge Management (CIKM 95)*, Baltimore, MD.

Gray, R. S. (1996). Agent Tcl: A flexible and secure mobile-agent system. In Diekhans, M. and Roseman, M., editors, *Proceedings of the Fourth Annual Tcl/Tk Workshop (TCL 96)*, pages 9–23, Monterey, CA.

Gray, R. S., Cybenko, G., Kotz, D., Peterson, R. A., and Rus, D. (2002). D'Agents: Applications and performance of a mobile-agent system. *Software – Practice and Experience*, 32(6):543–573.

Groves, T. (1973). Incentives in teams. *Econometrica*, 41:617–631.

Guttman, R. H., Moukas, A. G., and Maes, P. (1998). Agent mediated electronic commerce: A survey. *Knowledge Engineering Review*, 13(2):147–159.

Ha, V. A. and Haddawy, P. (1998). Toward case-based preference elicitation: Similarity measures on preference structures. In *Proceedings of the 14th Conference on Uncertainty in Artificial Intelligence (UAI-98)*, pages 193–201, Madison, WI.

Hamblin, C. L. (1970). *Fallacies*. Methuen and Co Ltd, London.

Hardin, G. (1968). The Tragedy of the Commons. *Science*, 162:1243–1248.

Harré, R. and Secord, P. F. (1972). *The explanation of social behaviour*. Basil Blackwell, Oxford.

Harsanyi, J. C. (1967). Games with incomplete information played by Bayesian players, i-iii. part i. The basic model. *Management Science*, 14(3, Theory Series):159–182.

Harsanyi, J. C. (1968a). Games with incomplete information played by Bayesian players, i-iii. part ii. Bayesian equilibrium points. *Management Science*, 14(5, Theory Series):320–334.

Harsanyi, J. C. (1968b). Games with incomplete information played by Bayesian players, i-iii. part iii. The basic probability distribution of the game. *Management Science*, 14(7, Theory Series):486–502.

Harsanyi, J. C. (1973). Games with randomly distributed payoffs: A new rationale for mixed strategy equilibrium points. *International Journal of Game Theory*, 2:1–23.

Hayes-Roth, B. and Doyle, P. (1998). Animate characters. *Autonomous Agents and Multi-Agent Systems*, 1(2):195–230.

He, M., Jennings, N. R., and Leung, H.-F. (2003). On agent-mediated electronic commerce. *IEEE Transactions on Knowledge and Data Engineering*, 15(4):985–1003.

He, Q., Sycara, K. P., and Finin, T. W. (1998). Personal security agent: KQML-based PKI. In *Proceedings of the Second International Conference on Autonomous Agents (Agents 98)*, pages 377–384, St. Paul, MN.

Helin, H. and Laukkanen, M. (2003). Jade goes wireless – gearing up agents for the wireless future. *Exp – in search of innovation (TiLab Technical Magazine)*, 3(3):20–31.

Herlocker, J. L., Konstan, J. A., Borchers, A., and Riedl, J. (1999). An algorithmic framework for performing collaborative filtering. In *Proceedings of the 22nd Annual International ACM SIGIR Conference on Research and Development in Information Retrieval (SIGIR'99)*, pages 230–237. Berkeley, CA.

Herlocker, J. L., Konstan, J. A., and Riedl, J. (2000). Explaining collaborative filtering recommendations. In *Proceedings of the ACM 2000 Conference on Computer Supported Cooperative Work (CSCW 2000)*, pages 241–250, Philadelphia, PA.

Herlocker, J. L., Konstan, J. A., Terveen, L. G., and Riedl, J. (2004). Evaluating collaborative filtering recommender systems. *ACM Transactions on Information Systems*, 22(1):5–53.

Hewitt, C. (1977). Viewing control structures as patterns of passing messages. *Artificial Intelligence*, 8(3):323–364.

Hewitt, C. (1986). Offices are open systems. *ACM Transactions on Office Information Systems*, 4(3):271–287.

Hewitt, C., Bishop, P., and Steiger, R. (1973). A universal modular Actor formalism for artificial intelligence. In *Proceedings of the Third International Joint Conference on Artificial Intelligence (IJCAI-73)*, pages 235–245, Stanford, CA.

Higgins, C. W. (1998). Legal issues of electronic commerce: Activity policies, intelligent agents and ethical transactions. In *Proceedings of the SGML/XML Europe 1998 Conference, From theory to New Practices*, Paris, France.

Hilpinen, R., editor (1971). *Deontic Logic: Introductory and Systematic Readings*. Reidel Publishing Company, Dordrecht.

Hitchcock, D., McBurney, P., and Parsons, S. (2001). A framework for deliberation dialogues. In *Proceedings of the Fourth Biennial Conference of the Ontario Society for the Study of Argumentation*, Windsor, Ontario, Canada.

Howard, J. and Sheth, J. (1969). *The Theory of Buyer Behavior*. John Wiley and Sons, Chichester.

Howden, N., Rönnquist, R., Hodgson, A., and Lucas, A. (2001). JACK Intelligent Agents – Summary of an agent infrastructure. Available at http://www.agent-software.com/shared/resources/reports.html.

Hughes, G. E. and Cresswell, M. J. (1996). *A New Introduction to Modal Logic*. Routledge, London.

Huhns, M. N., editor (1987). *Distributed Artificial Intelligence*. Pitman London and Morgan Kaufmann, San Mateo CA.

Huhns, M. N. and Singh, M. P., editors (1997). *Readings in Agents*. Morgan Kaufmann, San Mateo, CA.

Huhns, M. N. and Stephens, L. M. (1999). Multiagent systems and societies of agents. In Weiss, G., editor, *Multiagent Systems: A Modern Approach to Distributed Artificial Intelligence*, pages 79–120. The MIT Press, Cambridge, MA.

Iglesias, C. A., Garijo, M., Centeno-Gonzalez, J., and Velasco, J. R. (1998). Analysis and design of multi-agent systems using MAS-CommonKADS. In Singh, M. P., Rao, A. S., and Wooldridge, M. J., editors, *Intelligent Agents IV: Agent Theories, Architectures, and Languages (ATAL)*, LNAI Volume 1365, pages 313–327. Springer, Berlin.

Iglesias, C. A., Garijo, M., and Gonzalez, J. (1999). A survey of agent-oriented methodologies. In Müller, J. P., Singh, M. P., and Rao, A. S., editors, *Intelligent Agents V: Agent Theories, Architectures, and Languages (ATAL)*, LNAI Volume 1555, pages 317–330. Springer, Berlin.

Jackson, P. (1986). *Introduction to Expert Systems*. Addison-Wesley, Reading, MA.

Jafari, A. (2002). Conceptualizing intelligent agents for teaching and learning. *Educause Quarterly*, 25(3):28–34.

Jansen, W. and Karygiannis, T. (1999). Mobile agent security. Technical Report NIST Special Publication 800-19, National Institute of Standards and Technology. Available at http://csrc.nist.gov/publications/nistpubs/.

Jason (2006). See http://jason.sourceforge.net/.

Jehle, G. A. and Reny, P. J. (2001). *Advanced Microeconomic Theory*. Addison-Wesley, Reading, MA.

Jenks, J. M. and Kelly, J. M. (1985). *Don't Do, Delegate!* Franklin Watts, New York.

Jennings, N. (1993). Commitments and conventions: The foundation of coordination in multi-agent systems. *Knowledge Engineering Review*, 8(3):223–250.

Jennings, N. R., Faratin, P., Lomuscio, A. R., Parsons, S., Wooldridge, M., and Sierra, C. (2001). Automated negotiation: Prospects methods and challenges. *Group Decision and Negotiation*, 10(2):199–215.

Jennings, N. R., Mamdani, E. H., Corera, J. M., Laresgoiti, I., Perriollat, F., Skarek, P., and Varga, L. Z. (1996). Using Archon to develop real-world DAI applications. *IEEE Expert: Intelligent Systems and Their Applications*, 11(6):64–70.

Jennings, N. R. and Wooldridge, M. (1998). Applications of intelligent agents. In *Agent Technology: Foundations, Applications, and Markets*, pages 3–28. Springer, Berlin.

Jeon, H., Petrie, C. J., and Cutkosky, M. R. (2000). JATLite: A Java agent infrastructure with message routing. *IEEE Internet Computing*, 4(2):87–96.

Johansen, D., Lauvset, K. J., van Renesse, R., Schneider, F. B., Sudmann, N. P., and Jacobsen, K. (2002). A TACOMA retrospective. *Software – Practice and Experience*, 32(6):605–619.

Juan, T., Pearce, A. R., and Sterling, L. (2002). ROADMAP: extending the Gaia methodology for complex open systems. In *Proceedings of the First International Joint Conference on Autonomous Agents and Multiagent Systems (AAMAS'02)*, pages 3–10, Bologna, Italy.

Juan, T., Sterling, L., and Winikoff, M. (2003). Assembling agent oriented software engineering methodologies from features. In *Proceedings of the Third International Workshop on Agent-Oriented Software Engineering (AOSE 2002), Revised Papers and Invited Contributions*, LNAI Volume 2585, pages 198–209. Springer, Berlin.

JumpingBeans (1999). Jumping Beans White Paper. See http://www.JumpingBeans.com. Ad Astra Engineering Inc.

Kaelbling, L. P., Littman, M. L., and Cassandra, A. R. (1998). Planning and acting in partially observable stochastic domains. *Artificial Intelligence*, 101(1-2):99–134.

Karjoth, G., Lange, D. B., and Oshima, M. (1997). A security model for Aglets. *IEEE Internet Computing*, 1(4):68–77.

Keeney, R. L. and Raiffa, H. (1993). *Decisions with Multiple Objectives: Preferences and Value Tradeoffs*. Cambridge University Press, Cambridge.

Kephart, J. O. and Greenwald, A. R. (2002). Shopbot economics. *Autonomous Agents and Multi-Agent Systems*, 5(3):255–287.

Kim, W., Choi, D., Kim, J., and Jin, J. (2005). Development of a meta product search engine with web services. In *Proceedings of the Second Asia Information Retrieval Symposium (AIRS 2005)*, LNCS Volume 3689, pages 571–576. Springer, Berlin.

Kiniry, J. and Zimmerman, D. M. (1997). A hands-on look at Java mobile agents. *IEEE Internet Computing*, 1(4):21–30.

Kinny, D. and Georgeff, M. P. (1991). Commitment and effectiveness of situated agents. In *Proceedings of the 12th International Joint Conference on Artificial Intelligence (IJCAI-01)*, pages 82–88, Sydney, Australia.

Kinny, D., Georgeff, M. P., and Rao, A. S. (1996). A methodology and modelling technique for systems of BDI agents. In Van de Velde, W. and Perram, J. W., editors, *Agents Breaking Away: Proceedings of the Seventh European Workshop on Modelling Autonomous Agents in a Multi-Agent World (MAAMAW-96)*, LNAI Volume 1038, pages 56–71. Springer, Berlin.

Klemperer, P. (1998). Auctions with almost common values. *European Economic Review*, 42(3-5):757–769.

Klemperer, P. (2004). *Auctions: Theory and Practice*. Princeton University Press, Princeton, NJ.

Klusch, M. and Sycara, K. P. (2001). Brokering and matchmaking for coordination of agent societies: A survey. In Omicini, A., Zambonelli, F., Klusch, M., and

Tolksdorf, R., editors, *Coordination of Internet Agents: Models, Technologies, and Applications*, pages 197–224. Springer, Berlin.

Kollock, P. (1999). The production of trust in online markets. In Lawler, E. J., Macy, M., Thyne, S., and Walker, H. A., editors, *Advances in Group Processes*, volume 16, pages 99–123. JAI Press, Greenwich, CT.

Konstan, J. A., Miller, B. N., Maltz, D., Herlocker, J. L., Gordon, L. R., and Riedl, J. (1997). GroupLens: applying collaborative filtering to Usenet news. *Communications of the ACM*, 40(3):77–87.

Kornfeld, W. (1979). ETHER: A parallel problem-solving system. In *Proceedings of the Sixth International Joint Conference on Artificial Intelligence (IJCAI-79)*, pages 490–492, Tokyo, Japan.

Kotz, D. and Gray, R. S. (1999). Mobile agents and the future of the Internet. *Operating Systems Review*, 33(3):7–13.

Kotz, D., Gray, R. S., Nog, S., Rus, D., Chawla, S., and Cybenko, G. (1997). AGENT Tcl: Targeting the needs of mobile computers. *IEEE Internet Computing*, 1(4):58–67.

Kowalczyk, R., Brown, P., Mueller, I., Rossak, W., Franczyk, B., and Speck, A. (2003a). Deploying mobile and intelligent agents in interconnected e-marketplaces. *Transactions of the Society for Design and Process Science*, 7(3):109–123.

Kowalczyk, R., Ulieru, M., and Unland, R. (2003b). Integrating mobile and intelligent agents in advanced e-commerce: A survey. In Kowalczyk, R., Müller, J. P., Tianfield, H., and Unland, R., editors, *Agent Technologies, Infrastructures, Tools, and Applications for E-Services, NODe 2002 Agent-Related Workshops, Revised Papers*, LNCS Volume 2592, pages 295–313. Springer, Berlin.

Kraus, S. (2001). *Strategic Negotiation in Multiagent Environments*. The MIT Press, Cambridge, MA.

Kraus, S., Sycara, K. P., and Evenchik, A. (1998). Reaching agreements through argumentation: A logical model and implementation. *Artificial Intelligence*, 104(1-2):1–69.

Krause, P., Ambler, S., Elvang-Goransson, M., and Fox, J. (1995). A logic of argumentation for reasoning under uncertainty. *Computational Intelligence*, 11:113–131.

Kreps, D. M. and Wilson, R. (1982). Sequential equilibrium. *Econometrica*, 50:863–894.

Krishna, V. (2002). *Auction Theory*. Academic Press, San Diego, CA.

Krulwich, B. and Burkey, C. (1996). Learning user information interests through the extraction of semantically significant phrases. In *Proceedings of the AAAI Spring Symposium on Machine Learning in Information Access*, pages 110–112, Stanford, CA.

Krulwich, B. and Burkey, C. (1997). The InfoFinder agent: Learning user interests through heuristic phrase extraction. *IEEE Expert: Intelligent Systems and Their Applications*, 12(5):22–27.

Krulwich, B. T. (1996). The BargainFinder agent: Comparing price shopping on the Internet. In Williams, J., editor, *Bots and other Internet beasties*, pages 258–263. SAMS.NET, Macmillan.

Labrou, Y. and Finin, T. (1997). Semantics and conversations for an agent communication language. In Huhns, M. and Singh, M., editors, *Readings in Agents*, pages 235–242. Morgan Kaufmann, San Mateo, CA.

Labrou, Y. and Finin, T. (1998). Semantics for an agent communication language. In Singh, M. P., Rao, A., and Wooldridge, M. J., editors, *Intelligent Agents IV: Agent Theories, Architectures, and Languages (ATAL)*, LNAI Volume 1365, pages 209–214. Springer, Berlin.

Labrou, Y., Finin, T., and Mayfield, J. (1997). KQML as an agent communication language. In Bradshaw, J., editor, *Software Agents*, pages 291–316. The MIT Press, Cambridge, MA.

Labrou, Y., Finin, T., and Peng, Y. (1999). Agent communication languages: The current landscape. *IEEE Intelligent Systems*, 14(2):45–52.

Lai, K., Rasmusson, L., Adar, E., Sorkin, S., Zhang, L., and Huberman, B. A. (2004). Tycoon: An Implementation of a Distributed Market-Based Resource Allocation System. Technical Report arXiv:cs.DC/0412038, HP Labs, Palo Alto, CA, USA.

Lang, K. (1995). NewsWeeder: learning to filter netnews. In *Proceedings of the 12th International Conference on Machine Learning (ICML'95)*, pages 331–339, Tahoe City, CA.

Lange, D. B. and Aridor, Y. (1997). Agent Transfer Protocol – atp/0.1. Available at http://www.trl.ibm.com/aglets/atp/atp.htm.

Lange, D. B. and Oshima, M. (1998). *Programming and deploying Java Mobile Agents with Aglets*. Addison-Wesley, Reading, MA.

Lange, D. B. and Oshima, M. (1999). Seven good reasons for mobile agents. *Communications of the ACM*, 42(3):88–89.

LeBaron, B., Arthur, W. B., and Palmer, R. (1999). Time series properties of an artificial stock market. *Journal of Economic Dynamics and Control*, 23:1487–1516.

Lee, J. and Moray, N. (1992). Trust, control strategies and allocation of function in human-machine systems. *Ergonomics*, 35(10):1243–1270.

Lieberman, H. (1995). Letizia: An agent that assists web browsing. In *Proceedings of the 14th International Joint Conference on Artificial Intelligence (IJCAI-95)*, pages 924–929, Montreal, Quebec.

Lieberman, H., Fry, C., and Weitzman, L. (2001). Exploring the web with reconnaissance agents. *Communications of the ACM*, 44(8):69–75.

Linden, G., Smith, B., and York, J. (2003). Amazon.com recommendations: Item-to-item collaborative filtering. *IEEE Internet Computing*, 7(1):76–80.

Lindley, D. V. (1971). *Making Decisions*. Wiley-Interscience, London.

Linketscher, N. and Child, M. (2001). Trust issues and user reactions to e-services and e-marketplaces: A customer survey. In Min Tjoa, A. and Wagner, R., editors, *Proceedings of the 12th International Workshop on Database and Expert Systems Applications (DEXA 2001)*, pages 752–756, Munich, Germany.

Luce, R. D. and Raiffa, H. (1957). *Games and Decisions*. John Wiley and Sons, Chichester.

Luck, M., Ashri, R., and d'Inverno, M. (2004). *Agent-based Software Development*. Artech House, London.

Luck, M. and d'Inverno, M. (1995). A formal framework for agency and autonomy. In Lesser, V. R. and Gasser, L., editors, *Proceedings of the First International Conference on Multi-Agent Systems (ICMAS-95)*, pages 254–260. San Francisco, CA.

Luck, M., Griffiths, N., and d'Inverno, M. (1997). From agent theory to agent construction: A case study. In Müller, J. P., Wooldridge, M. J., and Jennings, N. R., editors, *Intelligent Agents III: Theories, Architectures, and Languages*, LNAI Volume 1193, pages 49–63. Springer, Berlin.

Luhmann, N. (1979). *Trust and Power: Two Works*. John Wiley and Sons, Chichester.

Luhmann, N. (1990). Familiarity, confidence, trust: Problems and alternatives. In Gambetta, D., editor, *Trust: making and breaking cooperative relations*, pages 94–109. Basil Blackwell, Oxford.

Lybäck, D. and Boman, M. (2004). Agent trade servers in financial exchange systems. *ACM Transactions on Internet Technology*, 4(3):329–339.

MacKenzie, J. D. (1979). Question-begging in non-cumulative systems. *Journal of Philosophical logic*, 8:117–133.

Maes, P. (1994). Agents that reduce work and information overload. *Communications of the ACM*, 37(7):30–40.

Maes, P. (1995). Artificial life meets entertainment: Lifelike autonomous agents. *Communications of the ACM*, 38(11):108–114.

Maes, P., Guttman, R., and Moukas, A. (1999). Agents that buy and sell: Transforming commerce as we know it. *Communications of the ACM*, 42(3):81–91.

Magerko, B., Laird, J. E., Assanie, M., Kerfoot, A., and Stokes, D. (2004). AI characters and directors for interactive computer games. In *Proceedings of the 19th National Conference on Artificial Intelligence, 16th Conference on Innovative Applications of Artificial Intelligence (AAAI/IAAI)*, pages 877–883, San Jose, CA.

Marik, V. and McFarlane, D. (2005). Industrial adoption of agent-based technologies. *IEEE Intelligent Systems*, 20(1):27–35.

Markopoulos, P. M. and Kephart, J. O. (2002). How valuable are shopbots? In *Proceedings of the First International Joint Conference on Autonomous Agents and Multiagent Systems (AAMAS'02)*, pages 1009–1016, Bologna, Italy.

Marsh, S. (1994). *Formalising Trust as a Computational Concept*. PhD thesis, Department of Mathematics and Computer Science, University of Stirling, UK.

Martin, D. L., Paolucci, M., McIlraith, S. A., Burstein, M. H., McDermott, D. V., McGuinness, D. L., Parsia, B., Payne, T. R., Sabou, M., Solanki, M., Srinivasan, N., and Sycara, K. P. (2004). Bringing semantics to web services: The OWL-S approach. In *Proceedings of the First International Workshop on Semantic Web Services and Web Process Composition, (SWSWPC 2004), Revised Selected Papers*, LNAI Volume 3387, pages 26–42. Springer, Berlin.

Martin, D. M. (1998). Internet anonymizing techniques. *;login:Magazine*. Available at http://www.usenix.org/publications/login/1998-5/martin.html.

Mas-Colell, A., Whinston, M. D., and Green, J. R. (1995). *Microeconomic Theory*. Oxford University Press, Oxford.

Massive (2006). See http://www.massivesoftware.com/feature.html.

McAfee, R. P. and McMillan, J. (1987). Auctions and bidding. *Journal of Economic Literature*, 25(2):699–738.

McBurney, P. and Parsons, S. (2001). Representing epistemic uncertainty by means of dialectical argumentation. *Annals of Mathematics and Artificial Intelligence*, 32(1-4):125–169.

McBurney, P. and Parsons, S. (2003). Dialogue game protocols. In *Communication in Multiagent Systems: Agent Communication Languages and Conversation Policies*, LNAI Volume 2650, pages 269–283. Springer, Berlin.

McBurney, P., van Eijk, R. M., Parsons, S., and Amgoud, L. (2003). A dialogue-game protocol for agent purchase negotiations. *Autonomous Agents and Multi-agent Systems*, 7(3):235–273.

McCabe, K. A. and Smith, V. L. (1993). Designing a uniform-price double auction: An experimental evaluation. In Friedman, D. and Rust, J., editors, *The Double Auction Market: Institutions, Theories and Evidence*, SFI Studies in the Sciences of Complexity, pages 307–332. Addison-Wesley Longman, Reading, MA.

McCarthy, J. (1958). Programs with common sense. In *Proceedings of the Symposium on Mechanisation of Thought Processes*, volume 1, pages 77–84, London. Her Majesty's Stationery Office.

McCarthy, J. (1979). Ascribing mental qualities to machines. In Ringle, M., editor, *Philosophical Perspectives in Artificial Intelligence*, pages 161–195. Humanities Press, Atlantic Highlands, NJ.

Menczer, F., Monge, A. E., and Street, W. N. (2002a). Adaptive assistants for e-shopping. *IEEE Intelligent Systems*, 17(6):12–19.

Menczer, F., Street, W. N., Vishwakarma, N., Monge, A. E., and Jakobsson, M. (2002b). IntelliShopper: a proactive, personal, private shopping assistant. In *Proceedings of the First International Joint Conference on Autonomous Agents and Multiagent Systems (AAMAS'02)*, pages 1001–1008, Bologna, Italy.

Menezes, F. M. and Monteiro, P. K. (2005). *An Introduction to Auction Theory*. Oxford University Press, Oxford.

Michalakopoulos, M. and Fasli, M. (2005). On deciding to trust. In *Proceedings of the Third International Conference on Trust Management (iTrust)*, LNAI Volume 3477, pages 61–76. Springer, Berlin.

Milgrom, P. (2002). *Putting Auction Theory to Work*. Cambridge University Press, Cambridge.

Miller, B. N., Albert, I., Lam, S. K., Konstan, J. A., and Riedl, J. (2003). MovieLens unplugged: Experiences with an occasionally connected recommender system. In *Proceedings of the 2003 International Conference on Intelligent User Interfaces (IUI)*, pages 263–266, Miami, FL.

Milnor, J. (1954). Games against nature. In Thrall, R. M., Coombs, C. H., and Davis, R. L., editors, *Decision Processes*, pages 49–60. Wiley and Chapman & Hall, New York and London.

Milojicic, D. S., Breugst, M., Busse, I., Campbell, J., Covaci, S., Friedman, B., Kosaka, K., Lange, D. B., Ono, K., Oshima, M., Tham, C., Virdhagriswaran, S., and White, J. (1998). MASIF: The OMG Mobile Agent System Interoperability Facility. *Personal and Ubiquitous Computing*, 2(2).

Milojicic, D. S., Douglis, F., and Wheeler, R., editors (1999). *Mobility: Processes, Computers, and Agents*. ACM Press, New York, NY.

Mitchell, T. M. (1997). *Machine Learning*. McGraw-Hill, Boston, MA.

Montaner, M., Lopez, B., and de la Rosa, J. L. (2003). A taxonomy of recommender agents on the Internet. *Artificial Intelligence Review*, 19(4):285–330.

MovieLens (2006). See http://movielens.umn.edu/login.

Müller, J. P. (1997). A cooperation model for autonomous agents. In Müller, J. P., Wooldridge, M., and Jennings, N. R., editors, *Intelligent Agents III: Agent Theories, Architectures, and Languages (ATAL)*, LNAI Volume 1193, pages 245–260. Springer, Berlin.

Müller, J. P., Pischel, M., and Thiel, M. (1995). Modelling reactive behaviour in vertically layered agent architectures. In Wooldridge, M. and Jennings, N. R., editors, *Intelligent Agents: Agent Theories, Architectures, and Languages (ATAL)*, LNAI Volume 890, pages 261–276. Springer, Berlin.

Muthoo, A. (1999). *Bargaining Theory with Applications*. Cambridge University Press, Cambridge.

Muthoo, A. (2000). A non-technical introduction to bargaining theory. *World Economics*, 1(2):145–166.

Myerson, R. (1981). Optimal auction design. *Mathematics of Operations Research*, 6:58–73.

MySimon (2006). See http://www.mysimon.com/.

Nash, J. (1950a). The bargaining problem. *Econometrica*, 18(2):155–162.

Nash, J. (1950b). Equilibrium points in n-person games. *Proceedings of the National Academy of Sciences*, 36:48–49.

Nash, J. (1953). Two-person cooperative games. *Econometrica*, 21(1):128–140.

Ndumu, D. and Nwana, H. (1997). Research and development challenges for agent-based systems. *IEE Proceedings On Software Engineering*, 144(1):2–10.

Negroponte, N. (1995). *Being Digital*. Alfred A. Knopf, New York.

Neumann, D. and Weinhardt, C. (2002). Domain-independent eNegotiation design: Prospects, methods, and challenges. In *Proceedings of the 13th International Workshop on Database and Expert Systems Applications (DEXA'02)*, pages 680–686, Aix-en-Provence, France.

Newell, A. (1962). Some problems of basic organization in problem solving programs. In Yovits, M. C., Jacobi, G. T., and Goldstein, G. D., editors, *Self Organizing Systems*, pages 393–423. Spartan Books, Washington, DC.

Newell, A. (1982). The knowledge level. *Artificial Intelligence*, 18(1):87–127.

Nicosia, F. (1966). *Consumer Decision Processes: Marketing and Advertising Implications*. Prentice Hall, Englewood Cliffs, NJ.

Nilsson, N. J. (1996). Introduction to machine learning. Available at **http://ai.stanford.edu/people/nilsson/mlbook.html**.

Nisan, N. (1999). Algorithms for selfish agents. In *Proceedings of the 16th Annual Symposium on Theoretical Aspects of Computer Science, (STACS'99)*, LNCS Volume 1563, pages 1–15. Springer, Berlin.

Nisan, N. (2000). Bidding and allocation in combinatorial auctions. In *Proceedings of the Second ACM Conference on Electronic Commerce (EC-00)*, pages 1–12, Minneapolis, MN.

Nisan, N. and Ronen, A. (2001). Algorithmic mechanism design. *Games and Economic Behavior*, 35:166–196.

Nodine, M. H. and Unruh, A. (1998). Facilitating open communication in agent systems: The InfoSleuth infrastructure. In Singh, M. P., Rao, A. S., and Wooldridge, M., editors, *Intelligent Agents IV: Agent Theories, Architectures, and Languages (ATAL)*, LNAI Volume 1365, pages 281–295. Springer, Berlin.

Norman, D. A. (1990). The "problem" of automation: Inappropriate feedback and interaction, not "over-automation". In Broadbent, D. E., Baddeley, A., and Reason, J. T., editors, *Human factors in hazardous situations*, pages 585–593. Oxford University Press, Oxford.

Norman, T. J., Preece, A. D., Chalmers, S., Jennings, N. R., Luck, M., Dang, V. D., Nguyen, T. D., Deora, V., Shao, J., Gray, W. A., and Fiddian, N. J. (2004). Agent-based formation of virtual organisations. *International Journal of Knowledge Based Systems*, 17(2-4):103–111.

North, D. C. (1990). *Institutions, Institutional Change and Economic Performance*. Cambridge University Press, Cambridge.

Noy, N. F. and McGuinness, D. L. (2001). Ontology development 101: A guide to creating your first ontology. Available at **http://www.ksl.stanford.edu/people/dlm/papers/ontology101/ontology101-noy-mcguinness.html**.

Nwana, H. S., Ndumu, D. T., Lee, L. C., and Collis, J. C. (1999). ZEUS: A toolkit for building distributed multiagent systems. *Applied Artificial Intelligence*, 13(1-2):129–185.

Oates, D. (1993). *Leadership: The Art of Delegation*. Century Business, London.

Odell, J. (1998). Agents and emergence. *Distributed Computing*, pages 45–50.

Odell, J. (2000). Agent technology. Green Paper. OMG – Agent Platform Special Interest Group. Available at **http://www.jamesodell.com/ec2000-08-01.pdf**.

Odell, J. (2002). Objects and agents compared. *Journal of Object Technology*, 1(1):41–53.

Odell, J., Van Dyke Parunak, H., and Bauer, B. (2000). Representing agent interaction protocols in UML. In Ciancarini, P. and Wooldridge, M., editors, *Proceedings of the First International Workshop on Agent-Oriented Software Engineering (AOSE 2000)*, LNAI Volume 1957, pages 121–140. Springer, Berlin.

OMG (2006). Object Management Group. See **http://www.omg.org**.

onSale (2006). See http://www.onsale.com/.

Osborne, M. J. and Rubinstein, A. (1990). *Bargaining and Markets*. Academic Press, San Diego, CA.

Osborne, M. J. and Rubinstein, A. (1994). *A Course in Game Theory*. The MIT Press, Cambridge, MA.

Ostrom, E. (1990). *Governing the Commons: The Evolution of Institutions for Collective Action*. Cambridge University Press, Cambridge.

Ousterhout, J. K. (1994). *Tcl and the Tk Toolkit*. Addison-Wesley, Reading, MA.

OWL (2006). The OWL Web Ontology Language. See http://www.w3.org/TR/owl-features/.

OWL-S (2006). OWL-S: Semantic Markup for Web Services. See http://www.w3.org/Submission/OWL-S/.

Padgham, L. and Winikoff, M. (2002). Prometheus: A methodology for developing intelligent agents. In *Proceedings of the First International Joint Conference on Autonomous Agents and Multiagent Systems (AAMAS'02)*, pages 37–38, Bologna, Italy.

Padgham, L. and Winikoff, M. (2004). *Developing Intelligent Agent Systems: A Practical Guide*. John Wiley and Sons, Chichester.

Paolucci, M., Kawamura, T., Payne, T. R., and Sycara, K. P. (2002). Semantic matching of web services capabilities. In *Proceedings of the First International Semantic Web Conference (ISWC '02)*, LNAI Volume 2342, pages 333–347. Springer, Berlin.

Papadimitriou, C. H. (2001). Algorithms, games and the Internet. In *Proceedings of the 33rd Annual ACM Symposium on the Theory of Computing (STOC 2001)*, pages 749–753, Heraclion, Greece.

Parkes, D. C. (1999). *i*Bundle: an efficient ascending price bundle auction. In *Proceedings of the First ACM Conference on Electronic Commerce (EC-99)*, pages 148–157, Denver, CO.

Parkes, D. C. (2001). *Iterative Combinatorial Auctions: Achieving Economic and Computational Efficiency*. PhD thesis, University of Pennsylvania.

Parkes, D. C. (2006). Iterative combinatorial auctions. In Crampton, P., Shoham, Y., and Steinberg, R., editors, *Combinatorial Auctions*, pages 41–77. The MIT Press, Cambridge, MA.

Parkes, D. C. and Shneidman, J. (2004). Distributed implementations of Vickrey-Clarke-Groves mechanism. In *Proceedings of the Third International Joint Conference on Autonomous Agents and Multiagent Systems (AAMAS'04)*, pages 261–268, New York, NY.

Parkes, D. C. and Ungar, L. H. (2000). Iterative combinatorial auctions: Theory and practice. In *Proceedings of the 17th National Conference on Artificial Intelligence and 12th Conference on Innovative Applications of Artificial Intelligence (AAAI/IAAI)*, pages 74–81, Austin, TX.

Parsons, S., Sierra, C., and Jennings, N. R. (1998). Agents that reason and negotiate by arguing. *Journal of Logic and Computation*, 8(3):261–292.

Patil, R. S., Fikes, R. E., Patel-Schneider, P. F., McCay, D., Finin, T., Gruber, T., and Neches, R. (1997). The DARPA Knowledge Sharing Effort: Progress report. In Huhns, M. and Singh, M. P., editors, *Readings in Agents*, pages 243–254. Morgan Kaufmann, San Mateo, CA.

Patrick, A. S. (2002). Building trustworthy software agents. *IEEE Internet Computing*, 6(6):46–53.

Paul, D. B. and Baker, J. B. (1992). The design for the Wall Street Journal-based CSR corpus. In *Human Language Technology Conference (HLT'91). Proceedings of the Workshop on Speech and Natural Language*, pages 357–362.

Pechoucek, M., Riha, A., Vokrinek, J., Marik, V., and Prazma, V. (2002). ExPlanTech: applying multi-agent systems in production planning. *International Journal of Production Research*, 40(15):3681–3692.

Peine, H. (2002). Application and programming experience with the Ara mobile agent system. *Software –Practice and Experience*, 32(6):515–541.

Peine, H. and Stolpmann, T. (1997). The architecture of the Ara platform for mobile agents. In Rothermel, K. and Popescu-Zeletin, R., editors, *Proceedings of the First International Workshop on Mobile Agents (MA'97)*, LNAI Volume 1219, pages 50–61. Springer, Berlin.

Pekec, A. and Rothkopf, M. H. (2003). Combinatorial auction design. *Management Science*, 49(11):1485–1503.

Pennock, D. M., Horvitz, E., Lawrence, S., and Lee Giles, C. (2000). Collaborative filtering by personality diagnosis: A hybrid memory and model-based approach. In *Proceedings of the 16th Conference in Uncertainty in Artificial Intelligence (UAI'00)*, pages 473–480, Stanford, CA.

Petersen, S. A., Divitini, M., and Matskin, M. (2001). An agent-based approach to modelling virtual enterprises. *Production, Planning and Control*, 12(3):224–233.

Petersen, S. A. and Greninger, M. (2000). An agent-based model to support the formation of virtual enterprises. In *Proceedings of the International ICSC Symposium on Mobile Agents and Multi-agents in Virtual Organisations and E-commerce (MAMA'2000)*, Woolongong, Australia.

Petrie, C. J. and Bussler, C. (2003). Service agents and virtual enterprises: A survey. *IEEE Internet Computing*, 7(4):68–78.

Pine, B. J. (1999). *Mass Customization*. Harvard Business School Press, Boston, MA.

Pine, B. J., Peppers, D., and Rogers, M. (1995). Do you want to keep your customers forever? *Harvard Business School Review*, 2:103–114.

Poslad, S., Buckle, P., and Hadingham, R. (2000). The FIPA-OS agent platform: Open source for open standards. In *Proceedings of the Fifth International Conference and Exhibition on the Practical Application of Intelligent Agents and Multi-Agent Technology (PAAM-00)*, pages 355–368, Manchester, UK.

Poslad, S., Charlton, P., and Calisti, M. (2002). Specifying standard security mechanisms in multi-agent systems. In Falcone, R., Barber, K. S., Korba, L., and Singh, M. P., editors, *Trust, Reputation, and Security: Theories and Practice, AAMAS 2002 International Workshop, Selected and Invited Papers*, LNAI Volume 2631, pages 163–176. Springer, Berlin.

Prins, J. E. J., Ribbers, P. M. A., van Tilborg, H. C. A., Veth, A. F. L., and van der Wees, J. G. L., editors (2002). *Trust in electronic commerce: The role of trust from a legal, an organizational and a technical point of view*. Kluwer Law International, The Hague.

Protege (2006). See http://protege.stanford.edu/.

Puterman, M. L. (1994). *Markov Decision Processes*. John Wiley and Sons, Chichester.

Rabelo, R. J., Camarinha-Matos, L. M., and Afsarmanesh, H. (1999). Multi-agent-based agile scheduling. *Robotics and Autonomous Systems*, 27(1-2):15–28.

Rahwan, I., Ramchurn, S. D., Jennings, N. R., McBurney, P., Parsons, S., and Sonenberg, L. (2003). Argumentation-based negotiation. *Knowledge Engineering Review*, 18(4):343–375.

Raiffa, H. (1997). *Decision Analysis: Introductory Lectures on Choices Under Uncertainty*. Addison-Wesley, Reading, MA.

Rajiv, V. and Aggarwal, P. (2002). The impact of shopping agents on small business e-commerce strategy. *Journal of Small Business Strategy*, 13(1):62–79.

Rao, A. S. (1996). AgentSpeak(L): BDI agents speak out in logical computable language. In Van de Velde, W. and Perram, J. W., editors, *Agents Breaking Away: Proceedings of the Seventh European Workshop on Modelling Autonomous Agents in a Multi-Agent World (MAAMAW-96)*, LNAI Volume 1038, pages 42–55. Springer, Berlin.

Rao, A. S. and Georgeff, M. P. (1991). Modeling rational agents within a BDI-architecture. In *Proceedings of the Second International Conference on Principles of Knowledge Representation and Reasoning (KR'91)*, pages 473–484, Cambridge, MA.

Rao, A. S. and Georgeff, M. P. (1998). Decision procedures for BDI logics. *Journal of Logic and Computation*, 8(3):293–343.

Rasmusen, E. (2001). *Games and Information*. Blackwell Publishers, Malden, MA.

Reddy, D. R., Erman, L. D., Fennell, R. D., and Neely, R. B. (1973). The Hearsay speech understanding system: An example of the recognition process. In *Proceedings of the Third International Joint Conference on Artificial Intelligence (IJCAI-73)*, pages 185–193, Stanford, CA.

Reichheld, F. R. (1993). Loyalty-based management. *Harvard Business School Review*, 2:64–73.

Reichheld, F. R. and Sasser Jr, W. E. (1990). Zero defections: Quality comes to services. *Harvard Business School Review*, 5:105–111.

Resnick, P., Iacovou, N., Suchak, M., Bergstorm, P., and Riedl, J. (1994). GroupLens: An Open Architecture for Collaborative Filtering of Netnews. In *Proceedings of ACM 1994 Conference on Computer Supported Cooperative Work (CSCW)*, pages 175–186, Chapel Hill, NC.

Resnick, P., Kuwabara, K., Zeckhauser, R., and Friedman, E. (2000). Reputation systems. *Communications of the ACM*, 43(12):45–48.

Resnick, P. and Varian, H. R. (1997). Recommender systems. *Communications of the ACM*, 40(3):56–58.

Rhee, M. Y. (2003). *Internet Security: Cryptographic Principles, Algorithms and Protocols*. John Wiley and Sons, Chichester.

Rieder, B. (2003). Agent technology and the delegation paradigm in a networked society. Presented at the New Media, Technology and Everyday Life in Europe Conference 2003. Available at http://www.lse.ac.uk/collections/EMTEL/Conference/papers/Rieder.pdf.

Riegelsberger, J. and Sasse, A. M. (2001). Trustbuilders and trustbusters: The role of trust in interfaces to e-commerce applications. In *Proceedings of the First IFIP Conference on Towards The E-Society: E-Commerce, E-Business, and E-Government (I3E 2001)*, pages 17–30, Zurich, Switzerland.

Riley, J. G. and Samuelson, F. W. (1981). Optimal auctions. *The American Economic Review*, 71(3):381–392.

RoboShopper (2006). See http://www.roboshopper.com/.

Rodríguez, J. A., Noriega, P., Sierra, C., and Padget, J. (1997). FM96.5 A Java-based electronic auction house. In *Proceedings of the Second International Conference on the Practical Application of Intelligent Agents and Multi-Agent Technology (PAAM-97)*, pages 207–224, London, UK.

Rosenbloom, A. (2000). Trusting technology: Introduction. *Communications of the ACM*, 43(12):31–32.

Rosenchein, J. S. and Zlotkin, G. (1994). *Rules of Encounter*. The MIT Press, Cambridge, MA.

Rosenfield, R. (1994). *Adaptive Statistic Language Model*. PhD thesis, Carnegie Mellon University.

Roth, A. E. and Ockenfels, A. (2002). Last-minute bidding and the rules for ending second-price auctions: Evidence from eBay and Amazon auctions on the Internet. *American Economic Review*, 92(4):1093–1103.

Rothkopf, M. H., Pekec, A., and Harstad, R. M. (1998). Computationally manageable combinatorial auctions. *Management Science*, 44(8):1131–1147.

Rotter, J. B. (1980). Interpersonal trust, trustworthiness and gullibility. *American Psychologist*, 35(1):1–7.

Russell, S. and Norvig, P. (2003). *Artificial Intelligence: A Modern Approach*. Prentice Hall, Englewood Cliffs, NJ.

Sadek, M. D. (1992). A study in the logic of intention. In *Proceedings of the Third International Conference on Principles of Knowledge Representation and Reasoning (KR'92)*, pages 462–473, Cambridge, MA.

Sadri, F., Toni, F., and Torroni, P. (2001). Logic agents, dialogues and negotiation: An abductive approach. In *Proceedings of the Symposium on Information Agents for E-commerce, Artificial Intelligence and the Simulation of Behaviour Conference (AISB-2001)*, York, UK.

Salton, G., Fox, E. A., and Wu, H. (1983). Extended Boolean information retrieval. *Communications of the ACM*, 26(11):1022–1036.

Salton, G. and McGill, M. J. (1983). *Introduction to Modern Information Retrieval*. McGraw-Hill, New York, NY.

Sander, T. and Tschudin, C. F. (1998). Protecting mobile agents against malicious hosts. In *Mobile Agents and Security*, LNAI Volume 1419, pages 44–60. Springer, Berlin.

Sandholm, T. (1999). Distributed rational decision making. In Weiss, G., editor, *Multiagent Systems: A Modern Approach to Distributed Artificial Intelligence*, pages 201–258. The MIT Press, Cambridge, MA.

Sandholm, T. and Huai, Q. (2000). Nomad: Mobile agent system for an Internet-based auction house. *IEEE Internet Computing*, 4(2):80–86.

Sandholm, T., Larson, K., Andersson, M., Shehory, O., and Tohme, F. (1999). Coalition structure generation with worst case guarantees. *Artificial Intelligence*, 111(1-2):209–238.

Sartor, G. (2002). Agents in Cyberlaw. In Sartor, G. and Cevenini, C., editors, *Proceedings of the Workshop on the Law of Electronic Agents (LEA 2002)*, Bologna, Italy.

Sarwar, B. M., Karypis, G., Konstan, J. A., and Reidl, J. (2001). Item-based collaborative filtering recommendation algorithms. In *Proceedings of the 10th International World Wide Web Conference, (WWW 2001)*, pages 285–295, Hong Kong, China.

Schafer, J. B., Konstan, J. A., and Riedl, J. (2001). E-commerce recommendation applications. *Data Mining and Knowledge Discovery*, 5(1/2):115–153.

Schein, A. I., Popescul, A., Ungar, L. H., and Pennock, D. M. (2002). Methods and metrics for cold-start recommendations. In *Proceedings of the 25th Annual International ACM SIGIR Conference on Research and Development in Information Retrieval*, pages 253–260, Tampere, Finland.

Schelling, T. C. (1960). *The strategy of conflict*. Harvard University Press, Cambridge.

Schmidt-Schauß, M. (1988). Implication of clauses is undecidable. *Theoretical Computer Science*, 59:287–296.

Schneider, J., Kortuem, G., Jager, J., Fickas, S., and Segall, Z. (2000). Disseminating trust information in wearable communities. *Personal and Ubiquitous Computing*, 4(4):245–248.

Schoder, D. and Eymann, T. (2000). The real challenges of mobile agents. *Communications of the ACM*, 43(6):111–112.

Searle, J. R. (1969). *Speech Acts: An Essay in the Philosophy of Language*. Cambridge University Press, Cambridge.

Sen, S. and Weiss, G. (1999). Learning in Multiagent Systems. In Weiss, G., editor, *Multiagent Systems: A Modern Approach to Distributed Artificial Intelligence*, pages 259–298. The MIT Press, Cambridge, MA.

Senicar, V., Jerman-Blazic, B., and Klobucar, T. (2003). Privacy-enhancing technologies: Approaches and development. *Computer Standards and Interfaces*, 25(2):147–158.

Shafer, G. and Pearl, J., editors (1990). *Readings in Uncertain Reasoning*. Morgan Kaufmann, San Mateo, CA.

Shapiro, S. P. (1987). The social control of impersonal trust. *American Journal of Sociology*, 93(3):623–658.

Shapley, L. S. (1953). A value for n-person games. In Kuhn, H. and Tucker, A. W., editors, *Contributions to the Theory Games II*, volume 28 of *Annals of Mathematical Studies*, pages 307–317. Princeton University Press, Princeton, NJ.

Shardanand, U. and Maes, P. (1995). Social information filtering: Algorithms for automating "word of mouth". In *Proceedings of the ACM Conference on Human Factors in Computing Systems (CHI'95)*, pages 210–217, Denver, CO.

Shehory, O. and Kraus, S. (1998). Methods for task allocation via agent coalition formation. *Artificial Intelligence*, 101(1-2):165–200.

Sheth, B. and Maes, P. (1993). Evolving agents for personalized information filtering. In *Proceedings of the Ninth Conference on Artificial Intelligence for Applications (CAIA'93)*, pages 345–352, Orlando, FL.

Shneiderman, B. (2000). Designing trust into online experiences. *Communications of the ACM*, 43(12):57–59.

Shoham, Y. (1993). Agent-oriented programming. *Artificial Intelligence*, 60(1):51–92.

Shoham, Y. (1997). An overview of agent-oriented programming. In Bradshaw, J. M., editor, *Software Agents*, pages 271–290. The MIT Press, Cambridge, MA.

Shortliffe, E. H. (1976). *Computer-based Medical Consultations: MYCIN*. Elsevier, New York, NY.

Sierra, C. and Noriega, P. (2002). Agent-mediated interaction: From auctions to negotiation and argumentation. In d'Inverno, M., Luck, M., Fisher, M., and Preist, C., editors, *Foundations and applications of Multi-agent systems: UKMAS Workshops 1996–2000, Selected Papers*, LNAI Volume 2403, pages 27–48. Springer, Berlin.

Silva, A., da Silva, M. M., and Delgado, J. (1998). An overview of AgentSpace: A next-generation mobile agent system. In *Proceedings of the Second International Workshop on Mobile Agents (MA'98)*, LNAI Volume 1477, pages 148–159. Springer, Berlin.

Singh, M. P. and Huhns, M. N. (2005). *Service-oriented computing: Semantics, Processes, Agents*. John Wiley and Sons, Chichester.

Skarmeas, N. (1999). *Agents as objects with knowledge base state*. World Scientific Publishing Co., Inc., River Edge, NJ.

Smith, R. G. (1977). The CONTRACT NET: A formalism for the control of distributed problem solving. In *Proceedings of the Fifth International Joint Conference on Artificial Intelligence (IJCAI-77)*, page 472, Cambridge, MA.

Smith, R. G. (1980a). The contract net protocol: High level communication and control in distributed problem solving. *IEEE Transactions on Computers*, 29(12):1104–1113.

Smith, R. G. (1980b). A framework for distributed problem solving. UMI Research Papers.

Smith, R. G. and Davis, R. (1981). Frameworks for cooperation in distributed problem solving. *IEEE Transactions on Systems, Man and Cybernetics*, 11(1):61–70.

SOAP (2006). Simple Object Access Protocol. See http://www.w3.org/TR/soap/.

Stallings, W. (2003). *Network Security Essentials: Applications and Standards*. Prentice Hall, Upper Saddle River, NJ.

Stanford-Smith, B. and Kidd, P. T., editors (2000). *E-business: Key Issues, Applications and Technologies*. IOS Press, Amsterdam.

Steels, L. (1990). Cooperation between distributed agents through self organization. In Demazeau, Y. and Müller, J.-P., editors, *Decentralized AI – Proceedings of the First European Workshop on Modelling Autonomous Agents in a Multi-agent World (MAAMAW-89)*, pages 175–196. Elsevier, Amsterdam.

Stone, P. (2000). *Layered Learning in Multiagent Systems: A Winning Approach to Robotic Soccer*. The MIT Press, Cambridge, MA.

Sun, J. and Sadeh, N. M. (2004). Coordinating multi-attribute procurement auctions subject to finite capacity considerations. Technical Report CMU-ISRI-03-105, e-Supply Chain Management Laboratory, Institute for Software Research International, School of Computer Science, Carnegie Mellon University.

Suri, N. (2001). State capture and resource control for Java: The design and implementation of the Aroma virtual machine. In *Proceedings of the First Java Virtual Machine Research and Technology Symposium*, Monterey, CA.

Suri, N., Bradshaw, J. M., Breedy, M. R., Groth, P. T., Hill, G. A., and Jeffers, R. (2000a). Strong mobility and fine-grained resource control in NOMADS. In *Agent Systems, Mobile Agents, and Applications, Proceedings of the Second International Symposium on Agent Systems and Applications and Fourth International Symposium on Mobile Agents (ASA/MA)*, LNAI Volume 1882, pages 2–15. Springer, Berlin.

Suri, N., Bradshaw, J. M., Breedy, M. R., Groth, P. T., Hill, G. A., Jeffers, R., Mitrovich, T. S., Pouliot, B. R., and Smith, D. S. (2000b). NOMADS: Toward a strong and safe mobile agent system. In *Proceedings of the Fourth International Conference on Autonomous Agents (Agents 00)*, pages 163–164, Barcelona, Spain.

Sutton, R. S. and Barto, A. G. (1998). *Reinforcement Learning: An Introduction*. The MIT Press, Cambridge, MA. Available at **http://www.cs.ualberta.ca/ sutton/book/the-book.html.**

Sycara, K. P. (1990). Persuasive argumentation in negotiation. *Theory and Decision*, 28(3):203–242.

Sycara, K. P. (1998). Multiagent systems. *AI Magazine*, 19(2):79–92.

Sycara, K. P., Lu, J., and Klusch, M. (1998). Interoperability among heterogeneous software agents on the Internet. Technical Report CMU-RI-TR-98-22, Robotics Institute, Carnegie Mellon University, Pittsburgh, PA. See **http://www.ri.cmu.edu/ pubs/pub_1440.html.**

Sycara, K. P., Paolucci, M., Van Velsen, M., and Giampapa, J. A. (2003). The RETSINA MAS infrastructure. *Autonomous Agents and Multi-Agent Systems*, 7(1-2):29–48.

Sycara, K. P., Widoff, S., Klusch, M., and Lu, J. (2002). LARKS: Dynamic matchmaking among heterogeneous software agents in cyberspace. *Autonomous Agents and Multi-Agent Systems*, 5(2):173–203.

Sztompka, P. (1999). *Trust: A sociological theory*. Cambridge University Press, Cambridge.

TAC (2006). Trading Agent Competition. See **http://www.sics.se/tac/.**

TAC Reports (2006). Trading Agent Competition: Research reports. See **http://tac. eecs.umich.edu/researchreport.html.**

Thirunavukkarasu, C., Finin, T., and Mayfield, J. (1995). Secret agents–A security archi-tecture for the KQML agent communication language. In *Proceedings of the Intelligent Information Agents Workshop* held in conjunction with the *Fourth International Conference on Information and Knowledge Management (CIKM'95)*, Baltimore, MD.

Tijms, H. C. (2003). *A First Course in Stochastic Models*. John Wiley and Sons, Chichester.

Trastour, D., Bartolini, C., and Gonzalez-Castillo, J. (2001). A semantic web approach to service description for matchmaking of services. Technical Report HPL-2001-183, HP Laboratories Bristol.

Tschudin, C. F. (1999). Mobile agent security. In Klusch, M., editor, *Intelligent Information Agents: Agent-Based Information Discovery and Management on the Internet*, pages 431–446. Springer, Berlin.

Tsvetovat, M., Sycara, K. P., Chen, Y., and Ying, J. (2000). Customer coalitions in electronic markets. In *Agent-Mediated Electronic Commerce III, Current Issues in Agent-Based Electronic Commerce Systems (AMEC)*, LNAI Volume 2003, pages 121–138. Springer, Berlin.

Tsvetovatyy, M., Gini, M. L., Mobasher, B., and Wieckowski, Z. (1997). MAGMA: An agent-based virtual market for electronic commerce. *Journal of Applied Artificial Intelligence*, 11(6):501–523.

UCITA (2006). Uniform Computer Information Transactions Act. See http://www.law.upenn.edu/bll/ulc/ucita/citam99.htm.

UDDI (2006). Universal Description, Discovery and Integration protocol. See http://www.uddi.org/.

UECA (2006). Uniform Electronic Commerce Act. See http://www.ulcc.ca/en/us/index.cfm?sec=1&sub=1u1.

UETA (2006). Uniform Electronic Transactions Act. See http://www.law.upenn.edu/bll/ulc/fnact99/1990s/ueta99.htm.

Ulfelder, S. (June 2000). Undercover Agents. *Computer World*. Available at http://65.221.110.98/news/2000/story/0,11280,45452,00.html.

Uschold, M. and Grüninger, M. (1996). Ontologies: principles, methods, and applica-tions. *Knowledge Engineering Review*, 11(2):93–155.

van der Torre, L. and Tan, Y.-H. (1999). Rights, duties and commitments between agents. In Dean, T., editor, *Proceedings of the Sixteenth International Joint Conference on Artificial Intelligence (IJCAI-99)*, pages 1239–1246, Stockholm, Sweden.

Van Dyke Parunak, H. (1987). Manufacturing experience with the Contract Net. In Huhns, M., editor, *Distributed Artificial Intelligence*, pages 285–310. Morgan Kaufmann, San Mateo, CA.

van Slyke, G. and Belanger, F. (2003). *E-business Technologies: Supporting the Net-enhanced organization*. John Wiley and Sons, Chichester.

Varian, H. R. (2006). *Intermediate Microeconomics: A Modern Approach*. N.W. Norton & Company, New York.

Vázquez-Salceda, J., Padget, J. A., Cortés, U., López-Navidad, A., and Caballero, F. (2003). Formalizing an electronic institution for the distribution of human tissues. *Artificial Intelligence in Medicine*, 27(3):233–258.

Vega-Rodondo, F. (2003). *Economics and the Theory of Games*. Cambridge University Press, Cambridge.

Vickrey, W. (1961). Counterspeculation, auctions and competitive sealed tenders. *The Journal of Finance*, 16:8–37.

Vlassis, N. (2003). A concise introduction to multiagent systems and distributed AI. Available at **http://www.science.uva.nl/vlassis/cimasdai**.

von Neumann, J. and Morgenstern, O. (1964). *Theory of Games and Economic Behaviour*. Science Editions J. Wiley, New York, NY.

von Wright, G. H. (1951). Deontic logic. *Mind*, 60:1–15.

Voyager (2006). See **http://www.recursionsw.com/Products/voyager.html**.

Vulkan, N. (2003). *The Economics of E-commerce*. Princeton University Press, Princeton, NJ.

W3C (2006). See **http://www.w3.org/**.

Walras, L. (1874). *Eléments d'économic politique pure*. Allen and Unwin, London. Lausanne, L.C. English translation. William Jaffé (1954) Elements of Pure Economics.

Walton, D. N. (1989). *Informal logic: A handbook for critical argumentation*. Cambridge University Press, Cambridge.

Walton, D. N. and Krabbe, E. C. W. (1995). *Commitment in dialogue: Basic Concepts of Interpersonal Reasoning*. State University of New York Press, Albany, NY.

Wavish, P. (1996). Situated action approach to implementing characters in computer games. *Applied Artificial Intelligence*, 10(1):53–74.

Wavish, P. and Connah, D. (1997). Virtual actors that can perform scripts and improvise roles. In *Proceedings of the First International Conference on Autonomous Agents (Agents 97)*, pages 317–322, Marina del Rey, CA.

Weiser, M. and Brown, J. S. (1997). The coming age of calm technology. In Denning, P. J. and Metcalfe, R. M., editors, *Beyond calculation: The next fifty years*, pages 75–85. Copernicus, New York, NY. See **http://www.ubiq.com/hypertext/weiser/acmfuture2endnote.htm**.

Weiss, G., editor (1999). *Multiagent Systems: A Modern Approach to Distributed Artificial Intelligence*. The MIT Press, Cambridge, MA.

Weitzenböck, E. M. (2001). Electronic agents and the formation of contracts. *International Journal of Law and Information Technology*, 9(3):204–234.

Weitzenböck, E. M. (2002). Electronic agents and contract performance: good faith and fair dealing. In *Proceedings of the Law of Electronic Agents Workshop (LEA-02): Selected Revised Papers*, pages 67–73.

Weta Digital (2006). See **http://www.wetadigital.com/**.

Wettig, S. and Zehender, E. (2004). A legal analysis of human and electronic agents. *Artificial Intelligence and Law*, 12(1-2):111–135.

White, J. E. (1994). Telescript technology: the foundation for the electronic marketplace. White paper, General Magic, Inc., 2465, Latham Street, Mountain View CA 94040.

Winkler, R. L. (1972). *An Introduction to Bayesian Inference and Decision.* Holt, Rinehart and Winston, New York, NY.

Wong, H. C. and Sycara, K. P. (2000). A taxonomy of middle-agents for the Internet. In *Proceedings of the Fourth International Conference on Multi-Agent Systems (ICMAS-00)*, pages 465 –466, Boston, MA.

Wooldridge, M. (1999). Intelligent agents. In Weiss, G., editor, *Multiagent Systems: A Modern Approach to Distributed Artificial Intelligence*, pages 27–77. The MIT Press, Cambridge, MA.

Wooldridge, M. (2000). *Reasoning about Rational Agents.* The MIT Press, Cambridge, MA.

Wooldridge, M. (2002). *An Introduction to Multiagent Systems.* John Wiley and Sons, Chichester.

Wooldridge, M. and Jennings, N. R. (1995). Intelligent agents: Theory and practice. *The Knowledge Engineering Review*, 10(2):115–152.

Wooldridge, M. and Jennings, N. R. (1999). The cooperative problem-solving process. *Journal of Logic and Computation*, 9(4):563–592.

Wooldridge, M., Jennings, N. R., and Kinny, D. (2000). The Gaia methodology for agent-oriented analysis and design. *Autonomous Agents and Multi-Agent Systems*, 3(3):285–312.

WordNet (2006). See http://wordnet.princeton.edu.

Wurman, P. R., Walsh, W. E., and Wellman, M. P. (1998a). Flexible double auctions for electronic commerce: Theory and implementation. *Decision Support Systems*, 24(1):17–27.

Wurman, P. R., Wellman, M. P., and Walsh, W. E. (1998b). The Michigan Internet AuctionBot: A configurable auction server for human and software agents. In *Proceedings of the Second International Conference on Autonomous Agents (Agents 98)*, pages 301–308, St. Paul, MN.

Wurman, P. R., Wellman, M. P., and Walsh, W. E. (2001). A parameterization of the auction design space. *Games and Economic Behavior*, 35(1):304–338.

XML (2006). The Xtensible Markup Language. See http://www.xml.org.

YahooAuctions (2006). See http://auctions.yahoo.com.

Youll, J. (2001). Agent-based electronic commerce: Opportunities and challenges. In *Proceedings of the Fifth International Symposium on Autonomous Decentralized Systems (ISADS)*, pages 146–148, Dallas, TX.

Yu, B. and Singh, M. P. (2002). An evidential model of distributed reputation management. In *Proceedings of the First International Joint Conference on Autonomous Agents and Multiagent Systems (AAMAS'02)*, pages 294–301, Bologna, Italy.

Zambonelli, F., Jennings, N. R., and Wooldridge, M. (2000). Organisational abstractions for the analysis and design of multi-agent systems. In Ciancarini, P. and Wooldridge, M., editors, *Proceedings of the First International Workshop on Agent-Oriented Software Engineering (AOSE 2000)*, LNAI Volume 1957, pages 235–251, Berlin. Springer.

Index

$(M + 1)$st price rule 229

A

AAII   66
abstract agent program   27
access control   371, 372
active objects   59
Actor model   6
agenda   283
agent communication   84
  languages   85
  layered model   95
agent register   391
Agent Tcl   332
agent types   197, 307
Agent UML   66
agent-oriented methodologies   62
agent-oriented programming   68
AGENT0   68
agentification   69
AgentSpeak   68
Aglets   335
allocation   172, 178, 223, 281, 287,
  316
Anglo-Dutch auction   246
anonymity   383
anonymization   383
anonymizer server   384, 385
antagonistic agents   81, 168
anthropomorphism   25
APRIL   68
Ara   333
argumentation   288
  logic-based   293
  modes   288
  persuasive, *see* persuasive
    argumentation
argumentation-based negotiation   288

arguments
  classes   294
  persuasive   289
  rebutting in   293
  undercutting in   293
Aroma   334
Arrow's impossibility theorem   282
Artificial Intelligence (AI)   5, 8, 41
ascending auctions   218
assessment   203
asymmetric cryptosystems   375
asymmetric information   185, 254
AuctionBot   239
auctions   215
  disadvantages   225
  objections   247
  terminology   216
auditing   371, 373
authentication   339, 343, 344, 371, 372,
  377
authorization   339, 344, 346, 372
authority relations   365
autonomy   23, 58, 59, 120, 346, 352,
  366, 382, 386, 389
availability   371, 372

B

BargainFinder   121
bargaining   252, 262
  axiomatic theory of   255
  power   253
  situation   252
  strategic models of   256
Bayes' rule   156, 197, 198, 202, 398
Bayesian game   197, 198
Bayesian Nash equilibrium   198, 200
behavioural approach   6

belief system   201
belief-desire-intention (BDI) architecture
    49
believable agents   10
Bellman equation   36
best-response function   188, 189
binary protocol   282
blackboard systems   6
Borda protocol   284
broadcaster agents   135
broker agents   79, 134
budget balance   213, 313, 315, 316, 319
bundling   13, 15
business models   13, 14
business-to-business (B2B)   116, 119,
    244
business-to-consumer (B2C)   14, 119,
    243, 244
buying clubs   273

C

calculative rationality   45, 46
call markets   228
capability description language   137
certification authority   380, 390
characteristic function games   267
Clarke mechanism   314, 315, 318
client-server model   326
closed multi-agent systems   79
coalition   83, 108, 267
    applications   273
    formation   267
    payoff division   271
    protocols   275
        post-negotiation   277
        pre-negotiation   278
    structure   268, 269
code-on-demand   326
cognitive systems   6
coherence   77
cold start problem   158
collaborative-based filtering   155
    problems   158

systems   159
collusion   221, 227, 245
combinatorial auction problem (CAP)
    238
combinatorial auctions   217, 236
    iterative   237
    price setting   237
    quantity setting   237
commitment games   185
commitment tactics   254
commitments   24, 50, 53, 211, 259,
    295, 365
common knowledge   182, 184, 259
common value auctions   219, 226
competition   82
competition games   185
competitive
    equilibrium   179, 180
    market   171
complete preferences   281, 311
computing with encrypted functions
    347
Concordia   334
Concurrent METATEM   68
Condorcet protocol   282
confidentiality   371, 377
conflict resolution   84, 211
connection problem   104, 128
constraint-matching   143
Consumer Buying Behaviour model   116
consumer-to-consumer (C2C)   14, 15,
    116, 215, 243, 244
consumption bundles   173, 175, 177
content language   86, 93
content-based filtering   153
context
    Aglets   336
    mobile agents   328
context matching   140
continuous environment   29, 30
ContractNet   7, 104
    limitations   106
    messages   105

roles   105
contracts   17, 366, 388
contractual capabilities   389
contractual liabilities   388
conversations, *see* dialogue
convexity   176
cooperation   48, 82, 192, 252, 370
    reputation for   193
cooperative agents   81, 103
cooperative games   185
cooperative problem-solving   103, 104
Core   271
correlated value auctions   219, 226
credit card model   380
cross-selling   162
cryptography   373
customer coalitions   273
customer loyalty   163

D

DARPA Agent Markup Language
    (DAML)   100, 144
deception power   265
decision-making
    rules   401
    under certainty   395
    under noncertainty   395
    under risk   395
    under uncertainty   395
decoy task   265
delegation   4, 5, 7, 355, 359
deliberation   49, 51
demand   169, 171, 172, 178
    curve   170
denial of service attack   340, 341, 343,
    355, 372
deontic logic   364
descending auctions   218
DESIRE   67
deterministic environment   28, 33
dialogue   94
    games   95, 295, 299
    negotiation   94, 290

persuasion   94, 288
    types, of   94
digital certificates   380
digital divide   16
digital signatures   378
direct revelation mechanism   309
directory facilitator   136
discrete environment   29
discriminatory auctions   218, 219, 221,
    222
Distributed Artificial Intelligence (DAI)
    5, 8
dominant strategy   186, 192, 220–224,
    227, 279, 309, 314, 319, 321
    equilibrium   186, 192, 199, 309, 311
    implementation   309, 310
    incentive compatible direct revelation
        mechanisms   311
double auctions   228
Dutch auctions   221, 224, 227
dynamic environment   28, 30, 38, 76,
    116, 354, 360
dynamic games   194
dynamic pricing, *see* price
    discrimination
dynamic programming   36

E

e-business   11
e-commerce   11
    individuals, and   14
    organizations, and   12
e-Game   240
e-person   390
e-services   13, 17
eavesdropping   342, 379
eBay proxy agent   228, 243
economic efficiency   13, 15, 17, 212,
    238
electronic data interchange (EDI)   11
electronic signatures   378
emergent behaviour   49
encounter   261, 266

encryption algorithms   375
end agents   128
English auctions   220, 224, 227
entry deterrence   245
environment   23, 24, 26, 32, 39, 41, 46,
    50
    characteristics   27
    rate of change   29, 53
episodic environment   29
equilibrium path   202
equilibrium principle   169, 171
exact match   139
execution tracing   346
Expected Loss rule (EL)   403
Expected Payoff rule (EP)   403
expert systems and agents   59
extensive form   183
externality   180, 315, 369

F

feedback phase   131, 150
FIPA   7, 90, 136
FIPA Agent Communication Language
    (ACL)   69, 90, 93, 136
    communicative acts   90
    semantics   90
first-price auctions   218
first-price sealed-bid auctions   222, 224,
    227
first-rater problem   158
folk psychology   25
fraud   16, 119, 359, 368, 373, 381, 384
fully observable environment   28, 33, 35

G

Gaia   62, 65
game theory   181
    solution concepts   186
general equilibrium   179
Generalized Vickrey Auction (GVA)
    315
Gibbard–Satterthwaite impossibility
    theorem   311
goal states   31, 266

goal-directed behaviour   24
Grid   215, 349
Groves mechanism   313, 321

H

Hare protocol, *see* single transferable vote
    protocol
horizontal layered architecture   54
hybrid agents   54

I

ideal rational agent   32
illocution   85
impatience   253
incentive compatible
    auction   223
    mechanism   309
indifference   174
indifference curve   175
individual rational   213, 223, 244, 262,
    306, 315, 316, 360
individual rationality   213, 315, 319
information asymmetry   15
information overload   16
information set   183, 184, 191, 195,
    201, 202
inside options   254
institutions   356, 359–361, 365
    electronic   360, 365
    mechanism, *see* mechanisms
integrity   371, 372, 378
IntelliShopper   121, 384
intentional stance   25
intentional systems   25
interaction   77, 80
    elements   81
    modes   82
    protocols   83, 97
        communication   84
        cooperation   84
        negotiation   84, 211
interference   29, 266, 360
InteRRaP system   56

J

JACK Intelligent Agents   63, 65, 69
JADE   69
JATLite   69
Java   58, 59, 68, 69, 330, 331, 333,
    336, 337, 339, 344
joint plans   38, 56, 266

K

Knowledge and Query Manipulation
    Language (KQML)   69, 86, 93,
    136, 137
  keywords   87
  performatives   87
  semantics   88
Knowledge Interchange Format (KIF)
    93, 136

L

Language for Advertisement and Request
    for Knowledge Sharing (LARKS),
    137
  matching   139
  matching methods   140
  specification   138
layered architecture   54
learning   38
legacy systems   9, 69
legal persons   386
legal transactions   389
legislation   352, 386, 388
liability   352, 386, 387, 390, 391
location phase   131
locution   85, 297
logging   344, 354, 371, 373
logic-based architecture   41
logical arguments   293
lotteries   397, 404–408
lying auctioneer   226

M

majority rule   282
majority runoff protocol   285

market economy   168, 179
market equilibrium   179
Markov
  decision problem   34
  partially observable decision problem
    34
  property   33
MAS-CommonKADS   67
MaSE   65
masquerade   340–342, 369
matching   128, 145
  capability specifications   128
  engine   129
  request specifications   128
  similarity   129
matchmaker agents   132
Maximum Expected Utility (MEU)
    principle   32, 34, 406
means-ends reasoning   49, 51
mechanism design   211, 307
  assumptions   320
  computational issues   320
mechanisms   307
  centralized   320
  decentralized   321
mental attitudes   25, 53, 88, 93, 389
merchant brokering stage   116
middle agents   79, 128, 132, 134, 135,
    150
  functionality   131
  interaction   130
migration   330
mixed strategies, see strategies
mixed strategy Nash equilibrium   189
mobile agents   327
mobility
  logical   326
  physical   326
money   399, 404
  utility of   407
Monotonic Concession Protocol   262,
    264
monotonicity in preferences   175

Mth price rule   229
multi-agent environment   29, 30, 76
multi-agent systems   76
   challenges   78
   definition   76
   potential   77
multi-attribute auctions   217, 234
multi-unit auctions   217

N
Nash bargaining solution   255
Nash equilibrium   187, 199
natural persons   386
Nature   30, 184, 197, 200
negotiation positions   287
negotiation protocols   211
   desired properties of   212
neighbourhood-based algorithms
      156
NOMADS   334
nonrepudiation   344, 354, 371, 373,
      376
normal form   182
norms   360–365

O
objects and agents   58
ontologies   61, 80, 97, 124, 129
   axiomatization   99
   concepts   97
   conceptualization   99
   developing   99
Ontology Web Language (OWL)
      100
   specification document   102
   sub-languages   102
Ontology Web Language for Services
      (OWL-S)   144
open
   environments   30
   multi-agent systems   79
   systems   9
open auctions   217
optimization principle   169

organizations   9, 12, 107, 361, 365
outside options   254

P
paradigm shift   3
parallel auctions   217
Pareto efficiency   172, 212
Pareto efficient
      allocation/outcome/solution   173,
         179, 187, 192, 193, 212, 223,
         252, 262, 264, 272, 287, 319,
         367
partially observable environment   28,
      30, 34, 43, 77
patrimony   390, 391
payoff matrix   182
payoff table   399
payoffs   181, 399
Pearson's correlation coefficients   157
perfect Bayesian Nash equilibrium   202
performance measure   30, 32
perlocution   85
permissions   364, 365
personalization   15, 120, 162, 163
personalized services   13, 16, 17, 61,
      120, 162, 163
PersonaLogic   121
personas   122, 384
PERSUADER system   291
   types of argument   292
persuasive argumentation   94, 289
phantom task   265
planning   37
plug-in match   139, 140, 146
plurality protocol   284
policy   33
   optimal   34–36
policy iteration   36
practical reasoning   26, 49, 50, 53
predatory behaviour   245
preferences   31, 173, 182, 311, 404,
      405
   relations   281

strong   174

weak   174

price collusion   14

price discrimination   13, 16, 164, 165, 383

price tatonnement process   180

prisoner's dilemma   191, 193, 367

privacy   16, 118, 120, 352, 381, 383, 391

protecting   384

privacy-enhancing technology   385

private keys   376

private value auctions   219, 223

proactive

behaviour   24, 54, 55, 60

systems   24

proactiveness   24

probability theory   396

product brokering stage   116

profile comparison   141

Prometheus   63, 65, 69

proportional representation protocol   285

provider agents   128

pseudonymity   383

public key cryptography   375

public keys   376

Q

quasilinear

environment   312

preferences   312, 318

R

random variables   396

rank order protocol, *see* Borda protocol

ratings   155

rational agents   26, 32, 53, 180, 182, 193, 266, 319

rationality   26, 188, 258

bounded   32

ideal   32

reactive

agent   33

architecture   45

behaviour   56, 59, 60

reactiveness   24

relaxed match   140

representation/reasoning problem   45

repudiation   342, 378

reputation   356, 367

issues   369

systems   109, 119, 150, 159, 345, 347, 367, 391

requester agents   128

revelation principle   310

revenue equivalence theorem   224

revenue nonequivalence theorem   225

rights   363, 365

rings   221, 227, 364

risk

degree of willingness to   263

trust, and, *see* trust

risk of breakdown   254

risk premium   408

risk-averse agents   409

risk-neutral agents   216, 224, 410

risk-prone agents   216, 225, 410

risks of agent technology   353

ROADMAP   65

roles   63, 365

Rubinstein's bargaining solution   257

S

scenes   363

scoring function   235

screen-scraping   120, 124

sealed-bid auctions   217

second-price auctions   218

secret keys   374, 378

security   352, 370

in Aglets   338

in mobile agents   339, 348

services   109

self-interested agents   81, 168, 182, 306

Semantic Web   8, 60, 61

Semantic Web Services   62

sequential auctions   217, 236
sequential environment   29, 30
sequential equilibrium   203
sequential rationality   202
ServiceGrounding   145
ServiceModel   144
ServiceProfile   144
shadow of the future   193, 367
Shapley value   271
shills   226, 277
ShopBot   121
shopbots   118
shopping agents   118
    how they retrieve information   120
    limitations   122
signature matching   142
similarity matching   141
simultaneous auctions   237
single transferable vote protocol   285
single-agent environment   29
Situation Calculus   37
situation-action rule   46, 48
sniping   228, 244
social ability   25, 60, 62
social choice functions   307, 308
    dictatorial   311
social choice rule   281, 318
social commitments   365
social norms   24
social preferences   281
social welfare   212, 287
    function   212, 286
solution complexity   321
speech act theory   85
spyware   163
state-oriented domain   267
static environment   28
stochastic environment   28, 30, 31,
    33–35, 76
strategic equivalence   224
strategic game   181
strategic interdependence   181

Strategic Negotiation Protocol (SNP)
    258
strategies   181
    behavioural   191
    dominant, see dominant strategy
    dominated   186
    mixed   188, 264
    tit-for-tat   194
    totally mixed   203
STRIPS   38
strong mobility   330
strong preferences   174
subgame perfect Nash equilibrium   195,
    201, 257, 260
subsumption architecture   46
subsumption hierarchy   46–48
symbolic approach   6
symbolic representation   6, 41
symmetric cryptosystems   374

T
TACOMA   333
tampering   340–342, 345–347
task
    decomposition   104
    distribution   7, 104
    synthesis   7
task-oriented domain   260
tax   315, 318
Telescript   332
theorem provers   41
theoretical reasoning   49
threats in mobile agents   340
    agent to agent   341
    agent to host   340
    host to agent   342
tit-for-tat, see strategies
TouringMachines   55
Trading Agent Competition (TAC)   242
traffic analysis   342, 384
transaction phase   131
transactions twice-removed from the
    interface   358, 383

transduction problem   45
transition model   33, 34
Tropos   64, 69
trust   18, 159, 192, 288, 321, 352, 353,
    355–357
  coalition protocols   276–278
  control, and   358
  impersonal   355, 356
  management services   109
  personal   355, 356
  risk, and   353, 355

U
ubiquitous computing   4
UCITA statute   388
UECA statute   388
uniform auctions   218, 219, 221, 223
user profiles   16, 154, 158, 163, 382
user-item matrix   155
utility   31, 34, 404
  cardinal   178
  expected   31, 186, 198, 199, 202,
    406, 408, 410
  maximum expected   32, 36, 406
  monotonic transformation of   178,
    406
  ordinal   177
utility functions   177, 197, 404, 405
  additive   35
  multi-attribute   235, 411
  separable   35
  Strategic Negotiation Protocol (SNP)
    259

V
value iteration   36
value-added networks   11
vertical layered architectures   56
Vickrey auctions   222, 224, 227
virtual enterprises, *see* virtual
    organizations
virtual organizations   12, 17, 107, 280,
    360
voting   158
  protocols   282
  truth telling   318
Voyager   334

W
weak mobility   330
weak preferences   174
web of trust model   381
web services   8, 60, 124, 144, 326
winner determination   235, 238
winner's curse   225
worth-oriented domain   266

X
X.509 standard   380
XML language   60, 100–102, 144

Z
ZEUS   68
Zeuthian strategy   264